HOUSING FINANCE

DAVID GARNETT

Chartered Institute of Housing
Policy and Practice Series
in collaboration with the
Housing Studies Association

The Chartered Institute of Housing
The Chartered Institute of Housing is the professional organisation for all people who work in housing. Its purpose is to take a strategic and leading role in encouraging and promoting the provision of good quality affordable housing for all. The Institute has more than 16,500 members working in local authorities, housing associations, the private sector and educational institutions.

Chartered Institute of Housing
Octavia House, Westwood Way
Coventry CV4 8JP
Telephone: 024 7685 1700
Fax: 024 7669 5110

The Housing Studies Association
The Housing Studies Association promotes the study of housing by bringing together housing researchers with others interested in housing research in the housing policy and practitioner communities. It acts as a voice for housing research by organising conferences and seminars, lobbying government and other agencies and providing services to members.

The CIH Housing Policy and Practice Series is published in collaboration with the Housing Studies Association and aims to provide important and valuable material and insights for housing managers, staff, students, trainers and policy makers. Books in the series are designed to promote debate, but the contents do not necessarily reflect the views of the CIH or the HSA. The Editorial Team for the series is: General Editors: Dr. Peter Williams, John Perry and Robina Goodlad, and Production Editor: Alan Dearling.

Cover photograph: Photodisc.

This publication has been sponsored by Dexia Public Finance Bank.

ISBN 1-900396-83-1

Housing Finance
David Garnett

Published by the Chartered Institute of Housing © 2000

Printed by the Charlesworth Group, Huddersfield

Contents

Preface

This book is intended for those who wish to acquire an up-to-date overview of housing finance. This means that it will be of interest to all those working for and with public and private housing agencies as well as those who are seeking to work in this field, whether in a professional, voluntary or political capacity. In producing the text, particular attention has been paid to the needs of that growing group of students on qualifying or exempting diploma and degree courses that lead to membership of the Chartered Institute of Housing, the Royal Institution of Chartered Surveyors, and the Royal Town Planning Institute. The text will also be of interest to those following academic courses in social and public administration and to the general reader concerned with issues relating to the built environment and public affairs.

The text provides a mixture of analysis and description; it is not intended to be a manual but an introduction and guide to the subject. As well as outlining the details of the current finance regimes operating in the different housing sectors, the book offers a way of understanding the basic, unchanging issues and principles that lie behind these transitory arrangements. To this end, it consciously takes both an historical and a conceptual approach to its analysis of housing finance. The present is grounded in the past. To understand the social, economic and political significance of what is happening now to the production, distribution and consumption of private and social housing requires some reference to history and theory.

The text is intended to provide the reader with a simple and clear conceptual framework based on what can be termed a *functional analysis* of housing finance. This approach makes the point that financial resources and arrangements are a means to an end rather than an end in themselves. It is how finance is used rather than what finance essentially is that is of consequence. A functional analytical approach does not simply address the technical question 'How does it work?', but also poses the socio-economic questions, 'Does it work well?', and 'In whose interests does it work?'

The descriptive elements of the text focus on how the financial regimes operate at the time of writing. Procedural changes are occurring all the time and the reader should use the publications and web-sites of the appropriate government departments, non-departmental public bodies, and professional and voluntary organisations to keep up-to-date. It should be recognised that the United Kingdom is experiencing a measure of political and administrative devolution that means in future, increasingly divergent practices will emerge in the various national regions. Further reading is indicated at the end of each chapter and a list of useful addresses is included as part of the bibliography at the end of the book.

Writing a book on housing finance that seeks to cover all tenures and all parts of the United Kingdom has been a daunting task – a task that has been made even more daunting by the constitutional and legislative changes that have occurred since the 1997 General Election. The original publication date was put back to allow the main features of the government's latest Housing Green Paper to be included in the text. Together with the Scottish Green Paper on Housing published in February 1999, this document sets in place a large part of the 'housing agenda' for the next few years. In writing this edition of the book I have sought to embrace this agenda.

Every effort has been made to ensure that the factual information included in the text is accurate and appropriately comprehensive. However, given its ambitious scope, there are bound to be mistakes and omissions. Many people have helped and guided me through the task of producing this text but I take full responsibility for any factual errors. Similarly, the opinions expressed in this book are my own and do not necessarily represent those of the Chartered Institute of Housing. The book was not written as a practice manual and should not be used as such.

Of the many people who have spared time to read and comment on various draft chapters, I owe a special debt to the following: Sam Lister (CIH) and Andy Monkley (Bristol City Council) who helped steer me through the intricacies of the current housing benefit system; and Dr Peter Williams for his comments on the chapters covering owner-occupation. I also wish to thank several colleagues who helped fill in a number of missing details: Jim Patman and Ailsa Daykin (East Midlands HA), Paul Roberts (Cadarn Housing Group), Philip Jones (Berwickshire HA), Irene Dillon (Cairn HA), Richard Bramley (consultant), Professor Robina Goodlad (Glasgow University) and Mark Lupton and Marian Reid of CIH. I am particularly indebted to John Perry for contributing the final chapter and for his tireless help and sympathetic encouragement. The help of all these, together with the encouragement of my wife Julie, played an important part in enabling me to complete the book.

David Garnett
Bristol
July 2000
David.Garnett@uwe.ac.uk

'Housing is a basic requirement for everyone. Our homes influence our well-being, our sense of worth, and our ties to our families, communities and work. If we live in decent housing we are more likely to benefit from good health, higher educational attainment and better-paid work.'

('A Housing Strategy for the 21st Century', in *Quality and Choice: A Decent Home for All*, DETR/Department of Social Security, April 2000).

PART ONE

Housing finance: conceptual context

Introduction to Part One

The first four chapters of this book provide a conceptual introduction to the more descriptive and analytical material that follows. By drawing on aspects of economic theory and social policy, these early chapters seek to establish a way of thinking and talking about housing finance that will help the reader to develop a critical understanding of some of the enduring problems and issues that surround the topic. The more 'factual' material that constitutes Part Two makes constant references back to the ideas and definitions outlined in Part One. This means that the impatient reader may, if they wish, initially skip Part One and turn straight to the book's substantive content that is located in Part Two. The serious student of the subject is, however, encouraged to begin at the beginning.

CHAPTER 1:
Housing and value

Finance is not an end in itself, but a means to an end. It is an instrument of action that allows modern societies to produce, consume and exchange the range of goods and services people demand and need. With respect to housing, finance provides the means to design, construct and acquire new dwellings, to maintain, repair and renew existing dwellings, and meet the day-to-day running costs associated with occupancy. Because, for any particular household or housing agency their means are limited, people are concerned to make the best use of the financial resources at their disposal. Be they occupiers, landlords, politicians or practitioners, the primary concern of those with an interest in housing finance is to achieve value-for-money. It is for this reason that we will begin by confronting the question of what is meant by *value* in the context of housing provision, consumption and exchange.

In this introductory chapter we will consider the nature of housing as a commodity by analysing the legal, economic and social characteristics that distinguish it from the other things we produce and use. *Proprietary analysis*[1] will be used to make the point that it is not what housing is that matters, so much as how it is valued. In other words, our ultimate concern is with the question of what housing does for and to people. We will consider this question by seeking to understand how people value the housing in which they have some sort of interest.

Before beginning our discussion we must define some basic terms.

Agreeing a vocabulary

Because the term 'family' carries such strong social and cultural connotations, it is the convention to refer to the occupiers of housing as 'households'. A household can be an individual or a group. In either case, what distinguishes it as a distinct and separate household is its exclusive use of a sitting-room and its joint catering and general housekeeping arrangements.

The terms 'housing', 'houses' and 'house' are sometimes used generically to cover all types of residential unit. However, they can be used more specifically to describe a particular class of domestic property; in this way houses are sometimes

---

1   The notion of *proprietary analysis* used in this book is based on work done at the Department of Land Economy in the University of Cambridge. Readers interested in this approach to analysis might refer to Denman, Prodano and Sylvio, (1972), *Land Use: An Introduction to Proprietary Land Use Analysis,* Allen and Unwin; or Denman, D.R., (1978), *The Place of Property*, Geographical Publications Ltd.

distinguished from bungalows, maisonettes, flats, etc. To overcome this potential confusion, governmental and other official publications use the term 'housing' to describe habitation in general or the stock of accommodation in a defined area and they use the term 'dwelling' to describe an individual unit of accommodation; we will follow this convention.

In using the term 'dwelling' we will take it to apply to any building or part of a building used as a unit of habitation and which has its own separate entrance. To be a 'self-contained' dwelling it must afford the occupier access to the outside world without having to invade some other household's private living space. If a dwelling is shared by more than one household, it is said to be in 'multiple occupation'.

A dwelling can be in a number of *physical forms* and, in the UK, these are generally classified as houses, either detached, semi-detached or terraced, bungalows, maisonettes, flats, high or low rise, or mobile homes, sometimes called park homes. Dwellings in multiple occupation can include bedsits, old people's homes, student residences, homeless persons' hostels and hotels. The legal terms on which a dwelling is held as property is referred to as its *tenure*. For the purposes of our analysis we will distinguish between three broad tenure arrangements: owner-occupation (freehold or long leasehold[2]); short leasehold; and rented (secure, assured, and assured shorthold). These three broad tenure sectors can be classified further by reference to the *proprietary interests* that individuals and organisations have in a particular dwelling.

The socio-economic nature of a dwelling

The three primary characteristics of a dwelling

We are going to argue that a dwelling is at one and the same time a consumer commodity, private investment, and a social good. These primary characteristics exist simultaneously in all dwellings irrespective of tenure.

Figure 1.1: The socio-economic characteristics of dwellings

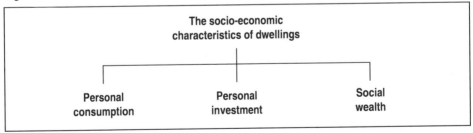

The socio-economic
characteristics of dwellings

Personal
consumption

Personal
investment

Social
wealth

---

2   Legally leaseholders are tenants; however, in this text we are classing long leaseholders along with freeholders as owner-occupiers because typically they pay for their occupancy rights by means of a single 'purchase' payment rather than by periodic 'rental' payments. We will take the term of a 'long lease' to be a period long enough to make the exchange value of the lease more-or-less the same as the freehold value of the property.

That dwellings constitute both personal consumption and private investment highlights the point that people have *proprietary interests* vested in residential properties. The fact that dwellings can be partly or wholly funded from the public purse and that society as a whole is concerned about what happens to the housing stock, highlights the point that there are also *non-proprietary interests* vested in residential properties. Proprietary interests refer to the concerns of those who have a direct and private stake in a property – such as tenants, landlords and owner-occupiers. Non-proprietary interests refer to the concerns that the wider community have for the property. These indirect, wider public interests are sometimes referred to as *externalities* (see Figure 1.2).

Figure 1.2: The socio-economic characteristics of dwellings

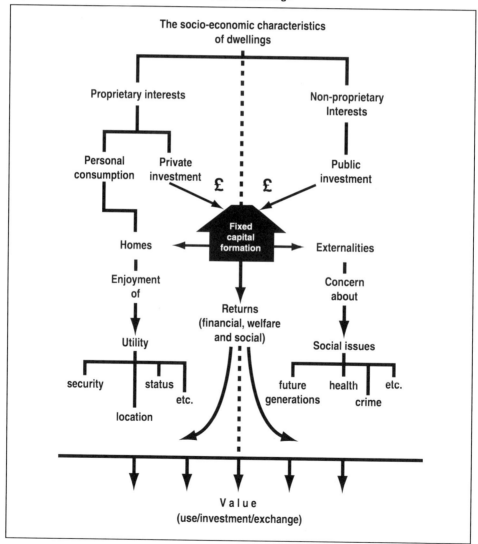

Proprietary interests

When considering the legal and economic relations associated with land and landed property it is more useful to talk of 'proprietorship' than of 'ownership'. This is because people or organisations other than just the freeholder may have some sort of stake in an individual plot or building.

Legal proprietorship is about tenure. In legal terms, a proprietor is someone who has a right or title to something that enables him or her to hold it as property. Although in everyday speech the term 'property' is commonly used to indicate the physical object to which various legal rights relate, in proprietary analysis the word is used to denote the legal relations appertaining to such an object. In this way, property is not conceived of as a concrete 'thing' but as a condition of belonging to some person or persons and is best thought of as comprising a bundle of rights relating to the possession, use and disposal of an object such as a building.

There may be a number of different legal proprietary interests attached to a particular dwelling. In addition to the freehold interest (*fee simple*)[3], individuals may possess leasehold or tenancy interests in the dwelling[4] and neighbouring households may have rights to use, enter or cross part of land or building(s) in order to carry out certain functions[5]. See Figure 1.3.

As well as a legal interest, a proprietor will have private welfare and economic interests vested in the property. Whereas a legal interest specifies the nature and scope of a proprietor's *rights and authority* to use or physically alter a particular

---

3   The term 'fee' comes from the Anglo-Saxon *feoh* meaning cattle – cattle being in early times a chief part of a man's possessions and a common medium of barter or exchange and, as such, came to signify transferable property. A freehold interest is the nearest thing to an 'absolute, transferable ownership' of real estate.

4   A leaseholder has temporary possession of the land and building(s) for a term of years from a freeholder or superior leaseholder who may be a private individual or an organisation, a local authority or a housing association. The term could be *specific* (e.g. for '99 years') or *periodic* (i.e. recurring – renewable monthly, annually, etc.). This means that we are reserving the term 'tenant' to apply to those who pay a regular rent and whose tenancy rights are defined by Act of Parliament. Leaseholders whose tenancy rights extend into the distant future are here treated as owner-occupiers and those with a short or 'periodic' lease agreement are regarded as a separate category. All new local authority residential tenancy agreements are classed as *secure tenancies* under the provisions of the Housing Acts 1980 and 1985. Private sector residential tenancies that began before 15 January 1989 are still protected by the Rent Act 1977: e.g. if the tenant is given notice to quit she does not have to leave because she has a *statutory tenancy*, a periodic tenancy lasting for the rest of her life plus two successors – e.g. her spouse and one child. Under the provisions of the Housing Act 1988 new housing association tenancies are on an *assured* basis. An *assured shorthold tenancy* is a hybrid: specific for six months and then periodic. Such tenancies were created by the Housing Act 1988.

5   For example, rights of *easement* establish rights of way or access (e.g. to maintain pipes, wires, fences); and rights of *profits a prendre* establish rights to take something from the property (e.g. grazing rights). Rights and restrictions may also be established by positive or restrictive covenants.

Figure 1.3: Proprietary interests

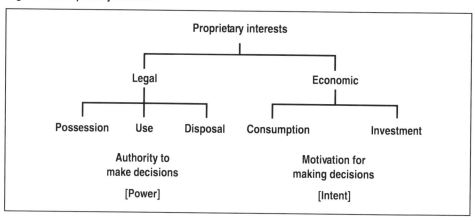

dwelling, a welfare/economic interest determines his or her *motivation* for using or altering it in some way. It can be said that legal proprietary interests are about *power* and welfare/economic proprietary interests are about *intent*.

It is welfare/economic interests that underlie a proprietor's attitude towards the property and provide the rationale for making use of it or looking after it in a particular way. The welfare/economic stake that someone has in a dwelling can take the form of a *consumption interest* or an *investment interest*.

Housing as consumption

A dwelling is a consumer item in that it generates utility in the form of a stream of housing facilities that individuals and families need or want. Indeed, the primary reason that most people seek access to housing is to consume and enjoy all the various things it provides that together go to constitute a 'home'. These include *shelter* in the form of protection from the elements, *location* in the form of convenient proximity to work, shops, schools, countryside, etc., *physical security* in the form of safety and security from the outside world and, less tangibly, benefits such as *status* that may relate to the siting, size or design of the dwelling.

It is sometimes said that housing, like food and clothing, is a *primary* consumer good because without it a reasonably decent life is not possible. In other words, it is argued that housing is no ordinary consumer item, but a *consumer necessity*. This argument is, however, limited as the quantity and quality of the housing enjoyed by many better-off households is more than that needed to satisfy what society currently regards as its minimum housing standards. Over the last hundred years or so society has used central and local government machinery to establish and enforce minimum housing standards and it is the desire to maintain such standards that is often pointed to as an underlying explanation of why housing is subsidised.

Another reason given for subsidising the consumption of housing is that it is expensive relative to disposable incomes. The price of a dwelling is almost invariably equivalent to a multiple of the purchaser's annual income, and for those who rent, the rental charge is likely to represent a high proportion of their expenditure relative to other items in their household budget.

The recognition of the fact that some minimum standard of housing is necessary for all people, and that it is expensive relative to income, has had a profound effect on the way in which the system of housing finance has evolved. When households with a preference for ownership are unable to purchase outright they must either rent their homes from landlords or borrow the money for purchase. Two consequences resulting from the nature of housing as a consumer commodity have been the establishment of a rented sector, and the development, alongside the market for owner-occupied housing, of a parallel money market providing long-term loans to purchasers in the form of mortgages. In subsequent chapters we will describe how, at different times, the State has intervened in different ways to encourage housing consumption by reducing both the price of renting and the price of borrowing.

In making a decision about where to live, a household will judge each dwelling's utility features in relation to its rental or purchase price. It is important to note, however, that to some extent, these features will be valued in terms of personal preferences. Just as different people like different types of music, different people like different types of home. This means that in choosing a home, a household will seek to balance a number of factors. On the one hand they will take account of the price or rent of the dwelling and its utility features, and on the other hand they will consider whether it suits their needs and expectations and whether or not they can afford to occupy it.

As well as being a home and generating utility, a dwelling will also have the features of an investment and, as such, have the potential to generate a financial or social 'return' on the money capital committed to its production or acquisition.

Housing as real capital investment

Investments can be held in the form of paper titles such as share certificates or bonds, or in the form of physical, utilisable artefacts such as plant, machinery or buildings. This latter category of investment is sometimes referred to as *real capital* or *fixed capital formation*. The term *fixed capital formation* is used to distinguish real capital from other, more liquid, types of assets such as stocks and shares. Although buildings are usually immobile, the word *'fixed'* here is not meant to imply that the asset itself cannot be moved but refers to the fact that the investor's money capital is 'tied up' and is in a sense 'fixed into' the physical asset. We therefore say that a building such as a house is an item of 'fixed capital' – that is, if needed, it will take the proprietor some time to 'unlock' the money he or she has invested in it.

A dwelling can be regarded as an item of *personal investment* in so far as it is a durable asset with a potential to earn a yield in the form of a rental income or a capital gain. A dwelling can be regarded as an item of *social investment* in so far as it has a potential to yield social gains valued by society. In either case, the value of the investment is determined by its potential to generate utility to some current or future end user. This means its type, size, condition and geographical location will affect an asset's relative value.

Housing yield and the concept of 'capital value'

In the housing field, private and public investment generates additions to real capital in the form of improvements and additions to the existing stock of dwellings.

Consumption and investment are related categories that are linked through the concept of value. The word 'value' comes from the Latin *valere* – to be strong – to be relied upon – to have worth. So the 'value' of something is that attribute that makes it, in some sense, worthy of use. If something has no use it is worthless and if it is worthless, it has no value.

The economic value of any capital asset is composed of three interrelated factors; namely, its potential selling price, or its *exchange value*, its potential usefulness, its 'utility' or *use value*, and its potential to yield a return on money capital committed, its *investment value*. At any time, a building's exchange value will be determined by the perceptions of potential purchasers about its current use and/or future investment value. *The real, underlying, fundamental economic value of a building is determined by what it does – its usefulness*, and in the final analysis, it is this that determines both its investment value and its exchange value. In the end, all economic value is grounded in current or potential use – value.

The *exchange value* of a building is represented by its selling price. Exchange is the mechanism by which use or investment value is realised. By selling the proprietary interests in a property, its use and investment values are exchanged for cash; that is, they are 'liquidated'.

Proprietorial motivations

The potential of a unit of accommodation to generate utility and a financial or social return affects a proprietor's attitudes towards spending money on its acquisition, improvement or maintenance. What people or organisations choose to do with or to a dwelling depends partly on their financial resources and partly on the nature of their proprietary interests. If the property is regarded as an item of consumption the proprietor will weigh up the price of buying, renting, repairing or maintaining it and compare this with the utility he or she would expect to acquire in return for such an outlay. If, however, a dwelling is regarded as a private or social investment then the proprietor will weigh up any proposed expenditure and compare it with the anticipated yield resulting from the investment outlay.

A tenant will have a predominantly consumption interest in a dwelling and will tend to be motivated to spend money on it with a view to gaining or maintaining its utility as a *home*. In contrast, a private landlord will have a predominantly investment interest and will be largely motivated to spend money on a dwelling with a view to maximising its rental income or capital value. An owner-occupier has a consumption and an investment interest in a property and will tend to bear both of these characteristics in mind when purchasing, improving or maintaining it. An understanding of the nature and scope of these private proprietary interests is a key concern of this text and will be considered in subsequent chapters.

Like other proprietors, local authorities and housing associations have clear legal interests in the stock they manage. In contrast with other proprietors, however, their economic *raison d' être* emphasises the need to generate politico-welfare returns for public expenditure and charitable investments. These returns are not simply measured in terms of rental flows and capital appreciation, but also take account of how the housing stock serves the needs of low-income or vulnerable households.

The provision, allocation and maintenance of decent, affordable housing constitutes the welfare/economic interest of local housing authorities and registered social landlords. The aims and policy pronouncements of the authority or association will determine the precise nature of this proprietary interest. Public sector and charitable landlords may regard the return on investment in social and political, rather than commercial, terms. To the extent that these 'returns' are specified (e.g. in the form of statutory duties, mission statements, performance targets, etc.), their achievement constitutes part of the organisation's proprietary interest. Because such agencies have to balance a number of objectives, such as the well-being of prospective as well as actual tenants, their proprietary interests will not necessarily be the same as those of their current tenants. The identification, creation and measurement of politico-welfare returns to social landlords are key concerns of this text and will be considered in detail in subsequent chapters. For the time being we will simply say that local housing authorities and housing associations have an interest in providing cost-effective housing for households deemed to be in some form of 'housing need'.

The social returns on housing investment extend beyond the specific concerns of the landlords and tenants of social housing. People and organisations that have no immediate, direct legal stake in a dwelling may still have concerns about its use or condition. These other-party concerns we term *non-proprietary interests* or *externalities*.

Non-proprietary interests

To say that someone has an 'interest' in a property is to say that they have some *stake in* or *duty for* the way in which it is produced, used and looked after. To the extent that its provision, use and maintenance is seen to be of concern to the wider community, housing possesses characteristics that can lead to it being classified as a *social commodity* in which non-proprietary as well as proprietary interests are vested.

Society as a whole may have concerns about the housing stock that go beyond, or are even in conflict with, the interests of those with proprietary stakes in the properties. For example, a housing association or a private company may wish to pursue their welfare or commercial objectives by developing a plot of land with a view to providing dwellings to let. The resultant development might obscure a view, create traffic congestion, destroy a wildlife area, or in some other way affect the interests of others.

Other examples of the ways in which we might consider housing to be a social good include the following.

1. Because nearly all dwellings in all tenures are built to a standard that ensures that they outlive their initial occupiers, housing production caters for future as well as current housing needs and demands. In this sense housing can be regarded as a national social asset, held in trust by one generation for the next.

2. Research findings have long demonstrated a clear link between homelessness, poor housing and people's health and vulnerability to crime.[6] Furthermore, there is a recognised, albeit ill-defined, link between housing conditions and educational performance. The research report, *More than somewhere to live* (1996), commissioned by the National Housing Forum with sponsorship from the Joseph Rowntree Foundation, produced evidence showing that these problems are particularly acute in the rented sector and among the poorest and most vulnerable.[7]

3. Together with roads, schools, hospitals, etc., housing constitutes part of an area's infrastructure and as such, plays a part in the promotion of its economic growth and prosperity. In particular, an appropriate supply of good quality housing is needed to attract a skilled and qualified workforce.

---

6 For selected examples of nineteenth century Parliamentary reports see Pike, E.R., (1966), *Human Documents of the Industrial Revolution*, Unwin. Refer also to commentaries on the influential report into *Inequalities in Health* by Sir Douglas Black and others: e.g. Anderson, J. and Ricci, M. (Eds), *Society and Social Science: A Reader*, The Open University, 1990.

7 There has been an historical reluctance on the part of governments to accept the links between poor housing and social issues. When the Black Report on inequalities in health was completed in 1980 the government rejected its findings on poverty and argued that its recommendations for housing were unrealistic. However, after the Black Report other evidence mounted and in 1994 the Health Secretary, Virginia Bottomley announced a research project into the links between poverty and health, paying particular attention to socio-economic conditions, geography, and ethnicity.

4. Because the condition of an individual dwelling has a 'spill-over effect' on the use values and exchange values of neighbouring properties, how one proprietor maintains or uses his property can affect the interests of neighbouring proprietors. It is in recognition of the interconnected nature of property interests that society gives local planning authorities powers to approve both new construction and alterations to existing buildings. In some instances, the externality interests of neighbours are internalised into the legal interests of a proprietor by means of positive or restrictive covenants.

For all these reasons it is possible to argue that there exists community interests in the housing stock that are external to those of proprietors. The existence of external, non-proprietary, community interests in the size and condition of the housing stock is pointed to as yet another reason for directing public expenditure into the housing system.

Housing as a social service

We will end our discussion on the nature of housing as a commodity by considering the extent to which it might be regarded as a social service. It is often argued that some basic goods and services should be made available to every household irrespective of their ability to pay. This discussion normally focuses on the proposition that the State needs to provide what economists refer to as 'public goods' and 'merit goods'.

Public goods. Pure public goods and services are those things that are provided collectively by the State because individuals operating in a market cannot sensibly pay for them. In other words, by their very nature, their consumption is indivisible: in providing them for one they become available to all. Good examples would be national defence, sewers, and street lighting. Some goods and services *could* be marketed to individuals but society may decide that such an arrangement would be administratively cumbersome or in some other way inconvenient or inappropriate. These are referred to as 'quasi-public goods and services' and might include roads, a police and fire service, and education. The extent to which quasi-public goods and services are financed or administered by the State will to some extent depend upon the political ideology of the government in power.

Dwellings, whether rented or owned, and housing services, such as advice, repairs, maintenance and improvements, are capable of being supplied on an individual basis and therefore do not display the features of pure public goods and services. This means that whether they are provided by the State or by the price system will be a matter of political judgement. Council houses are therefore quasi-public goods and a local authority's housing advice centre is providing a quasi-public service.

Merit goods. These are quasi-public goods and services which society regards as being too important to be left to market forces to provide. The State intervenes to subsidise or regulate their provision or to provide them directly because the community regards them as being particularly meritorious. If left to the market they might be 'under-consumed' or be of an 'inappropriate' type or standard. Education is a good example of a merit service. Society has come to believe that it is in the national interest that all children be educated to some minimum standard and in ways that society, rather than the market, decides.

It might be argued that some minimum standard of housing should be regarded as a *merit service* because the quantity and quality of housing affects the general national interest. This is so because the under-consumption of decent housing impinges on such things as health, educational performance, crime, and the mobility of labour.

The case for State intervention

The case for State intervention in the housing system is usually made in terms of the following logical argument. A completely free-enterprise system of market provision and consumption is inappropriate because the housing market is intrinsically imperfect. Furthermore, some minimum level of 'shelter' is a *necessity* for a humane and civilised life and therefore welfare *ideology* dictates that we should guarantee a basic level of housing to all. In addition to the welfare argument, an agreed minimum level of housing for all should be provided because it is *meritorious*: that is, it is in the general national interest that all people are decently housed. This national interest relates to such issues as public health, civil stability, and an effective economy.

In contemporary Britain there is a general consensus that for social, political and economic reasons, it is desirable that everyone should have access to some minimum level of shelter. However, it follows from what has been argued above, that housing at the level which most people consume it, cannot be regarded as a 'necessity'. Just because food and shelter are basics to life, it does not follow that my steak dinner or my penthouse apartment should be regarded as necessities.

Summary

Housing is an unusual and complex commodity in that it simultaneously possesses the features of personal consumption, private investment and social capital. Various proprietary and non-proprietary interests are associated with each of these features. As we will see in subsequent chapters, these characteristics, together with their associated interests, have important consequences for the ways in which we finance the production, consumption, management and exchange of housing.

CHAPTER 2:
Housing finance, accountability and value-for-money

Because the operational practices and procedures associated with the financing of owner-occupation and the various forms of renting all differ somewhat, much of the later material of this book is organised around a tenure framework. However, we need to recognise that the underlying principles governing the provision, distribution and utilisation of housing finance are independent of tenure. This chapter will therefore consider various ways of categorising housing finance that are not tenure specific and it will confront the central issues of 'accountability' and 'value-for-money'. These ways of thinking about, and assessing the effects of, housing finance need to be grasped at the outset because they permeate the tenure analysis that follows and they provide a cross-tenure coherence to our subsequent descriptions and arguments.

The system of housing finance

One way of appreciating the nature and scope of housing finance is to regard it as a mechanism for linking money inputs (sources of finance) to money outputs (expenditure). Treating housing finance as a system of bridging money inputs and outputs is useful on two counts. Firstly, it highlights the functions to which the finance is eventually put and thereby acts as a reminder that raising and spending money are not ends in themselves; it underlines the point that financial arrangements exist to facilitate proprietary plans and public policies. Secondly, it provides us with a simple conceptual framework and vocabulary that can be used to discuss the financial arrangements associated with all types of housing in all types of tenure.

Figure 2.1 illustrates the idea that *housing finance is a system of money and credit that operates to enable all types of residential property to be produced, managed, acquired, maintained, repaired, renewed and exchanged.* In the diagram a key distinction is made between finance that is used for *capital purposes*, finance that is used for *revenue purposes* and finance that is used to *augment incomes*.

Capital expenditure. Capital expenditure is that incurred for the purpose of acquiring fixed capital formation. Fixed capital formation is composed of assets of a relatively permanent nature and, in a housing context, can be thought of as anything that increases the quantity or quality of the stock. It includes payments made to lawyers, surveyors and other professionals in connection with the purchase of land and existing buildings as well as all the material, labour and other costs incurred in connection with the erection of new buildings. Money spent on

Figure 2.1: Housing finance as a monetary system

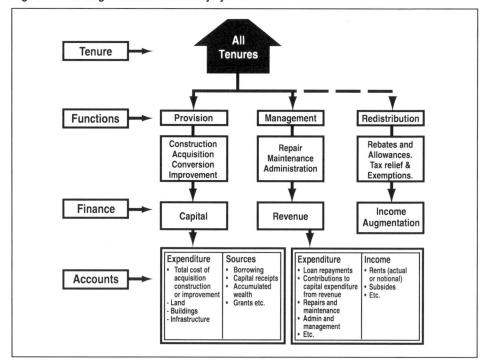

converting or improving, as against maintaining and repairing, the existing stock of dwellings results in more or better quality housing being available and is therefore regarded as capital expenditure in the same way as money spent on constructing new units is so regarded.

Sources of capital. Housing capital expenditure is typically financed by borrowing and/or by the use of accumulated savings, or reserves. It is often financed through the reinvestment of capital receipts from asset sales. Revenue income, grants, and gifts can supplement such sources.

Revenue expenditure. Revenue expenditure is that expenditure incurred in acquiring consumable and other non-permanent goods and services. This type of spending can be referred to as *current* or *consumption* expenditure and is sometimes termed 'running costs' or 'costs-in-use'. In a housing context, it refers to those recurring payments on general administration, loan interest and debt redemption together with those payments made for the purpose of maintaining, repairing and managing the housing stock. In other words, housing revenue expenditure comprises all outgoings incurred as part of the day-to-day provision of housing services together with that incurred in maintaining the real capital assets in a habitable state. Because the costs of servicing loans taken out to purchase capital items are regarded as part of revenue expenditure, capital expenditure decisions can have significant revenue consequences.

Revenue income. Revenue income pays for revenue expenditure. In a housing context, revenue income is derived from rents and/or other trading or employment earnings together with any available investment income or subsidy entitlement. In extreme cases, when a household or agency is unable to pay its recurring revenue costs, creditors may require them to generate the money by liquidating some of their assets.

The relationship between capital and revenue expenditure

The difference between capital and revenue is a theoretical one and, in practice, accounting procedures and conventions sometimes blur the distinction. What gets counted as capital or revenue may, for example, be determined by what funds are available. This has to be kept in mind when considering how various institutions actually classify their expenditure: for example, capital works may be financed from revenue. It is also worth re-emphasising the point made above that *capital expenditure decisions will carry with them future revenue commitments.*

Income augmentation. We have stressed the point that, for most households and agencies, housing is expensive relative to disposable income (i.e. income net of tax). This fact, coupled with society's desire to make it possible for everyone to be housed to some acceptable standard, has led governments at different times to introduce various subsidy arrangements that allow an increase in housing consumption by certain households. The idea is to provide financial help that will enable qualifying households to acquire and enjoy housing or housing-related services that they could not otherwise afford. Such financial help can take the form of rebates and allowances or tax relief and exemptions. There is some debate amongst practitioners and theorists about whether this type of support really is an element of housing finance or whether it should be classified as part of the Social Security system. It is in recognition of this debate that the diagram in Figure 2.1 ties income augmentation into the system of housing finance with a broken rather than a solid line.

Housing functions and housing finance

Having broadly categorised housing finance in terms of capital, revenue and income augmentation, we are in a position to look more closely at the various purposes to which money and credit is put.

Provision
The function of *capital finance* is to pay for new dwellings and for the acquisition, conversion and improvement of existing ones. It is needed to build and to buy: it pays for 'provision' in the widest sense of the word.

Dwellings may contain certain items of relatively expensive equipment such as central heating and double-glazing that are generally regarded as integral elements of the building. In new dwellings they are treated as part of the capital formation.

When such items are installed in existing dwellings they are, in practice, often paid for out of revenue income. Despite this, because they clearly add to, rather than simply maintain, the quality of the property, they are, in principle, real capital investment. This means that accounting practice does not always mirror the economists' theoretical distinction between capital and revenue used in this chapter.

Acquisition finance is required to purchase dwellings that are already in existence. Owner-occupiers and private landlords are the main purchasers of second-hand dwellings, although most local authorities and housing associations acquire properties that they usually improve or convert before letting on to their tenants. Private developers sometimes acquire blocks of dwellings or individual units that they convert or improve and then sell on to private buyers. Much conversion activity takes the form of altering large dwellings into a greater number of smaller units.

Management
Once the real capital formation has been built or acquired, capital expenditure ceases, with the exception of any later improvements, and the proprietor is then faced with all the recurring 'cost-in-use' that we have classified above as revenue expenditure. These costs stem from the need to manage the asset on a day-to-day basis.

Administration forms a major part of the management function, and revenue finance has to be provided to deliver the range of supervisory and support services landlords provide for their tenants and others. In a housing association or local authority housing department administration costs will include office consumables and expenses and the salaries of specialist staff. Some of the employees will operate at a professional level as housing officers and take responsibility for administering the procedures associated with allocations, rent collection, the management of maintenance and providing aid and advice to committees, tenants and the general public. Others will be employed to provide specialist services such as warden support for the elderly, while others will operate at a more technical level to provide such facilities as cleaning and caretaking.

Because over time dwellings and their fixtures and fittings deteriorate or become in some other way obsolete, the management function includes repair, maintenance and renewal services. Most private and social landlords operate a mixture of response and programmed maintenance and repairs.

Whether carried out in-house or contracted out to some other organisation, all housing management functions have to be paid for out of revenue flows. All dwellings have to be managed irrespective of tenure and, in this sense, private landlords and owner-occupiers are just as much housing managers as are the employees of housing associations and local housing authorities. Some day-to-day housing management functions, such as decorating or minor repairs, may be carried out by tenants. Indeed, some specific managerial responsibilities may be identified in a lease or tenancy agreement.

Income augmentation

Alongside the housing finance system, the Social Security system operates to alleviate poverty by redistributing real incomes. Broadly speaking, this works by the central government collecting taxation, part of which it then redistributes in the form of housing and Social Security benefits. In the case of housing benefits and allowances, local authorities act as agents of redistribution for the central authorities. Historically, owner-occupiers have received taxation concessions rather than direct payments or reduced charges.

Redistribution in the form of subsidies, payments, rebates and allowances occurs for two broad reasons. The historic reason has been to help low-income households meet their accommodation expenses. The subsidisation of housing can take many forms and these will be examined in subsequent chapters. At this point we will simply observe that, in recent years, there has been a shift towards fiscal welfare measures (income augmentation), and less reliance on supply-side ('bricks and mortar'), subsidies. The second reason that redistribution may occur is because the government of the day wishes to encourage a particular tenure. The Conservative administrations of the 1980s and 1990s, for example, wanted to encourage owner-occupation and accordingly maintained the system of mortgage tax relief.

Accounting and audit

The records of expenditure and income for a given period are kept in accounts. Periodic account can also be kept of the balance between an organisation's assets and liabilities. The production of audited accounts is an important aspect of the procedure by which those who manage an organisation are made accountable for their actions to some authority such as a body of shareholders, a management committee, councillors, a funding agency or local tax payers.

Types and styles of accounts

Most organisations produce annual accounts and some are legally required to do so. During the year, the organisation will record all of its financial transactions, and at the end of the year these records will be used to produce the final accounts.

The final accounts consist of records that show the income and expenditure for the year and a balance sheet that lists the assets and liabilities held by the organisation at the year end. The assets held will include such things as buildings and land, stocks of goods and debts owed to the organisation. The liabilities will include the amounts owed by the organisation to others in respect of capital (e.g. loans outstanding), and revenue commitments (sundry creditors).

Although all organisations produce accounts and balance sheets, this does not mean that these all look alike or contain the same sort of information: the style of the accounts used will be determined by the needs of the organisation. For example, the accounts of a company contain details of its trading activities, profits made and distributions to shareholders. The accounts of a local authority detail expenditure and income associated with the various services that it has a duty or power to provide, together with local tax receipts and Exchequer subsidies. Owner-occupiers are not required to keep accounts as they are not responsible to others for their housing decisions, but they may choose to keep records for their own information.

The nature and interpretation of accounts

While accountancy and account keeping demand professional skills and qualifications, accounts are no more than the recording in financial terms of the activities undertaken by the organisation over a given period, usually a year, together with an end of period balance of that organisation's outstanding assets and liabilities. From properly prepared annual accounts it should be possible, even for the uninitiated, to comprehend the nature of an organisation's transactions during the period covered and its financial worth as at the end of that period.

Accounts are prepared according to the *prudence principle*. This means that, as far as possible, accountants work with facts rather than opinion, and with past events rather than with future ones. Most accounts are prepared on an *historic* basis and use market-related values. The period for which the accounts are prepared, usually a year, is called *the accounting period*. Because accounts do not deal with the future directly, those wishing to make use of them for planning purposes can only use them to identify trends from transactions that have taken place in previous accounting periods.

Most people who use accounts are not so much interested in being able to do the book-keeping involved in their preparation, as being able to understand and interpret the information recorded in them. As well as allowing for the appraisal of past results, accounts are a source of financial and statistical information that can be used to provide guidance for policy. By careful analysis of accounting records it may be possible to bring to light data that will assist in identifying waste and inappropriate management decisions and help to suggest reforms and economies. In order to use and make sense of accounts it is important to have an appreciation of the organisation's aims.

There is currently much debate about how accounting procedures might be reformed so that the records can be used more effectively as resource management tools, rather than simply as book-keeping entries charting and dating cash flows. This shift in approach is called 'resource accounting' as against 'cash accounting'.

Can 'cash' accounts measure success?

If the organisation's aims can be expressed simply in terms of money flows, then cash accounts can easily be designed to show whether these aims are being achieved. For example, they can show clearly whether the rent charged by a landlord is sufficient to cover the costs of providing the accommodation and earn profit. However, current accounting practice cannot give clear guidance about whether or not the stock is being managed in a business-like way, hence the shift to resource accounting. It is not possible to rely on the accounts alone to determine whether or not an organisation's more complex concerns are being adequately addressed. For example, it is not possible to find out from the accounts whether the rate of juvenile crime will be reduced as a result of the refurbishment of a run-down estate or whether homeless families will be better off in a hostel or in bed-and-breakfast accommodation. Because of their historic nature, cash accounts can only demonstrate in a limited way whether or not an organisation is making the 'best' use of its limited and valuable resources.

Resource budgeting and accruals accounting

In recent years, housing agencies have been expected to become more business-like and to demonstrate that their financial decisions are commercially as well as socially justifiable. This has opened up a debate about the nature of public sector accounting. Traditionally, public sector agencies have tended to record their financial transactions on a simple *cash-flow* basis, rather like a bank statement. Cash-flow accounting allows the organisation to track the periodic balances, the surpluses and deficits, that exist in specific accounts. However, some critics argue that this approach provides a rather restricted form of accountability and public sector spending should be open to more rigorous scrutiny. In particular, they argue the need for an accounting system that provides the sort of information that allows us to judge whether or not the organisation is making the best use of scarce public resources. By the mid-1990s, the Treasury was arguing the need for government departments and public sector agencies to reform their accounting methods to allow for what is termed *resource accounting and budgeting* (RAB). The government plans to introduce RAB fully into the administration of public spending by 2001 as a way of reinforcing its fiscal strategy of clarifying the distinction between capital and current spending (discussed further in subsequent chapters). Resource budgeting will enable the application of cost-benefit analysis to the appraisal of proposed public investments. The Treasury has said that such analysis can even be used to measure the benefit of relatively small-scale discrete investments such as refurbishing a block of housing or acquiring a school playing field.

The idea of RAB is that the accounting records should be kept in such a way that the information they contain helps organisations make decisions about how best to allocate scarce resources between competing ends. That is, resource accounting seeks to present information in a way that will enable managers to make optimal decisions about the use of the valuable and limited resources under their control. Optimal decision-making requires clarity about the objectives of the decision-makers. It cannot be understood simply by reference to the records of cash flows that have been made in a given accounting period: it needs to consider the actual results of spending and investment decisions. In particular, it requires managers and auditors to be able to assess the *actual outcomes* of their decisions against the *planned-for outcomes*. RAB should seek to provide information that will help the organisation to judge the extent that its investment of funds has been effective. In this context the notion of 'effectiveness' has a particular meaning and this is discussed below (see Figure 2.3.).

In a commercial setting 'profitability' is often used as the measure of successful resource budgeting. Housing agencies, however, are usually more concerned with managerial effectiveness than with crude commercial profitability. As we have said, in attempting to optimise the use of resources, we need to match inputs and outputs. The shift towards resource accounting practices involves *matching* costs and revenues to one another as far as their relationship can be established, and recording financial transactions on an *accruals* rather than on a *cash* basis.

To measure the commercial or social viability of a project or individual asset, accounts need to be kept in accordance with what is known as the *matching principle*. This states that, as far as possible, costs should be set against the revenue that they generate at the point in time when this arises. If they are not so matched then it becomes difficult to calculate the true return on the committed expenditure. The idea of the *matching principle* is that in order to determine the social or commercial return, revenue must be compared or 'matched' with all the costs that have been incurred in earning it. We are simply trying to answer the question, 'Did we make the best use of our limited and valuable resources?' In addressing this crucial question, we need to engage in resources accounting so that we can balance inputs with outputs, match effort with accomplishment, and compare what we planned for with what actually happened.

As well as embracing the *matching principle*, the effective measure of commercial or social profit and loss also requires accounts to be kept in accordance with the *accruals concept*. This states that to acquire a true profit and loss picture for a specific period (e.g. a financial year), we should recognise revenues and costs as they are earned or incurred, rather than as they are received or paid out, as occurs in the cash-flow approach. In accruals calculations, expenses are recognised, although not necessarily recorded, in the period in which they are incurred rather than in that in which money happens to be paid for them. For example, if it costs £10,000 a year to rent a building then there is an expense of £10,000 to be recognised each year regardless of how or when the rent is paid. If, for example, it is paid biannually in advance, the accruals principle states that it would be inappropriate to charge £20,000 as an expense for year one. An *accrued charge* is an expense that has been incurred as at a particular date but not yet invoiced or paid. An *accrued revenue* is an income that has been earned but not yet recorded.

An important effect of the accruals approach is that capital expenditure is not all recorded as a cost in the year in which the asset is acquired. The front-loading of capital costs into the year of acquisition can act as an investment disincentive. Accruals accounting has the effect of reducing the recorded cost in the first year of investment and enables a longer-term rational view of the project's viability to be taken. Some argue that the change will remove a large part of the advantage that private landlords have over social landlords in accounting for investment, and thus will reduce the bias against investment in the public sector (England, M., 1997 p70).

The Treasury is considering the proposition that once resource accounting procedures are established in central and local government departments and public sector agencies, a move should be made to the next logical step which is *resource budgeting*. Resource budgeting involves establishing techniques for appraising how to make the best use of available financial resources. In terms of the total sums involved, some of the most significant financial corporate decisions involve expenditures to acquire capital assets.

Accounting for the provision of capital assets

The process of planning and evaluating proposals for investment in fixed assets is called *capital budgeting*. Capital budgeting is about investing in the future and involves either committing the organisation's accumulated savings to the acquisition or improvement of an asset or the borrowing of funds so to do. The process of appraisal entails the use of *opportunity costing* techniques that are designed to ensure that the available money capital is being put to its best possible use. These techniques are necessary because *historic* accounts are designed to record the past rather than appraise the future. Before identifying the sort of techniques that might be used in capital budgeting, we need to be clear about the nature of the problem that they are seeking to overcome.

The problem: What we spend now on plant, buildings and equipment will have significant consequences for the long-run financial health of the organisation. Organisations can benefit from good capital budgeting decisions and suffer from bad ones for many years. Decisions are complicated by the fact that appraisals have to be made from estimates of future operating costs and returns which, by their nature, involve a considerable degree of uncertainty and cannot be deduced from accounts that have been produced on the *prudence principle*. It also has to be recognised that, compared with revenue spending, capital budgeting often commits relatively large amounts of money for relatively long periods of time. Furthermore, capital investment decisions tend to be difficult or impossible to reverse once the funds have been committed and the project begun.

In common with other welfare agencies, housing organisations need to take account of a wide range of non-financial factors when making capital budgeting decisions. Housing investment produces valued social returns that are reflected in the findings of tenant satisfaction surveys and in reduced levels of urban disutility such as crime and disease. However, restrictions on the growth in public expenditure, together with shifts in emphasis towards public/private partnership arrangements, means that social housing investments are also expected to generate some quantifiable financial return. Without this return, investors will not be willing to make funds available to finance schemes and the agencies themselves will not be able to generate sufficient funds for their own future investment projects.

The techniques: There are a great number of sophisticated techniques for identifying and evaluating the financial and non-financial aspects of capital budgeting. These techniques are often used in combination. The choice of technique(s) will largely depend on the nature of the proposed investment and what it is that the organisation is seeking to achieve by the commitment of funds. Investment appraisal is a complex field and we will here simply point to four commonly used techniques by way of illustration.

1. *Cost-benefit analysis.* This technique seeks to value all the relevant gains and losses resulting from a proposed investment, including those of an intangible nature. A CBA operates within a specified time profile and discounting techniques are used to put a present value on future costs and benefits.

2. *Pay-back period.* This technique focuses on the length of time necessary to recover the entire cost of the investment from the resulting annual net cash-flow.

3. *Return on average investment.* This technique assesses viability by reference to an assessment of the expected average annual net income from an investment expressed as a percentage of the average amount invested.

4. *Discounting future cash flows.* Discounting is the process by which we seek to determine the present value of future cash flows. The present value of a future cash-flow is the amount that a knowledgeable investor would pay today for the right to receive that future amount. This will depend on the amount of the future payment, the length of time until the future payment will be received, and the rate of return required by the investor.

Accounting for the use of capital assets

Compulsory competitive tendering and the increasing tendency for public agencies to compete with the private sector, has made it necessary to know the true cost of a service, including the costs of managing and maintaining the stock of fixed assets. This, coupled with political pressure for public agencies to be more commercially orientated, has led a number of local authorities and other agencies to introduce a system of capital accounting that enables them to estimate the value of their fixed assets, make appropriate asset-use charges to revenue, and make allowances for depreciation.

Over time fixed assets can have their values eroded by wear and tear or obsolescence. The accruals principle states that this loss of value should be accounted for in the accounting period in which it occurred. This necessitates an adjustment to be made before calculating the profit or loss for the period in question. This adjustment is termed *depreciation*. Depreciation is a real cost of service provision and the matching principle requires a profit or loss calculation to compare revenue earned with *all of the costs* that have been incurred in earning it.

Audit and financial accountability

Investment appraisal decisions are the responsibility of management and, because the returns are long-term, their effectiveness cannot be submitted to an annual audit. However, financial accountability does require the annual auditing of historic accounts. This means that external accountants specialising in audit work check the accounts and certify that they have been prepared in accordance with legislation and good accounting practice. The external auditors must be independent of the organisation whose accounts are being checked and they cannot be employees of that organisation. Large organisations also have internal auditors who are employees with responsibilities for ensuring that the financial systems of the organisation are properly designed and implemented.

Book-keepers and auditors record and check how money flows in and out of an organisation. Accountants rarely introduce evaluative goals into published accounts even when quantification of such goals would not be controversial. Their primary concern is to ensure clarity, transparency and probity with respect to financial transactions. It is for policy-makers and managers to determine criteria for measuring an organisation's success and to find evidence of achievement from a wide range of sources of which the published accounts will be just one.

Accountability and value-for-money

We will now turn to a different level of accountability by moving our attention from the records of financial flows, the accounts, to the operational results of financial employment, the functions (see Figure 2.1). Finance is put to work with a view to generating some form of return or yield; so the question arises, 'How is that return measured and accounted for?'

If the financing of housing could be treated simply as a free-enterprise, commercial activity, questions of accountability and yield would be fairly straightforward. Where market ideology prevails, market forces are relied upon to establish accountability, and returns are equated with trading profits and capital appreciation. Firms operating in the unsubsidised, free-enterprise sector of the economy are directly accountable to those proprietors who have a freehold, share or stock-holding interest in the company. Economic theory assumes that, under competitive conditions, the proprietary interests of the freeholder, sole trader, partners or shareholders automatically coincide with those of consumers[1]. Under such arrangements, profit, including capital appreciation of assets, is assumed to be the measure of success.

---

1   In market theory this idea of the coincidence of interests is encapsulated by the phrase 'consumer sovereignty'.

The notion that commercial competition is conducive to the generation of value-for-money led the Conservative administrations of the 1980s and 1990s to introduce a process of compulsory competitive tendering (CCT), into a range of local government services that included housing. Under CCT, authorities were not allowed to carry out work using their own employees unless the work had first been exposed to competition, and the in-house workforce met centrally determined specified financial objectives each year. In 1997 the in-coming Labour administration modified the process of CCT by introducing what they termed the 'best value' concept. This states that councils should not be forced to put their services out to tender, but will be required to obtain what they termed 'best value'. The idea of best value is that an authority that puts people first will seek to provide services that bear comparison with the best. Not just the best that other authorities provide but with the best that is on offer from both the private and public sectors.

In introducing the idea of best value, the Labour Party manifesto stated that *'We reject the dogmatic view that services must be privatised to be of high quality, but equally we see no reason why a service should be delivered directly if other, more efficient means are available.'* This means that the notion of best value is an aspect of the government's partnership philosophy which argues that *'to maximise investment in the renewal of our infrastructure, public and private sectors must work together in a more modern and effective partnership.'* (Chancellor's Statement on the EFSR, HM Treasury News release 96/98, June 1998). The recent White Paper, *Modern Local Government: In Touch with the People*, (1998) made it clear that best value is seen by the government as the key to making councils more efficient. Under new legislation, councils now have a duty to deliver services such as housing to clear standards – covering cost and quality – by the most effective, economic and efficient means available. In addition, best value is seen as a vehicle to make councils more accountable to local people and to provide a framework within which to tackle difficult 'cross-cutting' issues that require co-ordinated action by a number of different services or agencies. The notion of best value is considered in more detail in Chapter 8 which looks at local government finance.

As we have seen (Chapter 1), housing cannot simply be treated as a commercial activity; because of its social and welfare outputs, criteria other than profit need to be taken into account in assessing returns on monies directed to its production and consumption. For this reason the question, 'How is the return to be measured and accounted for?' usually takes the form, 'How do we know whether we are getting value-for-money?' To answer this question we need to be clear about who constitutes the 'we' and what constitutes the 'value'.

We began to address these questions in the previous chapter by arguing that capital and revenue finance is employed to serve the interests of those with some form of proprietary stake in the dwelling or dwellings. We also pointed to the existence of non-proprietary interests in housing investment and consumption. Money spent on the provision and consumption of housing can enhance or damage the interests of a range of people and organisations including occupiers, landlords, neighbours, local and national taxpayers, and future generations. So any attempt to measure value-for-money has to begin by clarifying the issues, 'whose money?' and 'whose value?' By identifying the proprietary and non-proprietary interests involved in the employment of housing finance we automatically confront the question of what it is that constitutes value. In identifying who gains and who loses in the employment of housing finance, we necessarily have to differentiate between use value, investment value (both financial and social) and exchange value (see Figures 1.2 and 2.2).

Figure 2.2: Unpacking the notion of value-for-money

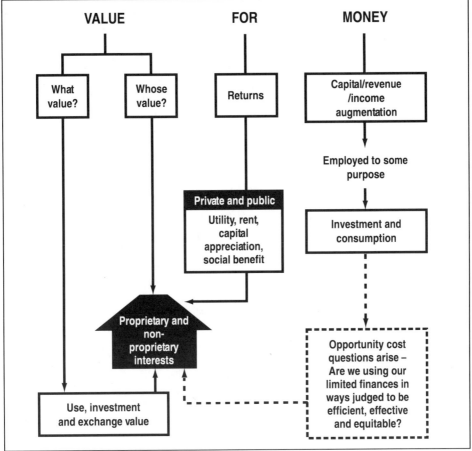

Figure 2.2 illustrates that it is proprietary interests that are at the heart of any analysis of value-for-money (VFM) in housing. That is, any VFM analysis must begin by clarifying who it is that pays the money and who it is that receives the value. Once this is established, the key question then arises, 'Given our concerns about these particular proprietary responsibilities and interests, are we making the optimum use of our limited funds?' In a specific context, this important question might be expressed as, 'Is the company's money being employed to the best

advantage of the shareholders?' Or perhaps, 'Is the housing association achieving its mission by spending this money in this way?' Or, 'Would the local authority be better advised spending its capital receipts repairing its housing stock rather than repaying debt?' Such questions emphasise the importance of what economists refer to as *opportunity costs*. An opportunity cost is a cost conceived of in terms of the best alternative foregone. It is a concept used by economists to underline the fact that financial and other resources are limited and that once used up in one way they are no longer available to be used in some other way.

The notion of *opportunity cost* emphasises the point that achieving value-for-money involves making the 'best' use of what we have. However, because so many interests are associated with housing, the determination of what counts as the best use of financial resources in this field is far from straightforward. One way of dealing with the issue that is advocated by bodies such as the Audit Commission and the Chartered Institute of Housing is to assess the extent to which the proprietary and/or non-proprietary objectives are being achieved in ways that can be judged to be efficient, effective and fair.

Figure 2.3: Efficiency, effectiveness, equity and experience

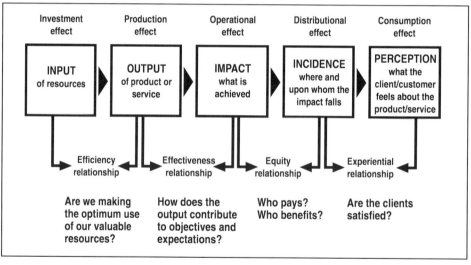

Measuring VFM

Because it is a relative notion, within an organisation, VFM is usually assessed against a set of agreed benchmarks. Publicly announced performance indicators will inevitably influence what employees do and how they do it – what you say you are going to measure is what you tend to get. For this reason, it is important for the organisation to select its indicators with care and to be clear about the relative importance that is attached to each. There is now an expectation that all social landlords who receive public subsidy must establish procedures that set quality and performance standards against which it is possible to measure the extent to which they are delivering their services in a way that delivers VFM.

Public sector service providers that have tax raising or precepting powers have a duty to provide *best value* (see above). This systematic approach to giving VFM is discussed in Chapter 8. In the particular case of housing authorities, the government has introduced an inspectorate that is intended to help improve the management of council housing, set standards for performance and guarantee high quality of investment.

Efficiency and VFM

Figure 2.3 indicates that efficiency is determined by considering the relationship between inputs and outputs. The idea of efficiency has its roots in engineering where the efficiency of an engine is calculated in terms of how much energy input is needed to generate a unit of power output[2]. Like an engine, an organisation is deemed to be operating below its optimum level of efficiency if either it could produce the same output with fewer resources or if, with the same resources, it could produce a greater output. It must be remembered that in the context of providing goods and services, quality as well as quantity is an aspect of output. This means that a better quality service or product would constitute an increase in output just as much as would a service expansion or an increase in the number of units produced.

Figure 2.4: The concept of 'efficiency'

Ways of viewing efficiency				
Business management	Economic	Theory	Business accountancy	Public sector planning
Output	Goods & services	Marginal social benefit	Yield	Social return
Input	Resources	Marginal social cost	Investment	Public investment

Given its concern with opportunity costs, economic theory equates output with the results of economic activity, such as goods and services, and inputs with the factors of production, the limited resources. An assumption is made that if, measured in terms of market values, any additional employment of resources, the marginal costs, produces a more than proportional increase in goods and services, a marginal benefit, then some improvement in efficiency has taken place. In the public sector the marginal benefit might be seen as some form of social return (e.g. better health or less crime), and the marginal cost is invariable seen as public expenditure.

---

2   Indeed, some contemporary management theorists use the word 're-engineering' when referring to the process of restructuring corporate arrangements with a view to enhancing an organisation's efficiency.

It is sometimes argued that, in the context of public and welfare services, current debates about the need for greater efficiency has a hidden political dimension. The contention is that as a justifying notion, 'efficiency' is intellectually sympathetic to free-enterprise market attitudes and many of those who are calling for 'more efficiency' in the running of public services are seeking to ally themselves with the core values of the private sector. In this way the notion of efficiency has been used to impose business management and budgetary arrangements on public sector and other welfare agencies. The concerns here are twofold. Firstly, when welfare organisations are reformed with efficiency 'savings' in mind, this occurs in a *managed* rather than a *free-enterprise* market, and when detached from the discipline of real market forces, the application of business management ideas can become procedural and unresponsive. A managed market is insulated from the warning bells of falling profits and other market signals that exist under proper free-enterprise arrangements and, as a result, there is a danger that, swept forward on an unconstrained wave of management ideology, the reforms may go too far. The second concern is that efficiency criteria tend to measure success in a relatively short-term time frame, giving undue weight to current cost savings and under-valuing longer-term effectiveness.

Effectiveness and VFM

Concerns like those mentioned above mean that the achievement of VFM involves more than making an efficient use of scarce resources. Most organisations are concerned to assess the output against its impact as well as against the quantity of resources used up in its production. The effectiveness of an output is assessed in terms of how well it contributes to the key objectives and expectations of those with some interest in the organisation's operations (see Figure 2.3).

Increasingly, effectiveness criteria are prescribed by society in the form of explicit expectations, regulations, laws and externally imposed performance targets. In the case of permanent organisations, like local authorities and housing associations, that utilise durable assets, effective performance has to be put into some time profile. We need to assess the future consequences as well as the current outcomes of putting money into housing.

Effective financial management of any organisation involves *meeting* proprietary plans and prevailing societal expectations (non-proprietary interests), in the near future, *adapting and developing* to accommodate changing needs and demands in the intermediate future, and *surviving* into the distant future.

Equity and VFM

Any consideration of effectiveness is likely to bring to the fore questions of equity. In cases where public money or the public interest is involved there is likely to be a particular concern about the distribution of costs and benefits that result from an employment of resources. Most major decisions made by social housing agencies have to be demonstrably fair as well as effective and efficient.

Economic and financial decisions change situations – they have an impact. As a result, some people are made better off and some people are made worse off. The positive and negative outcomes of such decisions, the marginal social costs and benefits, are distributed differentially to different interest groups. So when we change things by spending money we should be clear about who is going to gain and who is going to pay or in some other way lose out.

Assessing the impact of financial decisions again brings up questions of time and inter-generational justice. Costs and benefits associated with housing decisions often come on stream at different times so it is possible for one generation of tenants or occupiers to enjoy or pay for the spending decisions made at some other time. This can be illustrated by reference to the issue of paying for major repairs. If future repairs are paid for by means of a sinking fund, then the burden will fall on current rent payers. If, on the other hand, they are paid for by a loan taken out at the time of the works, then future loan charges will displace the cost burden onto the rents of future tenants.

Experience and VFM

There is an old Swiss proverb that says, 'Don't ask the doctor, ask the patient'. We should never lose sight of the fact that consumption is the ultimate purpose of all economic activity. What the customer or client feels about the service or product is of prime importance. In the free-enterprise sector of the economy, market forces operate to reward those firms whose output is in demand and commercially punish those whose products are not in demand. In recent years public sector and other welfare organisations have made a conscious effort to monitor user satisfaction and feed the results into their policy-making processes. The argument here is that if users are unsatisfied there must be doubts about whether the organisation is achieving value-for-money. In recent years a number of sophisticated but easy-to-use computer packages have been developed to help social landlords collect, organise and evaluate tenant priorities.

Economy and VFM

In discussing value-for-money, some commentators make reference to the need for 'economy'. In so doing, they are referring to the act of acquiring resources and are making the point that raw materials and other factors of production should be bought as cheaply as possible so long as they are commensurate with minimum specifications. As economy is concerned with the price of inputs, it is more sensible to treat it as an aspect of 'efficiency' than as a separate category.

Conclusion

This chapter has defined housing finance as a system of money and credit that operates to enable all types of residential property to be built, acquired, improved, maintained, repaired, renewed, and exchanged. It has categorised the elements of the system in terms of the functions to which the money is put. It has made the point that the application of finance to housing brings to the fore important issues about accountability and value-for-money and it offers a way of thinking and talking about these issues.

The real life system of housing finance is sometimes referred to as *the housing finance regime*. The current regime has evolved over a long period and within this evolution has come a wide range of financial practices and procedures that give the appearance of great complexity. The best way of dealing with this apparent complexity is to hold to models of the overall system that are clear and coherent. In this way, and only in this way, will it be appreciated that, in essence, housing finance is a straightforward subject.

In subsequent chapters the models we have built here will be used as conceptual frameworks to describe and discuss how housing finance currently operates in the different tenures. In so doing, we will find that accountability and value-for-money are constant themes.

CHAPTER 3:
The need-price dilemma and the affordability gap

In Chapter 5 we will consider the wider political, social and economic reasons lying behind the arguments for State involvement in the housing finance system. This chapter will focus on reasons for intervention that are associated with proprietary interests. In particular, we will consider the argument that one key reason for State intervention is to provide appropriate accommodation for those households who are unable to pay for it out of their disposable incomes.

The 'need-price' dilemma

The 'need-price dilemma' arises because everyone requires some minimum standard of residential accommodation in order to enjoy a dignified and healthy life, but for many low-income households access to such accommodation is not possible under free market arrangements. The 'need-price dilemma' can be summarised thus:

Dwellings are primary consumption goods but are expensive relative to disposable incomes.

It is said that housing, along with such things as food, clothing and health care, is no ordinary consumer commodity. It is of primary importance because a home is central to a decent human existence. This idea was clearly expressed by the Royal Institution of Chartered Surveyors in its evidence to the Inquiry into British Housing in the 1980s.

'The principal objective of national housing policies should be to ensure that, as far as possible, every household shall be able to occupy a dwelling of a size, type, standard and location suitable to its needs, free from nuisance, harassment or arbitrary eviction.' (NFHA, 1986, p151).

A broad statement of this kind is no more than a hope statement indicating a general policy direction. As the Inquiry itself pointed out, it raises more questions than it answers (NFHA, 1985, p7.). In particular, it raises the following fundamental questions.

- What is housing need?
- What is an affordable rent or price?
- Are rent structures equitable?
- To what extent can market forces be relied upon to achieve society's housing objectives?

- If market forces fail to achieve the objective of a decent home for everyone at a price they can afford, what should the State do about it?

The first four questions will be considered in this chapter. The last question provides a focus for much of the rest of the book.

What is housing need?

Although in the second half of the nineteenth century there was a good deal of official and Parliamentary concern shown about the living conditions of the poorer working classes, there was no meaningful intervention in the housing market until the outbreak of war in 1914. Even then, the rent control measures that were introduced in 1915 were seen as a temporary wartime expediency rather than a fundamental policy shift towards a social service approach to housing provision.

After 1919, the Liberal Party's election campaign to build 'homes fit for heroes', opened up the debate about whether market forces alone could be relied upon to meet the housing objectives of post-war society. Once the idea of housing as a social service had been mooted, it brought to the fore the question of what distinguishes the social policy concept of *need* from the market economic concept of *housing demand*.[1] The twentieth century concept of *housing need* has gradually emerged as a result of this questioning. By the end of the First World War the idea was established that the basic housing requirements of the 'working classes' were, in some degree, a concern of central government and should not be left to the vagaries of market forces and the charitable instincts of individual benefactors and parish officials. By requiring all local authorities to prepare plans to meet 'local housing needs', the Town and Country Planning Act 1919 set in place a statutory framework that would allow the provision of basic housing to be treated as a social service.

Today, the primary responsibility for assessing housing needs still resides with the local authority (under Section 8 of the Housing Act 1985). As we will see later in the book, each local authority is currently required to demonstrate patterns of housing need within its area in order to support its housing investment programme and its bid for central resources and the right to borrow money. It is expected to act as an 'enabler' that identifies needs and establishes plans to close any gap in provision. This no longer means that the authority necessarily has to provide housing and housing-related services itself. Local housing associations and other registered social landlords are expected to work with the local authority to help it define its enabling role and to produce solutions to any local needs problem.

The notion of *housing need* can apply to an individual household or to a geographical area.

---

1   Jonathan Bradshaw has pointed out (McLachlan, 1972), that the concept of social need is inherent in the idea of social service. Indeed, the history of the social services is, in large part, the story of how society came to recognise the existence of social needs and then organise itself to meet them.

Defining the needs of a household

The efficient, effective and equitable provision of any social service is dependent upon an understanding of what constitutes the needs of those who qualify to receive it. 'Social need' is a *contested concept* in so far as it can mean somewhat different things in different contexts. Jonathan Bradshaw has usefully distinguished between four contrasting categories of social need as used by administrators, politicians and researchers (McLachlan, 1972).

1. *Normative need* is what some expert or authority defines as need in a given situation. It specifies some acceptable norm of provision to which everyone should have access, so that if an individual's or group's consumption falls short of this standard they become identified as being in need. This category is sometimes referred to as 'postulated need' because it defines the taken-for-granted minimum standard that the authority or expert declares should be available to all.

   Normative definitions underline the fact that the issue of need assessment is really an aspect of society's desire to establish minimum standards. Such definitions are specific to time and place and are tied to the values and attitudes of those who set the norms. These norms might be postulated by an Act of Parliament, by a local authority, a management committee, an administrator, a professional body, a research group, or some other agency claiming authority or expertise. Building regulations, Parker Morris space standards, fitness standards, and point assessment systems all provide housing norm reference points for assessing housing need.

2. *Felt need* refers to an individual's own assessment of his or her requirements. This category of need is assessed by survey techniques involving questionnaires and interviews. In the private housing sector, for example, the volume builders sometimes employ market researchers to carry out consumer preference surveys to find out what type or style of housing is likely to sell well in a particular area. In the social housing sectors, felt need surveys have been employed to guide those producing design briefs for special needs housing such as sheltered schemes for the elderly. Many social landlords use the returns of tenant satisfaction surveys to provide service performance measures that help to check whether the agency is giving value-for-money (refer to the notion of a *consumption effect* in Figure 2.3).

   The highly subjective nature of felt need means that although it can be used to inform both the strategic planning and the day-to-day operational decisions of social landlords, it cannot be used to establish allocation eligibility criteria.

3. *Expressed need* is manifested when a felt need is acted upon. The way most of us express our felt needs most of the time is by purchasing goods and services. Effective demand is thus a form of expressed need: it is a felt need,

or a 'want', expressed in a market by spending money. In the social rented sectors, where a limited supply of dwellings and tenancies are allocated rather than sold, would-be occupiers express their felt housing needs by filling in application forms and registering their names on waiting lists.

4. *Comparative need* is defined in terms of the characteristics of those who are already in receipt of the service. If other people in similar circumstances and with the same need characteristics are not in receipt of the service then they are defined as being in comparative need. This measure underlines the requirement for open and even-handed treatment in the distribution of services to applicants. That is, a housing agency should establish value-for-money indicators that assess the distributional effects of service provision (refer to Figure 2.3).

Defining the needs of a geographical area

The central authorities require local authorities to prepare housing strategies and operational plans before allocating grants and credit approvals (see Chapters 9 and 10). A local housing needs assessment should be the starting point for devising a housing strategy. Comprehensive and up-to-date information on the nature and scale of current and future housing needs across all tenures is needed as a basis for identifying priorities, evaluating options, developing programmes, and targeting investment.

The cheapest and easiest way of assessing the social housing needs of an area is to refer to the registers of *expressed* need. Although local waiting lists offer a readily accessible source of information, they provide an inadequate measure of need for a number of reasons. They are seldom up-to-date because when applicants move to some other district or solve their housing problems through the offices of other agencies, they may not bother to withdraw their applications. On the other hand, lists will fail to recognise the needs of those who are excluded from registering because they do not possess the appropriate qualifying characteristics. They fail to register those who are judged to be in need by some normative or comparative standard but who nevertheless do not feel in need. They also fail to account for those who feel in need of rehousing but who do not bother, or who mistakenly believe that they do not qualify to register.

As well as being out-of-date and incomplete, waiting lists are time-specific. Because they only register current expressions of need they cannot be used to assess future requirements. In assessing the future needs for social rented housing we have to employ a more dynamic methodology that allows us to project trends in household formation, tenure moves and private sector provision so that some crude figure for social demand can be estimated. This estimate can then be compared with current supply projections, planned new social output plus expected relets, to determine whether there is likely to be a crude surplus or deficit for the period under review. A more refined estimate of future need can then be sought by adjusting this crude residual to take account of such factors as stock condition and location, household fit, and affordability.[2]

A needs assessment typically involves:

- the collation and analysis of existing internal and external data on housing needs;
- a household survey to gather data on socio-economic circumstances and both normative and felt measures of need;
- an analysis of the local housing market and, in particular, its capacity to provide accommodation for private renting and owner-occupation.

This information is then used to produce:

- a household/stock balance;
- a measure of stock/needs mismatches (e.g. in terms of suitability, condition, and location);
- an assessment of the affordability of available accommodation;
- an assessment of the shortfall between market provision and overall need over the period covered by the strategy.

The *comparative* concept can be applied to the assessment of the needs of geographical areas. Part of the government's annual allocation of public funds to housing is distributed into the regions on the basis of an assessment of comparative local needs. Although the central authorities have a good deal of political discretion over which region gets what, their allocation decisions have been informed by indices of housing need that aim to ensure that limited resources are distributed in a way that is felt to be objectively fair. In this way, a major element of funding has been distributed to the local authority regions by procedures that make reference to indices of need.[3] The central authorities seek to measure and weigh the need for local housing expenditure by reference to these indices as well as to broader regional investment strategies. The indices include statistical series and survey data relating to local house conditions and

---

2   A review and critique of need assessment methods can be found in Whitehead, C. and Kleinman, M.A., *Review of Housing Needs Assessment*, The Housing Corporation, 1992. Guidance and examples of good practice are also given in the CIH *Good Practice Briefing, Issue 7*, April 1997. See also *National Housing Federation, Reinvestment Strategies: A Good Practice Guide*, 1997, Chapter 3.

3   In England, for example, The Generalised Needs Index (GNI), has been used to distribute grants and permissions to borrow to local authorities. Parallel allocations are distributed to the regional offices of the Housing Corporation by referencing the Housing Needs Index (HNI). The government is currently reviewing the allocation procedures with a view to constructing a unified approach to measuring the regional needs for additional social housing. This would initially take the form of a single consolidated New Provision Indicator (NPI), as a common element within both the GNI and the HNI. The intention is eventually to create a single NPI that can be used to calculate the need for all new social housing investment.

demographic characteristics that are deemed to reflect housing need. In the future it is likely that such formulaic mechanisms for distribution will become less influential. As we will see later in the book, the government is shifting the emphasis towards more flexible 'strategic' approaches to allocating resources and spending approvals.

The 'affordability' debate

Although the pricing question has long been at the forefront of the housing policy debate, there is no universally accepted definition of *affordability*. Without such a definition it is not possible to produce any officially accepted statistics measuring the number of households living in *unaffordable* housing.

The question of affordability arises from the fact that, for most people, good quality housing is expensive relative to their incomes.[4] Affordability only becomes an issue when the State normatively defines some minimum level of housing provision as a *merit need*. If the State was prepared to allow the poor to live in mean, insanitary and over-crowded hovels, the affordability question would not arise.

The problem of defining affordability

There are three broad ways of analysing affordability. These are; 1. the ratio approach, 2. the benchmark approach, and 3. the residual approach.

The ratio approach considers the percentage of income that is expended on housing. This was an established way of thinking about affordability by the end of the nineteenth century. At that time people often quoted a rule of thumb that said *one week's wages equals one month's rent*. In this way there was a popular belief that to be affordable, rents should not be more than 25 per cent of a household's income.

In the late nineteenth century, Hermann Schwarbe pointed to a significant statistical relationship between the income growth of households and their housing-related outgoings. Schwarbe was the Director of the Berlin Statistical Bureau and in that capacity brought together various statistical series that illustrated that the burden of housing expenditure was proportionally heavier for the poor than it was for the rich. The point he made was that, although the rich tended to spend more on their housing in *absolute* terms, the poor tended to spend more *relative* to their total disposable incomes. In 1867 he published his findings and presented them in a form that has become known as Schwarbe's Law of Rent. The 'law' states that; *a*

---

4   The production of housing involves the use of land, a wide range of materials and much craft and professional expertise. For these reasons most dwellings cannot be regarded as being expensive *per se*. That is, although they are expensive relative to income, they are not expensive relative to the resources that get used up in their design, manufacture, assembly, marketing and exchange.

household's proportion of disposable income devoted to housing falls as total disposable income rises.[5]

Schwarbe's Law points to a policy approach to the question of affordability that seeks to determine an 'appropriate' income-to-rent ratio. Taking this approach, Schwarbe himself argued that, in principle, no household should be expected to pay more than 20 per cent of their net disposable income on occupation costs.

Until recently the income-to-rent ratio approach dominated the debate about what constitutes an affordable rent for social housing. In particular, the National Housing Federation, previously the National Federation of Housing Associations, has commented at different times in terms of such a ratio (see below).

The benchmark approach considers what is affordable by reference to some fixed level of expenditure that is assumed to be reasonable.[6] Much of the twentieth century debate has focused on the benchmark idea. The 1919 Act required council house rents to be comparable with controlled rents in the private sector, and, since that time, market theorists have consistently argued that the rents charged for social housing should be related to, albeit less than, what the market would charge. Welfare theorists, on the other hand, have tended to look to some measure of subsistence income as a benchmark guide to affordable rent levels, by arguing that rents should be within the reach of those on benefit or those in low paid employment.

The residual approach takes into account that in recent years some people have argued that both the ratio and the benchmark approaches are inadequate and that a more appropriate approach would be to consider residual income. The argument here is that affordability is better assessed by reference to the financial resources that remain available to a household once the rent and other housing costs have been met. They argue the need to consider the overall financial predicament of the household so that the following key question can be posed: '*Is the residual income left over after meeting housing outgoings adequate to cover the other necessities of living?*'

Defining affordability for a particular household

It should be recognised that, when applied to a specific household, each of the approaches mentioned above has limitations as an instrument of needs analysis. A low ratio may be the result of living in poor standard housing. Similarly, a benchmark or residual measure will tell us little or nothing about the actual living conditions of those who are above the mark or seeking to survive on the residual.

---

5   In economic theory this situation would represent an income elasticity of housing demand of less than one.

6   The notion of a 'benchmark' is taken from surveying and refers to a fixed reference point on a stone or post against which other elevations can be measured.

As well as price and income, issues of 'quality' need to be considered. In this context, quality may include more than the physical condition of the dwelling. It could include such factors as overcrowding, security of tenure, accessibility to neighbourhood facilities, and travel-to-work costs.

In any particular case, the determination of what should count as an affordable payment will turn on our view of what is reasonable bearing in mind the household's circumstances and financial resources. Although the general notion of *affordability* is easy enough to grasp, over the years there has been much discussion and little agreement about how to define precisely what should count as affordable for a particular household at a particular point in their housing career.

Whether they are defining affordability by reference to a ratio, a benchmark, or a residual, there is little consensus amongst academic and practitioner commentators about what costs of occupation should be included in the calculation. Any workable definition will involve making judgements about whether or not to include such items as heating, maintenance, depreciation, insurance, etc. Affordability calculations could, but seldom do, take account of the fact that occupation costs interact. For example, money spent servicing a loan, or in higher rental charges, taken out, or imposed, to improve the dwelling's energy efficiency, will add to direct housing costs but will enhance the property's value and reduce fuel bills. Similarly, over a given period, the higher rental charges of a centrally located dwelling may be more than offset by travel cost savings. It is interesting that travel-to-work costs are usually seen as significant in housing location theory but are usually excluded from affordability studies.

Because a particular household's needs can vary over time and needs vary as between households, an effective affordability policy must establish, not one, but a range of normative standards. Such a policy will seek to give every household access to housing appropriate to its needs at a price that does not impose an unreasonable burden on its disposable income. Personal and official attitudes to affordability are, to some extent tenure-dependent.

Owner-occupation and affordability

A crude house price-to-earnings ratio is sometimes used as a general measure of affordability in this sector. Reference to such a measure helps to emphasise the cyclical nature of house price inflation and shows that the point at which the household gained access to the tenure in part determines the costs of home-ownership. The point needs to be made, however, that because most owners acquire their first homes by taking out a variable interest mortgage loan, interest rates, as well as purchase prices, affect the month-by-month costs of occupation. Indeed, to make meaningful cross-tenure or inter-household comparisons, we need to conceive of the costs of owner-occupation not so much in terms of the purchase price but rather in terms of the week-by-week outgoings that the household has to pay in order to maintain its occupancy. In addition to loan interest payments these outgoings will include building insurance premiums. The costs of owner-occupation might also be considered to include the opportunity costs of any capital invested in the property and some actual or notional annual sum that is assumed to be set aside for repairs and maintenance.

Interest rate fluctuations mean that in the medium term, affordability tends to be a more unpredictable and volatile factor for owners than it does for renters. In the last quarter of 1993, for example, the TSB Affordability Index indicated that a typical first-time buyer would need to spend 26 per cent of net income on mortgage payments compared with 67 per cent in the first quarter of 1990. It should be noted that a relatively small change in mortgage interest rates could have a significant *real income effect* for the household. This means that for people with modest incomes and relatively large mortgages, even a change in interest rates of less than one per cent will make a noticeable difference to the affordability of their mortgages.

When people first enter owner-occupation there is often an expectation that they will pay more in mortgage and other housing-related outgoings than they would to rent an equivalent unit of accommodation. This reflects the fact that an owner household has an investment, as well as a consumption interest in the property they occupy. People may also be willing to pay more for home-ownership in order to avoid certain perceived consumption disadvantages associated with the imposition of tenancy agreement restrictions.

Renting in general and affordability

Although in more recent times both ministers and the various funding bodies have staunchly refused to give a clear definition of an affordable rent, in 1988 the then Minister of Housing, William Waldegrave set out broad criteria relating to a somewhat imprecise benchmark that later became enshrined in the Tenants' Guarantee for affordable rents. He said that rents should be 'set and maintained at levels within the reach of those in lower paid employment' (Cope, 1990, p106). As with changes in mortgage interest rates for the owner-occupier, changes in rent will have a *real income effect* on the household. It is this *real income effect* that needs to be considered when determining whether or not the rent increase is affordable.

Local authority renting and affordability

Local councils have some discretion when setting rents (see Chapter 11). The current financial regime is founded on the Local Government and Housing Act 1989 and this legislation makes no direct reference to the question of affordability[7]. However, the consultation paper that preceded the Act, *A New*

---

7   Although Section 162 refers to the notion of 'proportionality' which is an expression denoting an intention that local authority rents should bear a relationship to assured tenancy rents in the other rented sectors.

Financial Regime for Local Authority Housing in England and Wales (1988), identified the following objectives of the regime: (a) to strike a fair balance between the interests of tenants and charge payers and (b) to be fair as between tenants in different areas. To accommodate charge payer interests, the legislation imposed a duty on local authorities broadly to structure their rents in a way that both takes account of local market rent levels and also the capital values of the properties, calculated with reference to right-to-buy prices. Such considerations had the intention of raising average rents while still keeping them at levels that could be regarded as affordable.

> *'Rents generally should not exceed levels within the reach of people in low pay employment, and in practice they will frequently be below market levels. They should, however, be set by reference to these two parameters: what people can pay and what the property is worth, rather than by reference to historic cost accounting figures.'* (DoE Consultation Paper, 1988).

Other social renting and affordability

Each registered social landlord enjoys a degree of freedom to develop its own rental policy, establishing the level of rent that should be charged and how that rent should be levied across its stock. However, it is required to do so within a complex framework of guidance (Gibbs, 1992, p12).

The initial definition used by the NFHA was in line with Schwarbe's ceiling and they suggested a maximum of 20 per cent of net average income to be reasonable so long as it took into account such factors as floor area, location and type of accommodation. This 20 per cent ratio was gradually raised in line with official guidelines. Social landlords are now expected to reflect the guidance given in the various circulars and performance standards that are published annually.

The *Tenants' Guarantee* adopts a benchmark approach with respect to the setting of affordable rents in this sector. It suggests that social rents should be set below market rents for assured tenancies in the private sector. The rent charged should take into account the size, amenities and location of each dwelling. However, where the property has been provided with the help of public subsidy, the Housing Corporation, in England, expects the rent to be set and maintained at a level within the reach of those in low paid employment. Landlords should not discriminate in their rent setting between those who are eligible for housing benefit and others.

The various housing federations have attempted to provide guidance on what constitutes an affordable rent. In England, for example, the National Housing Federation (NHF), publish *indicator rents* that give guidance to English associations about what levels of rent are affordable in terms of the Federation's current affordability policy with respect to various tenant income levels. The current policy, under review, states that rents are affordable if the majority of working tenants are not caught in the housing benefit poverty trap (refer to

Chapter 17); or paying more than 25 per cent of their net income on rent. They also publish projected cost rents that take account of the full cost of developing, managing and maintaining a property. In addition, they publish actual rents through their continuous recording (CORE) system (SCORE in Scotland). In the late 1990s these figures indicated that about 70 per cent of new assured tenants were paying rents above the 'affordable' level as defined by the then current Federation policy. This policy stated that rents are affordable if the majority of tenants are not caught in the poverty trap, because of dependency on housing benefit, or paying more than 25 per cent of their net income in rent.[8] The current policy of the Scottish Federation (SFHA), states that a rent is affordable only if (a) no working household is obliged to pay more than 25 per cent of net income, including housing benefit, on rent; and (b) no working household is left with less than 140 per cent of the appropriate income support amount. In Wales the WFHA has no formal statement on affordability, but has looked at rent-to-income ratios, housing benefit dependency and residual income measures in its evaluations of rent policies.

Private renting and affordability

In England and Wales, the commonest forms of renting arrangements for private houses and flats are *assured* and *shorthold* tenancies and these are explained and discussed more fully in Chapter 16. In the private sector rents are negotiated and set as part of a contractual agreement. Under these arrangements rent levels are really a matter of 'comparability' rather than 'affordability'. The landlord can charge a full market rent for an assured or a shorthold tenancy. The timing of any rent increase is normally determined by the nature of the contract, and disputes over rent increases can be referred to a rent assessment committee who will decide what rent the landlord could reasonably expect for the property if he was letting it on the open market under a new tenancy on the same terms.

In this sector questions of affordability are addressed entirely by the housing benefit scheme that provides means-tested *rent allowances* to private tenants on low incomes (see Chapter 16 for more details.).

Affordability and equity

The issue of affordability highlights the question of equity within the housing system. If regional rent variations are more pronounced than regional income variations an unregulated housing system may create locational horizontal inequities. That is, it may create different financial outcomes to people on similar incomes resulting from renting similar properties but in different parts of the country. In so far as people on relatively lower earnings commit a higher

---

8   Figures published in 1997 indicate regional variations with the South West of England being the region in which rents were least affordable and the North region proving to be most affordable.

proportion of their disposable incomes to housing expenses than people on relatively higher earnings, vertical inequities may exist. That is, there may be a lack of fairness as between different income groups. The fact that different tenures are taxed and subsidised in different ways can also lead to vertical inequities. Horizontal equity involves the similar treatment of people in similar circumstances. Vertical equity involves treating people in different circumstances differently in order to reduce the negative consequences that stem from these differences.

The social housing system attempts to address the question of locational horizontal equity through the operation of needs indices (see above), that guide the distribution of finite national funds into local authority and housing association housing projects in accordance with a formulaic assessment of differentiated normative need.

The question of vertical inequity is constantly discussed by social policy theorists and is an issue that has led to calls for the system of housing finance to be reformed in line with the principles of tenure neutrality and proportionality.

Affordability and the economy

There is some evidence that higher rents charged by local authorities and other social landlords damage the economy by increasing inflation and public spending. Rent rises will lead to losses for the public purse when tenants claim back a proportion of such increases through housing benefit. It should also be noted that in recent years rents have been used in calculating the retail price index which is then, in turn, used to increase government payments for pensions, certain Social Security benefits, index-linked gilts, and National Savings. It is also probable that rent inflation has fed into the wider economy by depressing demand for consumer purchases thereby adding both to unemployment and a fall in tax revenues.[9]

The recognition of housing market failure

If unfettered free-enterprise market arrangements were seen to achieve the housing policy objectives pointed to at the start of this chapter, there would be no calls for government intervention in the housing finance system. In large part, it is the failure of market forces to deliver these objectives that has brought about State involvement in this field. This 'failure' of the market has been recognised by historians, market theorists, and social policy analysts.

The historian's view of housing market failure. In the nineteenth century, particularly in times of trade recession and falling wages, many tenants would take

---

9   This argument is based on the Joseph Rowntree Foundation report, *The Impact of Higher Rents, Housing Research 109*, 1994. The Rowntree research indicated that a 10 per cent rise in social rents would reduce GDP by up to 0.2 per cent and increase unemployment by more than 25,000. It would also raise retail prices 0.3 per cent and cost the Treasury around £100 million a year.

in lodgers to help cover the rent charges. In other cases, the market reacted to low wage levels by depressing rents, which, in turn, reduced the normal profits received by landlords. Under such conditions many landlords protected their investment returns by cutting back on repairs and maintenance. In this way, the unregulated market adjusted to low incomes by creating over-crowded, poor quality accommodation. Eventually these conditions were judged to be unacceptable and the State intervened to establish minimum standards for both existing and newly-built dwellings.

The economist's view of housing market failure. Economists point out that for markets to work efficiently there must be a high degree of competition. Competition depends on the existence of large numbers of producers and consumers so that no group of market participants can influence the market price through their actions. Competition also depends on the participants being knowledgeable about the nature of the product and the workings of the market. Furthermore, if for some reason it is difficult for new producers to set up in the market or for consumers to compare prices, this will also have the effect of diminishing competition. In a sense everything in the market-place is competing with everything else. However, the more alike two products are, the stronger will be their competitive relationship. On the supermarket shelf, a bar of chocolate is in a competitive relationship with a packet of sweets, but it has a much stronger competitive relationship with a similarly sized bar of chocolate produced by a rival chocolate manufacturer. We might say that it has a *perfectly competitive* relationship with an identical bar in identical wrappings, produced by the same chocolate company and stacked right alongside it. In other words, the more compact and coherent the market is and the less the products can be differentiated from each other, the stronger will be the degree of competition.

Many of these characteristics of competition only have a weak presence in the housing system.

Professional bodies, trade unions, employers' organisations, large and influential construction companies, multi-national development companies, planning authorities, etc., all exercise a degree of monopoly power or influence and in so doing inhibit competition.

For all sorts of reasons it is difficult for participants in the housing system to possess complete knowledge of the product and its market. Housing is technically complex. For example, recognition of building defects or awareness of any future planning proposals likely to affect the property, or the existence of legal constraints on the way in which the property can be used, all require a degree of skill and information that most buyers and sellers do not possess. Furthermore, it takes time and effort to get a feel for a particular local housing market. In these various ways the market participants have an imperfect knowledge both of the product and its market and this clearly inhibits competition. It is because of this lack of knowledge that many people employ exchange professionals such as surveyors, lawyers and estate agents to help them with their buying and selling arrangements. We might say that the very existence of these exchange professionals is witness to the imperfectly competitive nature of the housing market.

The market's competitiveness is also weakened by the fact that house-building is a highly capital intensive activity which also requires very specific skills of a craft, technical and professional nature. These factors act as barriers that make it difficult for new suppliers to enter the market to compete.

Competition is also inhibited by the fact that dwelling units are immobile and spatially separated. Because buildings are geographically fixed, a surplus in one area cannot be used to alleviate a shortage in some other area.

Finally, competition is inhibited by the way in which the housing system is fragmented in terms of tenure and dwelling type. Two geographically close and identically designed dwellings in similar states of repair will nevertheless have a weak competitive relationship with each other if they are being marketed under different tenure arrangements. Similarly, two very different types of dwelling in the same area and tenure sector are not likely to be in serious competition with each other. A surplus of large detached family houses in an area cannot be readily used to alleviate a shortage of bed-sits for students in the same district.

For all these reasons, economists argue that the housing market is *imperfectly competitive* and thus it cannot be relied upon to work automatically in the interests of consumers.

In addition to the housing market's *technical* failure to approximate to the conditions of *perfect competition*, it can be said to fail to meet society's housing objectives in another important respect. Namely, it has too restrictive a view of what counts as 'housing need'.

The social policy analyst's view of housing market failure. Social theorists argue that market arrangements fail to take proper account of the housing needs of low-income and other vulnerable households. Market theory equates need with the notion of *effective demand*. In so doing, it is said to recognise only those needs that are expressed in the market place. *Effective demand* is defined as a want or need backed by cash. This means that under market arrangements needs can only be made 'effective' by purchasing the required goods or services from a market provider at a price set by the forces of supply and demand. Under such arrangements those without sufficient purchasing power are unable to make their wants and needs effective. The much-lauded freedom of choice denoted by the market notion of *consumer sovereignty* is restricted to those with sufficient income to pay the market price. Thus, in a free market economy everybody is free to sleep under a railway arch but only those with sufficient money can purchase a warm, dry room for the night.

Over time, to any one household, a particular type of housing can become more or less affordable. This will depend on *comparative* changes between the price of occupation of the dwelling in question (e.g. rent or mortgage repayment), and the disposable income of the household in question. Social analysts point out that we can only rely on the operation of market forces to accommodate the interests of low income households if it can be demonstrated that the comparative price and income changes are such that good quality housing is becoming more rather than less affordable to this group.

Some market apologists argue that the market will provide for low income groups through a process of *filtering*. This argument says that over time dwellings tend to decline in value and thus become accessible to people on lower incomes. Social analysts, however, point out that the effectiveness of 'trading up' or *filtering* as a means of raising housing standards hinges on the speed of value-decline relative to quality-decline.

> *'If the value of the standing stock depreciates so rapidly that even low-income households can afford units which are still above the quality standards of social adequacy, the private market is a satisfactory instrument of public policy.'* (Lowry, 1960, p364).

Because a coherent definition of social need has to be a prerequisite to the establishment of a social service, twentieth century policy makers have sought to identify broader definitions of housing need than that provided by the concept of *effective demand*. In subsequent chapters we will see that these normative definitions have tended to be tied to tenures and are constantly modified over time.

Summary

In this chapter we have made the point that housing policy seeks to resolve the dilemma that, although some minimum standard of accommodation is a necessity for all, housing is expensive relative to the disposable incomes of certain households. We have argued that both historical experience and economic theory indicate that an unregulated housing market would fail to achieve society's objective of providing all households with a decent and affordable home.

In the next chapter we will look at how subsidy arrangements have sought to bridge the gap between people's housing needs and their abilities to pay. In subsequent chapters we will make the point that housing subsidies and other interventionist measures are a response, not only to the market's failure to support the consumption interests of low-income households, but also its failure to support the broader non-proprietary interests that are vested in housing. In Chapter 5 we will draw particular attention to the question of public expenditure control and its effects on housing finance.

Further reading

Angus Freeman, Alan Holmans and Christine Whitehead, *Evaluating Housing Affordability – Policy Options and New Directions*, LGA for CIH, LGA, NHF, 1999.

Tim Brown and Jon Passmore, *Housing and Anti-Poverty Strategies*, CIH/Joseph Rowntree Foundation, 1998.

CHAPTER 4:
Rent-setting principles and the concept of subsidy

In the context of rent-setting policy, the 'need-price dilemma' (Chapter 3), manifests itself as a concern to balance affordability with sufficiency. In other words, the problem facing the social landlord is to set a rent that is sufficiently high to cover the costs of provision yet low enough to be affordable by those deemed to be in housing need.

Figure 4.1: Principles of rent-setting

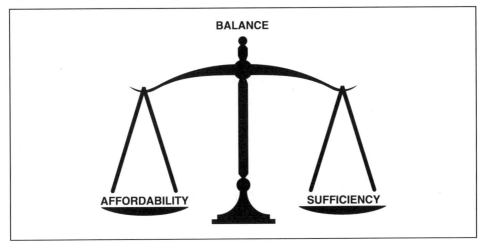

Rental sufficiency

Rent is a stipulated sum paid periodically by a tenant to a landlord in return for specified occupancy rights associated with the use and enjoyment of land or landed property. The rent may also pay for specified services provided by the landlord. From the tenant's point of view the rent is a *price* that is paid in order to acquire these rights of occupancy and associated services. From the landlord's point of view the rent is an *income* received in return for making these rights available and providing the services. Whereas the question confronting the tenant is, 'Given my income can I afford this rent?', the landlord has to consider the question, 'Given my outgoings is this rent sufficient?'

In any particular case, what will count as a sufficient rent will depend in large part on the landlord's motives for being in business. A social landlord, such as a housing association or a charitable housing trust, may consciously seek to set a rent that is less than would be charged for the same property by a profit-seeking commercial landlord. Any particular social housing rent level will also be affected by the existence or otherwise of supply-side grants and subsidies. This of course means that, if existing financial support is reduced or withdrawn this will automatically put an upward pressure on rents.

The total sufficiency rent

The following constitutes a list of items that a landlord conceivably could, although in practice may not, regard as legitimate financial costs to be covered by the rent charge.

- Loan service charges (LSC).
  These are paid on loans taken out to acquire, construct, improve or repair the dwelling. They would include an element to cover the repayment of the principal and an element to cover interest charges. They could include an element for mortgage insurance cover.

- Major repairs (MP).
  Major repairs might be paid for by taking out additional loans, in which case the costs will be added to LSC. An alternative approach is for an element of rent to be paid into a sinking fund and invested so that over time it accumulates into a balance that can be used to pay for or reduce (i.e. 'sink') the costs of such works. Calculated over the life of the dwelling, sinking funds are likely to be more cost-effective than loans. The choice between sinking funds or loans brings up questions of equity as well as financial efficiency as sinking fund charges will increase the rents of current occupiers while future loans will have to be serviced out of future rents.

- Other reserves (R).
  In addition to accumulating funds for future major repairs, an organisation may wish to set aside part of its income flow for other purposes. Contingency reserves may be established to cover any unexpected future expenses. Special reserve accounts may be set up to accumulate funds to cover future taxation liabilities. Reserve accounts may be set up to accumulate future investment capital. Investment reserves may distinguish between *replacement capital,* needed to cover the depreciation in the value of fixed assets due to wear and tear or obsolescence, and *expansion capital,* needed to increase or improve, rather than repair, the stock.

- Management (Mgmt).
  The rent might be expected to pay for the wages and associated administrative costs of running the range of housing functions and services offered by the agency.

- Maintenance (Mtnc).
  As defined by BS 3811, maintenance comprises all of the technical and associated administrative actions intended to retain a building and its facilities in a state that will allow it to perform its required functions.[1]

- Asset returns (AR).
  As items of fixed capital formation, dwellings have locked into them an investment value. The landlords may expect a financial return on this investment representing the opportunity cost of their money capital. In other words, if a dwelling is worth, say, £80,000, the landlord agency may require the rental income to generate a financial yield on that sum just as they would if they had invested it on the stock market or in some other commercial venture.

- Building insurance (BI).
  Some risks are insurable and some are not. Insurable risks are those that are associated with probabilities and include such misfortunes as fire, theft, vandalism and premature component failure. Non-insurable risks are associated with unquantifiable uncertainties such as changed market conditions, fluctuating interest rates, new restrictive legislation, and 'acts of God'.

- Profit (P).
  In a commercial business, profit represents the reward accruing to the successful entrepreneur and is held to be the motivating factor behind commercial, non-insurable, risk-taking. This means that in the case of the commercial landlord, some measure of profit is regarded as a normal cost of production and, as such, has to be provided for by the rental income.

- Bad debts (BD).
  In a housing context, the bulk of bad debts are in the form of rent arrears. If income from some properties is not being received then the consequential fall in the flow of income may have to be recovered in the form of higher rents in general. The profile of rent arrears over a period is often used as a performance indicator on the assumption that a well managed housing agency will have in place procedures for maintaining its flow of rental income.

- Voids (V).
  When a dwelling is unoccupied it is not generating an income and thus the costs of managing and maintaining the void stock have to be covered by other sources of income including the rents levied on other properties. At any one time it is inevitable that part of the stock will be unoccupied to allow post-occupancy surveys and checks, major repairs and so on. It might also be argued

---

1   Maintenance work is usually classified as 'reactive' and 'planned'. Reactive maintenance is characterised by low value and high volume with an emphasis being placed on relatively fast response times. Planned maintenance can be divided into 'condition-dependent', prompted by condition surveys, and 'condition-independent', prompted by schedules based on life-cycle data.

---

that a certain level of voids has to be maintained if new tenants are to be offered a degree of choice in the allocation of their homes. As with rent arrears, the level of voids is usually looked to as a performance indicator on the assumption that a well managed agency will not have an unnecessarily high number of empty properties at any one time.

- Service charges (SC).
  These are charges that are made for services to tenants that are in excess of normal housing management functions for such activities as caretaking, landscape and garden maintenance, warden services, etc. Strictly speaking, service charges are additions to, rather than part of, the rent. However, from the tenants' point of view they are experienced as part of the rent and we will, therefore, include them in the full sufficiency rent formula. The Housing Corporation's concept of *Housing Plus* (1995), points to a growing awareness that many social housing tenants need a wide range of services to support their tenancies and in the future the social landlord's core functions may be more widely viewed than they are at present.

A completely unsubsidised total sufficiency rent (TSR), would need to cover all of the above, viz:

$$TSR = LSC + MP + R + Mgmt + Mtnc + AR + BI + P + BD + V + SC$$

In any real life situation, the actual rent charged may be less than the TSR because of the receipt of subsidies. Actual rents will also deviate from the TSR because particular landlords may set their rents in accordance with principles that do not require them to pursue a policy of total rent sufficiency.

Rent-setting principles provide the rationale for rental policies. Different tenures tend to look to different principles when determining rents, and within a particular tenure, the underlying logical principles guiding rent-setting can change over time. At any one time in any particular tenure, rents can be set with reference to one or more of the logical principles discussed below.

Rent-setting principles

The following constitute a set of contrasting rent-setting principles that could be used to guide the pricing policies of providers of rented accommodation. They are each grounded in a different socio-economic logic.

1. *Marginal cost pricing* is the principle that stipulates that rents should be closely related to the costs of production at the margin in order to promote the efficient use of scarce resources. This means that if we produce an extra (i.e. marginal), unit of housing output we should charge a price that covers the extra (i.e. marginal), costs of producing it.

It is the price that economic theory says will be charged in an unregulated, perfectly competitive market[2]. The marginal cost price is thus the *perfectly competitive economic price*. The theoretical argument runs as follows. We should charge rents that cover the costs of production including 'normal' (i.e. competitive) profit[3]. If consumers are not prepared to pay this price this indicates a lack of demand and we should not waste resources in producing goods and services that are not in demand.

Of course, in reality, a lack of effective demand may be due to a lack of disposable income rather than to people not wanting, needing, or valuing the accommodation. For this reason, if marginal cost pricing is used as the guiding principle for setting rents in the social housing sectors, it may have to be accompanied by some form of income augmentation in order to make such rents affordable.[4]

2. *Market pricing* is the principle that stipulates that rents should be freely negotiated and determined by market forces. All real markets are more or less imperfectly competitive so that, in contrast with the marginal cost rent, the real market rent may be inflated by such things as scarcity and consumer ignorance of alternatives. In the real world landlords are often in a position to exercise a degree of monopoly power that enables them to charge more than the marginal cost price for a particular property.

3. *Historic cost accounting* is the principle that stipulates that rents should be set at levels that generate an income that is just sufficient to meet the historic costs of providing the service. Under this principle rents are simply set to recover actual costs and no account is taken of what the market would charge. In the extreme version of this principle no account is taken of either the property's current use or investment values.

Because the burden of debt diminishes over time, under a system of historic cost accounting older dwellings will tend to have lower loan service charges attached to them than equivalent properties that have been built or acquired more recently. Eventually the mortgage debt will be amortised so that the LSC

---

2   See Chapter 3 for a discussion on the conditions of perfect competition.
3   Normal profit is that level of profit that is just sufficient to persuade the supplier of a good or service to stay in the competitive market. It is treated as one of the costs of production, along with wages, interest payments, and the costs of raw materials, etc. Profits above this level are called 'excess'. In a perfectly competitive market excess profits cannot be maintained in the long-run. This is because the opportunity to receive excess profits will encourage competitors to increase their outputs and this, in turn, will force prices back down to a point where, once again, only normal profits are made.
4   Indeed this was the case in 1972 when the government extended the concept of 'fair rents' to the residential sector. Fair rents were set by a rent officer who sought to establish what the rent would be if the conditions of perfect competition existed (i.e. no shortages). It was recognised that such market-related rents would not be affordable by all those in housing need and therefore a parallel system of rent rebates and allowances was introduced at the same time.

element in the total sufficiency rent will disappear altogether. The reduced or liquidated debt burden associated with certain properties can provide an opportunity to let them at less than market rents and still cover the historic costs of provision.

The existence of differential historic costs has in the past allowed social landlords to allocate low-cost housing to low-income households thereby moving some way towards reconciling the claims of *sufficiency* and *affordability*. Where the stock was built or acquired over a long period, the differential costs between individual dwelling units can be significant. This means that if historic cost rents were to be set in a way that tied each dwelling's rent to its particular historic costs, the standard deviation within the overall rent structure could be unacceptably high. For this reason, where historic cost accounting principles have been adopted, they have been used to spread the cost savings across the stock as a whole by a process of *rent pooling*.

Rent pooling focuses on the relationship between the aggregated historic costs of providing the whole stock of dwellings and the aggregated flow of rental income generated by that stock. The idea is that, rather than charging rents that cover the historic costs of providing individual dwellings, the authority seeks to collect rents that cover its costs in total. Having determined the required income flow, the authority then has to devise a method of setting the rents of individual dwellings in a way that the unit price charged is felt to be reasonable when compared with others. Over the years social landlords who adopted historic cost accounting, have used three main methods of differentiating the rents of individual properties. Under the old rating system, individual dwellings were periodically valued for rating purposes. This value was termed the *gross value* and was assumed to represent the annual rent that the dwelling would generate when let. Councils used to refer to these values when deciding how to differentiate between the rents of individual dwellings. Point and formula systems have also been used to guide what constitutes a 'reasonable' rent (see below).

Rent pooling has been commonly used to even out historic costs over the total housing stock where older properties are cheaper to service than newer ones. It is recognised that the differentials that emerge as a result of historic cost accounting are in large part the result of not taking account of the current values of the properties. Since 1972, council house rents that have traditionally benefited from historical cost savings, have been set in a way that also makes some reference to the property's capital value.

4. *Capital value pricing* is the principle that stipulates that rents should be set in such a way that they provide a specified return on the capital values. The operation of capital value rents requires two figures: an estimate of the capital value with vacant possession, and an agreed rate of return. The former might be set by reference to private markets and the latter either to private markets or

to the official government discount rate.[5] The capital value might be arrived at by reference to the owner-occupied property market. The rate of return can be set by reference to current yields in the finance market.

It would, of course, be possible to discount the market figures to reflect the welfare nature of social housing. Because of its mission to house the poor, a social landlord may, for example, be prepared to accept a lower rate of return than it could get on other investments. This has tended to be the case when this principle is applied to social housing: even in the nineteenth century the 'five per cent philanthropy' movement sought a reasonable rather than a commercial return on its 'charitable' investments. The idea of social housing rents reflecting capital values is not so much about maximising investment returns as using financial disciplines to encourage the efficient financial management of public or charitable funds. It is more about accountability than profitability. Those who advocate using capital values as the basis for setting rents argue that affordability concerns can be addressed through some separate administrative mechanism.

5. *Consumption expenditure pricing* is the principle that stipulates that tenants should only pay for what they receive. As a principle it is grounded in the philosophy of the welfare state. It is based on the argument that the capital costs of providing a service should be paid by the taxpayers who then become the long-run owners of the school buildings, hospital equipment, council housing stock, or whatever. Under this principle, the receivers of a social service might legitimately be asked to pay towards the provision of consumables they enjoy, such as school meals, prescribed medicines, housing maintenance, etc., but would not be expected to pay for the servicing of debt associated with the acquisition of fixed assets that remain in the ownership of the education authority, hospital board, local authority housing department, etc.

This principle has never been fully applied to the British social housing system and the principle's welfare-statist logic is unlikely to be accepted by contemporary social commentators and politicians who are increasingly sympathetic to establishing rent regimes that reflect market prices and capital values.

Although consumption pricing is not normally used as the over-riding principle for setting rents, it is used by social landlords to differentiate the 'price' of one unit of accommodation from another. Social landlords do for example, use points systems to value the different utilities generated by different types of dwelling. The aggregated points for a particular dwelling are then used to fix its 'appropriate' rent. This is looked at in more detail in Chapters 11 and 13.

---

5   Most advocates of capital value pricing argue the need to determine a rent that will produce a rental income stream that is sufficient to provide landlords with a return on the capital invested comparable to other investments in the economy. The current government discount rate on new investment might apply in this case.

All rents are normally rationalised and legitimated by reference to one or more of the above principles. Rents tend to be rationalised differently in different tenures, and in any particular tenure the balance of rationalisations can change over time.

Rent-setting in practice

There is much talk amongst policy-makers and academics about the desirability of harmonising the rents of council houses and those of registered social landlords (RSLs), and relating them both to local private sector rents. At the moment, however, significant differentials exist between the rents charged by the various types of landlord. With all its faults, the old *fair rent* regime established in the early 1970s did point to a common approach to price setting across the whole rented sector. The shift away from *fair rents* in the late 1980s resulted in the abandonment of a common approach, and in the 1990s rent levels have tended to be rationalised differently in different tenures. Deregulation in the unregistered private sector has allowed private landlords to charge assured and assured shorthold rents that are more or less in line with market pricing. RSLs with assured tenancies are expected to take the incomes of their tenants into account so that the rents they charge are seen to be affordable. Their ability to do this is helped by the receipt of Social Housing Grant and other fiscal aid. It is also aided by their ability to incorporate historic cost accounting into their projected business costs. In local authorities pressure on rent levels is also eased by the dampening effect of historic costs: indeed, because of the generally older age profile of their stocks, the historic cost effect tends to be more significant in this sector. However, the 1990 finance regime for local authorities established the principle of aggregate guideline rents and required councils to take some account of both property values and how rents are set by the private sector locally when formulating their rent policies.

How rents have actually been determined in the different tenures is described and discussed in detail in subsequent chapters.

Ways of subsidising

All of the following have been used as *mechanisms* for subsidising housing:

- Price control and regulation.
- Tax relief and exemptions.
- The provision of grants to the providers of housing.
- Rent rebates and allowances (income augmentation).
- Right-to-buy discounts.
- Rent pooling.

The precise operational form of a subsidy will largely be determined by its intended function(s). This means that in seeking to assess the effectiveness of a subsidy we have to start by determining its function.

The function of a subsidy

We can identify the following possible functions of a subsidy:

1. To overcome demand deficiency. This centres on the affordability debate discussed in Chapter 3. Housing's characteristics as primary consumption provide a necessary but not sufficient reason for providing subsidy. The issue is not simply that basic housing is a necessity but that it is a necessity that not everyone can afford. In short, some minimum level of housing consumption is regarded as a *merit need*. Subsidy is the mechanism by which society has sought to bridge the gap between a sufficient and an affordable rent so that this *merit need* can be met. The concepts of *merit need* and *demand deficiency* are discussed fully in Chapter 17.

2. To redistribute the benefits of good housing to all, so that areas of poverty are not further worsened by poor housing standards. The argument here is that society as a whole has an interest in ameliorating the social and economic costs associated with bad housing. Where the issues of acceptability and affordability are brought together in housing policy, the question of 'subsidy' is bound to arise.

3. To influence proprietary behaviour (as an aspect of 2 above). In particular, to encourage individual investment in housing that would not otherwise take place. That is, to help pay for private investment that generates positive externalities. A positive externality is a benefit from economic activity for which no compensation is paid. The argument here is that non-proprietary interests may result from encouraging owners and tenants to renovate, or in some other way improve, their properties. These non-proprietary interests, or positive externalities, may include such factors as environmental enhancement, safer communities, and economic growth.

4. To establish a degree of vertical and horizontal equity with the housing finance system. A policy commitment to tenure neutrality may be associated with this objective.

5. To foster the development of a particular form of tenure. A policy commitment to influence tenure preference may be associated with this objective.

6. To offset market failure – e.g. the failure of historical markets to provide for today's needs; the inability of the market to react quickly enough to changes in demand; the inflexibility of the market due to its fixed locational nature in relation to demand; and problems of financing (Refer to Chapter 3 and Hills, 1991).

It has to be recognised that a subsidy may have consequences beyond those that have been planned for. In particular, subsidies in one tenure are likely to have implications for other tenures. The ultimate beneficiary of a subsidy may turn out to be other than that for whom it was intended, or it may produce an unintended undesirable effect in another sector of the economy.[6]

Defining 'subsidy'

Originally the word subsidy simply meant a 'payment'.[7] In English history the term became used specifically to describe financial grants made by Parliament to the Crown to pay for wars or other special needs. From this it was extended to apply to any Parliamentary grant in aid including those made to commercial agencies, public bodies and individual citizens. The term was then applied to any financial support to suppliers or consumers of goods and services, whether from Parliament or from other sources. In contemporary financial parlance the word has come to have a more focused technical meaning that is derived from economic theory.

Economic subsidy

In market theory a subsidy is said to exist if a good or service is sold below its market price. Thus the term 'subsidy' is used to describe a deficit between the price that *is actually charged* for a good or service and the higher price that *would have been charged* by the market. The idea here is that if a good or service is sold at a price that fails to cover its costs of production, including profit, the consumer is said to be enjoying an 'economic subsidy'. This is a rather theoretical view of subsidy and, in practice, it is difficult to determine the extent of economic subsidy when goods and services are provided outside of competitive markets. The social housing system has evolved out of welfare rather than market arrangements and, for this reason, it is often more sensible to conceive of subsidy in this sector as a money transfer.

---

6   The possibility of creating undesirable knock-on effects by subsidising housing has been discussed for many years.
    No thoughtful man will advocate the letting of houses below their economic rent, by means of subsidies...because...wages follow rents, and therefore that policy would only result in providing capitalists with cheap labour at the expense of the general body of ratepayers. (Nettlefold, 1908, p55)
7   The etymology of the word 'subsidy' shows it to be linked to the word 'subside'. Subside comes from the latin *subsidere* – *sub* meaning below/under and *sidere* meaning to sit down or settle. The word 'subsidy' comes from the latin *subsidium*, a word that originally referred to troops stationed in reserve in the third line of battle. The front-line troops would be at the battle front; the second-line troops would be the reserves that could be quickly called upon to support the front-line; and well behind the front-line, settled down and waiting, would be the third-line troops – the auxiliaries or *subsidium* (from *subsidere* – in waiting/to settle down). From this application it came to be applied to a sum of money paid by one prince or nation to another to purchase the services of auxiliary troops. It was then used more generally to mean extraordinary aid in money rendered by subjects to a sovereign, usually to pay for wars.

Money transfer or cash-flow definition

The cash flow approach to defining subsidy seeks to measure and track money transfers between people and organisations. This is the way subsidy is measured and traced in official statistics and accounts. The most common transfers take the form of public sector grants or allowances to certain qualifying housing providers or consumers. We must recognise, however, that some important housing subsidies do not involve a tangible transfer of funds; mortgage interest tax relief and rent pooling are two notable examples of economic subsidies that do not involve direct cash payments.

Ways of categorising housing subsidies

Subsidies that are derived from the State and are an aspect of government policy we can term *fiscal subsidies*.[8] Subsidies that arise as a result of one private citizen or organisation aiding the production or consumption of some other private citizen or organisation and are not directly derived from government policy, we can term *non-fiscal subsidies*. In the field of housing, examples of non-fiscal subsidies are rent pooling (tenant-to-tenant subsidies), and grants from charities to help provide or manage dwellings for special needs groups such as the elderly or the disabled.

Subsidy as an aspect of fiscal policy

Fiscal policy embraces both taxes and subsidies. It must be understood that fiscal policy is not simply concerned with raising funds to pay for public activities and to support the worthy and the needy. Throughout history governments have used taxes and subsidies to achieve wider economic and social objectives by deterring certain activities through taxation and encouraging other activities through subsidisation.

Subsidies may be used to influence market behaviour. That is, where the market fails to promote society's politically determined objectives subsidies may be used to promote greater *social efficiency,* by altering patterns of production or consumption, and/or *social justice*, by altering the distribution of real income. In this way, politicians see subsidisation as a policy instrument for altering what gets produced and consumed and by whom.

Because housing finance policy has developed in the context of political and administrative concerns that are tenure specific (e.g. concerns to encourage owner-occupation, concerns to make social rented housing more affordable, etc.), most subsidies are tied to specific tenures. Although understandable, this tenure specificity has inhibited rational discussion about how the subsidy system might be reformed with a view to enhancing cross-tenure efficiency, effectiveness and equity. To liberate our thought and understanding from this limitation we will end

---

8   Fiscal means 'of or relating to the finances of the State', from the latin *fiscus*, meaning public money.

this chapter by briefly considering ways of classifying housing subsidies that are not tenure specific. In subsequent chapters subsidies will be described and analysed on a tenure by tenure basis.

Classification by financial category

In Chapter 2 (Figure 2.1), we drew a key distinction between finance that is used for capital purposes, finance that is used for revenue purposes, and finance that is used to augment incomes. Within the context of any particular tenure it is possible to provide subsidy to support any or all of these functions. Social Housing Grant is an example of a capital subsidy going to housing associations and other social landlords. Housing Revenue Account subsidy is an example of revenue support to local authorities, if entitled. The housing benefit system provides income augmentation to tenants who qualify to receive it[9] and mortgage interest tax relief is used to provide income augmentation to owner-occupiers purchasing their homes by means of a loan.[10]

The incidence of a subsidy

Gibb and Munro, (1991), distinguish between the *formal* and the *effective* incidence of a subsidy. The distinction enables us to make the point that those who formally receive the benefit can pass its financial impact or 'effect' on to others. A social landlord, for example, may receive a capital grant that reduces the total scheme costs of a housing development (formal incidence), and as a result, the tenants enjoy lower rental charges (effective incidence).

In the owner-occupied sector, the formal receipt of mortgage interest tax relief enabled some house purchasers to bid higher prices for the homes they purchase thereby effectively passing on the financial benefit to house builders and land owners. Where subsidies get transformed into higher house prices we say that the subsidy has been 'capitalised'.

Cross-subsidy

Cross-subsidy occurs when administrative arrangements require one housing account, activity or group to aid some other housing account, activity or group.

Before 1990 local authorities could make transfers from the General Fund to the Housing Revenue Account (HRA), and vice-versa. Many councils used this power to lower rent levels without the HRA being forced into deficit. This ability to cross-subsidise one account with another was made illegal by the Local Government and Housing Act 1989.[11]

---

9   See Chapter 17.
10   MITR was abolished in April 2000 – see Chapter 7.
11   This is discussed fully in Chapters 8 and 11.

The old municipal principle of *rent pooling* is an example of cross-subsidisation of one group of tenants by another. Under rent pooling arrangements tenants living in established dwellings with small or no debt charges attached to them have their rents increased beyond the historic costs of provision so that tenants occupying newer properties with relatively high historic costs (debt charges) can have their rents reduced to more affordable levels.

Planning gain is another example of cross-subsidy. Under a development proposal requiring planning permission, it is possible for a local authority to grant permission, subject to an agreement with the developer that part of the profits from the sale of the properties on the open market will be used to subsidise the provision or improvement of a number of social housing units that are associated with the primary development. Such compacts are termed 'section 106 agreements' after the section in the Town and Country Planning 1990 that gives them legislative force. Section 106 agreements are often made in partnership with housing associations who, subsequent to the development, manage the low-cost dwellings that are let or part sold to households deemed to be in housing need.

Visible and hidden subsidies

A subsidy can be said to be 'visible' if its existence and nature are widely known and understood. All direct grants and benefits, or money transfers, are openly publicised, reported on and accounted for in expenditure statistics that are in the public domain (see Chapter 5). Not all subsidies are so clearly perceived and understood. If a subsidy's existence is obscured by administrative arrangements or its cost to the Exchequer is not openly discussed, it is said to be 'hidden'. It is sometimes said that subsidy received through tax exemption is less obvious than subsidy provided through the receipt of grant or benefit. It may be that the 'hidden' nature of mortgage interest tax relief and capital gains tax exemptions protected the main subsidies going to owner-occupation from the scrutiny and criticism to which more 'visible' subsidies have been subjected.

By controlling or regulating prices at the point of consumption the old Rent Acts effectively required landlords to provide a hidden economic subsidy to their tenants.

Universal and targeted subsidies

A subsidy is said to be 'universal' if it is available to a whole class of people (e.g. a tenure group), irrespective of their individual incomes or normative needs. As the term implies, 'targeted' subsidies are aimed at specific households on the basis of some assessment of need and/or income and savings.

When the Exchequer provides a development grant to help pay for the capital costs of a social housing scheme, the formal incidence of that subsidy is universal.

By reducing the need for a residual loan, the grant lowers the historic costs associated with the scheme and as a result the rents are universally lower than they otherwise would have been. The exemption from capital gains tax enjoyed by owner-occupiers is an example of an economic subsidy that is universally available to all owner-occupiers irrespective of their circumstances.

The means-testing involved in the distribution of targeted subsidies makes them relatively more complex to administer than universal subsidies. However, by concentrating limited funds on those in most need, they are usually regarded as being more rather than less *socially efficient*. Although housing benefit is the most prominent targeted aid available to help with housing costs, the social efficiency argument has led to a whole range of other subsidies being means-tested. Home improvement grants, for example, are distributed by local authorities in accordance with a means-test formula.

As well as targeting financial support at individual households through the application of means-tests, it is also possible to target State resources at specific geographical areas through the application of needs indices. (See discussion on comparative need in Chapter 3.)

Supply-side and demand-side subsidies

Throughout the twentieth century there has been a continuous debate about the most appropriate way of subsidising the housing needs of low-income tenants. In essence this is a debate about whether it is better to subsidise supply or demand. Any support measure that has the effect of influencing production and provision can be termed a *supply-side subsidy*, and any measure that influences consumption can be termed a *demand-side subsidy*.

Figure 4.2: Supply and demand-side subsidies

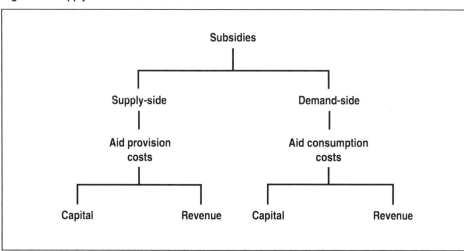

Financial aid to providers is sometimes referred to as a *supply-side subsidy* and financial support to consumers is referred to as a *demand-side subsidy.*

Provider (supply-side) subsidies are formally directed at landlords or developers with the intention of aiding them to provide quality accommodation at less than market rents. Where the grants in aid are provided to help cover the capital development, or redevelopment costs, they are sometimes referred to as 'bricks and mortar' subsidies. Provider subsidies can take the form of either capital or revenue aid. Such subsidies invariably take the operational form of a *money transfer.* For example, local authorities can receive capital grants and HRA subsidy. They may also receive various specific grants, including supplementary and special grants, and specified capital grants to help them fund such things as house renovations. Significant sums are provided to other social landlords in the form of SHG. These and other supply-side subsidies are described in subsequent chapters.

The supply-side arguments. Market economists tend to argue that supply subsidies to housing are only really justifiable in times of national emergency such as periods of war or post-war reconstruction. This is because, at such times, national priorities are such that the free market economy is abandoned or severely disrupted by a shift towards command economics. If housing is needed at these times, then the State may have to intervene directly and help pay for its production. In contrast, advocates of the welfare state tend to argue that, at all times, the housing needs of some vulnerable groups have to be guaranteed by the State and, consequently, suppliers should be aided to ensure that such needs are met.[12] Proponents of this approach point out that the universal nature of supply subsidies makes them less complex to administer than means-tested personal assistance. It is also argued that they are less socially divisive because, as a general subsidy, they are less inclined to stigmatise the recipients.

Consumption (demand-side) subsidies are directed at the users of housing with the intention of giving qualifying recipients additional income with which to pay for a standard of accommodation that would otherwise be beyond their means. They are sometimes referred to as 'personal' subsidies. By far the largest amount of personal subsidy is channelled through a form of assistance called *housing benefit* which is a government sponsored scheme designed to help people on low incomes with their rents (see Chapter 17 for details). Some home owners also receive consumption support in the form of mortgage income tax relief (see Chapter 17).

The demand-side arguments. Critics of supply-side subsidies argue that they are inefficient and distort the market. They are deemed to be wasteful of public money because their universal nature gives help to people whether they are in need or not. They distort the market by producing rents that are not related to

---

12   This is the *merit need* argument – see Chapter 17.

either the true costs of provision or to the current value of the property. By contrast, means-tested demand-side assistance (e.g. rebates), can be tightly targeted at those in most need and also allow the authorities and associations to set rents that are more in line with provision costs or current values. In this way, the flow of rental income into the housing system is not diminished as a result of policies designed to aid low-income households.

Some commentators argue that by not directly distorting opportunity costs or market prices, income support measures are not, strictly speaking, housing subsidies at all but part of the Social Security system. However, because such measures as housing benefit and mortgage interest tax relief have the same income effect as a subsidy and, in any case, indirectly *do* affect costs and prices, we will classify them as 'housing subsidies'.

The shifting balance of assistance

Since 1980 there has been a gradual but emphatic change in policy emphasis towards the demand-side arguments that has resulted in a shift from supply-side, particularly 'bricks and mortar', subsidies to demand-side, or 'personal' subsidies. As a consequence of this shift in emphasis rents have risen and the housing benefit budget has expanded. Between 1980 and the mid-1990s social housing rent levels increased at a rate greater than inflation while during the same period the number of people claiming housing benefit in the form of rebates and allowances more than doubled.

Summary and conclusion

In this chapter we have made the point that a rent has to be *sufficient* as well as *affordable* and that any deficit between these two primary objectives may have to be made up by the provision of *subsidy*. In economic theory a subsidy is thought of as the difference between what is actually charged for a good and what would have been charged. In practice, many subsidies take the form of a cash payment or a tax concession. Subsidies tend to take different forms in different tenures. We have made the further point that a gap between affordability and sufficiency may not be the only reason for subsidising the provision or consumption of housing.

We will end by making the point that the current systems of rents and subsidies were not so much designed as that they evolved. This has produced a number of irrationalities and inequities that can be identified and analysed by reference to the ideas in this chapter. One barrier to reforming and rationalising the system is the *subsidy ratchet effect*. By this we mean that there is usually only limited resistance to the introduction or extension of subsidies because they tend to create identifiable beneficiaries. Once these beneficiaries have been created, however, they have a vested interest in seeing the measures retained and this creates a political resistance to reforms that require the reduction or abolition of subsidies.

Further reading

Jill Gibbs, *Rent Structures and Affordability*, CIH, 1992.

CIH *Good Practice Briefing No.11 – Rents and Service Charges*, December 1997.

PART TWO

Housing finance: the regime

Introduction to Part Two

Part One of this book sought to establish a way of conceptualising the policy issues that surround what might be termed the 'housing finance debate'. Part Two seeks to provide the reader with an up-to-date description and critical analysis of what might be termed the 'housing finance regime'. It also considers some aspects of 'financial management'. It begins by considering why and how the central authorities seek to support and control housing spending. It then turns to an analysis of the capital and revenue funding arrangements as they operate in the various tenures. The penultimate chapter considers the fiscal arrangements that exist to support those households that have difficulty in meeting their basic housing costs. The final chapter points to some of the housing issues that are likely to dominate the housing finance policy agenda over the next few years.

This part of the book makes constant reference back to the cross-tenure ideas and issues that were outlined in Part One.

CHAPTER 5:
The State and housing finance

We have stressed the point that housing is a commodity that is of central importance both to the social and economic well-being of individuals and the wider community. Recognition of this importance underpins much of the State's involvement over the years in the housing system and its associated financial arrangements. This involvement has a political, social and economic context. Although politics, economics and social concerns are fundamentally entwined, for the purposes of analysis we will consider them separately.

Political context

Much State activity is straightforwardly pragmatic and takes the form of responses to social and economic factors that are not directly under the control or influence of the government. For example, the nature of State involvement in the provision of housing, health, and education will, to some extent, be affected by such things as the changing structure of the population, divorce rates, world commodity prices, and people's expectations of the 'welfare state'. However, despite this, much of what governments say and do is consciously planned for in the sense that it stems from political aims and manifesto pledges.

It should be recognised that government policies are not arbitrarily plucked out of the air but are derived from the values and attitudes of policy-makers. In the twentieth century history of housing it is possible to detect two broadly distinct and competing approaches underlying the various policy changes that have occurred throughout the period. Simply put, some policy enactments have been derived from what might be termed a *market ideology* and others from what might be termed a *welfare ideology*.

Two historical agendas

Although it is beyond the scope of this book to describe the detailed history of housing policy, it is useful for the student of housing finance to be aware that, broadly speaking, legislative changes have been driven by two competing political views about society's social and economic objectives.

Market ideology is grounded in the belief that free-enterprise tends to be naturally efficient and fair and that the activities associated with the provision, consumption and exchange of housing should, as far as possible, be conducted by private individuals or firms rather than by the agents of central and local government. Market ideology tends to favour rent policies related to market prices and replacement costs rather than to people's ability to pay or to historic costs. It also tends to advocate subsidy arrangements that put purchasing power into people's pockets rather than those that are designed to lower or suppress market prices. That is, it tends to favour welfare arrangements that augment the incomes of poor households so as to give them more effective market power, rather than promoting policies that subsidise production or impose price controls. This is because both production subsidies and price controls are seen as distorting the market and keeping prices 'artificially' low by inhibiting or preventing them from rising to their 'true' market levels. Because it embraces the notion of 'self-reliance', market ideology is sympathetic to the idea that owner-occupation is deemed to be the 'natural' and 'normal' tenure arrangement for most people.

Welfare ideology is grounded in the belief that certain commodities have a social importance that is so great that the State should guarantee some minimum standard of provision for everyone. It emphasises the notion of *need* rather than that of *demand*, and it represents the value system that underlies what is popularly referred to as 'the welfare state'. It has been instrumental in developing the concept of *welfare rights*, and in the housing field is associated with the proposition that every household should have a decent home at a price they can afford. It tends to be sympathetic both to price control or regulation arrangements and to the provision of production subsidies designed to reduce the price of housing for people on low incomes. In general, it sees an active role for central and local government in the housing system. The welfare approach to housing provision and consumption is often reinforced by the argument that the housing market is so imperfectly competitive that it cannot be relied upon to achieve society's objectives.[1]

The following schema, Figure 5.1, illustrates how the two ideologies lead to different housing finance practices depending on the policy adopted. As a generalisation, market ideology tends to lead to demand-side income augmentation measures while welfare ideology tends to be more sympathetic to the provision of supply-side 'bricks and mortar' subsidies.

Figure 5.1: Market and welfare ideologies

MARKET	THEORY PRACTICE	WELFARE
Ideology Notion of 'self-reliance' within an enterprise culture		*Ideology* Notion of 'entitlement' and 'welfare rights'
Policy Emphasis on 'effective demand' and market mechanisms		*Policy* Emphasis on 'social need' and ability to pay (administrative mechanisms)
Delivery Market-related tenancies and rents Income support in the form of tax relief, rebates, allowances, etc. Measures to encourage owner-occupation		*Delivery* Regulated tenancies and rents Production subsidies (e.g. Exchequer grants to local authorities and SHG) Measures to support public provision of housing

---

1   See Chapter 3 for a discussion on *housing market failure*.

Although market ideology is generally associated with the political 'right' and welfare ideology with the political 'left', it would be an over-simplification to say that these two worldviews have exactly mirrored the party political divide in Britain over the years. For example, the Conservative administrations of the 1950s directed large-scale financial support in the form of production grants towards the provision of council housing while at the same time pursuing a market approach by relaxing controls on private sector rents. In recent years, despite its general commitment to welfare ideology, the Labour Party has, for politically pragmatic reasons, supported measures designed to increase access to owner-occupation. For such reasons it is more useful to think of two *ideological* rather than two strictly *party political* agendas competing for prominence in the housing policies of the twentieth century.

The market agenda of recent Conservative administrations has resulted in the gradual shrinking of the amount of economic activity carried out by local government and public corporations. Between the elections of Margaret Thatcher in 1979 and Tony Blair in 1997, General Government Expenditure on housing fell in real terms by some 71 per cent (see table 5.2). Although this represents a dramatic cut in capital spending on housing it over-states the amount by which housing expenditure in total was reduced in this period. This is because the expenditure category 'housing' does not include the rising costs of housing benefit – nor does it include the costs of a number of other measures designed to support owner-occupation (e.g. mortgage interest tax relief and discounts on right-to-buy sales).

Figure 5.2: The changing balance of subsidy

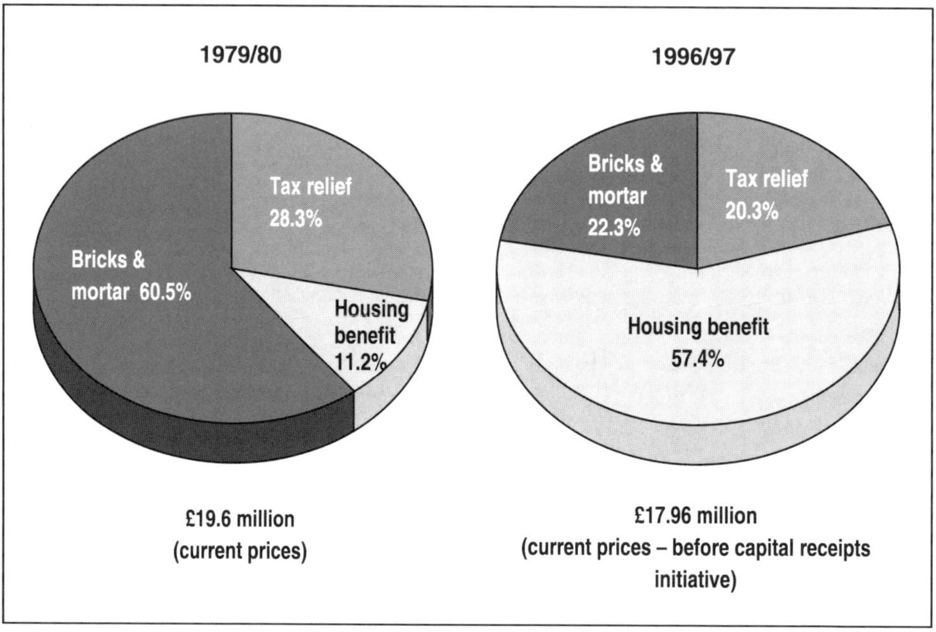

1979/80

Tax relief
28.3%

Bricks & mortar 60.5%

Housing benefit
11.2%

£19.6 million
(current prices)

1996/97

Bricks & mortar
22.3%

Tax relief
20.3%

Housing benefit
57.4%

£17.96 million
(current prices – before capital receipts initiative)

The current political agenda: a 'third way'?

In May 1997 a 'New Labour' government was returned to office with a policy agenda that was bedded in a philosophy that stemmed from the work of the Commission on Social Justice. The Commission was based at the Institute for Policy Research, the left-of-centre think tank. It was set up in 1992 while the Labour Party was in opposition. It was established on a date that coincided with the fiftieth anniversary of the publication of the immensely influential Beveridge Report, *Social Insurance and Allied Services*, which became the foundation of the post-war welfare state in the UK. The final report was published in 1994 (Commission on Social Justice, 1994), and it set out a broad policy agenda that centred on the following four propositions.

- There is a need to transform the welfare state from a safety net in times of trouble to a springboard for economic opportunity.
- There is a need to invest in people and radically improve access to education and training.
- There is a need to promote real choices in the balance of employment, family, education, leisure and retirement.
- There is a need to reconstruct the nation's social wealth and reform its social institutions so as to provide a dependable social environment in which people can lead their lives.

The 'New Labour' group of opposition politicians led by Tony Blair and Gordon Brown were also influenced by the early Clinton thinking about the so-called 'third way' that embraced policy programmes relating to welfare to work and social inclusion.

In office, the new government's commitment to the ideals of the Commission and the 'third way' found early expression in the form of declarations to enhance education spending and, where appropriate, to move people from welfare dependency to employment and economic independence. The new Prime Minister also established a Social Exclusion Unit to help co-ordinate the policies of government departments, local authorities and other agencies around the notion of 'best value', and to recommend changes in spending priorities.

To ensure that the priority reassessments were considered in a thorough and systematic way the government set up a *Comprehensive Spending Review* that was informed by the overriding principle that public spending should produce 'stability and investment for the long term'. The review covered all aspects of public expenditure and, in all, there were 43 separate departmental reviews carried out within Whitehall. The CSR altered the old control climate in one important respect. It shifted the measurement emphasis away from *costs* and *inputs* and towards the auditing of *quality* and *outputs*, relating to improving school reading ages, crime and illness being reduced, housing conditions up-graded, etc. The idea is that the output targets should be achieved in ways that are judged to be cost effective. To this end a policy commitment emerged to replace traditional cash accounting with a system of *resource accounting* by the year 2001. Widely used in the private sector, resource accounting requires departments and public bodies to know what assets they hold and to acknowledge that they are not 'cost free' simply because they are paid for, but that they cost money to keep running. The intention of resource accounting is to encourage public bodies to manage their assets in a more business-like fashion by making sure that the accounts record how much the asset is costing in the current period. This contrasts with cash accounting that records when the capital is *paid for* rather than when it is *used*.[2]

Under the CSR, the scrutiny of housing spending was co-ordinated by the DETR and the DSS, and alongside an analysis of mainstream housing expenditure, separate appraisals were made of the tax and benefit system and of spending on urban and community regeneration. The initial findings of the reviews were published in the summer of 1998 and their implications for housing are described and discussed at the end of this chapter and at various points throughout this book.

Although it may be inappropriate to refer to these changes as a new ideology or 'third way', they nevertheless provided an over-arching policy coherence to the new government's reshaping of the old historical divide between the ideals of Beveridge's welfare state and the principles of the market. As we will see later in the book, these New Labour postulations are clearly informing the present government's views about how best to finance housing consumption and production.

Implementing central government housing policy

Central government operates mainly through legislation, through regulations and by controlling the allocation of resources. To implement its policies it works with and through the following.

1. Four national housing bodies, referred to collectively in this book as 'regulators': the Housing Corporation in England, the Welsh Assembly (formerly the Welsh Office), Scottish Homes and the Northern Ireland Housing Executive. These currently act as agents for the distribution and allocation of capital grants and revenue subsidies to housing associations and other registered social landlords (RSLs).[3]

---

2   The idea of resource account predates the Labour government. The idea was introduced, for Whitehall departments, in the Treasury White Paper of July 1995. At that time, the then Chancellor, Kenneth Clarke, explained the basic idea of resource accounting by saying that it would allow auditors finally to get to grips with the quality of service provided, instead of 'measuring our performance by the rate at which we burn £10 notes'. (Reported by Michael White in *The Guardian*, April 1998).

3   In Wales and Scotland they are being restructured so that the Westminster Departments of State and the National Assembly for Wales and the Scottish Parliament can more effectively influence and co-ordinate regional housing policies (discussed below).

2. Local authorities, which are responsible for preparing local housing strategies, have important statutory duties, and own a significant proportion of the stock of social homes.
3. The private sector, in the form of housing associations, house builders, private landlords and lending institutions.
4. Voluntary bodies and agencies.

The Departments of State responsible for housing and local government

In England central-local relations centre on the Department of the Environment, Transport and the Regions (DETR)[4]. The DETR has the ultimate responsibility for developing and administering local government's structure, powers, conduct and finances. In this capacity, it has overall responsibility for the development and administration of the government's housing policy. The DETR also supervises the government's area regeneration and urban/rural programmes (See Chapter 10).

In the principality, since the mid-1960s, it was the Welsh Office and the Secretary of State for Wales that had general responsibility for housing and local government matters.[5] Significant changes have resulted from the creation of the Welsh Assembly. Under the Government of Wales Act, the Assembly has established a Partnership Council to ensure that the role of local government is safeguarded and that the Assembly and the 22 unitary Welsh local authorities work together in an effective way. The powers and responsibilities held by the Secretary of State until recently have now been transferred to the Assembly, although primary legislation remains a Westminster responsibility. One of the first tasks for the Assembly will be to approve and adopt a new Standard Spending Assessment formula, which sets the amount central government thinks councils should spend on a service.

A new co-ordinating housing agency originally called the Welsh Office Housing Department came into existence in November 1998 by merging Housing for Wales (Tai Cymru) with the Welsh Office Housing Division. This integrated Department is expected to bring the policy and financial, the operational, and the regulatory arrangements of all social landlords together into one supervisory organisation. It is intended that this will facilitate a more strategic approach to social housing provision. This reconstructed department will have its policy objectives set by the ministers and the National Assembly for Wales. As well as policy, finance and operational sections it will have a performance unit that has,

---

4   In 1997 the Department of the Environment and the Department of Transport were amalgamated to form the DETR as a single co-ordinating department of State.
5   The Welsh Office was established in April 1965, following the creation of the office of the Secretary of State for Wales in October 1964. As well as housing and local government matters, other Whitehall powers were delegated to the Office including those relating to roads, health, industry, agriculture, and economic policy.

amongst other things, taken on the regulatory functions of Tai Cymru. The new body also assesses local authorities' housing strategies and operational plans, allocates funding to registered social landlords on the basis of best value-for-money in meeting needs, and allocates development funding. The new body now serves the National Assembly for Wales directly, and goes by that title.

The Scottish Office Development Department (SODD), was responsible for developing and administering policy on housing and local government in Scotland.[6] It also supervised the government's area regeneration and urban/rural programmes (see Chapter 10). With the advent of the Scottish Parliament, its functions have been incorporated in the Scottish Executive, which reports to the Parliament through the Minister responsible for housing.

In Northern Ireland, plans for devolution are stalled at the time of writing because of the breakdown in the peace process. Under the plans, the Northern Ireland Department of the Environment, responsible for housing, would report to a new Assembly.

The establishment of a Scottish Parliament, Welsh Assembly, and Northern Ireland Assembly are all part of New Labour's blueprint for devolving power to the regions. English regional government is discussed but, as of yet, not acted upon. The government's argument appears to be that what the English regions need is economic rather than political regeneration. To date, ministers have argued that the best way to deliver this is through effective, streamlined co-ordinating agencies in the form of non-departmental public bodies. (See Chapter 8 for discussion on Regional Development Agencies).

Co-ordination versus devolution

Under New Labour it is possible to detect two somewhat contradictory tendencies. The government has established multi-departmental arrangements co-ordinated by the Cabinet Office with a view to establishing what the civil servants refer to as 'cross-cutting' policies to tackle issues of high political priority. The Social Exclusion Unit is the highest profile example of this approach. The idea of the Unit is to bring ministers together from across Whitehall, together with representatives from business and the voluntary sector, to deal with the multiple

---

6   The Scottish Executive's primary housing aims are to ensure an adequate supply of housing in Scotland, that allows for consumer choice and to bring about an effective use of resources, including the encouragement of private finance. The Scottish Executive sponsors Scottish Homes, the national housing agency whose purpose is to assist owner-occupation and to promote the development of a diverse rented sector by funding and supervising housing associations and other landlords who provide new and modernised housing to rent. The Executive provides advice and guidance to local authorities and other agencies on securing an adequate supply of housing for community care groups as part of the government's policy for Care in the Community, and for homeless people in priority need.

chronic deprivation that disfigures the poorest parts of Britain. It is generally accepted that the Unit might be seen as a pilot project that can set an example for future joint actions in other areas of concern.

However, this cross-cutting approach stands in sharp contrast to the devolution philosophy of the government. Once the Scottish Parliament, the Welsh and Northern Ireland Assemblies, and the English Regional Development Agencies are fully established, an increasing number of administrative issues will be devolved to regional institutions. It is inevitable that the devolved powers will embrace matters of finance. This is bound to work against the 'joined-up' approach to policy formation and implementation being looked for by the Cabinet. One of the most effective ways of achieving 'joined-up' policy is to provide parcels of public money that are ring-fenced and accounted for by reference to specific cross-cutting activities that focus on special areas of concern. This is difficult to achieve if the accountability patterns are complex and multi-faceted, and purse-holders are independent of Whitehall.

Social context

The emergence of social concern

Nineteenth century *laissez-faire* market attitudes remained largely unchallenged until a coherent and systematic welfare agenda began to emerge in the last quarter of the century. By that time there was much official and journalistic comment linking over-crowded and squalid living conditions with such social and moral evils as incest, prostitution and petty crime. But government intervention was most of all stimulated by the growing contemporary awareness of the relationship between insanitary housing and the incidence of communicable diseases such as cholera and typhoid.

Once the State began to intervene to establish minimum standards of housing provision as part of its drive to improve public health, the question of housing subsidies became an issue. The law prevented free market forces from adjusting housing standards downwards in line with the limited incomes of working class people. As a result, a more obvious gap emerged between the rent paying capacity of many households and the rent levels that needed to be charged by the market to provide less over-crowded and better quality dwellings. Simply put, once the State had intervened to improve housing standards, it brought to the fore the question of how the improved conditions should be paid for. It became clear that to realise fully the government's health and housing policy objectives would require additional interventionist measures in the area of housing finance.

After 1914 three broad strategies were adopted: rent control and regulation; the public provision of subsidised housing for the 'working classes'; and the encouragement of area based slum-clearance schemes. In addition, later in the century, financial assistance was also directed to the housing association movement and tax concessions and income augmentation measures were introduced to help people meet their housing-related expenses. In this way it can be argued that the social rationale for intervention was tied to society's desire to increase both the quantity and quality of the nation's housing stock and to help low-income households gain access to decent homes that are necessary for them to live healthy and active lives.

The qualified achievements of intervention

In many respects the interventionist measures have been successful and some recent commentators have argued that a prominent feature of Britain's recent housing history has been the closing of the post-Second World War gap that existed between the number of households and the number of dwellings. Between 1951 and 1980 the rate of growth of housing units was faster than the rate of growth of households, thereby creating an officially recorded crude national surplus of stock. Figures based on census and other official data indicate that a deficit of some 800,000 dwellings in 1951 had been transformed into an apparent surplus of 200,000 by 1971, and that this small crude surplus had been increased to about one million by 1980. The figures suggest that since 1980 the rates of growth of the housing stock and of households have remained more or less equal. By the late 1990s there were some 25,000,000 dwellings in the UK (Wilcox, S., 1999, Table 17C, p112), which more or less matched the officially recorded number of households (*Social Trends* 28, 1998 edition).

Although the apparent balancing of supply and demand has led some commentators to argue that, in general terms, housing need in Britain has been satisfied, such a crude comparison between the size of the total stock and the total number of households does not by itself show whether there are sufficient dwellings, and it certainly tells us nothing about the adequacy of the stock in terms of quality. There is currently a great deal of concern that the housing stock is deteriorating at a faster rate than it is being maintained. Estimates about the size of the repairs backlog associated with social housing vary but figures in excess of £20 billion are often quoted by researchers and practitioners.

Apart from crucial questions about the fitness of the stock, the apparent balance masks the existence of severe local and regional shortages and takes no account of the thousands of 'concealed households' made up of young adults, couples and one-parent families who live as part of someone else's household, often a parent's. It does not tell us anything about the relationship between housing costs and the ability to meet them, nor does it take account of the fact that not all of the dwellings are available for occupation, such as second homes, temporary voids and unlet properties held vacant with a view to sale. All of these qualifications mean that housing problems persist and that many households remain in housing need. We will consider the implications of this later in the chapter (refer to section *The need for future investment in housing as measured in 1996*).

Despite these important qualifications, the global figures do indicate that, as an historical trend, over the last one hundred years, general housing conditions for the mass of the British people have greatly improved. Much of this achievement has been the result of the financial provisions associated with the various forms of government intervention into the housing system.

These provisions constitute an important part of the mechanism by which money and credit pass through the housing system so as to enable all types of residential property to be built, improved, bought, rented, maintained, renewed and redeveloped. The arrangements operate within a legal and administrative framework established by Acts of Parliament and ministerial directives, and since the end of the First World War this framework has been subjected to a continuous stream of reforms and modifications that have stemmed from changes and shifts in government policy.

Throughout this period government policy has been concerned to utilise the system of housing finance to provide systems of support that are judged to be productive, efficient and equitable. In addition, there has been an overriding concern that the State should maintain a degree of control over the housing finance system to ensure that housing is regulated in the interests of the government's macro-economic policy objectives.

Economic context

The government's declared central economic objective is '*to achieve high and stable levels of economic growth and employment, which will promote greater fairness and social cohesion, while also respecting the environment*' (*Economic and Fiscal Strategy Report*, 1998). The pursuit of this objective gives central government a legitimate interest in influencing the nature and scope of public expenditure.

Defining public expenditure

There is no single definitive meaning of the term 'public expenditure'. Indeed, there is potential for confusion arising from the fact that a number of terms are used by journalists and commentators. These include, for example, 'State spending', 'government spending', and 'public spending', and it is not always clear from the context what the term being used precisely means.

The definitions of public expenditure used in official British publications that reference the Public Expenditure White Papers and the various fiscal reports all stem from accepted national accounting concepts that, in turn, broadly follow international guidelines. These official definitions can be rather confusing because of their technical nature and because they are periodically redefined or relabelled. Until 1999, the aggregate often referred to in official tables was 'GGE' which stands for General Government Expenditure.[7] GGE measures public expenditure for the government sector as a whole and is composed of three broad elements.

1. Central government spending.
2. Local government spending.
3. Subsidies to nationalised industries and public corporations.

---

7   In this calculation monies spent on cyclical Social Security (jobseekers' allowance and income support), and central government debt interest are included, as is spending financed from the National Lottery's contribution to the Exchequer. Privatisation proceeds are netted off rather than counted together with other general government receipts. This means that GGE treats privatisation receipts as a negative expenditure. Any self-financing expenditure of public corporations is not included. GGE(X) stands for Adjusted GGE and, under the previous Conservative Administration, this aggregate set the government's medium term spending strategy. It was calculated by excluding from GGE both privatisation proceeds and expenditure financed from the National Lottery. Receipts of interest and dividends from the private sector are also excluded from the calculation.

GGE(X) set a planning total or target expenditure to be aimed at by the Treasury. By attempting to control expenditure within this target cash total the government sought to achieve its wider medium term economic objectives. In this way the Chancellor of the Exchequer announced in his Financial Statement and Budget Report the government's commitment to controlling public expenditure by limiting growth in spending to a fixed average per year.

To help achieve the target set by GGE(X), the government sought to control expenditure by reference to a different measure called the *Control Total*. This focused on that part of GGE(X) that is under the direct control of the spending departments and agencies. This is now referred to as DEL and is discussed below. *The Control Total* was used in the control procedures operated by the Treasury and its officials who served on the Public Expenditure Survey Committee (PESC). The Control Total was described and analysed in a series of departmental publications that together constitute the annual White Paper on the Government's Expenditure Plans. As the name suggests, the Control Total excluded exogenous elements of GGE(X) that are not susceptible to direct governmental control (now referred to as AME). In particular it excluded such volatile components as central government debt interest, that cannot be tied to any specific spending agency or programme, and those parts of Social Security expenditure that are largely determined by the trade and employment cycles, such as the jobseekers' allowance and income support payments. It also ignored a number of accounting adjustments that appeared in GGE(X) as these also had nothing to do with the spending plans of departments. The following were also excluded on the grounds that they are independent of governmental control: depreciation allowances, pension increases paid to State employees, interest and dividend receipts of local authorities, and that part of the borrowing of nationalised industries and public corporations that have external finance treatment.

The Control Total definition brought together the major elements of the expenditure of central and local government and public corporations over which the government believed it *could* exercise a degree of control. It included the following:

• Central government's own expenditure.
• The capital and revenue grants that central government provides to local authorities.
• Credit approvals issued by central government authorising local authorities to incur capital expenditure financed by borrowing and other forms of credit.
• Local authority expenditure financed from the council tax.
• Non-domestic rate payments. Unlike the council tax, non-domestic rates are set nationally rather than by individual local authorities and are also included. Although local authorities collect payments, they do so as agents of central government.

Since 1999, the official total of public spending has been known as the Total Managed Expenditure (TME). TME is split into two categories: cyclical and non-cyclical. Cyclical spending, called Annually Managed Expenditure (AME), which includes much of Social Security spending, is assumed to be subject to changeable forces and events outside the control of the various spending departments, and is therefore subject to annual reviews rather than to longer-term plans. Non-cyclical expenditure, sometimes called 'The Control Total', is planned three years in advance under a procedure that sets Departmental Expenditure Limits (DELs). These are discussed and explained more fully below (in the sections *Public expenditure planning and control* and *Total Managed Expenditure*).

The extent of public expenditure

Total public spending currently amounts to more than £333 billion (1998). This represents about 40 per cent of national income and is equivalent to over £5,000 for every man, woman and child in Britain. Some of this spending is used to provide a wide range of services such as housing, health care, education, law and order, and defence, and some takes the form of transfer payments. For example, the government spent £96bn on Social Security in 1997/98.

Categorising public expenditure

There are various ways in which public expenditure might be classified. For the purposes of analysis it is useful to distinguish between the following categories: spending authority, function or programme; capital and revenue; economic activity and transfers.

Spending authority. The annual fiscal reports that set out the government's spending plans, discussed below, identify three broad spending authorities: central government, local authorities and public corporations. Central government is by far the largest spender, followed by local authorities.

Function and programme area. Social Security is the largest programme area at over a third of the total, followed by health and social services, about 18 per cent, and education, about 14 per cent. In recent years housing's share, measured as a proportion of total GGE, has fallen from 6.7 per cent in 1978/79 to 1.5 per cent in 1996/97.

- The external financing requirements of public corporations.
- A reserve to provide a margin for uncertainties. This is intended to cover any future net additions to items within the Control Total whether these result from policy changes, new initiatives, contingencies, or revised estimates of demand-led programmes such as winter shortfalls in health care provision.

The Control Total was the definition that was used when allocating funds between spending authorities and programme areas. The total was arrived at through an annual process of departmental negotiation that was co-ordinated by the Public Expenditure Survey Committee. The spending of a department such as the Department of the Environment, Transport and the Regions (DETR), was eventually set within the aggregate figure and specific budgets were also set within the departmental total. In this way the total standard spending (TSS), for local authorities and the grants and subsidies to other social housing agencies could be seen to form part of the Control Total.

Capital and current spending. The broad definition of *capital spending* used in the fiscal reports covers payments by the public sector either to renew or increase the nation's stock of physical assets. It covers expenditure on fixed assets (net of certain asset sales), stockbuilding, capital grants and net lending to the private sector, for capital projects. The wages and salaries of certain people in planning and supervising capital projects are included, and for local authorities it also includes the capital value of assets acquired under financial leases, property leased for more than 20 years and all vehicles leased for more than one year. The broad definition of *current spending* used in the fiscal reports covers payments made by the public sector on providing services, and largely consists of the wages and salaries of central and local government employees and the purchases of consumable goods and services by public sector organisations. In this context the notion of 'consumable' normally signifies that the purchase will be used up in the current financial year. It includes local authority payments of such things as mandatory student awards and rent rebates and allowances as part of housing benefit. Both local authority and central government spending is measured net of VAT.

Economic activity versus transfers. The aggregate figure for public expenditure falls into two distinct economic categories:

1. expenditure to generate economic activity; and,
2. expenditure on transfer disbursements.

Expenditure on economic activity produces real wealth and consists of all current and capital spending by central and local government and public corporations that directly contributes to the output of goods and services. Such expenditure absorbs real economic resources to produce housing, health, defence, education, and transport services, etc. In other words, it represents a measure of the State's direct financial engagement in economic activity.

By contrast, transfer disbursements involve a redistribution of money wealth from one set of private hands to another set of private hands and, as such, they are not directly used to finance public sector economic activity (see Figure 5.3). They include such items as student grants, housing benefit payments, subsidies to the private sector, State pensions and other Social Security payments.

Figure 5.3: Transfer disbursement

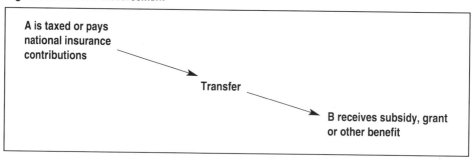

If we make the assumption that those who pay the most taxes and contributions do not receive the most disbursements, then we can say that such payments *redistribute* rather than *absorb* resources. Transfer expenditure has a direct *income redistribution effect* but only an indirect *economic effect*. The indirect economic effect results from the fact that the less well-off receivers of transfers will have a tendency to spend a higher proportion of their income than the better-off givers. This means that the transfers will affect the nature and scope of consumer spending and savings in the economy.

This way of categorising public expenditure allows for a more penetrating analysis of the global figures. It underlines the point that figures that show the growth in total expenditure may be masking a number of interesting social, economic and political issues. For example, it is sometimes argued that increases in public expenditure result in a redistribution of resources away from the private towards the public sector of the economy. This is not necessarily true: transfers, which in recent years have been the fastest growing element of public expenditure, may simply have the effect of redistributing resources between individuals within the private sector.

The argument for controlling public expenditure

Given the sums involved, central government has a legitimate interest in seeking to obtain value-for-money in its spending. Furthermore, the quality of public sector spending is bound to have an impact on the overall performance of the economy.

In the post-war period, British governments have instigated fiscal and monetary measures designed to establish an economic climate that will stimulate growth in output, employment and trade. Controlling the rate of inflation has been a central theme in the economic policies of all recent governments. Stable prices are seen to be a prerequisite to the maintenance of both long-run business confidence and international competitiveness. Inflation is also seen as being particularly damaging to the interests of vulnerable groups living on low and fixed incomes. Contemporary economic orthodoxy identifies a strong link between public expenditure and inflation and it is for this reason that controlling the level of public expenditure has become a key aspect of macro-economic policy. Simply put, the argument runs as follows. Public expenditure has to be paid for either by public sector borrowing or out of taxation. Increased borrowing involves an expansion of credit and thereby, effectively an increase in the money supply. If the increased money/credit base is not matched by an equivalent increase in national output, additional money demand will bid for roughly the same volume of output, and prices will rise as a result. If instead of borrowing, the public expenditure is paid for by raising indirect taxes (VAT, etc), this additional financial burden to suppliers is likely to be passed on to consumers in the form of higher prices. If, on the other hand, the increased expenditure is paid for by means of direct taxation (income tax, etc), this may lead to compensatory wage claims that will add to both consumer demand and production costs and this would also put upward pressure on prices.

When political arguments in favour of small government and low taxation are added to the economic reasoning outlined above, it can be understood why recent administrations have made the control of public expenditure such a prominent part of their strategies for regulating the economy.

Cash-limiting public expenditure on housing as an expressed part of government economic regulation began with measures introduced in 1976 by the Labour Chancellor, Denis Healey, and then became firmly embedded in the policies of the Conservative administrations that followed the general election of 1979. In comparison with other welfare programmes such as education and health, housing expenditure is capital intensive. This means that, unlike these other programmes, significant short-term savings in housing expenditure can be made by cancelling or postponing proposed building, improvement and repair works. In more labour intensive programme areas substantial savings can only be made by laying-off personnel. Of course, reducing the level of building activity creates unemployment in the construction industry and its related professions, but it does so in a less specific and obvious way than by sacking identifiable teachers, social workers, nurses, doctors and administrators. Furthermore, unlike much other welfare provision, social housing is used by a minority of the electorate thereby limiting the political impact of any cutbacks. For all these reasons it has proved to be politically easier to cut housing expenditure than most other big spending programme areas.

Sources of public finance

To pay for public expenditure central and local government collects revenue and borrows money. Currently, just over a third of revenue receipts are taken by the Inland Revenue in the form of income tax, corporation tax, petroleum revenue tax, capital gains tax, inheritance tax and stamp duties. About a third is collected by Customs and Excise in the form of VAT, fuel and tobacco duties, etc. Almost a third is raised by the combination of Social Security contributions, business rates, council tax, oil royalties and vehicle excise duties. Interest, dividends, rent, etc. contribute about six per cent of total receipts. In the recent past, privatisation receipts brought in about one per cent of the total general government receipts (HM Treasury,1996 and Wilcox, 1995, table 11b). The shortfall gap between total public spending and collected revenues creates a requirement for the public sector to borrow from other sectors of the economy and from overseas.[8]

---

8   For details see Wilcox, 1999, table 12b, p101.

European Structural Funds

Some housing projects are part funded from the European Regional Development Fund (ERDF). The ERDF is one of three European Union Structural Funds, the others being the European Social Fund and the European Agricultural Guidance and Guarantee Fund. While ERDF grants are additional to national expenditure, in the UK they are treated as public expenditure because the UK is a net contributor to the European Union budget. Provision for this is included in the public expenditure programmes of the departments co-ordinating funded projects.

Measures of public sector debt

The gap between what the government collects, in taxes and other revenue receipts, and what it spends, sets the public sector's net cash/credit requirement. In the published finance tables this requirement is referred to as *Public Sector Net Borrowing* (PSNB). PSNB is an accruals-based measure[9] that is calculated net of privatisation receipts and excludes certain other financial transactions that would be included in a 'cash-flow' but not in an 'accruals' calculation. It embraces the market and overseas borrowings of UK public corporations as well as the deficit spending of central and local government. The PSNB is the primary measure of the government's budget deficit.

The cash/credit gap always used to be measured in terms of a broader, cash-flow financial indicator known as the *Public Sector Borrowing Requirement* (PSBR), which, despite its title, does not exactly match what the government has to borrow. The PSBR, which is still used, measures the public sector's net cash requirement rather than its actual borrowing requirement. The shift from the PSBR to PSNB was made in 1998 to give greater accuracy and prominence to the recording of public sector debt. (*HM Treasury News Release 101/98*, 11 June 1998). The change was based on the assumption that this stricter measure of public sector indebtedness gives a better indication of the underlying budgetary position. By being an accruals-based measure, PSNB excludes privatisations and other financial transactions that affect cash measures of borrowing such as the PSBR. This means it is more consistent with the national accounts and internationally agreed measures of the deficit, and is not distorted by year to year cash movements.

In recent years both the Chartered Institute of Housing and the Local Government Association have advocated the use of a different measure of public sector indebtedness called the *General Government Financial Deficit* (GGFD). This is the measure that has been adopted by the EU to establish the economic convergence criteria for European Monetary Union[10]. The key feature of GGFD is that, unlike

---

9   The distinction between an accruals-based and a cash-based approach to recording financial transactions is discussed in Chapter 2 (refer to section *Making good use of scarce resources*).

10 The government will have to use the GGFD to show it has met the Maastricht Treaty criteria. The requirement is that a participating member State's GGFD must be less than three per cent of its GDP.

the PSNB and the PSBR, it does not include borrowing by *public corporations*. The CIH/LGA argument in favour of the employment of this measure centres on the fact that it would allow for investment in *local housing corporations* without technically adding to the government's total borrowing. This argument is discussed more fully later in the chapter (see also Chapter 10).

The principles and rules governing public finances

The presentational framework for analysing, planning and controlling the nation's public spending is broadly structured in line with national and international accounting conventions. The precise nature of the current format was introduced by the Chancellor, Gordon Brown, in the first *Economic and Fiscal Strategy Report* in June 1998. The current fiscal procedures are based on an over-arching commitment to a financial management framework that will support long-term planning; focus on outputs rather than inputs; recognise the essential difference between current and capital spending; and promote prudence, stability and investment for the long-term (HM Treasury News Release 97/98, 11 June 1998). This commitment has produced public expenditure planning and management arrangements that are grounded in a five-point fiscal code and three key fiscal rules. In the near future public expenditure planning and management will also be operated in line with revised accounting rules known as *resource accounting and budgeting* (RAB).

The five-point fiscal code

1. *Transparency* in the setting of fiscal policy objectives, the implementation of fiscal policy and in the publication of the public accounts.
2. *Stability* in the fiscal policy-making process and in the way fiscal policy impacts on the economy.
3. *Responsibility* in the management of the public finances.
4. *Fairness*, including fairness between generations.
5. *Efficiency* in the design and implementation of fiscal policy and in managing both sides of the public sector balance sheet.

Three key fiscal rules

The present Chancellor has established two key operational rules, one applying to current spending and the other to capital spending. He has also confirmed the continued operation, for the time being, of a third long-established Treasury dictate known as the 'financing rule'.

1. Current spending, cyclical and non-cyclical, is subject to a fiscal edict called *'the golden rule'* which states that departments must meet all current expenditure out of current revenue over the economic cycle. Put another

way, this means that, in the medium term, the government will borrow only to invest and not to fund current spending. This is part of the government's commitment to see that debt is normally only generated to cover capital investment (that can generate long-run returns to help service that debt). The surplus on current budget, current receipts minus current spending, is called the 'current balance' and is used to determine whether the golden rule is met over the economic cycle. The golden rule promotes *fairness* between generations by ensuring that the bill for today's current spending, which mainly benefits today's taxpayers, will not be passed on to future generations. It promotes *responsibility* by highlighting the distinction between the nature of current and capital spending – thus pointing to a duty to maintain the level of investment required to meet the economy's needs and to ensure that the public capital stock is kept in good condition.

2.   Borrowing to fund capital expenditure is constrained by the second of the Chancellor's key fiscal rules. The '*sustainable investment rule*' states that net public debt as a proportion of national income (GDP), should be held over the economic cycle at a 'stable and prudent level', currently set at 40 per cent. The rule was introduced to help contain the level of interest payments on the public debt by bearing down on the debt to GDP ratio.

3.   The third fiscal rule is a long-standing Treasury edict called '*the financing rule*'. This is a simple Treasury regulation that states that *for an organisation to borrow outside of the PSNB (previously the PSBR), it must be under private ownership and control.* How this rule affects the ways in which housing is funded is discussed in some detail later in this chapter. (see section; *An alternative to the PSNB and PSBR and the case for local housing corporations*)

Delivering the five-point fiscal code

The golden rule is being implemented using a definition of the current balance that is in line with the concept used in the national accounts (that are themselves published according to the definitions set out in the European System of Accounts 1995 – ESA95). In terms of this definition, depreciation is counted as current rather than capital spending. This ensures that current taxpayers meet the costs of maintaining the capital stock. Using agreed and recognised definitions helps to make performance against the golden rule more *transparent*. The new code requires governments to report regularly on progress in meeting their fiscal objectives. Since 1998 the familiar *Financial Statement and Budget Report* has been supplemented each year by an *Economic and Fiscal Strategy Report* that sets out the government's long-term strategy and objectives. The code now also requires a *Pre-Budget Report* to be published that will allow the skills and expertise of others to be drawn upon when formulating policy. Together, these reports are intended to allow Parliament, in particular, the Treasury Select Committee, and the public, to scrutinise the government's fiscal plans.

The principle of *responsibility* is manifested in the government's commitment to keep debt at levels that are judged to be 'prudent'. A *responsible* approach involves holding public debt to a 'sustainable' proportion of GDP[11]. In this context, 'sustainability' exists if, on the basis of reasonable assumptions, the government can be expected to maintain its current spending and taxation policies indefinitely while continuing to meet its debt interest obligations. The *responsibility principle* is based on the assumption that 'excessive' borrowing has detrimental economic effects. This assumption produces the intention that borrowing should be used only to fund value-for-money investment. The *Comprehensive Spending Review* (CSR), was the mechanism chosen by the New Labour government as the key method of determining what counts as a value-for-money investment. (The CSR is discussed at the end of this chapter).

This *responsibility* approach is consistent with the principle of *fairness*. By funding current spending from current revenue over the economic cycle, today's taxpayers bear the full cost of the public sector current spending from which they benefit.

By design, the fiscal rules are intended to lead to greater economic and fiscal *stability*. The new strategic approach is meant to allow decision-makers to plan and invest for the longer-term, confident in the knowledge that the public finances will not be managed in a 'profligate' fashion that might necessitate a sudden adjustment at some point in the future.

In pursuit of resource *efficiency*, the National Assets Register has been established to provide an indication of the extent and location of public sector assets. Departments are being encouraged to dispose of assets that are not contributing to service objectives. The principle of *focusing on outputs* rather than inputs is exemplified by the current rationalisation of the private sector's role in public service provision. With increasing use of Public/Private Partnerships (PPP), and especially the Private Finance Initiative (PFI), the public sector is moving more to being a sponsor, as against a direct provider of investment, where this offers a more effective way of delivering public services. In the new fiscal framework, the benefits of PFI and other forms of PPP are now seen in terms of securing the best value-for-money, rather than producing a temporary reduction in the PSNB (or PSBR). The argument here is that a simplistic focusing on the PSNB does not give a true indication of investment *efficiency*. In order to evaluate the true economic consequences of public investment we need to consider how that investment affects both sides of the public sector balance sheet. This in turn requires a shift to resource accounting and budgeting.

---

11   To a large extent the 'prudent' level of debt depends on the size of the economy since it becomes possible to sustain a higher money level of debt as national income grows. This is why the fiscal rule is specified in terms of the ratio of public debt to GDP.

Resource accounting and budgeting (RAB)

In the near future, RAB will underpin the operation of *the golden rule* and the drive towards better stewardship of public assets. Based on accruals accounting and making a clear structural distinction between current and capital spending, RAB will capture the full cost of resources consumed in the production of outputs in each reporting period. It is also expected that the introduction of *capital charging* for government departments will provide strong incentives to use capital productively.

The public sector balance sheet

The PSNB and PSBR focus on the public sector's net financial liabilities. The government is now beginning to pay more attention to movements in the public sector balance sheet, which includes tangible assets as well as net financial liabilities. There are, however, data and conceptual difficulties that need to be addressed before the balance sheet can be given a more formal role in the fiscal framework. In particular, the shift to Resource Accounting and Budgeting will provide more accurate balance sheet data as well as underpinning the golden rule.

By recognising that certain forms of public expenditure constitute capital investment, resource accounting establishes a public sector 'balance sheet' that allows policy-makers to consider properly the long-run economic and financial consequences of investing or not investing in capital projects. It makes clear for example, that if taxes were raised and invested in more or improved council housing, then the public sector's asset base would have increased without any additional debt being incurred. It would make clear that if council houses were built with borrowed funds then both local government debts and assets would have increased. Such an approach would also show that if council houses were sold and the receipts used to pay off public sector debts, it would have the effect of reducing the stock of built assets and thus the ability of local authorities to generate future rental income flows. The implications for local government finance of such a shift are discussed more fully in subsequent chapters. The implications for housing management are discussed at the end of this chapter (see below, *An alternative to the PSNB and PSBR and the case for local housing corporations*).

Public expenditure planning and control

The government's task can be thought of as comprising two broad activities:

1. making a political decision as to what total should be planned for and how that total should be allocated between different programmes; and
2. controlling and accounting for the actual spending outturns so that the outcomes match the plan and the constitutional requirements of Parliamentary control over spending of public money are fulfilled.

The planning process now includes a pre-Budget statement by the Chancellor of the Exchequer in the autumn that sets out his early thinking. [12] The process culminates in the *Financial Statement and Budget Report* that the Chancellor presents to Parliament in the spring prior to the passage of the Finance Bill. Once enacted, the Finance Bill gives statutory force to the provisions of the annual unified Budget.

Reliance on cash limits

For their plans to be realised governments need to establish procedures that influence the behaviour of those institutions and organisations that do the front-line spending. Cash limits are the main control mechanism. Cash limits quite simply set a ceiling on the amount of cash the government proposes to spend or authorise on specific services or blocks of services during a particular financial planning period.

The majority of cash limits are based on the Supply Estimates (see below), and cover direct expenditure by central government and its voted grants and lending to other public sector bodies. In this way, the bulk of public expenditure is cash limited including the amount of money the government contributes towards local government finance (called Aggregate External Finance) and capital expenditure financed by borrowing.

The emphasis on cash limiting as a control mechanism has focused attention on cash-flow management in the public sector and sharpened up procedures for controlling costs. However, it has been criticised for undervaluing long-term investment, as discussed above. It is also regarded by some as a 'surrogate pay policy' for the public sector because in setting a limit, the government seems to be taking a view about the appropriate level of salaries and wages in the coming year.

Total Managed Expenditure

The relationship between the three categories of public spending can be expressed by the formula: DEL + AME = TME. The move to a three-year planning period is part of the government's general commitment to get away from procedures that emphasise 'short termism' (see earlier section, *Defining public expenditure*).

---

12   In the 1998 Finance Act the government legislated for a Code for Fiscal Stability which requires more open and comprehensive reporting of the public accounts. Among other things, the fiscal strategy's key assumptions are examined and tested by the independent National Audit Office. Under the *Code for Fiscal Stability*, that was given the force of law in the 1998 Finance Act, an *Economic and Fiscal Strategy Report* (EFSR), has to be prepared and laid before Parliament each financial year. This sets out the government's fiscal strategy and planned spending totals and explains how the government's new fiscal approach seeks to achieve the central economic objective of 'high and stable levels of growth and employment' (EFSR, 1998, Chapter 1). The EFSR is accompanied by a series of Treasury press releases designed to communicate the government's spending intentions to a wider public and amplify the thinking behind its fiscal strategy.

That part of TME that is subjected to Parliamentary scrutiny is called *supply expenditure*. The term *supply expenditure* refers to that expenditure that is directly financed by money voted by Parliament in the Supply Estimates. Voted expenditure covers most of central government's own expenditure and central government support for the expenditure of local authorities. The main category of expenditure within the TME which is not covered by the Supply Estimates is expenditure related to the National Insurance Fund which provides over half the spending on Social Security.

Within TME, capital and current expenditures are planned and managed separately to ensure that the fiscal rules are met, and to prevent capital investment being cut back to meet short-term pressures on current expenditure. This is part of the government's general commitment to draw a distinction between the need to manage day-to-day spending prudently and the need to invest wisely in the future. As we made clear earlier in this chapter, the distinction between capital and current expenditure is seen to be of some economic significance. Capital investment in industry, commerce and the social fabric is regarded as an essential element in the maintenance of long-term economic prosperity and social well-being.[13]

Departmental planning and control: spending inside the DEL

The public spending round has been a feature of British economic life since the early sixties. It has established an annual cycle of year-on-year incremental bids by spending departments.[14] The planned spending totals are arrived at by a process of negotiation between the Treasury and the various spending departments and are discussed in Parliament as part of the Budget debate before being enacted via the provisions of the Finance Act. These negotiation arrangements are under review. (The pre-1997 arrangements are described in Appendix 5B at the end of this chapter). The present government's criticism of the established public spending round, i.e. pre-1997, is that settlements were reached by bargaining over inputs rather than by an analysis of outputs and efficiency. This, it is argued, has led to excessive departmentalism; an unrealistic and unhelpful split between private and public provision; and a bias towards consumption today rather than investment in the future.

Under arrangements established in June 1998, non-cyclical programmes, including housing, are set 'firm and realistic' plans and fixed capital budgets for

---

13   The importance of capital investment has been reinforced by the creation of the Investing in Britain Fund designed to modernise the nation's infrastructure and social assets.

14   Since 1978 the allocation of increases or decreases in public expenditure in Scotland has focused on a population-based mechanism rather than relying on the conventional approach of political bargaining between departments and the Treasury over their totals. This mechanism is known as the 'Barnett Formula'.

three years at a time.[15] Where possible, similar agreements will be made for the associated current running costs. The planned-for limits reference performance targets and are set in cash terms to provide a clear incentive for departments to control their costs and they are reviewed only if inflation varies substantially from forecast. In this way, the new system moves from an annual cycle to multi-year plans. To ensure that the Chancellor's fiscal rules are met, and to make possible long-term investment in the nation's infrastructure, departments are given distinct current and capital budgets and are expected to manage them separately. The idea is that investment plans are not squeezed out by pressure of current spending. As well as a clearer distinction between current and capital spending, service expenditures have to be justified by 'proper analysis' of their effectiveness rather than bargaining over inputs.

These multi-year plans are drawn together in a new aggregate, Departmental Expenditure Limits (DEL).[16] The revised arrangements put an emphasis on the co-ordination and integration of services rather than departmentalism and a piecemeal approach to spending. The idea of this *planning approach* is to move away from a procedure of *incremental budgeting*, in which a department is given a bit more or a bit less than before, to the laying down of departmental targets for efficiency and performance (i.e. *resource budgeting*). Under the old arrangements the Treasury and individual spending departments engaged in 'bilateral' bargaining meetings (see Appendix 5B). Under current arrangements interdepartmental consequences of spending, or not spending, have to be analysed. The new system is also based on a 'proper understanding' of the role and limits of government: *'a shift from the state only as owner, manager and employer to the state as also facilitator and partner'* (EFSR 1998, Introduction).

To bring a degree of flexibility into the planning approach, since 1999 departments have been given extended powers to carry budgets over from year to year. Departmental agents, such as local authorities, are given the same flexibility to carry over year-end under-spends. Resources are consciously allocated and monitored on the basis of agreed outcomes, and departments and their spending agents are set clear quality standards. In local government this takes the form of a duty to provide *best value*. As part of the best value regime, an inspectorate of housing has been established to help improve the management of council housing, set standards for performance and guarantee high quality of investment. It operates under the Audit Commission and will carry out regular inspections of housing departments. (This is discussed fully in subsequent chapters).

About one half of TME is within DEL. The remaining half is made up of Annually Managed Expenditure (AME).

---

15   Rolled forward for a further three years when RAB is introduced in 2001.
16   DEL includes spending funded by the Capital Receipts Initiative and spending on 'welfare to work', which is administered through an inter-departmental budget that is subject to special control arrangements.

Annually Managed Expenditure: spending outside the DEL

Firm multi-year limits are not seen to be appropriate for the large demand-led (i.e. cyclical) programmes that are brought together in Annually Managed Expenditure (AME). AME is subject to annual scrutiny as part of the Budget process and taken into account when the government sets its plan for TME and DEL. The main elements in AME are Social Security expenditure, local authority self-financed expenditure (LASFE), self-financing public corporations, Scottish expenditure financed by the Scottish variable rate of income tax and non-domestic rates, payments under the Common Agricultural Policy, and net payments to EU institutions, the National Lottery, and central government gross debt interest.

The relative position of housing in total public spending

Public expenditure by function. The main programme areas identified in the White Papers and fiscal reports are shown in Table 5.1.

Table 5.1 Percentage shares of general government expenditure

Year	1978-79	1989-90	1994-95	1998-99
Social Security	26.0	30.3	34.5	34.9
Health and social services	14.2	16.8	17.7	19.6
Education and science	14.5	14.2	13.4	13.5
Defence	11.5	11.6	8.5	7.8
Law and order	3.9	5.0	5.9	6.1
Transport	4.6	3.9	3.9	3.0
Trade and industry	6.4	4.0	3.3	3.0
HOUSING	**6.7**	**2.1**	**2.1**	**1.3**
Agriculture, fish and food	1.6	1.3	1.5	1.7

(Sources: based on Government Expenditure Plans 1990-91 to 1992-93 and Wilcox, 1995, 1996 and 1999. Note: GGE is defined earlier.)

If shares of public expenditure are measured against the total value of national output (Gross Domestic Product), rather than against General Government Expenditure, the order of public spending priorities is not altered. Public sector spending on housing as a proportion of GDP in 1995-96 was 0.7 per cent. The relative national decline of the programme area is illustrated by the fact that in 1981-82 its share of GDP was as high as 1.6 per cent (HM Treasury, 1996). Measured in absolute terms, some £7 billion was set aside for social housing in 1975. To have kept up with inflation, by the late 1990s this figure would have had to have risen to something like £24 billion, but was in fact less than £4 billion.

Current national investment in housing

The level of housing investment can be measured in a number of ways – gross fixed housing capital formation as a percentage of GDP, dwellings constructed compared to population size, or net additions to the stock. Whichever measure is used, research indicates that housing investment in the UK is low by the standards of other developed economies[17]. In recent years the UK devoted on average 3.6 per cent of GDP to gross fixed capital formation in housing which is less than the USA, Ireland, New Zealand and Sweden who invested over four per cent, and significantly less than Italy, France, Germany and Canada who invested about six per cent in house-building and improvements. Between 1980 and 1997 General Government Expenditure on housing fell by nearly 68 per cent in real terms which was the most severe drop in expenditure for any government service during that period. Whereas household numbers increased by 280,000 per annum in the period 1981-93, the number of dwellings increased only by about 200,000. Social housing completions fell from an average of 134,000 per annum in the 1970s to about 34,000 in the early 1990s.

Figure 5.4: Gross fixed investment in residential buildings as a percentage of GDP[1]

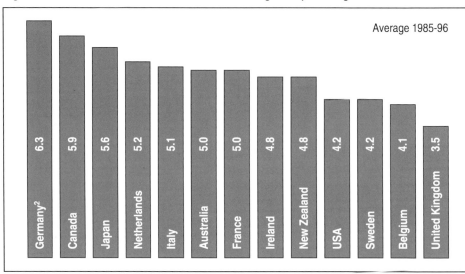

Source: Wilcox (1999)
Notes: 1. Gross fixed investment in dwellings and Gross Domestic Product are at market prices.
        2. The Federal Republic as constituted before reunification for the years until 1990.

The dramatic decline in housing's share of public expenditure is illustrated by the following table of comparisons. (Wilcox, 1999, p106, Table 15b.).

---

17   Research funded by Avebury International, Michael Oxley and Jacqueline Smith, *A European Perspective of Housing Investment in the UK*, Avebury, 1996. See also Wilcox, 1997, p70, Table 7.

Table 5.2: Real growth in percentage share of GGE 1980-81 to 1998-99

Law and order	88.3
Social Security	79.0
Agriculture, fish and food	35.7
Health and social services	73.7
Education	31.2
Culture, media and sport	86.1
Overseas aid	15.9
Environmental services	11.9
Transport	-13.5
Trade and industry	-23.4
Defence	-15.3
HOUSING	**-71.5**
Misc. expenditure	21.1
Total expenditure on services	39.4

The cuts in the housing programme have been particularly heavy in the local government sector. By 1999, Housing Investment Allocations to councils had dropped to a quarter in real terms of what they were in 1979. Although dramatic, the cutbacks in the housing programme area have to be seen against wider commitments in public spending in this period on housing benefit, mortgage interest tax relief, capital gains concessions, discounts on right-to-buy sales, and other financial aid given to support home-ownership and urban renewal. Financial support for these housing-related measures either do not appear in the public accounts or are counted as elements of other programme areas. Taking these measures into consideration we can argue that Table 5.2 somewhat over-states the real cuts in government support to housing and that in recent years there has not so much been a huge cut on housing expenditure as a redistribution of support away from bricks and mortar subsidies towards housing benefit and support to home-ownership.[18] The nature and scope of this redistribution is discussed in subsequent chapters.

The need for future investment in housing as measured in 1996

Between the budgets of 1993 and 1996 the government cut its commitment to housing development programmes by some £1.3 billion: the CIH estimate that these cuts alone represent a loss of 220,000 social rented homes (Wild, 1996, p14.). Of equal concern is the state of the existing stock. The physical state of the stock is officially measured by reference to the findings of periodic condition surveys. The seventh English house condition survey was published in May 1998 and describes conditions in 1996. The Scottish 1996 survey was published in

18   The 1995 White Paper *Our Future Homes* indicated that total housing expenditure on all rented housing in real terms was about the same in 1994/95 as it had been in 1979/80.

October 1997, Northern Ireland's in August 1998 and the Welsh was published in 1999.[19]

The English survey shows that although over 90 per cent of households were satisfied with the state of their homes in 1996, there was little change in the condition of the worst housing since the previous survey in 1991. In the 1996 survey 7.5 per cent of the English stock was classified as unfit, at about 1.5 million dwellings, compared with 7.6 per cent in 1991. The housing fitness standard, called the 'tolerable standard' in Scotland, consists of a set of minimum requirements deemed to be necessary for a dwelling to be regarded as fit for habitation. A dwelling is classified as 'unfit' if, in the local authority's view, it fails any one of the requirements. The standard is currently being reviewed in England and Wales. The Scottish standard uses slightly different technical references. The number of occupied dwellings in Scotland which were below the tolerable standard fell from 4.7 per cent in 1991 to 1 per cent in 1996. This figure has been contested by a number of local authorities who argue that, because of changes in the measurement criteria, the official figure significantly over-estimates the improvement between 1991 and 1996.

Table 5.2 indicates how badly housing has fared in recent years in comparison with other programmes. The most obvious practical effects of these substantial cuts have been rising rent levels, a reduction in public sector house-building, and a reduction in the frequency of repairs and maintenance of the existing public stock.

There is a general consensus that Britain needs to invest more in social housing. More than 1.7 million homes in Britain are classified as unfit and many more provide inadequate living conditions. There is a shortfall in provision and the existing council stock is under-maintained. In the late 1990s the Commons Environment Committee estimated that an extra 90,000 affordable rented homes would be needed each year for 20 years and the Environment Secretary stated that 4.4 million homes would be needed by the year 2016.[20] However, on trends apparent in 1997, by the year 2000, only 42,000 will be provided. The estimated shortfall between official estimates of the requirements for, and the likely provision of, affordable homes to rent is one crude measure of the scope of national housing need. However, any measure of this shortfall inevitably masks significant regional variations.

Although estimates of the size of the investment backlog vary, the Chartered Institute of Housing and others have called for a building programme of some 100,000 affordable rented houses per year to satisfy unmet need, and has estimated the backlog of disrepair and improvement work in British council housing to be £20 billion (see Moody, 1998). It is now accepted that there is no

---

19   For a summary of findings and further references see Wilson, I.,'Fact File', in *Housing*, September 1998, p46.

20   More recent DETR press releases compare a 3.8 million household growth over 25 years to 2021 with the earlier 4.4 million projection over the 25 years to 2016.

'quick fix' way of making good a shortfall on this scale: releasing capital receipts and allowing local authorities to borrow more within current borrowing rules would not deal with the backlog of construction and repairs within any reasonable timescale. What is needed is a multi-million pound injection of borrowed funds. There is an argument that such an injection has been inhibited by Treasury public spending rules.

How housing investment has been inhibited by Treasury rules

Although housing associations have been given the freedom to borrow against the value of their rental flow or on the equity in their built assets, different rules apply to local authorities. It has long been argued that adequate investment in council housing is inhibited by the way the Treasury has treated public sector debt. As we have seen, in planning and controlling levels of public expenditure in the 1980s and 1990s, the Treasury used a particular financial model that lumps all economic activity in the public sector into one category that is defined and measured by reference to the PSNB/PSBR.[21] The assumption has been made that, in the medium term, any addition to public spending involving borrowing will increase the PSBR. Control has then been established by making reference to the Treasury rule that states that, '*for an organisation to borrow outside of the PSBR/PSNB it must be under private ownership and control.*' This is the so-called 'financing rule' (the Treasury rules are discussed above).

This deficit measure has been favoured by the Treasury partly because of the straightforward cash-flow basis of its calculation that accommodates easy comparison with monies that have to be raised to finance public activities. It fits in particularly well with the government's traditional expenditure control mechanisms that focus on the setting of cash limits. It has also been favoured because it embraces the whole of the public sector thereby covering all forms of spending and all types of spending agency. By the 1990s, these very 'strengths' were being pointed to by some as problematic and other 'more appropriate' indices were being advocated. We will now return to the critique of the financing rule and look at the argument in more detail.

The broad argument runs along the following lines. If the public sector borrows, it immediately counts as part of PSBR and affects the PSNB. No distinction is made between monies borrowed for consumption or investment. It is argued that a clear distinction needs to be made between these two broad spending purposes. Indeed, the argument normally goes further and suggests that we also need to recognise a difference between public sector borrowing to invest in the infrastructure and borrowing for investment in trading operations, where the investment will generate a calculable commercial return. These distinctions between the nature and purpose of public borrowing are made in most other countries.

---

21   Since 1998 the PSBR is no longer used as the key measure of the level of borrowing. The Treasury now focuses on what is called Public Sector Net Borrowing (PSNB). See above for an explanation of the distinction between the two measures.

The use of the PSBR as a major financial indicator was not established in Britain until the 1970s and it is not used by any other EU government, all of whom tend to focus primarily on the deficits of central and local government in their attempts to monitor and control their levels of public expenditure. The use of the PSBR in Britain was given added significance in the 1980s when it featured as the centrepiece of the Treasury's medium term financial strategy. Since that time, controlling the PSBR has been seen as an alternative to putting up interest rates as a way of restricting the growth in the money supply and thus curbing inflation.[22]

An alternative to the PSNB and PSBR and the case for local housing corporations

Critics argue that, as an economic indicator, the PSBR inhibits public sector enterprise by failing to distinguish between different forms of expenditure. For example, it makes no distinction between borrowing to run the health, education and Social Security services, borrowing because the national accounts do not balance, and borrowing for investment purposes such as building and improving houses or re-equipping public corporations to enhance their commercial effectiveness. The assumptions behind the PSBR/PSNB control model are encapsulated by the simple Treasury rule that all spending by local government and public corporations counts as public expenditure. Traditionally the PSBR model made no distinctions between forms of expenditure, and critics argued that by headlining a single cash-flow figure of public sector indebtedness, it tends to discourage much needed capital investment in our social infrastructure. For this reason, in 1997, the New Labour government established the 'golden rule' that over the economic cycle net government borrowing should be restricted to investment projects.

Some commentators argue that to encourage appropriate levels of investment, we need to move completely away from the *cash-flow* approach of measuring public expenditure that is associated with the PSBR and embrace the *resource accounting* approach to public sector financial management that is pointed to by the GGFD measure (refer above and Chapter 2).

We have already made the point that by recognising that certain forms of public expenditure constitute capital investment, resource accounting establishes a public sector 'balance sheet' that allows policy-makers to consider the long-run economic and financial consequences of investing or not investing in capital projects. The shift to RAB and a balance sheet approach to the management of public finances will help to establish a fiscal framework that considers the real long-run economic consequences of public investment. In recent years there has

---

22   The argument here was grounded in the assumptions of 'monetarist' economics that there is
     a direct connection between the size of the PSBR and inflationary pressure in the economy.
     This notion is based on the fact that government borrowing expands the credit base and thus
     expands the money supply.

been a strong housing lobby arguing for a shift away from policy that simply focuses on the PSBR (net financial liabilities), to one in which consideration is also given to the tangible asset base (net balance sheet).

The change being suggested by the Chartered Institute of Housing and others is to move away from the PSBR towards a more appropriate measure of public sector indebtedness. The measure being advocated is the *General Government Fiscal Deficit* (GGFD). This measure is used in most of the rest of Europe. Unlike the PSBR, it treats any self-financing or commercially orientated expenditure of public corporations, including those that might be run under the auspices of local authorities, as being different from the normal expenditure outgoings of central and local government (i.e. such expenditure is counted as being outside the measure). It further differs from the PSBR by not treating privatisation receipts as a deduction from public sector indebtedness. The advocates of the GGFD model argue that the deduction of such receipts from the PSBR is an anomaly as it tends to give a false picture of the nation's underlying fiscal position. This is because privatisation results in the sale of revenue-earning public assets and this, in turn, increases the likelihood of future deficits (Hawksworth and Wilcox, 1995, p10.).

GGFD is the most appropriate measure to use when making international comparisons, as it is the closest to the aggregates used by most other countries. As the British economy becomes more involved with other European economies the case for using the same economic measurement tools as our European partners becomes stronger. However, the main argument for using the GGFD model is that the PSBR is too restrictive and stifles rather than stimulates public sector commercial enterprise by inhibiting investment growth plans. These constraints are seen as particularly damaging when they affect the commercial operations of public corporations. Under GGFD, borrowing by public corporations is not included in the calculation of public expenditure.

This issue came to the fore in the 1990s when the privatisation of the railways and the Post Office was being considered. The argument focused on the commercial freedom of such organisations. It was pointed out that, as part of the public sector, their investment plans would be curtailed as they would be constrained by the Treasury *financing rule*. However, it was seen to be in the national interest that they be commercially effective and, in the case of the Post Office, able to compete with international rivals in the complex field of information exchange. To do this would require significant investment in new technology and modern equipment. Because the Treasury paradigm regarded all expenditure by a public corporation as falling within the PSBR, it made no distinction between revenue and capital or between different types of capital programmes. In other countries, investment by a public corporation to make it more commercial, competitive and prosperous would *not* be treated as part of the public expenditure control figure. The choice seemed to be either to take the Post Office and the railways out of the public sector or to keep them in the public sector but lift the investment restrictions so that they could equip themselves to meet the challenges of changing technologies and customer demands.

The point about public corporations such as the Post Office is that they invest in order to trade and generate an income. The same might be said about social housing. Social housing agencies provide a public service, the quality of which crucially depends on a continuous stream of capital investment. This form of public expenditure creates debt, or the need for higher taxes. However, unlike other types of expenditure, it also creates capital assets that have a long-term life and generate a continuing flow of income in the form of rents. A shift to the GGFD model would pave the way to establishing an accounting framework that recognises this important distinction between, on the one hand, public spending in the form of capital investment, such as buildings and equipment, etc., and on the other hand, public spending on the day-to-day running of government, like public sector salaries and consumables, etc., or transfer payments, as in pensions, welfare benefits, etc.

From a housing perspective the shift to a GGFD model would enable a *local housing corporation* to invest in its stock of dwellings without breaking the Treasury control rules. Rigid adherence to the PSBR means that to achieve the required level of housing investment an authority would have to give up its landlord function completely (LSVT), or lose control of its stock by setting up local housing companies (refer to Chapter 10). The GGFD model would allow authorities both to control and invest in their stock by borrowing under similar rules to those governing housing associations. This would involve the authority setting up a local housing corporation (LHCo), to take over the control and management of its stock.

In contrast to local housing companies, a LHCo would be fully owned by the local authority and thus directly accountable to the local electorate. They would, however, have separate legal identities and operate as not-for-profit organisations that would be free to use the housing stock as an asset base against which to borrow from the private sector. Although they would still be caught in the PSBR/PSNB, this would become irrelevant as the new control measure would have shifted to the GGFD. This would mean that any investment decisions they make would not be regarded as being in competition with other public sector spending priorities. There is no reason why local housing corporations should not run alongside local housing companies and LSVT housing associations, thereby providing local councils with a range of options for meeting their housing investment needs.

To date, the case for adopting the GGFD in this context has not been accepted by the government (see above *Measures of public sector debt*), who remain concerned about the wider economic effects of allowing public bodies greater freedom to borrow. In the short-term it is more likely that current borrowing rules will be relaxed to allow some increase in housing investment. However, given the drive for European harmonisation, it is likely that in the longer term, Britain will shift to the internationally recognised accounting standards and expenditure control definitions. Indeed, the government has committed itself to continue to publish the GGFD and to give it prominence in the Budget documentation. We will return to this important topic when we consider local authority housing investment strategies (Chapter 10).

Controlling housing expenditure

The precise mechanisms for cash-limiting public expenditure on the provision and consumption of housing will be discussed in subsequent chapters. We will see that they involve the use of direct controls such as credit approval arrangements, capping and establishing eligibility criteria for subsidies and benefits. They also involve indirect 'accounting' controls that operate by establishing notional rather than actual money flows. By these mechanisms public funds are allocated against notional rather than actual expenditures. These notional figures are set by the central funding authority and this allows them to manipulate the level of support they give. For example, the *housing revenue account subsidy* of a local authority is based on notional calculations of income and expenditure, and in the social landlord sector notional *total cost indicators* are used to assess grant qualifying costs.

Regional supervision of housing expenditure

Although in recent years the governance of Britain has seen a trend towards centralisation, the administrative structure recognises the different traditions and needs of Britain's national regions. Scotland, Wales and Northern Ireland each has had its own Secretary of State, and Scotland has its own minister for housing. In addition, England, Wales and Scotland each has had its own social housing agency acting as a supervising intermediary between the Secretary of State and non-local authority social landlords. The Housing Corporation has operated in England, Scottish Homes in Scotland, and Housing for Wales (Tai Cymru), in the principality. In subsequent chapters we will describe how the role of these agencies is changing in response to the devolution of power to the Scottish Parliament and the National Assembly for Wales, and also to emergence of Regional Development Agencies in England.

Public expenditure control in Northern Ireland

Over recent years, central government control in Northern Ireland has been exercised through the DoE (NI), and operated in a way that seeks to ensure a broad compliance with the thrust of a centrally determined policy while maintaining a degree of independence and local discretion (Connolly and Knox, 1991, p309). The financial powers of the Northern Ireland Housing Executive (NIHE), (refer to Chapter 8), are based on the provisions of the 1977 Housing

Finance Order (No. 597, Northern Ireland). The Executive receives a public expenditure allocation in the form of an annual grant negotiated with central government and based on a budgetary analysis produced by the Executive's Finance Department. Rent levels are fixed as part of the grant allocation negotiations and the central authorities retain the power to instruct the Executive to alter the rents it charges.

Summary

In this chapter we have made the point that the workings of the housing system help to determine the nature and scope of the 'welfare state', and because of this the ways in which housing is produced and consumed are of political interest to the government of the day. The State has also intervened in the housing finance system because it recognises that the economic and social well-being of the nation is influenced by how we deliver and manage housing and housing-related services. A third broad reason for intervention is that the financial arrangements associated with the housing system have a significant impact on the ability of a government to fulfil its macro-economic policy objectives.

A tension exists between the need to invest public money in maintaining and improving the nation's stock of dwellings and the government's need to control public expenditure in order to pursue its economic objectives. This tension has led to a call from housing practitioners and academics to make a sharper distinction between capital and revenue expenditure. In June 1998 fiscal arrangements were reshaped around the Chancellor's two new fiscal rules – to finance current spending from taxation and to keep net public debt below a fixed percentage of GDP, currently 40 per cent. The 1998 reforms reflect the government's belief that *'Britain must have sustainable public finances, not just for the odd year or two, but throughout the economic cycle'*. (Chancellor's Statement on the EFSR, HM Treasury News Release 96/98, 11 June 1998).

In the chapters that follow we will see that the government's desire to control public expenditure plays a crucially important part in determining the nature and scope of the various housing finance regimes that operate in the different tenures.

Appendix 5A

The Comprehensive Spending Reviews

In 1996 the New Labour government came to office with a commitment initially to hold public spending broadly within the limits set by its predecessor. Immediately after the election, public spending patterns were altered to some limited extent within the PSBR totals to benefit health and education. In addition, some £5 billion of extra money outside the PSBR was found from the windfall tax on utilities to enhance education and employment opportunities for younger people. In the field of housing expenditure, a £1 billion sum was found from accumulated capital receipts which were also over and above the PSBR totals. To establish its longer term priorities the government set up a series of Comprehensive Spending Reviews that completed their work in July 1998 and set the scene for adjusted public spending plans to be introduced from 1999. The Review announced a significant increase in capital spending on public sector services, with particular emphasis on health and education.

The Comprehensive Spending Review reinforced the government's commitment to the Private Finance Initiative and Public Private Partnerships. This means that in the housing field local authorities are expected to explore ways in which to attract private funding to renovate their housing assets. To aid this process they were given borrowing approvals to spend an addition £3.6 billion of accumulated capital receipts. In the housing world there was much relief that over 90 per cent of the capital receipts was earmarked directly for housing and housing-related initiatives. The ability to borrow against the released receipts should enable significant amounts of private finance to be levered into the public housing sector. In announcing the release, the Chancellor claimed that the money could renovate 1.5 million homes, around £2,400 per property, over a three-year period, but the CIH called this 'an exaggeration' and expects the funding to refurbish only some 250,000 homes.

The Review also announced the government's intention to allocate £800 million to the year 2002 to the most deprived neighbourhoods through further rounds of the Single Regeneration Budget. This had the effect of reshaping the SRB so that the old Estates Renewal Challenge Fund, that granted money to help councils sell housing stocks to RSLs, became absorbed within the broader New Deal for Communities Budget. Although much of this New Deal money will be spent on business start-up projects and skills training and education, some will be put directly into housing. These 1998 changes set in motion a policy decision to create greater strategic coherence by merging housing's capital funding into a single stream from 2000, that is, a *single pot* of capital resources for housing. Under the new merged arrangements the housing investment programme and renovation grants will be combined. To underline a more strategic approach to council housing planning and management, resource accounting will be introduced to the Housing Revenue Account.

The Chartered Institute of Housing regards the additional resources stemming from the Review to be relatively small compared to the minimum £20 billion repairs backlog. There is also concern amongst professionals that, after the year 2002, mechanisms will be in place that enable housing investment to continue at levels that will enable the repairs backlog to be dealt with. The Institute's favoured option is the establishment of local housing corporations that would allow councils to borrow private finance to invest in their own housing stock. The whole question of public/private finance is considered in more detail in other chapters (see in particular Chapter 10 for further discussion of local housing corporations).

Appendix 5B

The work of the Public Expenditure Survey Committee prior to 1997

The Public Expenditure Survey Committee (PESC), is an interdepartmental committee of officials chaired by the Treasury. The Committee's function has been to provide the basic facts upon which ministers make their decisions. Under the PRSC system, the analysis prepared by officials was designed to provide ministers with answers to the following general questions.

1. What is the state of the existing expenditure plans? Practice was to define the existing position as the plans in the preceding White Paper, amended to take account of subsequent policy decisions.
2. Where could reductions be made? This provided ministers with some indication of priorities within their programmes, i.e. the question was asked even when there was no intention to cut a particular programme.

The expenditure plans were considered against forecasts prepared by the Treasury for the growth of the economy over ensuing years, and decisions were then made on the basis of such predictions.

The PESC planning process began with the Treasury having discussions with the departments about their spending proposals. Each department carried out its own review on a basis approved collectively by ministers beforehand. The Treasury issued instructions to each department giving the basic working assumptions upon which plans would be made and the department produced provisional estimates covering a five-year period which were sent to the chief secretary to the Treasury.

The chief secretary reported to a special Cabinet meeting at which ministers went through the ritual of pledging their allegiance to an agreed planned expenditure total. Individual negotiations between spending ministers and the chief secretary, referred to as 'bilaterals', then took place which attempted to resolve any conflicts between the departments and the Treasury. Under the Conservatives, if they were unable to reach agreement, the problem was dealt with by a small group of ministers chaired by a senior member of the Cabinet and popularly referred to as the *Star Chamber*. On entering office, Gordon Brown, the New Labour Chancellor, dispensed with the 1997 Star Chamber round and simply embraced his predecessor's spending totals for the first two years, while retaining his right to shift resources around within those totals. Once the CSR is fully completed, the government will have to determine its own ways of negotiating across departments. Once the departments and the Treasury were reconciled, the Cabinet met again and the final decision on public expenditure was taken.

The expenditure plans were detailed in the White Paper which outlined the assumptions of the planning exercise and analysed expenditure in terms of who plans it (department), who spends it (spending authority), where it goes (function and territorial area), and what it is spent on (economic category). The White Paper is really a collection of volumes or 'chapters', most of which are produced by the spending departments themselves as a sort of prospectus and 'financial report'. One chapter, for example, contains the DETR's plans for housing in England while others cover Scotland, Wales and Northern Ireland. These chapters usually include information on historical trends as well as projected expenditure. In addition to the DETR chapters, the housing practitioner and student will find much of interest in the chapter covering DSS estimates which includes plans for housing and other personal benefits.

The White Paper covers a specified three-year planning period and is titled, for example, 'The Government's Expenditure Plans 1997-98 to 1999-2000'. It contains firm programme decisions for the financial year ahead and more tentative plans for the remainder of the planning period. Plans for a new terminal year are added annually and the plans for any given year firm up as that year approaches; so, the plans for the year ahead are firm, while those for subsequent years are increasingly provisional.

Further reading

Steve Wilcox, *Housing Finance Review 1999-2000* (or latest edition), CIH/JRF.

Coopers and Lybrand, *Consensus for Change – Public Borrowing Rules, Housing Investment and the City*, CIH, 1996.

David Curry, *Lobbying Government – A Guide to Lobbying on Housing Issues*, CIH, 1999.

CHAPTER 6:
The nature and growth of owner-occupation

During the twentieth century, owner-occupation developed from being a restricted way of holding residential property that catered largely for the housing needs of the upper echelons of society into the nation's predominant tenure arrangement.[1] This growth has been particularly prominent over the last 20 years. During the 1980s the proportion of households that owned their own homes rose from about a half to two-thirds. By the end of the 1990s the proportion had risen to about 68 per cent. Housing equity now represents about a quarter of all personal wealth held in the UK.[2] The dominance of this tenure has important implications for society. It has implications for the wider economy because changes in the perceived value of this asset wealth (movements in house prices) can have a significant impact on household confidence and hence spending and saving decisions. It also has important implications for the distribution of wealth among households and for the transfer of wealth between generations.

The concept of ownership

Proprietary analysis, referred to in Chapter 1, makes the point that a house is not 'owned' in the same way that consumer durables such as cameras and refrigerators are 'owned'. In purchasing a dwelling the owner-occupier does not so much gain absolute possession of the building and the land, as acquire a bundle of legally enforceable *freehold or leasehold rights* relating to their use and disposal. This is an important point because it underlines the fact that others may also 'own' legal rights or interests in the same property, such as tenancy rights, or rights of easement. Such legal interests have a market value of their own and their existence can therefore affect the exchange value of the freehold or leasehold.

Figure 6.1: Ownership rights

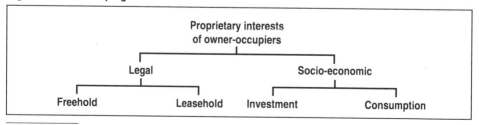

---

1   One of the reasons that conveyancing is such a convoluted business involving the employment of legal advisers is that until quite recently, property transactions were largely restricted to the landed classes and involved the transfer or break-up of complex estates.
2   The total value of private housing assets is estimated to be well in excess of £1,200 billion (1999).

The fullest individual, legal ownership of real property is called 'fee simple'. Fee simple is associated with freehold rights and it is the form of ownership that most of us think of in relation to owner-occupation. It is the strongest form of legal ownership and, subject to any underlying rights of the Crown, and any mortgage encumbrances, planning laws and health codes, the fee simple holder has absolute ownership of the property. These rights can be left to the owner's heirs forever, or until such time as they dispose of the property.

Leasehold is an agreement whereby a 'buyer', sometimes called a 'tenant', 'leaseholder' or 'lessee' acquires the right to use the landed property for a specific period in return for a land rent to the fee simple owner, the 'lessor'. At the end of the period, which can be up to 999 years, all the property rights revert to the party that holds title in fee simple. Leaseholders can be thought of as a class of owner-occupier. The term owner-occupier carries no legal weight and 'long' leaseholders usually consider themselves to be owners; indeed, they are considered as such by virtually everyone else, including the government.[3] They are, however, subject to regulation by third parties, the lessors, who can influence their expenditure, their ability to sell the house or flat, and its market value. Ultimately, these third parties can also influence the right of the occupier to remain in the home they have bought. The issue of leasehold reform is discussed later in the chapter.

The imagery and culture of ownership

During the second half of the century, the aspiration to own one's own home and thereby become part of the 'property-owning democracy', was actively encouraged both by the rhetoric that accompanied government housing policy and by the commercial advertising that was part of the rapidly expanding property and mortgage markets.[4] In addition, as home-ownership became more and more accessible to a wider section of society, the advantages of owning one's own home were increasingly pointed to in the organs of the popular media.

The case for expanding owner-occupation is grounded in the presuppositions of market ideology (refer to Chapter 5). In so far as it embraces voluntaristic, demand-led market mechanisms that operate to fulfil 'natural' domestic desires in ways that enhance life chances, the tenure can be said to encapsulate the values of a free-enterprise culture. In the minds of those who are ideologically predisposed towards owner-occupation, its growth is also seen to foster individuality and

---

3   See for example, *Discussion Paper – Leasehold Reform: Joint submission by LEASE and the British Property Federation* (November, 1999).

4   These views are typified by the following two statements. (1) 'Buying a house or flat is a sound financial investment – buying a home is also an investment in your quality of life'. (Nationwide Building Society, *The Home Buyers Handbook*, October, 1986. (2) 'Apart from the financial security, home-ownership gives a tremendous feeling of pride and achievement' (National and Provincial Building Society, *A Guide to Mortgage Management*, 1990).

personal responsibility.[5] In terms of this view, home-ownership is assumed to be 'good' for the individual, enhancing self-fulfilment, personal independence, financial security, etc., and also 'good' for the wider community, by spreading capital wealth and thereby cultivating 'responsible' attitudes towards property in particular and society's socio-economic structures in general.

By the 1980s the popular discourse on home-ownership was characterised by pronouncements that carried a distinct cultural symbolism of responsibility and self-fulfilment. This helped to create a political climate in which the government could argue that it virtually had a moral duty to make home-ownership more widely available. That as many people as possible should be encouraged to own their own homes was presented as a common sense proposition.[6] Although attitudes to home-ownership were modified by the sharp downturn in the property market that occurred after 1989, in Britain today there still exists a powerful ideological advocacy of owner-occupation. Politicians, mortgage providers and the press still commonly employ such housing imagery as 'castles' (of security), and 'ladders' (of mobility), and many commentators still point to the moral imperative of most people becoming home owners in line with their 'natural' desires and interests.

The popularity of owner-occupation

Recent attitude surveys indicate that aspirations for owner-occupation continue to be strong.[7] However, the desire to own one's own home in the short-term does

---

5.   A generation ago the basic philosophy underlying this advocacy was summarised by the chairman of the Building Societies Association when he claimed that home-ownership *'satisfies a basic human need to surround oneself with something that is absolutely personal and private'*. (Quoted by Saunders 1990, p.59). In 1980 this sentiment was reiterated by the minister piloting through the legislation giving council tenants the right to buy their homes. In commending the new legislation to Parliament he stated that there is *'a deeply ingrained desire for home-ownership'*. (Michael Heseltine, quoted by Saunders, 1990, p59). Several years later Margaret Thatcher is reported as having declared that *'the desire to have and to hold something of one's own is basic to the spirit of man'*. (Quoted by Saunders, 1990, p59). Some commentators have argued that in post-war Britain the political and popular debates about the benefits of home-ownership brought about a somewhat uncritical acceptance of the desirability of pursuing policies to stimulate the growth of this tenure.

6   This compares with what we might term an 'uncommon sense explanation' of the growth of the tenure. This non-ideological explanation accepts that the advantages of home-ownership can be tangible but argues that they are not intrinsic in the tenure. That is, it argues that they do not naturally occur in all places when a certain stage of socio-economic development is reached, but rather that they are largely the consequence of financial, fiscal, legal and other arrangements that are specific in terms of time and space.

7   In a recent Gallup poll (1996), owner-occupation was shown to be by far the most popular form of housing tenure across all sectors of society. The findings showed however, that in comparison with an earlier MORI poll published in 1993, its lead over other tenures had diminished. In answer to the question 'Given the choice, how would you prefer to pay for your housing?' – 72 per cent of respondents answered 'buying with a mortgage' compared with 78 per cent in 1993. For the full breakdown of the results of both polls see ROOF, March-April 1996.

seem to have stabilised during the late 1990s (Smith, 2000). The slight preference shift towards renting can in large part be explained by the downturn in the housing market that occurred between 1989 and 1995. As well as resulting in thousands of repossessions, the changed conditions after 1989 left many households with problems of negative equity and burdensome mortgage debts. This is discussed more fully below.

The size and structure of the tenure

As a tenure arrangement, owner-occupation has expanded continuously since the end of the First World War. Some 68 per cent of Britain's housing stock is now owner-occupied, compared with about 55 per cent in 1979 and less than 10 per cent in 1914. The trend of increasing home-ownership was significantly accelerated by the policies of the post-1979 Conservative administrations. During their terms in office, from 1979 to 1997, an additional 3.8 million households gained access to the tenure, an increase of some 38 per cent. The rate of increase has now slowed down and there is much current debate about the extent to which there is scope to expand owner-occupation in the future.[8] Future growth is likely to depend largely on economic factors. Given the current demographic structure in the UK, there is probably scope for further growth particularly if there is a period of low general inflation and stable interest rates.

The current figure conceals a marked social stratification and significant national, regional and local variations. Over 90 per cent of the professional/managerial class are now home owners compared with about 30 per cent of unskilled manual workers. Home-ownership is more prominent in Wales and the South East and South West of England than it is in Scotland and the North of England. Within particular towns and cities, significant variations can also exist at the district level.

Less traditional forms of home-ownership: park homes

Some 100,000 British households live in residential park homes. Their construction and their tenure distinguish these homes from other types of owner-occupied property. Although generally owned by their occupiers, these dwellings are usually sited on land that is owned by someone else. The relationship between the home owner and the park owner is governed by the Mobile Homes Act 1983. This legislation gives the occupier the right to a written statement setting out both the 'implied' and the 'expressed' terms of the agreement. Most importantly, the statutory rights implied by the Act include matters relating to security of tenure. The legislation also establishes the principle that the park owner has a right to take a commission[9] when a park home is sold on site, by means of a transfer agreement. The expressed terms outline the local details of the relationship

---

8   See, for example, Alan Holmans' article 'Owner-occupier households: recent trends in England and the USA, Australia, Canada and New Zealand', in *Housing Finance* No.45, February 2000, pp30-35.

9   Currently a maximum of 10 per cent of the sale price.

between the parties. They cover such things as the rules about pitch fees and their review. They also cover any other rules relating to the specific responsibilities and rights of the parties.

The dual nature of the owner-occupier's proprietary economic interests

As indicated in Figure 6.1, owners have both consumption and investment interests vested in the dwellings they occupy. To the owner-occupier the dwelling possesses both the characteristics of a home and an asset. As we will see, the dual nature of the occupier's economic interests in the property has, over the years, led to much debate about how this tenure should be treated with respect to taxation liability and subsidy support. This dual interest (consumption and investment) also has to be borne in mind when analysing questions relating to the affordability and sustainability of the tenure.

The affordability and sustainability of owner-occupation

Throughout most of the 1980s the market for owner-occupied housing was sustained by a combination of factors. These included: a growth in real incomes, an expanding mortgage market, following the general deregulation of financial services, and continued fiscal support in the form of mortgage interest tax relief and exemptions from both capital gains tax and Schedule A income tax.[10] We will look at the nature and scope of the mortgage market in some detail in Chapter 7, and the various tax arrangements covering this sector are also discussed in Chapter 7.

As the dominant tenure, it is clear that the government expects owner-occupation to play a significant part in the nation's overall housing strategy. Early in 1998 the government outlined a series of plans for dealing with Britain's housing needs for the early part of the following century. At that time it was estimated that a further 4.4 million homes would be needed by 2016. This projection has since been modified and the latest DETR releases suggest a 3.8 million household growth over the twenty-five years to 2021. Whichever statistical series is used, one thing is clear – the meeting of national supply targets will involve a continued expansion of owner-occupation.

Supply-side constraints: stock adjustment models

There is much debate about the extent to which this tenure can, or should, be relied upon to close the gap between future housing needs and probable supply

---

10   Before 1963 the Inland Revenue treated owner-occupied dwellings as assets that had the potential to generate an income. This potential income was calculated as an 'imputed rent' and taxed under Schedule A of the income tax schedules. The collection of Schedule A income tax on the main residences of owner-occupiers was abandoned after 1963. This is discussed more fully later in the chapter.

outturns. Some commentators make the point that there are severe supply-side constraints on private house-building.[11] By deducting demolitions from completions, we can calculate the net additions to the private housing stock. By projecting recent net additions up to the year 2021, it would appear that the required increase in building is well beyond the capacity of the construction industry at the current time, based on existing policies. The ability and willingness of the building industry to respond to the challenge will depend, to a large extent, on the general long-run performance of the economy. New house sales depend on transaction rates in the housing market and, in turn, these tend to increase in times of economic growth and decrease in times of economic slow-down.

Even if there is continued economic growth and a consequential general sustained demand for owner-occupied housing, the construction industry's response to any such increase may be inhibited by a variety of specific factors that reduce what economists refer to as the *price elasticity* of housing supply. The price elasticity of supply measures the responsiveness of producers to a given increase in price. If prices rise by a certain percentage, and supply adjusts more than proportionately, we say that the response is 'elastic'. Conversely, if the output response is less than proportionate to the increase in price, we say that it is 'inelastic'. In the future, the price elasticity of supply may be inhibited by the following variables.

- The capacity of the construction industry.
- Shortages of land.
- Planning restrictions, including political constraints on the use of greenfield sites.

Demand-side constraints: affordability and other proprietary perceptions

Any demand-side analysis has to begin by recognising the interrelated nature of housing tenures. Attitudes towards owner-occupation will be affected, to some extent, by the government's policies towards other housing tenures. If a household acts rationally, it will seek that form of tenure that gives it the greatest utility in return for the money it spends on housing. If owner-occupation is taxed and subsidised generously in comparison with other tenures this will add to its popularity, and vice-versa.

Individual perceptions of the desirability of owner-occupation are particularly influenced by the question of *affordability*. In the owner-occupied sector, the question of affordability is made more complex by the dualistic nature of the occupier's proprietary interests, as discussed above. Unlike a tenant, an owner-occupier has an investment as well as a consumption interest in the property.

---

11 See, for example the commentary, 'Supply and sustainability: home-ownership in Britain', by Geoffrey Meen, Duncan Maclennan and Mark Stephens in Wilcox, 1997, pp17-22.

This means that an owner-occupier household may be prepared to pay a premium over and above what they would expect to pay in rent for the dwelling because they appreciate the fact that they will eventually acquire a valuable asset.

Housing analysts point to two key ratio measures of owner-occupier housing affordability (e.g. Wilcox, 1996). Because of the dualistic nature of the owner-occupier's proprietary interest, it is possible to consider affordability in this sector both in terms of the *real cost of capital*, relating to the proprietary *investment* interest, and in terms of a *cost-to-income ratio*, relating to the proprietary *consumption* interest.

The real cost of capital. Because owners have a long-run investment interest in their dwellings, affordability in this sector is sometimes discussed in terms of the ratio between the *nominal* and the *real* costs of borrowing and investing. This approach enables analysts to make the point that capital appreciation and house-price inflation can work to the long-term financial advantage of owners so that, over time, the acquisition costs can become more and more affordable. If, over a given period, interest rates are, say, six per cent, and over the same period, the asset's exchange value has appreciated by the same amount of six per cent, then, although the nominal cost of the loan, or the opportunity cost of the money capital withdrawn from savings to purchase the property, is six per cent, the *real capital cost* is zero. In recent years, and up to the year 2000, the real cost of borrowing was further reduced by the ability of home owners to offset some of the interest charges on their mortgage debts against their income tax liabilities. By focusing on the real cost of capital, it is possible to argue that, over the longer period (e.g. since the 1930s) the cost of acquiring owner-occupied housing assets has fallen.

The cost-to-income ratio. Because owners have a continuing consumption interest in their dwellings, affordability in this sector is sometimes discussed in terms of the ratio between the household's disposable income and its occupancy costs. For new entrants to the tenure, mortgage repayment costs often constitute a high proportion of these outgoings. This means that existing owners experience a *real income effect* when mortgage interest rates go up or down. The real income effect measures how much the household's disposable monthly income changes as a result of an alteration in interest charges. An apparently 'small' change in interest rates, say one per cent, can bring about a significant *real income effect* on some households, thus it can alter the household's disposable income by a greater proportion than the interest rate change.

Although interest rates can fluctuate over time the mortgage debt itself is fixed. That is, loan service charges are governed by the principles of *historical cost accounting*.[12] This means that the original debt is gradually repaid, either directly

---

12   See Chapter 4 for an explanation of historic cost accounting.

or via an endowment arrangement. This means that for most households the mortgage 'burden' tends to diminish over time. For those who remain in the tenure long-term, the debt is eventually extinguished (amortised), when the mortgage is 'paid off'.

The continuing commitment to sustainable home-ownership

Chapter 4 of the 2000 DETR Green Paper is entitled 'Encouraging sustainable home-ownership' and makes the point that in the future the government will continue to support the tenure through its general economic policies and by providing specific financial support in the following forms.

- By helping the less well-off and those who live in areas where house prices are high relative to earnings, to gain access through shared ownership and low-cost home-ownership initiatives.
- By helping existing owners who encounter unforeseen difficulties through benefit assistance with payments of mortgage interest.
- By helping poorer owners to meet the costs of repairing, adapting and maintaining their homes through renovation grants, disabled facilities grants and related assistance.

As in other tenures, the affordability of owner-occupied housing has been, and will continue to be, affected by a variety of financial support measures. Some of these measures have been designed to ease the financial burden of *being* an owner-occupier whilst others have been designed to ease the financial costs of *becoming* an owner-occupier. Before looking at how the tax and subsidy system affects existing owners we will look at the range of measures that have, in recent years, been put in place to encourage access to the tenure.

Measures designed to encourage the expansion of owner-occupation

One important feature of recent policy in the UK has been a declared intention to assist those on the affordability margins of owner-occupation to gain access to the tenure through a variety of 'low-cost home-ownership' initiatives.[13]

Within the Conservative Party there has been a long-standing political commitment to expand home-ownership. As early as 1971 the then Conservative government related home-ownership to 'a deep and natural desire' on the part of households to have independent control over their living spaces (White Paper,

---

13   For an outline and analysis of these initiatives see Bramley, G. and Morgan, J., (1998).

July 1971, *Fair Deal for Housing*).[14] In the years that followed, the Conservative Party continued to espouse this ideal in all its election manifestos. Its 1979 manifesto devoted more space to this topic than to Social Security, education or health.

The 'right-to-buy' (RTB)

This initiative has enabled many occupiers to purchase their rented homes with discounts. Councils have always had the right to sell their dwellings to their tenants. The 1979 manifesto pledged to convert this 'right-to-sell' into a 'right-to-buy' that would give council tenants the opportunity to purchase their homes with generous discounts. The RTB has been by far the largest home-ownership initiative.

The right-to-buy policy was included in the Housing Act 1980 and the Tenants' Rights etc., (Scotland) Act 1980.[15] The statutory right-to-buy (RTB) formed the centrepiece of the 1980 legislation. Although previous legislation had granted

---

14   The notion of a 'property-owning democracy' being a part of the Conservative Party's political programme was given early expression in 1951 by Harold Macmillan, the then Housing Minister, when he stated the following. '*We wish to see the widest possible distribution of property. We think that, of all forms of property suitable for such distribution, house property is one of the best. Of course, we recognise that perhaps for many years the majority of families will want houses to rent, but, whenever it suits them better or satisfies some deep desire in their hearts, we mean to see that as many as possible get a chance to own their own house.*'(House of Commons, *Parliamentary Debates*, 5th series, vol. 494, session 1951-2, Cm2251.)

Two years later this position was given formal and official expression in the 1953 Green Paper on Housing. '*One object of future housing policy will be to continue to promote by all possible means, the building of new houses for owner-occupation. Of all forms of ownership this is one of the most satisfying to the individual and the most beneficial to the nation.*' (Ministry of Housing and Local Government, *Houses: The Next Step*. Cm8996, HMSO, November 1953, para 7, pp3-4.)

By 1977, the official commitment to owner-occupation was expressed in even more propositional terms.

'*A preference for home-ownership is sometimes explained on the grounds that potential home owners believe that it will bring them financial advantage. A far more likely reason for the secular trend towards home-ownership is the sense of greater personal independence that it brings. For most people owning one's home is a basic and natural desire, which for more and more people is becoming attainable.*' (1977 Green Paper, *Housing policy: A Consultative Document*, Cm6851, HMSO, 1977.)

A similar view was reiterated in the 1987 White paper. '*Clearly, the majority of people wish to own their own homes. This wish should in the government's view be supported. Home-ownership gives people independence; it gives them a sense of greater personal responsibility; and it helps to spread the Nation's wealth more widely. These are important factors in the creation of a more stable and prosperous society....*' (*Housing: The Government's Proposals*, Cm214, HMSO September 1987.

15   The scheme's success led it to be extended under the Housing and Building Control Act 1984 which expanded the scope of RTB eligibility, reduced the qualifying tenancy time to two years and raised the maximum discounts available. These discounts were further increased by the Housing and Planning Act 1986 (up to a maximum of 60 per cent and 70 per cent for flats). Although the House of Lords introduced an amendment excluding dwellings suitable for the elderly, RTB quickly proved to be a runaway success from the government's point of view.

local authorities discretionary powers to sell, in practice few transfers occurred so that the statutory obligation to offer for sale was an important change in emphasis. The new legislation established the principle that a secure tenant opting to purchase is entitled to a discount on the market value of the property, and that this discount should be dependent on the previous length of the tenancy.[16] The idea is that those who have been paying rent over many years should be able to purchase their homes more cheaply than short-standing tenants. The regulations require a minimum residency period and they put a ceiling on the total amount of discount that can be granted to any one purchaser.[17] RTB discounts can be thought of as *purchase grants* to those who enter owner-occupation by this route.[18] The right to a discount is like having a gifted cash deposit; it gives automatic equity in the property – something that takes years to accrue in the private sector, and/or it enables the purchaser to borrow more to carry out improvements.

The effect of RTB on capital receipts and the 'buy-back' issue

The right-to-buy is acknowledged to have been the greatest and most far-reaching act of privatisation of the Thatcher years. Over a million and a half sales have taken place under the legislation, generating some £28 billion – more than the combined sales of British Gas, Electricity and British Telecom. The bulk of these receipts went to pay off debt or was clawed back by the Treasury. However, several billions of pounds were held by local authorities as 'housing capital receipts'. (Refer to Chapters 8 and 9.)[19] Under the provisions of the 'exchange

---

16 At this date (1980) the right was given to the majority of council and housing association tenants – coupled with discounts of up to 50 per cent of the valuation dependant on length of tenancy (at least three years).
The 1980 legislation gave council tenants with houses the right-to-buy the freehold of their dwellings and tenants with flats the right to purchase a long lease (125 years). As part of its drive to stimulate the tenure, the Conservative government made higher discounts available after 1984 and then extended them to flatted units in 1986. These reforms had the effect of raising the average level of discount from about 40 per cent at the start of the 1980s to about 50 per cent by the end of the decade. It is estimated that the annual cost of this 'grant' in net present value terms was something like £400 million (1997 values). (DETR calculation reported by Colin Jones and Alan Murie in 'The Key to a Fair Deal', *Housing Today*, 25 March 1999, p19.)

17 Under current provisions, a two years tenancy gives an immediate 32 per cent discount, with a further 1 per cent allowed for every extra year's tenancy up to a maximum of 60 per cent. The discount is higher on flats and maisonettes. Currently, discounts on flatted units start at 44 per cent on qualification and rise to 70 per cent after 15 years. When a local authority transfers tenanted stock to an RSL as part of a transfer agreement, the occupying tenants retain their right-to-buy under Section 171A-H of the Housing Act 1985.

18 When a unit of social housing is purchased at a discount by the occupying household, we can regard the discount received as an implicit subsidy to owner-occupation. However, this subsidy may be partly offset by future housing benefit foregone.

19 Although the discounted sales produced a substantial flow of capital receipts the government's commitment to reducing the PSBR prevented all of these financial resources being reinvested in the council stock. Indeed, the legislation setting up the 1990 capital finance regime specifically required authorities to hold the bulk of the receipts in reserve or to redeem debt. It is estimated that by 1997 local authorities had accumulated some £7.5bn in 'set-aside' receipts (KPMG, 1996).

sale scheme' introduced in 1995, it is possible for local authorities to buy back properties that they had previously sold to individuals. It is now proposed (DETR discussion paper December 1999), that councils be given an added incentive to buy back ex-council flats and houses by modifying the 1995 arrangements. The proposal is to allow authorities to reduce the amount they have to set aside from sale receipts when, in the same accounting period, they repurchase properties.[20] This will have the effect of reducing the costs of the buy-backs.

The future of RTB

As a result of the 1998 Comprehensive Spending Review, the value of discounts in England were reduced by changing the maximum discount that could be obtained from £50,000 to a lower figure that depended on its regional location. Some commentators have pointed out that this reform begins to break the link between the residency term and the level of granted discount. Over time more and more households will be affected by the lower ceiling so that the principle of the discount being related to years of tenancy will be weakened. Jones and Murie argue (*Housing Today*, 25 March 1999), that it may be appropriate at some point to acknowledge this fact and to scrap the idea of discounts related to years of tenancy and move to a straightforward purchase grant. Such a grant could be allocated against other, arguably more sensible criteria, so as to encourage the sale of specific property types or to stimulate sales in specific localities. By such methods it might be possible to use public funds to encourage mixed tenures on those estates and in those neighbourhoods where such a result might help to achieve other policies related to the government's broader social exclusion objectives.

In the 2000 Green Paper, the government declared that it does not intend to make any further significant changes to the RTB scheme.

---

20   The issue of set-aside is discussed in Chapter 9. Generally, a local authority has to set aside at least 75 per cent of a capital receipt from selling council housing in order to pay off, or pay interest on, its debts. It can use the remaining 25 per cent for capital spending, such as building or repairing homes. Reducing the amount it has to set aside has the effect of increasing the amount it can spend on capital projects. This increases the amount of housing debt it is assumed to have when the government calculates its Housing Revenue Account subsidy (refer to Chapter 11). This increases the authority's entitlement to subsidy. The new scheme will work by reducing the amount that has to be set aside from capital receipts. The relevant receipts will be those from selling any council housing and they must be reduced by 25 per cent of their spending on buying back ex-council houses or flats. That part of their spending would be like a pool that can be used to reduce the receipts as and when they arose. In other words, the government proposes to allow authorities to reduce the amount they have to set aside by 25p for every £1 spent on buying back an ex-council property. This will effectively cover 25 per cent of the cost of the buy-back.

The voluntary purchase grant

The voluntary purchase grant scheme (VPG), was introduced in England in 1996. It is designed to enable tenants of housing associations or other registered social landlords, who, on the whole, are excluded from RTB, to buy their existing homes at a discounted price.[21] In this way, VPGs have been available to social housing tenants with assured rather than secure tenancies. Unlike RTB, these grants are discretionary and cash limited. Associations have to apply, or bid, to take part in the scheme. Under the arrangements, a participating registered social landlord (RSL), that sells a home is able to claim a grant equivalent to the amount of discount from the central funding body (the Housing Corporation).[22] It is a condition of the grant that all the proceeds from the sale must be placed in a separate Disposal Proceeds Fund. This fund can only be drawn upon to provide replacement social housing assets. The VPG scheme is not yet well-established and research shows that many landlords are concerned about the financial implications and difficulty of replacing properties 'like with like'.[23] Social landlords are generally more at ease with helping tenants to acquire homes in the private sector than purchasing their existing homes. They are generally concerned not to dispose of units that were specifically designed as social housing. More particularly, they are concerned about the possibility of losing their 'best' stock, that is, good quality units that are in popular locations.

Transfer from social renting: Homebuy, TIS, CIS, DIYSO and 'rent-to-mortgages'

In recent years various *cash incentive schemes* have been in operation. These schemes have been devised to encourage tenants in the social rented sector with higher incomes to move into the owner-occupied private sector thereby freeing up social tenancies for someone else who is deemed to be in 'greater need'. The current scheme is called 'Homebuy'. This is designed to help tenants of RSLs and local authorities and people on the waiting list in priority housing need, to purchase a home. The scheme arranges for a housing association to administer an interest free loan covering 25 per cent of the market value. The applicant is required to top this up with a mortgage that covers the remaining 75 per cent. The loan is repaid when the dwelling is sold. Although the scheme does not charge interest to the applicant, if the price of the property rises, the amount repaid will be higher than the starting loan because 25 per cent of the sale price has to be repaid. Eventually Homebuy will replace the Tenants' Incentive Scheme. This scheme (TIS), currently provides a cash grant to enable people to move into owner-occupation thereby relieving the waiting list pressure on certain types of

---

21   The current discounts range from £9,000 to £16,000
22   The work of the Housing Corporation and nature and scope of RSL activity is described and discussed in Chapter 12.
23   DETR Housing *Research Summary: Voluntary Purchase Grant – The First Year* (No.73, 1998).

housing association and council homes.[24] Both the TIS grant and the Homebuy loan effectively form a deposit that enables tenants eligible for a suitable mortgage to switch from renting to buying a home.

The Housing Act 1988 empowered local authorities, under certain conditions, to give grants to their tenants to help them obtain accommodation in the private sector. The primary purpose of the scheme is to create vacancies in the council stock for those in housing need. The existence of housing need has to be demonstrated before permission is given to run the scheme by the Secretary of State. In 1996/97 some £60 million was made available in credit approvals to English authorities for the Cash Incentive Scheme. In conjunction with contributions from the authorities themselves, these funds released over 5,000 dwellings for reletting.

The government is also considering the idea that Homebuy should replace the Do-It-Yourself-Shared-Ownership scheme (DIYSO). This scheme allows people who rent their homes from an RSL or a council, or who are on the local authority waiting list, to find a property on the open market and buy it jointly with a housing association.[25] Under the arrangement, the association purchases the dwelling and then leases a share to the purchaser, ranging from 25 per cent to 75 per cent, for which a mortgage was obtained. A reduced rent is then paid for the remaining

---

24 TIS developed out of the notion of 'portable discounts'. It was originally intended that the RTB should include tenants of charitable associations. This provision in the 1980 Bill was vigorously opposed by the associations who argued that it would undermine the very essence of their charitable status: the provision was withdrawn after a defeat in the House of Lords. In 1984 the Housing and Building Control Bill again attempted to extend the RTB to tenants of charitable associations, and again the draft provision was not enacted after a defeat in the House of Lords. However, the 1984 legislation did introduce a 'portable' discount scheme known as 'HOTCHA' (Home Ownership for Tenants of Charitable Housing Associations). This was designed to give certain tenants of charitable associations in England and Wales, but not Scotland, an equivalent benefit to the RTB. Under these arrangements several thousand tenants were given cash equivalents to the eligible discounts to help them buy dwellings on the open market either as an outright purchase or by a process of shared ownership. It worked by the association purchasing properties on the tenants' behalf. The cost of the discount was claimed from the Housing Corporation via the mechanism of Housing Association Grant. In this way, the Housing and Building Control Act gave tenants of charitable associations an opportunity to become owner-occupiers on much the same basis as RTB tenants in other agencies while, at the same time, preserving the rented stock of such associations for the purpose of social renting. The HOTCHA arrangements were replaced in 1990 by a similar, albeit more restrictive, procedure known as the Tenants' Incentive Scheme (TIS). This scheme aims to provide home-ownership opportunities to tenants who do not qualify for RTB: this includes assured tenants and tenants of charitable associations. The TIS arrangements involve associations bidding for funds to operate an approved scheme of tenant transfer and therefore the portable discount is only available to tenants of associations with such an allocation. In 1994 new rules were introduced to prevent housing association tenants using the scheme's resources to buy homes outside the UK. The argument here is that the original idea behind the scheme was, in part, to stimulate the UK housing market.

25 In 1996 the DIYSO rules were relaxed so that people on local authority waiting lists could join council and housing association tenants in applying for DIYSO.

---

proportion. The shift from DIYSO to Homebuy would have the effect of reducing access to owner-occupation. This is because the DIYSO scheme allows households to secure a mortgage for as little as 25 per cent of the market value, but the new scheme requires the households to earn enough to service a 75 per cent mortgage. This particularly disadvantages households in high-price areas such as London and the South East of England. The National Housing Federation estimates that in such areas, over half of the households who would formerly have been eligible for DIYSO will be excluded. Until they are phased out, probably by 2002, TIS and DIYSO will be funded out of local authority resources where they will have to compete with other budgets.

Despite the success of the RTB provisions, there still remained some tenants who could not afford to buy even with discounts. Therefore additional incentives were introduced as part of the Leasehold Reform, Land and Urban Development Act 1993. This legislation introduced a nation-wide *rent-to-mortgage scheme* that was based on a number of earlier pilot schemes in Scotland, England and Wales. Under this programme, the rent that a tenant would normally pay is converted into a mortgage and used to buy a portion of the equity in the property. Tenants are entitled to the same discounts as RTB applicants but this is calculated on the proportion being purchased rather than the value of the whole property. The important difference between this scheme and other shared ownership arrangements is that rent-to-mortgage occupiers are excused paying rent on the proportion of the equity remaining unpurchased. In this way the occupier is able to acquire an element of equity without increasing their monthly outgoings. The rent-to-mortgage scheme did not really take off and has had little impact on the transfer of social housing into owner-occupation.

Scottish initiatives

Scottish Homes operates the TIS. In Scotland, housing association tenants are also able to qualify for £10,000 grants under the tenant ownership purchase scheme that helps them purchase their current housing association rented home.

In Scotland GRO grants are available to stimulate new build homes for owner-occupation.[26] These are given to private developers to help fund the cost of new or improved homes, particularly for first time owners. Grants of up to 40 per cent of total project costs have been available, although the average grant (1999) is about 25 per cent. Rural home-ownership grants are available to individuals in rural areas of Scotland towards the costs of building or buying their own home. These are available to people on low incomes who would otherwise find it impossible to own their own home in a rural part of Scotland because of high building costs, lack of utility services, or inflated home prices. These grants are designed to

---

26   The post-war growth in owner-occupation was less marked in Scotland than elsewhere in Britain. In response, GRO grant was introduced in 1990 with a view to contributing to Scottish urban regeneration in a way that also stimulates the growth of owner-occupation. By 1996 GRO constituted 16 per cent of new provision.

facilitate the general policy of Scottish Homes to develop more homes for sale.[27] In Scottish rural areas, Rural Home Ownership Grant (RHOG), has been available to assist people into the tenure in locations where there is a lack of suitably priced accommodation.[28]

In Scotland, by the mid-1990s, low-cost home-ownership had grown to be a significant proportion of new provision, accounting for over 40 per cent of new and improved Scottish Homes' funded stock (1995/96).

Northern Ireland initiatives

In recent years, the main low-cost home-ownership initiative in Northern Ireland has been an equity sharing scheme called 'co-ownership'. The arrangements operate through a housing association on a DIYSO basis.[29] By 1997 'co-ownership' purchases had surpassed 14,000, with nearly 10,000 of these having subsequently staircased to full ownership (Bramley and Morgan, 1998).

Shared ownership

The idea of shared ownership was pioneered in the 1970s by the Notting Hill Housing Trust and Birmingham City Council. These early schemes were based on what was termed a 'community leasehold' arrangement in which the occupier acquired *a fixed equity share* in the dwelling. This meant purchasing a fixed 50 per cent share and paying rent on the remaining 50 per cent. Under such a community leasehold arrangement, the occupier never owned the property outright, since it remained a 'community asset', and when they wanted to move, the occupiers were obliged to sell their fixed share (that may well have appreciated in value) to a nominee from the local community.

In the 1980s the Conservative government sought to underpin their RTB initiative by developing the idea of shared ownership so that it could be used to help people become full and outright owners of their homes.[30] The 1980 legislation provided clear terms governing how local authorities and housing associations might

---

27 Since 1990 Scottish Homes has used the grant to assist private developers to build or improve housing for sale in two kinds of area. In regeneration areas the grant bridges the gap between low market values and the costs of building. In some rural areas, where demand is more buoyant, the grant has been used to reduce selling prices for 'priority' purchasers. For an evaluation of the scheme see Scottish Office, *An Evaluation of GRO Grant for Owner Occupation*, HMSO 1997. Refer also to Keith Kintrea, 'Growing Pains' in *Housing* July/August 1997, p40.

28 RHOG accounted for less than 1 per cent of Scottish Homes' funded provision in 1995/96 (Bramley and Morgan, 1998).

29 This scheme replaced a NIHE equity sharing scheme in the early 1980s.

30 The RTB provisions were part of a broader initiative called 'The Tenants' Charter'. This sought to give tenants the right to retain their council tenancy or to plan a move into owner-occupation. Those planning to transfer were to be offered a range of support options. Amongst these were the right to a mortgage from the landlord and the right to a shared ownership lease.

provide this more radical form of shared ownership agreement. Initially, shared ownership was restricted to local authority and non-charitable housing association new build schemes, but was eventually also offered to existing tenants under the provisions of the Housing and Building Control Act 1984. Shared ownership is defined in England, Wales and Northern Ireland as housing schemes where the social landlord has granted a shared ownership lease as defined in Section 622 of the Housing Act 1985. In Scotland shared ownership schemes have to be approved in accordance with Scottish Homes Guidance Note 1990/03.

By the mid-1980s procedures existed that allowed occupiers to acquire up to 100 per cent of the equity in their properties by a process of gradual purchase called 'staircasing'. Under these arrangements, the householder typically begins by purchasing between 25 and 75 per cent of the total equity. They then pay rent on the unpurchased share. Unsold equity normally remains with the organisation that built or previously owned the dwelling, e.g. the council or housing association. Occupiers can subsequently purchase additional shares up to a level determined by the particular agreement. The total cost of rent plus mortgage is normally less than the total cost of outright ownership and this fact means that the arrangement can open up access to owner-occupation to people on moderate incomes. When the 'owner-occupier' wants to sell they have to contact the 'owner-landlord' who will then match the property with people on their waiting list. If at the end of three months they have been unable to find a purchaser, a private sale (e.g. through an estate agent) can be sought. Currently the supply of shared-ownership properties is not sufficient to meet the demand and access to such a tenure arrangement is usually through registration on a waiting list.

As well as helping tenants to acquire their existing homes, in recent years social landlords have helped tenants and others in housing need to buy homes on the private market (see discussion above on DIYSO).

By the mid-1990s, it is estimated that the total stock of shared ownership in England stood at about 70,000 units.

Collective ownership

Collective ownership is different from shared ownership. Whilst shared ownership schemes are designed to give individuals a 'personal' stake in their homes, housing co-ops are designed to give groups of people a 'collective' interest in the homes they occupy. Housing co-operatives can take two tenure forms:

1. Tenant management co-ops (TMCs). These are currently favoured by the Housing Corporation. Under these arrangements the occupiers do not have a stake in the equity of their estates but are delegated management responsibilities by their landlords who typically will be a council or housing association. Strictly speaking, this form of co-op should not be classified as a form of owner-occupation as no equity is transferred.

2. Ownership co-ops. These contrast with TMCs in that the occupiers collectively own the equity in the properties. This gives them a form of collective proprietary interest in the properties that make it appropriate to classify them as 'owners'. The housing association manages the co-op on behalf of owners. They collect rents, carry out repairs and maintenance, allocate homes which become vacant, deal with disputes and generally run the co-op's affairs in the interests of the collective membership.

New initiatives

The 2000 Green Paper signalled the government's intention to provide further support for people on the threshold of home-ownership. They propose to introduce a new *Starter Home Initiative* that would operate on a competitive basis, with innovative proposals invited from registered social landlords and others. The initiative is planned to be flexible and capable of adapting to local circumstances and needs. It is aimed to be of assistance to people on low incomes who live in areas where house prices are relatively high. The proposal is to provide particular help for 'key' workers such as schoolteachers, nurses, and firefighters.

Developing owner-occupation through leasehold reform

One other way in which owner-occupation might be developed is through leasehold reform. A lease is a contract by which property is conveyed to a person for a specified period for a stated consideration, a rent. The contract creates a 'leasehold estate' that can be thought of as a personal property interest. In addition to a purchase price, the terms usually require the leaseholder to pay a periodic ground rent to the freehold landlord. A 'lease option' is an arrangement whereby the lessee has the right to purchase the freehold either during the lease term or at its end.

In the UK some houses and many flatted units are let under leasehold contracts and currently there is some concern about the financial predicament of those people whose leases come up for renewal or who want to sell at a time when the lease is close to its expiry date. The transfer or renewal price depends on a controversial calculation that involves taking account of what is called the *marriage value*. The marriage value is based on a calculation that links together the freehold and the leasehold interests. It is a complicated calculation made up of the rise in property prices and the declining value of the lease. Over time the marriage value will tend to increase thereby generating an element of 'profit'. In some cases this value increase, or 'profit', can be considerable, amounting to tens, or even hundreds, of thousands of pounds. Surveyors often disagree about the valuation and tenants can challenge the landlord's claim at a tribunal. Some argue that the complicated nature of the calculation and difficulties of challenging the landlord's figure, gives the freeholder an unfair advantage in the negotiation.

Leasehold relationships are grounded in ancient laws that many now regard to be anachronistic. In particular, it is felt to be inappropriate in modern times for a landlord, who only has a limited equity stake in a property, to be in a position to manipulate the law in ways that restricts the proprietary interests that owner-occupiers have vested in their homes. In opposition the Labour Party pledged itself to reform this arrangement which they saw as a relic of the feudal age. The current debate has centred on how the *marriage value* 'profit' should be split between the two proprietary interests, the freeholder and the leaseholder. In the past, the landlord has been able to claim up to 100 per cent of the marriage value and to be guaranteed a minimum of 50 per cent. In November 1998, the government acted on its manifesto pledge and produced a consultation paper in which it restated its intention to reform the system. It is seeking to alter the arrangements so that any value increase will be shared equally between the two parties or according to a 'fair' formula that relates to the length of the lease.

As part of their commitment to reform arrangements so that leaseholders enjoy the same degree of security and control over their homes that other owner-occupiers expect, the government has committed itself (2000 Green Paper para.4.17), to introduce a new form of tenure called *commonhold*. This will give the owner of each home in a block a proprietary interest similar to freehold, in that it will not be time limited. Unlike a lease, commonhold value will not decline over time. Owners will be members of a commonhold association that will own and manage the common parts of the development. Commonhold will be available for new schemes and it is intended that leaseholders in existing developments should be able to convert to commonhold if all parties agree.

Sustaining the 'marginal' owner-occupier

Whilst rents will generally continue to increase over the life of a tenancy, it is expected that mortgage repayments will account for a progressively smaller percentage of income over the lifetime of the mortgage. Research indicates that tenants can expect to pay about twice as much as owner-occupiers in cash terms over a twenty-five year occupancy period. (NFHA, 1990, p12). However, it is still possible for individual owners to experience life changes that can suddenly make it difficult for them to fulfil their mortgage obligations. Owners who have difficulty meeting their mortgage obligations may be entitled to receive help in the form of Income Support for Mortgage Interest. This, together with mortgage payment protection insurance, is described and discussed in Chapter 17.

Some 11 million people in the UK now have mortgages. In recent years there has been much debate amongst economists, social theorists, housing practitioners and mortgage lenders about how the radically changing nature of the labour market is affecting the long-term security of marginal home owners. The shift towards short-term contracts and part-time employment for a wider range of occupational groups brings to the fore important questions about how the mortgage and insurance markets need to be restructured to allow for more flexible personal repayment plans.

Owner-occupiers are currently denied access to housing benefit that is operated through the Social Security system. By operating through the tax system, it is expected that the *working families' tax credit*, introduced in 1999, will have a significant impact on the financial position of some low-income home buying households. (Wilcox, 1998b). Not only will the scheme be more generous, but it could also lead to a significant improvement over the earlier take-up rate of family credit by home-buyers (which was about 50 per cent).

Improvements, added value and the idea of a 'valuations gap'

Because of its primary function as a home, most decisions to improve an owner-occupied dwelling are designed to add utility, that is, comfort and convenience. However, an improvement is also likely to add to the property's exchange value. Precisely how much is added to the exchange value will depend on the nature of the improvement and the location of the property. Estate agents often make the point that it is possible for an owner to 'over invest' in their homes. In making this point they are considering the improvement expenditure from a strictly investment point of view. The argument centres on the notion of what land economists refer to as the *neighbourhood effect value* (NEV). The NEV is defined as that part of a property's total value that is determined by its location. Because location is such a powerful determinant of property value, it may turn out that an investment in improvement will not be fully capitalised into the dwelling's exchange value. This means that if the purpose of the improvement is to increase the market value of the property, account has to be taken of the neighbourhood in which the dwelling is located. For instance, a £40,000 annex on a house worth £90,000 in a district where the maximum selling price is £100,000 is unlikely to upgrade the property's value to £130,000. The extent to which improvement expenditure gets capitalised into the exchange value depends on the nature of the expenditure, as well as the location of the property. Some property experts suggest that central heating is the principal improvement that is likely to guarantee recoupment of outlay and the modernisation of a kitchen or bathroom is also likely to add value, although with these types of improvement, the owner is unlikely to get back all the expended costs.[31]

Finance is arguably the single largest barrier to owners repairing their properties, and an effective well-resourced grant system is essential to many home repair projects. The reader should refer to Chapter 10 for information on, and discussion of, improvement and repair grants. Certain categories of owner-occupier qualify for help in, and advice on, undertaking building repairs and improvements (refer to Chapter 7 and discussion on Home Improvement Agencies).[32] It might be argued

---

31 Midland Bank, 'Move or Improve?', in *Your Money*, Issue 4, Winter 1995.
32 The government currently provides nearly £7 million annually to support local authority funding of Home Improvement Agencies.

that other strategies such as government guaranteed fixed rate loans, changes in inheritance tax and capital gains tax may provide some added incentive for repairs (see Chapter 7 for discussion on capital gains and inheritance taxation).

In the leasehold sector, repairs and improvements are normally managed through a third party. It is usual for there to be a repairing covenant under the terms of the lease that places a duty on the lessor to keep the dwellings in a good state of repair. Services charges can be made to cover future repairs and maintenance costs. These have to be held in a sinking fund that under Section 42 of the 1987 Act have the status of a trust fund. Lessees have a statutory right to inspect the management accounts and any supporting documentation. It is intended that future reforms will give the leaseholders the right to appoint their own managing agents, thereby giving them more direct control of the administration, maintenance, and improvement of their homes.

Summary

The primary forms of ownership are freehold and leasehold. Within these broad categories others may 'own' certain legally enforceable rights relating to tenancy agreements and easement.

Owner-occupiers have both a consumption interest and an investment interest vested in their dwellings.

The *price elasticity of housing supply* is a way of analysing the supply-side constraints affecting the sustainability and continued growth of the sector.

The two key ratio measures of owner-occupier housing affordability are the *real cost of capital* and the *cost-to-income ratio*.

Recent governments have introduced a variety of measures designed to encourage the growth of the tenure. Foremost amongst these have been right-to-buy discounts and other 'purchase grants'. Shared ownership schemes are aimed at low-income households who cannot afford outright purchase even with the help of a discount or a grant.

Further reading

Tim Dwelly, (Ed), *Sustainable Home ownership – The Debate*, CIH/JRF, 1997.

CHAPTER 7:
Owner-occupation: capital and revenue finance

Having considered the nature and scope of owner-occupation and the various measures designed to encourage its growth and development, we will now analyse the basic financial and fiscal arrangements that surround its acquisition, exchange and consumption. In this analysis we will make a clear distinction between capital and revenue finance.

Acquisition, exchange and capital finance

Sources of capital finance

Money capital is used to purchase new and second-hand homes and to make improvements to such dwellings. Money capital is the key to both gaining access to owner-occupation and to increasing the quality of such housing once access has been achieved. Initial access usually involves either having sufficient funds for outright purchase or the taking out of a loan. The gaining of a loan usually depends upon a combination of factors including the borrower's income and prospects of income and the capacity of the property to act as a sound security against the advance.

The changing nature of the mortgage market

Since 1980 it is possible to detect two broad categories of change affecting the mortgage market. They are both the consequence of increased competition. Firstly, the institutional framework has been restructured with the emergence of new providers and by the transformation of many building societies into banks. Second, the industry has developed a wider product range.

In the 1970s the market was dominated by the building societies that regularly provided up to 90 per cent of lending in any one year. In the early 1980s the commercial banks, together with a number of specialised mortgage institutions entered the market and for a time, annexed over 40 per cent of the market. By the late 1980s the market stabilised with the societies providing about 60 per cent and the banks a little over 35 per cent of total lending. In the 1990s a number of significant 'mutual' building societies converted into 'commercial' banking institutions. Before looking in more detail at the institutional changes, we will consider the various types of house purchase loan that are currently available.

An aspect of the new competitive environment has been an increasing tendency to respond in a more flexible way to the particular needs of borrowers. In the 1970s the institutions tended to see themselves as providing a fairly standard product to a fairly typical group of borrowers. This typification can be characterised as *a twenty-five year repayment or endowment loan to young or middle-aged couples in secure employment wishing to acquire a not-too-dilapidated detached or semi-detached house in a not-too-run-down neighbourhood.* The institutions now see themselves as providing a fuller service and a broader range of products to a wider group of people. They have become aware that they are operating in a complex market where single people form a substantial group of borrowers, lower income households have expectations to become owners, divorced and separated couples need to form new households, and retired people wish to take out new mortgages for specialised housing.

Mortgages

Houses that are not inherited or bought outright are usually acquired by means of a loan. Where the property itself is used as a security for the repayment, the loan is referred to as a mortgage. A mortgage is a form of loan that is secured by pledging a piece of real estate as collateral. The word 'mortgage' is made up of the two French words – *mort* meaning dead and *gage* meaning pledge. This is because the pledged estate becomes *dead* or entirely lost to the lender if the borrower defaults on the agreed terms.

Some people get confused about the use of the terms *mortgagor* and *mortgagee*. What has to be remembered is that it is the householder who makes over the title to the house as security for the loan and is therefore classed as a 'mortgagor', just as someone who makes available employment is an employer. Conversely, it is the lender who receives the title and is therefore classed as a 'mortgagee', just as someone who receives employment from someone else is an employee. Because with mortgage arrangements the property is pledged as security, the mortgagee retains the title deeds until the loan is repaid. Mortgages are made up of two basic elements: the outstanding debt or 'principal' and the interest charges. How these two elements are treated depends on the type of mortgage agreement entered into.

Types of mortgage

Repayment mortgage
The most straightforward type of house purchase loan is the *repayment* or *annuity* mortgage. This is sometimes referred to as a 'capital and interest mortgage'. These arrangements involve the borrower making periodic payments, usually monthly, to the lender, partly of interest on the outstanding loan and partly of capital to repay the loan. In the early years, most of the monthly payment goes toward paying off the interest, but as the outstanding loan is

gradually repaid the interest element reduces and eventually the major part of the payment is used to repay the principal. The actual monthly payment will depend on the size of the loan, the length of the repayment period, known as the 'term', and the prevailing rate of interest. The typical arrangement involves a *level payment mortgage* that requires the repayment of a fixed monthly sum that only varies with changes in the rate of interest. In Britain the mortgage term is usually no longer than 30 years.

Some lenders offer *low-start repayment mortgages* that are technically known as 'gross profile mortgages'. With such an arrangement the monthly payments are lower in the early years of the term but gradually increase each year so that during the later years they are higher than they would otherwise have been with an ordinary repayment mortgage. These loans are designed for people who, at the time of taking out the loan, are on a tight budget but have expectations of a rising income. Over the full term of the loan such arrangements are usually more expensive than conventional repayment mortgages. Low-start mortgages should be distinguished from 'discounted' mortgages. Some lenders promoted these in the late 1990s as a way of attracting new business. They involve the mortgagor paying a reduced rate of interest for an initial period, typically a year or so, without the penalty of having to pay higher rates later in the term. We will say more about the different ways in which interest can be charged later.

With straightforward repayment mortgages it is possible to make an arrangement to pay a monthly *voluntary excess payment* and thereby shorten the loan term. Whether or not such a decision is worthwhile is sometimes difficult to determine and will depend on individual circumstances. A financial advisor, for example, may suggest that the mortgagor would be better advised to invest the voluntary payment in some form of 'tax-efficient' pension top-up or an Individual Savings Account (ISA). [1]

Interest only mortgages

The principle of an interest only mortgage is that the mortgagor makes monthly payments to cover the interest on the loan and is then responsible for arranging alternative means to pay off the capital amount of the loan at the end of the term. This is often achieved by using the proceeds of a life assurance policy, but some other savings and investment scheme could be taken out in parallel to the mortgage. These days the scheme can be associated with an ISA or pensions plan (see below).

A well-established approach is to take out an *endowment policy* that is arranged by the mortgage lender. This involves the borrower paying two separate payments each month. They pay interest directly to the lender together with a premium to an insurance/investment company. These premiums generate a fund that is designed to repay the principal on maturity. In this way, the capital is repaid at

---

1   Individual Savings Accounts were launched in 1998 to replace Personal Equity Plans.

the end of the term using the proceeds of the matured policy. The endowment policy is deposited with the lending institution throughout the duration of the mortgage term. As well as providing an investment element, an endowment also generates life assurance protection for the purchaser. There are various types of endowment mortgage, all with built-in life cover but with somewhat differing arrangements and potential benefits.

Low-cost endowment mortgage

A low-cost endowment mortgage is designed to keep the monthly payments to a minimum. It brings together a term assurance policy that will repay the loan should the mortgagor die prematurely and an investment-type endowment insurance policy to produce a sum of money on maturity which should be enough to pay off the debt at that time. It may, in addition, provide a lump sum over and above the debt liability. In cases where the investments turn out to perform less well than was anticipated, mortgagors may be required to increase their premiums part way through the term. Under a normal low-cost endowment mortgage the premiums payable are the same each month. Some companies offer low-start, low-cost endowments that allow the premium payments to be reduced in the early years.

Full endowment mortgage with profits

A full endowment mortgage operates in a similar way to the low-cost model, but the life cover is provided entirely by an endowment policy rather than partly by a term assurance. As well as guaranteeing a sum to pay off the loan, the policy incorporates a planned savings scheme that seeks to produce a sum of money at the end of the term that may be significantly greater than that needed to cover the debt. This is done by bonuses being added to the initial sum so that at the end of the term, the policyholder should receive a lump sum over and above the mortgage loan repayment.

The way it works is that the company regularly credits the policy with 'reversionary' bonuses and on maturity with a 'terminal' bonus. The size of these is determined by the profits that the insurance company makes by investing the premium payments. Once declared and added, the bonuses cannot be removed; they will add to the value of the policy and revert to the policyholder at the end of the term. The company will only take into account the reversionary bonuses when calculating the amount needed to cover and repay the mortgage; the terminal bonus acts as a sort of 'safety buffer' that guarantees that the loan will be more than repaid.

Compared with repayment mortgages, endowment policies are less flexible. In the case of a repayment mortgage the borrower can normally lengthen or shorten the term of the loan to suit changing circumstances. By contrast, an endowment mortgage is a long-term contract, including automatic life assurance, and once the agreement is made, the parties are normally committed to it for the full term. If the policy is cashed in early the mortgagor may not get back all the premiums they have paid. All endowment policies are 'portable' and the policyholders are able to take them with them when they move house.

Pension linked mortgages

These schemes are usually aimed at the self-employed or people who do not belong to a company pension scheme. The principle involves building up a fund that will repay the loan as well as provide the policyholder with a retirement pension. They work in a way that is similar to that of *with profits endowments*, but instead of an endowment policy, the mortgagor takes out a retirement annuity which, as well as providing a pension, pays a lump sum on retirement, or thereabouts, which is intended to pay off the mortgage. As contributions attract tax relief at the individual's marginal tax rate and are invested in funds that accumulate on a gross basis, free of taxation[2], these schemes are particularly tax efficient and therefore attractive to high earners who are eligible to join them.

Under present rules, when policyholders retire they are able to take a quarter of their personal pension funds as a tax-free lump sum to pay off their mortgages. Mortgage pensions may be tax efficient but can be restricting: they rely on the mortgagor having a personal pension throughout the life of the mortgage and as many people move in and out of company schemes, such personal pensions may be difficult to manage efficiently. The rules do not allow people to hold a personal and a company pension at the same time; nor do they allow them to use their occupational pensions to fund their mortgages. This means that pension mortgages are inflexible for people moving in and out of self-employment. By tying together these two financial assets, the mortgagor/policyholder may create a financial conflict of interest and at some future date, the interests of one may have to compromise the other. In an uncertain world, in which people increasingly have complex career patterns, it is often sensible to separate mortgage management from retirement planning. Despite the above argument, because of the tax advantages, pension mortgages have been popular with high earning executives and self-employed groups who have considerable control over their own pension arrangements.[3]

Unit linked mortgages

Compared with ordinary with profits policies, these schemes have a greater element of risk associated with them; their values will tend to fluctuate with the stock market. They operate in a similar way to endowment assurances in that the cash sum produced by the policy at maturity is credited to the mortgage account

---

2   However, by the provisions of the Finance Act (No.2) 1987, the Inland Revenue has imposed limits on the amount of tax-free benefits on such schemes, including an absolute limit of £150,000 per arrangement.

3   Pension managers have tended to have a rather paternalistic attitude and argue that it is not in an employee's interest to reduce a pension entitlement to pay off a mortgage. However, with the introduction of radical new pension arrangements in 1988 and the consequential intensification of competition in the pension plans market, attitudes are changing.

and any surplus is then paid to the policyholder. The savings element of the policy is channelled into an investment fund by the purchase of 'units'. The fund may deal in British or overseas property and stocks and shares, and the value of the units will fluctuate in line with how the fund prospers. The cash amount at maturity will be dependent on the value of all of the units held at that time. The company may sometimes review the value of the units to ensure that they are increasing at a rate sufficient to repay the mortgage, and if they are not, they may request additional premiums in order to acquire further units. If the value of the policy matches the mortgage debt at a time prior to the maturity date, the policy holder may choose to repay the mortgage at that time; in this way, unit linked schemes provide an additional element of flexibility over other endowment schemes.

Specialist savings arrangements

Some mortgage lenders offer a range of other vehicles for tying savings into a mortgage deal. Some of these will seek to utilise the relatively new government sponsored ISAs that are designed to provide a degree of tax efficiency to the 'saver'. These tax-efficient 'savings' mortgages are now quite popular and are increasingly being offered as an alternative to the more traditional repayment and endowment arrangements. Like an endowment they involve taking out an interest only loan and at the same time paying a monthly premium. The premiums are paid into an *individual savings account*. That cash will then be invested, probably in bonds and shares. The principle is that this will create a fund that will be big enough to pay off the mortgage at the end of the term. One drawback does exist however: anyone with such a mortgage is likely to be disqualified from receiving income support if the fund is valued at more than the qualifying capital allowance, currently £8,000, when they claim. (Benefit entitlements are discussed more fully in Chapter 17).

Varying interest rates

Interest rate 'deals' are wide-ranging. The following represent the main options that are currently available.

Standard variable rate. With this option the monthly repayments will fluctuate as lenders periodically alter their loan interest charges.

Fixed rate. A fixed interest is normally negotiated for a specified period, typically two years, rather than for the full term. Although a fixed interest charge gives the mortgagor a degree of certainty with respect to future housing costs, whether or not it is cheaper in the long-run will depend on how interest rates fluctuate over the fixed period. Fixed interest mortgages often include a 'lock-in' clause in the small print. This means that at the end of the fixed period the mortgagor may be required either to transfer to a variable rate mortgage, or pay a penalty surcharge to transfer to some other fixed mortgage scheme.

Capped rate. This guarantees the borrower that the interest will not rise above a pre-set rate, the 'cap', for a specified period.

Tracker rate. This provides the option to pay an interest rate that will rise and fall in line with rates set by the Bank of England for a specified period.

Discounted rate. This offers the borrower a reduced rate for a short initial period. It is really a marketing ploy (see discussion above on *repayment mortgages*).

Annual review schemes

The real income effect of a relatively small change in interest rates can be significant (see Chapter 6). If mortgagors wish to plan their outgoings on an annual basis they may opt for an *annual review scheme*. Under these arrangements the interest rate is fixed for a year so that if there is a change in rates during the year it will be ignored until the following review period, that is, the following year. If during the current review period interest rates are raised, there will then be a 'postponed' under-payment owing at the end of the period. In the following review period the repayments are adjusted to take account of this under-payment.

Mortgage protection and indemnity insurance

In recent years, both the government and lenders have placed more emphasis on *mortgage payment protection insurance* (MPPI). Indeed, there is now an explicit expectation that all home owners should take more responsibility for protecting themselves through private insurance and the industry is aiming to achieve take up of MRRI by 55 per cent of new home-buyers by 2004. The reasons for this pressure partly stems from the changing socio-economic profile of mortgagors, more of whom are now on temporary contracts of employment or are in jobs that do not provide the sort of stable, secure incomes that have historically underpinned owner-occupation. The pressure to take out MPPI also stems from the general shift in government policy away from sole reliance on the State for safety net provision[4] to forms of partnership provision with the private sector. Under MPPI policies, if the mortgagor loses his or her job through ill health or redundancy and cannot make the payments, the policy will normally cover them.[5] This policy expectation has proved to be problematic for all sorts of reasons.

---

4   The key difference between Income Support for Mortgage Interest (discussed in Chapter 17) and MPPI is that the former is largely tax funded whilst MPPI is funded by premiums paid by mortgagors themselves.
5   However, experience shows that some of these policies fail to cover self-employed work, jobs with fixed contracts or contracts that run for a shorter period than the term of the loan, so that when the borrower's circumstances change they are no longer covered.

A particular problem relates to how the benefits system treats the payout income derived from such policies.[6] If mortgage protection policies pay out so that money is transferred to the lender this has never been regarded as 'income' in the calculation of entitlement to State benefits. Some policies pay out direct to claimants rather than to lenders and, until recently, there had been some confusion about whether such payments should be treated by the DSS as 'income' in benefit calculations. After much lobbying, the situation has been clarified and payments to claimants are, since June 1998, now also disregarded when assessing benefits. For a fuller discussion of mortgage interest protection see Chapter 17.[7]

A mortgagor may be asked to pay a *mortgage indemnity premium* that safeguards the lender against the value of the property not covering the value of the outstanding debt in the event of default. Although these are being phased out by a number of the larger lenders, they are still quite common. They are normally required when a borrower is unable to put down a deposit of more than a specified percentage. Indemnity insurance plans should be distinguished from mortgage protection policies. Although both are charged to the mortgagor, the former are primarily designed to benefit the lender and the latter are primarily designed to protect the borrower.

The changing nature of employment, negative equity and repossessions

Many feel that the mortgage industry and the Social Security system have been slow to respond to the changing nature of employment and that this has added to the problem of insecure owner-occupation. The 1980s and 1990s saw a restructuring of the labour market so that by the end of the 1990s some ten million Britons relied on part-time work, fixed-term contracts, low pay or self-employment. Job security is also an important factor in determining the risk of repossession. During the 1990s, a significant number of heads of repossessed households were not in work when they lost their homes, either because of redundancy or because they were looking after a family full-time.[8] People in full-

---

6   Confusion has also surrounded the question of capital calculation for benefit purposes. Endowment policies have been classified differently from strict 'saving-related' schemes because of the way the benefit authorities regard the nature of the cover. If the surrender value of the endowment is over £8,000, the current saving limit for income support, it has not disqualified claimants from receiving benefit. This is because the DSS regards endowments as life insurance-related rather than income-related and the value of life insurance policies has always been disregarded in calculating income-related benefits. This has meant that endowment policies have been disregarded whether or not they were linked to mortgages. PEPs and ISAs have no life insurance content, and are taken into account in the usual way as capital. So a PEP or ISA without built-in life insurance cover is seen as an investment rather than as part of the mortgage and will therefore count as capital. The whole question of benefit entitlement to owner-occupiers is discussed fully in Chapter 16.

7   See also article by Deborah Quilgars, 'High and dry down Acacia Avenue', *Roof* March/April 1999, pp22-23, Chapter 16. Refer also to Janet Ford, 'MPPI take-up and retention: the current evidence', in *Housing Finance* No.45, February 2000, pp45-51.

8   See also article by Deborah Quilgars, 'High and dry down Acacia Avenue', *Roof*, ibid.

time employment headed only a third of repossessed households. Two out of ten heads of repossessed households were self-employed.

Suggestions have been made for restructuring the mortgage industry and the fiscal support system so that they are more in tune with the current realities of the contemporary employment market and the needs of those owners who are finding it financially difficult to remain in the tenure. The most persistent policy suggestion has been the call for a unified housing benefit scheme covering low-income owners as well as tenants (see Chapter 17). Other proposals are aimed at the industry rather than the government. They include the following.[9]

- More flexible mortgages in which repayment periods, payment schedules and interest rates can be varied according to the mortgagor's ability to pay. This would involve encouraging mortgage deals in which people pay more in prosperous periods and less when earnings fall.
- To reduce the impact of falling income, introduce a system of 'stair-casing-down' from home-ownership, on a similar basis as part-owners can gain access to the tenure by 'stair-casing-up'. This would produce a more flexible tenure in which those leaving home-ownership can retain occupation of their homes instead of having them sold over their heads (often at a fraction of their market values) while they become homeless.
- The introduction of a statutory code of practice for any lending that is based on the security of someone's home. The code would be designed to ensure that, so long as the mortgagor paid a debt serving figure that was in line with the market rent, they could not be forced out of their home.

Positive equity and equity release schemes

Equity represents the value of a mortgaged property after the deduction of any charges against it. In other words, it is that part of the property's value that is 'owned' by the occupier, as against the mortgage provider. Over the years, there has been much debate about the extent to which equity growth in the owner-occupied sector leaks out into the wider economy, thereby causing increases in money demand. The question is important because increases in money demand will induce inflationary pressures that could cause damage to the government's broad macro-economic policy objectives (refer to Chapter 5).

There are a number of ways in which residential property equity can be unlocked and spent on general consumption. As the market value of an occupier's dwelling increases over time it may be possible to borrow against the equity growth. If the mortgagor borrows from the institution with which he or she has a mortgage, the interest charged will usually be the same as the standard variable mortgage rate. This means that the new loan will cost significantly less than taking out an

---

9   Data produced from *Roof* magazine – derived from 57 lenders who between them account for 73 per cent of all mortgagors.

ordinary personal loan. If the mortgagor borrows from a different lender, there is likely to be an arranging fee and the rate of interest is likely to be slightly higher than the standard variable mortgage rate. Nevertheless, over the term of the loan, total charges will normally still be less than they would be for a personal loan. Equity release loans tend to be for a minimum amount, £5,000, and the total amount that can be borrowed will depend on the mortgagor's income, the value of the property, and the level of outstanding debt. Equity release loans are often used to finance home improvements. Many households unlock part of their accumulated housing equity later in life by 'trading down'. This typically involves selling the family home and then purchasing a smaller, and less valuable, retirement property. Equity can also be unlocked when the occupier dies and their estate is inherited by people who then sell the fixed assets with a view to acquiring liquid assets.

The mortgage industry currently provide a number of products that are designed to release equity. The most common mechanisms include the following.[10]

- *Interest only loans* This is the most straightforward method of tapping into home equity. These loans have largely been aimed at older people who tend to have more debt-free equity than younger households and therefore more potential for utilising this as collateral against further borrowing. Under these arrangements no repayments of capital are made until redemption by the borrower through his/her estate.
- *Home income plans* These are a well-established specialist equity release product. The most common form of plan involves a secure *fixed interest only* loan that is used to purchase a lifetime annuity providing fixed periodic payments until death. The cost of the annuity and the income which flows from it are based on life expectancy. The income from the annuity is used to pay the interest repayments on the loan and the balance remaining is available to the borrower.
- *Home reversion* These arrangements are also well-established and typically involve an older home owner selling all or part of their property to an investor either for an annuity income for life or a discounted cash sum while retaining life occupancy rights. The return to the investor, that is, the effective cost to the occupier, is equivalent to the difference between the discounted purchase price and the final sale price when vacant possession is obtained. The level of discount on market value is mainly determined by the life expectancy of the client.
- *Shared appreciation mortgages* These were piloted by the Bank of Scotland in the late 1990s and are gradually becoming available through other banks. They were initially targeted at older people (established owner-occupiers) who want to release some of the equity tied up in their properties. They involve the owner-occupier agreeing to give up a certain increase in the value of the property in exchange for releasing some of that

10 Based on the Council of Mortgage Lenders Briefing Paper, *Equity Release*, April 1998.

cash, thus any equity growth is shared with the mortgagee. The principle of shared appreciation mortgages is now being extended so that new, younger, buyers can take out smaller, and therefore cheaper, mortgages in return for sharing any future capital appreciation with the mortgagee. The issue of equity accumulation and equity release is discussed in more detail below.

The institutional framework

The lending institutions

New entrants into the owner-occupied market acquire their dwellings by means of inheritances, savings, gifts or loans. The lump sum necessary to acquire the asset and cover the transaction and relocation costs may, of course, be assembled from more than one source. Banks and building societies are by far the most important source of mortgage finance. Over the years other providers have included local authorities and insurance companies.[11] After 1981 the banks began to make a significant contribution to the total provision of home loans and have, since that date, been an important but volatile influence in the mortgage market.

The traditional distinction between building societies and banks

The commercial banks are public limited companies operating under the auspices of the Registrar of Companies. They are owned by shareholders whose shares are quoted on the Stock Exchange. Traditionally, building societies have operated in a separate financial sector. Since the first comprehensive Building Societies Act in 1874[12], they have been treated as mutual co-operative organisations and, until recently, they have been set apart from the controls and regulations of the banks and other finance institutions. Their special legal powers were derived from a succession of statutes that were eventually consolidated into the Building Societies Act 1962 and the Building Societies (Northern Ireland) Act 1967, which recognised their mutual, non-profit-making nature by requiring their overall supervision to be administered by the Registrar of Friendly Societies.

The societies have traditionally secured the bulk of their funds in the 'small savers' market, sometimes referred to as the 'retail savings market', by issuing

---

11 A number of insurance companies have traditionally engaged in the mortgage market and they have also been a source of top-up loans when a first mortgage offer is insufficient to meet a purchaser's needs. Local authority mortgages played a significant part for a short period after the return of a Labour government in 1974. They were usually given for older properties for which traditional mortgage finance was not so readily available. Council funds are now severely limited since the government restricts the amount they lend through the Housing Investment Programme process.

12 The first building society was formed in the UK in 1775 when workers formed a co-operative to pool their savings.

shares to investors. Although shares confer membership of the society, they are not transferable and are therefore not comparable with shares in a public company. Normally the investor is issued with a passbook in which is recorded the share value standing to his or her credit. This can be added to and withdrawn from with little fuss and at immediate or short notice. Some societies also offer 'bond' or 'term' shares that have to be held for a fixed period in order to obtain a higher rate of interest. Members have voting rights in relation to elections to its board of directors. As well as receiving money from investing members, societies may, subject to the provisions of the statutes, receive deposits and borrow money from other sources. Depositors who are not members do not have voting rights but do have a prior claim on the assets should the society be wound up.

Concern about the financial instability resulting from the unwise use of funds for property speculation by a few societies after the Second World War led to the imposition of various restraints on building society activities. The 1960s legislation required building societies to concentrate their lending in the form of mortgages and it prevented them from offering the range of financial services provided by the clearing banks. Because mortgages involved them lending over relatively long periods while taking deposits which could be withdrawn at short notice, care was taken to underpin both their general financial stability and their short run liquidity.[13] They were required to hold a proportion of their total assets, prescribed by the Registrar, in the form of cash and gilt-edged or local authority securities. They were also obliged to hold a proportion of securities with a fairly short maturity date so that, if necessary, liquid funds could be realised to cover any abnormal level of withdrawals with a minimum risk of capital loss.

The common features of building societies and banks

In a housing context building societies and banks can be thought of as playing a similar role: namely, they act as financial intermediaries bridging the savings and mortgage markets. In recent years, the distinction between building societies and banks has become increasingly blurred. Under powers given them by major legislation in 1986, the societies now offer a range of financial services formally the province of banking institutions. As deposit-takers, building societies have traditionally been regarded as savings institutions and their share and deposit accounts have been regarded as safe and accessible refuges for money balances which depositors wish to accumulate and keep for some future use such as the deposit on a dwelling or on a holiday. However, nowadays societies offer a range

---

13 The practice of borrowing 'long' and lending 'short' contravenes one of the basic principles of sound financial management. It allows for the possibility of a liquidity crisis if ever there is a loss of confidence in the society and savings are withdrawn at short notice. Because of this, building societies have tended to be conservative in their lending and investment policies. It also helps to explain why their investment policies have been supervised by external agencies.

of banking-type facilities that have led to deposits with them being increasingly used as *transactions* rather than *savings* balances. The most significant developments have been the linking of building society deposits to instant access accounts with chequebook and cheque guarantee card facilities and the provision of high street cash points. In parallel with these developments, the banks have greatly expanded, and aggressively marketed, their mortgage lending facilities. It can be argued that banks and building societies are now competing in the same markets both as lenders and deposit-takers. Because of their growing functional similarities, since 1984 the Inland Revenue has treated building societies and banks on a more or less equal basis.[14]

The growth of competition and the changing structure and role of building societies

As we have seen, the institutions playing the most dominant part in the mortgage market have traditionally been the building societies. Essentially they have acted as financial intermediaries standing between the retail savings market and the housing system. In this position they have channelled funds from savers to borrowers, and in so doing have played a crucial part in the striking increase in owner-occupation that has taken place since the end of the war. In the period between 1945 and the mid-1980s the societies became bigger and fewer in number.[15]

By 1981 the societies were experiencing serious competition from the clearing banks in the field of mortgage provision.[16] The societies tended to charge higher rates of interest on their more substantial loans, whilst the banks tended to offer flat rate mortgages whatever the size of the advance. Because of this, the banks made significant inroads into the more expensive end of the housing market and this in turn encouraged the societies to liberalise their attitudes to lending on 'down market' properties.

---

14 Between 1984 and 1991 savers in both types of institution received interest net of a composite rate of tax which was less than the basic rate. The reduction was not reclaimable by savers who were non-taxpayers. From April 1991 composite rate tax was abolished, with basic rate now applying, and non-taxpayers were able to arrange to obtain gross interest on their accounts. In addition, savers can claim back from the Inland Revenue any tax deducted by the bank or building society that is in excess of their total tax liability for the year.

15 By 1986 the five largest societies controlled 56 per cent of total assets, compared with 45 per cent in 1960.

16 There had already been a significant shift towards more competition between the societies themselves. The most prominent manifestation of this shift was the breaking up of the so-called *building societies' cartel*. The cartel arrangements, which operated throughout the 1970s, involved the trade body for the movement, the Building Societies Association, setting recommended rates of interest for both savers and borrowers. The arrangement was 'official' in that it operated with government approval and thereby became exempted from the provisions of the Monopolies and Mergers Act 1976, which is legislation designed to prevent restrictive trade practices. Over time the cartel was criticised from within and without the movement, and in any event, by the end of the decade, market pressures were undermining the arrangements. The cartel was gradually dismantled in the early 1980s.

The Building Societies Acts 1986 and 1997

Despite their attempts to respond to external competition, the 1962/67 legislation prevented the building societies from competing effectively with rival institutions in the banking and insurance sectors. They were, for example, prohibited from offering overdraft facilities and cheque guarantee cards on their newly introduced cheque book accounts; in addition they were only permitted to offer insurance services in conjunction with a mortgage loan. Both the 1984 Green Paper *Building Societies: A New Framework* (Cm9316), and the Building Societies Association's own discussion paper published a year earlier[17] were critical of this situation. They argued that, whilst societies should remain mutual finance organisations, they should be allowed a wider range of powers in order to meet the growing competition from the banks and other institutions. The consultation process eventually led to a major piece of reforming legislation in the form of the Building Societies Act 1986. This Act repealed all previous legislation regulating building societies.

Under current legislation (the Building Societies Act 1986 as modified by the Building Societies Act 1997), building societies have the choice of two distinct courses of development. They can convert to, or be taken over by, a public limited company, and so become a bank, or they can remain as a mutual society with additional operating powers.

The new Acts of Parliament and their related measures have expanded building society powers. Whilst their prime activity remains the provision of first mortgages, the legislation has gone some way towards removing the distinctions between societies and other banking-type institutions. By easing the restrictions on the provision of unsecured loans and on investment in land and property development, the reforms also allow societies to become directly involved in partnership schemes to provide low-cost housing to purchase, rent or make available on a shared equity basis. The legislative reforms have encouraged the building society movement to undergo significant structural changes. By 1998, a number of its largest members, including its flagship society, the Halifax, had followed the lead of the Abbey National, and merged with, or converted to, banks. These changes have transferred an estimated 75 per cent of the total assets previously held by the building societies sector into banking.

The question of regulation

In recent years the home loans industry has been regulated by a voluntary code of practice. This mortgage code sets out minimum standards that lenders and intermediaries have to meet so as to provide protection for borrowers. The code embraces a list of commitments that seek to give protection with respect to

---

17   The John Spalding Report, *The Future Constitution and Powers of Building Societies*, Building Societies' Association, January 1983.

(a) how the mortgage should be arranged, (b) what information should be presented by the mortgagee prior to agreement, and (c) how the loan will be managed once it is in place. Despite the existence of the code, the Office of Fair Trading has published concerns about the level of customer complaints to trading standards officers and citizens' advice bureaux about mortgages. MPs' post bags and items in the press have also highlighted complaints against a small number of 'rogue' mortgage providers. In 1999, as a result of such stories, the influential committee of MPs and peers who were scrutinising the legislation for the new Financial Services Authority (FSA) called on the government to bring home loans, and long-term care insurance, within the scope of the regulating Authority's terms of reference. Steps are being taken to integrate the regulation of all financial services so the FSA now takes responsibility for supporting the Building Societies Commission, the Friendly Societies Commission and, in relation to credit unions, the Chief Registrar of Friendly Societies.[18] The idea of this transfer of authority is to promote early integration of financial regulation and help achieve the benefit of a single regulatory culture ahead of the new legislation. The legislation will seek to create arrangements that bring consistency and coherence to the regulation of all financial sectors, including banking, insurance, mutual societies, and other financial services.[19]

The Treasury announced the outcome of its review of mortgage regulation in January 2000.[20] Briefly the government has decided the following.

- Not to regulate mortgage advice along the lines of the approach taken for investment advice under the Financial Services Act.
- The FSA will require lenders to disclose all the main features of loans clearly and openly. In effect this means that lenders, but not mortgage intermediaries, will need to be authorised by the FSA, whose remit will cover mortgage advertising, a standard disclosure regime, commission disclosure, and compensation arrangements.
- A new CAT standard for mortgages should be introduced, covering Charges, Access and Terms. This would seek to create a format for providing a straightforward, easy-to-understand mortgage that would appeal to borrowers who want a 'transparent' deal with no complex 'strings' attached.

These proposed provisions were signalled strongly in the 2000 Green Paper and mean that the government will now develop new stronger regulatory measures that

---

18 It will also act on behalf of the Treasury in the conduct of insurance supervision under the Insurance Companies Act.

19 Further controls are opposed by the industry that warns that they would increase the cost of home loans and would threaten the existence of hundreds of independent mortgage brokers. The lenders also point out that endowment policies, the area where much concern has focused, are already regulated as investment products.

20 Circular No 1233, dated 26 January 2000.

will build on and complement the Council of Mortgage Lenders' Voluntary
Mortgage Code.

The Green Paper also considered encouraging the development of a more active
secondary market in mortgages through a process of *securitisation*. The
securitisation of home loans is common practice in the USA. It involves lenders
selling on mortgages by issuing bonds. Because the market judges the bonds to be
a relatively low risk investment, they can generate funds at relatively low rates of
interest. It is argued that the securitisation process also increases competition by
breaking up the mortgage process into its component parts, marketing, processing
applications, raising finance, and servicing mortgages, and allows mortgage
providers to out-source those components that can be provided more effectively or
cheaply by others.

The exchange process

It often takes several months to complete the sale of a property. A number of
exchange professionals can be involved. These typically include an estate agent, a
solicitor, a surveyor, and a mortgage institution. Because a contractual agreement
is at the heart of the process, solicitors, or commercial conveyancers, usually play
a key role in driving the arrangements towards completion. Most solicitors use the
Law Society conveyancing code as a reference for appropriate practice and this, to
some extent, has the effect of standardising the process. Special forms are used
that include an information questionnaire that the seller completes. This sets out
details about the property and acts as a checklist of what is being sold. The seller's
solicitor then provides a pre-contract package for the prospective buyer, which is
essentially a draft contract with documents relating to the client's title to the
property. The buyer's solicitor obtains *searches*. These investigate public records
to check whether the property is subject to any legal liabilities or encumbrances.
Once the searches have taken place, the conveyancer will formalise any necessary
amendments to the draft contract. Meanwhile, the buyer will normally arrange a
survey and, if necessary, a mortgage loan. Once these transactions have been dealt
with, a completion date is set and contracts can be exchanged. Between exchange
and completion, the purchaser's solicitor arranges for the mortgage funds to be
released and prepares a transfer document so the contract's financial consideration
can be passed over.

For years the home buying process has been criticised for being unnecessarily
lengthy and cumbersome. Outside Scotland, where legal obligations are
established on the exchange of contracts, the process has also been criticised for
allowing the would-be purchaser to be 'gazumped', or the seller to be confronted
with a withdrawn or reduced offer weeks into the negotiations. New measures are
currently being considered that are intended to reduce the time lag between offer
acceptance and exchange of contracts. By shifting more of the responsibility and
cost of the exchange process on to the vendor it is planned to reduce the risk of
last minute renegotiations. After testing in a number of pilot areas, it is expected

that new legislation will be introduced that will require the seller to prepare an information pack for prospective purchasers. It is proposed that the pack will include draft contracts, title deeds, an independent surveyor's report on the condition of the property and its energy efficiency, warranties and guarantees for any work carried out, the results of searches and answers to commonly asked questions. Under these arrangements, the survey would be to a standard format prescribed by the government, and the surveyor would be liable to both the seller and the buyer for its contents. Although developers will not be required to include a survey report in their packs, they will have to include copies of planning consents, warranties and guarantees.

The above proposals will have implications for social landlords who are involved with property sales. As an extension of existing 'best value' principles, social landlords involved in sales will be expected to adopt performance targets ensuring that those with whom they deal receive a fast and efficient service.

Exchange costs

The following constitute the main exchange costs associated with residential property transactions. They do not all apply in all cases.

- *Estate agents' fees.* Most agent's tariffs differentiate between a 'sole' and a 'multiple' agency. A higher fee is usually charged if there is more than one agent commissioned to sell the property. Some agents charge a flat fee and then additional charges for the erection of a board and placing advertisements in the press, whilst others have an overall marketing agreement with no additional charges.
- *Legal fees.* Legal fees are paid for the services of a solicitor or conveyancer. The final bill will be broken down into various charge categories. The contract administration charge is normally calculated as a percentage of the purchase price plus VAT. In addition to a charge covering contract administration and legal advice, the following might also be included in the final account.
- *A Land Registry fee.* This is a charge to check the nature and scope of the seller's title to the land and buildings.
- *A local authority search fee.* This is charged to check the existence of any current or proposed planning restrictions or other factors that might affect the occupier's consumption or investment interests.
- *Stamp duty.* Stamp duty is a sales tax that is charged to higher priced real estate transactions.[21] Although the tax has only a limited affect on the housing market, it is criticised by housing economists as a tax on mobility.

---

21 The stamp duty rates currently stand, from April 2000, at one per cent on properties sold for more than £60,000 but for less than £250,000; three per cent where the sale price is above £250,000 and less than £500,000; and four per cent where the price is more than £500,000. Land Registry figures indicate that, in 1997, of the total residential property sales, about two per cent were for dwellings valued above £250,000, and the majority of these were in the South East of England.

It is also criticised as a fiscal anomaly with no clear social or economic purpose. It is simply a revenue raising measure and, at the time of writing, real estate stamp duty raises some £500 million annually with about 25 per cent of the yield coming from residential property sales and the rest from the transfer of land and commercial properties.[22]

- *Property survey fees.* When a mortgage loan is involved, the lender will normally require a surveyor's report and mortgage valuation. This is usually a simple visual inspection that is designed to confirm that the property's value is sufficient to cover the debt liabilities. This survey report is not designed to provide a detailed condition survey and therefore a purchaser may choose to commission a fuller structural survey before making a final offer.

Taxation and capital finance

Capital gains tax

Britain, like many other countries, does not tax capital gains on an owner-occupied dwelling where it is classified as the 'only or main residence' of the occupier.[23] In strict economic terms this concession may be criticised as bringing a distortion into the wider capital market. The argument here is that dwellings are capital assets and the tax privilege will attract funds away from other, more productive, classes of asset, thereby inhibiting investment efficiency and general economic growth in the economy. Despite this economic argument, it is possible to justify the tax concession in social policy terms. The case here is that private residences should be treated as 'domestic' rather than 'commercial' assets. It is argued that the tax system should not penalise the acquisition of those forms of real property that most owners regard as capitalised 'savings' to be inherited by their children or used to fund their own declining years.

With some exceptions[24], if someone owns a second home the Inland Revenue treats this as a taxable investment. This is true even if it is not let out on a commercial basis, but it is held as a holiday home. In its first Budget, the New Labour government altered the capital gains tax rules as they apply to second homes. The old rules were based on the idea that the tax was levied on sale on the basis of 'proceeds less costs'. This provided an indexation allowance, or inflation protection, in the calculation of the 'gain' and the seller was then allowed an

---

22 It might be argued that recent stamp duty rises, in 2000, were introduced in an attempt to dampen down house price inflation, particularly in the South East of England. Stamp duty also applies to documents transferring other types of property such as shares and other securities.

23 If two or more main residences are held simultaneously, the individual may select which property they wish to qualify for exemption.

24 For example, if an individual disposes of a residence previously occupied by a dependent relative, rent free and without other consideration, capital gains tax exemption will normally be granted.

annual exemption before the tax was levied. Under the new rules there is still an annual exemption[25], but other aspects of the computation have changed significantly. Indexation has ceased so there is now no inflation protection built into the system, and the new regime tapers away the gain, depending on how long the asset has been held.[26]

The Inland Revenue estimate that the cost to the Exchequer of the capital gains tax concession in 1998/99 amounted to £1,350 million. In 1985/86, when the housing market was unusually active, the estimated loss to the Exchequer was as high as £2,500 million. It should be recognised that, some at least, of this 'lost' Exchequer revenue is eventually recouped through inheritance tax.

Inheritance taxation

To introduce a capital gains tax charge on ordinary housing transactions would be politically difficult. It would also be inconvenient and expensive to administer, given the volume of transactions. It is more convenient to tax capital appreciation on domestic assets through the mechanism of inheritance tax. Inheritance tax is payable on death and is charged as a flat rate percentage of the value of the estate over an exempted figure.[27] The tax is not payable if the deceased's spouse inherits the estate and other exemptions are possible if the estate is willed to a charitable foundation. The 'estate' upon which the tax is charged covers all cash and assets including residences, cars, any life assurance benefits and investments, and valuables such as antiques and jewellery, minus any outstanding debts. Inheritance tax raised £1.7 billion in revenue in 1997/98.

Occupancy and revenue finance

The idea of housing expenditure and revenue

As managers of their homes, owner-occupiers are responsible for meeting all the associated costs-in-use. They are responsible for all the recurring revenue charges with respect to interest and debt redemption on mortgage or other loans taken out to acquire their properties, together with all the payments made for the purpose of maintaining and repairing the fabric of the dwellings once they have been acquired.

In practice, the day-to-day revenue expenses of owner-occupation are met out of the household's total disposable income, which is generally derived from

---

25 Currently 6.8 per cent.

26 The taper works over a ten-year period. Under current regulations, the capital gains taxed is initially charged at the taxpayers marginal rate, so that, for instance, a 40 per cent marginal taxpayer would go in at the 40 per cent band for a three-year holding period. It then steadily tapers away so that after ten years it has fallen to 24 per cent.

27 At the time of writing this tax is chargeable at 40 per cent on that part of the estate's value in excess of £234,000.

employment earnings, or any welfare benefits to which they are entitled. However, in its strictest sense, the housing revenue of an owner-occupier stems from his or her ownership of the dwelling as an economic asset. This means that, in theory, it is conceived of as the revenue benefit that is generated by the asset and then enjoyed by the owner. This benefit takes the form of a stream of housing services and can be thought of as an *income in kind*. This income in kind is referred to as *imputed rent* or *imputed income*.

Revenue income

As with the case of landlords, owner-occupiers can be said to receive 'incomes' that are directly derived from the dwellings they own. Also, like housing organisations, owner-occupiers can be said to receive these incomes in the form of 'rents' and 'subsidies'. However, the difference between the housing income of an owner-occupier and that of a landlord is that in the case of the former, the 'rent' is not paid by a tenant but is conceived of as an *imputed rent*. Because no cash is actually received, the idea that owners pay themselves 'rent' is counter-intuitive and rather difficult to grasp. However, it is important to understand the notion of *imputed rent* because it features strongly in the general debate about the nature and scope of owner-occupier subsidies.

The non-taxation of imputed rental income

An owner of a dwelling may either let it out to another person or occupy it as a home. If they let it out, the rental income he or she receives after allowances will be taxed as part of his or her income. It will be taxed under Schedule 'A' of the income tax schedules, which deals with income from land and landed property. If, on the other hand, the owner chooses to occupy the dwelling, he or she receives a benefit that can be thought of as an *income in kind*, and this benefit is not now subject to income taxation, although it was prior to 1963 – see below. In this way, an owner-occupied residence might be thought of as a durable asset that yields a flow of untaxed housing services that are consumed by the owner-occupant. The term 'imputed income' is used to describe the monetary value that is attributed to these services.[28]

The abolition of Schedule 'A' income tax and the changing nature of mortgage interest tax relief

As a general taxation principle, if taxpayers take out loans to acquire consumption items, such as family cars, holidays, jewellery, etc., they cannot offset the cost of servicing such loans against their income tax liabilities. By contrast, if taxpayers take out loans to acquire investment items (e.g. fleet cars, plant, machinery, etc.), they may, under certain conditions, be entitled to claim income tax relief for

---

28 It is possible, of course, for an owner-occupier to take in a lodger or let out part of the dwelling. In such circumstances, that owner would receive actual revenue income in addition to the imputed rental income.

interest paid. In this way, the Inland Revenue treats consumption and investment expenditure differently when it comes to allowing tax relief in loan interest charges. One of the long-standing debates in housing finance is whether owner-occupied housing should be treated, for tax purposes, as consumption or investment.

Prior to 1963, owner-occupied dwellings were treated for tax purposes as though they were investments. The imputed income benefit received was taxed, but certain costs, including that of servicing the mortgage loan were granted as allowances. This means that, at that time, mortgage income tax relief (MITR), was not technically a 'subsidy', but rather a legitimate tax allowance set against investment earnings. As such, MITR was on a par with similar allowances in the business world.

The reason that the main residences of owner-occupiers were exempted from Schedule 'A' income taxation after 1963 was largely political and was the result of the rating revaluation that took place in that year. The tax was assessed on the assumed letting value of the property net of repairs and maintenance, and rateable values were used as the basis of the assessment. However, residential properties were only periodically revalued for rating purposes, and at the time, it was the 1936/37 rating valuations that were being used to calculate the imputed incomes. A long overdue rating revaluation was to take place in 1963/64 and, if the Schedule 'A' tax had been retained, it would have meant that, in many areas, the tax burden would have trebled or quadrupled. This would have had damaging political consequences for the government at a time when more and more of the electorate were becoming owner-occupiers.[29]

When Schedule 'A' income tax was abolished, a political decision was made to allow owners to continue to set their mortgage interest costs against their income tax liabilities. The changes had the effect of converting MITR from a legitimate allowance, on a tax charge that was actually paid, into an effective housing subsidy. Many commentators argued that once the tax was scrapped, MITR became an anomalous, tenure-specific, fiscal benefit.

Mortgage income tax relief (MITR) and the introduction of MIRAS

In recent years, the Treasury has not treated mortgage income tax relief (MITR), as a 'subsidy', preferring to regard it as a 'tax forgone'. This failure explicitly to recognise the real income effect of the tax privilege has produced what might be termed a 'hidden subsidy' for the tenure. The concession, and therefore the 'subsidy', has now been phased out (see below).

---

29 As well as exempting owner-occupation, the Finance Act 1963 altered the whole way in which Schedule 'A' tax was assessed. Before the 1963 Budget the tax had been charged on an annual value related to the rateable value. After the 1963 Budget the taxation of income from land and buildings (Schedule 'A'), was based on the actual profit arising, i.e. receipts less allowable expenditure.

Before 1983 the relief was granted by means of the Inland Revenue adjusting the borrower's tax coding and assessment. This system was changed in 1983 with the introduction of new administrative arrangements known as *Mortgage Interest Relief at Source* (MIRAS). Under the MIRAS scheme, borrowers paid the monthly interest on their mortgage loans net of tax relief.[30] MIRAS cost the Exchequer some £2.7 billion in lost revenue in 1997/98 and £1.9 billion in 1998/99 and £2 billion in 1999/2000 (estimated) – from a peak of £7.6 billion in 1990/91.

The rise and fall of mortgage interest tax relief

Income tax was first introduced in 1799 and the idea of giving income tax relief on the interest element of personal debt dates back to the early nineteenth century. Under the provisions of the Income Tax Act 1803, borrowers received relief on the interest portion of all personal loans including charges on house purchase mortgages. Initially, the extent of the relief was calculated by multiplying the mortgage interest charge by the borrower's marginal tax rate. This meant that the original MITR system was distinctly regressive in so far as the relief granted was relatively higher for those with big loans, living in big dwellings, and for those earning larger incomes, and paying relatively higher marginal tax rates. After 1974 tax relief on interest paid by individuals was restricted to loans for the purchase or improvement of property. [31] From that date it was not possible to set the interest on non-property personal loans against income tax liabilities.

1974 saw a further rule change that marked the beginning of the long, slow death of MIRAS. Up to 1974 the relief was available for the full cost of the mortgage loan. In that year, however, a debt ceiling was fixed at £25,000. In practice, this had no effect on the tax position of the overwhelming majority of home owners as, at that time, the average mortgage, at about £6,500, was well below the ceiling.[32] By the time MIRAS was introduced in 1983, the tax concession had played its part in spurring on house price inflation. During the thirty-year period prior to the introduction of MIRAS house prices rose at twice the rate of inflation. Partly in response to this rise, in 1983 the debt ceiling was raised to £30,000, a level at which it remained fixed thereafter. In the early 1980s, the interaction between continuing rapid house price inflation and the fixed ceiling meant that eventually the real income effect of the relief was systematically diminished.

Concerns about the need to establish tenure neutrality led the mid-decade *Inquiry into British Housing*, chaired by the Duke of Edinburgh (NFHA, 1985), to advocate the replacement of MIRAS and housing benefit with a single needs-

---

30 The reader needs to be clear that MIRAS is the allowance 'process', and MITR is the 'concept'. Under the MIRAS process, the lender had to calculate the borrower's periodic repayments and then work out the tax relief at the qualifying rate on the interest element. This saved a great deal of work for the Inland Revenue because, for standard rate taxpayers, there was no longer a need to deal directly with the local tax office.

31 The concession was abolished in 1969 except for interest paid on mortgages, although it was reintroduced briefly between 1972 and 1973.

32 Average house prices at that time were in the region of £11,500.

related allowance. But royal patronage was not enough to overturn the Conservative Party's commitment to use the fiscal system to expand home-ownership, and MIRAS lived on.

Up to 1989 unmarried couples living in the same dwelling and sharing the burden of the mortgage charge, could each claim personal relief up to the ceiling of £30,000 against their income tax liabilities. This was seen as discriminating against married couples, or as even a fiscal incentive to 'live in sin'. The dual tax relief was abolished in 1989. Because the change was signalled several months beforehand in the Chancellor's Budget speech, this reform led to a sudden surge in demand in the housing market. People advanced their purchasing plans so as to avoid the in-coming restriction. This helped to spin house prices upwards and in so doing, helped to burst the 1980s housing boom.

Successive Finance Acts systematically reduced the impact of MIRAS. With politicians finding it increasingly difficult to justify the concession in social and economic terms, it was phased out as the principal subsidy to owner-occupation. In the 1990s the real income effect of the tax concession was significantly diminished by a sequence of Budget changes that reduced the rate of tax against which the allowance could be claimed. After 1990 it was no longer possible to claim the relief at the borrower's marginal tax rate, and relief was limited to the standard rate of income tax no matter how much the mortgagor earned. In 1994 allowances were restricted to a 20 per cent rate (i.e. less than the standard rate of income tax). In 1995 the rate of relief on payments of mortgage interest was reduced to 15 per cent, and after April 1998 they were reduced to 10 per cent. The death of MITR was finally announced in the 1999 Budget in which the Chancellor declared that relief on mortgage interest payments was to be removed altogether from 6 April 2000. MITR for those aged 65 and over who take out a loan to buy a life annuity (a mortgage home income plan) ended in March 1999. Existing loans of this kind continue to qualify for relief for the remainder of the loan period.

Maintenance costs

Debt servicing charges are not the only recurring housing costs confronting home owners. Indeed, many owner-occupied dwellings are owned outright.[33] Owners have to spend money to maintain their properties in a state of good repair whether or not they are buying with the help of a loan.

The distinction between 'primary maintenance' and 'improvement'

Primary maintenance work is undertaken to prevent or arrest the building's structure and fabric from deteriorating and is therefore concerned with

---

33 Census figures indicate that about 68 per cent of dwellings are owner-occupied (England and Wales). This breaks down to 43 per cent owned with mortgage debt attached and 25 per cent owned outright.

maintaining the building envelope. In other words, primary maintenance is carried out to ensure that the building is 'safe and sound'. This type of maintenance might occur in response to some form of unexpected structural failure or it might be planned and budgeted for in advance. Improvement work is undertaken to add to the building's size or quality rather than to maintain it in working order. This may involve building some kind of extension to the property or converting it to a different use (perhaps from a large house into flats) installing some feature or facility it previously lacked, or refurbishing it to bring it up to some higher standard of accommodation. In this way, improvement works can be said to be adding to the capital value of the dwelling rather than simply maintaining its value.

In Chapter 2 a theoretical distinction was made between 'capital' and 'revenue' finance. It was made clear that, in theory, capital finance is used to add to the quantity or quality of the housing stock and revenue finance is used to maintain the stock in a reasonable state of repair. On this basis, 'maintenance' can be thought of as requiring revenue finance and 'improvement' can be thought of as requiring capital finance. In financial practice, however, the distinction between 'primary maintenance' and 'improvement' can be blurred. Some primary maintenance work, such as a major roof repair or the reinforcing of foundations to arrest subsidence, may require as much or more money than some improvement work such as installing central heating. Furthermore, like much improvement work, some primary maintenance jobs may qualify for grant aid or require loan finance. In other words, improvements and primary maintenance works may be financed in similar ways and from similar sources.

The distinction between 'primary' and 'secondary' maintenance

In contrast to 'primary' maintenance, 'secondary' maintenance tends to be paid for more on a month-by-month basis and includes repairs of non-structural building elements and components. It includes non-essential external redecoration and nearly all internal redecoration, as well as the various minor jobs around the house. Most do-it-yourself (DIY) activity falls into this category of secondary maintenance. Whether carried out by a contractor or on a DIY basis, these activities are typically paid for out of current income or savings rather than by means of a grant or loan.

Factors affecting the level of maintenance

The amount of money an owner-occupier spends on maintenance over a period will be affected by: (a) his or her financial resources and priorities; (b) the age and condition of the building; (c) the level of wear and tear to which it is subjected; (d) the owner's ability and inclination to do work him or herself on the property; (e) the quality of the building and the nature and quality of previous improvement and maintenance work; and (f) the way the market values maintenance work. We will say something briefly about each of these.

(a)   The primary element of a household's financial resources is its disposable income. Because dwellings are costly to repair, low-income households are likely to suffer relatively poor housing conditions in the absence of government aid. In this way, it has long been argued that 'housing decay is one manifestation of poverty'[34].

As we saw in Chapter 6, recent governments have done much to encourage the growth of owner-occupation. In particular, since 1979 there has been a series of measures aimed principally at those who, before that date, would not have considered owning their own homes. In addition to specific policies aimed at low-income households, the decline in expenditure on public sector rented housing (see Chapter 5), combined with the continual shrinkage in the availability of private rented housing (see Chapter 16), has served to persuade large numbers of people to become owner-occupiers. Many of these will have been relatively poor households that have competing demands on their limited resources and who, as a result, will have chosen to 'under-maintain' their homes, that is, maintain them to a level that is below the minimum standard deemed desirable by government policy and established professional practice.

In higher income households, maintenance also has had to compete with other budget items. In any household, what actually gets spent on maintenance will, to a large extent, depend upon the priority it is given over the other claims on the household's savings and disposable income. In other words, money spent on the dwelling will have an *opportunity cost* (see Chapter 2), in the form of the sacrifices of some other household need or demand. In the case of a relatively wealthy family, living in a well-maintained house, the sacrifice may have only a limited effect on their collective lifestyle; it might, for example, involve saving less for a short period or taking less expensive holidays for a year or two. However, in the case of a low-income family, living in a poorly maintained house, the sacrifice needed to repair it to a satisfactory standard may involve a considerable reduction in their general standard of living over an extended period.

With the reduction in grant expenditure and the curtailing of the area based improvement programmes (see Chapter 10), owner-occupiers have been increasingly placed in the position of having to rely more and more on their own resources. There are considerable difficulties in obtaining meaningful information on how much home owners spend on repairs and maintenance. This is partly because only a limited amount of research has been done on the topic, and partly because researchers have found that owners do not usually keep records of such expenditure. Furthermore, much of the maintenance work is done on a DIY basis or by someone else working within the informal economy. Researchers in this field find that the problem is further compounded by the fact that most owners find it difficult to cost work done by themselves or by friends or relatives (Mackintosh *et al.*, 1988).

---

34   NEDO 1986, p19.

(b/c) It is self-evidently true that buildings decay through time and use: accordingly, the annual maintenance costs tend to increase as the building ages. In this respect, it is of general interest that in most regions of Britain over 20 per cent of the housing stock was built before 1919 (Wilcox, 1997, p105).

(d)   Other factors affecting the level of maintenance in this sector are the knowledge, skill and energy of owners together with their inclination to do or organise maintenance work themselves. In other words, resources other than finance will be available to some households. Where it exists, household expertise and energy can be combined with finance to carry out certain maintenance tasks. However, it is difficult for most home owners to acquire substantial experience in maintenance; few will ever undertake a major job, like a roof replacement, and of those who do, very few indeed will re-use the expertise gained, (Mackintosh *et al.*, 1988). This contrasts with professional housing agencies, such as local authorities or housing associations that continually accumulate or re-use such knowledge.

One form of direct help is the support of *agency services*. Home Improvement Agencies (HIAs), provide independent advice and help to elderly and disabled people and people on low incomes to undertake building repairs, improvements and adaptations to their properties. They help vulnerable people to stay put in their homes rather than be forced to move into an institutional setting. HIAs are usually small schemes, staffed by three or four people, operating within a particular district. They are managed by a variety of organisations, often housing associations, but also local authorities and independent bodies such as Age Concern. Grants, of up to 50 per cent of revenue costs of HIAs, are channelled through local authorities who are responsible for assessing the need for HIA services in their areas and for bidding on their behalf.[35]

(e)   Decisions aimed at determining best financial practice in the field of building maintenance and renewal centre on what might be termed the *time-cost dilemma*.[36] This poses the following decision question: *Is it better to spend more on the works now and thereby achieve relatively low future costs-in-use; or is it better to spend less now and instead pay for relatively higher costs-in-use sometime in the future?*

The time-cost dilemma highlights the point that the nature and quality of previous renewal and maintenance works can affect current and future maintenance costs. This relates to the points made in (a) and (d) above.

---

35   This means that at the time of writing HIAs are funded through specific grant that has to be matched by local authority money. Specific grants are explained in Chapter 9. In 1998 the government paid grants worth £5.2 million to a total of 163 agencies.

36   The time-cost dilemma arises because buildings are durable assets and money has a 'time value'. This poses a dilemma for those making decisions about how much to invest in any building project. For a full discussion and explanation of the dilemma see Garnett, 1996.

That is, some owners may 'under-maintain' through choice, ignorance or lack of income. From the point of view of a professional builder, surveyor or housing manager, some private owners may decide to carry out building work in the 'wrong' way. It may be that some owners create future maintenance problems by doing jobs in an inappropriate sequence, with inappropriate techniques, with inappropriate materials or by employing an inappropriate contractor. The use of the word 'inappropriate' here is intended to indicate a situation in which conventionally accepted 'good practices' by a local authority or registered social landlord would have resulted in things being done differently.

(f)   The way the housing market operates tends to militate against providing owners with an incentive to maintain the structure of their properties in accordance with conventionally accepted 'good practice'. More precisely, it tends to discourage owners from undertaking primary maintenance. The housing market seems to operate in a way that emphasises the value of decorative work (such as painting, kitchen fittings, etc.) more highly than less visible primary maintenance work to the building's fabric and structure. In other words, market weaknesses in the form of imperfect buyer knowledge, may affect the rational maintenance behaviour of owners so as to emphasise short-term consumption goals relating to the appearance of the dwelling, rather than the longer-term investment goals relating to the physical life of the building.

Furthermore, where property prices are depressed, maintenance may be neglected as the costs may not be recouped in the resale value of the property. Where prices are rising, more owners may be encouraged to maintain or improve their dwellings but, on the other hand, it may also make economic sense for them to downgrade maintenance in order to increase their 'yield' as property prices reflect location factors rather than house conditions. This market phenomenon is referred to as the *valuation gap* and it offers an economic explanation for 'under-maintenance'.[37]

Management and insurance costs

In the case of owner-occupation, most supervision and administration costs are counted in time rather than in money terms. Insurance is, however, a financial cost that most private households have to meet. Although there is no legal obligation for an owner-occupied dwelling to be insured against damage or destruction, a prudent owner will take out appropriate cover and all lending institutions insist on such cover before approving a mortgage loan. Insurance policies vary in terms of cover provided and premiums charged, but all will be based on a calculation of value that relates to the costs of replacement rather than to the purchase price. Because the rebuilding costs of a dwelling can be in excess

37   The valuation gap is discussed further in Chapters 6 and 10.

of its market value, the owner may have to insure the property for a larger amount than its potential sales price. Most insurance companies provide index-linked policies in which the sum insured and premiums automatically rise in line with rebuilding cost inflation.

New building insurance and warranties

The National House Building Council (NHBC), offer a ten-year warranty on newly built dwellings to cover defects after hand-over. If the dwelling is covered by the warranty and defects appear within the first few years, the NHBC will arrange for an inspection of the property and, if defects are found, they will set a deadline within which the repair work has to be started. They also offer what they term 'catastrophe insurance' to cover serious structural faults that appear between years three and ten. Cover can also be provided for the roof coverings, rendering and internal floors.

Summary

Most owner-occupied dwellings are acquired with the aid of a mortgage loan.

The occupier's *equity* is represented by that part of the property's value that is unencumbered by debt.

Banks and building societies are the primary providers of house-purchase finance. In recent years the interplay between competition and legislation has reduced the distinctions between 'mutual' building societies and 'commercial' banks.

In the climate of enhanced competition, a wide range of mortgage 'products' are now available. However, an important distinction still remains between 'interest-and-capital' mortgages and 'interest only' mortgages.

The government is introducing statutory regulation by giving the FSA responsibility for regulating key aspects of mortgage selling. We are moving towards a unified system of regulation for all financial services.

When sold, the main residences of owner-occupiers are not subject to capital gains taxation. But they may be subject to inheritance taxation.

Prior to 1963 MITR was classified as a *tax allowance* rather than a *subsidy* because the Inland Revenue treated the main residence of a taxpayer as an investment asset that generated a flow of 'income' that could be legitimately taxed. After 1963 MITR has to be classified as a subsidy because Schedule 'A' income tax was abolished. MITR has now been phased out.

In analysing the broad management costs confronting the owner-occupier we should distinguish between the following: debt service charges, primary maintenance, secondary maintenance, improvement expenditure, and insurance premiums.

Further reading

Sustainable Home Ownership – New Policies for a New Government, CIH, 1997.

CHAPTER 8:
Local government and housing finance: an introduction

The importance of local government

Local government is seen to matter because it is the one public institution that, through its democratic mandate, can empower citizens locally. It provides a range of major services to local residents and firms either alone or in partnership with central government, the private sector, or voluntary groups. Currently in the UK more than 20,000 councillors and 2 million employees are responsible for spending some £75 billion each year from taxes and charges. This represents a quarter of all government expenditure (DETR, Cm6646, 1998). The government helps meet a large part of this cost through grants and business rates. The rest comes from the council tax that is levied on local residents. Northern Ireland is not dealt with in detail in these chapters as its remaining local government has no housing responsibilities.

The basic structure of local government

In many parts of England the responsibility for providing major local authority services is divided between county councils and district councils. Where this two-tier model applies, the counties, often referred to as the 'shire counties' because they broadly correspond to the historic county boundaries, are responsible for the wide-scale services such as education, highways, police, social services, libraries, waste disposal, and trading standards. The district councils administer the more local-scale services such as housing, environmental health, building control, waste collection, cemeteries, parking, parks, leisure and recreation, roads and footpaths. In this two-tier model, some responsibilities, such as planning, traffic management, tourism, architecture, galleries and museums, may involve both tiers.

The other model for local government is the unitary council in which a single authority has responsibility for providing and delivering the full range of local government services to a designated area. The whole of local government in Scotland and Wales is organised on a unitary basis. In England, all the London boroughs are unitary authorities as are the metropolitan districts. Following recent reviews, many more unitary authorities were established after 1995. Usually, but not always, these new unitary authorities are based on large or medium sized cities such as York, Bristol, Hull, Portsmouth, Southampton or Plymouth. However, they also include areas such as South Gloucestershire, North Somerset, Rutland, and the

Isle of Wight. Details of the changing structure of local government can be found in Appendix 8.A.

Responsibility and accountability: the twin pillars of local government finance

The system of local government finance has its roots in the seventeenth century Poor Law. This legislation, which dates from 1601, established the two basic principles of local government finance: (1) that a monetary amount or '*rate*' should be levied from local residents to help pay for local services, and (2) that those who administer such services should be accountable to the elected representatives of those who have to pay these rates. Contemporary local government functions, including housing, are administered by authorities that are popularly referred to as 'councils'. The term 'council' reflects the fact that an assembly of locally elected 'members' or 'councillors' is the embodiment of local government's democratic authority.

The periodic reforms of local government that have taken place in response to the expanding range and volume of municipal services have transformed the old arrangements designed to deal with seventeenth century pauperism into a large-scale modern complex business.[1] Throughout these structural transformations, however, the traditional twin principles of *local responsibility* and *local accountability* have been maintained. Indeed, the present government was elected on a manifesto (1996), which said that local decision-making should be less constrained by central government and more accountable to local people.

Current principles of local government finance

The present government has said that it expects the local government finance system to reflect 'the nature of modern councils' relationship with their communities and with central government' (DETR, Cm6646, 1998, p7). This means that they should be accountable and responsive to their local taxpayers, be increasingly responsible for raising expenditure locally, have an open and soundly based system of business rates, and receive a fair distribution of government grant.

Local relations

Because of their wide range of responsibilities, their democratic mandate and their tax raising powers, the government sees councils as having a unique role to

---

1   Expenditure on local government in the UK is now approximately 10 per cent of GDP and in Scotland almost half the funds allocated each year to the Scottish Office are automatically reallocated to local authorities. (Kerley, 1994, p29.). Local government spending in Northern Ireland is relatively less significant as the Northern Ireland Office is a central government department and is directly responsible for many of the functions carried out by local authorities elsewhere in Great Britain.

interpret the priorities and aspirations of local people and translate them into action. *'In short, leadership is at the heart of modern local government'* (DETR, Cm6646, 1998, p35).

Central-local relations

By international standards, British local authorities are heavily dependent on central government financial support. The bulk of local spending is financed by the national taxpayer and this in itself establishes a high degree of interconnection between central and local decisions on councils' finances. Central government seeks to ensure that public spending is carried out in ways that are supportive to macro-economic policy objectives such as the control of inflation and minimising public sector debt. It is also responsible for managing total public expenditure in a way that is judged to be financially 'sound'. Local authority spending makes up around a quarter of total public expenditure and has to be subject to the same constraints as other areas of spending. Central government also has a political interest in ensuring value-for-money and the efficient use of resources in the delivery of local services, while keeping the overall burden of taxation as low as possible. For all these reasons, it has a strong interest in local government's taxation and spending decisions. In recent years, central control has focused on the government's powers to cap revenue charges, to allocate grants to local authorities, and to restrict their ability to borrow and to utilise their capital receipts.

Local authority net revenue and capital expenditure, including debt interest, for the UK in 1996/97 amounted to nearly £76 billion. Local government spending represents about 10 per cent of national income. Put in more personal terms, we can say that local government spending amounts to approximately £1,300 per head of the population for every man, woman and child (CIPFA, 1997a, p39). Given the value of their assets and the volume of their annual spending at 25 per cent of all public spending, the current government has placed a new duty on local authorities to achieve 'best value' outputs (refer to Chapter 2). This takes different forms in different parts of the UK. [2]

Value-for-money and the notion of 'best value'

In England and Wales, authorities are required to produce *best value performance plans* that are backed up by Audit Commission monitoring. Best value constitutes a major change in the way local authorities contract local services and supersedes

---

2   At the time of writing, there is much discussion about the need to alter the regulatory arrangements in Scotland. In particular, the regulatory role of Scottish Homes is being brought into question with calls for a new national housing 'super regulator' of all landlords, including councils. In Wales the functions of Tai Cymru were amalgamated with those of the Welsh Office prior to Welsh Assembly control. A National Consultative Forum on Housing Consultation Forum for Wales has been established to inform the agenda for the new Welsh Assembly.

the earlier system of *compulsory competitive tendering* (CCT), the rigid and restrictive nature of which sometimes failed to guarantee value-for-money in contracts. In its far-reaching 1998 White Paper on local government reform (Cm4104), the government made it clear that it would honour its manifesto pledge and abolish the legalistic CCT regime and let councils decide how to provide services so long as they give 'best value' to the public they serve. These provisions are now contained in the Local Government Act 1999. The new duty places a requirement on local authorities to 'deliver the quality of service that people expect at a price they are willing to pay'. The government sought to clarify this rather vague commitment by identifying a number of key principles, announced in June 1997, that were subsequently used as the basis for developing a best value framework. Together, these principles amplify the point that local authorities owe a duty of best value to local people both as taxpayers and as consumers. This duty applies to all local authority service, not just those previously covered by CCT.[3]

The best value duty requires authorities in England to demonstrate that they are operating in line with the following tenets.

- Each authority should seek to provide services that bear comparison with the best on offer from both the private and public sectors.
- Although competition remains an important consideration in management planning, it is not the sole criterion for demonstrating a best value approach.
- The decision as to whether a service is provided in-house or privately must be judged against efficiency, effectiveness, equity, and experiential criteria (refer to Figure 2.3 in Chapter 2), rather than by reference to dogma; i.e. 'what matters is what works'.
- Councils must seek to address 'cross-cutting issues' facing their citizens and communities, such as community safety and sustainable development, which are beyond the reach of a single service or service provider.
- Local accountability to deliver value-for-money must be monitored against published performance plans and targets.
- Local targets will be judged against a basic framework set by central government so that performance comparisons can be made between local authorities.
- Good management information on performance should be the basis of both national and local targets.
- The integrity of performance information should be confirmed by independent inspection and audit, and requires certification.

---

3   The education service was the first to develop a workable framework for ensuring quality enhancement. This involved, in part, the establishment of a powerful external inspectorate (OFSTED). In June 1998 the government announced its intention to set up a Housing Inspectorate that would operate under the umbrella of the Audit Commission in England. In July of the same year, it announced its intention to introduce legislation that will give central government new powers to take control of housing from poorly performing authorities, and also to give tenants a more effective say in how their homes are managed.

- Where an authority is judged to have failed to provide best value the Secretary of State can direct intervention and this can take the form of greater competition or external management support.

A campaign is gathering momentum for the government to include equal opportunities under the principles of best value. This would be in line with the *equity relationship* discussed in Chapter 2 (refer to Figure 2.3). This campaign has been given voice in a report by the Local Government Information Unit (*Best Value and Equal Opportunities*, LGIU, 1998), that argues that public services cannot be delivered effectively unless they are underpinned by equal opportunities.

A provisional best value administrative framework was developed from the guiding principles (excluding equal opportunities) prior to establishing a legally enforceable system in England in April 2000. Some thirty authorities were selected to participate in a pilot scheme designed to test the extent to which improvements in quality and performance have occurred as a result of the new approach. All local authorities were encouraged to move towards the best value framework whether or not they were selected to take part in the pilot scheme.

Performance indicators are to be used as the main way of demonstrating best value. These should incorporate challenging, clear, and realistic targets for service improvements that relate to an overall plan for quality enhancement within the local authority. These indicators might include some or all of the following.

- User satisfaction surveys and consultation exercises. These can be used to gather information pertinent to specific aspects of the *experiential relationship* referred to in Chapter 2 or to monitor year by year trends in user satisfaction.
- Complaint monitoring and the establishment of mechanisms that record what action has been taken to deal with complaints.
- Comparative cost analysis. This would involve comparing costs against those of other private or public sector providers, including other authorities, who are offering services of a similar type and quality and on a similar scale. Comparative cost analysis focuses on the question of the *efficiency relationship* discussed in Chapter 2.
- Cost-benefit analysis. This is a technique designed to measure best value in a way that takes a wider and longer-term view of what counts as the relevant costs and benefits associated with a proposed investment of resources. A shift away from a cash-flow towards an accruals approach to accounting will make CBA more practicable (see Chapters 2 and 5 for discussion on accruals accounting).
- Voluntary competitive tendering, in contrast to the old CCT method favoured by previous Conservative administrations.

- Process benchmarking. This involves setting target standards of performance and measuring outcomes against those targets. Process benchmarking focuses on what in Chapter 2 we referred to as the *effectiveness relationship* (see Figure 2.3).
- The balanced scorecard approach. This is a methodology developed by the Harvard Business School that seeks to take account of the fact that running a large, complex organisation requires the managers to keep in view four important 'perspectives' relating to: (1) how customers see the establishment – client perspective; (2) decisions about priorities and how best to operate – internal business perspective; (3) decisions about how to improve and create value – innovation and learning perspective; and (4) how the organisation is viewed by those who have a proprietary financial interests in the organisation – financial perspective.

As part of its best value initiative, the government announced in June 1998 its intention to set up an inspectorate for housing within the Audit Commission that will report on the work of local authorities in England. The inspectorate will draw up and carry out a programme of cyclical inspections covering each local authority. It will assess performance on all requirements of the best value framework and undertake out-of-cycle inspections as directed by the Secretary of State. In cases of performance failure, it will undertake follow-up inspections to ensure that its directives have been acted upon. It will also promote the dissemination of best practice initiatives across local authorities. In terms of process, inspection will examine whether target setting and performance plans are sufficiently exacting; whether the authority's comparative analysis with other public and private providers is convincing; whether they have properly assessed the possibility of competition; and to what extent and in what ways community involvement has been secured. In terms of outcomes, the inspectorate will assess how the needs of service users are met.

In Wales, the National Assembly for Wales will direct the work of the Audit Commission in relation to best value inspections and the housing inspectorate will operate in Wales. The National Assembly for Wales will have powers of intervention where authorities are failing to deliver best value.

Best value in Scotland has followed a similar but not entirely parallel route to that of England and Wales. The legislation for the establishment of unitary authorities in Scotland in April 1996 had already placed on local authorities the statutory duty to seek efficiency, effectiveness and economy in the use of resources. Following the general election, a task force of representatives from the Scottish Office, CoSLA, and the Accounts Commission was set up to develop thinking on the shape of best value for Scotland. On 27 May 1997, the Secretary of State announced that authorities who could demonstrate a significant degree of commitment to, and compliance with, the essential elements of the best value framework would be able to apply for extended exemption from compulsory competitive tendering (CCT). This was followed by the release of Scottish Office Circular 22/97 requiring councils to submit to the Secretary of State a self-assessment checklist on their ability to meet best value, along with a corporate implementation plan for best value. More recently, councils have been required to submit to the Scottish Executive details of how they intend to develop a *public performance reporting framework*, intended to show how councils will report on performance to a wide range of stakeholders.

The Scottish Executive has yet to clarify detailed arrangements for the scrutiny of best value, although the current monitoring provisions of the Accounts Commission remain. The Scottish Executive has announced its intention to establish a single framework for the regulation of housing, to be included in the forthcoming Scottish Housing Bill, whereby Scottish Homes will regulate all social landlords, including local authority landlords.

The Northern Ireland Housing Executive (NIHE) is applying the principles of best value to its activities on a voluntary basis. Delivering a high quality housing service in accordance with the government's principles of best value is one of the Executive's key strategic objectives for the future.

Although the structure of local government seeks to ensure that local services are provided under local democratic control and run in accordance with local knowledge of local needs, the United Kingdom is a unitary state in which, subject to certain legal restrictions set by the Treaty of Rome, all authority ultimately stems from the Westminster Parliament, although now in Scotland the Scottish Parliament has powers to define the powers and duties of local authorities so far as they fall within its own devolved powers. The principle of *the supremacy of Parliament* means that local authorities are created and controlled by central government and their functions are determined by statute. It also means that the ways in which councils raise and spend money are largely prescribed by central government. If in its financial dealings a local authority fails to operate within its derived powers it is said to be acting *ultra vires*.[4] On matters of financial irregularity, the auditor is usually best placed to establish the facts. In such circumstances officers and/or elected members can be sanctioned and disciplined.[5]

---

4   Meaning 'beyond its authority' (literal Latin, *beyond strength*).

5   In the past councillors involved in financial misconduct have been surcharged. The Nolan Report recommended that surcharging should be abolished and, pending the introduction of a new statutory offence of 'misuse of public office', replaced matters with a procedure in which the auditor applies to the courts for a ruling and the court has the power to order compensation and/or impose disqualification from office. More generally, the 1998 White Paper (Cm4014), points to the government's intention to establish a new ethical framework within which disciplinary arrangements would be centred on a new independent body – a 'Standards Board'. This body would handle all substantive allegations that councillors have failed to observe their council's Code. Under these arrangements, each council would have a duty to establish and maintain a 'Standards Committee' that would have responsibility for setting and enforcing an appropriate ethical Code of practice for councillors.

The Local Government Finance Review

In July 1997, the government announced a wide-ranging review of local government finance, the findings of which were to be set alongside those of the Comprehensive Spending Review (see Appendix 5A). The review considered the balance between central direction and local discretion and in so doing, took a critical look at the following.

- Ways of improving local accountability for spending and revenue-raising decisions.
- The current arrangements for local authority revenue raising.
- Ways of encouraging cost-effective and efficient delivery of services.
- The rationale for, and effectiveness of, measures to reduce needs and resources inequalities.
- Possible improvements to the capital finance system.

The review involved wide consultation. In England, the Central-Local Partnership Group has been established to bring together cabinet ministers and local government leaders. In Wales, a Central Local Partnership has likewise been set up, and in Scotland the government has established the Commission on Local Government and the Scottish Parliament to consider what ought to be the appropriate relationship between local government and the new Scottish Parliament. The first results of these consultations were brought together in the form of a White Paper in the summer of 1998 (Cm4014). Subsequent to the review, the Scottish Office Green Paper on Housing in February 1999 signalled the government's intention to introduce a range of reforms. These would include the introduction of a new single tenancy, a single unified system of regulation for all landlords, including local authorities, a common housing register, and a new Scottish Housing Advisory Panel. The proposals placed particular emphasis on the intention to develop a new range of mechanisms for the allocation of public resources to housing, amongst which are a single unified housing budget, new procedures for allocating housing resources to local authorities, and a new unitary grant mechanism in the form of a 'Social Housing Grant' to replace Housing Association Grant. The detailed implementation of this programme of reforms will be worked out by the Executive of the Scottish Parliament.

The 1998 White Paper sought to address the question of how central-local relations might be restructured so as to push forward the government's commitment to 'modernise' local government. These proposed changes to the relationship between councils and their communities, and to the relationship between local and central government will be reflected in the system of local government finance. In a recent consultation paper (Cm7257), the government argued that the following broad changes to the system are needed:

- to promote partnership and greater co-operation between local authorities and all those with a stake in local matters;

- to enhance local accountability, and reduce central government's involvement in local tax and spending decisions; and
- to encourage the better planning of local services, and widen the range of choices available to authorities as to how those services might be delivered.

Regional Development Agencies (RDAs) and regional chambers

In addition to establishing a Scottish Parliament and National Assemblies in Northern Ireland and Wales, the government is progressing its manifesto pledge to create new forms of regional representation for England. However, with the exception of London, full constitutional devolution for England is not on the current political agenda. It has been suggested that the new constitutional arrangements elsewhere in the kingdom should be balanced by creating assemblies in the English regions. It is now clear that such a reform will not be introduced unless there is strong political demand for it, and in any case it will not happen until it has been placed before the electorate at a general election. Compared with Northern Ireland, Scotland and Wales, devolution in England has started much more tentatively.

Following consultations and the publication of the 1997 White Paper, *Building Partnerships for Prosperity*, The Regional Development Agencies Act 1998 brought into being nine Regional Development Agencies (RDAs) in England. RDAs are expected to co-ordinate regional economic development by promoting business efficiency and competitiveness within their regions, maintaining or safeguarding employment, enhancing skills, and encouraging inward investment. They will act as a focus to develop sustainable regional economic strategies. They are to be business-led, but with full participation by other regional players including the local authorities, the Government Offices for the Regions, and other government departments with an interest in the social and economic development of the area.

In line with the Labour Party's commitment to 'joined-up' government tackling 'cross-cutting' issues, the original plan for the RDAs was to create 'all-singing, all-dancing one-stop regional shops' with considerable development and planning powers devolved down from other government departments. However, following concerns expressed by members of the select committee and by other departments of State with a stake in the regions, it was decided that, initially at least, the powers of the RDAs should be more limited. They will advise, but not decide, on the allocation of development grants. They will work alongside, rather than absorb, other governmental regional actors and players such as the Training and Enterprise Councils. Despite this, the RDAs are likely to bring more administrative coherence to regional planning and development by encouraging new corporate initiatives and by gradually co-ordinating and controlling the work of the existing agencies that have been operating in their areas such as, for example, English Partnerships and the Rural Development Commission.

To bring a degree of representative democracy and public accountability into the processes of regional planning and development, *regional chambers* have been established to work alongside the RDAs. These will have strong local authority representation and devolutionists see them as prototypes for directly elected assemblies with real powers. The Local Government Association wanted the chambers to have political control over the agencies, but at present their powers are limited to a right to be consulted. Both the agencies and the chambers are financed by and answerable to central government.

Wider relations

Following the Rio Earth Summit of 1992 local authorities are now seen as key agents in establishing a 'sustainable' approach to economic development, resource use and poverty reduction. These three interrelated issues were at the heart of the Summit's Agenda for the 21st Century ('Agenda 21'). The Rio delegates argued that policies have to be planned and delivered locally if they are to be effective; they also recognised that they must be based on local knowledge, awareness and consent if they are to be regarded as being truly 'sustainable'. Around the world, local authorities were asked to formulate and publish Agenda 21 strategies.[6]

In many areas, the most visible results of Agenda 21 have been the establishment of such things as household waste recycling arrangements and protected wildlife areas. However, it is important to recognise that the Rio delegates intended that Agenda 21 issues should be addressed in all aspects of service planning and delivery. This means, for example, that an authority's housing strategy (see Chapter 10) should consciously consider, among other things, how it will contribute to poverty reduction and 'sustainable' economic development.

The Departments of State responsible for housing and local government

The current and future roles of the Department of the Environment, Transport and the Regions, the National Assembly for Wales and the Scottish Parliament are discussed in Chapter 5. In the future, the new Welsh and Scottish national tiers of government will have statutory duties to develop schemes for sustaining and promoting local government. However, Welsh and Scottish local government will need to maintain links with the Secretaries of State who will retain responsibility for primary legislation affecting Wales and, to a much lesser extent, Scotland. The restructuring of the government departments in Cardiff and Edinburgh is designed

---

6   These strategies are to comprise the following six elements: (1) managing and improving the authority's own environmental performance; (2) integrating sustainable development aims into its various service delivery policies; (3) raising the local level of awareness of the importance of Agenda 21; (4) consulting and involving local people in developing strategies and policies for pursuing Agenda 21; (5) working in partnership with local firms, voluntary bodies and other local agencies; (6) monitoring and measuring the success or failure in achieving Agenda 21.

to allow the National Assembly for Wales and the Scottish Parliament to develop policies that integrate programmes across tenures.[7]

The provision of local authority housing services

The power to provide a service is given by Act of Parliament or by instruction from the central government department responsible for the national planning of that service. Such powers are usually given to a particular class of local authority. Where there is no unitary authority, housing services are provided by the second tier of local government. Local authorities have a duty to establish the nature and scope of the housing needs in their area and to review the need to use their repair/improvement powers. The law *requires* the unitary or second tier councils to help the unintentionally homeless find suitable accommodation and *empowers* them to provide council housing for rent. As well as being landlords themselves, councils provide grants for the improvement of privately owned dwellings and they support other social landlords, such as housing associations, in the provision of accommodation for people on low incomes or with special needs. Local authorities also administer the distribution of housing benefit

New public management: the changing role of local government

Although politically and administratively important, the structural changes to local government have not, in themselves, significantly affected the nature and scope of local authority housing management and finance. However, the same cannot be said of the changes in internal organisation and culture that have evolved alongside these reforms.

Throughout the 1980s and 1990s changing views about the role of local government developed that have led to the emergence of a 'new orthodoxy' (Stewart and Stoker, 1995, p199) about how best to run public services. This reformed view places a strong emphasis on a 'partnership' approach to service provision in which elected local authorities work through and with a range of other local agencies. The changes that have stemmed from this revised view have tended to produce a more organisationally fragmented system of responsibilities that is sometimes described as 'new public management' (NPM), and which some commentators suggest has features that are more in line with the notion of local *governance* than that of local *government* (Lowndes, 1997).

NPM embraces the following interrelated features.

---

7 Scotland's housing comes within the remit of the Minister for Communities and the future framework for strategic planning, programme approval and funding, and regulation is still under discussion. There is, however, a strong move to see closer integration of local authority priorities, as the statutory housing agencies, with the funding consents currently approved through Scottish Homes. There is already greater coherence between the two.

- An increased emphasis on the notions of efficiency and effectiveness (refer to Chapter 2).
- The introduction of competition and the pursuit of best value.
- The development of partnership arrangements with private sector firms, voluntary bodies and other agencies.
- A greater use of private finance.
- A greater internal use of business methods such as *total quality management* and *performance monitoring.*
- A commitment to cultivate user satisfaction (see Chapter 2).

Administrative and financial barriers to NPM

Although the principles of new public management were laid down by the Conservative administrations of the 1980s and 1990s, they were developed with enthusiasm by the in-coming Labour government in 1997. Speaking at the first Treasury taskforce/Capita conference on the Private Finance Initiative in April 1998, the Paymaster General emphasised the point that ministers wanted to enable local and central government to progress rapidly with public/private partnership projects. Progress with such projects has been inhibited by accountability rules and regulations that restrict how public monies can be used on private ventures. For example, councils have been prevented from trading with non-public sector bodies, and regulations have prevented post-development revenue support finance being available when there is a private interest associated with the scheme. Furthermore, when councils transfer their assets to non-public ownership, they have only been free to reinvest a proportion of the capital receipts. It is argued that the effective development of NPM partnership arrangements will involve a change in the regulatory environment within which such schemes operate. The government is currently addressing this issue.[8]

NPM and housing

In the specific field of housing, the shift in emphasis away from *government* towards *governance* has produced a change in emphasis away from direct service provision to 'enabling'.[9] The role of local authorities as direct providers of social housing has been systematically diminished by such measures as 'right-to-buy' and stock transfers.[10] Although in many areas, local authorities still own relatively

---

8   It has already been agreed that the regulations surrounding the Private Finance Initiative should be altered to allow non-HRA housing schemes more ready access to private funds. The Private Finance Initiative is discussed in Chapter 9.
9   For a thoughtful analysis of this trend see Goodlad, (1994).
10 In Scotland, although the development of the RTB exactly paralleled that in England, there was no clear lead from the Scottish Office towards the transfer of council stock. However, the belated (compared with England) requirement to use a large proportion of capital receipts to pay off debt, established a situation that made stock transfer more attractive, although by 1999 only one Scottish council had transferred all of its stock. Throughout this period, as in England, there was a steadily growing emphasis on local authorities establishing housing strategies that did not involve direct provision, an emphasis that was reinforced by the economics of RTB.

large stocks of residential property, their landlord role is gradually being superseded by their strategic role as assessors of housing need and 'enablers'.

The first clear signal of this change was given by the 'right-to-buy' (RTB) provisions of the Housing Act 1980. It was further articulated in the 1985 Report of the Inquiry into British Housing that had a separate section on 'The local authority as co-ordinator and enabler' (NFHA, 1985, Chapter 7). It was then given more explicit expression in the 1987 White Paper that declared that *'Local authorities should increasingly see themselves as enablers who ensure that everyone in their area is adequately housed; but not necessarily by them.'* (DoE, 1987a, p3). From this point the government made it clear that it expected the primary role of a local housing authority to be a strategic one that focused on the identification of housing needs and demands, encouraged 'innovative methods of provision' by other bodies to meet such needs, maximised the use of private finance, and encouraged participation by the independent rented sector, (DoE, 1987a and 1987b). From 1990 onwards ministers made it clear that the government expected local authorities to be explicit about how they intended to fulfil this wider enabling role in their Housing Investment Programme (HIP) submissions (e.g. DoE, 1990 paras. 2-3.). In this way the departments of State responsible for housing explicitly related central government financial support to the willingness or otherwise of local authorities to change their housing functions in line with the principles of NPM. The combined effects of local government restructuring and purpose redefinition pose important questions about how a local authority housing service should be financed and organised. However, before we consider these housing-specific issues, we need to say something about how housing finance relates to local government finance in general.

Local government housing finance: an overview

Financial accountability

As with most other organisations, councils have to be accountable for both their day-to-day revenue spending and their longer-term investment spending (refer to Chapter 2). A local authority's budget is therefore divided into *current* and *capital* expenditure. Current expenditure mainly pays for the day-to-day running costs on such items as salaries, fuel bills, office consumables, etc. Although strictly speaking, revenue spending does not provide long-term physical assets, in practice some revenue monies can be used for this purpose. In such cases, the revenue transfer becomes redesignated as 'capital spending'. Capital expenditure produces assets that have an extended physical life. Examples include the acquisition of land and buildings and the construction and improvement of housing.[11] About

---

11 Expenditure on improvement is classified as 'capital' if the works amount to 'enhancement' of the asset. This means that they are intended to lengthen substantially the physical life of the asset or increase substantially its exchange value. See Chapter 9 for a fuller explanation. Housing capital investment is currently the single biggest capital spending item in local government.

eight times as much is spent annually by local government on current running costs as on capital investment. This gap has widened in recent years as central governments have actively sought to restrict the capital spending of authorities.

Financial accountability is achieved by a process of audited accounting. Accounts receive money from various sources, such as grants, tax levies, rents, charges, fees, and transfers, and make outward payments to cover the costs of providing a service or acquiring an asset. Some transaction accounts may not actually 'hold' funds but they will record financial in and out flows that are associated with particular activities. Unlike other services, some housing transactions are ring-fenced within special transaction accounts.

Until recently local authority accounting was based on what accountants refer to as the 'fund and entity approach' (CIPFA, 1995). This approach treated the authority as an entity comprising separate service departments, like housing, education, etc., each with its own funds and accounting records. The costs of providing each service were recorded in the departmental fund accounts. The separate revenue accounts paid the running costs of the services including the debt charges, the interest and repayment of principal. In this way, each service could be seen to be bearing the costs of the debt associated with the fixed assets owned by that fund.

Although financial activities were recorded in separate accounts, in practice all borrowed money was normally pooled into a consolidated loans fund so that service accounts in surplus could 'lend' funds internally to service accounts in deficit. This system of internal borrowing, called 'loans pooling', allowed the authority to make the best use of its cash so that it only needed to borrow externally and incur interest charges if the consolidated fund was insufficient for its needs. Under loans pooling most authorities tied the loan costs to services and projects. Typically, individual capital projects were amortised internally over a sixty-year period, although the external borrowing period could be flexible. This means, for example, that large-scale housing projects were typically financed from the consolidated loans fund over a sixty-year period, but the fund itself borrowed from external sources over a variety of shorter periods. Some authorities did not operate a system of internal advances but simply accounted for debt at the corporate level, thereby treating loan service charges as a cost to the authority as a whole. Whichever internal accounting method was used the overall financing costs remained the same, so it was just a presentational difference. This meant that it made no difference to the eventual burden falling on the local taxpayers. This system of loans pooling allowed the authority to develop a balanced portfolio of loans and to take advantage of borrowing opportunities as and when they arose.

The 'fund and entity' approach to local authority accounting in England and Wales was abolished by the provisions of the Local Government and Housing

Act 1989. This Act did not have the same effect in Scotland where housing revenue accounts (HRAs), were already partially ring-fenced.[12]

After 1990 housing revenue accounts were universally 'ring-fenced' so that the costs of providing council housing always had to be recorded separately from all the other local authority services. The other, non-council housing, services ceased to have separate revenue accounts; these were replaced by a combined revenue account usually referred to as the 'General Fund'. More recently, further changes have occurred. Starting in 1994, a system of *resource accounting* has gradually been introduced to local authorities. This relatively new development has altered the way in which the costs of acquiring and managing assets are accounted for. Resource accounting simply seeks to lay out the accounts in a way that allows managers, members and the Audit Commission to assess the full and proper costs of providing an aspect of services provision, so that a judgement can be made about the extent to which value-for-money is being achieved. Resource accounting still operates within the general legislative constraints of the 1989 Local Government and Housing Act. (Resource accounting is discussed further in Chapters 2, 5 and 11).

The shift to resource accounting means that authorities no longer keep consolidated loans funds. However, the treasurer is still expected to manage the authority's overall finances in a way that is prudent and efficient. This means that, in practice, much of the authority's borrowing will still be consolidated and managed at the corporate level. This will normally be achieved by having some form of loans and investment unit that is chaired by, and answerable to, the treasurer.

The most important accounts used by a housing authority are:

- *Housing Revenue Account* (HRA) that records the income from council house rents and any housing subsidies designed to pay for the running costs of council housing provision. These include management and maintenance costs, council tenants' housing rebates (except in Scotland) and capital financing charges on HRA capital schemes. HRA capital schemes are projects that contribute to the quantity and quality of the council's housing stock. They would include any investments in new house building and all the major repairs and improvements that are made to the existing stock. Since 1990 the HRA has been *ring-fenced* which means that the account cannot be subsidised by transfers from the General

---

12 Although Scottish HRAs were technically ring-fenced until the mid-1980s, some level of rate support was permitted. Rate fund contributions were reduced to zero in the 1980s through the application of the Housing Support Grant formula and the requirement on councils to keep the HRA in balance. Unlike in England, housing benefit never formed part of the HRA. In Scottish district councils all non-HRA spending was from the 'General Fund' (from 1975) though clearly there were always functional budgets.

Fund. It is a one-way ring-fence in so far as HRA surpluses can, in certain cases, be applied to non-housing activities. With the introduction of resource accounting, the whole issue of ring-fencing the HRA is currently under review.

- *The Consolidated Revenue Account* (CRA) which is a fund account that makes and receives payments with respect to all of the authority's revenue income and expenditure. It will include a recorded summary of the financial transactions of the Housing Revenue Account (HRA). This means that the HRA is not a separate 'fund' but a ring-fenced 'transaction account' recording the financial transactions associated with provision of the council housing service.
- *General Fund* (GF) The authority's General Revenue Account is normally referred to as the 'General Fund'. It collects local taxes and central government grants to pay for services to electors. Revenue payments are made from this account to meet the costs of providing services other than council housing. It thus records payments made for housing matters that affect the wider community – such as the assessment of local housing needs and some services for the homeless, advice to private tenants and landlords, the administration of housing benefits to private tenants and the tenants of registered social landlords, and capital financing charges on GF capital schemes (i.e. non-HRA investments). GF capital schemes will encompass housing projects other than those that are related to the council's own housing stock. They would include spending on such things as advice centres, help for the homeless, the purchase of land for the purpose of building for sale or disposal for housing development, slum clearance, abatement of overcrowding, supervision of houses in multiple occupation, the provision of Disabled Facilities Grants, and loans and grants to other social landlords, in England, for capital purposes.
- *Capital Receipts Accounts* which collect the sales proceeds of liquidated assets. Capital receipts are kept separately because they can only be used for capital purposes, either to pay for capital works or to repay debt. This means that these funds can be used to help finance capital housing projects, but only within prescribed limits (see Chapter 9).

In the next three chapters we describe the financial framework for local authority housing. Before proceeding to the detailed study of local authority housing finance, the reader needs to be aware that the government proposes to make significant changes to current arrangements, procedures and practices. Following the *Comprehensive Spending Review* in the summer of 1998, ministers proposed a package of measures with the aim of improving the efficiency with which local authority housing is managed, and ensuring better value-for-money from future investment. Part of the package involves the establishment of the new housing inspectorate operating within a best value framework, discussed above. The three other interrelated elements of the package are:

1. strengthening the assessment of performance by authorities of their housing management functions within the Housing Investment Programme;
2. encouraging authorities to take a more strategic and 'corporate' approach to housing investment, and the introduction of a single pot for housing, and
3. introducing a new financial framework based on a form of resource accounting for the HRA.

The first two points will be considered in Chapters 9 and 10, and we will return to point 3 in Chapter 11.

Summary

Every part of Britain is covered by one, and sometimes two, major local authorities. In recent years the structure of local government has been reformed in a way that has created a greater number of unitary authorities. This has helped local government to take a more strategic, and regional approach to the provision of local services. This approach has been enhanced by an expectation that local authorities will work in partnership with other local agencies to provide local services. This has brought about a somewhat changed view about the nature and scope of local government that increasingly sees local authorities acting as assessors of need and enablers rather than as direct service providers. Their role is increasingly being seen to be strategic: assessing local housing needs, planning how these needs are to be met (often by others) participating in the funding of projects to meet those needs, and monitoring the effectiveness of implementation policies.

Housing transactions are split between the Housing Revenue Account, the net costs of which are met by council tenants through their housing rents, and those transactions in the General Fund where the net costs are met by council tax payers. The requirement to ring-fence the HRA produces an important distinction between two classes of social housing spending. These are sometimes referred to as 'HRA housing' and 'non-HRA housing'. In this way a clear administrative distinction is made between the financial management of the council's own housing stock[13] and monies spent on other types of housing project.

The present government is seeking to establish a best value framework within which all local authority services will be encouraged to meet local needs in ways that take account of local opinion and are judged to be efficient and effective.

---

13 Despite the changing nature of local authority housing departments, collectively they remain large-scale landlords. Total gross spending on HRA housing planned by local authorities in England and Wales in 1997/98 amounted to £12.3 billion. The figure for Scotland was £1.2 billion.

Appendix 8A

The changing structure of local government

The basic structure before 1995

Until the mid-1990s, in most areas of the UK, there existed a basic two-tier local government structure. Outside London, England and Wales were divided into counties (the first tier) and districts (the second tier). Mainland Scotland was divided into regions (first tier) and districts (second tier). The London boroughs and the Scottish Islands were designated as single-tier 'unitary' authorities. Also in some metropolitan districts, service provision was combined under the auspices of one unitary authority. Northern Ireland was and is a special case (see below).

In the non-metropolitan parts of England and Wales the upper tier authorities were constituted as non-metropolitan county councils. In Scotland regional councils constituted the upper tier. These 'first tier' authorities were responsible for providing major county wide, or regional, services such as education, strategic planning, social services, traffic management and highways.

The second tier authorities were designated as 'districts', although some had the title 'city' or 'borough' for historic reasons. England and Wales were divided into thirty or so metropolitan district or borough councils and over three hundred non-metropolitan district councils. In Scotland there were 53 district councils operating beneath the nine regional councils. These second tier authorities provided more locally orientated services including housing.

Some districts, and metropolitan districts, also had parish councils within them that had limited powers and acted as 'sounding boards' on local issues. In the best cases they also instigated worthwhile local initiatives. These third tier authorities continue to exist under the reforms instigated after 1995. They have particular responsibilities for providing and maintaining such parochial facilities as playgrounds, footpaths and village halls. In Scotland the third tier comprises community councils.

The shift towards regionalism and single-tier authorities after 1995

The structure of local government has been regularly subjected to programmes of reorganisation. For example, the two-tier system described above, was the result of a major restructuring that took place in 1974, and 1975 in Scotland. In March 1991, the Secretary of State for the Environment announced that a commission was to be set up to advise on a further restructuring with the preferred option being a system of nation-wide unitary authorities in England. This restructuring is now more-or-less complete and has resulted in some remapping of boundaries and, in many areas, to a shift from two-tier to unitary provision.

At the same time as the DETR announcement, a similar statement was made by the Secretary of State for Scotland and this has resulted in the wholesale restructuring of the Scottish local government system. Since April 1996 Scottish local government has operated as a system of unitary authorities that are responsible for the provision of all local government services, while the three island councils of Orkney, Shetland and Western Isles already had unitary status. Scottish local government now comprises 32 all-purpose authorities. From the same date Welsh Unitary Councils became responsible for all local government services in the principality.

Since April 1997 a number of district councils in England, along with the counties of which they were part, were converted into unitary authorities. A hybrid arrangement now exists in some county areas in which a unitary authority runs the county council functions in part of the area while the remainder operate under the earlier two-tier system. The continuous reorganisation of local government structures has produced rather a *hotch potch* system of different types of authority operating in different parts of the nation.[14]

The special case of Northern Ireland[15]

No intermediary like the Housing Corporation exists in Northern Ireland because the Northern Ireland Housing Executive operates as an all-powerful local housing authority throughout the province. In the late 1960s there were concerns that the allocation and management of public sector housing were being influenced by sectarian factors. In response to these concerns, the 1969 Joint Declaration of Principles called for a complete restructuring of the province's housing administration. This restructuring took place in 1971 with the creation of the Northern Ireland Housing Executive (NIHE) that was set up to operate as a single regional authority. The establishment of the NIHE distanced housing administration from the hothouse politics of local government. The new body took over all of the province's 150,000 local authority homes and then operated as a non-sectarian builder and manager of affordable social housing. In addition, it was charged with responsibility to develop a strategic view of housing development in

14 From 1 April 1997 UK local government structure took the following form: 35 English County Councils, 32 London Boroughs, 1 Corporation of London, 36 Metropolitan Districts, 260 English Districts, 27 English Unitary Councils, 22 Welsh Unitary Councils, 32 Scottish Unitary Councils, 26 Northern Ireland Councils.
15 The information in this section is drawn from Ian Evan's brief history of and commentary on the Executive published as part of an *Inside Housing* supplement, Connolly, M., (1996). See *Inside Housing*, 21 March 1997, pp17-18 and *Local Government Studies*, Winter 1996, pp77-91. See also Chris Paris's article on the Northern Ireland housing policy review in Wilcox, 1997, pp30-36.

the province by undertaking research and providing housing advice to others including private sector providers.

The Executive operates as a quango with devolved powers from the Department of the Environment to whom, under the provisions of the 1981 Housing Order (NI), it ultimately remains answerable. In recent years, the NIHE has been accountable to the Permanent Secretary of the DETR (NI) who, in turn, is accountable to Parliament. The NIHE is headed by a Chief Executive with ten Board members, all of whom have to be approved by the DETR. The Executive is supported by a professional management team. A degree of local democratic accountability is established through the Northern Ireland Housing Council that has one representative from each of the province's 26 local government bodies or district councils. The Council has regular meetings with the Executive and nominates three members of the Executive Board. The Executive is organised into six regional offices with its headquarters in Belfast.

From the late 1980s pressure was mounting to bring Northern Ireland's broad housing policy more in line with that operating in the rest of Britain. In particular, consideration was given to shifting the Executive's role away from direct provider towards that of enabler. This means that responsibility for the new-build programme is gradually being transferred to a number of developing associations with the NIHE's role becoming more regulatory and strategic. (Refer NIHE, 1994, *Housing Strategy 1995-1998: The Case for Programme Funding*, Belfast NIHE). Such a shift in emphasis is in line with political reforms that are taking place elsewhere in Britain.

Political reform

At the time of writing there is a good deal of debate about the need to bring about further constitutional reforms that would reshape the political structure of local government in Britain. This debate centres on principles associated with the Hunt proposals that appeared in a private members Bill that failed to complete its passage through Parliament.[16] Because the Labour government is sympathetic to many of the Bill's ideas, it is expected that modified versions of the Hunt proposals will appear in future White Papers. Such political arrangements as elected mayors and 'cabinet committees' are likely to become established features of the British system of local government sometime after the year 2001. Reforms similar to those in the Hunt Bill are being considered for Scotland and Northern Ireland (see above). In particular, it is clear that reforming the political structures of councils is high on the agenda of the Scottish Parliament.

---

16 The Local Government (Experimental Arrangements) Bill 1996. This bill began life in the Lords. It was sponsored by the president of the Local Government Association, Lord Hunt of Tamworth before entering the Commons.

Further reading

Housing and Best Value – A Guidance Manual, CIH (published in installments).

Douglas Johnston and Marian Reid, *Best Value for Housing Services in Scotland*, CIH, 1998.

Robina Goodlad, *Creating a New Future – The Strategic Role of Scottish Local Authorities*, CIH, 1998.

Robert Smith, Tamsin Stirling and Peter Williams, *Housing in Wales: The Policy Agenda in an Era of Devolution*, CIH, 2000.

CHAPTER 9:
Local government: the capital finance regime

The capital finance system governs local authorities' spending on the construction, improvement and major repairs of such social assets as council housing, schools, roads, community and leisure centres, and on regenerating local areas. Although some of this spending is funded from the authorities' own resources, including the proceeds of asset sales, much is supported directly by central government in the form of subsidy towards the costs of borrowing.

Defining capital finance

We have discussed the concept of capital in Chapter 2 (in particular refer back to Figure 2.1). In the local government sphere what counts as capital finance is defined in legislation, as in Part IV of the Local Government and Housing Act 1989. To prevent authorities from avoiding revenue controls by designating revenue expenditure as capital (other parts of the legislation prevent authorities from running deficits on their revenue accounts) the legislation requires all expenditure to be charged to revenue unless it is used for:

> *'the acquisition, construction, preparation, enhancement or replacement of roads, buildings and other structures; where enhancement means the carrying out of works which are intended:*
> * *to lengthen substantially the useful life of the asset; or*
> * *to increase substantially the open market value of the asset; or*
> * *to increase substantially the extent to which the asset can be used for the purposes of or in connection with the functions of the local authority concerned.'* (Adapt the asset to make it more useful).

Subsequent regulations and supplementary guidance notes have clarified the definition.[1] The following are included in the definition and are pertinent to the provision of housing services:

* construction, improvement, and major repair of dwellings;
* making grants to third parties for capital purposes;

---

[1] Further guidance was given in DoE circular 11/90 on Local Authority Capital Finance. Later amendments to the Capital Finance Regulations are incorporated in the *Local Authorities (Capital Finance) Regulations 1997*, effective from 1 April 1997.

- increasing substantially the thermal insulation of a building or to the extent that it can be used by elderly or disabled people;
- reducing substantially the fire risk in a building;
- acquiring or writing computer software.

What counts as 'substantially' in any particular case is left to the judgement of local authority accountants and their auditors. Pragmatic intuition may seek to distinguish between capital and revenue expenditure by reference to some financial benchmark so that, say, expenditure over £5,000 is treated as capital. This could clearly lead to classifying expenditure in a way that contravenes the intention of the legislation. For example, relatively small 'cosmetic' repairs made to a large number of properties would not constitute capital as defined in the Act, even if the total sum spent turns out to be relatively large. In an attempt to overcome such problems and establish a degree of consistency of practice, the statutory definition is intentionally similar to that used by professional accountants and the Act requires authorities to follow accounting conventions at all times except where these conflict with specific provisions of the Act.

There is a government intention to move away from crude statutory, sector-specific accounting rules towards more reliance on established accounting conventions that are used in other sectors of the economy. This shift in emphasis, as explained later, will gradually transform the way in which the government monitors and controls the capital spending of local authorities.

Capital spending and control

Central government capital support to local authorities

The government currently provides capital support to local authorities in a variety of different ways. Capital allocations are made in accordance with the following general principles.

- Sharing out support according to 'needs' formulae. For example, social services funding is partly given according to numbers of elderly people in the area and a Generalised Needs Index is referred to in the initial distribution of housing resources in England.
- Assessments of social efficiency and managerial effectiveness, so that support for housing is partly judged against the quality of the authority's strategic programmes.
- Through a process of competitive bidding that emphasises commercial and economic efficiency and effectiveness, as in much regeneration funding and the major New Housing Partnerships programme in Scotland.

These general allocation methods seek to embrace the principles of equity, efficiency and effectiveness discussed in Chapter 2. In the context of these general principles, the current government is particularly concerned to improve the ability of the capital finance system to influence strategic and corporate planning within local authorities and to give them the incentive to develop *local performance plans* that focus on cross-cutting issues such as social exclusion/inclusion, employment, and youth crime as well as producing 'best value' approaches to service provision and asset management.

> *'Decent housing is one of the most basic requirements for individuals and has a direct effect on their self-esteem. It is a linchpin in tackling social exclusion.'* (Hilary Armstrong, Housing Minister, July 1998, commenting on the outcome of the Comprehensive Spending Review).

The Scottish Housing Green Paper, *Investing in Modernisation – An Agenda for Scotland's Housing,* also calls for high quality housing which *'supports the integration and regeneration of communities rather than dividing them'*.

Aims for the capital finance system

The present capital control and allocation arrangements for England and Wales were established in 1990. Before describing them we need to make the point that they are currently under review and that the government is consulting about how they might be amended so as to deliver its broad objectives for local government more adequately. The following have been identified as the objectives of an 'ideal' system governing local authority capital expenditure.[2] Such a system should seek to:

- maximise the value of local government investment within public spending constraints;
- tackle needs and resource inequalities between authorities;
- strike the right balance between local discretion and the government's priorities;
- encourage authorities to take an integrated, corporate approach;
- be inherently stable;
- be simple, open and accountable;
- encourage prudent financial behaviour; and
- be economical to administer.

In describing the current arrangements, we will make constant reference back to these aims as a way of highlighting criticisms of the present system and of pointing to possible reforms and future shifts in emphasis.

---

2   Based on research carried out by the Audit Commission and set out in DETR Cm7257, p11, para.2.7.

The current capital control and allocation arrangements

The system of control

The present capital finance system for England and Wales was laid down in Part IV of the Local Government and Housing Act 1989 and subsequent regulations that have been made under it. It governs local authorities' capital spending on council dwellings, other community assets, and on regenerating local areas. The basic principle of control is that local authorities must ensure that their capital expenditure does not exceed their 'credit cover'. Authorities' credit cover comprises spending on capital that is paid for from borrowing, or some other form of credit arrangement, from grants, or from capital receipts. Controllable capital spending is thus defined as the sum of the following:

- usable capital receipts, including those carried forward;
- permissions to borrow and enter into credit arrangements – called 'credit approvals' in England and Wales and 'borrowing consents' in Scotland;
- government grants and contributions.

Other sources of capital finance include the following:

- revenue used to finance capital projects, that can be referred to as 'contributions from revenue' or 'direct revenue financing' – but usually referred to as revenue contributions to capital outlay (RCCO), or in Scotland as 'capital from current revenue' (CFCR); and,
- contributions from the private sector.

These five elements can be thought of as the 'types' of capital finance available to local authorities. The first three are directly controlled by central government via procedures established by the 1989 Act. These procedures are collectively referred to in England and Wales as 'the 1990 capital financing regime'.[3]

The 1990 regulatory system only applies in England and Wales and a somewhat less regulated system of capital controls applies in Scotland. A Scottish authority's capital spending is controlled by reference to a 'total allocation' consisting of a net permission to borrow called a 'borrowing consent' and an amount for capital receipts. The key difference is that Scottish authorities have, in the past, been able to use all of their capital receipts during any year unless specifically forbidden to do so by the Scottish Office (see below and footnote 18). By contrast, in England and Wales a clear distinction is made between 'usable' and 'reserved' receipts.

---

3   The Department of the Environment recently issued a consolidated set of regulations relating to the regime entitled *Local Authority (Capital Finance) Regulations 1997 S1319* and a *Guide to the Local Government Finance System.*

Capital receipts

A capital receipt is a sum of money in excess of £5,000 received from either (1) the disposal of land or some other capital asset such as a council house, or (2) the repayment by a third party of a grant or loan that was made to that party to enable them to invest in capital. Grants received from central government or other bodies are not classified as capital receipts.

Under the Local Government and Housing Act 1989, local authorities have been required to set aside a specified proportion of most types of capital receipts. In recent years, the majority of receipts by councils has come from the sale of housing. As part of its expenditure control mechanism in England and Wales, the government does not allow the whole of a capital receipt to be reinvested. Each receipt is deemed to comprise a *usable* and a *reserved* element and only the usable element can be employed to fund new capital spending. The remaining (reserved) percentage has to be 'set-aside' as provision for future credit liabilities and/or used to repay current debt. In practice, the money will be invested (see below).

The regulations currently set the standard 'usable' proportions as follows:

- 25 per cent for council houses; and
- 50 per cent for most other assets.[4]
- 0 per cent for repayments by the Housing Corporation of a loan by an English council to a Registered Social Landlord.

Although the terminology is slightly different, these percentages also now apply in Scotland; Scottish authorities have only recently moved from the position where they were allowed to re-use 100 per cent of their receipts.

An authority's set-aside receipts can be used to repay debts or pay off credit arrangements. Until they are used, they are generally held in approved investments or invested internally by being used as an alternative to short-term borrowing. Authorities with no long-term debt are not required to set aside part of capital receipts and may spend them as they wish. For those with loan debt, the above proportions can be, and have been, altered for specified periods by central government regulation in order to promote particular policies.[5] The 1996 Budget relaxed the capital receipts rules for certain types of property sales by English authorities, including unoccupied dwellings, shops and derelict land, so that the liquidated resources can be used on regeneration projects in designated 'deprived' wards so long as the investment is matched by private finance. The receipts can be

---

4   Special regulations called 'in-and-out rules' apply to certain transactions that involve an authority in expenditure which is closely linked to a capital receipt. For example, an authority selling an old school building for (say) £1 million and building a new school for (say) £3 million, is able to use the whole £1 million receipt to help finance the project rather than just 50 per cent.

5   For example, to stimulate investment most receipts received by councils between 13 November 1992 and 31 December 1993 were classified 100 per cent usable.

used to fund housing association development. In order to calculate the capital charge to the HRA, annual housing capital receipts have to be recorded separately from general receipts. However, usable receipts may be employed for any capital purpose, which means that usable HRA receipts may be invested in non-HRA projects and vice-versa.

If instead of selling a capital asset for cash, an authority disposes of it in a barter arrangement, it may be deemed to have received a 'notional receipt'. In such a case, it must calculate what the reserved element would have been if it had been sold conventionally and charge an appropriate amount to its usable receipts or revenue.

The proportion set for different types of asset may be changed by ministerial directive and the government has used this flexibility on occasions either to influence the level of local authority spending or to encourage sales of particular types of asset.[6] An authority may spend its usable receipts at any time and on any service. However, under the Conservative administrations of the 1980s and 1990s there was a disincentive to retain usable receipts because the government took them into account when issuing credit approvals (see next section). Furthermore, it should be noted that any financial benefit that arises to the authority as a result of repaying loans from its reserved receipts or investing the set-aside, is deducted from its HRA subsidy (see Chapter 11). The current government has given local authorities extra borrowing permissions based on the national total of accumulated capital receipts. It is also considering the abolition of set-aside on non-housing receipts[7] as a way of simplifying the system and reducing the disincentive for authorities to sell assets.

Accumulated capital receipts constitute a valuable financial resource and should be managed as such. About 160 authorities have now appointed private sector fund managers to administer the proceeds raised from the sale of council assets such as RTB house sales and stock transfers to housing associations.[8]

Capital receipts initiative

As part of its manifesto commitment the Labour government pledged itself to the phased release of accumulated capital receipts. The case was based on the report *Boosting Housing Investment through Capital Receipts* (CIH, 1996) which

---

6   In the 1992 Autumn Statement, for example, the Chancellor announced that, as part of a strategy to boost the economy, authorities would be able to spend all proceeds from capital receipts from midnight on 12 November 1992 to 31 December 1993. In January 1994 the previous proportions of 25 per cent for council housing and 50 per cent for other assets were reinstated.

7   Provided the potential increase in public spending were offset by a reduction in the amount currently allocated as credit approvals (DETR Cm7257, 1998, p28).

8   Guinness Flight Hambro alone manages around £1.32 billion of cash reserves on behalf of 76 councils (*Public Finance*, Feb 6-12, 1988).

persuaded the (then) opposition of the case and of the amount, about £5 billion, subsequently 'released'. In fulfilment of this pledge, the Local Government Finance (Supplementary Credit Approvals) Act 1997 authorised Ministers to issue Supplementary Credit Approvals (permissions to borrow for particular projects or services – see below) to English authorities with accumulated set-aside receipts. These additional 'permissions to borrow' can produce financial resources that have to be used specifically for housing and housing-related regeneration schemes (refer to next chapter).[9] This initiative also benefited Scotland, Wales and Northern Ireland, but in these cases the receipts were not distributed to local authorities by a national formula.

Borrowing and credit arrangements

Loans and credit arrangements are an element of an authority's credit cover. Borrowing is, and always has been, the most important way of financing local authority spending. Borrowing allows projects to go ahead for which there would otherwise be no funding. It also spreads the capital costs of provision over future years in a way that more-or-less matches the benefits received. Unlike private sector borrowing, local authority loans are not usually secured against individual assets or groups of assets. Consequently, the amount borrowed for expenditure on a stock of council housing is not directly attributable to any one advance or loan.[10] The debt relating to each property, or group of properties, is therefore a notional calculation based on an apportionment of the total debt across the whole stock.

Local authorities are permitted to borrow funds for any purpose relevant to their functions. However, the 1990 capital funding regime established a control mechanism whereby each local authority's annual level of borrowing for capital purposes requires government approval, closing the few remaining loopholes in the pre-1989 regime. This means that the total amount of a local authority's long-term borrowing is effectively limited to the value of credit approvals issued by the central authorities.

As well as taking out loans, authorities can enter into delayed payment contracts that involve commissioning capital works or acquiring capital assets in the current financial year and then paying for them in subsequent years. Such 'buy now – pay later' contracts are known as *credit arrangements* and they have the same economic impact as expenditure financed by borrowing. Control over such credit

---

9   Current CRI resources (1999/2000) are allocated on a similar basis as the HIPs allocation. Two-thirds is allocated in line with a needs assessment and the rest in accordance with relative performance.

10 Another consequence is that there is no automatic check on the repayment regime that is needed to amortise the debt. This can lead to rents and rational repayments getting out of synch. The useful life (social benefit) of a new house may be fairly described as 60 years (perhaps), but that does not make it sensible to repay the loan over that period because of other factors such as life-cycle renewals. The capital financing regime for local authorities has tended to ignore this issue.

arrangements is exercised by requiring authorities to identify a prescribed amount of *credit cover* when the contract is signed. Such cover has to take the form of credit approvals, usable receipts, or revenue.[11]

Annual Capital Guidelines (ACGs)

An authority's total credit limit covers both its loans and its credit arrangements. In determining the appropriate credit limit, the relevant government department begins by assessing the assumed local need for capital spending on the particular service in question. A service by service capital allocation is seen to have a number of advantages. In particular, allocation criteria can take account of a wide range of service-specific factors influencing the need for capital spending which can vary significantly from authority to authority. It also enables the central authorities to take account of performance measures that are specific to the service in question. In its assessment the government takes into account the previous year's expenditure and the assumed need for the service, bearing in mind the circumstances of the residents in the area. This assessment is known as an *Annual Capital Guideline* (ACG).

Although the ACG service-based approach to allocations can deliver improvements in service performance it does, to some extent, work against the government's intention to provide incentives for effective corporate planning and working. In particular, it does not naturally encourage cross-cutting initiatives that are now an important aspect of government policy. (See discussion below on *The move towards a single funding mechanism.*).

ACGs constitute broad guideline estimates of what central government thinks an authority needs to spend on capital projects in the next financial year relative to the needs of other authorities. The department of State responsible for each service area sets its own criteria for arriving at an authority's individual ACG figure. As well as a comparative needs element, these criteria tend to include competitive elements to reward efficient performance, and elements that give recognition for particularly persuasive bids.

ACGs are issued for housing, transport, education, personal social services and 'other services'. This means that a unitary authority will receive five ACGs covering the full range of service provision, whilst other authorities will receive ACGs relevant to their range of responsibilities.[12] The housing ACG is determined

---

11 The amount of credit cover required is prescribed in regulations. In general it amounts to a discounted value of the total contract payments. There are a number of exceptions: for example, no credit cover is required for leases of property of less than 10 years duration or for the short-term leasing of equipment. In Scotland, the control method is more straightforward and direct and allows for individual arrangements for each capital amount (i.e. HRA and General) and a maximum size of outlay (e.g. £5 million).

12 An English District Council, for example, will receive only two ACGs: housing and 'other services'.

following the submission of an annual housing investment programme, sometimes referred to as the 'HIP bid' and discussed below.

In determining how much to allow an authority to borrow – the so-called 'Basic Credit Approval' – all the ACGs allocated to that authority are aggregated and then offset by a figure that represents a proportion of its usable capital receipts. In this context, this figure is referred to as the *receipts taken into account* (RTIAs – usually pronounced 'RITAs').[13] Special 'in-and-out' rules apply to certain receipts. Where, for example, an authority replaces an obsolete or run-down asset, such as an old school or office building, with a new one, the monies received from the sale of the old property can be used in full to help pay for the new one.

The idea is that what, in the government's view, the authority needs to spend (its ACG) should in part be paid for out of its own accumulated resources, its RTIAs. This amount is then clawed back from the ACG allocations of individual authorities. This clawback creates a central 'pot' of resources (some £275 million for 1998/99). The pot then provides the government with a mechanism for operating the BCA/borrowing consents system in a way that *redistributes* funds between authorities as well as *controlling* their levels of spending. The overall allocation of credit approvals and capital grants is determined as part of the public expenditure survey round (refer to Chapter 5). The national total allocation of ACGs is determined by adding together the national provision for BCAs and the national planned RTIA total. In line with the principle of comparative need (Chapter 3), the aggregated ACG figure is then allocated in a way that shifts resources from 'receipt-rich' to 'receipt-poor' authorities. A resource clawback takes place where an authority is receipt-rich but judged to have a relatively low need to spend.

There has been much criticism of the RTIA system, particularly amongst those authorities who lose out and who perceive the arrangement as a tax on their useable capital receipts. However, the present government takes the view that the allocation system will be demonstrably fairer and more efficient if it continues to take some account of resources raised locally so that scarce public resources can be targeted to those areas of greatest need (DETR, Cm7257, 1998, p25, para.6.1.). Nevertheless, the system may be reformed and currently views are being canvassed about the advisability of taking account of a three-year average of useable receipts or using an asset register rather than usable receipts information.

Basic Credit Approvals (BCAs)

As we have seen, the key to achieving an equitable inter-authority resource redistribution lies in the richer authorities having their share of the fixed total

---

13 The RTIA comprise the authority's useable capital receipt holdings and represent the additional resources a LA is assumed to have available as a result of selling assets such as land and buildings.

allocation reduced by a proportion of their particular balance of usable receipts. In this way, authorities with low access to usable receipts can be given higher credit approvals and vice-versa. After the RTIAs are deducted from the ACG, the resultant amount is then issued to the authority as its *Basic Credit Approval* (BCA) – or *Borrowing Consent* in Scotland. The BCA/Borrowing Consent is calculated on an all-service basis, but authorities are able to calculate how much has been allowed for housing and in practice, actual housing spending will tend to be more or less in line with this official allocation. The idea of allowing a degree of discretion about how an authority's all-service credit approval should be committed stems from the principles of local government identified at the start of Chapter 8. These principles say that local knowledge and accountability should play the dominant part in determining how the money is spent. The principles of local democracy indicate that the central authorities should be more concerned with controlling overall spending levels than with dictating local priorities. The government has made it clear that in future, 'when possible resources will be allocated as basic credit approvals' (DETR, Cm7257, p14). It is felt that the flexibility associated with BCAs underpins the ability of the capital finance system to influence strategic and corporate planning within authorities and gives them the incentive to focus on cross-cutting issues such as social exclusion and youth crime.

The discussion so far has been rather technical. It can be simplified and summarised as follows.

- At the national level:
  Provision for BCAs + RTIAs = ACGs

- For each authority:
  Aggregate service ACGs – RTIAs = BCA

- An individual authority's BCA is thus calculated as the sum of its service ACGs minus RTIAs.

If the amount of an authority's usable receipts taken into account is higher than the total of its ACGs, it will be allocated a zero BCA. A zero BCA implies that an authority has enough usable receipts to cover the whole of its ACGs. A BCA cannot be less than zero.

In Scotland, a somewhat simpler system has been in operation, where there is a fundamental distinction between HRA capital finance and capital allocated to General Fund investment. In the latter case, non-HRA capital used to be separately identified, but has now been rolled into a single General Fund 'pot' not unlike what is proposed in England. HRA capital finance consists of borrowing permissions for investment in the council's own stock, and cannot be used for other purposes. There is no explicit redistribution mechanism for capital receipts as there is in England, but the set-aside arrangements, though different in formulation, are the same in effect. HRA capital finance is effectively unsubsidised for most authorities, because very few are eligible for Housing Support Grant. At the same time, there has been no central constraint on the growth of rents. Revenue funded capital investment (CFCR – see above), is consequently more important.

Capital finance for special initiatives: specific grants and Supplementary Credit Approvals

The government offers local authorities a dual system of credit approvals. In addition to its BCA, a council may be given a *Supplementary Credit Approval* (SCA), (*Supplementary Borrowing Consent* in Scotland), for specific, government-approved projects and initiatives or if government considers the original borrowing consent should be supplemented during the year. It may also give a capital grant to such projects. The BCA issued to each authority is expected to cover the regular annual capital works. If the government wishes to encourage authorities to direct funds towards certain types of investment, it may offer extra borrowing/credit arrangement powers through an SCA or it may give a specific grant for such purposes. Both capital grants and SCAs are given only for specific projects or types of expenditure. In this way, each year, the government encourages investment in special schemes by making funds available in the form of SCAs and grants. Also, in recent years, authorities have been allowed to bid for additional resources for housing projects under the Housing Partnership Fund, the Cash Incentive Scheme, and the Single Regeneration Budget. In Scotland Supplementary Borrowing Consents have been used, for example, to encourage rural development, empty homes and rough sleepers initiatives.[14]

To attain an SCA or grant an authority has to bid within the context of a particular initiative. This means that allocations over and above the BCA can only be used for the purposes for which they were granted and within the time period for which they have effect. They can be issued for expenditure taking place in any period, but in order to help central government keep track of local authorities' expenditure, they are normally issued for a single financial year. In the housing field SCAs have recently been granted in England to encourage the Cash Incentive Scheme to enable tenants to buy properties, and thus release public sector stock; the housing partnership programme that was introduced in 1993/94 for schemes with matching private finance and contributions from the councils' own capital resources; and projects that focus on energy efficiency or the use of empty properties. Prior to 1997/98 SCAs were also issued for all private sector renovations, but are now only retained to provide Disabled Facilities Grants (discussed in more detail in the next chapter). SCAs used to be used to finance the Estates Action programme, but since 1994/95 resources for this have been provided within the new Single Regeneration Budget (see below).

---

14 These are all examples of the key initiatives favoured by the government at the time of writing. The government encourages different initiatives at different times and the reader should investigate what is in favour at the time of reading.

The SCA and grant arrangements, and comparable Scottish arrangements, should be thought of as a mechanism by which central government exercises additional influence over local government spending patterns. During the 1990s there was a shift in emphasis away from BCA to SCAs and grants, which meant that the central authorities exercised more and more control over local authority spending patterns. The supplementary approvals and consents are funded by a process called 'top slicing'. This involves, prior to distribution, setting to one side a proportion of the total allocation of credit approvals. These 'top-sliced' approvals and consents are then distributed, directly or through competitive bidding, in a way that reflects government priorities.

Grants from central government are always associated with specific projects or types of expenditure and are therefore referred to as 'specific grants'. The term 'specific grant' thus describes all government grants to local authorities, including supplementary and special grants, other than Revenue Support Grant and HRA subsidy (Housing Support Grant in Scotland). In the past these have helped to pay for such things as house building, housing renovation, slum clearance, and area improvement. Capital grants form part of an authority's credit cover. This means that along with capital receipts and loans, grants and contributions can be used to pay for capital projects. That part of an authority's grant aid that comes directly from central government is automatically controlled by the central authorities. This control is extended to EC funding (e.g. grants from the European Development Fund) by allocating such funding to specific local authorities in the form of SCA issues.

The term 'specified capital grant' is reserved for a particular type of Exchequer transfer. Specified capital grants (SCGs) contribute to particular types of capital spending that all authorities are likely to have to confront, such as the provision of house renovation grants to disabled people. Authorities are required to apply a special accounting treatment to these grants so that their credit approvals are reduced by the amount of the grant received. This means that the receipt of SCG reduces the need for the authority to borrow but does not add to the overall level of spending. SCGs all relate to housing.

In the next chapter we will see that local authorities often provide a good deal of help to upgrade sub-standard dwellings in the private sector. In certain circumstances they have a mandatory duty to improve facilities for disabled people. As with discretionary renovation grants, the government meets 60 per cent of any expenditure incurred subject to the authority not exceeding its approved HIP allocation. However, this is not the case in Scotland where housing grants are supported through the revenue block grant to the General Fund.

Financial support for local authority expenditure on Disabled Facilities Grants comes in the form of a specified capital grant (SCG) in England and Wales. This support is linked to the allocation of SCAs because the expenditure has to be incurred and financed before the grants are paid. Local authorities must apply a special accounting treatment to these grants so that their credit approvals are reduced by the amount of the grant once it is received. This means that, initially, receipt of the SCG involves the provision of matching SCA up to the guideline figure in the authority's HIP/HSOP allocation. So we can say that, for private sector renewal, Exchequer support is provided in the form of a cash limited grant known as Private Sector Renewal Support Grant; and a non-cash limited grant for mandatory works associated with the award of a disabled facilities grant to a local resident. Central government Exchequer support meets 60 per cent of the cost of works, or where there is a cash limit (works other than those associated with a mandatory award to provide facilities for a disabled person) 60 per cent of expenditure within that limit.

The central authorities can alter the mechanisms through which public expenditure support is channelled into local authority capital projects. Estate Action projects designed to up-grade council estates, for example, used to be financed through BCAs and SCAs but were subsequently altered to take the form of capital grants. One of the reasons for the shift in emphasis towards grants is that it allows the government to provide support to projects involving participation by other providers who cannot legally receive SCAs.

How are ACGs, SCAs and government grants allocated?

In England, the methods used to allocate central government financial support to local authorities are complex and vary significantly from service to service. The bulk of this support, some two-thirds, goes to three service areas: housing, transport and education. Housing's share is distributed to local authorities on a basis that is partly formulaic, reflecting regional and local needs, and partly based on an assessment of relative performance.

The total housing resources available (determined as part of the public expenditure planning and control process and discussed in Chapter 5) are distributed in two stages. The distribution of the total resources *between regions* is made in proportion to the sum of the relevant needs index scores of the local authorities in each region. The distribution of regional resources *between authorities* in the region is currently determined on a fifty-fifty weighting between a calculation of their needs index scores and an assessment of their relative performance made by the Government Offices for the Regions.

In Scotland, there is no formal system of index scores and capital allocations are distributed according to the Scottish Executive's informal assessments of need, although this is likely to change. In practice, HRA capital allocations at the level of individual authorities have been relatively constant year-on-year, with additional resources now allocated to the majority of councils to fund specific initiatives through the New Housing Partnerships programme. Non-HRA capital allocations have been subsumed into overall General Fund investment and the effect has been a drastic reduction in councils' spending on private sector renewal.

Non-departmental capital grants and contributions

As well as receiving support from government departments, local authorities can receive capital grants or contributions from non-departmental government bodies, such as the National Lottery distributors, the Rural Development Commission, or English Partnerships, the private sector, and the European Community (EC).

A 'capital contribution' is a financial contribution to capital spending from a third party that has the same effect as a grant without technically being a grant. Planning gain agreements, for example, can direct financial resources from developers into local authority housing projects but are not classified as 'grants'. Under current ministerial guidelines, local authorities may require developers seeking planning permission for housing developments above a certain size to reserve a proportion of homes for social housing.[15] Developers may avoid this requirement by offering councils a *commuted payment* which can then be used to develop social housing on a different site. In general, there is no limitation on the use of non-departmental grants and contributions to finance capital expenditure: they will usually provide additional funds to those generated by credit approvals, usable receipts and revenue transfers.

How local authority debt is treated in the accounts[16]

Taken together, all the credit approvals, also known as net *capital allocations* in Scotland, can be thought of as central government 'borrowing permissions': they establish the maximum sums a council can borrow to invest in capital projects.[17] For government accounting purposes, in England and Wales, local authority 'debt' has, since 1990, been defined by a 'credit ceiling' that takes into account the annual amount borrowed (the credit approvals) the appropriate proportion of capital receipts that have arisen from the disposal of housing assets and a notional sum for repayment of principal which is defined in government terms as the 'minimum revenue provision' (MRP). Although rather complex, in essence, the process can simply be thought of as central government determining the annual credit ceiling for each authority by subtracting the amount of capital receipts taken into account in that year from the annual capital guideline and then adding in the authority's entitlement to SCAs. The process can be summarised thus:

- credit limit = (ACG – RTIA) + SCA.

15　The 1999 Rogers Report, *Towards an Urban Renaissance*, the Report of the Urban Task Force, DETR, advocates the levying of standardised impact fees as a substitute for planning gain agreements for smaller developments.

16　Information in this section is based on Hall, 1997.

17　Note that credit approvals are used to authorise other forms of credit, such as leasing as well as borrowing, see above.

In Scotland, set-aside receipts and housing (HRA) debt are treated as separate accounting terms which means that the accounting treatment of debt is not based on credit ceilings.[18]

There are three types of credit ceiling in England and Wales:

- overall credit ceiling: this is the overall debt of the council;
- HRA credit ceiling: this is the amount of debt that is tied to HRA dwellings;
- subsidy credit ceiling: this is the amount of HRA debt assumed for subsidy purposes (called 'HRA eligible debt').

What determines the level of debt?

At any one time, the actual level of external debt will depend on three broad factors: internal Treasury policies; the structure of the authority's historic costs (refer Chapter 4); and the authority's ability to attract grants and contributions. To become debt-free an authority must (1) have no long-term borrowing, and (2) have set aside reserves sufficient to meet their outstanding liabilities.

Debt management policy

By being statutory authorities, council debts are automatically underwritten as local authorities cannot be declared bankrupt. However, treasurers and controllers of finance must seek to balance financial efficiency with prudence. They will try to manage the authority's profile of debt in a way that balances the need for flexible access to funds with the need to minimise service charges, while at the same time ensuring that the authority is not taking on unnecessary financial risks. The level of outstanding debt will vary at different times. This is because at certain times, even if the funds are in the reserves, it will be inappropriate to repay loans if they have been secured at low interest and/or where early repayment would incur a penalty charge.

Under the provisions of the 1989 Act, authorities with debt must set aside an amount from their revenue resources every year to ensure that some provision for repayment is in place. At present, English authorities are required to make minimum revenue provision (MRP) of 2 per cent of their borrowing arising from

---

18 In Scotland, receipts have not been 'set aside' in the same way as they have been in England. The different approach required the reserved portion of the receipt to be used to repay debt in the year in which it was generated. It appears that England got a different system because the original proposal (for treatment of RTB receipts) was so aggressively opposed by Conservative local authorities that the government came up with the concept of set-aside receipts. In contrast, Scottish (largely Labour) authorities were told that one year was quite long enough to spend a capital receipt, even if generated in March. In response, Scottish authorities learned how to reinvest in capital programmes in short time-scales. In this way, the Scottish arrangements became (apparently) more flexible.

council housing and 4 per cent of all other debt – DETR, Cm7257, p39. An authority may charge more than this to the revenue account in any one year, but not less. The MRP rules are part of the 1990 capital finance regime. The MRP regulations are about financial prudence and are designed to ensure that authorities set aside sums from revenue to repay debt and meet other credit liabilities. Before MRP, authorities made provision on a more discretionary basis. It has been suggested that the current statutory requirement might be replaced with a mandatory code of practice set by CIPFA. A change of this type would allow a significant reduction in the volume of capital finance regulations and a code might be more practical for authorities, and it would be easier to adapt in line with developing accounting practice.

For reasons mentioned above, not every authority with the potential to become debt-free will choose to do so. However, by being debt-free an authority enjoys the privilege of no longer having to set aside part of its capital receipts and it also allows it to utilise previously set-aside reserves.[19]

Historic costs

The actual amount of the HRA credit ceiling (HRA debt), varies considerably from authority to authority, depending on the amount that has been borrowed historically and the amount of capital receipts that have been set aside since the introduction of the current regime. For some urban authorities, the HRA debt is many thousands of pounds per unit, whereas for some other authorities, mainly district councils, the HRA debt is already nil or close to nil. (Hall, 1997, p7).

Revenue used to finance capital projects

In addition to the types of finance already discussed, local authorities may also use *revenue resources* for capital spending. This practice is sometimes called 'Revenue Contribution to Capital Outlay' (RCCO), and 'Capital From Current Revenue' (CFCR), in Scotland. Revenue financing is one element of its credit cover that does not fall within the capital control system. This means that, in theory, a council can invest as much as it likes of its council house rent income on building and improving its housing stock (HRA schemes). Similarly, it is theoretically free to build what it likes in the way of community projects (General Fund schemes), from its council tax revenues. Although local authorities are technically free to finance capital spending directly from their revenue flows, their ability to do so in England and Wales is limited by the government's reserve powers to place a cap on revenue budgets. It is further inhibited by any negative political impact that such a decision would have on council tax and rent levels. In

---

19   59 non-metropolitan shire districts, 2 shire counties and one London borough were debt-free as at 30 September 1997. Many of the districts have become debt-free following transfers of their housing stock to registered social landlords such as housing associations (DETR, Cm7257, p40).

any event, because of the 'ring-fence' around the HRA, they are not allowed to take resources from the General Fund to finance council housing projects or to systematically finance General Fund projects out of the HRA. Such constraints have not applied in Scotland where revenue funded capital spending has recently grown in response to declining capital allocations and the imposition of controls over re-use of capital receipts. Although, under the ring-fence principle councils are not normally expected to finance GF projects directly from the HRA, in certain circumstances both North and South of the border, HRA surpluses can be used for GF purposes (i.e. to mix metaphors, the 'ring-fence' is not 'water-tight').

As rents are a major source of revenue finance, good practice points to the need to involve tenants in any decision to use their rents to fund capital projects. This means that tenants need to be consulted, and not simply informed, about the resultant rent increase. In particular, they should be consulted about whether they think rents will remain affordable, and given an opportunity to say whether they would prefer to do without the proposed scheme and keep their rents down.[20]

Challenge funds and private sector sources of capital funding

The elements of credit cover already described constitute the primary sources of capital funding for local authority housing projects. In recent years the methods of allocating the public expenditure elements have changed somewhat. In line with the partnership principles of the *new public management* (NPM), mentioned in Chapter 8, the government operates a competitive allocation process whereby authorities can submit project bids for capital allocations and grant resources that are judged against bids from other authorities. Challenge funding was introduced by the Conservatives as a means of distributing limited State funding on the basis of 'guided competition'. This involves top slicing the overall budget and then inviting authorities to bid for a share of the top sliced element against specific project criteria established by ministers. From the point of view of an individual authority, this process can lead to uncertainty about the level of future funding, and it can be complex and expensive to administer. Challenge funding is discussed further in the next chapter in the context of local authorities' housing strategies.

Authorities are also starting to explore the possibility of funding housing schemes through a government sponsored programme called the *Private Finance Initiative* (PFI). This initiative seeks to lever private sector funds into public sector projects usually by means of a *design, build, finance and operate* contract (DBFO). How the PFI is likely to impact on housing provision is also discussed in more detail in the next chapter. Housing projects that contribute towards area renewal and improvement are now largely funded through the Single Regeneration Budget in England.

---

20 The same might be said about loan-financed capital expenditure. However, consulting tenants on the desirability of financing projects through debt creation is fraught with difficulties relating to financial accountability and technical competence. Such an approach requires effective tenant forums to be in place.

Single Regeneration Budget (SRB) in England

The SRB is one of the challenge funding arrangements. It is a single budget that subsumed many former grant and credit approval allocations to allow authorities to bid for comprehensive schemes to address defined issues in partnership. SRB funding is not restricted to housing schemes and, as we will see in the next chapter, it plays an important part in providing funds for urban regeneration. Together with the English Partnerships Investment Fund, the SRB currently constitutes the main public funding source for urban regeneration in England. Now that Regional Development Agencies have been made responsible for the SRB and English Partnerships, there is an argument for integrating these sources into a single 'pot' that can be used in creative and flexible ways in support of integrated physical and social regeneration initiatives. There is also a strong logical argument for extending the precedent set by the New Deal for Communities so that funding programmes have the flexibility to run over longer time-scales of up to ten years. Best value principles also point to the logic of ensuring that funding is tailored to the needs of the project rather than the other way around.

The European Regional Development Fund (ERDF)

The ERDF is one of the three European Union Structural Funds, the others being the European Social Fund and the European Agricultural Guidance and Guarantee Fund. The ERDF is an international initiative that operates outside the SRB, and the Departments of State are responsible for co-ordinating ERDF programmes. The programmes are carried out by the Government Offices for the Regions in partnership with local authorities, TECs, other local bodies, and the European Commission.

The Structural Funds have a number of objectives, of which the following are relevant to the EDRF.

- To promote the development of regions lagging behind the rest of the European Union (Objective 1).
- To redevelop regions that are seriously affected by industrial decline (Objective 2).
- To promote the development of rural areas (Objective 5b).

An ERDF grant normally pays up to 50 per cent of the eligible costs of a project, but can be more in Objective 1 areas. The rest, called 'matching funding', must be found by the prospective ERDF recipient, either from within its own resources, or from other public or private sector organisations. An important source of matching funding is from central government through the SRB. Because 'housing' is not a specific European competence, pure housing projects are difficult to fund by these means. Housing projects will normally need to be linked to one of the funds' objectives if the bid is to be successful.

Having considered the 'types' of capital finance available to local authorities, we now need to say something about the 'sources' of such finance.

The lending institutions

The Public Works Loans Board (PWLB)

Much local authority borrowing is acquired through the Public Works Loans Board (PWLB). This is a government backed fund that borrows on behalf of the public sector. By being government sponsored, it is able to acquire funds from the capital market at competitive rates of interest. The Board usually only adjusts its own rate once a week. It is controlled by the Treasury and is really an agent of central government. For this reason it is, to some extent, influenced by central government policy. Money from the Board is allocated to authorities on a quota basis that takes account of their capital programme commitments and debt profiles. It does not usually advance funds to councils who are sitting on receipts. The PWLB also underpins the financial stability of local government by acting as the 'lender of last resort' to local authorities. In this capacity it will provide short-term loans to authorities that are temporarily short of funds.

When the quota is used up, or if an authority is not entitled to a quota allocation, or if it thinks it can borrow on better terms than those offered by the Board, it may consider going directly into the finance markets by issuing deposit receipts, bills and bonds. To beat the PWLB rate is difficult, but at different times authorities have gone into the market on their own or in collaboration with other authorities.

The market for local authority short and long-term finance

Since the 1950s, local authorities have periodically turned directly to the city institutions to raise funds. Over the years a range of monetary instruments (paper assets) have been developed that can be traded in the money and capital markets in order to raise both short and long-term finance. (See Appendix 9A).

Capital spending: Housing Investment Programmes

Having looked at the types and sources of local authority capital funding and discussed the mechanisms of central government control and redistribution, we now need to consider how the spending is planned for locally and where the money goes.

Local planning of housing investment

The description of the credit control system described above seems to reduce local government housing investment to a mechanical formula. We now need to make the point that, although the central authorities exercise considerable power, the system does allow for a degree of influence to be exercised by the local authorities themselves. The system seeks to reconcile local perceptions of local needs with the wider national concerns of central government. Although in recent years central government has extended its control over local government spending, the twin principles of local government finance pointed to at the start of Chapter 8 (local responsibility and accountability) require the system to take some account of local views about local needs. We therefore need to explain how the allocation system works and how local authorities seek to influence its operation. In Chapter 10 we will consider the elements of a successful housing strategy and investment plan. As a precursor to this discussion, we will end this chapter by describing the regulatory procedures that surround the local investment decision-making process.

As we have seen, the annual BCA/Borrowing Consent is an all-service allocation that gives local authorities the power to raise credit for capital purposes. Although the BCA can be used to justify capital expenditure on any service (in theory it could be used exclusively for housing projects, for example) it is calculated from a number of sub-BCAs that are service specific. The housing specific BCA, together with any grant and SCA allocations, is called the *housing investment programme* or *HIP allocation* in England.[21] In Wales the terminology used is *housing strategy and operational plan* or *HSOP allocation*. In Scotland the terminology used is *capital programme allocation* but, as we have seen, this operates in a different way from in England.

HIP/HSOP and capital programme allocations

Investment allocations currently have three components: a general purpose housing ACG allocation; an allocation of grant for private sector renewal projects *(the private sector renewal support grant)*; and a guideline allocation of SCG to help pay for the awarding of *disabled facilities grants*. The details of how these all operate within the context of an authority's investment programme are discussed in the next chapter where we consider the question of strategic planning and implementation.

The strategy document

As part of the process, the authority has to produce a strategy document. In the context of best value, ministers have indicated that local authorities will have considerable discretion to determine local priorities and policies in consultation with local people. Different circumstances exist in different parts of the country and these differences should be reflected in the strategy documents.[22] However,

---

21 The HIP allocation was introduced in 1978 and replaced the previous system of individual project loan sanctions.
22 Housing Plans have been required in Scotland since the 1970s, supplemented in the 1990s by Housing Management Plans. These are now being merged into the best value framework.

there are some processes that are an essential part of developing *any* good strategy. These are:

(a) needs assessment;
(b) objective setting;
(c) resource identification;
(d) deciding priorities and appraising options;
(e) defining policies, programmes and outcomes.

These are not expected to be section or chapter headings but points that should be addressed in the document. The document should be focused (up to 30 pages) be forward looking, covering at least a three-year planning period. Given the central importance of strategic planning, we will return to it in more detail in the next chapter.

The capital allocation process

These allocations are, in effect, the culmination of an annual bidding round. In recent years, the process has been determined largely by the appropriate DETR Regional Office or the Welsh or Scottish equivalents, and have been based on an assessment of each authority's strategy statement, HIP/HSOP submission and other performance indicators. In Scotland and Wales, the government continues, at present (1999), to provide the capital programme allocation based on a local needs assessment. The use of the so-called 'Barnett formula' is being reconsidered in the light of the creation of the Scottish Parliament and the National Assembly for Wales. It is has become a wider political issue since April 1999 when the nine English RDAs began to operate.[23] (The National Assembly for Wales, the Scottish Parliament and the English RDAs are discussed in the previous chapter.)

In England, the process of allocation begins with the national aggregate of ACGs being divided amongst the ten administrative regions. In determining this division the government makes reference to estimates of relative regional need based on a formula known as the Generalised Needs Index (GNI). This formula is subject to discussion with the local authority associations and depends, for example, on the profile of the housing stock within each authority and on measures of overcrowding. Even quite small changes in the formula can produce relatively large sums of capital being moved between regions.

Once the regional distribution has taken place, the Government Office for the Region (GOR), allocates an ACG to each local authority in its area. This individual allocation of the available resources is only partly informed by the GNI formula. The remainder is distributed, not in accordance with the housing needs of

---

23 The Barnett formula was created in the 1970s. The pressure for change has escalated because of concern in England that the Scottish Parliament and the Welsh Assembly will further enhance their ability to attract inward investment.

the area, but in line with the government's assessment of the council's efficiency and effectiveness.

The local needs element, based on the GNI, weights factors to do with the local authority stock condition (about 60 per cent) the private sector stock condition (about 10 per cent) and the need for new provision (about 30 per cent). In this last category measures of concealed and over-crowded households will be included, as will measures of the need for affordable, sheltered and special needs accommodation. The 'objective' measure of generalised housing need is modified to take account of local variations in costs and conditions.

In assessing a council's efficiency and effectiveness, a judgement is made about the extent to which the service is providing 'best value'. This means that although the individual allocation is informed by the GNI it is unlikely that an authority will receive support that is based solely on a measure of its relative needs. The GOR will have a good deal of discretion to allocate resources in a way that allows for the development of a regional strategy that is in line with best value principles. In determining the distribution of resources, the GOR will certainly take account of how authorities have been performing. Authorities that can demonstrate that they have been relatively efficient and effective (refer to Chapter 2), in carrying out their housing strategies can expect to receive more than their formulaic ACG, while those that are judged to have performed less well can expect to receive less.

Authorities are placed in one of four performance bands by the GOR, with top performers in the 'well above average' band. In recent years, middle band authorities have received broadly the amount of ACG indicated by the GNI. Higher band authorities have received up to 120 per cent of their GNI-based allocations, and lower band authorities have been restricted down to 75 per cent.

We will now summarise the allocation process with specific reference to the English 'HIPs' model. The reader should bear in mind that, although the principles of allocation are similar, somewhat different terminology is used in Wales and Scotland – refer above.

The bidding process

The key elements of the HIP process are as follows.

- In the autumn, before the national allocation decision process starts, regional officials from the government department discuss the written submissions with the authorities themselves and other interested parties such as the Housing Corporation. This cross-section of local knowledge is taken into the national level decision process to help inform the government about how best to distribute the regional allocation of grants and credit approvals.

- The regional distribution is in part informed by an assessment of need. The formula used to measure housing need is the Generalised Needs Index (GNI). Ministers have a great deal of discretion in determining the assessment criteria but a degree of objectivity is meant to be provided by the GNI standard formula. The GNI is an example of a mechanism for accommodating geographical comparative need (refer to Chapter 3). The GNI was originally used as the prime determinant of resource allocation. Over the years, however, central government has increasingly over-ridden the 'objective' measure of relative need in order to impose a distribution that reflects its own priorities. In its last year of office for example, the Conservative government, in the 1997 round, required authorities to be explicit about how they intended to transfer stock to the private sector. During the 1990s authorities became increasingly adept at wording their strategy statements in ways that emphasised their commitment to central government priorities.

- Each GOR then uses its discretion to distribute its local allocation between competing local authority HIP bids using the authority's specific GNI as a guide. At the regional level, the needs assessment is subject to discussions with representatives from the local authorities and others in which consideration is given to such things as the profile of the housing stock within each authority and measures of overcrowding.

- On behalf of ministers, GORs assess performance and efficiency aspects of each HIP against guidelines that are meant to provide the competitive process with a degree of objectivity. These criteria will include an assessment of the extent to which 'good practice' has been adopted. In this context, 'good practice' might include such things as effective liaison with local partners and the effective use of information about the condition of the housing stock.

Subject to the requirement to fulfil its mandatory duties, the authority is free to use the borrowing and credit approvals associated with its HIP allocation as it sees fit.

The authority's BCA/Borrowing Consent has to be issued before the start of the year to which it applies and, in practice, is usually announced just before Christmas. SCAs can apply to any period but, in practice, are normally issued for a single financial year. They can be issued at any time up to six months after the year to which they apply. So that their plans can have some influence on the finally declared allocations, the authorities need to develop their housing strategies much earlier in the year. They begin by devising a Housing Strategy Statement, and this is then submitted with a financial analysis of how the strategy is to be implemented. Together, the statement and the financial plan constitute the authority's capital bid for a share of the regional ACG.

The current debate and likely direction of future change

A proposed new option

The 2000 Green Paper, *Quality and Choice: A Decent Home for All*, proposes an additional option for financing capital investment in housing that remains in local authority ownership. The key feature of this option would be that some authorities, the best performing in terms of 'best value', would be able to retain and use more of their rental income to finance borrowing for investment in stock improvements. This would involve establishing an arm's length management body to manage its housing stock and associated investments. This idea has been championed by the CIH who refer to such proposed bodies as 'local housing corporations' (LHCos). These are discussed more fully in Chapter 10.

Resource accounting and the need to value the stock

The topic of resource accounting is discussed fully elsewhere in the text. In particular, in Chapter 11 we consider its consequences for the Housing Revenue Account (HRA). In this chapter we must emphasise the need to provide a consistent approach to housing valuations, and other HRA assets, on the introduction of resource accounting.

If councils and RSLs are to prepare effective business plans and demonstrate that they are making good use of their housing assets, they must have 'proper' valuations and condition information. Although there has always existed general, centralised information based on the periodic house condition surveys carried out in the national regions, there is no tradition in local government of collecting this kind of 'business' information at the local level. Right-to-buy and LSVT valuations are not appropriate because they were never intended to provide 'business plan' data. Professional surveyors have always made it clear that the quality of data relating to property values and building repair and maintenance is heavily dependent on location. This means that meaningful resource accounting will require authorities to carry out their own local valuations and condition surveys in order to provide appropriate information that can be used in the context of the long-run management of their assets.

The book value of an asset will, to some extent, depend upon how it is valued. In other sectors (private housing, housing companies and housing associations) the three main methods used have been open market value (OMV), existing use value (EUV), and existing use value as social housing (EUV-SH). OMV is based on what the property would sell for on the open market. It includes development potential and therefore does not presume that the land/property will be retained for housing purposes. When applied to social housing, it produces a discounted market value that recognises its tenanted nature. EUV seeks to determine what the property would sell for on the open market but assumes it will continue to be used for housing, but not necessarily social housing. EUV-SH seeks to deduce how much another social landlord might be willing to pay in order to acquire the asset and continue to let it at 'affordable' rents (not necessarily current rents). Although technically the most difficult to assess, because of its orientation to social returns, the government now argues that EUV-SH best reflects the impact of any new investment that takes place.[24]

The move towards a single funding mechanism

The systems for allocating capital resources have been criticised for giving too little assurance over future funding and too little flexibility to reallocate resources. They have also been criticised for imposing artificially rigid deadlines on the take up of funds (DETR, Cm7257, 1998, p23, para.5.1.). Furthermore, the shift in emphasis towards challenge funding has increased both uncertainty in planning capital expenditure and administrative complexity.

As we have seen, the ACG assessments are essentially service-based. A service-based approach has a number of advantages (refer to the section on ACGs above for a summary of these advantages). However, following recent research by the Audit Commission, the government is now giving serious consideration to creating a single 'pot' covering a large proportion of all capital resources currently allocated to local government. The idea behind this suggestion is that it would help to deliver a number of the declared aims of the 'ideal' capital finance system identified at the start of this chapter. In particular, this approach might achieve an extra degree of local autonomy, increase local accountability, allow investment decisions to be made more on broad economic factors, and allow greater opportunity to mobilise resources to tackle cross-cutting issues. It might also provide more stability (with less year-to-year variability in allocations) and be simpler and more economical to administer. However, it would not lend itself to identifying highly specific service related needs and for this reason, many housing practitioners fear that it would result in a shift of resources out of front-line housing provision.

If and when such a pot is established, it is likely to include most of the resources currently distributed through service ACGs, and would probably also include some resources currently allocated through SCAs and grants. Indications are (DETR, Cm7257, 1998), that resources from this pot would be allocated partly by reference to a simple needs-based formula and partly by competitive assessment of authorities' service and corporate capital strategies, together with a reference to their performances in delivering their plans. In this way, an authority that consistently performed well would then be able to predict its minimum allocation of resources with reasonable certainty.

---

24 This is a highly technical subject and the DETR provides extensive guidance notes on 'Stock Valuation for Resource Accounting'.

The shift away from housing specific to single pot investment

There is a trend in government thinking that favours future capital investment operating on a cross-service basis. In England the initial step towards a single pot investment was taken in the 1999 HIP round. From that date the centrally provided housing capital resources have been allocated to councils through the ACG mechanism which, as we have seen, feeds through into the BCA. This single allocation now replaces what was previously three separate allocations; namely, the capital receipts initiative, credit approvals, and grants for private sector renewal. Only capital grants for disabled facilities now remain clearly differentiated. (See next chapter for fuller discussion). The shift to single pot allocations is expected to be extended, so that by 2003 there will be a general single capital allocation with the implication that housing investments will have to compete with other capital projects for funds.

The idea behind single pot funding is that it allows for greater flexibility and encourages strategic planning. However, the shift may have dangers for future housing investment. The danger of merging housing investment into a single pot is that long term housing priorities may be downgraded in attempts to find resources for other projects that bring high local short-run political gains. Because housing is capital intensive it is likely to be a major item in any total local capital spending. This makes it vulnerable to political 'raids' when funds are being sought for other purposes. Some commentators have pointed out that the precedent from merging the Estate Action programme into the Single Regeneration Budget a few years ago is not encouraging for the survival of a strong level of housing investment.[25]

Emphasising the corporate financial strategy

As well as housing strategies, authorities are required to provide spending and financial management plans based on the previous year's ACG allocation and operational data.

To be viable and coherent, the local authority's housing strategy must be consistent with its overall financial strategy. The key double-edged question is, 'What funds and physical resources are required to support the housing strategy and are they likely to be forthcoming?' This question points to the need for the authority to carry out an assessment of available resources so it can evaluate investment options and decide realistic spending priorities. As a way of making their priorities explicit, they are required to show how they would cope if their ACG was less than in the previous year, and what they would do if their allocation were to be larger.

---

25   National Housing Federation, *Six big pictures and social housing investment*, 1999, p11.

The authority's financial strategy should aim to achieve the following:

- Make effective use of its own funds, including capital receipts from the sale of housing and land.
- Make effective use of its non-financial resources such as land and buildings.
- Identify potential sources of public and private funding and explain why particular options have been chosen or rejected.
- Consider opportunities to raise private finance and evaluate the long-run revenue consequences of so doing.
- Seek to make its spending a catalyst to attract investment by other agencies in support of the strategy.
- Present a convincing, well-researched bid for its capital allocation to the DETR, the Scottish Executive or the National Assembly for Wales.

It might be said that these considerations are essentially short-term in nature. In Chapter 15 we make the point that any financial plan should seek to be 'sustainable'. In particular, financial planners need to think through how the investment can be paid for over the longer-term and balanced against other likely commitments. It is likely that in future, the corporate financial strategy will be judged against 'best value' criteria. Under a best value capital strategy, the government would expect to see evidence that each major project had only been included if it had been subjected to an objective needs assessment and a business case appraisal. There would also have to be some assessment of the medium and long-term financial implications of the investment of funds and a performance outcome measure that specifically takes into account such factors as whether it was completed on cost and on time and to what extent the original objectives were achieved.

It is clear that in the future, more rather than less emphasis will be placed on the coherence and quality of authorities' investment strategies. For this reason, in the next chapter we will give this topic special attention.

Summary

Over the years councils have been concerned with various types of housing capital spending projects, some of which have involved investing in the private sector. These have included slum clearance; new building and acquisitions; repairing and improving their own stocks of dwellings and upgrading the environments surrounding them; purchasing land; providing renovation grants to private landlords and home owners to improve their homes or provide special facilities; giving loans to housing associations for them to build or renovate properties; providing and under-writing mortgages for those aspiring to become home owners; and providing house purchase grants to allow council tenants to buy a home in the private sector.

There are three main sources of finance for spending on capital projects: credit approvals; capital receipts; and the HRA.

The capital finance regime regulates the financing of local authority capital expenditure from sources other than revenue grants. It covers expenditure that is paid for from borrowing and other forms of credit arrangement, or capital receipts. There are two kinds of credit approval: BCAs and SCAs. Capital receipts are monies received when property or land is sold or a loan is repaid. Only a proportion of capital receipts can be reinvested in the housing service. The rest has to be held in reserve or used to pay off debt. The new Labour government has relaxed these regulations and has allowed for the planned release of some of the receipts for investment purposes. In so doing, there has been a degree of resource redistribution between authorities. The third major source of capital funding is the HRA. There are no legal restrictions on councils using revenue income to pay for capital schemes. There are, however, political constraints on this financing route.

Each year the council has to submit a capital 'bid' to the government department responsible for housing. This submission has two elements: a housing strategy statement and an analysis of its proposed funding plans. These have been assessed partly on need and partly on the council's performance.

Since the mid-1980s, central government has introduced a number of special funds upon which housing can draw. Each of them was designed to produce a particular investment result at the local level, and each required councils to bid against each other for the limited funds being offered. Most of the resources for these special programmes were produced by a process of 'top slicing' the total public expenditure commitment to BCAs and grants. In the near future, much of this system is likely to be replaced in England with a 'single pot' system of capital support.

Appendix 9A

The local authority finance markets

The market for local authority short-term finance

Local authorities can borrow very short-term, typically from 2 to 91 days, and evidence the debt by issuing an instrument called a *temporary deposit receipt*. Longer short-term debt can be evidenced by issuing *local authority bills*. Bills are financial assets with less than one year to run until the date that they will be redeemed by the original borrower. All bills are traded in what is known as the 'discount market'. Local authority bills are classified on the same basis by the Bank of England as Treasury bills. Local authority bills are technically *local government promissory notes* and are sometimes called 'revenue bills' or 'money bills'. Specialist institutions called *discount houses* create a market by trading in them (along with commercial bills issued by private companies). To be discountable, the issue needs Bank of England approval. The tender procedure is similar to that for Treasury bills (the promissory notes issued by central government) and, as with Treasury bills, most local authority bills are taken up by discount houses and the clearing banks. Treasury bills and local authority bills constitute about 25 per cent of the total bill market and are referred to, along with bills issued by large 'blue chip' companies, as 'first class bills' because they carry negligible risk. This, plus their liquidity, make them attractive assets to short-term lenders looking for a high degree of security. Prior to maturity, they can be sold at a discount to their face value. The price differential will reflect the waiting time to maturity, and it is through the operation of this discount that the discount houses make a profit.

The market for local authority longer-term finance

Local authorities can go directly into the capital market and raise longer-term funds by issuing their own bonds. A bond is a kind of IOU acknowledging a debt to the holder of the certificate. The bondholder treats the IOU as a financial asset and they become a creditor to the issuing organisation. The raising of capital in the form of a bond carries an obligation to pay interest just as it would in the case of a bank or building society loan. A local authority bond is a form of fixed-term loan of normally one to ten years duration. Investors can also lend money to the local authority sector through *negotiable yearling bonds*. These are issued by a number of local authorities every week for one year, two years or longer periods.

All these paper commitments to repay a specific sum on a particular 'maturity' date are called 'transferable instruments' because the holder can redeem them prior to the maturity date for less than their face value, that is, at a 'discount', in the finance markets. This tradability enhances the liquid nature of the loan and makes them attractive to certain types of lenders, particularly finance institutions who themselves may be called upon at short notice to settle debts or lend on to clients. Certain categories of lender are also attracted by the secure nature of the debt. From the investor's point of view, local authority bonds are low risk. No council has ever defaulted on a balance sheet loan and loans raised by a local authority are secured on all its rates and revenues. Furthermore, provided the authority has drafted a legal budget, the PWLB will always act as 'lender of last resort' in times of difficulty.

Bonds are sometimes referred to as 'loan stock' or 'local authority stock' and they can be traded on the stock market. Instead of receiving capital appreciation, the holder is entitled to a stream of coupon payments. So that if, say, a bond is issued at £100 and it makes an annual coupon payment of £10, the rate of interest is calculated as follows.

Annual coupon payment over price of bond times 100 = 10 over 100 times 100 = 10 per cent

Long-term bonds

Bonds can be issued for periods in excess of ten years and thereby provide loan finance for the much longer term (i.e. up to 30 years). This long-term local authority debt market was relaunched in January 1994 when three councils jointly issued long-term bonds arranged by a City broker.[26]

Long-term bond issues can be structured with a partly paid feature. This means that, although the terms and the price of the entire issue are determined on the day it is placed on the market, the proceeds are split so that some will be paid on other agreed dates in the future. This allows the authorities to maintain a proportion of their debt linked to short-term interest rates knowing that the refinancing rate is secured. The attractiveness of bond issues will depend on Treasury views about long-term interest rates – the idea is to take out an issue on a date that turns out to be offering historically low rates of interest.

Local authority mortgage bonds

Local authorities that have the power to levy council tax are able to issue 'mortgage bonds' that are secured against their revenue flows. Mortgage bonds are aimed at smaller investors. They normally specify a minimum investment, and will usually be for a relatively small amount (i.e. less than £1,000). They are issued for a fixed-term, typically two to seven years, and unlike local authority stock, they are not negotiable instruments and cannot be marketed on the Stock Exchange.

The European Investment Bank (EIB)

For some years UK local authorities have had access to a range of EU funds and grants. In the past a number of local authority linked deals have failed to attract European backing because of the difficulties of packaging relatively small projects to make them viable. European funding arrangements are now becoming formalised with the EIB acting as the co-ordinator for a growing range of 4P investment projects (refer to Chapter 10 for explanation of 4P). The EIB is based in Luxembourg and, by being backed by the EU member states, it possesses a 'triple A' credit rating. It uses this rating to borrow funds cheaply in the international capital markets. It then lends these funds on to its sponsored projects. As well as being mandated to act as a catalyst for economic and monetary union,

---

26 Salford City Council, Dudley Borough Council and Leicester City Council. They acquired funds at 7 per cent on 25-year bonds. The success led Salford to join with Coventry City Council in 1995 to raise a further £80 million in the form of a bond issue. A few other councils have also entered the local authority bond market, mainly through club deals. The merchant banking arm of NatWest raised £85 million for the London Borough of Enfield, York District Council and Manchester Metropolitan District Council, while UBS raised £73 million for Carlisle, Brentwood, Colchester, Gravesham, Eastbourne, East Hertfordshire and Selby district councils. (*Public Finance*, 15 Dec. 1995)

the Bank is expected to support regional development and infrastructure projects. In 1997, its total lending reached about £40 billion, with the UK accounting for £3 billion. To date, the Bank has focused on transport projects such as the Channel Tunnel rail link and investment in the utilities sector. However, it is noted that, following the approval of the Amsterdam Special Action Programme (1998), the EIB is now expanding beyond its traditional areas of involvement into projects associated with health, education and housing.[27]

Further reading

KPMG, *Boosting Housing Investment through Capital Receipts*, CIH, 1996.

---

27   Doug Cameron, *Public Finance*, Jan-Feb 1999.

CHAPTER 10:
Local government: investment strategies

The national policy context

The broad strategic framework within which local authorities develop their individual local housing strategies is set by central government. The present government's priorities were clarified in July 1998 when the results of the housing spending review for England were announced by the Deputy Prime Minister (see Appendix 5A). The key policies were identified as follows:

- To encourage a more strategic approach to the production of local housing investment programmes.
- The reinforcement of a strategic approach through the establishment of a single capital pot for housing and eventually a single pot for all capital works.
- The separation of a council's strategic and housing management functions.
- The development of best value approaches to service delivery and the establishment of a Housing Inspectorate.
- The shift to resource accounting for the Housing Revenue Account (discussed in Chapter 11).

This current policy framework should be seen as a development of an approach to local housing planning and management that has been in place for a number of years. It was the 1987 White Paper (DoE, 1987a) that first clearly articulated the principle that local authorities should see themselves as *enablers* who ensure that everyone in their area is adequately housed; but not necessarily by them.[1] From that date, ministers have made it clear that they expect the primary role of a local housing authority to be a strategic one. In particular, they expect authorities to focus on the identification of housing needs and demands, to encourage innovative methods of provision by other bodies to meet such needs, to utilise private finance, and to encourage participation by the independent rented sector. None of these objectives have been abandoned as a result of the housing spending review. The 1998 review simply gave a sharper focus to some of the already established

---

1   In Scotland, this trend was apparent as early as the mid-seventies when Housing Plans were introduced. The late eighties saw the establishment of Scottish Homes with a remit to introduce more private finance into housing, which was mirrored by promotion of the 'enabling' role of housing authorities.

priorities.[2] In particular, it is clear that the present government expects each authority to improve its performance by showing a greater ability to plan strategically, take an integrated 'corporate' approach, and deliver high quality services with clear and meaningful involvement of tenants, residents and other local 'stakeholders'. In this chapter we will give an overview of these expectations and in so doing, identify the various elements that go to make up an effective local housing investment strategy.

Although the substantive issues pointed to in this chapter are of long-term universal concern (i.e. are likely to be of continuing interest to all authorities), the detailed legal and financial frameworks that surround them vary between the different parts of the United Kingdom. They are also subject to continuous adjustment and change. Because of this and because the range of issues embraced by a strategic housing plan is so wide, we will not be able to examine every element in detail. The object of this chapter is to identify what key issues need to be addressed by a strategic housing plan. Readers wishing detailed up-to-date information on specific topics (such as the system of home improvement grants, the regulations appertaining to houses in multiple occupation, or the legislative framework for urban renewal), should consult specialist texts and current guidance notes. Having said this, some topics will be looked at in more detail because they feature strongly in the current debate about the future of social housing, e.g. large-scale voluntary stock transfer and the private finance initiative.

The need for a planning frame

A successful housing strategy should seek to use scarce public resources in a way that is judged to be efficient, effective, equitable and in line with the needs and reasonable expectations of local people (refer to Figure 2.3 in Chapter 2 for a summary of this philosophy).

Each year the DETR, National Assembly for Wales and Scottish Executive publish their guidance notes for councils bidding for a capital allocation. Each has slightly different requirements and the terminology used also varies slightly. In England the DETR now expects authorities to produce a housing strategy looking at least three years ahead. The main elements are set out in a *housing strategy statement* which is required as part of the housing investment programme (HIP) submission. The National Assembly for Wales requires authorities to prepare both a strategy and an operational plan (HSOP). The operational plan should have a three-year perspective and give details of resources and programmes. The Scottish Executive requires authorities to produce a five-year Housing Plan as part of the Capital Allocation System. It sets a four-yearly rota for plan submissions so that a

---

2   In Scotland, for example, the completion of the review saw the identification of additional funds for New Housing Partnerships, which offered resources for solving housing problems providing these were by way of a public-private partnership, whether for new development or by stock transfer.

proportion of authorities provide a plan each year, but as an exception Glasgow submits a plan every two years. In Scotland, authorities also submit a Housing Management Plan, on a similar cycle, dealing with the management of their housing stock and an Annual Policy Statement and a capital programme which together act as a bid for government funds and borrowing approvals (comparable to the HIPs bid in England). These arrangements are likely to alter as a result of the establishment of the Welsh Assembly and the Scottish Parliament.

The annual plan outlines the contribution to the strategy of next year's hoped-for programme of investment. In addition to the description of the proposed programme the return requires specific sectionalised comment and information. In the DETR 1998 HIP round, for example, councils were required to provide information under the following six headings.

Section 1:   Capital expenditure on housing within the HRA.
Section 2:   Capital expenditure on other housing.
Section 3:   Sources of finance for capital expenditure on housing.
Section 4:   Housing capital receipts.
Section 5:   Renovation of the local authority housing stock.
Section 6:   Commentary on housing capital programme.

The elements of a successful housing strategy

The strategy document should be *precise* (maximum 30 pages). It should seek to explicate the following in a *focused* way, and compress them into about six interrelated objectives.

1. How the housing authority will achieve its wider strategic role as an 'enabler', especially as an assessor of local housing need.
2. How housing investment can be seen as a coherent element of the authority's wider corporate strategy. In particular, how expenditure on housing will underpin other local strategies designed to expand employment and economic growth, encourage inclusiveness, enhance environmental quality, and reduce crime and the fear of crime.
3. The time profile within which the overall strategy is expected to operate, together with the resource costs of delivering the service.
4. How the authority has taken proper account of local wishes, including tenants' opinions.
5. How the authority will dispatch its mandatory and inferred duties to house the homeless, those living in sub-standard accommodation, and those with disabilities.
6. How housing plans can be seen to fit in to the authority's land-use planning priorities.
7. How the investment in housing will contribute to the improvement of private dwellings in its area.

8. How the authority's strategy for area improvement and urban regeneration will involve the resources, expertise and energy of others and embrace the principles of competition, challenge funding, and community involvement.
9. How the authority plans to maintain, repair, improve, and where appropriate, expand its own stock of housing.
10. Whether and why the authority should transfer all or part of its stock to another landlord.
11. How the authority intends to develop new approaches to public/private partnerships and, in particular, make use of the Private Finance Initiative.

All these strategic objectives clearly interrelate and reinforce each other in all sorts of ways. Bearing this in mind, we will now say something about each.

1. The authority as 'enabler' and 'assessor of need'

Local authorities are expected to act as enablers who seek to ensure that households in their areas are adequately housed. This means that the first step in any strategy must be an understanding of the wider local housing market and the identification of future housing needs. This usually involves providing brief background information about the local authority area. It will also involve the identification of differing district needs (urban versus rural, ethnic concentrations, etc.). It is also important to consider what the tenants and residents want, even though it may not be possible to meet all demands (see 4 below).

Most needs fall within one of three categories: (1) need for works to be done on the existing housing stock; (2) need for more dwellings; and (3) need for care and support. Robust and up-to-date information on each of these categories is required, and should be accompanied by an explanation of how data were analysed and used to inform decision-making.

Once an authority has assessed the need for itself or others to provide for new or improved housing, it must decide how it can best satisfy this need (refer to Chapter 3 for discussion on needs assessment).

The strategic role of local authorities has grown in significance in recent years as their role as 'enablers' has become more prominent. In particular, some authorities now see their role extending to the understanding of the wider housing market in their area, and the part that they might play in it. A housing strategy provides a framework for bringing together the various housing market participants. It should provide a co-ordinated, cross-tenure approach to dealing with local housing problems and issues. In partnership schemes, the local authority will often be expected to play the lead role and co-ordinate the work of the various contributing agencies, firms and voluntary bodies.

It is clear that in the future local authorities will be expected to play an increasingly important enabling role in delivering urban regeneration. The DETR has recently emphasised the point (The Rogers Report, 1999)[3], that there are many neighbourhoods where regeneration can only be achieved through comprehensive packages of measures to tackle not just the physical environment, but also the economic and social needs of local people (see 8 below).

2. The wider corporate strategy

An effective housing strategy should be treated as part of the authority's wider corporate plans rather than a self-contained arrangement belonging to the housing department. The housing strategy must be consistent with the authority's corporate objectives and overall financial strategy. It should embrace the aims and activities of every department insofar as these affect housing. Thus all departments, in particular planning, environmental health and social services, should contribute to the strategy and have a stake in it.[4]

Current guidelines from all the three departments of State make it clear that 'housing needs' should be seen as part of a wider corporate approach to service delivery that should be developed as part of the government's best value philosophy (e.g. DETR, Cm6988, 1998). Authorities are expected to be explicit about how housing investment impacts on other issues such as social and physical regeneration, community safety and welfare to work.

An important aspect of best value is that due consideration should be given to how investment and management activities in one area of service provision impact on other areas. This means that an effective strategy should involve some form of systematic optional appraisal that will help to schedule and prepare that mix of preferred projects and policies that will have the maximum combined beneficial effects on set outcomes. The authority should be able to explain how its strategy will bring together activities across service areas in a way that generates synergy and stimulates creative interactions. Assessment criteria must include issues that cannot be quantified in simple monetary terms. They should cover such economic, social and environmental factors as the maintenance of established communities, the improvement of security and safety, the elimination of anti-social behaviour, the enhancement of environmental quality, and the need for transport, shopping, leisure and social facilities. The appraisal should also analyse the extent to which the option selected will prove to be attractive to industry and commerce, thereby acting as a magnet for inward investment and employment. The strategy should also recognise that, to be coherent, corporate financial planning and management has to operate within clearly defined time profiles (see Figure15.1 in Chapter 15).

---

3 *Towards an Urban Renaissance*, the Report of the Urban Task Force, DETR, 1999. The Rogers Report proposes the designation of Urban Priority Areas (UPAs), in which planning and funding procedures can be streamlined and additional incentives be provided.
4 For outline guidance on this and other aspects of developing a local housing strategy refer to the CIH, *Good Practice Briefing Issue 7*, April 1997.

3. The strategic time profile and the shift towards a 'single pot' and resource accounting

The Comprehensive Spending Review requires each local housing authority to make a clear distinction between their longer-term 'strategic', and their shorter term 'management', functions. This means that in future additional resources will be dependent on the authority's ability to demonstrate that it is both planning for the longer-term by presenting a focused strategy, and currently delivering a 'best value' service. Underpinning the corporate strategy will be more detailed objectives and targets that will normally be set out in an *annual plan*.

Authorities need to identify all the resources available to them. *'This does not simply mean the likely levels of finance available, resources include land, partners and the tenants and residents themselves.'* (DETR, Guidance Notes, May 1998). The resource assessment should be realistic and take into account the economic climate, known public expenditure programmes, and the degree to which the private sector will be able to contribute.

Objectives should be as explicit as possible and include the timing of expected costs and outcomes. In all cases, local housing strategies should be informed by an assessment of the housing needs of the area (refer to 1 above and to Chapter 3). The principles of the new public management philosophy (see Chapter 8) require councils to take account of, and an interest in, all housing provision regardless of tenure. In each allocation round, the government departments provide guidance notes on how authorities should present their strategies and plans.[5]

The authority's strategy statement, together with a set of supporting documentation, has to be submitted annually. The strategy statement should identify, and where possible quantify, the locality's housing needs by making reference to the stock condition in all tenures, the need for new homes, the special needs of groups such as the frail, elderly and the disabled, specific technical needs such as those related to energy conservation, and community problems such as crime and vandalism on estates. The statement should present the authority's proposals for meeting and tackling these needs and problems within a specified time-frame.

In England, the reformed HIP system demands a longer-term (three to five years) *strategy document* underpinned by *annual plans* setting out investment priorities. Housing Plans in Scotland, established since the mid-1970s, are for five years, produced every four years, with annual plans setting out programme intentions. In Chapter 15 we will make the point that financial planners need to distinguish between different planning time profiles (see Figure15.1) and that a coherent strategy needs to distinguish between current and future costs and revenue streams.

---

5   Complaints about the lack of transparency in the way their bids were assessed led government departments and the regional offices to publish fuller summaries of the assessment criteria, from 1998 onwards.

There is now a move towards the development of universal five-year planning periods (on the Scottish model) that should create more stable strategies that encourage prudent financial management and prove to be more economical to administer. Under best value there is also an assumption that authorities will review their strategies every four to five years. The exact period covered by the strategy document will depend to some extent on the timing of stock condition surveys, the local development plan, and planned reviews of objectives and policies. It may be appropriate also for different parts of the strategy to cover different time-scales (see Figure 15.1).

Following the Comprehensive Spending Review in July 1998, the government announced its intention to allow local authorities more strategic control over their capital assets. It has been announced that from the year 2000 there is to be a 'single pot' in England of capital resources for housing, and eventually for all capital spending. By giving a single capital allocation, the intention is to give councils more flexibility and responsibility for the internal distribution of their resources and a greater opportunity to address cross-cutting issues such as social exclusion. Under the single pot arrangement, resources will be allocated partly according to a needs based formula and partly by competitive assessment of councils' strategies and performance delivery.[6]

To encourage a more strategic approach to the management of council housing in England, resource accounting is to be introduced to the Housing Revenue Account and a new inspectorate, under the Audit Commission, will oversee the longer-term management of council housing. (Refer to Chapter 2 for a general explanation of resource accounting). Resource accounting alters the strategic time profile within which the provision costs of an asset should be considered (see Chapters 2, 5 and 11 for further discussion on the principles of resource accounting).

4. Consultation

As part of its objective of making local authorities more accountable for the services they deliver, the central authorities are now pointing to the need to engage tenants and other stakeholders in the development of local strategies.[7] Current guidelines make it clear that councils must demonstrate that tenants have been involved in a range of housing issues, that their views have been taken into account and that feedback has been given on how these views influenced the authority's assessment of need. Tenants' groups and other interested parties must be involved from the start of the strategy formulation – it is not good enough to pass a completed strategy statement out for comment and observation.

---

6   In Scotland these allocation decisions are now a matter for the Scottish Parliament and currently under consideration.

7   For example, the government has declared a commitment to *'giving local people more choice in making decisions on capital spending in their community'* (DETR C7257, 1998, p10). Similarly the old Scottish Office Development Department declared that the New Housing Partnerships Initiative is intended to allow *'all parties to explore alternative and innovative models'*. (SODD note to directors of housing and other chief officers, December, 1997).

The Chartered Institute of Housing, however, make the point that consultation should not be seen as an alternative to adequate funding. In their recent report on the future financing of council housing (CIH, 1998), they argue that there is little point in involving tenants in housing investment strategies if the choices are how to allocate inadequate budgets. In these circumstances, it is more likely that disillusionment and discontent will be achieved than best value.

Best value principles make it clear that consultation has to embrace more than just the service users. Effective links between housing and social services, planning, education and transport departments will enable the local authority to achieve much more than can be delivered by isolated departments.[8] Liaison with neighbouring authorities also needs to be demonstrated. Outside the local authority, there are numerous bodies and interested parties that need to be involved, including registered social landlords, police and health authorities, and voluntary bodies, together with local builders, landlords, employers, and 'most important of all' tenants and residents.

5. Responsibilities to the homeless and the disabled

We have already made the point that over the years authorities have been mandated to provide various housing services and this fact establishes a degree of priority spending within their housing plans. In recent years, the two main areas of statutory responsibility have been for homelessness and the renovation of sub-standard private sector housing. After 1996, outside of Scotland, private sector renovation grants became discretionary except where a dwelling needs to be adapted to the needs of a disabled occupant. Mandatory disabled facilities grants are discussed in section 7 (below), in the context of local authority support for home improvements.

Accommodation for the homeless

Since 1977, local authorities have had the duty to provide accommodation for households who are unintentionally homeless. Most authorities have sought to exercise this duty by housing such households in permanent self-contained units within the council's own stock or that of some other social landlord. Where this is not possible, such households have to be housed in temporary (usually 'bed-and-breakfast') accommodation until suitable permanent homes become available.

In England and Wales the authorities' statutory duties were changed by Part VII of the Housing Act 1996. With effect from 20 January 1997, English and Welsh local housing authorities no longer have a duty to secure permanent accommodation for statutory homeless households: instead, they are required to secure temporary accommodation for a minimum period of two years. The Act provides that, where a local housing authority is satisfied that there is suitable alternative accommodation available in the district that it would be reasonable for a statutory

---

8   DETR *Guidance Notes*, May 1998. Similar guidance is given to Welsh and Scottish authorities.

homeless household to occupy, it can discharge its duty towards that household by giving advice and assistance to enable them to secure that accommodation.[9]

Homeless households accommodated in council dwellings become tenants and the costs of providing their homes and the income received by the authority from housing them is treated as revenue and recorded in the HRA. Temporary accommodation rents are charged on the General Fund. If the authority wishes to spend capital monies on providing accommodation for the homeless it has to do so within the capital funding constraints described in Chapter 9.

6. The land-use planning dimension

The local housing strategy must recognise that house-building has a spatial/planning as well as a financial/resource dimension. The 1998 White Paper for England made it clear that the need to continue to build new homes (an estimated 4.4 million by 2016) must take account of the widespread and growing public concern about protecting the countryside. Since 1998 it has been government policy that greater use should be made of brownfield sites (derelict urban areas) for new house-building. The White Paper of that year said that local authorities should aim for 60 per cent of new homes to be built on brownfield sites by 2008. The government has also proposed giving 'conferences' of English local authorities power to determine the number of homes to be built regionally and setting up a national database of recyclable land. In July 1998, a Commons select committee report argued for an even greater concentration of house-building activity on redundant urban land. However, the government recognises that not all new homes will be able to be built on brownfield sites, and that at least one million will have to be built on greenfield sites to meet the 2016 target. The select committee report argued that the majority of greenfield developments should be in the form of extensions to existing urban areas.

In recent years the tax system has operated to discourage this policy by discriminating against making better use of empty and run-down property. Value Added Tax is charged at the full rate of 17.5 per cent on renovating existing property, while newly built housing is exempt. This encourages developers to build on greenfield sites while appropriate land and buildings in nearby urban areas are left to decay. The Chartered Institute of Housing has joined with others in calling for equality of treatment in VAT terms for new build as compared with renovation.

7. Property improvement

Local authorities are expected to utilise their own resources and also to work in partnership with others to develop a strategy for property improvement that pays

---

9   This does not apply in Scotland. The Conservative government tried to introduce a parallel measure with a draft Code of Guidance. This led to a strong lobby against the change and eventually the general election meant it did not come into effect. There is now a new Code of Guidance in force.

---

particular attention to areas or individual dwellings that might be slipping into decline. In recent years, a clear distinction has been made between funding the improvement of HRA dwellings and council estates on the one hand and providing support to areas in which privately owned housing predominates on the other. However, the reader should be aware that, in the future, this distinction will become increasingly less relevant in England as the housing investment programme becomes merged with private sector renovation grants into a single capital stream.[10]

Local authority support to the private sector
Local authority support for the private sector includes providing information and advice to owner-occupiers, private landlords and tenants, and to a wide variety of would-be investors and voluntary agencies. More concretely, authorities provide financial help to promote access to owner-occupation, to improve private dwellings, and to help other social landlords provide accommodation. Increasingly they also work in partnership with others to regenerate areas that include poor quality residential properties.

Grant aid to other social landlords
An English authority may use some of its resources to provide grant funding to other providers of social housing (registered social landlords) through Local Authority Social Housing Grant (LA SHG). In Wales this sort of council support has been given in the form of SCAs. Any grants paid have been recoverable from the Housing Corporation or the National Assembly, but the recovered funds cannot then be recycled back into further grant aid as this would generate an endless loop of expenditure. In Scotland, where the Social Housing Grant is known as 'Housing Association Grant', the capital aid has been provided directly by Scottish Homes.[11] With Scottish and Welsh devolution, these arrangements are in the process of being reorganised.

Dealing with individual unfit private housing and aiding private sector renovations
An important part of a local housing strategy will be the council's plans to deal with unfit private sector properties in its area. For many years there has been in place a system of house renovation grants designed to provide financial support to residential property owners needing to up-grade their dwellings. The idea of providing grants to help private owners look after their properties can be justified on two 'strategic' counts. Firstly, as a durable 'social good' (refer to Chapter 1), the local community has an interest in seeing that the current stock is passed on to future generations of residents in good condition. Second, as a primary

---

10 An issue that will have to be addressed is how areas in public/private ownership are to be improved. Regeneration funds are not always available to private owners (e.g. Scottish New Housing Partnerships), and this inhibits the scope for any agency to carry out comprehensive improvement in areas with RTB properties, particularly flatted districts.

11 In addition, the local Government (Scotland) Act 1989 gives councils the power to assist any private landlord, which can include an RSL, subject to the consent of the central authorities.

'consumption good' (refer to Chapter 1) society has an interest in seeing that low-income vulnerable groups are living in decent conditions.

It is beyond the scope of this text to describe the detailed arrangements surrounding the allocation of home improvement grants. Indeed, these arrangements are constantly being revised and they vary from one part of the UK to another. Our concern here is to emphasise that all authorities need to take some account of the condition of the private stock when developing their housing strategies. A broad policy trend that has emerged in recent years has been a shift in emphasis away from mandatory to discretionary grants. Until recently house improvement grants were mandatory throughout the UK in cases where the authority issued an enforcement order to make good a failure to meet the 'fitness' standard.[12] During the 1990s the grant system in England and Wales was changed so that in most cases these grants are now discretionary in this part of the UK.[13] In Scotland, the terminology used is 'tolerable standards'. Scottish 'tolerable standards' are similar to, albeit a little less rigorous than, the 'fitness' definition used in England and Wales.

The shift in emphasis towards discretionary grants (particularly in England and Wales) is an aspect of a broad government policy to direct limited resources at those households and those properties most in need of help.[14] In the 2000 Green Paper (*Quality and Choice: A Decent Home for All*) the government stated the aim of current policy is to provide better opportunities for people to maintain and repair their homes from their own resources if they can, and to help those who cannot afford to do so.

> '*In the past, local authority help to homeowners has been driven by a desire to preserve properties. We believe that the focus should be on protecting people, and that priority should be given to those cases:*
> * *where the household is most at risk from poor housing and the owner cannot afford to repair the house;*
> * *where the poor condition of a house or group of houses is having a negative impact on the wider area; and*
> * *where the authority has a scheme to improve the area as a whole.*'
> (DETR/Social Security, April 2000, Chapter 4 para.4.8).

---

12 E.g. In England as set out in the Housing Act 1985 (S604A) as amended by the Local Government and Housing Act 1989, and clarified in Annex 'A' of DoE Circular17/96.

13 The Housing Grants, Construction and Regeneration Act 1996, introduced the discretionary system for England and Wales. Means-testing was also considered in Scotland by a review committee in 1995. The grant system in Scotland has not been reformed in the same way and is regulated by the Housing (Scotland) Act 1987.

14 This can be illustrated by the conditions surrounding the home repair assistance grants that replaced the previous minor works assistance grants. The new grant has a lower cost limit, narrower eligibility, and less broadly defined purposes. It is awarded on a discretionary basis to aid the repair, improvement or adaptation of private dwellings including mobile homes and houseboats. These awards have to be directed to the elderly, the disabled or to people in receipt of means-tested benefit.

In line with the philosophy of 'targeting' support, special grant levels and allocation procedures have applied to owners of houses in multiple occupation (HMOs). Local authorities are also expected to pay particular attention to the housing needs of those people in their areas who are disabled.[15] The majority of houses in multiple occupation are in the private sector where they provide an important source of rented accommodation for low-income households. However, some of the worst private sector housing conditions can be found in HMOs. Problems include disrepair, inadequate basic amenities and means of escape from fire. Furthermore, the living arrangements in HMOs necessarily place special demands on the management of such properties.[16] The 1996 Housing Act put these awards in England and Wales on a discretionary rather than a mandatory basis but at the same time gave landlords clearer responsibilities, and local authorities stronger powers, to take action. This usually involves requiring works to take place to rectify substantial disrepair, to make the property fit for habitation, as defined by the relevant legislation,[17] or works to make it fit for the number of occupants[18]. The 1996 Act also provides for a revised HMO registration scheme that allows authorities to adopt one of two model schemes and to charge HMO landlords registration fees for re-registering after five years to help meet the costs of HMO enforcement activity.

Common parts grants are available for similar purposes to a renovation grant but for those parts of a building that comprise the common parts, as defined in Section 58 of the 1996 Act. These include the structure and exterior of the building and the common facilities provided whether in the building or elsewhere. People whose proprietary interest in the building is such that they have a duty or a power to carry out or contribute to the cost of the works may apply. These may be the landlord and/or occupiers of one or more flats in the building.

Current legislation in England and Wales provides powers for authorities to adopt group repair schemes for exterior repair work or to give structural stability to groups of defective dwellings, including flatted units. Freehold owners and leaseholders with five or more years left to run may participate in a group scheme so long as they contribute to the cost of the works.

Under the provisions of the Housing Grants, Construction and Regeneration Act 1996, the only mandatory improvement grants currently operating in England and Wales are to provide for works to facilitate a disabled person's use of a

---

15 Renovation, HMO, and Disabled Facilities Grants are all part of an authority's capital expenditure authorised by the annual housing investment allocation (see above and Chapter 9).

16 In response to these factors, Part VIII of the LGHA89 introduced a new grant aimed at helping landlords bring dwellings in multiple occupation up to the minimum legal standards required by Part XI of the Housing Act 1985. The grant operated hand-in-hand with local authority enforcement action, and at that time were mandatory where a statutory notice was served under the 1985 Act. In Scotland the grant arrangements are governed by the provisions of the Housing (Scotland) Act 1987.

17 E.g. Section 604 of the 1985 Act in England and Wales.

18 E.g. as defined by Section 352 of the 1989 Act in England and Wales.

dwelling.[19] These provide aid only in limited respects prescribed by the statute and subsequent regulations. Emphasis is placed on works to improve heating, safety, cooking, and access facilities. Even if the proposed works fall within the prescribed categories, approval is not given to an application unless it can be shown that they are necessary and appropriate, and that it is reasonable and practicable to carry them out having regard to the age and condition of the building. Mandatory disabled facilities grants do not operate in Scotland and this has resulted in a lower volume of this kind of work being carried out north of the border. The remaining house improvement grants are now all discretionary, as are disabled facilities grants in England and Wales for works other than those prescribed for a mandatory award.[20]

Although there is no longer a mandatory entitlement to grant assistance across the UK, there is still an intention that all authorities will make use of the discretionary grants for the improvement of unfit private housing.[21] *'The Secretary of State would consider that a local authority was failing in its duty as a housing enabler and in its responsibility to consider the condition of local private sector stock if it did not have some provision for grant assistance.'* (Circular 17/96 para.5.2.1). The move to a mainly discretionary grant regime requires authorities to have a clear policy for considering grant applications. This policy should seek to have three key features. It should be:

- objective,
- fair and reasonable,
- open and transparent.

The reforms pointed to in the 2000 Green Paper are intended to reinforce the existing policy of 'targeting' resources at those in most need. The government is now seeking to establish an approach that will allow local authorities to use their resources more effectively as part of their strategic role in providing help to a wider range of home owners (Green Paper, Chapter 4). That help might take the

---

19 Exchequer support for private sector renewal in England and Wales (from 1998) involves separate resource allocations for disabled facilities grants (DFGs) and for expenditure on other types of improvement. For DFGs, specified capital grants are provided, which are not cash limited but on receipt of which, authorities are required to make equivalent reductions in credit approvals. Other private sector renewal expenditure used to be supported by a specific grant called private sector renewal support grant (PSRSG), up to an annually determined cash limit. This was, however, phased out (1999-2000) as part of the 'single pot' changes.

20 Since 1994, local authorities have had to contribute 40 per cent towards expenditure on renovation grants and the government contribution, currently 60 per cent, is dependent on the authority not exceeding its approved allocation for the period. The authority is obliged to find the balance from other sources of finance. Any over spend above its agreed allocation is not covered and also has to be financed by other means. Adaptations to the dwellings of disabled local authority tenants also have to be financed from the authority's existing resources.

21 Where there has been a breach of the grant conditions, authorities are normally required to demand repayment from the recipient. On recovery, authorities are required to repay the Exchequer contribution in line with the percentage payable at the time the contribution was paid (currently 60 per cent).

---

form of a grant or loan, the provision of a low-cost maintenance service through a home improvement agency, or advice or help in taking out a commercial loan. It is likely that new housing legislation will be introduced to reform local authority grant giving powers in England and Wales, currently under Part I of the Housing Grants, Construction and Regeneration Act 1996, to give them more discretion over how they allocate grants. It is also being proposed that the existing loan-giving powers of authorities (currently under Part XIV of the Housing Act 1985) be broadened to enable them to give preferential or interest free loans for home improvement. The Green Paper also suggests the possibility of giving authorities new powers to make payments to third parties such as Home Improvement Agencies to help lever in private finance for home improvement.[22]

8. Area improvement and urban regeneration

The local authority strategy must consider how it will deal with the renewal of run-down areas as well as with individual properties. Of course, these two aspects of renewal will often be linked as the up-grading of an area will normally involve repairing and improving individual dwellings.[23]

As well as providing a system of renovation grants, Acts of Parliament also provide a legislative framework for developing area based approaches to renewal. As with the arrangements for improvement grants, provisions for supporting area renewal are complex, constantly being reviewed, and are administered differently in different parts of the UK.[24] Area renewal and urban regeneration policies have a long history that can be traced through the general literature on housing policy and the interested reader is directed to these sources.[25]

---

22 Local authorities already have powers, under Part XIV of the 1985 Housing Act, to indemnify mortgages and to contribute towards mortgage costs.

23 For example, a new relocation grant has been introduced to help people displaced by a slum clearance scheme to purchase a replacement property in the same area. Such a scheme can only be adopted by an authority with the resources to fund the grants. The legislation also introduced an additional option for a local authority taking enforcement action on unfit property to allow it to defer remedial action for up to two years before reviewing the most satisfactory course of action. In this way, a council may serve a *deferred action notice* (DAN) if it is satisfied that to do so is the most appropriate thing to do in respect of an unfit dwelling. The notice identifies the nature of unfitness, describes the work necessary to make it fit, and advises the action the council might take if it remains unfit.

24 In England and Wales, for example, the current legislative framework for area renewal is based on the provisions of Part 2 of the Housing and Local Government Act 1989. This legislation replaced the old General Improvement Areas and Housing Action Areas with Renewal Areas. Area renewal strategies based on the declaration of Renewal Areas should be considered where there are geographical concentrations of unfitness and disrepair or where there is a perceived need to support neighbourhoods at risk from being sucked into a spiral of decline and for which concentrated area action might provide an effective solution. Small scale area renewal or group repair approaches, allowed for in the 1996 Act, are also appropriate for tackling disrepair and unfitness in rural village communities. Housing Action Areas still exist in Scotland.

25 See in particular Gibson, M. and Langstaff, M. (1982), Thomas, A. (1986), Leather, P. and Mackintosh, S. (1993), Mackintosh, S. and Leather, P. (1993), Anderson, K. (1996), and Leather, P. and Mackintosh, S. (1997).

The theoretical rationale for instigating an area approach centres on the idea of the *negative valuation gap*. The idea here is that without some form of intervention from the local authority, property owners with investment interests in run-down areas will not put much money into improving their housing units. This is because any expenditure they make will not be fully capitalised into the exchange value of their assets so that it will not be recoverable if and when they sell. This 'valuation gap' is likely to exist because of the power of what is termed the neighbourhood effect value. The *neighbourhood effect value* (NEV) is defined as that part of a property's value that is determined by its location. The powerful relationship between location and value can mean that it is not worthwhile, from an individual investor's point of view, to repair or improve a structurally sound property unless improvements are also made to nearby properties and to the local environment. Because proprietary investment decisions are atomised, the area can be blighted by an investment inertia resulting from the fact that no one proprietor sees it to be in his or her interest to make the first move to invest. However, if some individual owners can be persuaded to invest in concert, and other area improvements are put in place, then investment resistance from other property owners will be lowered. The expectation is that property owners will be motivated to invest in their dwellings once they become aware that the negative valuation gap is closing or becoming positive.

Current policy states that the replacement of worn out housing can be an important aspect of a local housing strategy and that authorities should consider renovation and clearance on an even-handed basis (*Circular 17/96* para.3.22). In recent years, clearance and redevelopment activities are increasingly seen as being part of a wider urban regeneration policy in which the local authority is expected to work in partnership with other agencies both in the public and private sectors, and with voluntary bodies. There is also a strong expectation that private as well as public funds should be invested in development and redevelopment schemes.

The 2000 Green Paper proposes (Chapter 4) that local authorities should be given more general discretion over how they carry out area renewal. Under current legislation renewal area powers are circumscribed by conditions that relate to the size of the area, the proportion of properties in private ownership, and the proportion of unfit properties within the area. To enhance the capacity of authorities to act 'strategically' it is now proposed that these requirements be relaxed.

Competition, challenge funding and the involvement of other agencies and the community

In the current political climate, an effective housing strategy is also necessary because so much government funding is now allocated by a process of competitive bidding. Although, in its enabling capacity, the authority will take the lead role in developing and implementing the strategy, it is expected to involve other local agencies such as registered social landlords, developers, private landlords, health authorities and social services departments. The strategy should provide a planning and action framework for all organisations concerned with local housing, and it is generally recognised that an effective, practical commitment from other agencies is more likely to be forthcoming if they are involved in the development of the strategy from the start.

Urban regeneration and challenge funding

Since the 1970s, both central and local government have placed a great deal of emphasis on tackling inner city problems and the regeneration of run-down areas. The existence of two different policy-making systems, local and national, has meant that, in many cases, local authority regeneration initiatives have been underpinned by national programmes of support. In recent years, there has been a shift in emphasis in how these two systems have been brought together. This change in emphasis has involved the creation of a mechanism called 'challenge funding'. The basic idea behind challenge funding is that limited and fixed central government support should be distributed on the basis of 'guided competition'. This involves top slicing the overall national allocation and then inviting authorities, and/or their partners, to bid for a share of the top-sliced element against specific project criteria established by ministers.

The English challenge funding approach to up-grading specific run-down areas began in earnest with 'City Challenge', later incorporated into the Single Regeneration Budget. This 'challenge' approach marks a shift away from the principles that underpinned earlier initiatives (e.g. Urban Development Corporations, Housing Action Trusts, Enterprise Zones and TECs). It embodies a shift away from the prime concerns of the 1980s, viewed in terms of the 'three Es', efficiency, economy and effectiveness, towards new public management's emphasis on the 'four Cs', co-operation, concentration, competition, and community involvement (refer to Chapter 2). The change in emphasis is based on the assumption that dealing with property by itself does not bring about sustainable regeneration. It emphasises the need for investment to take place in a way that encourages an integration of effort.

The introduction of the Single Regeneration Budget (SRB) for England in 1994 re-emphasised the Conservative government's commitment to the principle of challenge funding as a mechanism for distributing the government's fixed sum of regeneration resources. Under these arrangements authorities in England have been required to submit scheme proposals that are judged against other bids in the allocation of credit approvals or grant resources. In recent years the challenge fund philosophy in England has produced a number of bidding opportunities centred on such initiatives as City Challenge[26], the Housing

---

26   City Challenge committed £1 billion of government money to regenerating disadvantaged urban areas in England. City Challenge authorities have been designated by annual competition. They have been provided with core funding that was supplemented by resources from other established public sector programmes together with investments from the private sector. Under these arrangements the local authority and its partners have discretion to select the districts and priorities in which to invest, with the Department of State acting as the final arbiter on the overall five-year plan and its annual implementation strategy. The competitively determined and collaboratively implemented plans are expected to improve the quality of life for local residents and are administered through an agency that is independent from the local authority and capable of making rapid and effective decisions that are endorsed by all the partners.

Partnership Fund[27], Capital Challenge[28] and, most significantly, the Single Regeneration Budget. In 1994 the government amalgamated Estate Action with 19 other English budgets related to housing, training, education and economic development. These had previously been managed by five different departments and were pulled together to create a 'single pot' called the Single Regeneration Budget (SRB). The creation of the SRB was based on the Conservative Party's 1992 manifesto pledge to promote local economic, social and physical regeneration through investment in the infrastructure and in people's education and employment skills, particularly the young and the disadvantaged. In setting up the SRB, housing improvement was identified as a specific objective along with an increase in community safety, the enhancement of the environment, an expansion in community and tenant participation and an improvement in the industrial competitiveness of firms. The Fund was valued at £1.4 billion in its first year of operation and these public resources were

---

27   In 1996/97 the Housing Partnership Fund made available £30 million for 238 housing projects designed to meet local housing needs and boost economic and employment opportunities around England. Under this fund, bids were made to launch schemes designed to bring back into use both private and public sector empty dwellings, including properties over shops and other commercial premises. Authorities were also required to consider energy efficiency improvements as part of such schemes. In applying for such resources a bid had to demonstrate that the proposal has the following features.
  • It makes a significant contribution to meeting housing need in areas of housing stress.
  • It involves financial contributions from the private as well as the public sector.
  • It makes efficient and effective use of public funds.
  • It satisfies the normal criteria for statutory consent.
  • It is consistent with priorities already set by the LA's housing strategy and established community care and urban regeneration activities.
  The Fund helped local authorities to lever in over £100 million of private finance for their housing projects. This scheme was discontinued in 1997/98. Local authorities were, however, expected to continue to involve the private sector in housing schemes. This continued involvement was one of the objectives of the Capital Challenge pilot scheme introduced in 1996.
28   A pilot Capital Challenge scheme was introduced in May 1996 with the objective of exploring how best the challenge concept might be brought to bear on the allocation of government support for local authorities' mainstream capital spending. It was created by rationalising a number of former grant and credit approval allocations into a single competitive system. It allows authorities to bid for comprehensive schemes that seek to tackle defined local issues in partnership with other agencies and firms. The fund is aimed specifically at local authorities and is separate from the Single Regeneration Budget. Under the scheme, local authority departments, combined fire authorities, fire and civil defence authorities, magistrates' courts committees and probation committees were invited to submit bids for support for priority capital projects. The emphasis was on allowing authorities to set their own priorities in partnership with the local community and private sector. An initial fund of £600 million in credit approvals was made available over three financial years, departments contributing in proportion to their shares of the overall budget for government support for local authority expenditure. There were 189 winning pilot awards that varied in size from £30,000 to £26 million. The pilot scheme is being evaluated before a decision is made on whether to proceed to a fuller application of challenge principles to determine capital expenditure. It is unlikely to survive the rethinking that has stemmed from the Labour government's expenditure review exercises.

---

expected to act as a lever to encourage additional investments from the private sector.[29]

Current 'challenge fund' arrangements such as the SRB are intended to encourage partnership approaches to regeneration through joint working which means that individual projects by a single agency are not normally funded. They now increasingly also put a lot of emphasis on community involvement[30]. Although the policy of *regeneration partnerships* has been followed more assiduously in England than elsewhere, it is now a clear trend in government policy across the UK. Currently Welsh Capital Challenge provides a £30 million budget to support local authority regeneration strategies and projects in Wales through an annual bidding round.[31] This approach has also been recently imported into Scotland through the New Housing Partnerships.[32]

The objectives of *regeneration partnerships* can be summarised as follows:

- improving housing and housing conditions for local people through physical improvement, better maintenance, improved management and greater choice and diversity.

---

29 The unified budget is intended to allow for a greater degree of flexibility by allowing the transfer of funds from one programme to another in order to achieve a more coherent strategy. However, this has had the effect of shifting the emphasis that was placed on tackling poor housing by the Estate Action Programme and HATs towards wider socio-economic goals. These wider goals are emphasised by the fact that TECs were identified as joint lead bidders alongside the local authorities.
At the same time that the SRB was established, new Government Offices for the Regions were formed, integrating what were the regional offices of the five Departments of State. Up to 1999 the SRB will be managed by civil servants based in these Integrated Regional Offices. Under these arrangements the Regional Offices administer services and programmes previously delivered by what was the Department of the Environment along with the old Departments of Trade and Industry, Transport and Employment. Each Integrated Regional Office has been responsible for developing a regional regeneration strategy within which local authorities and TECs have been given the task of co-ordinating the submission of bids from local partnerships. The administration of the SRB is about to change. It is expected that about 50 SRB schemes will be supported in the fifth round (1999), and from that date, in England, the money will be administered by the new Regional Development Agencies (refer Chapter 8).

30 This contrasts somewhat with earlier initiatives such as 'renewal areas' that put more emphasis on economic factors and put less emphasis on a 'community' approach to neighbourhood regeneration.

31 The scheme focuses on encouraging regeneration schemes that create significant employment and training opportunities in the more disadvantaged areas of Wales.

32 The New Housing Partnerships initiative was established in 1999 with a view to fostering close collaboration between local authorities and their partners, including the private sector and tenants, to secure additional investment and promote and provide good quality housing in the social rented sector. In order to assist longer-term thinking on NHPs, the Scottish Executive, in consultation with Scottish Homes, CoSLA, SFHA and CIH, has identified three broad partnership approaches. These are (1) transfer partnerships, which involves transfers of council housing to new or existing social landlords; (2) development partnerships, that would be joint ventures with regeneration objectives and could also involve new or existing housing associations or housing companies; and (3) other joint venture partnerships between local authorities, the private sector and other parties.

In addition to this housing-centred objective, the following represent the sort of criteria needed to be met by successful bids.

- Enhancing the employment prospects, education and skills of local people, particularly the young and the disadvantaged, and to promote equality of opportunity.
- Encouraging sustainable growth and wealth creation by improving the competitiveness of the local economy, including support for existing and new businesses.
- Protecting and improving the environment and infrastructure, and promoting good design and landscaping.
- Promoting initiatives of benefit to ethnic minorities.
- Tackling crime and improving community safety.
- Enhancing the quality of life and capacity to contribute to local regeneration of local people, including their health, culture and sports opportunities.

Recent research by the Joseph Rowntree Foundation[33] has examined how to establish appropriate financial structures to support *regeneration partnerships*. The findings concluded that any additional financial mechanisms underpinning community involvement in neighbourhood regeneration should incorporate the following features.

- Regional decision-making, with national funding for umbrella organisations.
- Targeting community groups themselves, especially those excluded from other regeneration funding opportunities.
- Simplifying the application procedures, for example by using call centres.
- Flexible funding packages, recognising local diversity.
- Investment in long-term support, not short-term programmes.
- Ensuring that additional finance from other private and public sector sources is already available before community organisations apply.
- Avoiding duplication with existing funding regimes.
- Prioritising support funding of community-controlled bodies.
- Low administration costs.
- Effective evaluation.

Since 1996, many bids to support the improvement of housing have had to be subsumed into schemes with wider community objectives and this has reduced the amount of public funding going directly into housing projects. In England, for example, the amalgamation of Estate Action into the SRB not only reduced the volume of public resources being directed at housing regeneration, it also shifted the renewal emphasis away from council housing estates towards mixed tenure areas. Despite this, in the early rounds, over a third of all successful bids incorporated housing-related objectives.

---

33 Pete Duncan and Sally Thomas, *Neighbourhood Regeneration: Resourcing Community Involvement*, Rowntree and The Policy Press, Bristol, (2000).

An emerging regional dimension

The creation of the Scottish Parliament and Assemblies in Wales and Northern Ireland mean that in the future urban regeneration, and therefore a good deal of housing investment, will be partly planned for and administered at a regional level. In England this regional planning dimension will focus on the new Regional Development Agencies (RDAs).

Challenge funding and its associated administrative arrangements are continuously scrutinised as part of the government's on-going Comprehensive Spending Review. In July 1998, the Review announced the government's intention to allocate £800 million to the year 2002 to the most deprived neighbourhoods through further rounds of the Single Regeneration Budget. Although much of this will be spent on business start-up projects and skills training and education, some will be put directly into housing. A decision has already been made to make RDAs responsible for the SRB in England.

9. Investing directly in council housing estates

Although the shift in emphasis away from Estate Action[34] towards challenge funding has had the effect of reducing resources directed at council estates, it has

---

34 The current New Deal for Communities project was preceded by an English initiative called Estate Action. In 1985 central government influence over urban regeneration was tightened when the decision was made to top-slice the overall Housing Investment Programme to create resources for this new centrally controlled initiative. The Estate Action programme aimed to help local authorities transform unpopular housing estates into places where people would want to live. It provided central funds in the form of grants to encourage authorities to tackle the physical condition of such estates, improve housing management, secure greater tenant involvement, provide variety and choice in housing and create opportunities for training and enterprise. The objective of Estate Action was to upgrade areas of poor quality public sector housing through diversification of tenure, increased local, and particularly tenant, participation, selective refurbishment and the introduction of private finance. In the ten years that followed its introduction the programme created billions of pounds of spending on housing improvements in the form of credit approvals, grant allocations and private investments. More than half a million dwellings were improved with more than 90 per cent of the resources coming through public sector channels.
By 1994 Estate Action had developed into the government's most important policy tool to address the physical and socio-economic problems associated with residualised council estates. In 1994 the programme was subsumed into the Single Regeneration Budget (SRB), which was introduced in an attempt to take a more co-ordinated approach to area regeneration through the use of a single, flexible funding regime that allocated resources on the basis of competitive bidding. The inclusion of the Estate Action programme within the SRB had significant consequences for the larger urban local authority landlords. In 1994/95 the Estate Action budget accounted for more than a quarter of SRB resources and some 23 per cent of all credit and grant approvals made available to local housing authorities (Nevin in Wilcox, 1996, p24). Financial constraints in the second half of the 1990s, coupled with the need to share the fixed pot of resources with other programmes such as HATs, UDCs, English Partnerships and City Challenge, meant a systematic cut back on those projects that had relied on Estate Action funding. These constraints on the Estate Action programme were intensified by the shift in emphasis towards competitive bidding and challenge funding. The Estate Action programme is being phased out and now only funds the continuation of schemes that were started in 1994/95 or earlier.

---

allowed successful housing partnerships to develop a more holistic approach to the social, economic and physical problems associated with residualised council housing.

Part of the government's policy commitment to urban regeneration in England has had a specific council housing focus and expenditure has been targeted at those local authority estates in greatest need of investment through the Estates Renewal Challenge Fund, the Estate Action and Housing Action Trust programmes[35], and through housing expenditure as part of other Single Regeneration Budget schemes. Under the latest capital receipts initiative, £3.6 billion has been made available to English local authorities. Building on previous releases, this means a total of £5 billion capital receipts have been made available over the course of the first Labour Parliament. In the future, this will continue through programmes such as the New Deal for Communities (discussed below).

The Chartered Institute of Housing supports an estimate of £21-£23 billion for outstanding work to British council housing, with an on-going need to invest about £600 per unit each year to address the backlog of necessary major repairs and improvements. It is estimated that the current unsatisfactory state of the nation's local authority stock is adding some 20 per cent to councils' maintenance budgets. Of course, the intensity of the problem varies as between estates, authorities and regions.

It is important not to overuse nation-wide statistics to generalise about council housing, as many council dwellings and some estates are of a comparatively high quality. Others have developed into so-called 'sink estates' that have deteriorated into places with ingrained social problems. Allocation policies as well as under-maintenance have produced some estates that are difficult to let and have unusually long transfer waiting lists. Recent work by the Social Exclusion Unit has emphasised the point that to turn such estates around will require policies that

---

35 Housing Action Trusts: HATs were established under the provisions of the 1988 Housing Act. HATs are non-departmental public bodies which, with the agreement of their tenants, have taken over run-down housing estates from local councils. They are charged with regenerating the estates they take over with a view to creating 'sustainable local communities'. The aim of HATs is, over a ten-year period, to redevelop, refurbish and manage their housing stocks and to improve the physical, social and environmental conditions in their areas. In order to achieve these objectives, they can make grants available to individuals, organisations (including charities) and businesses. Their specific statutory objectives are as follows: (1) to repair or improve the housing they provide; (2) to manage and use their housing effectively; (3) to encourage diversity of tenure, including home-ownership, and in particular to give tenants a choice of future landlord, including the statutory right to return to local authority tenure; and, (4) to improve the living, social and environmental conditions in their areas.
While, in recent years, the majority of HATs' expenditure has been financed by grant-in aid under the SRB, the six remaining Trusts have been encouraged to explore opportunities for funding through other sources, including the PFI, and by developing partnerships with other local regeneration initiatives. All HATs work with Registered Social Landlords, schools and colleges, and local employers.

look beyond 'bricks and mortar' solutions. To improve the quality of life on unpopular estates will require a co-ordinated approach by a number of agencies that together address questions to do with poor employment opportunities, the fear of crime and anti-social behaviour, and the provision of retail, commercial and social facilities. All of this points to the need for future estate action policies to develop new approaches to housing management that are founded on interdisciplinary understandings and multi-agency responses. It also emphasises the need for local participation, particularly from tenants, so that potential 'solutions' are owned by those most affected by a policy's success or failure. Furthermore, the existence of both 'good' and 'bad' estates points to the need for there to be both national and local investment strategies so that limited funds can be targeted on those areas where they are most needed. A strategic approach to investment also points to the need to strike a balance between areas where funds are 'most needed' and areas where re-investment is likely to be 'preventative'. The first phase of the New Deal initiative focuses on 17 deprived communities that together constitute a pilot scheme for further action over the next 10-20 years.

The 'New Deal' projects embrace cross-cutting issues designed to tackle social exclusion on deprived estates. They concentrate on tackling problems of crime, low educational attainment, poor health, and the other symptoms of social exclusion. Many of these problems result from a lack of employment opportunities, but some can be ameliorated through carefully targeted housing investment. As Frank Dobson, the then Health Minister observed in 1998, *'Everybody with a grain of sense knows that it's bad for your health if you don't have somewhere decent to live.'* (CIH and Graham Moody Associates, 1998, p6.).

The New Deal for Communities is meant to provide linked (holistic) funding targeted on communities of up to 4,000 homes, while other funds, such as the SRB, provide regeneration resources for larger areas. The New Deal programme will be financed initially by top-slicing some £800 million from the phased release of capital receipts. The funds released by the second capital receipts initiative, announced in 1998, will be phased into the system between 1999 and the year 2002. The Scottish, Welsh and Northern Ireland Office comprehensive spending reviews have established the basis for spending plans to be inherited by the Scottish Parliament, the National Assembly for Wales and the new Northern Ireland Assembly. Each review provides for additional resources for public services over the next three years (Scotland £4.1 billion, Wales £2.2 billion, Northern Ireland £1.4 billion). Scotland will receive another £319 million specifically for housing, but in Wales resources from capital receipts have not, to date, been directed into housing.

Leasing from the private sector

If the regulations could be relaxed, councils might make more use of leasing arrangements to acquire capital assets. Leasing is a contractual arrangement whereby a council, in return for regular payment to the owner, gains the right to use a capital asset for a specified period. At the end of the period, the lease might be renewed, returned to the owner, or purchased by the council. Under current rules, local authorities can lease private sector homes for up to ten years, so long as they are only used to house homeless people.

Relaxing the restrictions on leasing would also allow councils to acquire the use of equipment such as lifts, heating and security systems that would improve the quality of their housing provision. The leasing costs would be recouped by charging higher rents. Leasing costs do not count against the council's credit approval and are not an element in the public sector borrowing restrictions, because the finance is raised by the private sector company. Two barriers exist to extending these sorts of arrangement. Firstly, the regulations require the equipment to be regarded as 'removable' and thus not part of the structural fabric. Secondly, HRA capping rules introduced in 1996/97 make it difficult to increase the rents in order to gain these benefits, even in cases where tenants approve.[36]

As we have already made clear, in broad financial terms, local government housing activities cover both HRA and non-HRA housing investments. An authority's strategy for housing investment has to embrace both of these areas of activity. The extent to which a council decides that the residents in its area require council rather than private housing will be a local political decision, but central government 'new public management' philosophy (refer to Chapter 8), manifested in the form of credit controls, can make it difficult for an authority both to expand and renew its own housing stock. This means that an authority will, reluctantly or otherwise, have to look towards the private sector and other social landlords to provide much of the accommodation local people need.

10. The transfer of estates to other landlords
One strategic approach to tackling the under investment in local authority housing within the constraints set by the public sector financial framework, has involved transferring estates to the ownership and control of private sector landlords. By transferring housing to private sector organisations that are not subject to public sector borrowing constraints, authorities may be able to allow for much needed improvement and repair to be undertaken on the transferred homes. However, a significant proportion of council housing will have a low or negative value and will require subsidy to facilitate the transfer deal. Until

---

36 The Scottish Office has given a lead in allowing a number of Scottish councils to use leasing agreements to install gas central heating. Tenants benefit from reduced fuel bills that offset the burden of increased rents that help pay for the leasing charges (England, M., 1997, p69). Some of the biggest and longest established leasing schemes are run by the City of Glasgow Council. Changes in the Budget (March 2000) will make leasing deals for heating easier to carry out.

recently English authorities could bid for special funding for this purpose through the now defunct Estates Renewal Challenge Fund.[37] Until recently this was not possible in Scotland, but now bidding through the NHP initiative has made this possible. This means that, somewhat contrarily, although it is now possible in Scotland, this special bidding arrangement no longer exists in England since the abolition of the ERCF, and, if subsidy is needed by an English authority, it now has to be accounted for in the authority's HIP bid.[38] The government has recognised that a minority of English authorities would be prevented from considering transfer as an option because the capital receipts from the transfer sale would be insufficient to cover their overhanging debt. As a result it is now possible to receive a one-off special payment to help the relevant authorities to redeem their debt (December, 1999).

The Conservative administrations of the 1990s positively encouraged authorities to include the transfer of ownership in their housing strategies.[39] Transfers may involve all or part of a local authority's housing stock. However, transfer of

---

37 These funds were set up to support stock transfers that could not proceed without central government financial support. Initially they operated outside the SRB. ERCF was available to English authorities and Estate Partnership operated on a similar basis in Wales. The schemes operated on the challenge fund principle (see above). This means that the extra resources that are distributed to the winning bids have been provided by top slicing (i.e. cutting) the capital allocations to all authorities. In Scotland the transfer of poor quality estates has been eased by the provision of Housing Association Grant from Scottish Homes. This particular form of challenge funding in England and Wales was designed to enhance the potential to transfer stock that was in demonstrably poor condition to new social landlords. In particular, it sought to compensate for low or negative valuations or poor asset cover. The funds were designed to provide the minimum level of public spending needed to draw in the necessary private finance. The funds, which provided both capital and revenue grants to local authorities were allocated through a bidding process. All bids had to involve the transfer of 200-12,000 homes to registered social landlords. The funding was to help towards the cost of making such transfers feasible and was payable only up to the minimum level needed to achieve transfer. Typical eligible costs included a 'dowry' for the new landlord (where the stock had a negative value) and costs of essential capital works undertaken by the authority in order to secure the transfer agreement. This could take the form of works carried out prior to the transfer, or as post-transfer works as an alternative to payments to new landlords. In addition, it could pay towards the set-up costs of the new landlord and, exceptionally, other elements of regeneration where these were essential to achieve a transfer agreement. The funding rules limited the possibility of demolition and renewal and this inhibited some planned transfers and led to some lobbying for more flexibility so that selective demolition could take place where it was judged to be appropriate. Questions relating to stock transfers are discussed in more detail below. To help deal with the issue of negative value, a 20 per cent levy is charged on all positive value transfers (from April 1999). There is an argument for investing some of the resources raised by this *stock transfer levy* in improving and remodelling the transferred estates as well as in paying off overhanging debt. The argument is that if such public investment was put directly into improving the physical quality of the stock, it would help to attract private funders.

38 However, in December 1999 the DETR announced plans to intervene on transfer values to help councils where the capital receipt from transfers failed to cover outstanding housing debt.

---

tenanted council housing cannot take place without the approval of a majority of relevant tenants voting in a ballot.[40]

Large-Scale Voluntary Transfer (LSVT)

The 2000 Green Paper makes it clear that the government sees stock transfer as an important option for improving the quality of social housing available at affordable rents, and for offering tenants a more diverse range of landlords to meet their needs.[41] The process of LSVT operates under powers largely contained in the Housing Act 1985, The Housing and Planning Act 1986, the Leasehold Reform, Housing and Urban Development Act 1993, and the Housing Act 1996.[42] In England and Wales, tenanted housing can only be transferred to RSLs. In Scotland, stock can be transferred to housing associations that are registered with, or companies that are contractually regulated by, Scottish Homes.

With the support of tenants and the approval of ministers, more than 100 local councils have transferred their dwellings to other agencies that have access to private sector finance. These new landlords receiving the transferred stock can be

---

39 Under the heading 'Rights for Council Tenants', the 1987 Conservative manifesto emphasised the Party's commitment to empower public sector tenants to exercise more direct control over their housing situations, including the right to choose whether or not their council tenancies should be transferred to some other approved landlord. In the White Paper following the general election *Housing: The Government's Proposals*, Cm214, 1987, it became clear that the proposed 'choose a landlord' scheme was intended to be part of the government's broader policy of diminishing the direct landlord function of local authorities. Together with the right-to-buy provisions of the 1980 Housing Act, these new tenant rights were part of the government's aim to transform local authorities from 'providers' into 'enablers'. The new rights were established under the provisions of the Housing Act 1988 and the Housing (Scotland) Act of the same year. This legislation extended the 'right-to-buy' council houses to 'approved' landlords and 'approved' Housing Action Trusts. Tenants were given the 'right to choose' their landlords and suitable prospective agencies were then invited to purchase council stock for rent. The purchase could only go ahead with the agreement of a majority of the tenants and the transfer had to be to a landlord approved by the national housing corporations.

40 The Scottish system is based on individual choice rather than ballot.

41 *Quality and Choice: A Decent Home for All*, DETR and Social Security, Chapter 7.

42 Initially, some authorities that were sympathetic to the changing role of local authorities, away from being direct landlords, responded by making plans to transfer the whole of their stock to an existing or specially formed housing association. Others who were not sympathetic to the 'choose a landlord' philosophy, but who nevertheless feared the piecemeal breaking up of established estates, considered doing the same. Other strategies involved efforts to get closer to tenants and to become more responsive to their needs by initiating decentralisation and participation programmes that were often tied to user satisfaction surveys. Some authorities used alarmist 'propaganda', warning their tenants of the 'perils' of transferring out of the public sector. The early transfers were thus a response to the perceived threat of Tenants' Choice in the 1988 Act. Research shows that, in later transfers, this fear was replaced by other concerns stemming from the implications of the new financial regime for local authorities, introduced by the Local Government and Housing Act 1989 (DoE, 1992). For many authorities, transfer was seen as the best way of continuing to provide an effective social housing service at affordable rents. This means that, although the 'choose a landlord scheme' acted as a catalyst for what has become termed 'large scale voluntary transfer', the idea itself did not so much stem from central government as from the local authorities themselves. As such it can be said to stand as a good example of 'bottom-up' policy making (Aughton and Malpass, 1994, p37).

existing housing associations who take the properties direct or sponsor subsidiaries to do so, or stand-alone local housing companies (see below). Between 1988 and 1999 LSVTs raised close to £6 billion in private sector funds and involved some 325,000 tenanted properties with a gross value of more than £3 billion. The New Labour government required local authorities to keep LSVT as a strategic option. *'We won't be forcing anyone to transfer, but we will expect everyone to consider it as one of their options'* (Hilary Armstrong, reported in *Inside Housing*, 19 September, 1997).

The financial principle behind LSVT is that of *equity release*. The objective is to improve the housing service by reinvesting the money capital generated by the sale in new building and in improving and modernising the existing stock. It becomes possible because the stock's asset transfer value is greater than its historic cost value (refer to Chapter 4). Put simply, because the outstanding debt associated with the stock is often significantly less than its exchange value, the new landlord is able to borrow on the strength of the difference (i.e. the unencumbered equity) and then invest the funds raised in improving the service. Research shows that active interest in LSVT was originally confined to those where the transfer valuation exceeds loan debt and can allow for the necessary 'catch-up' repairs (DoE, 1995). LSVT brought to the fore the question of how private lenders assess the value of social housing. How to value council housing assets is an important issue and is discussed in Chapter 9. A typical LSVT involves the council providing wide-ranging warranties to the new landlord as a way of easing the transfer process and reinforcing the funder's confidence in the deal.

In England, the DETR draws up an annual disposal programme. English authorities wishing to be in the programme submit applications in November along with a detailed financial appraisal of the public expenditure implications of the proposed transfer. Scottish authorities apply to the Scottish Executive and transfer consent is granted by Scotland's First Minister. In Wales the consent procedure operates in a similar way through the National Assembly.

One financial disadvantage of LSVT from the Treasury's point of view was that, unlike local authorities in England and Wales, housing associations and other RSLs are not liable for a proportion of their tenants' housing benefit.[43] This anomaly was addressed in 1993 when the government established the annual disposal programme for England. Since that date the Exchequer claws back some of this lost revenue in the form of a levy. A 20 per cent levy is now charged on the capital receipt arising from a transfer of 500 dwellings or more to a single purchaser in any one year. From April 1999 the 20 per cent *stock transfer levy* will be paid on all positive value transfers. The government is currently consulting on the details of any changes that might be made to the levy from 2001.

---

43 The government is planning to end the cross-subsidy paid by council tenants to pay for housing benefit. This reform is part of the move towards resource accounting.

The 1993 changes also set a limit to the number of properties that can be transferred to a single purchaser. This regulation resulted in a number of ballots for 'split transfers' to two new landlords. In England and Wales, the transfer of more than 500 homes to a single purchaser over a five-year period requires the consent of the Secretary of State. The New Labour government has relaxed the transfer limit and indicated that it regards 12,000 to be a reasonable maximum in most cases. There is no such limit in Wales. Consent is required for any property disposal in Scotland. The respective central authorities publish guidelines that explain the basis upon which consent will be granted.

As we have said throughout this book, present capital decisions invariably produce future revenue consequences. One of the revenue consequences of LSVT has been that conversions produced differentiated rents that are felt to be unfair to new tenants. As part of the transfer agreement, time limited rent guarantees were usually given to existing tenants, typically for a five-year period after LSVT. To cover the costs of this internal, short-term rent control measure, new tenants on the estate have often been required to pay relatively higher rent charges than they would have done had the guarantee not been made.[44] As we have argued (Chapter 2), along with efficiency, effectiveness and experience, equity is a key element in any value-for-money calculation, and the distributional consequences of policy decisions must always be addressed.[45]

The main purpose of a transfer is to benefit local authority tenants, but it should be remembered that leaseholders will also have a proprietary interest in the proposed deal. Many estates have a number of leaseholders or owner-occupiers who bought their homes under the right-to-buy. Although there is no statutory duty to consult leaseholders or owners before a transfer can progress, good practice requires that they be informed and be given information about how the proposals will affect their financial interests, for example, the expected effects on future service charge levels.

The case for housing transfer does not rest solely on financial advantage. It provides an opportunity to create new types of provider and to engage smaller bodies that are based in, or closer to, the communities where the homes are transferred. Transfer can help to improve the diversity of housing management. It also helps to separate out local authorities' strategic responsibilities from their landlord functions.

---

44 The rent differential actually pays for more than the rent guarantee. It is generally needed to help fund the promised improvements. It also feeds back into the public purse as a higher capital receipt for the local authority and Treasury because the transfer valuations are partly based on income/expenditure flows.

45 The 'equity' debate might be said to be more complicated than this. The strategy might need to take account of the interests of council tenants who have had to suffer substandard conditions or would-be tenants who have been denied access to decent quality housing because of the council's inability to repair, improve or build new.

The 2000 Green Paper states that, in England and Wales, the government will support the transfer of up to 200,000 dwellings each year. If local authorities submit transfer proposals at that level, and if tenants support them, RSLs will become the majority providers of social housing from 2004 onwards.

It must be remembered that LSVT does not absolve an authority from the need to develop a local housing strategy and it is therefore important that, if LSVT is the preferred option, proper consideration is given to how the decision will affect the authority's continuing strategic role in the period after transfer.[46] It may not always be sensible to transfer all of an authority's stock to one or more RSL. Often, the transfer of part of the stock will be the best option, at least initially. Where a council wishes to retain a significant measure of control, or chart a different course from RSLs in the area, they may prefer the transfer to be made to a local housing company. Company structures are now generally chosen because they offer more flexibility than industrial provident society structures (see below for more details on local housing companies).

The 2000 Green Paper points to the need to 'modernise' the stock transfer programme so that it can more adequately contribute to the government's wider objectives of providing choice and tackling social exclusion. It is proposed that in future the following criteria be given added emphasis.

- Transfers should be seen to aid community regeneration. This means that the receiving RSL should work closely with other key local players in forging and implementing plans for regeneration.
- The transfer should be regarded as part of a strategic approach to tackling changes in housing need and demand. This means that the local authority should develop a strategy and business plan for the new landlord to cope with the changing market.
- Competition and tenant involvement within the transfer process should be encouraged. This means that the government does not favour a single RSL being identified as the only route to transfer. There should be ample scope for RSLs to bid against each other for the chance to acquire and manage particular authorities' stock.
- The transfer should result in better services for tenants. This means that transfer proposals should demonstrate the improvements over the long-term in the services that will be available to tenants.
- Transfer should not substitute one large-scale 'monolithic' landlord with another. This is why the transfer guidelines limit the number of dwellings that can normally be transferred to one new landlord. The principle should be that a social landlord is big enough to be able to afford good quality staff but flexible enough to be responsive to local needs.

---

46 A more detailed critique of the operation of LSVT under recent rules can be found in the CIH report on the future funding of council housing (CIH, October 1998, paras. 317-325).

Stamp duty

New stamp duty reliefs are being introduced for transfers and leases of land and buildings to RSLs. Many such landlords are charities and benefit from the general stamp duty relief for charities. New concessions are being introduced that will also exempt the following.

- All transfers to resident-controlled RSLs from whatever source.
- Transfers between RSLs
- Transfers to RSLs from local authorities and Housing Action Trusts.
- Acquisitions by RSLs that are assisted by public subsidy (including Social Housing Grant).

The valuations question

Both the policy of stock transfer and the increasing use of fixed assets as collateral for private sector loans, has brought to the fore the tricky question of how to put an appropriate value on units of social housing. (This question is addressed more fully in Chapter 9). Transfer valuations are particularly sensitive to the cost of dealing with any catch-up repairs and future repairs. This is especially true of ageing estates in which the units were built at the same time and where building elements, such as windows, roofs, etc., may need renewing or repairing *en bloc* or over a short period. The transfer valuation also needs to confront the issue about whether particular sorts of work are to be treated as 'repairs' (the costs of which are usually offset against the price), or 'improvements' (the costs of which would normally be met by rent increases). Valuing non-traditional buildings can be particularly problematic because some necessary works might not be regarded as repairs in the usual sense (putting the building back to its original condition), but rather as correcting basic design flaws.

The transfer deal will need to take account of any shortfall between the value of the stock and the outstanding debt on the properties. The government allows the transfer of council housing that does not generate a capital receipt or where the receipt does not fully meet outstanding debt. Transfers were restricted solely to authorities where the price received cleared the outstanding debt until the principle of residual debt funding had been accepted. This was initially operated through the Estate Renewal Challenge Fund (see above). In cases of partial (rather than whole stock) transfer, the government has been prepared to make continuing subsidy payments to authorities to help them repay residual debt. The DETR and the Scottish Executive have both now indicated that they will meet the costs of outstanding debt left after whole stock transfers, where they are not covered by capital receipt.

Local housing companies (LHCs)

Local authorities are already encouraged to separate their strategic role from day-to-day management of stock. One way to achieve this would be to set up a company, controlled or influenced by the authority itself, to manage their housing. A local housing company is a form of not-for-profit social landlord established by the Housing Act 1996. LHCs are independent organisations that are normally created by local authorities to purchase and manage council housing. Such companies have to be genuinely private sector organisations, that is, less than 50 per cent local authority ownership, to avoid breaching the current Treasury public spending rules.[47] The housing company principle is that of 'continuing local authority influence without domination'. Council nominees or tenants can form up to 49 per cent of shareholders or board members, and organisations registered with the Housing Corporation or the National Assembly for Wales are deemed to have passed tests designed to ensure that they are free of 'dominant influence' by councils.

LHCs are able to repair, improve and renew the housing stock by raising capital resources unavailable to local authorities.[48] As well as taking over the traditional landlord role of the authority, they can also play a part in wider urban regeneration initiatives, either directly or in association with others. Housing companies need not restrict their activities to stock transfers; they can be involved in the building of new homes. Furthermore, they can be involved with dwellings other than those designated as 'social housing'. This makes them flexible vehicles for pursuing local housing policies.[49] An authority may decide that the interests of tenants and local taxpayers are best served by transferring parts of their stock to an LHC so they can concentrate their limited resources on managing and up-grading the retained units. In any event, a LHC transfer requires the majority support of councillors and a majority vote by tenants in a formal ballot. Part of the strategy might involve allowing properties becoming vacant to be 'trickle transferred' to the new landlord. Whatever decisions are made, they should be in line with the authority's wider corporate strategy and have the consent of those whose interests will be affected.

LHCs can be constituted as industrial and provident societies, companies limited by guarantee, or companies limited by shares. The Chartered Institute of Housing expects the company limited by guarantee to become the standard model. All transferred tenancies become assured with fewer statutory rights than council (secure) tenants. Although the RSL provisions of the 1996 Act do not apply in

---

47 Despite intensive lobbying by housing pressure groups, the Comprehensive Spending Review (July 1998), confirmed that these rules were to be maintained so that the spending of arm's length local housing companies still count as public expenditure unless the company is under the control of a RSL.

48 Local housing companies were seen by the Conservatives as another mechanism for levering investment from private sources into social housing and they were encouraged as another form of privatisation. Under Labour, the debate about their function has shifted somewhat. Because they have a significant level of councillor involvement, they are seen by some as a way of maintaining local authority influence over the management of the stock, and also of providing assurance of continuing social accountability to tenants. This has proved to be particularly important in Scotland and Wales where traditionally there has been a stronger loyalty among council tenants to the philosophy of council housing.

49 Although housing associations have similar powers, some councils will be more comfortable sponsoring a new LHC than a new housing association.

Scotland, significant Scottish stock transfers have taken place from local authorities, new towns and from Scottish Homes.[50] The New Housing Partnerships in Scotland recognises the possibility of transfer to a non-HA organisation but requires the organisation to opt for contractual regulation by Scottish Homes.

Existing registered housing associations may wish, or be encouraged, to convert to LHC status in order to change their constitutions to allow 'constituencies' such as tenants, community organisations, lenders and local authorities to have structured rights to representation. It is these aspects rather than any different powers of action of LHCs that have caused some councils to favour them over housing associations. Tenants can become shareholders of an LHC and will be represented on the board. Lenders might also have a place on the board. The local authority can also be a shareholder with the power to appoint board members. A possible membership structure might result in the tenants and the authority each appointing a third of the members, with the remaining one third membership being offered to lenders, housing associations or community groups.

Structure of post-transfer landlords
Whatever form of transfer is adopted, it will provide an opportunity to review the authority's whole approach to housing provision and to create a new structure within which to pursue its corporate strategy. The complex nature of local housing needs and plans, particularly the practical problems surrounding refurbishment and regeneration programmes, has meant that using group structures as part of an LHC strategy is proving to be attractive to many authorities. A group structure enhances a partnership approach by ensuring that one megalithic landlord, the local authority, is not simply replaced by another, the company. A group structure exists when one dominant organisation, referred to as the 'parent', sets the policy direction but works with a number of other organisations, referred to as 'subsidiaries', in delivering the service. Under these arrangements, the parent association or company will have a controlling share at membership level. The parent will also have the right to appoint and remove board members, though the exercise of these rights will be regulated by a procedure agreement that only allows the parent organisation to alter the membership in specified circumstances. Since 1997 Housing Corporation rules have been made more flexible so that parents no longer have to have full legal responsibility for the activities of their subsidiaries. This makes it easier for different types of organisation (e.g. charitable and non-charitable) to work together. National Assembly for Wales group structures policy is tighter than that of the Housing Corporation in that it still requires all members of a group to be RSLs registered with them.

---

50   However, to date, there has been only one whole stock transfer from a council. Although the RSL provisions of the Housing Act 1996 do not apply in Scotland, Scottish councils can consider the following options: (1) local housing companies incorporated under the Companies Acts; (2) joint venture developments with a private developer or housing association; (3) transfer of stock and/or land to an existing housing association or specially constituted subsidiary; a new housing association; or the private finance initiative. For a discussion of these options see Philip Sim, 'Highland Games', *Inside Housing*, September 1997, p27.

The parent organisation might be an already established association that then 'leads' a group of subsidiary LHCs and associations. This model can be particularly effective with smaller estate-based transfers. Small transfers into a LHC can be given added feasibility if a group arrangement produces economies of scale in the form of lower overheads. Research shows that forming an LHC as a subsidiary of an established housing association can make it easier to attract private finance and may lead to significant savings in interest costs (Halifax *Local Housing Companies Newsletter* No.2, Spring, 1997). An established housing association's track record and financial strength can be used to maximise access to essential sources of private finance. Asset pooling can allow housing associations to transfer their assets in a particular local authority area to a new community-controlled housing company in exchange for participation in the new body. Loans raised on the unencumbered assets could help to support the refurbishment of the transferred homes. Experience already shows that the strength of a group structure can make it easier to arrange borrowing and on-lending deals with lower costs and less restrictive loan covenants, and that this can bring advantages both to the new company and to established associations that become associated with it.[51]

Group structures are also being looked to by some authorities as a vehicle for larger whole-stock transfers. They are seen as being more attractive than conventional LSVT schemes partly because they involve a variety of agencies and partly because they allow the authority to maintain some direct influence over the future management of the transferred stock.[52]

In cases where authorities have secured substantial funding to deliver non-HRA as well as housing outputs (e.g. through the SRB), a group structure is likely to be a more effective way of managing the complexities of the mixed programme than centring control on a single stand-alone housing association or LHC.

These are still early days for experiments of this kind and there is to date only a limited experience of how they work. It has to be recognised that multi-agency working will inevitably bring with it new risks and added management problems. A successful arrangement will rely on the creation of jointly understood and jointly shared objectives that are built into a coherent business plan. It will also require the joint aspirations to be set into specific legal agreements and warranties that make it clear how the various subsidiaries are to be held responsible for each other's liabilities and how non-performing partners are to be dealt with.

Both LSVT and local housing companies involve a weakening of local accountability to the elected authority and for this reason, some commentators have argued the case for the Treasury rule to be relaxed so that local authorities

---

51 See, for example, article by Peter Lewis, Chief Executive of the Anglia Housing Association Group in *Inside Housing*, 20 September 1996, p26.
52 In the proposal for the transfer of Glasgow's stock, the 'group' is effectively one large landlord with a range of community-based service management boards.

themselves can directly invest borrowed funds in their stock of rented housing.[53] Indeed, some funders have indicated that they would prefer to lend to a local authority than to a private landlord (*Inside Housing,* 19 September 1997, p20), and if this can be shown to be a common reaction then local housing corporations, rather than companies, may prove to be a future way forward.

Local housing corporations and quasi-corporations

Local housing corporations (LHCos), are an idea that has been put forward by the Chartered Institute of Housing and described in the report *Challenging the Conventions* (Coopers *et al.*, 1995). The creation of a LHCo involves a transfer process similar to that in LSVT, including the mechanics of negotiating a transfer price and raising funds. The idea is to establish an organisation that would be local authority majority owned and controlled but with a separate legal identity, probably a registered company. LHCos could have a locally determined mix of councillors, tenants and independent board members.

In recent years consideration has also been given to the possibility of allowing local authorities to set up *housing quasi-corporations*. This option would allow for future ownership and investment in council housing by means of the local authority establishing a 'quasi corporation' as part of its own structure, but ring-fencing both capital and revenue expenditure and delegating management of the stock to a special board. Such an arrangement would allow the authority to manage its stock of housing at 'arms length' from the political agendas of the elected members.

For several years now the Chartered Institute of Housing has argued the case for the creation of some form of 'corporation' mechanism; but the Institute makes the point that the spending of such corporations should not be subject to the same rigid rules as apply to local authorities. They argue that disengaging long-term housing investment decisions from the short-term financial constraints of public expenditure control would give councils more scope to develop sustainable investment strategies by allowing them to invest directly in the improvement and expansion of their housing stock. This means that the development of such 'arm's length' local authority controlled 'corporations' will require a switch to the General Government Financial Deficit system of public expenditure control (as discussed in Chapter 5).[54]

---

53 In particular, see John Hawksworth and Steve Wilcox, *Challenging The Conventions: Public Borrowing Rules and Housing Investment*, Chartered Institute of Housing and Coopers and Lybrand, 1995. See also, Nicola Carroll's interview with John Perry, 'You Want a Revolution?', *Public Service and Local Government*, March 1996, p31.

54 As the Institute's 1998 report makes clear (*Council Housing – Financing the Future*), under present rules, there would be no financial advantage to this sort of arrangement as the borrowing of a LHCo would still count as public expenditure as defined by the Treasury's financing rule discussed in Chapter 5. For LHCos to play a significant role in the social housing system, there would have to be more emphasis placed on the GGFD measure of public spending (refer to Chapter 5). However, announcements made subsequent to the publication of the Comprehensive Spending Review (1998), make it clear that this approach to public sector investment has been rejected by the government for the time being. However, the ideas were revived in the 2000 Green Paper.

Along with other practitioners, the CIH see local housing corporations as a sensible mechanism for ensuring that, in the longer period, councils will be able to borrow adequate sums from the private sector to invest in their own housing stock. This ability is seen to be particularly important since the scrapping of the ERCF. It is further argued that the ability to raise money outside of the public expenditure control limit will become crucial in the period after 2002 when the capital receipts released as part of the Comprehensive Spending Review will have been utilised. Local corporations are seen as a possible way to tackle the backlog of council house repairs over the long period.

The government sees some potential for arm's length housing corporations helping to clarify the 'somewhat confused' distinction between the landlord and strategic roles of authorities. With this in mind consideration is currently being given to the establishment of pilot projects to test the viability of such arrangements. The idea was highlighted in the 2000 Green Paper (paras. 7.39-41).

11. New style partnerships: the Private Finance Initiative

The present Labour government has made it clear that it believes that *'to maximise investment in the renewal of our infrastructure, the public and private sectors must work together in a more modern and effective partnership'*. (Chancellor's statement on the EFSR, HM Treasury News Release 96/98, June 1998). On the face of it, this appears to be a continuation of the previous government's 'mixed funding' approach to public investment. As we have seen above, the Conservative administrations of the 1980s and 1990s established the practice of *Public-Private Partnerships*. Public-Private Partnerships (PPPs) encapsulate the principle of introducing private capital and expertise into the provision of infrastructure and public services. In the fields of housing, economic development and transport, joint ventures and partnerships had made a considerable impact by the time the New Labour government came to power. By that time, recent private investments had contributed something in the order of £10 billion to housing programmes and £6 billion to urban regeneration schemes. However, since the general election of 1997 it is possible to detect a change of emphasis on the expected nature of the private/public funding relationship.

> *'So this government will apply a public interest test. What is the best means, whether through private or public investment, of securing the highest levels of investment in Britain's future and so ensuring the best public services. Not demanding private ownership as a matter of dogma when it does not serve the public interest, nor maintaining State ownership when private and public partnership is the best way of advancing the public interest.'* (Chancellor's statement, June, 1998, ibid)

The present Chancellor has made it clear that the government believes that in the past, what is termed the 'Private Finance Initiative' (PFI), was not so much an effective inter-sectoral partnership as an ideological commitment to substitute private investment for public investment and thus an 'excuse for abdicating responsibility' by the State. In future, large local authority development contracts will not have to be 'PFI tested' prior to making a decision. The argument here is that straightforward substitution will not in itself produce efficiency and effectiveness gains – *true partnership involves a working together to produce a result that could not have been achieved by either party working apart.*

The Private Finance Initiative and the 4Ps

The Private Finance Initiative (PFI), is a scheme designed to encourage the private sector to finance, build and maintain the public services. It is a form of partnership arrangement that matches public need with private provision. Its proponents claim that it offers an effective and efficient way of paying for service expansion without contravening Treasury rules. It is also seen as a way of introducing private sector management skills into the public sector. Its appeal is likely to be maintained so long as control arrangements exist in which the PSNB/PSBR is the main public expenditure test.[55]

In April 1996, the local authority associations set up their own dedicated unit, the *Public Private Partnerships Programme* (the 4 Ps), to guide and assist local authorities to develop PFI projects and similar partnership initiatives. In the area of housing, projects might include the building or improving of dwellings, or their management and maintenance, or any combination of these.

In November 1997 the Treasury published a new guide to the Private Finance Initiative, *Partnerships for Prosperity,* that underlined the continuing importance of the PFI as a mechanism through which PPPs can secure improved value for money for the public sector. It was clear from the start that the present government, like its Conservative predecessor, is keen to support arrangements that produce investment in the nation's infrastructure without imposing extensive immediate charges on the public purse. Where credit approvals have been cut, such an arrangement allows for investment in public sector built assets that would otherwise not take place. From the public authority's point of view PFI provides a 'buy now – pay later' deal. From the private company's point of view, the arrangement provides a relatively low risk, long-term investment. Under PFI arrangements private firms bid for a contract not only to build roads, fire stations, hospitals, etc., but also to maintain them for an extended period (e.g. 30 years).

There is no one 'standard' approach to setting up a PFI agreement, but what might be termed the 'classic' model[56] has the following features:

---

55 The PFI was introduced by the Conservatives in 1992 and hailed by commentators at the time as a policy change that might prove to be even more radically transforming than privatisation. Prisons, hospitals, motorways, government computers, school buildings, and an extension to the Channel rail network are being financed through the PFI. There has even been talk of private companies leasing back tanks, aircraft and warships to the Ministry of Defence under PFI. On its election, the new Labour government appointed the Paymaster General as minister responsible for developing PFI.

56 The idea of a 'classic' model is taken from an excellent summary of the different approaches open to housing authorities published by Paul Buckland in *Public Finance*, 4-10 June 1999.

- The authority retains a long run legal proprietary interest in the land (refer to Chapter 1 for discussion on the nature and scope of proprietary interests).
- The authority retains a degree of managerial control over the assets by establishing a performance-related payments mechanism.
- Commercial risk and general managerial responsibility is passed to the private partner.
- There is limited (or no) capital resource funding from the authority or the public sector.

The 'classic' model might be modified by granting a lease to the private partner whereby the authority retains a long-run legal proprietary interest in the built assets themselves, that is, as well as the land. Under this kind of PFI agreement the freehold remains with the authority so that the assets are returned at the end of the lease, or before if the contractual conditions are broken by the private sector organisation.

It should be noted that PFI arrangements can be quite flexible and there is nothing to prevent a legal interest in the land, as well as the assets, being passed to the private sector organisation. Such an arrangement would be called a 'property PFI'. However, this is not a typical arrangement and many current PFI arrangements lease back the assets to the commissioning public body who provides concessionary agreements to the company, including paying for the service in instalments (usually in the form of an index-linked annual charge). This kind of contract is referred to in the regulations as a 'private finance transaction', but is popularly called a contract to 'design, build, finance and operate' (DBFO). Once elected, the Labour government began to give consideration to how the PFI might be extended to include council housing.

PFI and the long-run management of the stock
Public-private partnerships can be used radically to restructure the process of social housing management. One clear way of using PPP/PFI would to transfer the stock to a new owner under some form of LSVT arrangement (refer above). However, PFI is flexible enough to offer the authority a range of strategic options. Although stock transfers usually involve the passing of full ownership and responsibility to the private sector, as mentioned above, this need not be the case. In PPP/PFI schemes the property interests can be treated in a variety of ways. The authority could choose to retain ownership of the stock and remain the legal landlord whilst delegating responsibility for maintenance, repairs and refurbishments to the private sector. Under such an arrangement the delegation might be extended to include the housing management functions. In such a case the authority would make regular payments to the private partner, the amount of which could be dependent upon how well they perform these functions during the contract period. As well as allowing the private organisation to cover its revenue costs during the contract period, the capitalised value of these payments allows

the private organisation to recoup any investment it makes in repairing and improving the stock. The payments would typically be funded from the rental flow, together with any top-up funding the government may provide to support PFI projects.

Under normal (non-PFI) stock transfer arrangements an obvious difficulty arises because of a perceived mismatch of interests. Housing that is in a prime location and in good condition is likely to be of interest to registered social landlords and their private sector funders because both the assets and the land upon which they are sited will provide sound collateral. They are also attractive because they will be in demand from potential tenants and will be relatively easy to let and manage. In sharp contrast, private sector partners will be far less interested in acquiring run-down housing units in unpopular districts or deprived areas with above average unemployment and/or crime rates. It is, of course, just this kind of stock that would most benefit from a transfer of ownership. In such circumstances, a PFI arrangement may well help ease the transfer. Because PFI deals focus on the income generation rather than asset transfers, the value of the underlying land becomes less of an issue for the private party to the contract. This is not to say that the quality of the stock or the nature of the neighbourhood is of no concern to the private parties, but rather that such factors are of less concern than the reliability and value of the income streams that are due to be paid over the period of the contract. As a result, commentators point out that PFI/PPP is likely to be a valuable tool in the regeneration of some of the hitherto most problematic neighbourhoods, and sits comfortably with the New Deal For Communities initiative and the objectives of the government's Social Exclusion Unit. (Buckland, 1999, p23).

Barriers to PFI

Contract complexities:

PFI contracts have proved to be complex to arrange because there are no standard forms and they have normally involved an enormous number of clauses. The complexity is a reflection of the need to satisfy a range of public and private interests that are embedded in the design, build, management, and financing of a project. This balance of interests may have to be robust enough to last for several decades. The costs associated with bidding for such a contract is often several times higher than bidding for more conventional contracts. The Conservative government expected that over £14 billion of investment in PFI projects would be raised by 2000, but this has not been achieved as in practice a number of contractors have withdrawn from bidding because of the costs and complexities of the tendering process.

The ultra vires problem:

Initially, the legal capacity of local authorities (and other public bodies such as hospital trusts) to enter into workable long-term PFI contracts was far from clear. Some funders were reluctant to support proposed PFI projects because of legal uncertainties about the status of local authorities and other public bodies with respect to ventures that involve commercial, 'profit-making' activities. Banks and other financial institutions require assurance that local authorities can commit to, and be responsible for, contracts into which they enter. Legal uncertainty is the enemy of commercial enterprise, and PFI projects need to be founded on clear local authority powers. All parties need to be confident about the extent of the local authority's powers to enter into contracts. They also need to be clear about what will happen in the event of a legal challenge, and the extent to which contractors can be compensated.

The problem of capital control:
Public sector investment is part of Total Managed Expenditure (refer to Chapter 5) and is therefore subject to control by central government. This meant that, from the start, the PFI posed questions about whether or not this kind of joint investment contravened the Capital Finance Regulations. There was particular concern about how the PFI might legitimately become involved with council housing projects.

The revenue support problem:
Although the Capital Finance Regulations now permit the use of PFI in the refurbishment of council housing, there has been no general access to the government support needed to help pay for PFI charges. The problem stems from the Local Authorities (Capital Finance) Regulations 1997 that govern authorities' ability to access revenue funding (so-called 'PFI credits') from central government. Eligibility for such credits has been determined by the nature of the PFI contract that has to fall within the statutory definition of a 'Private Finance Transaction' (Regulation 16), and also achieve a statutory degree of risk transfer to the private sector partner (Regulation 40). By prescribing the nature of revenue-supported PFI contracts, these regulations have had the effect of inhibiting a number of potentially successful housing PFI deals. In addition, the regulations have excluded from the definition the construction of a new dwelling on HRA land. Indeed, the ring-fenced nature of the HRA has prevented authorities giving revenue support to private partners engaged in council housing stock management. As a result of such restrictions, only refurbishment and energy conservation projects have been legally eligible for PFI credits. These problems have now been addressed and the regulations are being amended so that PFI deals can reflect commercial realities and commercial practices. The new, more flexible, approach was outlined in the 1999 4Ps report *PFI and Social Housing: the Potential for Increasing Private Sector Investment*.

Differential interests:
There is a concern that the sorts of returns (the social returns) that the public sector is interested in do not coincide with the sorts of returns (commercial returns) that interest the private sector. Furthermore, there is evidence that contractors are more interested in projects that on completion guarantee a future stream of revenue through user charges (such as transport projects) than projects that rely on the costs in use being covered by revenue transfers from the public purse.

Overcoming the barriers:

In May 1997, the Paymaster General announced that Malcolm Bates, Chairman of Pearl Group, would review how the PFI was working. The Review reported in June 1997. It recommended that public sector structures be simplified and responsibilities be clarified. A Treasury Taskforce was set up to explore how these recommendations might be implemented. A new procedure aimed at streamlining the approval of local authority PFI projects has now been established.

Since the Review a succession of measures have been introduced, including a clearer and simpler framework within which to develop DBFO arrangements for virtually the full range of local services. A variety of partnership approaches can now be adopted by local authorities. Typically, the PFI provider will be a separate legal entity, and in many PFI arrangements, a Special Purpose Vehicle (SPV) has been set up as the PFI provider.

The capital control confusion has been eased by new regulations that make it clear that, given sufficient risk transfer, the PFI investment in the project will not score against an authority's capital spending limits.[57] The risks taken on by the PFI provider typically include time over-runs on building works, accommodating financing and other cost increases, and penalties for poor performance against the specification. The '4Ps', the body set up by the Local Government Association to promote public private partnerships in local government, now provides detailed guidance and helps develop 'pathfinder' projects with authorities. It also disseminates case studies to encourage successful approaches to be replicated elsewhere. In addition, the Central-Local Partnership Meeting has been established, bringing together Cabinet Ministers and senior local government leaders to discuss major issues affecting local government.

The *ultra vires* question has been addressed by the Local Government (Contracts) Act 1998. This legislation confirms and clarifies the powers of local authorities to enter into long-term contracts for the provision of assets and services; provides a certification procedure to establish a contract's enforceability; and provides for compensation to be paid if a contract is nevertheless rendered void by the courts. This legislation gives authorities and prospective private sector partners and financiers some of the legal reassurances they were looking for. Experience may show that further legislation will be required to clarify the position of local authorities with respect to their contractual obligations if PFI is to play a major role in social investment in the future.

---

57 In particular, there was initial confusion about the how the credit cover regulations (refer to Chapter 7) operated in the context of PFI arrangements. To overcome this, the regulations have been amended so that authorities entering into long-term contracts for the provision of non-HRA assets and related services are now not required to find credit cover at the time of contract signature, provided the contract meets the required standards of risk transfer to the private sector by satisfying the *contract structure test*.

The *revenue support* issue is particularly relevant to the question of whether or not it is appropriate to extend PFI to council housing projects. In their report *PFI and Social Housing – the potential for increasing private sector investment* (Public Private Partnership Programme, 1999) the '4Ps', put forward various models for both new provision and the refurbishment of existing social housing, and they outline the circumstances under which they might generate value for money for the public sector. The CIH and Graham Moody Associates have also explored a number of approaches to incorporating PFI into council housing provision and management in their report *Council Housing – Financing the Future* (CIH, 1998).

Approval has now been given for eight English 'pathfinder' PFI projects for refurbishment of council housing in Leeds, Manchester, N.E. Derbyshire, Sandwell, Reading and the London Boroughs of Camden, Islington, and Newham. Progress towards the more general availability of revenue payments towards PFI schemes is expected to depend on the outcome of these pilot projects.

The issue of *differential interests* brings to the fore the question of whether PFI provide *value-for-money* for the commissioning agency. There is a live debate surrounding the question about whether or not PFI projects represent value-for-money to the taxpayer. There is a clear potential conflict of financial interests between the desire of the public service provider to make reasonably low level payments over a long period, and the desire of the commercial contractor to receive a reasonably high and speedy return on its investment. This mismatch of financial interests is likely to be an issue in all PFI projects. What counts as value-for-money to the service provider crucially depends on the time frame being considered (refer to Figure 15.1). Over the long period, most PFI projects tend to be more expensive than publicly funded equivalents because commercial firms cannot normally raise finance as cheaply as the Treasury. This additional expense can be thought of as the 'cost' to the public sector of (1) acquiring up front private capital finance without adding to the PSBR, and (2) acquiring private sector management expertise in managing the asset over a large part of its physical life. A cost-benefit assessment of a PFI proposal involves the use of a *public service comparator* – a figure for how much the project would have cost in the long-run if it had been funded by government rather than the private sector. Critics of PFI make the point that it would be unnecessary if we moved towards the European model of public expenditure control, based on the GGFD. The argument here is that the PSBR approach fails to make a proper distinction between expenditure on consumption, expenditure on capital infrastructure projects and capital utilised commercially in public sector trading activities in which some commercial investment return can be expected.

Summary

Following the government's Comprehensive Spending Review there is now an expectation that every authority will need to demonstrate that it has a coherent investment strategy for meeting the housing needs and demands in its area. This involves setting out, as part of its housing investment programme, an annual plan that is clearly tied to longer-term strategic objectives.

In this chapter we have identified a number of themes and issues that would need to be considered in developing a housing investment strategy. It should be noted that we have not included any discussion on how an authority might develop a strategy for encouraging home-ownership. This issue is considered in Chapter 6.

Further reading

DETR/Social Security, *Quality and Choice: A Decent Home for All*, The Housing Green Paper, April 2000.

Readers wishing to explore how the shift towards a strategic role for local authorities is likely to impact in Scotland should look at The Housing Green Paper *Investing in Modernisation – An Agenda for Scotland's Housing*, February 1999.

Sue Goss and Bob Blackaby, *Designing Local Housing Strategies – A Good Practice Guide*, CIH/LGA, 1998.

Graham Moody Associates, *Council Housing – Financing the Future*, CIH, 1998.

Coopers and Lybrand, *Consensus for Change – Public Borrowing Rules, Housing Investment and the City*, CIH, 1996.

Jeff Zitron, *Local Housing Companies – A Good Practice Guide*, CIH, 1995.

Brendan Nevin, *Local Housing Companies – Progress and Problems*, CIH/JRF, 1999.

Keith Anderson, *Funding Local Authority Stock Transfers (Scotland)*, CIH, 1997.

Derek Joseph and Rachel Terry, *Private Finance – Initiatives for Affordable Housing*, CIH, 1997.

HACAS and Trowers and Hamlins, *New Structures for Council Housing?* CIH/LGA, 1999.

CHAPTER 11:
Local government revenue finance

The concept of revenue

As explained elsewhere (Chapter 2), the conceptual distinction made by financiers between capital and revenue mirrors the distinction made by economists between production (development) and consumption (use). Once a capital asset has been acquired, constructed, or improved, capital expenditure ceases; but of course the need to expend money on it does not. As we move from the production to the consumption phase of the asset's life, we are confronted with the financial problem of meeting the 'costs-in-use'. These day-to-day running costs constitute *revenue expenditure*. Revenue expenditure has to be met out of *revenue income*. As we will see, revenue expenditure and income are accounted for separately from capital finance.

Revenue expenditure

Where the asset's acquisition or construction was financed by means of a loan, the subsequent need to service that loan (pay interest and repay the principal) creates an obvious cost-in-use.[1] The financing costs of borrowing are classed as 'revenue expenditure'. In most cases, this expenditure is supported by government revenue grants. Almost all such support comes from two grants: these are the *Housing Revenue Account (HRA) subsidy* for borrowing to finance spending on council housing (*Housing Support Grant – HSG* in Scotland), and the *Revenue Support Grant (RSG)* for other borrowing. Loan service charges are, however, just one of many revenue expenses that have to be paid by local authorities. In the local government setting, physical assets are acquired in order to provide some kind of service to local people. This provision imposes a wide range of costs-in-use that include such things as staff salaries, office stationery, fire insurance, and building maintenance. These revenue expenses have to be met to keep the services running efficiently and effectively.

---

1   Debt servicing creates a charge against revenue that is variously referred to as a 'debt charge', a 'loan charge', or a 'capital financing charge'. It can also be referred to as an 'item 8 debit'. These regular charge payments will include an element of interest and an element of principal repayment. Over the life or 'term' of the loan, these payments will gradually diminish and eventually write off or 'amortise' the debt.

In practice, the distinction between capital and revenue is fuzzier than it is in theory: in particular, as we saw in the last two chapters, local housing authorities often use 'revenue' funds on 'capital' projects. However, local authorities are not normally permitted to sell assets and use the capital receipts to finance revenue activities; nor are they allowed to pay for revenue spending by establishing long-term debt.

Gross and net revenue expenditure

Revenue expenditure can be expressed as a gross or as a net figure. Gross expenditure measures the running costs of the service without taking any account of inward flows from such things as rental income, charges for the use of community facilities (such as swimming pools, function rooms, etc.), any fee income earned, and service specific grants received. Net expenditure is gross expenditure minus these receipts. When an authority sets its annual budget and the council tax, it will be concerned with the level of net expenditure because it is this that represents the financial gap that has to be filled by local taxation. Net expenditure is also the common yardstick for comparing spending on different services within an authority and for comparing spending on the same services by different authorities. However, it must be remembered that it is the gross level of spending that measures the total financial cost of providing the service. For the HRA the budgeted net expenditure must be no greater than zero, i.e. the account has to be at least in balance at the year end.

Revenue income

Potentially, revenue costs can be financed by a mixture of the following:

- Local taxation (national non-domestic rate plus council tax).
- Revenue support (RSG, HRA subsidy, service-specific revenue grants).
- Rents for council housing and associated properties such as lock-up garages and estate shops (that go into the HRA).
- Rents from other properties (that go into the General Fund).
- Income received from council mortgages (granted for RTB purchases).
- Interest earned from the investment of capital receipts.
- Fees and charges for council services.

General Revenue Support

Before turning to the specific question of housing revenue finance, we need to say something about how the central authorities provide general revenue support to local authorities. What follows is a simplified overview and largely uses the English arrangements by way of illustration. Although the detailed control and support mechanisms vary somewhat in different parts of the UK (particularly since devolution) the general support principles are UK-wide.[2]

Revenue support represents central government's contribution to council finance and is designed to ensure that the whole cost of local services does not fall on local taxpayers. It also ensures that the level of tax does not vary across the country simply because of differences in the needs and resources of individual local authorities.

Local taxation

In line with the 'local responsibility' principle mentioned at the start of Chapter 8, a significant part of the income of local authorities is raised in the form of local taxation. Two distinct types of 'rate' are levied locally: the business rate and the domestic rate. The business rate is variously referred to as the 'uniform business rate', the 'national non-domestic rate' or the 'non-domestic rate'. We will refer to it as the *non-domestic rate* (NDR). The domestic rate is referred to as the *council tax*.

Non-domestic rates

The non-domestic rate (NDR) is the council's share of the money paid into the nation-wide business rating pool by shops, offices and factories. It constitutes a levy on local businesses based on a national rate in the pound set by the government multiplied by a notional value of the premises they occupy referred to as the 'rateable value'.[3] These rates are the means by which local businesses contribute to the cost of providing local authority services.

The NDR is a nationalised system that is intended to be fair to businesses by exposing them to even-handed treatment wherever they happen to operate

---

2   Devolution means, for example, that in Scotland there are two tiers of democratically elected government. Local government now has to work with a Parliament that has general responsibility for all aspects of local government, including finance. This means that since the 2000/1 local government finance settlement the two tiers have to agree spending priorities. The Scottish Parliament is empowered to scrutinise and approve the Executive's overall proposals for support of local government spending. In Wales the Settlement is now operated through the Assembly, rather than the Secretary of State. The Assembly has limited discretionary powers to influence local authority spending plans. The method of allocations however has not, to date, much changed. Indeed, in its first three years, the Assembly will be tightly bound to a spending plan determined by the government's Comprehensive Spending Review.

3   Every five years all business properties are revalued: the last such revaluation was in 1995. The City of London is treated differently from other local authorities because its working population is so much greater than its residential population. The City can set its own non-domestic rate poundage, and can keep some of its rate income by offsetting a prescribed amount against its collection to the central pool. So far the City has always set its poundage in line with the national poundage.

nationally.[4] Before the start of each financial year, the Secretary of State estimates the amount in the pool that will be available to distribute to local authorities. This is called the *distributable amount* and once fixed, is shared out amongst all local authorities according to the number of residents in each local authority area.[5]

In addition, along with the Revenue Support Grant arrangements, the NDR system provides a degree of resource equalisation. Given the uneven distribution of rateable assets across the country, without this equalisation, councils would have to set widely different local tax levels in order to provide a similar level of service.

Most business rates are collected by 'billing authorities'[6] in line with national criteria. The centrally pooled funds are then redistributed back to the local authorities and police authorities on what is deemed to be an equitable basis that takes particular account of population sizes.[7] Once authorities receive notification of their NDR resources, they have to determine what they will need to levy from domestic ratepayers in the form of *council tax* to balance the budget for the year.

Council tax

The council tax is levied on households within its area and, together with the NDR, constitutes the local taxation base. Council tax is the means by which local residents contribute to the cost of providing local authority services. The amount payable depends on the valuation band of the dwelling, the number of adults who have their main residence in it, and whether any discounts or exemptions apply. The tax is levied on the occupants of the house, whether tenants or owners, and only if the house is empty does the landlord begin to bear a responsibility for payment.

---

4   At the time of writing there is discussion about once again giving local authorities some local discretion over business rate levels. In its 1997 manifesto the Labour Party talked about handing back to local authorities the power to set the NDR. However, once in office it announced (July 1998) that a uniform business rate, linked to inflation, will continue to be set by the Treasury, but with councils being given powers to vary the standard rate at the margins, by setting a supplementary local rate or rebating the national rate. This local discretion will operate within centrally prescribed limits. Furthermore, local authorities have been told that they must consult fully before using their new powers and ask businesses how they think the extra money should be spent. This means that any supplementary monies raised must help finance additional discretionary spending on priorities that have been agreed with businesses and the local community through a process of 'stakeholder meetings'.

5   Once the Distributable Amount has been fixed, the total amount distributed will not vary, even if more or less is actually paid into the pool in the following financial year. For 1998/99 the Distributable Amount was £12.5 billion. This represented about £250 per resident.

6   The Local Authorities (Contracting Out of Tax Billing, Collection and Enforcement Functions) Order 1996 gives authorities the freedom to use contractors to carry out most of the functions connected with the administration and collection of council tax and business rates.

7   The rates of certain large businesses are not collected by local authorities but are paid directly to the central authorities.

Council tax is levied on local households by the billing authority. The proceeds are paid into its collection fund for distribution to precepting authorities[8] and to its own General Fund. Councils are free to fix the overall level of council tax collected provided they do not exceed a limit set by central government that is related to, although not the same as, the Standard Spending Assessment.[9] If an authority attempts to exceed this limit it may be 'capped' by the government and prevented from so doing. In such a case it will be obliged to revise its proposed budget. In its 1998 local government White Paper (Cm4014), the government threatened that 'hit squads' would be sent to run 'failing' councils, while rewarding those providing best value by easing the capping regime that limits their spending powers (see below).

Because it only pays for 20 per cent of the total costs of local services, council tax has a high *gearing effect* on local tax levels. This means that to get a one per cent increase in council revenue the council tax would have to rise by five per cent. The high gearing effect limits the ability of a local authority to raise revenue finance in this way.

It is recognised that the strength of a property-based tax rests on the fairness of the valuation of property on which it is levied (Cm4014 para.5.23.). By using banded rather than individual property values, the council tax has proved to be more robust in the face of changing property prices than the earlier rates system. So long as the band differentials are judged to be fair, it makes it possible to extend the period between expensive and potentially disruptive revaluations. Current reforms (1998) point to the need for greater equity to protect low-income households while imposing a greater burden on higher income households.[10]

---

8   Precepting authorities are not responsible for collecting the local taxation. They comprise 'major precepting authorities' (the county councils in the two-tier system) and 'local precepting authorities' (parish, community and town councils). County councils in England have a SSA set by government. They receive grants directly from central government but raise money from ratepayers via the district councils. They levy a charge on each district authority *pro rata* within their boundaries for the income they need. Police authorities do likewise. As the 'billing' authorities, district councils take this commitment into account when assessing their overall expenditure. Unitary authorities in England, Wales and Scotland deal with all the income and expenditure and receive grants directly from central government.

9   Central government's assessment of what the authority needs to spend in order to provide a standard level of service.

10 This is to be done by changing the banding system. Proposals are to split the top (H) and bottom (A) bands to get a greater spread. Currently, band A in England covers those dwellings valued up to £40,000 and £30,000 in Wales. Band H is for properties worth over £320,000 in England and £240,000 in Wales. It is further proposed that the highest bands F,G,H, can only claim in band E – on the assumption that if they can afford to occupy an expensive house they can afford to pay more tax. As part of the redistribution arrangements, council tax reduction grant can be allocated to areas where a high percentage of residents live in council tax bands A, B and C. This fiscal support allows a maximum annual council tax rise to be imposed on people in these areas.

Revenue expenditure limitation or 'capping'

Expenditure limitation was first introduced by the Rates Act 1984. This legislation gave central government the power to impose direct controls on that part of local authority revenue expenditure that is financed from local taxation. This power works through a system of revenue expenditure limitation or 'capping'. The so-called 'capping powers' were revised by the Local Government Finance Act 1992 that gave the Secretaries of State the authority to designate a local authority for capping if they judge either:

- the amount that the authority calculates as its *budget requirement* to be 'excessive'; or
- the increase in the authority's *budget requirement* compared with its budget requirement for the preceding year to be 'excessive'.

An authority's *budget requirement* broadly represents its proposed expenditure charged to the General Fund net of any funding taken from reserves or any other income it expects to raise[11] (other than general funding from the government), and after taking into account the use of, or contributions to, general reserves (the balances that every authority must maintain as a matter of prudence).

Capping applies to General Fund expenditure only; different mechanisms, based on the provisions of the Local Government and Housing Act 1989 (in England), are used to control expenditure by the Housing Revenue Account, which relates to the provision of council housing. These HRA account controls are discussed below. In capping an authority, the ministers have to make their criteria explicit. In this context, 'excessiveness' is judged against the benchmark of the authority's Standard Spending Assessment (SSA). [12]

The government's ability to control General Fund expenditure in a direct way brings to the fore the whole question of local accountability discussed at the start of Chapter 8. With the introduction of best value and proposals to introduce new political structures and improvements to local democracy (1998 White Paper, Cm4014), the government has now decided to end 'crude and universal capping' so that councils are no longer told in advance what they may spend. Proposed legislation will repeal existing capping laws and give the government flexible reserve powers to limit local tax increases and spending in ways that are sympathetic to those local authorities working towards the achievement of best value.[13]

---

11 E.g. any fees or charges or any specific or special grants.

12 A council's budget requirement is currently judged to be excessive if it is 12.5 per cent or more above its Standard Spending Assessment.

13 These are identified in para.5.11 of the White paper Cm4014. Because it still has a strong interest in local government taxation and spending decisions, the government proposes to retain reserve powers that will enable it to control 'excessive' council tax increases if it wishes. However, so long as councils act in a responsible way, the use of these powers will very much be the exception rather than the rule (Cm4014 para.5.9.). The White Paper made it clear that the powers would be evoked if councils failed to provide 'best value'.

Critics of capping argue that it undermines the basic local government principle of local accountability and that it mechanistically ignores local knowledge of local needs. Some argue that a fairer system would be to place all councils within a fixed spending band analogous to the exchange rate mechanism while others argue the need for a more fundamental overhaul of local government finance to make it more adequately reflect differences in local needs.[14]

Controlling revenue spending in general: the Finance Settlement

Every summer the government decides how much it thinks local government should spend and how much it will receive in grants in the following year. In late November or early December, the Secretary of State announces a provisional Finance Settlement to Parliament and to the local authorities. At the same time, the Secretary of State sets out for each authority the amount by which it can increase its budget. After this announcement, there is a period of consultation, leading to the House of Commons approving a final Local Government Finance Settlement in late January or early February, in time for the authorities to set their budgets for the following year. If any authority sets a budget above the declared limit, the central authorities consider the case it puts forward following a process prescribed by law and then either confirm or revise the original set limit. The final Settlement has to be approved by Parliament before coming into effect.

So far as Westminster is concerned, there is no direct control of Scottish or Welsh local authorities, but the Scottish Parliament and the National Assembly have to stay within the allocated public spending totals for Scotland and Wales and decide the proportion available for local government.

Total Standard Spending (TSS). The process by which the Financial Settlement is approved begins with the government setting a level of revenue spending that it considers appropriate for local authorities to spend in aggregate; this is called Total Standard Spending (TSS). This figure is determined as part of the public expenditure survey process described in Chapter 5.[15] TSS is meant to represent the total amount that local government as a whole needs to spend in that year in order to provide a 'standard' level of service. The TSS has to be consistent with overall

---

14   Harding, (1997), ibid. The public sector spending rules (see Chapter 5) treat spending financed out of council tax revenues, non-domestic rates and Scottish variable rate of income tax, as demand-led cyclical expenditure rather than as 'planned for' non-cyclical expenditure. It is therefore not subject to the firm multi-year limits that are imposed on many other public spending categories. The Treasury argues that treating local taxation in this way is consistent with the relaxation of capping promised by the new Labour government and places a greater emphasis on local democracy. However, as we have said, the Treasury intends to hold on to strong reserve powers over this form of local authority spending so that capping and grant withdrawals are still possible if, in the future, ministers judge local authorities to be 'profligate'.

15   In the official statistics, police TSS is usually shown separately.

public spending plans.[16] TSS is used to help calculate the level of central government support to local authorities to help them provide such a level of service.[17]

Aggregate External Finance (AEF). The amount of support authorities receive from the government in respect of TSS (including police TSS) is known as Aggregate External Finance. Some 80 per cent of local government revenue finance comes from central government. In this way, the government helps meet a large part of TSS by distributing grants and business rates. Together, this income constitutes AEF. The difference between TSS and AEF is the approximate amount local authorities need to raise through council tax if they spend at the level of TSS.

AEF thus includes Revenue Support Grant (RSG), redistributed NDR, and a number of specific, special and transitional grants. Most expenditure not met by AEF is financed by the authorities' own resources, including the council tax.

Specific and special grants

The government pays for part of TSS by providing specific and special grants. These are designed to fund particular services that the government wishes to encourage. These grants tend to vary over time according to the government's policy priorities.[18] General funding needs, that is, TSS not covered by specific and special grants, is supported by the Revenue Support Grant.

Revenue Support Grant (RSG)

The bulk of central financial support comes in the form of RSG.[19] The purpose of the RSG is to bring about a more-or-less equal local tax burden between areas that have different needs and taxable capacities. Its calculation is tied to spending assessments called *standard spending assessments* (SSAs – see below). It is important to understand, however, that RSG support is *not* channelled into the running of the council housing service whose finances are ring-fenced from the authorities' general funding arrangements and are helped through a different mechanism called the *HRA subsidy* (discussed below).

RSG is simply that part of AEF that is not provided from business rates or specific and special grants. In line with the government's public expenditure control

---

16 For 1998/99 the government proposes the TSS should in excess of £48 billion.

17 It excludes expenditure funded by specific grants outside AEF and a small amount of other financing.

18 For example, there is an Under Five Education Grant that local authorities could apply for in 1998/99.

19 Revenue Support Grant replaced Rate Support Grant on 1 April 1990. It is paid to local authorities, including police authorities, to enable the council tax for a property in any given band to be set at broadly the same level throughout the country if each authority budgeted in line with its Standard Spending Assessment.

priorities, the allocation of RSG begins with the TME process (discussed in Chapter 5). This determines how much money in total local authorities will be permitted to spend (TSS). The government then determines the proportion of that TSS that will be financed by the Exchequer. By a process of residualisation, this then determines the proportion that authorities collectively will have to find for themselves. Having fixed the Exchequer's total commitment to support general local authority revenue spending, the government then turns its attention to the question of how best to distribute that sum.

The amount of RSG an authority receives is determined by the following formula:

RSG = its SSA *minus* its share of the NDR pool *minus* the amount it would get if it set its council tax at a national standard rate.

Standard Spending Assessments (SSAs)

The allocation of RSG centres on a calculation methodology referred to as *standard spending assessments* (SSAs).[20] Using a number of formulae, the government assesses how much it is reasonable for each local council to spend in providing its range of General Fund services for a given period. To date the SSA has been annual. However, in the 1998 White Paper (Cm4014), the government declared its intention to establish a three-year planning period for the distribution of grant aid.[21]

Although the allocation process allows for an assessment of particular local needs, it is, nevertheless, fundamentally resource driven in that the SSA system is used as a statistical device for sharing out the fixed pot of public expenditure. In this way, SSAs represent the amount that the government considers appropriate for each authority to calculate as its *budget requirement* (refer above) for a given period consistent with the amount that the government considers it would be appropriate for all authorities to spend.

SSAs are built up from seven major service blocks: education, police, fire, highways maintenance, personal social services, capital financing, and other

---

[20] The SSA was introduced in 1990. This was a further reform of a system that had begun in the early 1970s as Needs Assessment, which used a single formula to calculate how much an authority should get from central government to provide a standard level of service. Needs Assessment was regarded as too volatile as it generated wide variations in grant. It was therefore turned into Grant Related Expenditure that used more than sixty separate formulae to calculate an authority's needs. That also came to be regarded as too complex, hence the SSA with its dozen formulae. (Rory Maclean, Public Finance, CIPFA website).

[21] The idea here is that strong local financial accountability depends on people understanding better the link between their local council's spending decisions and the council tax bills that they face. It is felt that it will be easier for them to see this link if there is stability year on year in the funding which government gives to councils.

services[22] Whether the SSAs are judged to be fair depends crucially on what is included as an indicator and how they are weighted.[23] The SSAs are much criticised for being too crude and failing to reflect the subtle social, economic and cultural needs of different local authority areas[24].

The government is currently investigating, in partnership with local government, whether there is a better way of determining the distribution of revenue support grant that is simpler, more stable, more robust and fairer than the present arrangements for SSAs.

Housing revenue finance

The distinction between HRA and non-HRA housing revenue finance

In any discussion on local authority housing spending, we must always make a clear distinction between monies spent on, and derived from, an authority's council housing service, and monies committed to providing housing services to people other than council tenants. Revenue expenditure and income on council housing are recorded in a separate account known as the Housing Revenue Account (HRA). Revenue transactions relating to all other council services appear in the General Fund (see Chapter 8). It is particularly important to note that, since 1990, and earlier in Scotland, it has not been possible to make a contribution to the HRA from the General Fund.[25] With the introduction of resource accounting in April 2003, significant changes will be made to the structure of the HRA. Before looking at the changing format of the HRA, we need to consider the key issue of rent-setting.

---

22 Each SSA element is calculated by multiplying a unit cost by the size of the relevant client group (such as the number of pupils for education), with allowances such as the 'area cost adjustment' for additional costs that authorities might face in providing this service (e.g. relatively poor social conditions or the additional employment costs in London and the South East). In this way, each service assessment uses indicators which are then weighted to reflect the relative priority given to that element. For instance, in social services, indicators include age factors such as the number of children between 0 to 17 years or the number of over-65s, and cost factors such as the proportion of household residents living in shared accommodation and the number of children in non-white ethnic groups.

23 In 1996, for example, the index used to measure comparative social need placed Barnsley in 313th position, Runnymede in 38th, Kingston upon Thames in 53rd and Westminster in 4th. Critics argue that such comparative assessments are unfair because they give a relatively high weighting to such factors as the need for help to cope with in-coming visitors and a relatively low weighting to factors such as the need for help to cope with a declining local economic base. (See Harding, D. 'Share and Share Alike', *Public Finance*, 21 March 1997, pp18-20).

24 In any particular year, SSA Reduction Grant can be paid to those authorities whose SSA falls significantly as a result of changes in the calculation methodology.

25 This used to be compulsory if the HRA would otherwise have been in deficit.

Council house rents

The main rental income of local authorities is from council housing and this is recorded in the HRA. Other rents are recorded in the General Fund, as are fees and charges for the receipt or use of municipal services and facilities other than those directly associated with council housing.

Given its central importance to the whole debate about council housing finance, we need to begin our discussion on council housing revenue finance by considering the issues surrounding rent-setting in this sector.[26]

The nature of rent

In Chapter 4 we made the general point that a conflict exists between, on the one hand, the *social policy objective* of setting rents at levels that are *low enough* to be affordable to tenants and, on the other hand, the *commercial policy objective* of setting rents at levels that are *high enough* to cover the landlord's legitimate costs. What counts as 'legitimate costs' with respect to the provision of council housing lies at the heart of a long-standing debate. (Refer to the notion of *total sufficiency rent* in Chapter 4). In essence, the rent payment is the 'price' that the tenant pays in return for enjoying rights of occupancy together with the range of housing management services associated with the tenancy. In practice, rents have to contribute to the provision of those functions itemised in the HRA (see below). Although the rent constitutes a price to the tenant, from the council's point of view, it constitutes an 'income'. If an authority wishes to increase its expenditure on the HRA, this may well require an increase in price (i.e. rents) as the housing subsidy element of HRA income is fixed.

Council housing rents: the changing national policy framework

Before considering the essential elements of current rent policy we need to look briefly at how the debate about what counts as a reasonable social rent has brought about a reshaping of the national framework within which council housing rent policies operate. In the private business community, a landlord's legitimate costs would include a return on the current value of capital invested and a measure of *normal profit* (refer Chapter 4). In other words, the private landlord will expect the rental income to cover the opportunity costs of being active in the housing market. Business people will expect a reasonable return on the money capital that is 'locked' or 'fixed' into the asset, and to be rewarded for the energy, effort, time and risks associated with being a landlord. Private lenders to registered social landlords will also expect rent policies to be part of a viable business plan.

---

26   In the discussion that follows, the reader should be aware that different provisions apply in Scotland. Notably, there is no overall rent-setting formula in Scotland and no requirement for housing benefit for council tenants to be part funded by other council tenants.

In short, both private landlords and private lenders will expect the pricing system to be value based and market-orientated. In contrast, local authorities have traditionally been regarded as part of the 'welfare state' rather than as part of the business community.[27] For this reason, historically, they have taken a *cost/expenditure* rather than a *value/market* approach to setting rents. In their role as agents for the welfare state they have traditionally sought to set rents on the basis of pooled historic cost pricing (refer Chapter 4). This means that, traditionally, municipal pricing policies have not put an emphasis on making a profit or a return on capital, but rather have sought to provide affordable housing by ensuring that the rental income plus subsidy covers the current outgoings, including the servicing of debt. The ability to 'pool' historic costs goes a long way to explain why council rents have tended to be lower than those of other tenures.

By the 1970s, the introduction of *fair rents* in the private sector helped to bring about a sharper disparity between the prices being charged by private landlords and local authorities. These differentials became a cause for concern amongst those politicians and policy-makers who felt that the development of a fair and coherent social housing policy depends in part on cross-tenure price equivalence. Of equal concern was the fact that pooled historic pricing had produced council rents that varied considerably from one authority to another in a way that bore little or no relation to the type, condition or location of the stock. Historians also make the point that the traditional (pre-1970s) system of local authority housing finance distributed subsidies inequitably amongst councils and tenants so that scarce resources were not necessarily targeted at those in most need (e.g. Malpass, 1990, p69).

The Housing Finance Act 1972 was the first piece of legislation that attempted to address these issues, and in so doing it ruptured the basic principles upon which the old welfare statist system of local authority housing finance had been built. Although the 1972 Act was soon reformed, by radically challenging the traditional principles upon which local authority rents and subsidies policy had been founded, it marked out a framework for a subsequent policy debate that eventually led to the establishment of the current housing finance regime.[28]

The principles of local authority rent-setting

The old 'welfare statist' approach has now been abandoned in favour of a regime that consciously attempts to incorporate a degree of 'market/value' principles into council housing pricing policy. Over the last twenty-five years we can see the emergence of a general, cross-party consensus about the broad objectives that

---

27 It has to be said that in a 'best value' climate, lenders to local authorities will now also want assurance that the rent policies will be part of a viable business plan.

28 These principles should be seen as having emerged out of a process of policy development that Peter Malpass calls the 'reshaping of housing policy'. Readers wishing to explore the historical and policy backgrounds to these developments should refer to Malpass, 1990.

---

should form the basis of an appropriate public sector rent-setting policy. These objectives can be summarised as follows. Although there is considerable agreement about these objectives, how they should be balanced and linked is still a cause for considerable debate.

1. *Rents should not contribute a subsidy to or be subsidised by the General Revenue Account.* Prior to April 1990 it was possible for authorities in England and Wales to make a contribution to the HRA from what were then rates, now council tax. It was also easier to transfer council house rental income into the General Fund to subsidise local taxpayers. These interchanges produced a situation in which tenants occupying similar types of property but in different local authority areas, were charged different rents depending upon the extent to which these cross-subsidy transactions formed part of council policy. The ring-fencing of the HRA was introduced partly to impose an accounting discipline on the management of council housing, but it was also intended to establish a greater degree of inter-authority equity with respect to rent charges.[29]

2. *Rents should, to some extent, reflect current incomes and prices.* The point has to be made that implicit in this objective is the need to link rents to some kind of inflation or incomes index or housing market price index (Malpass, 1990, p70). The argument here is that this indexing would place a greater emphasis on equity of treatment between different forms of renting. Furthermore, by establishing a link between council rents and wider market forces, price distortions in the overall housing system would be reduced. We might also make the point that if future policies seek to attract private investment into the development of council housing, lenders will expect rents to bear some clear relationship to market forces. In the current housing finance regime there is an expectation that local authority rents are 'proportionate'. 'Proportionality' is an expression denoting an intention that local authority rents should bear a relationship to assured tenancy rents in the other rented sectors.[30]

3. *Rents should, to some extent, reflect the asset value and condition of the dwelling.* The argument here is that a measure of capital value pricing would place a greater emphasis on equity of treatment between different forms of renting and would lead to rent charges that more accurately reflect consumer preferences. Information collected on rents shows that many authorities have a relatively flat structure for their rents that fails to reflect the different size and characteristics of their dwellings. It could be argued that this objective would also impose a degree of inter-area equity into the rent-setting system. The point has also been made that adequate and stable resources for the

---

29 This is not to say that disparities no longer exist. Largely because of historic debt patterns, disparities are still particularly marked in Scotland.

30 This is made an explicit duty under Section 24 of the Housing Act 1985 that requires authorities to have regard to the pattern of rents for similar types of properties in the private rented sector when setting their rents.

improvement, maintenance and management of the stock are more likely to be generated through capital value rents, supported by needs-related housing allowances, than through reliance on *ad hoc* government subsidies (NFHA, 1995, p21). This point has become more relevant now that resource accounting applies to the councils' own stocks of housing. The 2003 reforms are expected to introduce a requirement for authorities to produce 'appropriate' profiles of their stock values and conditions. This improved information, collected as part of the resource accounting exercise, might prove to be useful when considering rent structures after the year 2002.

4. *Rents should not be unduly distorted by the relative holdings of capital receipts.* Authorities that have sold large numbers of dwellings and, as a result, have accumulated capital receipts are potentially in a position to spend more on their council housing service without having to increase rents proportionately. Conversely, authorities that do not have such accumulated reserves are, on the face of it, poorly positioned to invest in their stock unless they do so by hiking up rents. To prevent consequential inequitable rent differentials between authorities, it may be necessary to instigate a degree of resource redistribution. This is currently achieved via the capital finance regime that controls the use of, and to some extent redistributes, capital receipts (Chapter 9). It is expected that the introduction of a needs-related repairs allowance in 2003 will help to address this question.[31]

5. *Subsidy rather than rent should be treated as 'the residual'.* The implication of this is that general subsidies should be calculated on a deficit basis reflecting any shortfall in HRA income (Malpass, ibid.). The argument here is that rents should be set in line with rational principles and not simply be calculated as a residual to make up the 'cost/expenditure' shortfall that exists after the receipt of a standard subsidy.

6. *Rents should be affordable.* Objectives 2 and 3 above are founded on economic rather than social principles, and therefore take no systematic account of affordability. The declared affordability principle in this sector (DoE Consultation Paper 1988) is that rents generally should not exceed levels within the reach of people in low paid employment, and in practice will normally be below market levels (refer to Chapter 3). There can be no guarantee that rent levels that are determined by reference to proportionality and asset values will be within the means of low-income households. This problem has been addressed by the introduction of rent rebates that now take the form of a standardised, national, means-tested assistance procedure that is administered as part of the housing benefit system (see Chapter 17). The argument here is that those who cannot afford to pay the 'appropriate' rent for a decent home, should be helped through fiscal welfare, or rebates, rather than by generally suppressing rents, which would involve abandoning objectives 2

31　At the time of writing, there are no plans for a needs-related repairs allowance in Scotland.

and 3 above. The 2003 reforms will remove the burden of rent rebates out of the HRA so that the account can more clearly operate as a landlord asset management account (see below for details).

From principles to practice

Although the principles enunciated above are UK-wide, many of the mechanisms only apply to England. To establish a working system that is equitable, clear and coherent, these guiding principles have to be turned into detailed practice procedures. These rules of practice are grounded in legislation and can be thought of as a regulatory 'regime'. Because any deficit subsidy system (principle 5 above) derives from the relationship between rents and expenditure, central government will have an interest in how both these amounts are determined. This interest is exercised via the regulatory regime. The current finance regime for England was established in 1990 under the provisions of the Local Government and Housing Act 1989. They will be reformed under new legislation scheduled to be enacted before April 2003.

Setting council rents in practice

In setting their rents, English local authorities are currently required to comply with Section 24 of the Housing Act 1985 and Section 162 of the Local Government and Housing Act 1989. The legislation requires the authority to do the following.

1. Fix a 'reasonable' rent for the tenancy.
2. Carry out regular rent reviews.
3. In fixing and reviewing rents, have regard to the principle of 'proportionality' so that rent differentials for different types of council dwelling are more-or-less in line with the differentials charged for assured tenancies of similar types of dwelling in the non-council sectors in the locality.[32]

The government periodically produces guidance notes explaining how authorities are expected to achieve these broad legislative requirements. These indicate that any council price-setting mechanism such as a points system, does not have to achieve rents that are, in an absolute sense, the same as those charged by other types of landlord. They indicate that they should establish the same sorts of differentials that other landlords would charge for different classes of property (e.g. between a flat and a maisonette) or different conditions or forms of property of the same class (e.g. between an old and a new house, and between a two and a three-bedroomed house).

Towards convergence

At present, rents in the registered social landlord sector are around 20 per cent higher, on average, than rents in local authorities. This is seen to be both unfair and

---

32 Scottish legislation does not carry the same prescriptions.

confusing to tenants. In the latest Housing Green Paper, *Quality and Choice: A Decent Home for All* (DETR/Department of Social Security, April 2000), the government has declared its intention that in future, rents across the two social housing sectors should be based on the same principles. This is likely to mean that pressure will be applied to hold RSL rents to current levels while allowing average local authority rents to increase (within set limits).

Rent capping, guideline rents and current policy

The current rent capping regime means that English councils lose HRA subsidy if their rents are raised beyond 'guideline' figures. The guideline seeks to set average rents for each authority using an approach that balances regional earnings and property values. The guideline is a figure that is produced as part of the subsidy calculation (see below). Although councils will take notice of this figure when fixing rents, in practice, actual rent increases may differ from this official guideline. In 1997, about 60 per cent of English authorities set rent increases above guideline levels and some 27 per cent set rents below these levels.

The consultative document that preceded the Local Government and Housing Act 1989 made specific reference to the government's intention both to increase local government financial accountability and to establish a more business-like system of housing finance. The Act, which established the new financial regime, was unquestionably part of the Conservative government's ideological commitment to a more market-orientated and commercially driven public sector. One of the most prominent effects of the new regime was that it imposed an upward pressure on rents. The intention was twofold (1) to bring council rents more into line with private sector rents, and (2) to allow for a tighter control of public expenditure on housing.[33]

The present government does not have an ideological commitment to using market rents as a benchmark for setting council rents. It is more concerned to rationalise rent levels across the social housing sector as a whole. After the initial Comprehensive Spending Review (1998), the New Labour government declared its intention to diminish the differentials that exist between rents in the council and RSL sectors for similar dwellings. This means that, in general terms, current policy is to put downward pressure on RSL rents (RPI plus one per cent on new schemes and one per cent on existing schemes in England), while encouraging council rents to increase in real terms. Ministers have established a general guideline policy that will allow council rents to increase in real terms by one per cent in 1999, two per cent in 2000, and two per cent in 2001[34]. Generalised average increases are not the only issue associated with social housing rent

---

33 Although not part of declared policy, higher rents also made the Conservative Party's drive to expand owner-occupation more attractive and may also have encouraged some tenants to exercise their newly given rights to choose a non-council landlord.
34 These planned-for increases are linked to proposed changes in the financial administration of rent rebates (i.e. the restructuring of the HRA).

rationalisation. The government is also concerned to see that social rents within a locality to some extent reflect utility. That is, a particular rent should bear some relation to the type, condition and location of the dwelling. The emphasis in Scotland has been a little different where there is a general concern that rent levels should be kept more in line with incomes.

The changing format of the Housing Revenue Account

The HRA has to be kept in a prescribed form. This form was most recently laid down in the Local Government and Housing Act 1989 and subsequent regulations. It will be changed by the year 2003 as a result of the finance reforms that will come in with the shift to resource accounting. The fact that the form of the HRA was different before and after 1990 and will change again in 2003 needs to be borne in mind when HRA time comparisons are made. The format is different again in Scotland.

The HRA before 1990

It has long been recognised that in order to keep council housing rents at affordable levels, the HRA needs to be supported by extra money from elsewhere (historically from the government or from other parts of the council's finances). Such financial support takes the form of a *revenue subsidy*. This need for subsidy has, over the years, produced tensions between the interests of central government (national taxpayers), the council (local ratepayers) and tenants (service users). The question is, 'Who should bear the cost of the subsidy?' After 1972 councils were required to pay *rent rebates* to aid tenants on low incomes. Eventually the rebates were incorporated into the housing benefit system that is discussed fully in Chapter 17. Until 1990, councils were also allowed to move money from the Rate Fund to HRA to support council housing. Prior to the Local Government and Housing Act 1989, English councils had a degree of discretion over how the burden of the subsidy should be distributed, that is, the HRA was not ring-fenced, and different practices were established in different parts of the country.[35]

The pre-1990 system potentially provided four major categories of income to the HRA. These were:

- Rent – paid by the *tenants*.

---

35 By the late 1980s, there were large variations between councils with respect to the rents they charged, the extent to which they cross-subsidised the HRA, and how much of their HRA expenditure was directed to debt redemption. Some councils, typically urban authorities with accumulated debts and a repairs backlog, relied heavily on subsidy to make the HRA balance. Other councils, typically non-urban districts with small debts and a good quality stock, were at or near the point where the rental flow covered the HRA outgoings. Some councils were actually in surplus on the account and used such surpluses to cross-subsidise the Rate Fund. Councils' discretion was considerably more fettered in Scotland.

- Rent rebate subsidy – paid by the *government* to underpin the council's ability to charge a reduced rent to those on low incomes.
- Housing subsidy – paid by the *government* in general support of the housing service.
- Rate Fund contributions – paid by the *council* (from money received from the rate levy).

In Scotland, housing benefit was part of the General Fund accounts so the HRA accounted only for full rents. HSG was steadily minimised so that it was paid only to the highest debt landlords and RFCs were capped from the early 1980s and virtually eliminated by the end of the decade. In Scotland the HRA has therefore been substantially 'stand-alone' for several years.

Why the system was reformed in 1989

The government of the day wished to reform the English and Welsh systems in a way that would allow more central influence over local housing finance polices and to bring about greater uniformity of practice across the country. The government was particularly concerned about two aspects of the pre-1990 regime.

First, under the old regime, central government's ability to influence local rent and spending policies was limited because of the powers of councils to supplement the HRA from the Rate Fund. If for example, subsidy was reduced with a view to encouraging an increase in rents or to cut public spending, the gap in finances could simply be met by the council increasing its Rate Fund contribution. What happened to really focus the government's attention was that during the 1980s, for the first time ever, the aggregate level of rate fund contributions to HRAs came to exceed the aggregate Exchequer housing subsidy contributions. This was seized upon by ministers in the late 1980s as a major reason for reforming the system.[36]

The government's second concern related to the operation of the rent rebate subsidy. Because it was regarded as a 'welfare' rather than a strictly 'housing' subsidy, the old rebate subsidy was administered separately from the general housing subsidy. This separation meant that if and when a council moved into surplus it lost entitlement to general subsidy but it still qualified for the rebate subsidy that was designed to help it meet the costs of paying housing benefit payments to its less well-off tenants. The amount of rebate subsidy received was largely determined by the gap between the rent levels and the tenants' abilities to

---

36   It was also to do with the politics of specific localities. Some authorities, in particular a number of inner London boroughs, were paying very large rate fund contributions into the HRA. These councils were judged by ministers to be irresponsible 'loony left' authorities. It could be argued that the 1989 focus on ring-fencing was largely as an attack on a relatively small number of Labour local authorities who were seen to be 'working the system' for political ends and keeping rents down against central government policy.

pay. In order to get rents to rise, which was its intention throughout the 1980s, the government sought to withdraw subsidy.[37] However, the rent rebate subsidy element was received automatically when tenants could not afford the rent charges. As councils were free to determine their rent levels, once they moved into 'surplus', the central authorities effectively lost any influence over the council's HRA policy.[38] The crucial question then arose, '*How can the government exert influence over rents when there is no subsidy left to withdraw?*'[39]

The issue came to a head when it became apparent that, all over the country, authorities were increasing their rents by more than the guidelines. This meant that households qualified for rebates that were automatically supported by rebate subsidy. In this way councils were undermining the government's ability to pursue its legitimate interest in controlling public expenditure by influencing the volume of subsidy going into housing. Some authorities increased their rents substantially more than the guidelines and there were arguments about why they were doing this. In some cases it was quite clear that the councils were increasing their rents in order to give their tenants an incentive to vote for a *large-scale voluntary transfer* or to opt for the *RTB*. In some other cases, it was equally clear that they were increasing their rents in order to generate resources to spend on improving the stock (to compensate for losses in capital funding). The effect of local authorities increasing their rents above the guideline amount was that the tenants who were claiming housing benefit were entitled to more financial support in the form of rebated rent. This meant that the aggregate amount of rent rebate subsidy was going up in an uncontrollable way, as the rebate element of subsidy was an uncapped budget head. The Treasury is always wary of this kind of demand-led expenditure, and the dramatic increases in the overall housing benefit bill eventually resulted in this powerful ministry calling for action.[40]

The new regime introduced in 1990 was designed to meet these concerns and, in particular, to impose greater central influence over local decisions.

---

37 That is, assume when calculating the notional figures that rental income will rise more than expenditure.

38 In Scotland, the need for the General Fund to support housing benefit, plus a differential rate of subsidy for rent rebates and rent allowances, together with rate capping, meant that there was always some control on councils' rent fixings.

39 In the earlier 1980 system, the government tried to deal with this question by withdrawing the old block grant which the Treasury gave to local authorities to subsidise general services. The idea was that authorities would be expected to transfer surpluses from the HRA into the General Fund to make good these reductions in the block grant. This mechanism never really worked (for political reason relevant at the time). The government then came back in 1980 with another way of approaching this question of what to do when there is no housing subsidy to withdraw. On this occasion they went for the rent rebate subsidy.

40 Part of the increase was expected and was implicit in the reform that moved subsidy support from a general subsidy system to an income augmentation system, but part of it was unplanned and unexpected. This resulted in the Conservative Administration making a major U-turn in rents policy.

The HRA after 1990

The 1990 system introduced to England and Wales for the first time a single HRA subsidy consisting of two parts: the housing element and the rent rebate element. The housing element can become negative, and in most local authorities it is now a substantially negative amount. The rent rebate element will always be a positive amount because it is simply the aggregate entitlement of all the council tenants to housing benefit. The net HRA subsidy that a local authority receives is the sum of these two elements. So a large negative housing element will have the effect of reducing the size of the rent rebate element. This now means that most authorities do not receive all of their potential central government support to pay their rebates, and indeed, some get very little or none at all.

The second major change introduced by the 1989 Act was the ring-fencing of the HRA. Since 1990 the general principle has been that money spent on, and derived from, council housing has to be 'ring-fenced'. The HRA should now only deal with finances that relate to the authority's role as a housing landlord, and funds in the account cannot be used to subsidise any other part of the council's finances such as education, libraries or social services. Similarly, other service funds cannot be used to subsidise the HRA.[41]

In setting the boundaries of the 'ring-fence', there are certain grey areas. The costs of such functions as housing aid and advice and some homeless functions such as hostels have been treated differently by different authorities. A particular degree of confusion emerged with the passing of Section 127 of the Leasehold Reform, Housing and Urban Development Act 1993 which gave local authorities the power to charge certain welfare services to the HRA. It is now established that the costs of placing homeless families in temporary accommodation such as that leased from private landlords should not be charged to the HRA. The costs of employing staff to run the homeless service is typically split between the HRA and the General Fund. Any personal care costs associated with the running of sheltered housing for the elderly should not be charged to the HRA. In the period during which compulsory competitive tendering operated, ministerial guidance stated that the property and activities subject to CCT would normally be within the HRA, apart from short-term leases. Housing management CCT start-up costs and contract monitoring were also chargeable to the HRA. On the other hand, directives make it clear that the HRA should not be burdened with services such as estate-based employment advice or drug rehabilitation services. Although the 1994 guidance allowed road sweeping and children's play schemes on estates to be paid for from the HRA, the CIH argues that this should be resisted as it would mean that tenants are paying for these services twice: through their council tax and then again through their rents.

---

41 If a council has transferred all of its stock to the ownership of a housing association or some other landlord through LSVT, they can apply for permission to lift this provision.

The debate about where to draw the 'ring-fence' continues: the Labour government's social exclusion agenda and the notion of 'Housing Plus' both point to the need for a wider view to be taken about the nature of housing need.

The elements of the Housing Revenue Account (under current arrangements)

The main elements of the HRA in England and Wales can be summarised as follows:

Expenditure
Loan service charges, management costs, spending on repairs and maintenance, payments of rent rebates to those tenants qualifying for housing benefit, and 'other' outgoings such as revenue contributions to capital outlays (RCCOs), bought in services, including those from other council departments, provision for bad debts, and a contingency sum to cover any unforeseen expenses of shortfalls in income. In Scotland there are no housing benefit payments and RCCOs are called CFCR (capital funded current revenue).

Income
Rents and service charges paid by council tenants, HRA subsidy (HSG in Scotland), and 'other' receipts such as rents from council owned retail properties on the estate and interest received on council mortgages. Note that interest received from invested capital receipts from the sale of HRA assets has to be paid to the General Fund rather than the HRA.

Figure 11.1: Typical HRA (highly simplified) in the current format

INCOME	£m	EXPENDITURE	£m
Rent and service charges	35	Debt charges	15
HRA subsidy	10	Management	10
Other (see text above)	10	Maintenance	10
		Rent rebates	15
		Other (see text above)	5
Total	55	Total	55

The above represents the main elements of an HRA. In a real set of accounts the elements would be split into sub-categories and other items of income and expenditure would be included. The precise content of an account clearly depends on an authority's debt profile and the nature and scope of its activities.

Balancing the HRA
The Local Government and Housing Act 1989 allows a council to run a surplus on the account and to carry that surplus over to the next financial year. If, however,

the account moves into deficit it is required to take such 'reasonable steps' as it can to bring it back into balance. Any end of year deficit is carried forward and must be made up, or accounted for, when the budget is set for the following financial year.

Setting rents and balancing the budget

If the final subsidy settlement is such that the real, as against the nominal, HRA is potentially in deficit, there are only a limited number of choices open to the council in its attempt to balance the budget. This is because many of the expenditure items cannot be controlled by the council within the on-coming financial year. The level of rent rebates is fixed by law, and the loan service charges are contractual. This means that to close any budgetary gap, the council will have to consider raising rents, reducing staffing levels (or in some other way reducing management costs), rescheduling repairs and maintenance programmes, or find savings from the 'other' category in the account, or some combination of all of these.

HRA subsidy

The 1990 reforms in England and Wales replaced the two distinct subsidies with one unified subsidy called the *Housing Revenue Account Subsidy*. This, together with ring-fencing, meant that the four previous primary income flows into the HRA were reduced to two. These are:

- Rent – paid by the *tenants*.
- HRA subsidy – paid by the *government*.

It has to be remembered that the primary reason for introducing the reforms was to allow the government to exercise more effective control over local decisions. The government was particularly concerned to have more direct influence over the setting of local rent and expenditure levels. Because the HRA is now ring-fenced, if the government cuts the unified housing subsidy, the loss of income cannot be made up by transferring money from the General Fund. The shortfall has to be met either by increasing rents or by reducing expenditure.

Because central support for rent rebates in England and Wales is now subsumed into the single unified subsidy, the government is better positioned to influence the rent setting policies of those authorities that, under the old arrangements, would have been 'out of subsidy'. In other words, by combining the two subsidy elements into a single entitlement formula, any authority with tenants qualifying for housing benefit, might remain 'in subsidy' and thereby remain under the influence of the government, who control the subsidy.[42] Since 1990, in total, subsidy has shifted from supporting *general needs* to under-writing *rent rebates*.

---

42 Although now many local authorities are totally out of subsidy because they pay all their own housing benefit.

In recent years it has been the government's intention to use the subsidy system to provide incentives to 'better' management. The current HRA subsidy includes certain incentives for English authorities to manage their housing assets efficiently, for example the use of formulaic allowances in the calculation of management and maintenance expenditure and the voids allowance in the calculation of notional rent income. The idea is to reward authorities financially where their efficiency is greater than assumed in the formula. It is likely that this 'incentives approach' will be enhanced with the introduction of resource accounting that will judge subsidy entitlement, in part, by reference to an 'HRA Business Plan' (see below).

The cross-subsidy effect of rent rebates

The fact that currently the subsidy received in English and Welsh HRAs is the sum of two elements, the housing element and the rebate element, can have significant financial consequences for the authority and its tenants. Those authorities that have no requirement for housing subsidy will nevertheless be entitled to the rent rebate element of the combined subsidy. If the negative housing element exceeds the positive rebate element such an authority may find its support for housing benefit reduced. However, the rebate is a tenant entitlement and has to be paid for with or without central government support. This may mean that the shortfall has to come from the rents. In this way the system frequently produces a situation in which the better-off tenants, paying full rent, are subsidising the rebates of their less well-off neighbours, who qualify for housing benefit.

Although the cross-subsidy is unpopular with tenants' and residents' organisations, from the government's point of view, it generates a net surplus to the Treasury of some £1.4 billion a year (1998). To give it up would involve adding that sum to the public expenditure total. With most English authorities' HRAs now in surplus, housing professionals (LGA and CIH), would like to see this money re-invested in capital improvements in the housing stock. The Chartered Institute of Housing estimate the sum of money is close to the amount needed to finance the debt charges on the £21-23 billion of needed stock improvements (CIH, *Council Housing – Financing the Future*, 1998). Although ending the cross-subsidy has the potential to enhance spending on the stock, the money will have to come from somewhere. If it is not met from general taxation then the burden is likely to be shifted to the councils' General Fund. This may help placate council tenants, but the reform would then have the effect of inhibiting investment in regeneration and non-HRA housing schemes. Furthermore, the councils that would gain are in relatively affluent areas and have less need of new resources than councils in poorer areas. This points to the need to introduce a redistribution mechanism as part of the reform to ensure that any released resources were used to meet housing need in a way that would be effective and fair. The cross-subsidy effect will be partly addressed with the introduction of resource accounting to the HRA (discussed below).

The government's changing views about rent

A major reason for changing the subsidy system in England and Wales in 1990 was to give the government more central control over local rent-setting policies. At that time, the government's view was that council rents were too far below market levels and that there were undue variations from one council area to the next. The government also felt that 'unjustifiably' low council rents were damaging their wider housing policy initiatives. In particular, it was felt that low rents were discouraging tenants from exercising their 'right-to-buy' and inhibiting them from choosing to transfer their tenancies to another landlord. For all of these reasons, in the early years, the government sought to operate the system to bring about rent increases that were substantially above the general rate of inflation. The way in which it put upward pressure on rents was to assume, in the notional calculations, that rental income was going to increase by more than expenditure.[43]

In Scotland, the capital finance regime, which in effect allowed councils to utilise 100 per cent of their receipts if they were sufficiently adept to spend them all in the same financial year, did the job for the government. The extra investment meant that loan debt rose steadily year-on-year and the cost per tenancy increased further as RTBs continued to take place, reducing stock numbers year-on-year.

By the mid-1990s the government's views had changed. Once a general rise in rents had occurred the Conservative government's broad objective had been achieved and the political pressure to continue raising rents well above inflation moderated. The reversal of policy was stimulated by an awareness of the link between rent increases and the rapidly rising housing benefit bill. Between 1988 and 1997 there was a twofold increase in rent rebate expenditure paid to council tenants.[44] The poverty trap associated with the housing benefits system was seen as particularly damaging to the incoming Labour government's 'welfare to work' initiative and by 1998 the new government was firmly committed to a policy of low rent increases.[45]

HRA subsidy determination

Since April 1990, all local authorities can claim a unified *HRA subsidy* from central government. This is an annual payment that is designed to bridge the gap between the authority's 'notional income' and its 'notional expenditure' (see below). In Scotland this fiscal support is called *Housing Support Grant (HSG)*. An authority's entitlement is determined by aggregating two subsidy elements.

---

43 In the early years the government sought an annual 5 per cent real increase in rents.
44 There was a fivefold increase in rent allowance expenditure.
45 Over the years the structure of council tenancies has altered so that a higher proportion of tenants are benefit dependent. Furthermore the housing benefit system has become less generous and puts more emphasis on means-testing. This means that for many people, an increase in income by £1 a week can result in a loss of 97 pence in benefits.

1. *The housing element.* This provides general support to the HRA and is often negative. This is the sole element in HSG in Scotland where it is either positive or, in most cases, zero.
2. *The rent rebate element.* This helps to provide housing benefit to council tenants in England and Wales and is always positive.

Each year the government publishes what is known as the *HRA subsidy determination.* This is a formulaic assessment of how much subsidy the government thinks is appropriate for each authority to claim for the following financial year. Embedded in the determination formulae are assumptions about the authority's debt charges for the year, its need to spend money on managing and maintaining its stock, and the level of rents it will charge. By manipulating these assumed expenditure and income flows, the government is able to exercise a degree of control over the total amount of subsidy payable nationally and how that total is to be distributed regionally to different types of authority.

Central government influence is then extended by creating a *notional* HRA for each council. This is a combination of actual known costs and notional costs and income (based on central government assumptions about what they 'should be' for this sort of authority). This produces a notional account of income and expenditure. It is important to understand that these notional figures are not based on a 'need to spend'. The system works down from a national aggregate figure. It is grounded in concerns about controlling public expenditure rather than financing what local politicians judge to be local housing needs.

The 1990 system for England and Wales gave each authority its own guideline rent and its own management and maintenance allowance. In the early 1990s, guideline rents were calculated according to the government's objective of trying to move rents to levels that reflected the kinds of differentials that existed in the local housing markets. This was not to say that council rents should be equated with market rents, but that rent increases should reflect property values.[46]

Figure 11.2: Notional HRA (highly simplified)

INCOME	£m	EXPENDITURE	£m
Rent	20	Debt charges	12
HRA subsidy	8	Management	7
		Maintenance	9
Total	28	Total	28

---

46 Council rents have always tended to reflect property values (e.g. they have been higher in London than anywhere else). What the 1990 system did was to enable the government to influence rents through the subsidy system and to put particular pressure on councils in high value areas to increase their rents by more than authorities in low value areas. They do this by taking RTB valuations as a proxy for property values in different areas. Authorities are then expected to raise a share of the aggregate rental income in the country as a whole in proportion to the value their stock (as a share of the total national stock of council housing).

The two sides of the account have to balance. The central authorities make assumptions about each of the items (i.e. enters notional figures) and subsidy then fills any final deficit. By altering the notional entries, it becomes possible to alter the amount of subsidy entitlement. Clearly, this control mechanism can be used to influence local housing management policies. If the starting point is a reduction in subsidy, then the notional account can only be made to balance by putting up rents, reducing management and maintenance, or by some combination of all three.

Guideline rents and the local authorities' freedom to set rents

As described above, the current subsidy system allows the government to influence the level of rents through its assumptions about the notional HRA. In practice, this influence is exercised each year by the government announcing a 'guideline' rent increase for each council.[47] Local authorities have always had a great deal of freedom to set their own rents, apart from a short period in the 1970s. This freedom is something that they value and to which they have clung tenaciously. Both the 1980 and the 1990 regimes should be seen as central government attempting to devise mechanisms that simultaneously meet the local authorities' aspirations to keep control over rent-setting, and central government's desire to control subsidy levels and to have some influence over local rents. With this in mind, the system works by the government saying to every council what it regards as a reasonable guideline rent level for that particular authority. Each authority, in England and Wales, is given its own guideline rent and its own guideline rent increase every year. However, each authority is still free, in principle, to set whatever rent it likes – the guideline does not have to be followed. To deviate far from the guideline, however, will have consequences as the system is designed to put pressure on authorities to conform to the guideline.

Until 1997, the allocation of subsidy was not explicitly tied to rent increase decisions. If an authority increased its rent above the guideline it did not received any additional subsidy, but, of course, the additional rents would in themselves generate more income. In 1996/97 the government made a significant change to the subsidy rules by introducing a subsidy 'penalty' for English councils that increased rents above the guideline figure. Any council that increased its rents above the guideline would not get any increased rent

---

47 The arrangement works by the government setting guideline rents for each authority based on what it regards as being the necessary HRA expenditure for that authority (notional figures). It makes an assumption of the RTB sales in the year and calculates the interest on put aside sales money that can be part of the HRA. Thus: Rents plus interest = the gross income...minus...reasonable expenditure on rent rebates, management, maintenance, voids, revenue to capital, etc., (mostly notional figures). This information then enables the government to set a minimum lowest rent and a maximum rent increase for each authority. In the early years after 1990 the increases were well above what the authorities had been setting in previous years. At the time, the government wanted to raise general levels to realistic rents and to encourage tenants to buy.

rebate subsidy as a result. This provided a strong incentive for authorities not to increase their rents above the rate of inflation.

Management and maintenance

The management and maintenance allowances set by the government each year are less than what councils actually spend on administering and looking after the stock. If over time, the allowances are not increased to cover inflation, which in recent years has been the case, this will have the effect of reducing the subsidy for management and maintenance in real terms.

Elsewhere in this book we have made it clear that, whereas maintenance is clearly a 'revenue' function, spending on major repairs or improvements is technically classed as 'capital'. However, in practice, under the current rules, a council can also pay for major building, repair or improvements schemes from the HRA. These sums are sometimes referred to as Revenue Contributions to Capital Outlay (RCCO), or Capital From Current Revenue (CFCR) in Scotland. In recent years, the introduction of tighter borrowing controls have led many councils to invest in such projects via revenue contributions. Because these resources come largely from rents, tenants should be consulted about such a policy. This is particularly true if the council wishes to show that it is acting in line with the principles of best value. Best value requires the authority to ensure that users understand the policy and have expressed a willingness to pay more for such repairs and improvements. Since 1997 it has become more difficult for English councils to fund capital schemes in this way. This is because in the 1996/97 subsidy determination, the rules were changed so that subsidy is only payable on increased rents up to the guideline increase.[48]

Debt charges

Under the present accounting system, a share of an authority's *historic* debt charges (covering both interest and repayment of principal), together with the cost of managing that debt, are charged to the HRA. Most of these charges also attract HRA subsidy. Although these arrangements are effective and fair in so far as they ensure that the HRA bears a share of the authority's debt financing costs, it is now recognised that historic charges in the HRA do not reflect the true 'resource' cost of the capital employed in housing assets. The charges take account of the continuing capital financing costs of assets funded by borrowing, but _not_ of assets funded from useable receipts, grant or revenue contributions. Furthermore, the HRA is _not_ charged with a cost covering asset depreciation. It is argued that the present accounting arrangements fail to make clear the real resource costs and therefore mask the true level of subsidy. For all these reasons, a decision has been made to move to a system of *resource accounting* that will allow the accounts to record the full resource costs of managing and maintaining the authorities' housing assets.

---

48 This, in effect, imposed a penalty on rent increases above the guideline. The changed rules reflected the Conservative's changed attitudes to rent increases at the end of their term (discussed above).

The HRA after 2003: the shift to resource accounting in England

Why is resource accounting being introduced?

It is intended to enable local authorities to make better decisions about the use and maintenance of their housing assets, by making more transparent the cost of capital tied up in the assets and providing resources to maintain them. It will also bring council house costing closer to the charging regime used in PFI deals thereby helping to open the way to the use of private finance to provide and improve council housing.

What is resource accounting?

Resource accounting is gradually being applied across government. It is planned to extend it to council housing from April 2003 onwards (in England only). A key feature of resource accounting is that it assesses the cost of capital as the capital is 'used' rather than when it is 'paid for'. In this way, it is meant to record the 'true asset costs' of providing the service during the period covered by the accounts. By making the accounts more transparent, resource accounting should make it easier for managers to assess the extent to which the assets are providing value-for-money. Under these arrangements, the accounts include a *charge* for the capital, reflecting the fact that it is *tied up* (e.g. as in council housing) rather than *free* to invest and earn a return. Resource accounting encourages the organisation to think in a more business-like fashion by shifting the accounting focus away from its historic costs towards the current value of its assets. By making explicit the maintenance and repair costs associated with low-grade assets, it also draws attention to the consequences of a *failure to invest* and acts as a stimulus to longer-term planning. In council housing, this aspect will be reinforced by the setting up of a Major Repairs Allowance to help provide for future repairs.

The debate centres on how to alter public sector accounting rules so that they do not inhibit public sector authorities and agencies from investing in worthwhile capital projects. Reformers argue the case for moving away from a 'cash-based accounting' model that focuses on the balance of inward and outward cash flows in a single financial year, towards an 'accrual accounting' model that focuses on the balance of costs and benefits that accrue over time (e.g. over the physical life of an asset or the term of the loan taken out to build or acquire an asset). The argument is that cash based accounting produces a bias in favour of short-term solutions that may prove to be more expensive in the long-run. Take the example of providing social housing for the homeless. Cash based accounting shows that relatively large sums of public money will need to be committed in the development period causing a 'deficit' in the short-term 'cash' accounts. This may discourage the decision-makers from investing in such assets and instead choose what *appears* to be the 'cheaper' option of putting homeless households into bed-

and-breakfast accommodation. However, accrual accounting, by taking a cost-benefit approach, may show that in the longer period, providing new social housing makes more financial sense than putting homeless people into bed-and-breakfast accommodation.

The new accounting arrangements

The object of the new arrangements is to enable authorities to take better decisions about the use of their housing assets by moving the HRA and the calculation of HRA subsidy to a resource accounting, or 'capital charging', basis. The new regulations are intended to make it easier to determine how much money a council has got tied up in housing stock, how much it will cost to maintain it, and what level of subsidy is necessary to keep rents below market levels. This, it is claimed, will make the system more transparent for tenants and will also highlight the true extent of the backlog in repairs. Because the introduction of resource accounting is intended to be a step towards authorities taking a more commercial approach towards housing management, its introduction will require the following:

- rent rebates to be removed from the HRA to the General Fund;
- the stock of housing to be appropriately valued;
- the backlog of repairs to be surveyed and costed;
- a capital charge to the HRA based on an assumed percentage return on the value of the stock;
- the imposition of an asset depreciation charge;
- the provision of a flexible allowance for major housing repairs (that can be carried forward); and,
- more freedom to draw up an HRA Business Plan and to behave commercially.

Rent rebates and the end of the cross-subsidy effect

As part of the shift towards resource accounting, the government is proposing to end the cross-subsidy paid by English council tenants to fund housing benefit. In September 1998, a spokesman for the DETR said, *'The idea is to get rid of rent rebates from the Housing Revenue Account and to place them elsewhere'* (*Public Finance*, 2-8 October 1998, p9.). If rent rebates remain a charge on the HRA this will distort their effectiveness as operating (i.e. 'resource') accounts as such a charge has nothing to do with the business efficiency of the housing department and is unrelated to the costs of maintaining the department's assets. Furthermore, because such a charge is not a feature of housing association accounts, its retention makes it difficult to compare business efficiency between the two types of service provider. The new financial framework is designed to place councils in a similar position to registered social landlords. The removal of rent rebates from the HRA will allow the account to function as a quasi-commercial landlord account, based on the value of its housing stock, rather than as a social account that relates to tenants' incomes. In this way the new HRA should more accurately reflect financial flows relating to the provision of housing assets.

This reform brings up the question of how the rebates will be paid for in future. One option would be to fund them in broadly the same way as rent allowances are funded at present, with the majority of the expenditure being met through specific grant, and the remainder being reflected within the SSAs (used to determine entitlement to Revenue Support Grant – refer above).

Valuing the stock and surveying its condition

If councils are to prepare their own effective business plans, they must have 'proper' valuations and condition information. The question of stock valuations is discussed in Chapter 9.

The new capital charge

The government consultation paper, *A New Financial Framework for Local Authority Housing* (DETR, 1999) indicates that the new capital charge will have two elements. The first relates to the opportunity cost of the capital tied up in the assets and the second to the costs of depreciation and major repairs.

The *opportunity cost charge* reflects the *cost of capital* employed in purchasing and maintaining HRA assets and will be based on a percentage return (probably 6 per cent) on the asset value. By charging the account with the current opportunity cost of the tied up money capital rather than the historic debt cost should encourage authorities to see their housing units as valuable economic assets that need to be managed in an optimal way. It underlines the fact that even properties that are out of debt (paid for) are not 'cost free'. This is intended to encourage managers to think carefully about getting value-for-money from their repairs and maintenance programmes. It should also encourage them to maximise rental income by operating an efficient voids policy. Under resource accounting, HRA managers are still expected to be responsible for paying an appropriate proportion of the authority's historic debts. The HRA will therefore continue to make a contribution to debt servicing costs based on a notional assessment of the HRA's share of the authority's total outstanding debt.

The *depreciation charge* reflects the *cost of consumption* or the 'depreciation' of the HRA assets. Depreciation is the wearing out, using up, or other reduction in the remaining life of the asset through use, passage of time, or obsolescence. Depreciation can be measured as a straightforward calculation based on a specified percentage, e.g. one per cent, of stock value. Another, more meaningful, approach would be to set an allowance for major repairs (MRA) based on stock condition information and designed to indicate the resources needed to maintain the value of the dwellings. The latter is likely to be regarded as the favoured option as it fits in better with the idea of a Business Plan that charts expected future maintenance and renewal costs. The MRA approach would also help to emphasise the nature of housing as a continuing social asset that needs to be in existence in perpetuity (as against a commercial asset with a fixed life term).

This element will provide authorities with more explicit information on the need for expenditure to maintain the value of the stock. It is intended to encourage authorities to produce stock condition profiles with realistic maintenance and replacement expenditure projections that will allow the production of more coherent asset management plans. An annual allowance for depreciation and major repairs will be paid as part of the subsidy calculation. This will provide greater certainty of future resources and thereby help to underpin the drive for better asset management planning.

The introduction of a Major Repairs Allowance

The shift to resource accounting implies the need for authorities to be able to demonstrate that they are using repairs and maintenance money efficiently and effectively. The consultation paper signals the creation of a ring-fenced pot of money for structural repairs in the form of a new *major repairs allowance*. Under this system the backlog of repairs may be addressed through credit approvals but these 'residual' approvals will be phased out as the backlog recedes. It was announced in December 1998 that there would be more resources for dealing with urgent repairs. Once the stock is 'in order', the authority will then be expected to produce accounts that reflect the value of homes and the cost of maintaining them. The new system may allow councils to build up reserves to underwrite their repairs and renewal plans. Unlike credit approvals, the major repairs allowance would not necessarily have to be used up in the year in which it is received. As revenue, it would be outside a single capital 'pot' (unlike housing credit approvals). Authorities will be encouraged, or required, to keep separate Housing Repairs Accounts that would record both the annual contributions from the resource account and what was actually spent. Any unspent balances will be carried forward to future years to fit in with the planning approach to asset management.

This accruals approach will replace the practice of allowing for the finance of historic debt. The idea is that such a system can be used to ensure that authorities are targeting need, and spending money on the stock in accordance with the principles of best value. Such an allowance will give authorities greater certainty about future funding levels on repairs and maintenance. It will also allow for funds to be withdrawn from failing authorities, or face scrutiny from the new Housing Inspectorate. It could also allow for the rewarding of authorities that demonstrate effective stock management.

It is not yet clear how the allowance will be paid for. One option would be to allow the surpluses that will accrue to the HRAs as a result of removing rent rebates elsewhere to be pooled nationally and recycled in accordance with some kind of needs formula.

The freedom to behave commercially

The reforms are predicated on the assumption that the current accounting arrangements fail to encourage the production of business-like asset management decisions. Of course, it has to be recognised that a reformed accounting structure by itself cannot change behaviour. The intention is that the proposed changes will be reinforced by other policy initiatives such as the best value regime and the creation of a single capital pot. We might add that councils cannot be expected to be more business-like if they are operating in a supervisory environment that requires them to comply with a wide range of detailed regulations and procedures. Resource accounting seems to imply a greater degree of freedom to set rents and make investment decisions.

The structure of the resource account is simply a tool to allow sensible decision-making to take place. The new account structure should help authorities to draw up HRA Business Plans relating to the financial management of the stocks of housing.

Figure 11.3: Typical HRA (highly simplified) in the new format

INCOME	£m	EXPENDITURE	£m
Rent and service charges HRA Subsidy (including allowance for major repairs) Other income		Capital charge, comprising: (a) cost of capital element (b) contribution for major repairs to Housing Repairs Account Management Maintenance Revenue contributions to capital Other expenditure	
Total		Total	

HRA Business Plans

It is likely that in England, the basis of HRA subsidy will soon be a process incorporating HRA Business Plans submitted by authorities. To avoid duplication and unnecessary bureaucracy, it is envisaged that submission of these plans will be linked to the HIP/best value process. The plans will be concerned with asset management and will focus on the physical needs of the stock. They will provide proposed schedules of work covering the planning period and make clear how such work will be financed. They are likely to have a strong strategic element within them that clarifies how the authority plans to maintain or enhance the value of its housing assets, and how its plans to invest in the stock will contribute to wider corporate objectives, such as the reduction in estate-based crime and the promotion of social cohesion.

Summary

Revenue funds are used to pay for the day-to-day running of *services* rather than for the construction or acquisition of housing *assets*.

Local authority revenue transactions are recorded in two major fund accounts. The day-to-day spending on services other than council housing is met from the General Fund. Spending on the provision of council housing, however, must be charged to a separate Housing Revenue Account (HRA). The distinction between HRA spending and non-HRA spending is key to an understanding of local government housing finance.

Central government supports the General Fund through the Revenue Support Grant and by redistributing the national non-domestic rate pool. It supports the HRA through the provision of an HRA subsidy. The HRA subsidy entitlement is calculated by reference to a notional account and its purpose is to cover the deficit on that notional account. The notional account provides a control mechanism through which the central authorities seek to administer the distribution of subsidy. The subsidy is represented as having two elements – a 'rent rebate' element and a 'housing' element. In Scotland, only the latter element is included, as housing benefit for all tenants is charged through the General Fund.

Apart from central government support, the main sources of income are council taxes (to the General Fund) and council housing rents (to the HRA).

Since 1990 in England and Wales, and for longer in Scotland, the HRA has been ring-fenced. This prevents virement of money from the General Fund and restricts money transfers from council housing to support the council tax fund.

The current arrangements are under review and in England will be replaced by a system of resource accounting by the year 2003.

Further reading

Jill Gibbs, *Rent Levels, Rent Structures and Affordability*, CIH, 1992.

Good Practice Briefing No.11 – Rents and Service Charges, CIH, December 1998.

Graham Moody Associates, *Council Housing – Financing the Future*, CIH, 1998.

CHAPTER 12:
Housing associations and registered social landlords: an introduction

This chapter introduces the financial arrangements for housing associations and Registered Social Landlords. Whilst the term 'housing association' is still commonly used, the more recent term 'Registered Social Landlord' (RSL) is gaining currency and is now used increasingly in Scotland as well as England and Wales. It is therefore used freely in the following four chapters on this topic. This introductory chapter identifies the objectives of this housing sector and briefly describes its institutional framework of regulation and control. Chapter 13 describes the basic revenue finance regime for RSLs and says something about rents and the consumption interests of tenants. Chapter 14 describes and analyses the sector's capital finance regime and Chapter 15 considers some aspects of the financial management of social landlords. How social landlords pay for the provision of support services for people with special needs is discussed in Chapter 17.

What is the social rented sector?
Housing associations and registered social landlords are non-profit-distributing organisations who, along with local authorities, provide and manage dwellings that are allocated principally on the basis of need rather than on ability to pay. Over the last forty years, governments have encouraged the development of the housing association movement as a 'third force' in housing provision. This encouragement has in part been motivated by a desire to prevent the housing system from becoming polarised between pure private provision on the one hand and municipal provision on the other. Although technically independent from central and local government, most housing associations have received funds from the public purse and have been held accountable for how this money has been spent. Housing associations are included within the Neill Committee's definition of 'Local Public Spending Bodies'. These are conceived of as not-for-profit organisations that are rarely elected and whose members are not appointed by ministers, but which provide local public services that are wholly or largely funded by the taxpayer.[1] Housing associations can provide housing for rent, leasing, or part sale, and are established for the declared and limited purpose of giving housing advice or themselves acquiring, building, improving, maintaining,

---

1   The concept of Local Public Spending Bodies was used by the Nolan Committee, now the Neill Committee. (Second Report of the *Committee on Standards in Public Life*,1996).

or managing dwellings (including hostels), or helping others so to do. In line with the present government's policy of developing housing and housing services in ways that promote social cohesion, well-being and self-dependence, associations have been given wider permitted purposes. The 2000 Green Paper *Quality and Choice: A Decent Home for All*, (DETR and Social Security), makes it clear that the government expects RSLs to contribute to housing-related manifestations of social exclusion (such as unemployment, relationship breakdown and drug dependency) and help address other factors that affect the quality of life (such as area regeneration and community safety). Since the late 1990s associations have also been encouraged to develop group structures which allow sister organisations to be set up that can develop units for outright sale.

There is no such thing as a typical RSL and the sector is becoming increasingly diverse. As well as housing associations, the legislative definition[2] embraces a variety of organisations variously constituted as 'societies' (founded on principles of self-help or mutuality), or 'trusts' (founded on principles of charity or the concern for the welfare of others), or 'companies' (founded on principles of business enterprise). More specifically, such landlords can be organisations previously registered (pre-1996), under Part 1 of the Housing Associations Act 1985, industrial and provident societies (registered with the Registrar of Friendly Societies), charitable trusts (registered with the Charities Commission), or companies (registered at Companies House). Social landlords can be charitable or non-charitable organisations. In this context, the notion of 'charity' involves the organisation defining and declaring specific benevolent objectives together with a commitment to use its financial surpluses solely for such purposes. A 'non-charitable' social landlord is allowed to operate without having to declare charitable objectives, but it is nevertheless debarred from trading for profit.

Many of the more recently formed social landlords have been created as a result of transferring local authority housing to the ownership and management of new landlords. The Housing Act 1996 extended eligibility for registration in England and Wales to not-for-profit, non-charitable companies including local housing companies set up by local authorities (refer to Chapter 10). It should be noted that large-scale voluntary transfer (LSVT), of local authority stock to housing associations was already established before 1996 (allowed for under the Housing Act 1985). LSVT has helped to transform the balance of responsibility in providing social housing. Since 1988 more than 400,000 homes have been transferred from around 100 local authorities to RSLs. In the latest round (1999) the government has received bids to transfer a further 150,000 homes. On current projections, RSLs may well become the biggest provider of social housing before 2005.

---

2   Part 1, Chapter 1 of the Housing Act 1996. In the consultations that led up to the Act, the government pushed for profit-seeking companies to be embraced by the legislation, but these proposals were not implemented and all social landlords must still operate on a not-for-profit basis.

In Scotland, there is currently no provision for statutory registration of bodies other than housing associations, and so far there has been only one LSVT, in Berwickshire. However, government policy now advocates stock transfer. Because this policy is being actively pursued by the Scottish Executive, changes in the registration and regulation regime are expected in the near future. In Northern Ireland, the housing association sector is small (less than 3 per cent of the stock) and stock transfer has not yet been considered. In Northern Ireland there are 43 registered housing associations providing about 15,000 homes. These represent 10 per cent of the province's publicly funded stock.[3]

Registration and its obligations

For administrative purposes, social landlords are divided into registered and non-registered categories. Although we are primarily concerned with the contributions of the registered sector, the reader should bear in mind that some social landlords choose not to be registered. By not being registered, such associations, trusts and companies are not eligible to apply for a share of the grant aid that is channelled through the non-departmental public bodies (see below and next chapter). They do, of course, avoid the bureaucracy that comes with supervision. One reason for not registering is that it gives the organisation the freedom to operate on a co-ownership basis.

Financing RSLs: an overview

Later we will look in detail at the sources of finance, but for the time being we will simplify matters by saying that RSLs receive funding from three primary sources.

1. Rental income from *tenants*.
2. Grants from the *government*.
3. Loans from *private lenders*.

In addition to these primary resources, some social landlords receive financial support from associated charities and from private donations and bequests.

If registered with the appropriate regulator (e.g. the Housing Corporation, Scottish Homes, National Assembly for Wales or Northern Ireland Housing Executive), the organisation becomes eligible to take advantage of government subsidies. In recent years, about half of the capital finance for RSLs has come from the State in the form of grants and most of the remainder has taken the form of loans from banks, building societies or other institutions.[4] By investing this mixture of public

---

3   The three largest associations, Belfast Improved Houses, Fold, and Oaklee, together provide about half of all association homes in Northern Ireland.

4   In 1997/98, an average of £23,000 of public money was spent on providing a new rented home in England, with the remainder coming from private funds. (NHF(a) undated p10).

and private funds, RSLs have now become the main providers of new social housing in the UK. They have provided about half a million new dwellings over the last ten years. By the late 1990s they were managing well over a million homes and each year re-housing over 80,000 households. In 1996/97 they provided an additional 28,000 dwellings in the UK (Wilcox, 1999).

The term 'registered social landlord' was introduced by the Housing Act 1996 to cover both housing associations and local housing companies in England and Wales. In Scotland and Northern Ireland, the term 'housing association' is still appropriate, although the same terminology as in England is slowly being adopted in Scotland.

Within constraints, RSLs are allowed, indeed expected, to generate surpluses, but unlike pure commercial enterprises, these cannot be distributed as dividends. Given their welfare objectives and level of public funding, commercial shareholding and trading for profit are not allowed and the unrestrained principles of business free-enterprise are deemed to be inappropriate. Having said this, RSLs are expected to operate in a business-like fashion and to use their financial resources in ways that are seen to be efficient and effective (see Chapter 2 for discussion on the notion of *value-for-money*).

Before looking in detail at how RSLs acquire and manage their capital and revenue funds, we need to assess their contribution to housing provision and say a little more about how their activities are managed and supervised.

The size and structure of the sector

Social housing is now recognised as being 'big business'[5] with social landlords owning more than £30 billion worth of assets, managing an annual revenue turnover of several billion pounds, and receiving private finance in excess of £15 billion.[6] About four per cent of the stock of dwellings in Great Britain is rented from housing associations and other non-local authority social landlords.

Individual RSLs vary in size from relatively small non-development organisations managing a few dwellings and carrying out no new construction, to large active conglomerates managing 20,000 dwellings or more, operating a development programme, and employing hundreds of staff. Several hundred associations are actively engaged in the process of building and refurbishing houses; the rest restrict their activities to managing existing properties. The larger organisations, such as the Anchor Trust and the North British Housing Association, each own in

---

5   This is reflected by the title of the 1997 conference of social housing finance executives and staff organised by the National Housing Federation in York: 'Housing Finance – Big Business'.

6   The National Housing Federation, reported by Alison Barker in 'High Rise, High Risk' in *Public Finance*, 14 March 1997, p13.

excess of 20,000 units, but the vast majority of RSLs are much smaller. During the early 1990s the movement consolidated through a process of mergers so that by the middle of the decade the ten largest associations managed about a quarter of the movement's total stock and the largest 200 owned three quarters of the stock. Although the larger associations are now prominent, the majority of associations are still relatively small in comparison with local authority housing departments. Two-thirds of all associations manage fewer than 250 units. 92 per cent of associations in England and Wales manage more than 25 per cent of the sector's total stock. On average, associations in Scotland and Northern Ireland are smaller than those in England and Wales.

A concentration of development activity

Since 1989, as far as development is concerned, a sharper distinction has emerged between the relatively small and the relatively large associations, particularly in England. The emphasis on 'value for public money' (*grant stretch*), coupled with the need to raise a higher proportion of the capital funding from private institutions, has meant that development activity has increasingly centred on the larger, 'fast track' associations. The larger associations are better positioned to provide collateral for loans, enjoy financial and managerial economies of scale, and they can cross-subsidise more costly projects from surpluses (often generated from schemes developed during more favourable grant regimes). In contrast, smaller, specialist associations have less scope to demonstrate value-for-money in a development role. As a result, the total number of associations receiving grant allocations declined after 1989.

The aims and objectives of the sector

Despite the important structural and motivational differences that necessarily exist between organisations that have been set up at different times for different reasons, it is nevertheless possible to identify a number of general aspirations, activities, characteristics and objectives that are shared by RSLs as a whole. The common aim of the movement is to provide decent housing and related services for people on low incomes and in housing need. More particularly, the Housing Act 1996 sets as criteria for registration that RSL (in England and Wales) must be non-profit bodies providing rented housing and with the following additional permitted purposes:

- providing land, amenities or services, or providing, constructing, repairing or improving buildings, for their residents;
- acquiring, or repairing and improving, or creating by the conversion of houses or other property, houses to be disposed of on sale, on lease or on shared ownership terms;
- constructing houses to be disposed of on shared ownership terms;
- managing houses held on leases or other lettings or blocks of flats;

- providing services of any description for owners or occupiers of houses in arranging or carrying out works of maintenance, repair or improvement, or encouraging or facilitating the carrying out of such works; and
- encouraging and giving advice to other voluntary organisations concerned with providing housing or services related to housing.

Housing associations have increasingly moved into other areas of activity such as housing for sale, regeneration, care activities, etc., and this has led to a wider use of group structures and unregistered subsidiaries. The government has now moved to recognise this growing diversity by widening the permitted purposes of RSLs to include regeneration activities, and by instigating various changes to the regulatory regime.

Accountability

Although, unlike local authority housing departments, RSLs are not controlled by directly elected representatives of local taxpayers, they are subject to internal and external scrutiny and regulation. The internal control centres on the board that has general responsibility for the organisation's affairs. The financial effects of past activities are recorded in 'standard' accounts (see below and following chapters). End of period *financial statements* are produced which typically comprise the audited set of 'standard' accounts together with a report by the board, legal and administrative details, and an auditors' report.

External accountability

RSLs are independent in the sense that they do not operate as direct agents of central or local government. However, they do receive significant sums of public money and, because of this, their development and management activities are scrutinised and, to some considerable extent, controlled by the non-departmental public bodies that have been vested with statutory powers of supervision. They are also answerable to any external firms and agencies that have lent them money. Because they borrow a proportion of their development finance from private sources, RSLs need to demonstrate to lenders that they are properly managed and have adequate collateral to cover their debts. The issue of financial management is discussed more fully in Chapter 15.

Regulation and control

Together this diverse group of non-profit-making organisations are sometimes referred to as 'the voluntary housing movement'[7]. This is because they are usually directed by unpaid committees or boards whose members are drawn from all parts

---

7   Over the years there has been considerable debate about how to describe the sector (see Mullins, *'More Choice in Social Rented Housing'* in Marsh and Mullins, 1998).

of the local community, including their own tenants. This group of 'volunteers' takes overall responsibility for the organisation's policy and work but are not usually involved in the day-to-day management. Typically, each RSL is managed by a paid chief executive who heads a team of officers, many of whom will be qualified. The *voluntary housing movement* should be distinguished from *the independent rented sector* of which it is a part. The term 'independent rented sector' was first coined by the 1987 White Paper Cm214 (1987a) and was then used in the Housing Act 1988 to cover all those landlords, both voluntary and commercial, that the Act empowered to operate the newly introduced deregulated, assured and shorthold, tenancies (see Chapters 16 and 17).

RSLs across Britain originally had a common regulator but the picture is now more complicated because of devolved government in Scotland, Wales and Northern Ireland. In England, the regulator is a non-departmental public body, the Housing Corporation, responsible to the Department of the Environment, Transport and the Regions. In Scotland, the regulator is Scottish Homes, formed from the Scottish part of the Housing Corporation and the now-abolished Scottish Special Housing Association. It is answerable to the Scottish Executive.

In Wales, Tai Cymru, or Housing for Wales, was originally the regulator, having taken over responsibility from the Housing Corporation. However, prior to devolution it was absorbed into the Welsh Office and the regulatory function is now administered by the National Assembly for Wales.

The Department of the Environment has acted as regulator in Northern Ireland, but this function is being transferred to the Northern Ireland Housing Executive as it has now given up its role as a developer of new housing. The NIHE will be responsible to the Northern Ireland Assembly once its constitutional position has been clarified and reaffirmed.

These regulators have four broad roles.

1. *To monitor and regulate* the RSL's overall financial health, core performance indicators (i.e. measures of performance standards in the areas of governance and finance), risk management, rent levels, and non-core housing work (e.g. their work in areas such as community care).

2. *To channel public investment* to RSLs in a way that seeks to help meet local needs and achieve value-for-money.

3. *To promote good practice* by disseminating research findings, and publishing directives and guidance notes. In support of this role they distribute grants to encourage innovation and good practices.

4. *To apply the principles of targeting and proportionality* that have been established by the government's Better Regulation Task Force.

The role and duties of the regulators

Since their creation, the regulators have been charged with a general duty to develop and scrutinise, that is, to encourage, monitor and control, the activities of housing associations and other RSLs in their areas. The 1988 legislation also charged them with the responsibility to advise and register landlords wishing to manage any stock transferred from the public sector and to offer advice and guidance to tenants of public sector housing that might be subject to stock transfer.

Through legislation, ministerial directives and informal advice, the government has sought to use the non-departmental public bodies to instil market-led values and commercial principles into the sector's development and management activities. Exactly why and how it has sought to achieve this will be discussed in Chapter 14 when we consider the detailed financial operations governing the investment activities of RSLs.

England

The Housing Corporation's headquarters are in London but it operates through a network of eight regional offices whose boundaries are more or less coterminous with those of the central government's regional boundaries for England. The network of offices carry out the day-to-day liaison with the individual RSLs and play a key part in managing the distribution of development resources (refer to Chapter 14). The Corporation is accountable to a board of management and a chief executive, all of whom are appointed by the Secretary of State who also receives an annual written report from the Corporation.

The Corporation has a statutory duty to regulate the performance of over 2,200 English RSLs to ensure that the 857,000 homes they provide are efficiently and effectively managed. It channels public funds into the sector to help RSLs play a part in meeting the government's target for the supply of affordable homes for people in housing need. It is itself accountable to ministers and, through them, to Parliament for how this public money is employed.[8] Ministers expect to see that the grant aid is invested in ways that help to deliver the government's policies for the sector. Its regulatory activities are also expected to reinforce the government's broader policies relating to best value, urban regeneration, welfare to work, social exclusion, community safety, and energy conservation. As the sector's regulator it seeks to see that RSLs provide their tenants with substantial rights and a good quality of service. As a catalyst of good practice, it commissions research and sponsors an Innovation and Good Practice Programme, previously Promotion and Advisory Grants, that supports practical projects that test new ideas for the benefit of RSLs, their tenants and the wider community.

---

8   In recent years, the government has been ambivalent about the degree of control and influence it seeks to exert over the day-to-day operations of these agents. On the one hand, it has sought to encourage independence of action by no longer requiring them to provide the Secretaries of State with five-year corporate plans. On the other hand, it has sought to use them to encourage RSLs to follow ministers' policy priorities.

In England eight Regional Development Agencies were launched in March 1999. Although their main role is currently seen to promote economic development and tackle the perceived imbalance in economic growth between the English regions, at some time in the future they could become included in the government's plans for devolution. Their responsible bodies, the *regional chambers*, could evolve into full-blown assemblies like those in Scotland, Wales and Northern Ireland if voters so decide. In any event, because housing is intrinsically linked to economic development, these new strategic bodies are bound to exert increasing influence over how housing provision is planned and financed in England.

Wales

Tai Cymru (Housing for Wales), was the national body responsible for promoting the development of affordable homes by RSLs in Wales. It was set up by Parliament in 1989. Since its creation, it has invested more than £1.5 billion, and produced over 30,000 new and improved homes for people who could not afford to buy or rent on the open market. Like the Housing Corporation, Tai Cymru had a statutory responsibility to regulate RSLs. 98 Welsh RSLs manage some 52,000 homes.

Tai Cymru was absorbed into the Welsh Office immediately prior to devolution, but with the creation of the National Assembly for Wales it took over the regulatory and funding roles. These are dealt with in separate parts of the Assembly Office. Regulation is the responsibility of the Housing Performance and Finance Division within the Local Government Group, whilst funding falls into the Housing and Community Renewal Division of the Social Services and Communities Group.

Scotland

Scottish Homes was set up in April 1989 and, like the Housing Corporation in England, it receives government funding and provides supervision of, and support for, housing associations and other RSLs. Scottish Homes was created by amalgamating the Scottish Housing Corporation and the Scottish Special Housing Association (SSHA). Its primary purposes are to help provide good quality, affordable housing for those in need and to contribute to the regeneration of local communities. In pursuing these goals it sponsors a wide ranging research programme and works in partnership with local authorities, housing associations, the voluntary sector, private developers, economic development agencies, financial institutions and local communities. Back in the 1970s, the SSHA was involved with regional housing development and urban regeneration and this involvement has remained as a priority of Scottish Homes. This emphasis on regeneration was given particular practical significance with the Scottish Office's initiative in the late 1980s called 'New Life for Urban Scotland'. This shifted the policy emphasis of Scottish Homes and other agencies away from inner city areas towards the problems of the peripheral local authority housing estates. Recent policy has maintained the emphasis on integrative projects in which Scottish Homes seeks to co-ordinate partnership approaches to urban development and renewal. Policy is set to change further now that Scottish Homes is responsible, through the Scottish Executive, to the Scottish Parliament.

Historically, Scottish Homes has functioned as a social landlord in its own right[9] and it still owns about 15,000 homes (1999). At one stage, the agency owned over 100,000 dwellings, but it was decided to give tenants more choice over who should be their landlord. As a result, many have voted to transfer to organisations such as housing associations or co-operatives. The process of transfer is continuing so that the remaining tenants will be given the opportunity to choose a new landlord. This policy is in line with the long-standing commitment to use the agency as an instrument for achieving tenure diversification in Scotland where public sector housing has traditionally been dominant. More than most other UK housing agencies, Scottish Homes has had a tradition of operating across tenure boundaries.

In addition to its cross-tenure strategic role, Scottish Homes has a specific 'housing corporation' role with respect to the activities of RSLs. Like the Housing Corporation in England, it regulates and channels funds into the RSL sector. The profile of Scottish RSLs is rather different from those in England and Wales. Many were established in the 1970s as relatively small and locally based housing associations, and a significant proportion were established to implement improvement programmes associated with the tenement housing so prominent in many Scottish cities. More recently, Scottish Homes has actively supported local authority stock transfers, notably in Glasgow, to tenant orientated management co-operatives and associations.

The tradition of publicly supported housing has been stronger in Scotland than elsewhere in the UK, and as a result, although development grant rates (still called 'Housing Association Grant' in Scotland) have fallen, they have remained significantly higher than those in England and Wales. As in England, the 'corporation' activities operate through regional offices. The front-line support and monitoring work of the agency is carried out through five regional offices, based on Scotland's local authority areas.

The process of devolution has brought into question the status and functions of Scottish Homes. There is currently much discussion in Scotland about the need for a new national housing 'super regulator' of all landlords, including councils. Scottish Homes has been put forward for this role.

The special case of Northern Ireland

Policy in Northern Ireland has been to maintain firm central control of housing association capital funding by the Westminster authorities who, until recently,

---

9   The Scottish Special Housing Association was not a housing association in the conventional sense, but rather a central government agency answerable to the Scottish Office. Its brief was to provide social housing where it was not reasonable to expect this to be done by local authorities.

provided 100 per cent funding of schemes in the form of grants and loans, channelled through the Northern Ireland Office. Fear of sectarian influence and discriminatory practices made Westminster slow to encourage a shift to mixed funding arrangements and the greater independence of action that would follow. By the 1990s, however, mixed funded schemes were being promoted in the province albeit with a greater degree of central government scrutiny than elsewhere in the UK.

As we explained in Chapter 8, since 1971, responsibility for the provision of public sector housing has been in the hands of the Northern Ireland Housing Executive, which was formed as a non-sectarian body to overcome the discriminatory allocation practices that had long been associated with local authority politics. The province's local authority housing stock was transferred to the NIHE to manage and develop. In contrast to local authorities in other parts of the UK, the NIHE continued to have a significant house-building programme in the 1990s and by the middle of the decade its new build output constituted more than half of the UK's total public sector output. Currently, direct housing provision by the Executive is being wound down and the development role is being passed to housing associations. With the establishment of the Northern Ireland Assembly, the NIHE will take over the monitoring and regulatory functions from the Northern Ireland Department of the Environment. Its well-established position as a strategic trans-authority agency places it in a good position to carry this 'housing corporation' function. Unlike the case of Scottish Homes, there is currently no proposal to end the housing management role of the NIHE through stock transfer to other landlords. A common waiting list is used for the Executive and the province's housing associations.

The independent Housing Ombudsman

Tenants in England with a grievance against an RSL may seek support from the Ombudsman so long as they can demonstrate that all other avenues of redress have been explored.

The structure of RSL accounts

Since the early 1990s housing association accounts have had to be presented in 'plc format' in accordance with accounting policies detailed in the Statement of Recommended Practice (SORP), drawn up by the four national housing federations in England, Wales, Scotland and Northern Ireland. Prior to that date housing association accounting practices were rather idiosyncratic reflecting their historical detachment from normal commercial business. With the development of mixed funding and the requirement to work more closely with private sector partners and funders, it became increasingly important to present their accounts in a format that matched that required by the various Companies Acts. In particular, it was felt that RSL accounts should have the following features. They should:

- reflect sound contemporary accounting practices and procedures;
- allow for the development of accounting policies relevant to the movement and which can be constantly applied to all social landlords;
- be clearly understood by other organisations who have an interest in, or financial relationship with, RSLs.

The main objective of the SORP is to provide guidance to RSLs on complying with the Statutory Instruments (first introduced in 1992) that require RSL accounts to conform to the relevant Companies Acts. Auditors and civil servants are also concerned that accounting practices in this sector do not diverge significantly from those used in local authority housing departments. In future, the demands of government policy mean that there will be an increasing need to compare efficiency and effectiveness criteria across the whole of social housing provision. This points to the need for a degree of commonality in accounting practices across all social housing providers.

The need for professional financial management and the requirement to produce financial statements

The new financial regime enhanced the financial profiles of housing associations and increased the risks attached to their financial management. (See Chapter 15 for discussion on risk management). This pointed to the need for associations to follow a clear professional code of practice for treasury management. Such a code was put forward in 1994 by the public sector accountants' professional body (CIPFA). The voluntary code is broadly based on that used in local authority housing departments but amended to take account of the views of the regulatory bodies in England, Scotland and Wales as well as of the appropriate UK federations. The code seeks to establish a framework that recognises the processes of control, reflects the decisions that have to be made, and concentrates on the policy issues that result. It is intended to ensure that there are appropriate reporting lines and procedures to enable landlords to implement their policies while, at the same time, making those who make these decisions properly accountable for their actions.

The code emphasises the point that the effective employment of money always involves a degree of risk and that treasury management decisions need to be explicit about the relationship between financial risks on the one hand and returns and benefits on the other. A treasury policy statement is considered to be at the heart of sound and accountable financial management. Such a statement might be expected to give guidance on the following.

- The limits of approved treasury activity.
- How the financial management strategy is formulated.
- The approved methods of raising capital finance.
- The approved sources of finance.
- Policy on interest rate exposure.

- Policy on external cash managers.
- Delegated powers.
- Review and reporting arrangements.

As well as clarifying and bounding financial responsibilities, a treasury policy statement sets a clear and concrete structural framework within which financial policy can be developed.

Wider accountability: RSLs and best value

There is currently much talk about extending the Labour government's local government best value initiative to cover the work of RSLs. The precepts of the local government best value framework are discussed in Chapter 5. The creation of a specialist Housing Inspectorate to oversee the implementation of housing service provision in local government was announced in June 1998. The government has made it clear that in England the statutory duty to provide best value in local government should 'read across' to the RSL sector. This means that although there is currently no intention to put a statutory duty on RSLs to provide best value, the government and its regulating agencies have made it clear that they expect the principles of best value to embrace the services that such landlords provide. Public and private organisations are expected to play an important role in the local authority's approach to best value through partnership, contractual work and collaboration.

Best value involves the setting up and monitoring of 'performance standards'. The Government also expects its agencies to secure 'continuous improvements' in the performance of individual landlords and the RSL sector as a whole. These two objectives establish a degree of tension in the system because a best value regime aimed at continuous improvement of services does not necessarily sit easily with a housing management standards approach aimed at everyone aiming at a minimum standard.

In essence, the idea of best value shifts the emphasis in the value-for-money debate away from an obsession with *costs* to a consideration of the quality of *outputs*. This shift in emphasis means that the service users' opinions have to carry more weight in policy and management decisions. A best value regime therefore requires emphasis to be placed on tenant participation.[10] The best value approach will require RSLs to demonstrate that they are delivering cost-effective services that meet the aspirations of tenants and residents. The Housing Corporation in particular is leading the way by working with the NHF to establish 23 pilot projects that will test the methods RSLs can use to deliver best value.

---

10 In the local government sector, best value involves creating locally negotiated agreements between tenants and the authority, setting out how the service users will participate in decisions that affect their homes and community.

As well as surveying best value activity, the Corporation is establishing a linked process designed to guarantee that such activity occurs. This process requires RSLs to develop 'comprehensive' participation methods that are relevant to local circumstances. These are to be followed by 'comprehensive' service reviews that:

- Critically appraise the purpose of undertaking tasks and the ways in which they are carried out.
- Monitor, measure and then *compare* performance with that of others to see where improvements might be made.
- Compete with others to demonstrate that value-for-money is being achieved and the best interests of residents and others are being met.

The comprehensive service reviews will be followed by the preparation of service statements, and then the production of performance plans and performance reports.

This linked process from participation, through review and culminating in action plans for improvement constitutes the framework for RSLs to develop and deliver best value. Detailed information on the operation of this framework is outlined in *Best value for Registered Social Landlords*, The Housing Corporation, February 1999.

Although the government is serious about establishing best value practices in this sector, any extension of the Housing Inspectorate's powers to cover RSLs has so far been resisted. Such a proposal is in any case questioned by many practitioners and commentators who are concerned that the sector is already over regulated. For this reason, the Housing Corporation, and Scottish Homes are suggesting a 'softer' approach that will not, for the time being at least, enforce a rigorous compulsory regime. In Wales, however, the National Assembly has decided to make best value a requirement for RSLs from April, 2000 onwards. The Audit Commission carries out value-for-money studies jointly with the three nationally based non-departmental public bodies. The Registrar of Friendly Societies plays a role in monitoring the affairs of some housing associations, and the Charity Commissioners regulate the affairs of associations registered as charitable trusts.

The softer approach to best value in this sector involves the following.

- The regulators setting 'aspirational targets' that social landlords should seek to achieve on core functions.
- Consulting residents on such things as design and layout, how they see their communities developing, the need for non-core facilities, and what constitutes a fair and reasonable rent policy.
- Landlords 'signing up' to an implementation framework that involves the publication of annual performance reports and action plans (as described above).

The need to take a cost-benefit approach to financial management

Given the fact that many RSLs are relatively small organisations, the drive for best value may put an upward pressure on costs. Because the sector's regulators (e.g. the Housing Corporation) place an emphasis on both cost reduction and best value, some social landlords will be confronted with a conflict of objectives. This means that any best value initiative involving the utilisation of additional resources, should be analysed in ways that measure intangible, as well as tangible, costs and benefits. Both best value and resource accounting and budgeting point to the need for social housing strategists and managers to develop cost-benefit assessment techniques that enable proper account to be taken of such relevant intangibles as tenant empowerment and staff morale.

Summary

In recent years, RSLs have been the main providers of new social rented accommodation.

Although there is no such thing as a 'typical' RSL they share the following core values:

- a focus on need and affordability;
- a commitment to independence and voluntarism;
- a concern to create and maintain 'sustainable' social housing;
- a commitment to obtain added value from housing management and investment;
- a commitment to build partnerships with stakeholders in communities;
- an increasing commitment to act as housing-centred regeneration agencies.

Registration places an obligation of external regulation and control, but also qualifies the RSL to bid for centrally provided resources.

With the development of regional tiers of government, in future there is likely to be a more co-ordinated approach to the regulation and support of social rented housing.

Further reading

David Curry, *Lobbying Government – A Guide to Lobbying on Housing Issues*, CIH, 1999.

HACAS, *Housing Associations – A Viable Future?* CIH, 1999.

Jeff Zitron, *Winning Structures – Registered Social Landlords in a Changing World*, CIH, 2000.

CHAPTER 13:
Social landlords: rents and revenue finance

In the previous chapter we looked at the nature and scope of housing associations and other registered social landlords (RSLs), and we also described the framework of regulation within which they have to operate. In this chapter, we turn to the question of rents and revenue finance. Once we have defined revenue as a financial concept and explained how it is treated in the accounts, we will turn our attention to the various consumption interests that are vested in the sector. We will conclude by examining the revenue finance regime and considering the theoretical and practical questions surrounding rent-setting policies.

Revenue income and expenditure

Revenue finance is concerned with the day-to-day income and expenditure of the organisation. Revenue income is needed to meet the running costs of being in business. In calculating revenue income, allowance has to be made for voids and bad debts.

The income and expenditure account is one of the primary accounts that all housing associations and other RSLs have to have audited every year. The broad purpose of the account is threefold. It shows how the surplus for the year was arrived at. It charts any transfer to or from restricted and designated reserves. And it shows how the balance on the revenue reserve has changed from the previous accounting period (i.e. last year). See Figure 13.1.

The income and expenditure account can receive money inflows from rents, grants, interest earnings and private donations. In addition, in certain circumstances, some money can enter the account when assets are sold.

Income
The following constitute the primary sources of revenue income:

- *Rents*. Rent charges are the prime source of income for all social landlords. The rental flow represents the main business 'turnover' or 'trading income'. Housing associations can receive rents that are based on two distinctive types of tenancy contract. Contracts entered into before 1989 are typically based on 'secure' tenancy agreements. Under these agreements, the rent is determined by an independent rent officer and is calculated on a 'fair rent' basis. (The notion of fair rents is explained in

Figure 13.1 Income and expenditure account for the year ended 31 March XXX1 (Presented in the format of SORP March 1999)

	XXX1 £'000	XXX0 £'000
Turnover	X	X
Less: Operating costs	(X)	(X)
Operating surplus		
Profit/(loss) on sale of fixed assets	X	X
Interest receivable and other income	X	X
Interest payable and similar charges	X	X
	(X)	(X)
Surplus on ordinary activities before taxation		
Tax on surplus on ordinary activities	(X)	(X)
Grant receivable against taxation	X	X
Surplus for the year	X	X
Transfer from/(to) restricted reserves	(X)	(X)
Transfer from/(to) designated reserves	X	X
Revenue reserve brought forward	X	X
Revenue reserve carried forward	X	X

Notes

1. Turnover represents the income received during the period and is therefore shown net of rent losses from voids. Rent losses from bad debts are included within operating costs. Turnover comprises gross rents receivable plus service charges receivable plus revenue grants receivable[1] plus any other 'trading' income.

2. The operating costs record the running expenses of the housing services provided during the accounting period. They include depreciation, bad debts, cost of sales, staffing costs, overheads, property maintenance and repairs, management and other operating costs. Interest payable and similar charges are not classed as operating costs but appear as a separate item below the operating surplus. This is because interest is deemed to be part of the financing aspect of the business and as such, not tied to operations or turnover, even though a substantial part of the rental income is in fact used to meet loan interest charges.

3. Before calculating the surplus, or deficit, for the year, the effect of any corporation tax payable must be shown. Charitable organisations are not subject to corporation tax. Non-charitable RSLs are liable to pay tax but have, until recently, been able to receive a 'Section 54 grant' to help meet this liability. Other taxation (e.g. VAT) is included with the related expenditure. The tax liabilities of RSLs are looked at in Chapter 15.

4. Auditors, lenders and other readers of the account will pay particular attention to the figure representing the surplus for the year. It is important because it will determine whether or not the reserves can be added to. Loan covenants (see Chapter 15) often stipulate minimum surplus levels.

5. Restricted reserves are monies that have to be held for specific purposes that are decided by outside parties (e.g. the Housing Corporation). They include, for example, the grant element of a capital receipt from a dwelling that was originally part funded by public grant (e.g. HAG). This money has to be either recycled into new development or clawed back by the funding agency (e.g. the Housing Corporation). In the meantime it must be set aside in a 'restricted reserve'.

6. Designated reserves are monies that are held for specific purposes decided by the agency itself (e.g. a sinking fund for major repairs).

---

1   If SHG was used to fund the costs of major repairs during the year and these were included in expenditure, then SHG would form part of the annual turnover.

Chapter 16). Contracts entered into after 1989 are typically based on 'assured' tenancy agreements and are determined by the association itself. (The notion of assured rents is explained in Chapter 16 and the issues surrounding rent-setting policy are discussed at the end of this chapter). When secure tenancies are surrendered the re-lets convert to assured status. This means that over time, fair rent tenancies will be phased out.

- *Revenue grants.* These were significant before 1989 because the income from fair rents was insufficient to cover the normal running costs of associations and as a result many experienced a deficit in their revenue finances. For this reason Revenue Deficit Grant (RDG), can be claimed in England and Wales to help finance the running of pre-1989 general needs schemes. Allocated RDG will be reduced if the association is holding significant reserves and surpluses. The central authorities argue that the need for revenue grants is diminishing because fair rent levels have risen and assured tenancies (with higher rents) are becoming the normal arrangement.

  In recent times, supported housing (providing for special needs) has been given grant aid to contribute to the enhanced management costs associated with such schemes. In England this support is called Supported Housing Management Grant (SHMG); in Wales it is called Supported Housing Revenue Grant (SHRG); and in Scotland it is called Special Needs Allowance Package (SNAP). The way in which public funds are directed into supporting the management of special needs housing is currently under review (see below for fuller discussion on this topic). For supported housing schemes, RSLs have to set two elements of rent/service charge, as from April 2000. In setting the core accommodation element, they have to take account of rent levels for comparable general needs accommodation in the area. Higher management and support costs relating to the extra staff time required to work with vulnerable tenants has to be identified separately for the purposes of the transitional housing benefit scheme being introduced under the *Supporting People* policy.

- *Social Housing Grant (SHG).* SHG is usually classified as *capital* support and, as such, will be discussed fully in Chapter 14. However, if SHG was received to help finance major repair work, and these costs were treated as 'revenue', then the accountants' 'matching principle' requires the grant to be classified as revenue in such instances. The idea of the *matching principle* is discussed in Chapter 2.

- *Interest received.* Those RSLs with invested surpluses are able to generate an additional income flow from these cash investments.

- *Donations.* Some associations may also receive some financial support from associated charities and private contributions.

In addition to these primary sources of income, there can be an inflow of money into the expenditure account when assets are sold. As a general principle, when an asset is sold the disposal proceeds constitute a capital receipt (i.e. *capital* rather than revenue income). However, under certain circumstances, assets sales may produce financial resources that are counted as a contribution to income.

- *Current asset disposals.* Properties developed for outright sale or on behalf of third parties should be treated as current assets rather than fixed assets. This means that the development activity is regarded as part of trading activity. Where there have been current asset property disposals in the period, for accounting purposes, the disposal proceeds are included in turnover.

- *Surpluses on fixed asset values.* Dwellings held as part of the landlord's stock of rentable properties count as fixed, as against current assets. They are represented in the books at a value called the 'carrying value'. If they are sold and the proceeds are greater than the carrying value then the surplus is treated as a contribution to income. This is a rather technical point and is really a book-keeping nicety. Any such surplus cannot be regarded as a *bona fide* trading income, it is simply the result of a miscalculated value. And of course, it is quite possible for sale proceeds to be *less* than the carrying value so that the sale has a negative income effect. For these reasons the surplus or deficit is shown as a separate item on the face of the income and expenditure account below operating surplus and above interest (refer to Figure 13.1).

Expenditure

Revenue income is used to pay for the day-to-day running costs of the business. In social housing these so-called 'costs-in-use' include outgoings on the following.

- *Debt servicing.* This has become an increasingly significant factor since the introduction of the reformed finance regime in 1989. The new regime (described below and in the next chapter) requires associations to rely much more heavily on private sources of finance to fund their development activities. This produces loan debts that have to be serviced out of current income flows. Measured as unit costs (cost per tenancy provided) debt charges tend to be higher than those of local authority housing departments. This is because RSLs tend to have a relatively higher proportion of 'newer' dwellings that carry relatively higher debts.

- *Housing management.* These are the administrative costs of running the business. The main items of expenditure are staff salaries, and office expenses such as rent, heat, light, telephones, consumables, etc. Measured as unit costs, the administration costs of traditional housing associations tend to be higher than those of local authority housing departments. This is because most traditional associations tend to operate on a relatively small scale. Management economies of scale are more readily achievable in larger LSVT associations.

- *Property maintenance*. An issue here is defining what building works should count as revenue and thereby be charged to the income and expenditure account, and which should be capitalised. Generally accepted accounting practice says that works that result in an enhancement of the productive capacity of the asset, that is, an increase to the net rental stream over the life of the property, should be deemed 'improvements' and capitalised. An increase in the net rental stream may arise through an increase in the rental income, a reduction in future maintenance costs, or a significant extension of the life of the property. An item that results in this kind of outcome should *not* normally be charged as revenue. (For further discussion on this point see section below on *Accounting for income and expenditure*).

- *Major repairs provision*. Before 1989 capital grants, called Major Repair Grants, could be applied for to help bring sub-standard dwellings back to an appropriate fitness standard. With the withdrawal of this support after 1989, monies now have to be set aside in designated reserves for this purpose. The reserves are accumulated by making regular payments into some kind of sinking fund. The sinking fund payments are normally derived from a supplement to the rent charge. The statutory funding bodies make recommendations about the appropriate amounts that ought to be set aside in this way. (This is discussed further in Chapter 14).

Accounting for income and expenditure

Each social landlord is required to keep a record of its revenue finance transactions in an income and expenditure account. The standard format for this is set out in Figure 13.1. The income and expenditure account records the receipt of rental income. In commercial terms this represents the main item of business 'turnover' for the financial year. Operating costs are deducted from the turnover figure to display an 'operating surplus'. Other sources of income, such as any profit on the sales of fixed assets, interest received and other income, is added to the operating surplus to produce a 'surplus on ordinary activities before taxation'. Tax adjustments are then made to give the 'surplus for the year'. This surplus, which of course cannot be distributed as a dividend, has to be transferred into reserves which are part of the organisation's assets and are valued in the balance sheet. (The layout of a standard balance sheet is shown in Chapter 15).

As we have made clear in previous chapters, the distinction between revenue and capital is not hard and fast and is largely determined by accounting conventions and local practices. The distinction can be particularly murky in the area of property maintenance. With the level and pattern of spending changing and increasing pressures to demonstrate 'best value', social landlords need to ensure that they employ accounting practices that can be applied consistently to the expenditure incurred. These days they therefore follow generally accepted accounting practice in deciding which items of spending are capitalised and which items are charged to income and expenditure. As a general principle, expenditure that relates to maintaining a building in its present state or restoring it to its original condition should be treated as revenue. Revenue spending thus helps maintain current property values and rent earning capacity. In contrast, acquisitions and works that result in a real increase in the net rental stream over the life of the property are deemed to be 'productive' and thus counted as capital.

Rent Surplus Fund

One of the consequences of the 1989 revenue finance regime (discussed below) was that, in the early 1990s, social housing rent levels increased. This increase in rental income was an intentional outcome of the Housing Act 1988. In introducing the reforms the government intended that most associations would begin to make surpluses of income over expenditure. The legislation therefore required all housing associations that had been in receipt of capital grant aid to set up a special fund to receive such surpluses. The fund *only* applies to schemes built under the old finance regime (prior to 1989).[2] This fund is called the Rent Surplus Fund (RSF). The purpose is to show separately in an association's financial statements any surplus that has arisen from increased rental income on projects built under the earlier regime for which it had received 'generous' grant aid. In April 1992, the rules relating to this fund were liberalised and simplified. Under current arrangements the regulatory bodies may allow a proportion of the rent surplus fund to be retained to help finance future reinvestment. When this is allowed, the approved amount is transferred to a restricted reserve set up for that purpose. When the regulatory body has not prescribed the operation of the RSF in this way, a designated reserve should be used. Precisely how any rent surplus can be used varies as between rented properties and shared ownership properties.

Tenants and the consumption interest

The 1991 census indicated that, at that time, housing associations housed about three per cent of all households.[3] By 1997, housing associations had increased their market share to about 4.8 per cent of all households in the UK. By that date

---

2   In these schemes some tenants may be paying fair rents on secure tenancies and some may be paying assured rents, if the property has been re-let.

3   In 1997, of the 24,802,000 households in the UK, some 1,188,000 were renting from housing associations or some other form of RSL. This was less than half of the figure for the private rented sector, which housed about 2.5 households or 10.4 per cent of the total. Some 17.4 per cent rented from local authorities (4,323,000 households). 67.3 per cent of all UK households (16,702,000) were owner-occupiers. (Source: Wilcox, *Housing Finance Review*, Rowntree/CIH/CML, 1999).

they were providing over 1,188,000 homes for some two million people.[4] By 1999 not only had RSLs become the main provider of new homes to rent, but also they owned and managed as much as a quarter of the total stock of social housing (NHF(b) undated).

The letting conventions of this sector are embedded in notions of beneficence and tenant support that stem from the historical values of the housing association movement (see Chapter 12). This means that landlords in this sector have a long tradition, going back to the establishment of almshouses in the twelfth century, of providing homes for those who are unable to afford market housing. This tradition recognises that access to a decent home is a prerequisite for people to live a dignified life and to participate socially and economically in the community. Today, these traditional housing association values continue in that most RSLs actively seek to play a part in tackling what has become known as *social exclusion*.[5] In particular, they seek to deliver what the Housing Corporation terms 'Housing Plus'. This Corporation term is meant to encapsulate the idea that investment in housing should have more than 'bricks and mortar' outcomes. It demonstrates a commitment to *extra curricula* consequences of housing investment such as providing tenants with better health and employment opportunities, reducing truancy rates amongst their children, and generally providing safer and more stable communities.

Affordability

National Housing Federation figures (1997) indicate that by the late 1990s almost 70 per cent of rents charged in this sector breached its own definition of affordability. The Federation's definition utilises both a *benchmark* and a *ratio* measure of affordability (refer to Chapter 3). It states that *rents are affordable if the majority of working households are not caught in the poverty trap (because of dependency on housing benefit), or are paying more than 25 per cent of their net income on rent*. In Scotland, SFHA advocates a different measure of affordability and there is no formal measure in Wales. CIH has published, jointly with NHF and LGA, a new study, *Evaluating Housing Affordability: Policy Options and New Directions*.

By the early 1990s, nearly 75 per cent of housing association tenants were not in paid employment (i.e. they were retired, unemployed, or for some other reason 'at home'). Of the 25 per cent or so with jobs, most were in low paid employment with an average income of under £10,000 (1992). It is worthy of note that today about 82 per cent of the working population earn more than the average new housing association tenant. This means that a relatively high proportion of tenants

---

4   By this time, the private rented sector had also expanded to house over 10 per cent of households. (Source: *Housing and Construction Statistics* and NFHA).

5   'Social exclusion' is a declared political concern of the Labour government, and Tony Blair has highlighted housing as one of the 'seven pillars' of a decent society.

are in receipt of housing benefit. The incomes of tenants in social housing have been put on average at one third of the incomes of home owners.[6]

Entering and exiting the sector

Many tenants are nominated to an RSL by their local authority housing departments. Some will be referred by a specialist referral agency or a housing charity. Individuals can always apply directly to a local RSL for a tenancy. The movement's welfare commitment means that consideration is given to methods of exit from, as well as entry to, the sector. In particular, if a tenant wishes to become an owner-occupier and can afford to do so, arrangements exist to help this to happen. In this way a renter with ownership aspirations is aided while, at the same time, a social tenancy is made available to someone else who is deemed to be in greater housing need. Under certain circumstances it may be possible for the tenant of a social landlord to purchase their home. (These exit methods are described in more detail in Chapters 6 and 14).

Providing support services

A high proportion of RSL housing is targeted at people with special needs. There is a wide range of people who rely on such support. These include the frail elderly, people with learning disabilities, people with mental health problems, victims of domestic violence, people who suffer from alcohol or drug addiction, ex-offenders, and young people who are homeless or who are for some other reason at risk. The current provision of sheltered and supported housing seeks to help this wide range of vulnerable people to maintain stable and independent lives in the community by providing a range of specialist support services. Such services vary in scope and intensity and include general counselling and advice, assistance with administrative affairs, services provided by wardens, and liaison work with other agencies and individuals responsible for the person's welfare. At the time of writing, the government is proposing to introduce new integrated arrangements to help fund these services. These are discussed in Chapter 17.

Prior to 1989 special needs hostels were developed against specific design and staffing criteria and then received 100 per cent capital grant (HAG) funding. Once built, the costs-in-use that could not be met out of rental income were covered by a special revenue deficit grant.[7] This meant that so long as the costs-in-use met specific criteria and were approved by the funding agency, public money would ensure that these, like the capital costs, would be fully covered. Under the 1989 arrangements revenue support for this type of housing centred on a fixed bedspace formula that allowed associations running hostel-type accommodation to apply for a revenue allowance that contributed towards the higher management costs of

---

6   Information on tenants' incomes and rents is recorded by continuous recording systems (CORE in England and Wales and SCORE in Scotland). These systems are operated by the NHF and SFHA.

7   Hostel Deficit Grant paid the difference between revenue and qualifying actual costs.

schemes for people needing specialist help. In contrast to the earlier arrangement, the management allowance did not provide full deficit funding and only paid a contribution towards the additional costs. By the late 1990s the expectation was that the running costs of supported housing should be met largely out of revenue income rather than through additional revenue grants.[8] This has meant that in recent years much of the revenue burden has been carried by the housing benefit system (refer to Chapter 17).

Under government proposals due to be introduced across the UK in 2003, housing benefit will no longer meet the costs of service charges for support services. Instead, there will be more general grants administered by local authorities, and separate grants like SNMA and its equivalents will disappear. More details are contained in Chapter 17.

The revenue finance regime

Both the capital and the revenue financial arrangements for this sector were radically reformed in 1989. (The capital regime is described and discussed in the next chapter). To appreciate the nature and scope of the present revenue system, we need to understand the pre-1989 arrangements and why and how they were reformed. The arrangements are described for England but are similar in the rest of the UK.

The revenue finance regime before 1989

The earlier revenue regime was established in 1974 and its main features can be summarised as follows. (The pre-1989 capital finance arrangements that ran in parallel with the revenue regime are summarised in Chapter 14).

- In line with the policy for most private sector rents, housing association rents were *regulated* 'fair rents'[9] set by independent agents of central

---

8 Social landlords can have access to other sources of revenue funding for supported housing from a range of partner agencies. For example, Section 73 funding (1985 Housing Act) gives central or local government authority to help voluntary organisations concerned with the homeless or with matters relating to homelessness assistance by way of grant or loan. Home Office funding might be available to help with the running costs associated with the provision of housing for ex-offenders and people on probation. This normally involves the scheme setting aside an agreed quota of bedspaces – analogous to a local authority nomination agreement. Other resources can come from the Health Service and from charitable donations. Under new proposals, the additional public funding streams are likely to be pulled together into a unified support system, embracing housing benefit, that will be co-ordinated by the local authorities.

9 The 'fair rent' system was introduced by the Rent Act 1965 for the private sector and extended to public sector and housing association tenancies by the Housing Finance Act 1972. The provisions were consolidated in the Rent Act 1977 and subsequently amended by the Housing Act 1980. The provisions were again consolidated by the Housing Act 1985 and then further amended by the Housing Act 1988.

government known as 'rent officers'[10]
- Management and maintenance allowances were granted. These were designed to give associations some security of income so that they could plan their budgets and cover their basic administrative costs, including the costs of development.
- A flexible Revenue Deficit Grant (RDG) could be applied for. This helped associations meet the additional current costs they faced as a result of expanding their development activities. This grant was put in place in recognition of the fact that rent levels were not negotiable but pre-set by rent officers. Because an association was unable to meet any legitimate additional revenue expenses by raising its rents it was felt necessary to provide this addition grant aid.
- The Housing Corporation was given enhanced powers so that it could impose an appropriate degree of regulation and control over the use of this 'generous' public funding.

The 1989 revenue finance regime

The above arrangements were reformed by the provisions of the Housing Act 1988 which laid down the structure of the current revenue finance regime. The new regime came into force in January 1989. The current revenue regime has the following key features.

1. The replacement of secure tenancies with assured tenancies
The driving idea behind the revised tenancy arrangements was to shift housing association practices on to a more commercially orientated footing. The key element was the replacement of fair rent tenancies with assured tenancies. Under the provisions of the Act, existing secure tenancy agreements continued but new tenancies were to be 'assured'. In this way, over time, secure tenancies will be phased out. Rents for assured tenancies are required to be market-related and agreed between the landlord and the tenant. To all intents and purposes this means that they are set by the association. This provision means that RSLs can normally no longer look to rent officers to determine rent levels – they must have their own procedures for establishing and implementing rents. In setting rents they have to balance the requirements of *affordability* with those of *sufficiency* and *accountability* (see below *Rents and rent setting policy* and also discussion in Chapter 4).

---

10   These officials are required to set rents that ignore the personal circumstances of both the tenants and the landlords. Furthermore, the rents they set must assume that the properties are not in short supply; this means that they must not include any price element that reflects the scarcity value that a particular tenancy may possess. They must, however, take into account other relevant circumstances including the property's age, location, character and state of repair. Fair rents are 'registered' and remain fixed for a period of two years. Either party can appeal to the Rent Assessment Committee and subsequently to the courts if they wish to challenge the rent officer's decision. A fair rent may consist of two elements; one relating to rights of occupancy and the other to service charges.

2. A shift away from the 'welfare' principle of revenue deficit funding towards the 'commercial' principle of self-financing from rental income

The shift towards assured tenancies and the freeing up of rents reduced the expectation of deficits. Although assured tenancy rents were not expected to be as high as rents for equivalent properties in the private sector, they *were* expected to rise to a point where deficits diminished or disappeared. After 1989, rents became negotiable and were normally expected to cover all management costs. For this reason, under the new arrangements, the old Revenue Deficit Grant[11] was no longer normally payable to help cover the running costs of schemes that had been part funded by the private sector (called 'mixed funded' schemes). Such schemes were now expected to be largely self-financing from rents. Like the move from secure to assured tenancies, the move away from *revenue deficit funding* towards *self-financing* underlined the government's intention that associations should now operate less as welfare agencies and more as commercially viable organisations. Deficit funding is now only available for schemes that are fully financed by the public sector (called 'publicly funded' schemes).

3. Clear rules for how revenue surpluses can be used

By the 1980s it became clear that some of the well-established associations had managed to pay off the capital loans associated with their projects and the continued rental flows were beginning to generate revenue surpluses. In response, the government introduced the Grant Redemption Fund (GRF – created by the Housing Act 1980). The scheme, which became fully operational in 1983, established the principle that when a grant funded scheme made a surplus on the revenue account, the assessed surplus could only be used in prescribed ways. With ministerial approval, it could be utilised by the association itself on specified reinvestment projects. Alternatively, it could be used to offset any entitlement to Revenue Deficit Grant, which was then still widely available. If neither of these courses of action were deemed appropriate, the surplus was clawed back by the central authorities into a central fund for reinvestment elsewhere.

The 1989 regime replaced the Grant Redemption Fund with a new fund called the Rent Surplus Fund (RSF). Under these revised arrangements, associations have been allowed to retain a higher proportion of their surpluses. The bulk of any surplus generated from mixed funded schemes can now be retained so long as the money is used specifically to build up reserves or establish sinking funds to help meet future major repair costs. A proportion can now also be used for 'rent pooling' purposes. The scheme has worked slightly differently in Scotland where associations have been allowed to utilise more of the surpluses, usually to set up sinking funds for future repairs and replacements.

---

11   The object of RDG was that it should make good revenue deficits where it is clear from the application and from the accounts that the association had done its best to manage its stock and its revenues efficiently. In cases where, despite good management, a deficit arose, RDG might be awarded. Although RDG was phased out after 1989, a new one-off up front grant could be paid to associations who experience setting up problems and are unable to cover outgoings from rents.

Rents and rent-setting policy

The key revenue inflow for any landlord is rental income. Rents are set in accordance with the tenancy agreement and usually reflect the nature of the utility generated by the dwelling; that is, to some extent tenants pays for what they consume. Tenancy arrangements in this sector were reformed by the Housing Act 1988 in ways described above. Tenants whose tenancy agreements predated the Act will be paying rents under the old 'fair rent' regime, under which the rent is set by the rent officer and reviewed periodically. Under the post-1988 regime, associations are allowed to set their own rents so long as they meet their obligation to cover their costs. [12]

In Chapter 4 we made the general point that a potential conflict exists between the social policy objective of setting rents at levels that are low enough to be affordable to tenants, and the commercial policy objective of setting rents at levels that are high enough to cover the landlord's legitimate business costs. In exploring the tensions generated by this conflict we identified a set of contrasting rent-setting principles that could be used to guide the pricing policies of landlords. Marginal cost pricing, market pricing, historic cost accounting, capital value pricing, and consumption pricing were all identified as basic principles that could be used individually or in combination to rationalise and legitimate charging a particular rent for a specific property.

New tenancy agreements are now based on the 'assured' principle. The published Performance Standards of the regulatory bodies set out the principles that RSLs currently have to follow in setting their rents (and those elements of service charges that are eligible for housing benefit – see Chapter 17). Broadly, they require rents and charges to be set at levels that:

- are below those that would be set by unrestrained market forces;
- are affordable to the low paid employed;
- allow the landlord to meet its current financial commitments;
- allow the landlord to cover its historic costs; and
- allow the landlord to make appropriate provision for future repairs and other contingencies.

---

12 As we have already indicated, in recent times two different tenancy regimes have been used to fix housing association rents. Prior to January 15, 1989, housing association tenants had *secure tenancies* and rents were set on the so-called *fair rent* basis. Tenancy agreements entered into after that date were *assured* rather than *secure*, and rents were set in accordance with Section 35 of the Housing Act 1988. The existence of two different funding regimes has resulted in cases of different rents being charged on the same estate (bringing up questions of horizontal equity – refer to Chapter 2 for discussion on equity). For example: the houses built in and around Jenkin Road, North Sheffield, overlooking the Don Valley were built in two phases several years apart and under different funding regimes. They were all similar two storey, brick construction, three bedroomed houses and no distinction was or is made with regard to allocations. The rent difference of about £15 a week (1996) is entirely due to differences in the ways they were funded. (Judith Webster of North Sheffield Housing Association talking on Radio 4 *File on Four* programme on the Housing White Paper February 1996).

With the shift to assured tenancy agreements the basis was lost for developing a common approach to setting rents across all sectors. In the 1990s rent levels have tended to be rationalised differently and set differently in different tenures. Landlords with assured tenancies are expected to set rents that in some way reflect the different utility characteristics of individual properties, so that 'better' dwellings earn higher rents, while at the same time taking the incomes of their tenants into account, so that the rents charged are affordable. Their ability to do this is aided by the receipt of capital grants and other fiscal aid. (The capital grant arrangements are described and discussed in Chapter 14). Those RSLs whose stock has a mixed age profile are also aided by their ability to incorporate historic cost accounting into their current and projected business costs.

In recent years development-driven social landlords have needed to demonstrate that they are holding down their rents if they want to be successful in bidding for capital grant aid. In the 1980s the government signalled to housing associations that their rents were 'too low'; in contrast, by the mid-1990s they were being urged to curb any proposed increases. By the late 1990s RSLs in England were confronted with a contentious policy based on a Retail Price Index plus one per cent directive, under which they are asked to justify annual rent increases that are more than one per cent above inflation. This policy has put particular pressure on LSVT landlords who had made pre-transfer pledges to their existing tenants to encourage them to vote in favour of transfer. These pledges often required the new landlord to carry out a repairs and maintenance 'catch-up' programme within a certain time-scale while at the same time holding current rent levels for a period after transfer. For such RSLs, the ability to meet these pledges rested on an assumption that annual rent increases for new tenancies would be significantly above the level of inflation.[13]

Some commentators argue that the RPI formula is too blunt a control instrument as it takes no account of starting points and thus stands in the way of establishing rent changes that move towards fairer differentials. Another problematic consequence of this 'rent restraint' has been a disinclination to put aside enough funds into *designated reserves* to cover anticipated future costs such as those associated with major repairs. It also has to be remembered that rents have to reflect long-term interest rates if the association is to cover its long-run costs. Furthermore, the limit on rent increases tends to reduce the value of the stock and this can affect the security available for underpinning private sector loans. All of these tensions are manifestations of the basic *need-price dilemma* discussed in Chapters 3 and 4. Some of the practical consequences of these tensions will be discussed in the next two chapters.

---

13 The Housing Corporation accepts that rents charged to tenants who transferred will be relatively low because of rent guarantees and that, as a consequence, new tenancy rents may need to be higher than the guideline. However, there is still an expectation that total rent increases across the stock will be held to the guideline formula of RPI plus one per cent.

In Wales, Tai Cymru introduced 'rent bidding' on a local authority area basis. Any RSL charging more than ten per cent above the most competitive RSL lost its development programme. This was later replaced by 'rent benchmarking'. The National Assembly sets benchmark rents for different property types. Subject to limited exceptions, RSLs cannot charge more than the benchmarks. Doing so would mean losing Social Housing Grant. Increases in benchmarks have so far been below RPI, and for 2000/01 are likely to match RPI.

The drive to convergence

At present, rents in the RSL sector are around 20 per cent higher, on average, than those in local authority housing. This differential is seen to be unfair and confusing to tenants. The 2000 Green Paper, *Quality and Choice: A Decent Home for All*, makes it clear that reducing the gap between average rents in the two social housing sectors is now a key feature of government policy. This commitment to developing a more coherent approach to rent-setting could put increased pressure on RSL landlords to fix rents at current real levels (RPI plus 0 per cent), while allowing some limited real rent increases in the local authority sector.

Summary

As the tenants of social landlords are on relatively low incomes the question of 'affordability' is at the heart of the revenue regime's objectives. However, there is a tension between this objective and the recognised need for social landlords to set rents that enable them to remain financially viable.

In the 1980s the government put pressure on housing associations to raise their rents to be more in line with market levels. The pressure was formalised in the provisions of the Housing Act 1988 which brought in assured tenancy agreements. More recently RSLs have been urged to curb proposed increases and relate them to the general rate of inflation. The shift to assured tenancy rents after 1989 resulted in the withdrawal of Revenue Support Grant for mixed funded schemes.

It is important to note that RSL projects funded through mixed funding arrangements are not allowed to make claims on RDG, nor are they obliged to return surpluses to the RSF.

Future rent policy is likely to give a high priority to the question of 'convergence'.

Further reading

D. Gray, *What's it all about? Registered social landlord accounts explained*, NHF, 1999.

'Moving to a fairer system of affordable rents', Chapter 10 of the 2000 Green Paper, *Quality and Choice: A Decent Home for All* (DETR/Social Security).

Angus Freeman, Alan Holmans and Christine Whitehead, *Evaluating Housing Affordability – Policy Options and New Directions*, LGA/CIH/NHF, 1999.

Good Practice Briefing No. 17–Housing and Services for People with Support Needs, CIH, November 1999.

Jill Gibbs, *Rent Levels, Rent Structures and Affordability*, CIH, 1992.

Good Practice Briefing No. 11–Rents and Service Charges, CIH, December 1997.

Janet Ford and Jenny Seavers, *Housing Associations and Rent Arrears: Attitudes, Beliefs and Behaviour*, CIH/JRF, 1998.

HACAS Consulting, *Sustaining Success – RSLs, financial risk and low demand*, CIH, 2000.

CHAPTER 14:
Registered social landlords and capital finance

Capital expenditure and income

Capital expenditure is money spent on creating, acquiring or enhancing assets. As a general principle, to count as 'capital' the spending should produce a new asset, substantially increase the life or value of an existing asset, or add to the uses to which an existing asset can be put. Capital income is money received from the sale of assets.

Social landlords follow generally accepted accounting practice in deciding which items of spending are capitalised and which items are charged to income and expenditure. As a general principle, expenditure that relates to maintaining a building in its present state or restoring it to its original condition should be treated as revenue. Revenue spending thus helps maintain current property values and rent earning capacities. In contrast, acquisitions and works that result in real increases in the net rental streams are deemed to be 'productive' and thus counted as capital. An increase in the net rental stream may arise through any of the following, and they therefore all count as capital spending.

- Constructing or acquiring a new dwelling unit.
- Up-grading the rent category of an existing dwelling through improvement works.
- Reducing future maintenance costs through repairs and renewals.
- Extending the economic life of a dwelling through repairs and renewals.

In practice, social landlords have to interpret these accounting principles and produce a working list of which expenditures are to be capitalised and which are to count as revenue in the context of their own particular circumstances.

Sources of capital finance

The main sources of capital finance for housing association/RSL investment are as follows.

1. *Grants*
   The main grant available to the sector is Social Housing Grant (SHG), or Housing Association Grant (HAG) in Scotland. Grants are allocated through

the capital finance regime that is described below. As well as central government grant, social landlords may receive grant aid towards land and buildings from local authorities, the European Commission, Health Authorities, the National Lottery Charities Board and similar bodies.

2. *Accumulated reserves*
A key regulatory distinction is made between 'designated' and 'restricted' reserves. Designated reserves are unrestricted but are earmarked by the management board for a particular purpose, such as major repairs. The designation of reserves is an internal exercise and may be reversed by future board decisions. Restricted reserves are those reserves that are subject to external restrictions governing their use. Where an external body, typically a funder, requires that specific reserve funds be accounted for separately they are recorded as 'restricted'.

3. *Capital income*
Capital income is derived from the sale of assets. Since 1996, RSLs in England and Wales have been given more control over how they can dispose of properties and reinvest the resources thus generated. There is also the possibility of grant recycling from the sale of assets.

4. *Borrowing*
Loans can be short-term or long-term, carry fixed or variable rates of interest and secured against various types of collateral, typically property or rental income flows. The types of loan currently taken out by RSLs are described below and the question of loan planning and management is discussed in the next chapter.

The capital finance regime

The basic structure of the present financial regime was laid down in the provisions of the Housing Act 1988 and the Housing (Scotland) Act of the same year. Before describing this structure we will outline the capital funding arrangements that were in place prior to 1989 and explain why they were judged to be unsatisfactory and in need of reform.

The capital finance arrangements before 1989

The previous finance regime centred on the provisions of the Housing Act 1974. This legislation provided what, from today's perspective, would be regarded as a generous system of fiscal support. This support was intended to increase the capacity of housing associations so that they could act as a 'third force' in housing by supplementing local authority and market provision. The high level of fiscal support also implied that, despite their independent status, they operated *de facto* as agents of the welfare state.

The main features of the 1974 capital regime can be summarised as follows. (The pre-1989 revenue arrangements that ran in parallel with the capital regime are summarised in Chapter 13).

- Up to 100 per cent public funding for approved capital projects was available for registered associations. This public funding typically comprised two elements The main element was in the form of a high percentage capital grant called Housing Association Grant (HAG), and the balance took the form of a long-term fixed interest loan from the Housing Corporation. This high level of public funding underlined the 'social welfare' nature of the sector's mission. Because the projects were 'publicly funded', prior investment approval had to be sought from the regulator.

- Once approved, the funding body then guaranteed loan finance to help pay for the development. On scheme completion, a *fair rent* was set by independent rent officers. Fair rents were fixed for a period of two years. The annual income from these controlled rents was then offset against management and maintenance costs and an allowance was given for voids and bad debts. The remaining rental income was assumed to be available to service a loan that was typically provided by the funding body itself. All scheme costs over and above this 'serviceable loan' were then met by the grant allocation. Development cost over-runs were often eligible for additional HAG, so long as they could be justified.

- Major Repair Grants (MRGs) were available, up to 100 per cent, to contribute to, or to cover, the costs of major works on properties that were at least ten years old. To qualify, the properties had to have been originally funded through HAG. The idea behind MRGs can also be traced to the movement's 'social welfare' mission. Without the provision of this support, major repairs would have to have been funded in other ways (e.g. by loans) that would put upward pressure on rents. The existence of MRG ensured that a dwelling's physical integrity was maintained without penalising the tenant for living in a dwelling needing major works.

- The regulators were given enhanced powers so that they could impose an appropriate degree of regulation and control over the use of this 'generous' public funding.

The idea of 'mixed funding'

Schemes that were funded by HAG and government loans were termed *publicly funded projects*. At this time, HAG often covered more than 75 per cent of the total scheme costs. In the 1980s, as government macro-economic policies placed more and more emphasis on the control of public expenditure, pressure mounted for a significant proportion of scheme costs to be funded through the provision of private finance. By the middle of the decade the idea of *mixed funded projects* had taken firm root. After 1986, the old regime was modified so that there was an expectation that new schemes would be funded with a proportion of scheme costs being covered by private sector loans. The public sector money (HAG) was now conceived as 'challenge funding' rather than as a full development grant.[1] The 'challenge' was to use a limited (at that time 30 per cent) capital grant to lever in loans from private institutions such as banks and building societies. The shift to a policy of *mixed funding* signalled the government's intention to alter the whole basis of support for housing association development. This intention was given legislative force by the passing of the 1988 Housing Act and Housing (Scotland) Act.

Reasons for the reforms

The 1988 legislation radically altered the legislative framework within which the housing association movement operates. This 'new regime' was based on the government's revised view of how best to fund housing association activity. In particular the government wanted to expand the role of housing associations without putting any substantially increased burden on the public purse. It was also concerned to encourage associations to think and behave more commercially and it sought to provide incentives to achieve greater value-for-money.

As we have seen above, HAG was initially a subsidy to cover the bulk of the development costs. The remaining costs were then largely paid for by taking out a *serviceable loan*. This meant that the grant covered the estimated costs of building a scheme minus an amount that the association was assumed to be able to afford to contribute without putting up rents beyond the 'fair rent' levels. These arrangements meant that rents bore little or no relationship to actual scheme costs. This was out of line with the Conservative government's general 'market' philosophy that prices should reflect, but not necessarily match, the marginal costs of production.[2]

Prior to 1989, once the scheme was approved, its completion was guaranteed and the funding body covered the housing association against any unanticipated over-run costs on the development. Under these arrangements there was an implied assumption that housing associations were operating as a quasi-public service. At that time, HAG was seen as a subsidy to reduce the cost of the development loan finance to a point where it could be serviced by 'fair rents'. Ministers seeking to reform the system argued that these arrangements did not encourage associations to be sufficiently commercial in their outlook and failed

---

1   The idea of challenge funding is discussed in Chapter 10.
2   See Chapter 4 for discussion on the theory of marginal cost pricing.

to encourage cost consciousness. The new capital funding arrangements, which came into force in 1989, addressed these points by fixing a predetermined grant at the outset of the development project and requiring the associations to take on the commercial risks of any cost over-runs. To facilitate this, fair rent tenancies, where rents are fixed by a rent officer, were abandoned in favour of assured tenancies, where rents are set by the association. There was now an expectation that rents would rise to levels that were more in line with marginal cost (i.e. competitive market) rents.

The post-1989 regime reversed the relationship between grant aid and rental income. Whereas, previously, rents were fixed at the outset and grant aid provided the deficit funding, the new system required the grant contribution to be predetermined with loans filling in any financial shortfall. Under the new arrangements rents had to be mutable so that any increases on loan service charges could be covered. There was now an implied assumption that associations should operate in a more market-orientated business atmosphere and that their dependency on HAG should be reduced.

The 1989 reform objectives and principles

The reform objectives were first outlined in the 1987 DOE Consultation Paper *Finance for Housing Associations: The Government's Proposals*. These interrelated objectives can be summarised as follows.

1. To tighten central government's control over public expenditure on social housing investment.
2. To 'stretch' the public investment in social housing so that each increment of grant produces more output.
3. To encourage the use of private capital finance.
4. To impel associations to behave more commercially.
5. To put upward pressure on rents so that they were more in line with the costs of provision.

The following operational principles lie beneath these objectives.

1. Total public spending should be capped within the financial planning period.
2. The fixed total spending should be allocated to those associations that would make the best use of it.
3. Social landlords should seek to work in partnership with private funders.
4. The commercial risks associated with development activity should be shifted away from the Exchequer and towards the associations and their funding partners.
5. Housing benefit would 'take the strain' of the rent increases that would follow the changes.

The operating principles of the 'new regime'

Capital grant and the principle of 'total public subsidy'

Since 1996, outside Scotland, the capital grant is referred to as 'Social Housing Grant' (SHG). In Scotland the capital support is still often called Housing Association Grant (HAG). The 1989 reforms sought to reinforce the government's ability to control public spending.[3] This objective has produced operational procedures that ensure that the grant allocation normally represents the *total public subsidy* going into this sector. Any public investment above the approved grant allocation now requires special approval. Generally speaking, if an RSL receives investment support from some other public sector source this will result in a proportional reduction in its grant allocation.[4] The *total public subsidy principle* means that the level of grant now has to be *predetermined* and *fixed* before the works begin rather than be given as *deficit funding* on completion.

The principle of *total public subsidy* is well illustrated by the regulations applying to the treatment of land donated by or transferred from central or local government (or some other public authority) at a price that is below market value. In such circumstances, the difference between the 'fair value'[5] and the transfer price has to be treated as a government grant.

Grant 'stretch' and competitive bidding

An objective of the post 1989 regime was to increase the volume of housing output for a given increment of public investment or grant. This is achieved by seeking to allocate available funds to those organisations that will make the most efficient use of them. In England this involves a process of local competitive bidding. How the bidding process operates is described below (see section on *The Approved Development Programme*). The effect of the bidding process has been that the average level of grant paid to English associations has been substantially below the maximum grant rate set by the Housing Corporation. More recently, the

---

3   The relationship between public expenditure management and the delivery of the government's macro-economic policy objectives is discussed fully in Chapter 5.

4   For example, it is not possible to circumvent the total public spending rule by doing land deals with sympathetic local authorities. The 1988 Local Government Act requires local authorities to obtain special consent of the Secretary of State to dispose of land at below full market value. It may be deemed to be appropriate for an association to work closely with an authority and, in line with the 'partnership' principle, to acquire cheap development land in return for nomination rights. In such a case the Minister may require the benefit to be valued and deducted from any grant allocation so as not to contravene the *total public subsidy* rule. Similarly, if a local authority decides to give revenue contributions instead, they may have to be capitalised and their net present value (i.e. discounted) deducted from the grant allocation. The restriction does not apply to any private sector subsidies, revenue contributions for non-housing costs, or any grants received to help restore historic buildings that are on the development site.

5   'Fair value' is defined as the amount at which an asset could be exchanged in an arm's length transaction between informed and willing parties, other than in a forced or liquidation sale.

emphasis has shifted away from competitive bidding, towards one of keeping rents down.

Encouraging commercial behaviour and shifting financial risks

In line with its market ideology, the Conservative government sought to encourage associations to think and behave less like publicly funded welfare agencies and more like privately funded commercial firms. The broad effect of the 1989 regime was that, although housing associations retained social objectives, the maximisation of resource use became the key driver to their operational management practices.

The revised arrangements had the effect of shifting the financial risks associated with development away from the Exchequer and towards the associations and private lenders. This more 'commercial' approach to investment was expected to provide an incentive to greater efficiency and to enhance value-for-money in the funding of social housing developments.[6] It might be argued, however, that it is the tenants who are the ultimate risk-takers when things go wrong financially because, under current arrangements, financial mismanagement may result in additional costs most of which will have to be covered by rent increases. Because the question of risk management is now an important aspect of financial management in general, we will return to this topic and look at it in more detail in the next chapter.

The abolition of Major Repairs Grants (MRGs) and the introduction of sinking funds

In line with the *total public subsidy* idea, the new regime abolished MRGs. After 1989 associations were generally expected to accumulate resources to pay for future major repairs out of current revenue streams. As well as seeking to control public expenditure, this change can also be seen to be a way of shifting the emphasis away from the principles of welfare provision towards the principles of commercial management.

Although limited grant assistance is still available, the costs of future major repairs are now normally planned for by setting up a *sinking fund*. Only RSLs with limited reserves can apply for SHG for repairs and improvements. By including an element to the rent charge, money can be set aside against future needs (such as

---

6   The reforms were an immediate success in this respect. After 1989, associations tightened up their development management procedures and practices so as to more rapidly progress schemes through to completion and thereby reduce the level of on-costs. Of particular concern was the need to minimise short-term interest charges and the risk of interest rate rises occurring during the development period. The speedier completion of projects led in 1990/91 to a cash crisis at the Housing Corporation who failed to forecast accurately the effect of the new system on development progress times.

major repairs). This money is normally invested in a fund in order to retain its value over time. We will return to the idea of sinking funds in Chapter 15 when we consider aspects of financial management. (Refer to section on *Resource accounting and the planning and paying for major repairs*).

The use of private finance and the declining reliance on grant aid

A declared objective of the 1989 reforms was to 'normalise' mixed funding arrangements. Indeed, since the late 1980s the government has expected associations to put less reliance on public funding and to look to the private sector for a significant proportion of their capital resources. As a consequence, in the ten years following the introduction of the new regime, average grant rates (for all schemes) fell from 72 per cent of total scheme costs to around 54 per cent in England. In Wales, particular emphasis has been put on limiting rent increases rather than cutting grants, and grants are currently fixed at 56 per cent. In Scotland, the figure is higher still, at 70 per cent.

It is estimated that in Great Britain gross investment expenditure in this sector for 1999/2000 will be £2,145 million. Of this, about £881 million will be provided by the 'regulators', £320 million will be channelled through local authorities, and some £944 million will have been raised from private sources (Wilcox, 1999). This means that over the country as a whole, ignoring regional variations, nearly 45 per cent of the capital funds invested annually in this sector come from private sources. Even in Scotland, where public funding has been more firmly entrenched, there is now a clear commitment to look more to the private sector for investment funds.[7] The effects of this policy have been particularly dramatic in England where the Housing Corporation's budget was cut from £2.1 billion in 1993 to just over £1 billion in 1997. In 1998 the figure fell to less than £600 million[8] As a result, fewer grants are being made and those that are, tend to be smaller.

In recent years RSLs have achieved significant success in gaining access to private finance and this has enabled them nearly to double the value of every pound provided through the public purse, thereby achieving the *grant stretch* objective.[9] Since 1988, private lending to RSLs has helped to provide 120,000

---

7   In February 1996, Scottish Homes launched a major drive to raise £1 billion from City financiers to support its social housing programme up to the year 2002. The agency sought £500 million of private cash to support its building programme and a further £500 million to aid transfers from public ownership to associations or local housing companies.

8   This figure would allow for some 30,000 new lettings in 1999 at a time when the DETR's own estimate of supply need for social housing to rent is 60,000 a year. In 1995 DETR research indicated that there would be 4.4 million more households in England in the 25-year period running from 1991 to 2016. This was almost a million more than the then current planning estimates. The Department argued that this pointed to a needed rate of provision of new social lettings of 60,000 a year.

9   In the early 1990s their success was fuelled by the collapse in the residential housing market which encouraged lenders to look for new markets.

more homes than would otherwise have been possible with government money alone. (DoE, Cm3607, 1997 p24). Since 1989, RSLs have raised more than £15 billion from the private sector. To achieve this success, RSLs have cultivated sophisticated approaches to financial management. These will be looked at in the next chapter.

In Chapter 12 we described how the 1989 reforms involved a shift from 'secure' to 'assured' tenancy agreements. The introduction of assured tenancies was seen to be a precondition for the required shift towards increased private funding. It was argued that social landlords must be freer to set rents on a more 'commercial' basis if they are to be expected to acquire funds from the private sector.

Private sources of capital finance

The total value of funding committed to the social housing sector is currently running at about £15 billion, of which some £11 billion has been drawn down.[10] The National Housing Federation estimate that over the period 1999-2002 the private borrowing requirements of RSLs for mixed funded schemes will be in excess of £6 billion. In recent years, banks and building societies have been the lead providers of committed funds, at some 80 per cent of the total, with the bulk of the remainder coming from a variety of institutional investors.

In recent years social landlords have reduced their reliance on variable rate funds so that by the end of the 1990s more than half of the private sector borrowing was based on fixed rates of interest. The sector has also shown a preference for long dated finance with nearly 80 per cent of committed funds having maturities of more than 14 years (*NHF Private Finance Loans Monitoring Bulletin,* March 1999).

The private finance initiative (PFI)

Introduced in 1992, the PFI encourages public/private partnerships on projects that receive a measure of public funding but where the main commercial risks are taken by the private partner(s) and where the assets do not appear on the balance sheet of the public sector agency. We have already discussed the broad principles of PFI in Chapter 10 when we were considering the question of local government investment strategies. Since the 1997 General Election, more emphasis has been placed on PFI projects that underpin the Labour government's wider agenda of economic regeneration, improved service provision (best value), and sustainable development. The expectation is that local authorities will take the lead in working up PFI proposals. These must now be progressed through a Project Review Group chaired by the Treasury Taskforce before any commitment can be given to housing associations or other RSLs.

---

10   Refer to the NHF *Private Finance Loans Monitoring Bulletin* for up-to-date estimates.

Partnership in regeneration and care in the community

Throughout the 1990s, RSLs developed strong and effective working relationships with local authorities and private sector partners to create thousands of new homes for households in various categories of need. Partnership activity also resulted in the refurbishment of existing estates and the regeneration of run-down areas. In addition, RSLs, together with other landlords in the independent sector, undertake a significant proportion of *care in the community* provision under contract from local authorities.

Because of the continuing constraints on public spending[11], both the government and the housing lobby organisations are now arguing the case for more comprehensive strategic partnerships in social housing. This will involve an even greater co-ordination of the scarce and valuable resources of the public, voluntary and private sectors. In the context of the current debate on diversification for RSLs[12] the present regulatory framework is likely to be systematically restructured to support the expansion of the housing association remit into a wider community role that takes them beyond their traditional social landlord functions. The 2000 Housing Green Paper *Quality and Choice: A Decent Home for All*, makes it clear that the government is keen to see public support to RSLs (SHG) being used in ways that consciously support regeneration projects (paras. 8.21 and 8.22).

Local strategies provide the means by which national objectives are achieved at the community level. As was made clear in Chapter 10, the ultimate responsibility for drawing up a local housing strategy rests with the local authority. However, in so doing, it will need to involve RSLs as closely as possible, together with private landlords, the construction industry and relevant voluntary advice agencies. By virtue both of their operational experience and their constitutions, RSLs are particularly well positioned to take a key role in the government's commitment to 'joined-up' policies for urban and rural regeneration.

Strategic agreements with the National Assembly for Wales and Scottish Homes

The National Assembly distributes all SHG in Wales. It does so with specific reference to local authority housing strategies and the broader strategic concerns of the Assembly. As part of their Housing Strategy and Operational Plans (HSOP), (refer to Chapter 9), Welsh authorities are invited to make a case for the level of investment required and provide detailed investment plans for working with RSLs. To help this arrangement work, the Assembly encourages authorities

---

11 By 1997/98 the Housing Corporation's Approved Development Programme was down to £516 million, compared with £2,199 million in 1992/93.

12 Such as the Housing Corporation's recent consultation paper, *Regulating Diversity*, and the draft statutory order initiated by the DETR that proposes wider objectives and purposes for RSLs.

to enter into Community Housing Agreements with their RSL partners. The agreement defines their respective roles and responsibilities and sets out a partnership framework for a co-ordinated strategy to provide affordable housing.[13] Similarly, Scottish Homes encourages the Scottish unitary authorities to enter into strategic agreements so as to create a partnership approach to investment in Scotland.

Local authority and other sponsorship

In recent years, not all SHG in England has been channelled through the Housing Corporation's Approved Development Programme. Non-APD funded schemes have been grant aided from sources such as City Challenge, Rough Sleepers and local authority SHG. Such schemes do not require the association to negotiate a funding agreement with the Corporation but, because of the principle of *total public funding*, such scheme submissions are recorded and monitored and the SHG they received is treated by the government as part of the public expenditure total. In the case of joint funded schemes, the pro-rata share of the overall scheme grant that comes from the ADP is included in the regulator's funding agreement arrangements.

In addition to central government funding channelled directly through the Housing Corporation, English local authorities are allowed to sponsor RSL housing developments from resources they acquire through their housing investment programme allocations. Local authority funding towards the capital costs of housing association schemes takes the form of a loan that the authority recovers from the Corporation in the form of Local Authority Social Housing Grant (LASHG). Local authorities seek to sponsor schemes that reinforce their own local housing strategies as declared in their HIP bids.

The 1998 Comprehensive Spending Review signalled the government's intention to maintain Housing Corporation direct programme funding at current levels (see below). This means that in many areas, any expansion in the development programme may depend on the provision of LASHG. LASHG currently contributes something in excess of £400 million to the English RSL development programme. This equates to about 16 per cent of total council expenditure. If this level of priority is to continue RSLs will need to receive more than £550 million in 2001/02. However, with the eventual introduction of the single capital pot for English authorities (refer to Chapter 9, *The move towards a single funding mechanism*), it may prove to be politically difficult to persuade local councillors to invest that level of resource in 'partner' organisations. The 2000 Green Paper reinforces the government's intention to see a continuing role for LASHG – particularly in areas where there is a high demand for social housing (para.8.14).

---

13 Blaenau Gwent and Wrexham councils were among the first authorities to sign such agreements.

Full public funding

Some schemes may be eligible for 'public funding', as against 'mixed funding'. Smaller associations may have difficulty in presenting adequate security to borrow from the private sector; where this is the case loan finance may be made available from the funding agency. This might occur in cases where the agency (e.g. the Housing Corporation) felt that a small specialist housing association was well positioned professionally to provide a particular type of supported accommodation but not well positioned commercially to raise funds from private sources.

The Approved Development Programme (ADP)

Public funds are allocated to RSLs through a bidding process that is similar in principle to the Housing Investment Programme procedures that operate for local authorities (described in Chapter 9). In England the investment programme is called the 'Approved Development Programme' (ADP). Like the local authority funding programme, the broad objective of the ADP is to distribute a fixed allocation of public expenditure to housing activity in a way that partly reflects local needs and is partly determined by value-for-money and best practice criteria.

Once the total public expenditure commitment to the sector has been determined by central government (refer to Chapter 5),[14] the allocation of funds into the English regions and then to individual housing providers is carried out by the Housing Corporation. The allocation processes differ somewhat for the other UK funding bodies (see below), and they are also subject to constant revision. Current moves towards regional devolution will inevitably alter how decisions will be made to this budget in the future. It is likely that the ADP will be tied in more and more closely with other budgets to underpin the social and economic objectives of the various national/regional authorities and agencies. Because of all of these factors, what follows should be seen as a general description of current arrangements. Although the following description focuses on the requirements of the Housing Corporation, the other funding bodies have many similar priorities and they operate many similar procedures.

The Housing Corporation's programme (ADP) is agreed annually by the DETR. [15] This sets the framework for the allocation of capital resources to RSLs in England.

---

14   The Corporation's capital investment programme is financed by Exchequer grant and capital receipts. Expenditure control is exercised through a net cash limit that takes account of receipts.

15   The Housing Corporation ADP investment in 1999/2000 is expected to be about £643 million (Wilcox, 1999). About three-quarters of the funds are directed to the rented stock and the rest goes to support the various home-ownership initiatives. In recent years larger associations, with over 2,500 dwellings, have been allocated nearly 60 per cent of the funds, while smaller associations, with less than 500, have received less than 10 per cent (*Public Finance*, 13 February, 1996). At its peak public investment was much higher. In 1992/93 Housing Corporation investment was well over £2.3 billion. In that peak year Housing for Wales allocated £163 million and Scottish Homes spent a further £255 million.

Its declared aim is to 'invest well' so that the funding makes a significant contribution to creating sustainable communities and reducing social exclusion. The Housing Corporation's approach to capital funding of RSLs is set out in its current National Investment Strategy which establishes broad output targets for the ADP.

Design and space standards

Between 1964 and 1981 local authority housing had to be built to set space and design criteria known as Parker Morris standards, after the chairman of the committee that devised them. Before 1989, housing association homes tended to be built to Parker Morris standards or above, although the standards were officially abandoned in 1981. After 1989, housing association building standards tended to be below Parker Morris levels. Subsequent detailed research by Valerie Karn and Linda Sheridan[16] reinforced by information from the National Federation of Housing Associations (now the National Housing Federation) indicates that both design and space standards continued to decline into the 1990s. Although cause and effect is not certain (standards may have declined despite the provisions of the 1988 legislation), most commentators suggest a direct link between meaner standards and the 1989 funding regime. Competitive bidding for grant allocations and the drive for development efficiency, coupled with the need to minimise commercial risks, have driven those associations engaged in development activities to reconsider the design and space standards of the dwellings they produce.

Largely as a result of these research findings, the question of minimum standards once again emerged as a cause for concern within the housing association movement. In 1995, the NFHA launched a project to look at the standards and building quality in association developments. An advisory group[17], sponsored by the Joseph Rowntree Foundation was set up to identify where current mandatory standards within the Housing Corporation Scheme Development Standards could be supplemented in order to identify standards below which value-for-money may be compromised. There is an understandable reluctance to return to a mandatory system of narrowly controlling crude dwelling size. The concern is more to consider whether or not the allocation of public funds to development projects should operate around advisory targets relating to such things as parking, furnishing quality, activity space and energy efficiency.

As part of the Corporation's current commitment to gaining value-for-money, it only supports projects that conform to its own scheme development standards. These were first introduced in October 1993 and are periodically revised. These standards pay particular attention to questions of accessibility, safety and security,

---

16   Karn, V. and Sheridan, L., (1994), *New Homes in the 1990s, A Study of Design, Space and Amenities in Housing Association and Private Sector Housing*, Joseph Rowntree Foundation.

17   The Standards and Quality Steering Group.

energy efficiency, good building practice and the long-term costs of maintenance. The most recent concern is with construction efficiency, following the work of the Egan task force. In Wales, Design Quality Requirements set basic layouts and specifications for SHG funded projects. In Scotland, there are no published standards but a particular requirement is that all general needs housing is 'barrier free', that is, accessible to people with disabilities.

Other priorities

In recent years, the largest share of ADP funding has gone to schemes providing family dwellings for households accepted as homeless, or in similar need, by local authorities. ADP investment in 1996/97 was approximately £1.1 billion, with £787 million devoted to rental projects and £259 million on home-ownership initiatives, including the new voluntary purchase grant scheme. Under the earlier Tenants' Incentive Scheme (TIS), a cash grant was paid to tenants of RSLs to help them move into owner-occupation and thereby release their tenancies for others in housing need. Many RSLs also run shared ownership schemes (part rent, part purchase) that help local authority and RSL tenants, and other first-time buyers, to become home owners. Dwellings for shared ownership have also been provided through new-build, rehabilitation, or Do-It-Yourself Shared Ownership (DIYSO) schemes whereby a property is purchased on the open market. A purchase grant scheme was introduced in 1996 to help RSL tenants buy the home they live in. For existing units (prior to 1997) the scheme is voluntary and RSLs opt in if they wish to. The Housing Act 1996 gives tenants of future publicly funded developments a statutory right to acquire their homes with the help of a purchase grant. The RSL receives the full value of the property and recycles the receipt to provide further social housing. In April 1999, it was announced that TIS and DIYSO were to be phased out and replaced with a new scheme called 'Homebuy' (described in Chapter 6).

The Corporation also funds the Housing Associations as Managing Agents scheme (HAMA), under which associations manage properties for private landlords. HAMA Plus is a scheme for funding capital works designed to bring sub-standard properties back into management. HAMA schemes are sometimes referred to as Housing Association Leasing Schemes (HALS). This is where the object is to utilise private sector properties to house the homeless, subject to a three-way arrangement between the landlord, a housing association and the local authority. Under such a scheme the properties are managed by the RSL and tenants are nominated by the local authority.

Many of these special initiatives do not exist in the same form in Scotland and Wales. For example, Homebuy has operated in Wales since 1996, but does not operate in Scotland. Scottish Homes does, however, have a range of schemes of its own to promote low-cost home-ownership. For example, in 1998/99, 79 private developers were funded through GRO grant to provide houses for sale.

The changing approach to investment in housing

The Corporation, in common with the other funding bodies, has to make decisions about how much and where to allocate its ADP. In the past it has relied heavily on formulae to guide these decisions. The two indices used to distribute resources to the English regions have been:

1. the Housing Needs Index (HNI) – a weighted basket of indices of housing needs constructed down to local authority level; and
2. the Housing Association Stock Condition Index (HASCI) – a measure of the relative condition of RSL stock in each region.[18]

It is now proposed to change this purely formulaic approach in favour of one that focuses more on those requirements for local housing investment that cannot be adequately measured simply by reference to standardised needs indicators. The pre-2000 system tended to allocate resources to a local authority area on the basis of past and current needs. This worked well when all areas had a shortage of housing and similar problems. But it is now recognised that the issues and challenges faced both between and within the regions of England vary considerably. For this reason the Corporation has devised a new allocation system that relies less on nationally devised formulae and takes more account of local and regional differences. The new approach will be implemented incrementally between 2000 and 2004. The key elements of the new approach can be summarised as follows.[19]

*   HNI will continue to be used to allocate the ADP between regions, but may be modified to reflect more accurately strategic housing investment priorities, such as future regional regeneration and development needs.

*   By 2004 the formulaic approach for determining the amount of SHG a local authority area receives will be modified. Every local authority area will be guaranteed to receive an allocation of not less than 80 per cent of that indicated by the HNI. The remaining element of allocation will be determined by a more sophisticated (less mechanistic) assessment that reflects the longer-term need for housing investment across a region. Consistency of application of this element will be ensured by making reference to three key objectives (see below), rather than by making reference to need and condition formulae.

*   The starting point for decisions about investment priorities will be *regional housing statements*. These are to be produced in partnership with

---

18   The nature and scope of the HNI, and the equivalent local authority index (the GNI) are constantly under review by the DETR.
19   The detailed proposals are presented in *The Housing Corporation's National Investment Strategy*, (2000). They are also headlined in the 2000 Green Paper (paras.8.17-20).

the Government Office for the region and, to ensure the fullest understanding and agreement on issues and priorities, they will be subject to a high level of consultation with other regional stakeholders. The *regional housing statements* will span three to five years[20] and are intended to provide an overview of priorities that takes account of the region's economic outlook and planning strategies as well as its demographic projections. This means that they will necessarily be tied in with the work of the new Regional Development Agencies (see Chapters 8 and 10).

- To guide RSLs to make appropriate proposals for funding that are relevant to local and regional circumstances, the Corporation's regional offices will produce their own *regional investment strategies* highlighting the areas and types of activity that they deem to be priorities for funding.[21] These will be issued to RSLs at the same time as invitations are made to them to bid for funding.

- At the core of these *regional investment strategies*[22] will be *key objectives*, currently three in number. By applying these key objectives to its allocation decisions, the Corporation seeks to ensure a consistent approach to its distribution of resources within and across regions. The key objectives have been specifically chosen to ensure that housing investment cross-cuts with wider government policies. The current key objectives are to:
  1. provide new affordable housing in areas of economic and demographic growth;
  2. aid the regeneration of deprived neighbourhoods by helping to fund the refurbishment or replacement of existing housing; and
  3. contribute to the funding of new supported housing to meet the needs of a wide range of vulnerable groups.[23]

- Within these broad objectives, other more detailed aims are set out, such as supporting rural housing, contributing to low-cost home-ownership initiatives, encouraging community capacity building, supporting 'foyer' initiatives or tackling rough sleeping.

- To ensure that the allocation decisions are understood, and 'transparent', they will be published, together with explanations of how and why they were taken, in the form of *regional allocation statements*.

---

20 With annual updates as required.
21 Where appropriate, they should break the strategy down to reflect the needs of sub-regions.
22 Formally known as *regional policy statements*.
23 Currently more than 12 per cent of grant confirmations for the rented programme go to schemes catering for supported housing needs. The largest proportionate provision is for people with mental health problems, followed by people with physical disabilities and the frail elderly.

Distribution to RSLs in England: the costs, grant and rent framework

Once the regional allocation of public funds has been made, local RSLs are invited to compete for a share of the available total. Successful bids acquire funding in the form of a capital grant called 'Social Housing Grant' (SHG).[24] The Corporation seeks to approve schemes that require the minimum public subsidy while still delivering high quality outputs to meet local housing needs at affordable rents that are related to, but normally below, free market levels. The allocation process is generally informed by the various *regional investment strategies* (see above).

The mechanism that controls the bidding process has three elements:

1. An eligible cost ceiling.
2. A maximum grant rate.
3. A commitment to cap rents.

1. The Corporation operates a system of benchmark costs to assess value-for-money. These nominal figures are called Total Cost Indicators (TCIs), and they represent the Corporation's estimate of the norm total cost of providing different types of housing in different parts of the country.[25] TCIs relate to current construction and development costs and act as a check that an estimated scheme cost is providing value-for-money at the time a project is approved for grant. Projects on which costs exceed TCI are subject to technical scrutiny prior to approval and may, if justified, be approved.[26]

   These indicators represent officially determined indicative scheme costs and they are issued by the regulatory body in an annual circular. It is important to understand that they do not represent actual scheme costs – they are *notional* figures that are simply used to regulate the allocation process by setting a ceiling on what can qualify as an eligible bid. The indicative costs appear in 'look-up' tables that are updated annually to take account of such things as changing building and borrowing costs.

   Because sites and dwelling units vary, the tables incorporate cost modifiers that operate by adjusting the allowable TCI percentage or applying a *multiplier* to the calculation. The calculation procedure starts by consulting the

---

24 The grant was previously called 'Housing Association Grant' (HAG) and was renamed as part of the provisions of the Housing Act 1996. The provisions of the Act do not apply to Scotland where the grant, until recently, was still referred to as HAG.

25 Broadly, the indicators assume that development costs will vary by: (a) location (local authority district); (b) the nature of the development (new build or rehab – high rise or low rise); (c) the type of need being met (general needs housing or supported housing); and (d) the size of dwelling (or numbers of people housed).

26 Normally schemes where costs exceed 130 per cent will not be approved.

---

tables to determine the notional average cost of the dwelling type being proposed. Once the base TCI (the indicative unit cost) has been determined, the guideline figure is modified by reference to a series of adjustments that are designed to take account of the fact that different types of project have different associated unit costs. Significant cost differentials exists, for example, between developing a rural 'greenfield' site and redeveloping an urban 'brownfield' site.[27] Likewise, the construction of high and low-rise buildings involves the employment of different technologies that, in turn, creates different unit construction costs. In addition, some schemes, like supported housing and elderly peoples dwellings, will require the inclusion of special features and facilities that will make the project more expensive. The various adjustments take account of these and other factors that have a bearing on the unit costs of development. [28]

Schemes that are sponsored by the local authorities through the local authority SHG process (refer above) also have to comply with the limits on scheme costs specified by the Corporation. This ensures that the same value-for-money criteria are used on schemes that are funded by different mechanisms.

The underlying principle behind some of the multiplier adjustments is that of *residual loan equalisation*. The logic behind this principle runs as follows. The special features of, say, supported housing can add a premium to the total development cost of a scheme (e.g. special adaptations for the elderly or wheelchair access). This can mean that the unit construction costs of such schemes will be higher than for similar accommodation designed for general needs. It is felt to be unfair for the tenant to have to pay more rent to service the bigger loan just because they are elderly or disabled, etc. – thus a multiplier adjustment is made. Special needs schemes are not only more expensive to build and manage but they also tend to carry higher development risks than general needs schemes. Because they are often individually designed there is also a greater risk of cost over-runs occurring. In general, private funders see them as being more risky compared with general needs

---

27 Standard Percentage Adjustments (SPAs) can be set by the Corporation to reflect particular high or low cost locations within a single TCI cost group area. These adjustments are intended to make the TCI more sensitive to local circumstances and are fixed within a fixed range (currently 80-120 per cent of TCI).

28 To bring some flexibility into the system key and supplementary multipliers are applied to the base TCI figures to allow for scheme variations. Key multipliers make cost distinctions between fundamentally different types of development, that is, between new build, off-the-shelf, existing satisfactory, and purchase and repair. These key multipliers are mutually exclusive, only one applies to any scheme. Supplementary multipliers are applied to reflect special cost features and can be accumulative, although certain combinations of multipliers are invalid. Supplementary multipliers adjust costs to take account of such things as wheelchair access, the provision of common rooms or communal facilities, the installation of lifts, supported housing and the provision of various categories of housing for the elderly. Adjustments can also be made by setting SPAs (see previous endnote).

projects and the additional grant aid that results from applying the multiplier helps to counteract this investment aversion.[29]

2. Grant rates represent, for each type of scheme in each area, the maximum percentage of total qualifying scheme costs that may be funded by SHG. The primary objective of the public capital subsidy is to allow quality dwellings to be produced and let at rents below market levels so that they are affordable to those in low paid employment. Like base TCIs, headline grant rates are determined by reference to dwelling and scheme type and location. Thus, if for example the TCI calculation indicated an allowable total scheme cost of £1 million and the appropriate grant rate for such a scheme of these dwelling types in that area was currently set at 55 per cent, then the project would be eligible for grant aid of up to £550,000.

In most cases, the actual grant paid will be below this upper limit. For any particular scheme the actual grant is negotiated by a bidding process. This means that there is no standard rate of grant contribution – it will vary significantly for different schemes, even if they are in the same local authority cost group area and are building similar types of dwelling. However, within particular periods, there does exist a general 'headline' level of grant that measures the overall average contribution of State funding committed to RSL projects. This 'headline' level of grant aid has systematically fallen from an average of 72 per cent in the 1980s, to 67 per cent in the early 1990s, and 56 per cent in the late 1990s.

3. The third element within the control framework is a system of rent caps. These represent the upper level of rents, including any housing benefit eligible service charges, that will normally be acceptable for new schemes. RSLs are expected to bid at rent levels that will not breach the appropriate rent cap.[30]

Those wishing to acquire more information on the cost, grant and rent framework should consult the Housing Corporation's *Capital funding system procedure guide* and the annual circular that provides details of the current TCIs, grant rates and rent caps.

---

29 In general needs schemes, much of the cost of private finance is passed on to tenants through the rents that have risen significantly since the introduction of mixed funding in 1989. Because building special needs housing tends to be more costly to construct and manage there is a danger that rents in this sub-sector will be particularly high. This problem is partly dealt with by allocating SHG in accordance with the principle of *residual loan equalisation* and partly through the provision of revenue support funding (such as a special needs management allowance – refer to Chapter 13).

30 The current condition of grant receipt is that RSLs must certify that the average rent increase after first letting, across their post-1996 Act stock, will not exceed RPI plus one per cent. The 2000 Green Paper points to the possibility of tightening this further by altering the formula to RPI plus 0 per cent.

Wales

The National Assembly will allocate £67.9 million in 1999-2000 to which RSLs will add about £5 million from reserves. Grant rates are set at 56 per cent. The equivalents to TCIs in Wales are Acceptable Cost Guidelines (ACGs). Rents are more tightly controlled for Welsh RSLs through rent benchmarking. Projects to be funded through RSLs are identified through the relevant local authority HSOPs (see Chapter 9).

Scotland

Scottish Homes will allocate about £167 million to associations in 1999-2000, to which £78 million will be added in private finance. These funds are distributed to Scottish Homes' regions principally on the basis of a series of social exclusion indicators, although performance is also taken into account. Individual associations submit *Strategy and Development Funding Plans* that set out proposals for a three-year period and form the basis of programme agreements with Scottish Homes' regional offices. Local authority strategies are considered as part of the allocation process at regional level.

Scottish associations' scheme costs are governed by a system of 'benchmark costs', the equivalent of England's TCI. Schemes that fall within these benchmarks are only lightly appraised. There are no rent benchmarks but rent levels are considered at regional level. Targets are set for leverage of private funding into the current investment planning period. The current target set is at 30 per cent on rented schemes.

The successful bid

The object of the funding body is to achieve value-for-money. In seeking to achieve this, they will bear a number of factors in mind.

- Grant stretch – is the bid attracting an appropriate level of private funding?
- Quality, standards and design – does the proposed scheme satisfy housing needs appropriately?
- Cost – does the scheme meet the cost ceiling guidelines?
- Affordability – will the rents be within the means of the target group of tenants?
- Wider policy objectives – does the scheme contribute to the principles of Housing Plus and will it help to create a 'sustainable' community?

The bidding process seeks to ensure that approved schemes provide the best public investment in *opportunity cost* terms (Chapter 2 explains the notion of opportunity cost). Quality, scheme costs and rent levels are the three key factors that are taken into consideration. In ranking competing bids an effort is made to take account of factors other than crude costs so that the cheapest bid may not, in the final analysis, be regarded as providing the greatest value-for-money. In discussions with the local authority and the government regional office, special local factors may be taken account of and this can result in a more expensive scheme being ranked higher than its less costly rivals. Such bid adjustment factors might take into account the track records of the bidders, the need to provide higher, and more expensive, standards relative to the objectives of the scheme, and the various community benefits of one scheme as against another. In some cases, programmes that are delivered through 'joint commissioning' (or partnership bids) may be favoured so as to encourage a more integrated use of public and private resources.

Local authority HIP decisions and housing association ADP decisions are taken within a co-ordinated framework locally. The two processes now operate to a common timetable in an attempt to co-ordinate the total local provision of social housing. In this way it is hoped that ADP resources can contribute to satisfying the local housing needs identified by local authorities in their three-year strategic housing plans.

A sustainable strategy for each RSL

In making bids, RSLs need to ensure that the discounts from norm grant they offer on individual proposals represent value-for-money and are competitive. At the same time they must demonstrate that they provide sufficient subsidy across their entire programme of works to allow for the provision of higher cost priority schemes and allow the association to meet any unforeseen cost over-runs. They are also expected to provide evidence of long-term demand/need for the proposed schemes and to demonstrate how they will promote community sustainability. No bid will be accepted that does not have an appropriate delivery plan in place.

Affordability

The bidding process now places a great deal of emphasis on the investment producing housing units that are affordable. In the period 1988 to 1994 rents in the housing association sector rose by 107 per cent, and the average weekly disposable income for tenants in work, moving into newly completed homes, fell from £41.00 to £35.00 after meeting rent and basic living costs.[31] Between 1990 and 1995 associations' rents increased by about three per cent per annum more than the private sector so that by the mid-1990s some were already higher than for equivalent private sector units.[32] Official concern about relatively high rent levels first manifested itself in Tai Cymru who, by 1995, had incorporated rent affordability into its bidding criteria for HAG allocation. By 1996 ministers were

31 *Solon Housing Association Newsletter* Oct, 1994, p4.
32 Chaplin, R. *et al.*, 'Rents and Risks', (1995), *Investing in Housing Associations*, Joseph Rowntree Foundation.

declaring a concern that rents were rising beyond the reach of many tenants and the Housing White Paper of that year advocated that projected rents be included as an element in the bidding process for SHG funding as a way of suppressing rent rises. In December 1997, it was confirmed that registered social landlords wishing to apply for capital grants would be expected to hold rent increases within the 'retail price index plus one per cent' formula.[33] The 2000 Green Paper reaffirms the government's concern that an ability to hold rents down to affordable levels should remain a key element in the bidding process. There are indications that the guide formula might be tightened to encourage static rents for a period (i.e. RPI plus 0 per cent).

Over-runs

The basic principle is that of 'predetermination' which means that over-runs will not normally be grant aided. The expectations are that such additional costs will normally be paid for through higher rents (hence deregulation and assured tenancies), from the landlord's reserves or, if adequate reserves do not exist, from the sale of assets.

The receipt of grant

The allocated grants are paid directly to associations rather than via an intermediary such as a solicitor. The payments are phased and received in *tranches* that coincide with specific 'events' such as site acquisition, the commencement of construction works, and on practical completion of the scheme. The RSL will spend the publicly provided funds in line with its funding agreement and its annual Cash Planning Target (CPT), that has to be submitted to the funding agency. The CPTs are meant to provide the funding corporations with realistic forecasts of when the RSLs expect to be able to take up allocated cash for both new allocations and committed schemes. This enables the funding agencies to plan their own cash targets for the year and then be held to account by central government, the ultimate paymaster, for the outcomes of the total public investment in this sector.[34]

Where a scheme has reached the trigger point at which a further tranche of SHG/HAG is receivable but the amount has not been received at the balance sheet date, the amount is included in 'debtors' as 'SHG receivable' (see Figure 15.2).

---

33 Under the pre-1989 arrangements some 60 per cent of tenants were on housing benefit. Of new tenants coming in 1996, the figure was 83 per cent. This concern to restrict rent increases can be seen as an aspect of the Labour government's political agenda on poverty and social exclusion (see Chapter 5). If low-income households are to escape the 'poverty trap' and avoid being dependent on benefits then rents will have to be prevented from rising too fast.

34 The funding body's ability to agree forward programmes is inhibited by ministerial directives that set forward commitment limits on expenditure. These are part of the public expenditure control mechanisms described in Chapter 5.

The right-to-buy or acquire

The 1980 Housing Act introduced a 'right-to-buy' (RTB) for secure tenants of non-charitable housing associations in England and Wales (as well as for local authority tenants). Equivalent rights were extended to housing association tenants in Scotland in 1986. These rights involved qualifying tenancy periods that carried entitlement to discounted sale prices. To encourage more tenants to avail themselves of these purchase rights, subsequent legislation[35] amended the original provisions to make them more generous.[36] This means that 'secure' (i.e. fair rent) tenants of non-charitable associations who became tenants before the operative date for the Housing Act 1988 kept the right-to-buy their homes at discounted rates.

The RTB arrangements were radically restructured by the provisions of the Housing Act 1988. This legislation replaced the fair rent/secure tenancy arrangements with 'assured' tenancies. These reforms set in place new financial arrangements that required the abandonment of fair rents and placed restrictions on the right to acquire.

Part 1, Section 16 of the Housing Act 1996 confers on certain tenants of housing associations and other RSLs the statutory right to purchase their homes, so long as the dwellings were provided or acquired with public money and have remained in

---

35 The Housing and Building Control Act 1984 and the Housing and Planning Act 1986.

36 It was originally intended that the RTB should include tenants of charitable associations. This provision in the 1980 Bill was vigorously opposed by the associations who argued that it would undermine the very essence of their charitable status: the provision was withdrawn after a defeat in the House of Lords. In 1984 the Housing and Building Control Bill again attempted to extend the RTB to tenants of charitable associations, and again the draft provision was not enacted after a defeat in the House of Lords. However, the 1984 legislation did introduce a 'portable' discount scheme known as 'HOTCHA' (Home Ownership for Tenants of Charitable Housing Associations). This was designed to give certain tenants of charitable associations in England and Wales, but not Scotland, an equivalent benefit to the RTB. Under these arrangements several thousand tenants have been given cash equivalents to the eligible discounts to help them buy dwellings on the open market either as an outright purchase or by a process of shared ownership. It worked by the association purchasing properties on the tenants' behalf. The cost of the discount was claimed from the Housing Corporation via the mechanism of Housing Association Grant. In this way, the Housing and Building Control Act gave tenants of charitable associations an opportunity to become owner-occupiers on much the same basis as RTB tenants in other agencies while, at the same time, preserving the rented stock of such associations for the purpose of social renting. The HOTCHA arrangements were replaced in 1990 by a similar, albeit more restrictive, procedure known as the Tenants' Incentive Scheme (TIS). This scheme aims to provide home-ownership opportunities to tenants who do not qualify for RTB: this includes assured tenants and tenants of charitable associations. The TIS arrangements involve associations bidding for funds to operate an approved scheme of tenant transfer and therefore the portable discount is only available to tenants of associations with such an allocation. In 1994 new rules were introduced to prevent housing association tenants using the scheme's resources to buy homes outside the UK. The argument here is that the original idea behind the scheme was, in part, to stimulate the UK housing market.

---

the social rented sector. This right only applies if the would-be purchaser has an assured tenancy, that is, not a tenant on an assured shorthold or long tenancy, or a secure tenant. He or she must also satisfy any further qualifying conditions applicable under Part 5 of the Housing Act 1985 (the right-to-buy). This so-called 'right to acquire' will only arise if the grant agency (e.g. the Housing Corporation) makes it clear that it is a condition in advance of making the grant. The RSL then has the opportunity to withdraw the grant application. Where the right to acquire is exercised, the RSL will received a capital receipt to provide a replacement dwelling. This provision reflects the public investment assumption that in a mixed funded scheme, the public money is intended to help create a *permanent* dwelling that will provide a series of social lettings to successive tenants.

Assured tenants whose agreements predate the 1996 Act do not possess the statutory right-to-buy but will, in many cases, also be able to acquire their homes with the help of a government grant called the Voluntary Purchase Grant.

The treatment of capital receipts

The new SORP makes provision for important changes in the treatment of capital receipts. In England, from 1999 receipts do not have to be returned (e.g. to the Housing Corporation), but can be recycled directly into their accounts. Such receipts are held as 'restricted reserves' (see model accounts in Figure 13.1 and 15.2). In Scotland, the use of capital receipts is controlled directly by Scottish Homes.[37]

The danger of falling reserves

The constraint on rents together with the reduction in public subsidy per unit of output, has meant that some RSLs have maintained their production levels by drawing down reserves. Imprudent use of reserves could reduce the funds available for future repairs.

Summary

The capital grant supporting this sector is called Social Housing Grant, previously Housing Association Grant. In Scotland it is sometimes still called Housing Association Grant. Initially, the grant was calculated in such a way that it covered virtually all of the scheme costs. Since 1989 it has been distributed on the basis of directed competition, covers only a proportion of total scheme costs, and is set as a predetermined amount. The remaining costs have to be met from private sector loans, accumulated reserves, or asset sales.

---

37 *'The Government which had forbidden Scottish Homes to use its capital receipts to build new homes from 1997/98, has softened the blow by allowing the agency to use £30 million of receipts received which exceeded its target for 1996/97.'* (Public Finance 7 March 1997, p4.).

The current capital funding regime is based on the following principles:

- The basic principle is that, because RSLs produce social housing, a percentage of the scheme cost should be covered by grant aid in the form of HAG/SHG.
- Because of the need to control total public expenditure, the level of grant should be predetermined and fixed before the works begin rather than be given as deficit funding on completion.
- Maximum grant is fixed by reference to standard cost limits, maximum grant rates, and rent caps, all of which are set by the funding agencies.
- Actual grant paid should represent an efficient use of public funds. 'Efficiency' in this context is judged by reference to the notion of 'grant stretch'.
- The 'grant stretch' principle is put into operation by a process of competitive bidding.
- As well as helping to provide good quality housing at affordable prices, the public funding is expected to aid RSLs to contribute to the government's wider policy objectives relating to sustainable communities, urban renewal and social inclusiveness.

Further reading

HACAS Consulting, *Housing Associations – A Viable Financial Future?* CIH, 1999.

The Housing Corporation, *Building A Better Future: Revitalising Neighbourhoods*. (The Housing Corporation's Three Year Strategy 1999/2000 – 2001/2002).

The Housing Corporation's *Capital Funding System Procedure Guide*. The annual circular providing details of current TCIs, grant rates and rent caps.

The Housing Corporation Consultation Paper, *Performance Indicator Framework for Registered Social Landlords*, January 2000.

DETR/Social Security, *Quality and Choice: A Decent Home for All*, the Housing Green Paper, Chapter 8, April 2000.

CHAPTER 15:
The financial management
of social landlords

Introduction: questions of time and opportunity costs

Before considering the practical elements of an effective financial strategy, we need to remind ourselves that the key objective of all financial planning is to make the 'best' use of limited resources. Before addressing the content of this chapter the reader is recommended to refer back to the discussion on *opportunity cost* in Chapter 2 (refer in particular to Figure 2.3). In that earlier chapter we stressed the point that the outcome of any financial spending has to be judged in terms of its contribution both to the declared corporate objectives of the organisation and also to the expectations of those who have some interest in the organisation's operations.

As earlier chapters have shown, the recent history of social housing has been characterised by change and uncertainty. Where uncertainty exists there may be a tendency to avoid mapping the future for fear of closing down options. However, so long as flexibility is consciously built into appraisals, it is generally agreed that in times of change financial planning is particularly important if an organisation wishes to make sustainable decisions and use its valuable resources to the best advantage. Because uncertainty is inherent in financial planning, the process has to incorporate procedures for monitoring, review and feedback. The well-managed social landlord is, among other things, a 'learning organisation'.

Focusing on the notion of opportunity cost, rather than the more limited notion of financial cost, helps to emphasise the point that financial management is not concerned with doing things as cheaply as possible; it is about getting value-for-money from limited resources. The notion of opportunity costs also helps to explain why financial management is not simply the responsibility of the treasury or finance section of the organisation. Because we are seeking to achieve specified objectives, financial management has to involve all those who make decisions that use up limited resources. As well as being a primary responsibility of the chief executive and the board of management, financial planning and control is also of concern to operational managers.

Aspects of financial management

What is financial planning and management? [1]

Financial management is a continuous process by which an organisation seeks to forecast and control its income, expenditure and cash-flow. As we will see, the overall process should be treated as a set of inter-connected plans, each operating within a specified time-scale and each producing documents that contain varying amounts and types of data and information. The process begins by establishing a coherent and logical *planning and control cycle*.

Planning describes the process by which an organisation decides (a) where it wants to be in the future and (b) how it intends to get there. *Control* describes the systems and procedures employed to ensure that the plans are (a) implemented appropriately, (b) monitored effectively, and (c) reviewed, refined and revised as necessary.

The need for a strategic approach to financial planning

Many of the features of the post-1989 revenue and capital regimes (described in the previous two chapters) point to the need to establish clear financial procedures and to employ effective financial management techniques. This is true for all social landlords but is particularly important for those engaging in development activities. The revenue and capital finance regimes create a need for social landlords to think strategically about how to manage their existing assets through the different planning time periods. Also underlined by these regimes is the importance for landlords to have in place sound policies for future borrowing and capital reinvestment.

Why is financial planning and control important?

Because housing associations and other RSLs are 'permanent' organisations with a responsibility to provide facilities to a succession of occupiers and service users, effective financial planning has to consider the future consequences as well as the current outcomes of putting money into housing. This means that effective financial management by social landlords involves:
- *adhering* to current regulations and *meeting* past promises *now*;
- *meeting* proprietary plans and prevailing societal expectations in the *near future*;
- *adapting* and *developing* to accommodate changing needs and demands in the *intermediate future*; and,
- *surviving* into the *distant future*.

This idea of a series of interrelated time profiles lies at the heart of strategic financial management. Such a series of time profiles is sometimes conceived of as

---

1   Based on NHF, *Financial Planning: a practical guide*, 1996, p vi.

an *integrated planning and control cycle* that links the organisation's long-term aspirations to its immediate activities. Converting the idea of the cycle into a management process involves asking different types of policy question and creating a cascade of documents differentiated by time, scale and specific detail.

Figure 15.1: Financial planning integrated over time: the planning and control cycle

The distant future period (up to 40+/- years)
Embraces the sorts of questions asked by the chief executive and management board. E.g. 'What is our growth strategy?' and 'What is our corporate mission?' This period also poses the question of how to account for the long-term replacement of the organisation's fixed assets (depreciation).

Requires the production of a *strategic plan* covering the physical life of an asset, the economic life of an asset, the period of a long-term loan, and beyond. During this period the organisation might be expected to grow or amalgamate, and/or redefine its mission.

The intermediate future period (up to 15 years+/-)
Embraces the sorts of questions asked by investment project managers, lending institutions, and the management board. Includes identifying objectives that need to be achieved to fulfil the mission and how best to acquire funds for development and renewal.

Requires the production of *business plans* and *project appraisals*.

The near future period (up to 5 years +/-)
Embraces the sorts of questions asked by service users and/or front-line managers about imminent rent changes, proposed maintenance and minor works schedules, and sources of short-term finance.

Requires the publication of *budgets*, *cash-flow forecasts* and *work schedules* relating to specific projects, and *committee minutes* confirming policy decisions relating to the *business plan*. It also requires the periodic publication of *performance indicators* that measure outcomes against the organisation's declared objectives.

The present and recent past periods (annual)
Focuses on the immediate concerns of auditors, front-line managers, and current stakeholders.

Requires the production of annual *accounts*, and *financial statements*.

Different landlords can take distinctly different approaches to financial planning and management and the above should be regarded as a broad schema rather than a set framework that is appropriate to all social landlords. In particular, the time periods are indicative only and they tend to merge into one another. However, in the discussion that follows the reader is encouraged to keep in mind this model of an integrated planning process. Sound financial planning rests on an awareness of these different planning time horizons, and throughout the chapter reference will be made to the various questions, concerns, and forms of documentation mentioned above.

Financial profiling

The strategic approach to financial planning involves establishing a 'rolling' analysis of future revenues, costs and investment needs that is termed 'financial profiling'. A financial profile charts anticipated costs and revenues based on present knowledge and current assumptions about the future. It provides a present day 'snapshot' of the anticipated financial future. The projection has to be based on a range of assumptions about such things as known and planned debt servicing charges, appropriate gearing ratios, building cost inflation, interest rates, expected maintenance, repairs and renewal needs (of the housing stock and other fixed assets), planned rental flows, and other anticipated sources of income. As the projection moves further into the future it moves away from a zone of relative certainty into zones of increasing uncertainty. We have to be more and more circumspect about our assumptions as we move away from a relatively certain present towards an increasingly uncertain future.

The profiling approach seeks to enable managers and decision-makers at a particular moment to:

- be certain about the immediate financial needs of the organisation, based on accurate information about the past, and firm assumptions about the current and near future accounting periods;
- be clear about the intermediate financial needs of the organisation, based on provisional estimates of incomes and costs relating to that period;
- have some conditional ideas about the long-term financial needs of the organisation, based on tentative assumptions about the distant future.

This static profile of the future, the 'snapshot', is made dynamic by establishing procedures that periodically check the assumptions. In this way, as time passes and we roll towards the future, financial plans can gradually firm up and become more concrete. At any point in time, different futures can be anticipated through appraisal techniques such as *discounting* and *sensitivity analysis*. (More about these later).

We will now turn to the key issues that contemporary social landlords have to consider when planning and managing their finances. These issues straddle the different planning time profiles that we have been discussing.

The key elements of financial planning and control

Sound financial management depends on achieving each of the following.

1. The presentation of relevant financial data to management committees in ways that allow informed decisions to be made about current management issues, prospective projects and longer-term strategic aspirations.
2. An appropriate policy for raising money from the private sector.
3. Clarity about how best to cover the costs of maintaining, repairing, improving and renewing the built assets over the longer as well as the shorter term.
4. An appropriate policy for assessing and managing the financial risks that come from operating in a commercial climate.
5. Effective tax planning.

The rest of this chapter is structured around these five key aspects of financial management.

1. Financial information

Strategic planning

Long-term overall goals are normally designed around mission statements. These tend to be written in language that is more aspirational than technical. Mission statements try to summarise, in a sentence or so, the overriding purpose of the organisation. The strategic plan is then grounded in this publicly declared mission. The strategic plan identifies four planning levels that can be represented by the acronym **MOST**.

Mission → Objectives → Strategy → Tactics

Objectives are specific goals that need to be achieved in order to fulfil the mission; they constitute the various priorities, projects and activities that naturally flow from the mission. The strategy describes *how* the objectives will be achieved and, in so doing, it specifies key policy directions and identifies the real and financial resources needed. Usually there are a variety of approaches to delivering policies and acquiring and using resources. The organisation therefore also needs to consider its tactics. Tactics determine *what* the organisation does on a day-to-day basis to achieve its objectives. Tactics determine actions.

Although they do not normally describe detailed financial arrangements, strategic plans should make some reference to how current loans are to be serviced, when fixed capital assets will need renewing or replacing, and how general institutional growth and change are to be paid for. Although the strategic plan takes the long view (say up to 40 years) it should be periodically revisited and revised in the light of operational experiences and changing circumstances.

Business planning

Intermediate-term decisions about specific projects and policy initiatives (such as a proposed stock transfer, major acquisitions or new building works) should be based on some form of business planning that typically begins with the presentation of an *option appraisal* report and culminates with *budgeting* and *cash-flow forecasting*.

An option appraisal report can be produced internally but is often commissioned from external consultants who will have had experience of working on similar projects with other organisations. Option appraisals are usually presented in a cost-benefit format that identifies, and in some way quantifies, all the relevant advantages and disadvantages of following one course of action as against others. The 'costs' and 'benefits' should encompass everything that is judged to be relevant to the corporate mission and strategy. This may mean that some rather intangible costs and benefits have to be included, such as staff morale and tenant satisfaction. Because costs and benefits come on stream at different times, the report has to be put into a clear time profile that discounts the value of future costs and benefits back to a present value. There are many difficulties and problems associated with the production of a cost-benefit report and over the years a number of techniques and conventions have been developed to standardise their production.[2] When commissioning a cost-benefit analysis (CBA), the housing practitioner, or the management board, needs to be aware of the strengths and limitations of this kind of appraisal. They also have to be clear that they, and not their consultants, have to be responsible for making the final decision. This means that such reports should not 'make' the decision about which option to follow, but rather act as a guide and source of information and analysis. A CBA should be regarded as a management tool that guides those who carry the ultimate responsibility for taking the option decision. Once decided upon, the selected option has to be budgeted for and cash flows have to be estimated.

Budgeting

Budgets are intended to help the organisation ensure that, over a specified budgetary period, expenditure is met by income. The budgetary period may cover more than one financial year. Budgets are used to monitor and authorise expenditure and the collection of income. The budget process also enables the organisation to set and declare priority spending and to establish a rational sequence of spending events. More broadly, budgets can be used to co-ordinate different functions and activities, set targets, and provide a recorded basis for measuring performance and reviewing the organisation's strategy.

There are a number of recognised approaches to budgeting. These include incremental budgeting, planning programming budgeting systems (PPBS), and zero-base budgeting. The incremental approach is commonly used in the preparation of revenue budgets. It involves making incremental adjustments to the previous period's budget by focusing on those items that need to be altered

---

2   For a fuller discussion of these see Garnett, D. 1994a and 1994b.

because of changing circumstances, like inflation, new service agreements, salary increases, withdrawal of revenue grants. This is a largely conservative approach to budgeting as it assumes that, although circumstances will change, basic service provision will continue much as before. It concentrates on making provision for changes in the *external environment*. In contrast, PPBS focuses on the *internal objectives* of the organisation and identifies alternative ways of achieving these objectives. This approach is more relevant for capital budgeting where particular investment and reinvestment plans might be achieved by a variety of different spending programmes. Zero-based budgeting takes a cost-benefit approach by comparing estimated outcomes with the costs of producing those outcomes. It extends the PPBS approach into a more overtly value-for-money analysis: as such, it is particularly appropriate where alternative levels of provision are possible for various functions. It takes a strictly opportunity cost approach to spending by seeking to make explicit what would be gained or lost by spending 'more here' and 'less there'. By giving a priority to value-for-money outcomes, this approach may point to the need to make significant changes to previous spending patterns. Although in line with the philosophy of resource accounting, zero-based budgeting can be relatively expensive and time-consuming to establish and operate. As with any CBA approach, it also involves making value judgements about the value of one course of action as against another, and is open to a degree of political manipulation.[3]

Budgets can be set at different levels (corporate, departmental, section). Once an organisation has reached a certain size, experience shows that some resource use decisions are best made by those who have direct managerial responsibility for spending outcomes. A *cost centre* is a sub-division of the organisation that is used for planning and accounting purposes. Typically the manager of the cost centre will be the budget holder and, as such, will be held responsible for controlling and justifying the devolved budget. The principle here is that devolved responsibility produces more informed decisions and a more intelligent and flexible use of limited resources, and is therefore less bureaucratic.[4]

Cash-flows

All businesses have to manage the month-by-month flow of cash in and out of the transaction accounts. This means that, once set, internal budgets have to be monitored and managed. For each cost centre, adjustments may have to be made during the budgetary period to ensure that receipts can cover payments. At certain times, it may be necessary to delay certain payments until the cash-flow situation improves, or reschedule spending programmes, or abandon or increase planned spending, or acquire short-term finance to cover impending costs. The analysis and monitoring of cash-flow is particularly important with respect to capital budgets where the sums of money are likely to be relatively large.

---

3   For a fuller discussion of types of budget and methods of budgeting refer to NHF, *Financial Planning: a practical guide*, NHF, 1996, pp11-19.
4   For a fuller discussion on planning for cost centres refer to NHF, *Financial Planning: a practical guide*, NHF, 1996, pp8-10.

Standard accounts and financial statements

Shorter term financial information is presented in the audited accounts, appended notes, and accompanying financial statements. Two key accounts have to be kept by housing associations and other RSLs: these are an Income and Expenditure Account and a Balance Sheet. A standard Income and Expenditure Account is set out and analysed in Chapter 13 (refer to Figure 13.1). A balance sheet is a statement featured in the annual accounts that indicates the value of the organisation's assets and liabilities at the end of the accounting period, and the ways in which these have been financed. The main purpose of the balance sheet is to show the state of affairs of the social landlord at the year end date.

Figure 15.2: Balance Sheet at 31 March XXX1 (Presented in the format required by the English 1997 Determination, and the Northern Ireland 1993 Order)

		XXX1 £000		XXX0 £000
Fixed assets				
Housing properties – depreciated cost				
Less	X		X	
SHG	(X)		(X)	
Other public grants	(X)		(X)	
		X		X
Investments		X		X
Other fixed assets		X		X
		X		X
Current assets				
Debtors	X		X	
Investments	X		X	
Cash at bank and in hand	X		X	
		X		X
Creditors: amounts falling due within one year			X	X
Net current assets		X		X
Total assets less current liabilities		X		X
Creditors: amounts falling due after more than one year				
Disposal proceeds and recycled capital grant funds	X		X	
Other creditors	X	X	X	X
Provisions for liabilities and charges		X		X
Capital and reserves				
Housing property revaluation reserve		X		X
Designated reserves		X		X
Restricted reserves		X		X
Revenue reserve		X		X
See notes on next page		X		X

Notes to Figure 15.2

1. Fixed assets are investments that are held for a long-term purpose. Current assets are those investments that are held as part of short-term treasury management where the intention is to realise the investment in the short-term without reinvestment of the sale proceeds, that is, use the proceeds for some planned expenditure purpose in the immediate or near future.

2. The item 'housing properties' should distinguish between dwellings held for letting and shared ownership.[5] Anyone reading the accounts should also be able to distinguish between completed schemes and properties under construction. Properties developed for outright sale or on behalf of third parties should be treated as 'current assets', rather than as 'fixed assets'.

3. Because any decision to dispose of housing properties is controlled by regulations, they cannot be valued in market terms. The balance sheet value of housing properties can be either: (a) historic cost less SHG and depreciation; or (b) valuation less depreciation. (Issues relating to the valuation and depreciation of social housing are discussed fully below).

4. The amount at which an item is included in the balance sheet is called the 'carrying value'.

5. If conditions change causing a reduction in the recoverable amount of a fixed asset below its carrying value, this is called 'impairment'.[6]

6. Designated and restricted reserves are explained in the note to Figure 13.1.

7. Where valuations are used, the properties should be periodically revalued at least every five years. Where housing properties are revalued and the valuation exceeds the carrying amount (net of capital grants and any depreciation) the difference should be credited to the revaluation reserve and reported in the statement of total recognised surpluses and deficits (see below). Where housing properties are revalued and the valuation is less than the carrying amount, the diminution should be recognised.

8. In deciding whether to include housing properties at valuation, the RSL will need to consider the balance of costs and benefits. Although a valuation provides more meaningful information to users of the accounts, periodic valuation exercises cost money.

9. When housing properties carried at valuation are disposed of, any amounts in the revaluation reserve relating to those properties should be transferred to the revenue reserve.

10. Fixed asset investments, other than housing properties, should be stated at their market value, or the Board's best estimate of market value. This is deemed the most appropriate basis of valuation because, unlike housing properties, there are no external restrictions attached to their disposal. Any upward or downward revaluations are accounted for in the statement of recognised surpluses and deficits (see below).

11. For all investments included at a valuation, the historical cost should be disclosed in a note to the accounts.

12. The above is just a simplified summary balance sheet. In practice, subsidiary accounts will also be referenced. For example, SHG to be recycled (i.e. after disposals) should be credited to the Recycled Capital Grant Fund within 'creditors'. A whole range of further detailed information is also given in notes to the accounts and by cross-referencing to the various financial statements.

---

5   In shared ownership developments, the proportion of the development that is expected to be sold as the first tranche should be shown as a current asset. The remainder should be shown as a fixed asset from which SHG should be deducted.

6   Examples of events and changes in circumstances that indicate impairment may have occurred include: (a) social, demographic or environmental changes resulting in a fall in property prices locally; and (b) significant adverse changes in the statutory or regulatory environment.

Financial statements

In addition to the two main accounts (Figures 13.1 and 15.2), each RSL has to produce a set of *financial statements* that give an indication to the management committee, and other interested parties, of the year's transactions and how the organisation has fared financially over the accounting period. The financial statements typically include the following.

(a) *A cash-flow statement.* This tracks and records the money transactions that occurred over the accounting period. It seeks to set out the organisation's financial activities in cash terms. It normally records the following.
   - Net cash-flow from operating activities.
   - Net cash outflow on investment and servicing finance (interest received and paid).
   - Net cash outflow from taxation (corporation tax paid less grants received).
   - Net cash outflow from capital expenditure (acquisition and construction of properties and other fixed assets net of receipts from sales and capital grants).

   As well as itemising the net cash outflow (the summation of the above), the statement should record the financing changes that have occurred, as in loan advances received, loans redeemed, and principal repaid during the period.

(b) *A statement of total recognised surpluses and deficits.* This sets out the recognised surpluses and deficits for the year. This is a sort of 'profit' statement, although it must be remembered that RSLs cannot make money to be distributed to shareholders. The surpluses can arise from three sources.
   - An operating surplus from their activities as a landlord.
   - Unrealised surplus/(deficit) on revaluation of housing properties (a bookkeeping annual charge reflecting any movement in the value of the stock – i.e. equity growth/decline).
   - Unrealised (deficit)/surplus on investments.

(c) *A note of historical cost surpluses and deficits for the year.* Despite the shift in emphasis towards resource accounting (see below), it can still be useful to have a note that records the overall financial picture in strictly cash terms. This note seeks to present the historical cost surplus for the year before and after taxation. It adds the surplus on ordinary activities to any property revaluation surpluses of previous years that have been actually realised in this accounting period. This note will also include the difference between an historical cost depreciation charge and the actual depreciation charge for the year calculated on the revalued amount.

The information presented in the accounts and their accompanying financial statements are necessarily detailed. The detailed requirements, published as the

Statement of Recommended Practice – SORP,[7] change periodically. What the general reader needs to bear in mind is that the presentation of all this information is designed to guarantee accountability (transparency) and to allow informed decision-making to occur. Later in this chapter we will consider the important question of risk management. It is worth making the point straightaway that the production and presentation of deficient, misleading or inaccessible information is bound to add to the risks of running a business.

2. Borrowing strategies

Broadly speaking, social landlords need recourse to private loans for two reasons: (1) to counteract the effects of the reduced grants rates described in the last chapter, and (2) to help finance the increased activity described in Chapter 12.

In broad terms, the costs of servicing a loan will depend on how much is borrowed, when the loan was taken out, the nature of the investment product, the term of loan, what security is being offered to underwrite the debt, and the status of borrower (including the quality of its management procedures).

Experience shows that success in raising private finance can often be traced back to sound planning long before approaches are made to lenders. (Button, 1993, p12). The objective of loan planning and management is to secure loan finance that balances in an appropriate way the following factors.

- Cheapness – low interest charges.
- Certainty – a degree of fixedness of interest rates.
- Coherence – matching cash-flow and debt service obligations.
- Renewability – an opportunity to extend the loan if this becomes necessary.
- Redeemability – an opportunity to cancel the loan if the needs arise.
- Security – a balanced loan portfolio in terms of loan type and term.

These features have to be negotiated with lenders whose priorities are somewhat different from those of borrowers. Lenders are primarily concerned with balancing the return on their investment with the risk of default. As a general rule, lenders tend to charge higher rates of interest for higher risk projects. This means that in negotiating a loan with manageable interest charges, the borrower has to underwrite the debt in some way that satisfies the lender's desire for an appropriate 'risk-reward' relationship.

---

7   The Accounting Standards Board (ASB), has approved the National Housing Federation, the Welsh Federation of Housing Associations (WFHA), and the Scottish Federation of Housing Associations (SFHA) – the three Federations – collectively for the purpose of issuing recognised Statements of Recommended Practice (SORPs). This requires the three Federations to follow the ASB's code of practice for the production and issue of SORPs. The code provides the framework to be followed by the three Federations.

Since 1989, the movement as a whole has been successful in raising more than £15 billion from private sources. Currently, a higher proportion of the total gross investment expenditure in this sector is provided by private financiers than by the 'housing corporations'. The initial success in levering in private funds can be explained in large part by the timing of the introduction of the new regime. In the early 1990s there was a shortage of commercial lending opportunities and this gave housing associations the chance to establish themselves as a significant borrowing presence in the finance markets. Since that time, their continued success has been founded on the following factors.

- The movement has presented itself as being professionally well managed. Social housing managers tend to be well qualified and their work is regulated by statute and monitored by the regulators. This gives potential lenders confidence in social landlords in general.

- In comparison with many pure private sector landlords, social landlords have a good quality stock and a low level of bad debts. This is partly because their development activities have been supported by grant and their rental flows have been underpinned by housing benefit. This support gives private lenders added confidence in the sector. This is, of course, a 'two-edged sword' in that reductions, or feared reductions, in central government support may rapidly diminish the willingness of private lenders to invest, particularly if the reduction occurs at a time when the economy is buoyant and other investment opportunities exist.

- Social landlords have learned market skills relating to financial opportunism. The principle here is to borrow at the 'appropriate' time (i.e. when a good deal can be clinched). The optimum time to borrow may not coincide with the moment when the money needs to be employed. Large financial savings might be made by borrowing ahead of need, reinvesting the borrowed resources (e.g. in easily redeemable gilts) and then drawing them down into housing projects when they are needed. As private sector organisations have long known, you cannot rely on capital markets providing what you want just when you want it. This means that, to some extent, borrowing should be planned around financial market trends. In the early days, housing associations found that opportunistic borrowing was inhibited by the committee cycle. Opportunities were lost because financial planning was too firmly driven by decision committee timetables. Commercially minded associations soon overcame this by establishing a knowledgeable *standing sub-committee* that had clearly delineated delegated powers to respond to borrowing opportunities as and when they arose. Effective opportunism depends on being prepared. Among other things, this involves early identification of which assets are going to be pledged as collateral and making sure that clear certificates of title are available and that these assets are valued in an appropriate way. (The question of asset valuation is discussed fully below).

- Social landlords have managed their financial affairs in ways that are seen to be coherent. Coherence in financial planning involves establishing a portfolio of loans that is structured in a way that allows the landlord to meet the debt servicing obligations without having continually, and erratically, to manipulate running costs and rents. As we made clear in Chapter 2, the question of 'equity' is a key aspect of value-for-money in social housing operations. This means that rent projections should seek to spread the costs of debt servicing fairly between different generations of tenants. It would not be acceptable to over burden one generation of tenants in order to meet relatively high interest charges operating at a particular time. In order to spread the burden fairly across a succession of tenants, debt managers may need to take out low-start mortgages, even if they are more expensive over the life of the asset. A variety of innovative funding instruments have been developed to help match debt costs with cash flows. Most involve meeting debt service charges from cash flows on a stepped interest basis. The two main mechanisms for creating low-start loans are (1) *deferred interest* arrangements, where the interest burden is back-loaded to a time when incomes from employment and rents will assumed to have risen; and, (2) *index-linked* arrangements, where the interest rates are tied to a prices or incomes index.

  By shifting part of the debt servicing burden into the future, low-start finance comes into conflict with the principle of resource accounting. For this reason the SORP regulations make it clear that where a social landlord uses such finance, a proper application of the accruals concept of accounting is to charge an annual interest cost that reflects the full rate of interest implicit in the loan, irrespective of the timing of the cash payments.

- Social landlords have expanded the financial mechanisms for borrowing funds. Most of their private borrowing is still in the form of traditional mortgages from banks and building societies, but over time they have sought new ways of borrowing. Housing association bonds are now well-established. A bond is simply an IOU agreement under which a sum is repaid to an investor after a fixed period. Bonds can be issued by anyone but their issuing costs are relatively high for small amounts of money borrowed for short periods.[8] For this reason bonds are normally issued by public bodies or companies wishing to borrow relatively large sums for relatively long periods. They can be thought of as loans that repay a fixed rate of interest over a specified time and then also repay the original sum *at par* in full after an agreed period – when the bond 'matures'. Bond debt appears in the balance sheet as a liability. The debt should be stated at its current value (net amount) in 'long term creditors'.[9]

---

8   For example, bond issues are sometimes guaranteed by what is called 'monoline enhancement'. This is a form of insurance policy that guarantees investors against any default on their interest payments.

9   The net amount is the gross redemption value less the discount net of amortisation. Immediately after issue, before any amortisation of the discount, the net amount will be equal to the net proceeds. Amortisation is charged to the income and expenditure account. Similarly, any significant early redemption costs (penalties for redeeming the debt) should be charged to the income and expenditure account.

Bonds can be traded (i.e. they are transferable instruments) so that the original investor can pass them on at a discount before the maturity date. The trading market for bonds is sometimes referred to as 'the debt capital market'. Bonds provide an appropriate form of finance for larger, more active landlords in that they produce long-term (i.e. 20-40 years) fixed rate funding that matches the economic life of the housing assets they help to fund. Where large sums are involved they can prove to be (incrementally) the cheapest form of secure funding. Local authorities have always sought to achieve financial economies of scale by financing housing assets over a 60-year period. By accessing the large pool of institutional monies available from pension funds and life companies, the LSVT landlord in particular can, like the local authorities, acquire longer-term financing than is available in the bank market.[10]

By the mid-1990s housing associations had become among the most active 'public sector' bodies in the bond market, raising some £5 billion between 1989 and 1996. After 1996, as LSVT plans gathered pace, an increasing number of social landlords looked to the capital bond market to provide the large amounts of development and redevelopment funding they needed. (Refer to Chapter 10 for discussion on LSVT and funding). Under the 1999/2000 LSVT plans, the government received 24 bids to transfer up to 150,000 homes with a combined value of more than £2.5 billion. Given the scale of this financial requirement, a large proportion of the funds will have to be raised on the debt capital market.

Increasingly, specialist bankers are arranging sophisticated packages for LSVT landlords that can include a core funding element in the form of a bond issue with complementary funding in the form of a long-term (e.g. 25 year) banking facility. This sort of arrangement establishes opportunities for renewing and extending loan facilities into the future, thereby achieving one of the key borrowing objectives mentioned above.

A number of social landlords have turned to specialist merchant banks to arrange highly flexible loan packages that cannot be provided directly by the more traditional clearing banks and building societies. These specialist institutions may be able to arrange 'designer loans' that include special features that allow the RSL to operate more finely-tuned treasury management. These specialist loans can include facilities such as a 'revolving arrangement', whereby the RSL borrows an agreed sum for an agreed period but is given the facility to reduce the debt (and thereby lower the interest charges) for set periods within the term. This can prove useful if sometime in the future, unexpected cash flows emerge or cheaper sources of finance become available, such as a newly introduced government subsidy. In such circumstances, part of the loan can be redeemed and then taken out again at

---

10   Institutional investors (such as pension fund managers) and social landlords are both concerned with long-term cycles of lending and borrowing. The fund manager is concerned that the fund's invested resources keep up with long-run inflation, and the RSL rents tend to rise with inflation.

some later date if the need arises. These specialist loans tend only to be available for longer-term loans (in excess of ten years) and will require more 'up front' time and money to arrange. However, they can prove to be cheaper in the long-run.

- Associations have developed trusted relationships with lenders that enable them to negotiate repeat issues and loan extensions. Loan set up costs can be high, therefore repeat issues can produce economies of scale.

- As part of their negotiations with funders, associations have developed imaginative ways of providing sound cover security for the loans they take out. Because of its importance, we will now look at this aspect of their success in more detail.

Negotiating loans

Loan negotiations involve making a contract that strikes an equilibrium between the borrower's and the lender's objectives. A key factor in this negotiation is the ability of the RSL to persuade the potential investor that the loan is secure over its term. This involves establishing the following:

1. The legal and managerial competence of the borrower.
2. What collateral is being offered and what cover ratio is allowed.
3. How the value of the collateral is to be measured.

Status and legal and financial competence

Lenders require evidence of the corporate status of the borrower and its capacity to service the loan over its term. The lender will want to inspect a current copy of the borrower's rules and constitution with evidence of its registered status. Having satisfied the lender that it has the power to take out the loan, the borrower must then show that it has carried out the necessary actions to exercise that power. The lender's solicitors are likely to require documentary evidence, such as minutes of an authorised committee of the borrower, that delegated powers are valid comprehensive and relevant to the loan conditions. Audited accounts will have to be presented for inspection so that the lender can be satisfied that the borrower is in a position to service the debt. Supplementary statements may be required from the borrower's auditors confirming that there has been no material change in financial status since submission of the last audited accounts.

Lenders will be interested in the borrower's overall debt profile and their ability to cover that debt if things go wrong. This means that they will wish to compare the loans outstanding with the total reserves. When expressed as a ratio this relation is called the *loan gearing*.

Lenders are always concerned with the managerial competence of those to whom they lend. For this reason the association should be able to demonstrate that it has in place mechanisms for maintaining the value of its built assets over the long term. For example, the financial planning of repairs and renewals is prudent in itself (see below), but it is also necessary if the organisation wishes to borrow investment funds. Lenders will want to see projections of future costs (such as repair costs) to ensure that the agreed (covenanted) loan interest cover ratios and revenue break-even points are not likely to be breached.

Covenant conditions including collateral and effective loan cover ratio

Covenants stipulate the loan conditions. In particular, they specify how the loan is to be secured, by collateral and effective cover ratio; penalties for default or for early redemption; and any penalties for changing the loan conditions. Covenants may also specify the financial performance borrowers are expected to achieve. For example, the lender may require the association to generate enough revenue to meet its interest charges one and a half or two times over. Covenants result from contractual negotiations and in practice they differ substantially.

Collateral constitutes the lender's security against default on the loan. It takes the form of an identified asset that is pledged as guarantee for repayment of money lent. Typically, property is put forward as the security, although in recent years some deals have been struck that pledge the organisation's rental income flow. The idea of pledging the rent flow, sometimes termed *securitisation of receivables* or *rental securitisation*, is an idea that was first developed in the USA. Under these arrangements, the rental income is paid direct to the lender, via a financial intermediary. This gives the rental income a 'first charge' status (see below) thereby providing sound collateral for the loan. Once the debt service charges have been deducted, the surplus rent is then paid back to the landlord.[11]

As grant rates fall, the proportion of cost met by private loans has had to increase. This has meant that the value of the new units being developed are often insufficient to under-write fully the debt, and lenders have sought further security from the existing stock (or the rental income flow). Where existing properties are pledged, security can be given by means of a 'fixed charge' or a 'floating charge'. If the loan is secured by a fixed charge, it is tied to specific, identifiable dwellings owned by the landlord and does not change over time. If the loan is secured by a floating charge, it may be covered by all or a range of the association's stock. A floating charge security may change over time as it can include any equity growth on properties already subject to fixed charges. Whether property or rents are put up as collateral, lenders to this sector typically look for fixed charge security to cover their loans. They will normally expect to have a fixed *first charge*. This means that they will want assurance that the asset is free from any existing prior claims so that they have first claim on the asset in the event of default. Because of lender aversion to floating charges, associations sometimes arrange consolidation of existing lenders' charges as a way of releasing the maximum amount of unencumbered asset cover.

---

11   For a clear explanation of the principles of rental securitisation see briefing by David Walker and Graham Brombley in *Inside Housing*, 17 February 1995, pp14-15.

The cover ratio stipulates what the lender is prepared to accept as a ratio between the value of the asset collateral and the agreed debt. So, for example, the lender may stipulate a 1.2 cover ratio meaning that a debt of £1 million will have to be covered by £1.2 million worth of assets. In the case of floating charge securities, lenders will normally require a greater effective cover ratio – something like 2.5. Clearly much depends on how the properties are valued. How to value and depreciate units of social housing are now important questions in social housing management. These days landlords need to put a value on their housing assets for a number of reasons. As well as the need to provide collateral for private borrowing, the whole principle of resource accounting is based on assumptions about the use of the financial resources that are locked into the fixed assets. For these reasons, the questions of valuation and depreciation will now be discussed as separate issues.

Social housing valuations

There is no one definitive way of valuing a unit of social housing. Broadly, the value could be measured against its costs of production or acquisition (historic cost value); or it could be measured against its vacant exchange value (open market value); or it could be measured against its tenanted transfer value (existing use value). In any case, a lender will require the value to reflect the social nature of the asset.

So long as social landlords were deemed to be located in the welfare sector of the economy and were publicly funded, there was little or no pressure put upon them to value their housing assets in terms of current values. As welfare agencies, so long as they covered their costs over the long-term, there was little concern about whether or not their assets had appreciated in value thereby generating equity. This meant that housing units were simply valued by reference to their historic costs of provision. However, the principles of best value and the requirements of resource accounting now require social landlords to estimate and record the current value of their fixed assets. The introduction of mixed funding made it imperative that associations knew the exchange value of their assets. Many private sector loans are secured against the equity vested in the stock and, in any event, lenders will wish to measure the current overall financial standing of those to whom they advance loans.

There are a number of ways in which a unit of social housing might be valued. For accounting purposes (i.e. balance sheet valuations), properties are normally valued in terms of existing use. The accounting principle behind giving a book value to a housing property is that it should represent the lower of replacement cost (i.e. of an identical development today) or recoverable amount (its net realisable value or value in use). Under normal circumstances social tenanted properties will only be disposed of to another social landlord. Therefore, for all intents and purposes, the value of such properties is limited to Existing Use Value for Social Housing (EUV-SH). For social landlords the Royal Institution of Chartered Surveyors has introduced the EUV-SH into its Practice Statement within its Appraisal and Valuation Manual. EUV-SH seeks to estimate what another RSL would be prepared to pay to acquire the asset and keep it in existing use. This involves valuing the asset(s) on a 'going concern' basis.[12] EUV-SH has now also been adopted as the basis for resource accounting for local authority housing.

The basis of valuation for secured lending purposes can differ from that for accounting purposes. The lender tends to be interested in the property as an 'investment asset'. Lenders are concerned with cover ratios (see above), and ease of acquisition and disposal in the case of default. Most lenders have private sector experience of securing loans against properties valued in terms of vacant possession open market prices. However, it has to be recognised that open market vacant possession is not a relevant basis of valuation for social landlords because the rights of the tenants have to be taken into account.

In the past, money has been lent to social landlords against housing assets that have been valued in rather rough and ready ways. Arguably the simple valuation would be 'discounted open market value' (OMV minus social discount). The discount is applied to reflect the continuing social nature of the asset. When this simple valuation has been used, the discount has tended to be fairly hefty (e.g. 50 per cent).

When an 'historical cost' approach to valuation is used, the question of how to represent any embedded capital grant (e.g. HAG/SHG), is brought to the fore. In such cases, associations have traditionally favoured the practice of deducting the grant element from the value but showing it in the balance sheet so as to record the extent to which government support contributed to an association's development.

Depreciation of the value of housing assets

Depreciation measures the reduction in the value of an asset with the passage of time, due in particular to wear and tear. In the past, social landlords often argued that regular maintenance and periodic refurbishment of their housing properties have the effect of maintaining values thereby eliminating the need to provide for depreciation. With the shift in emphasis towards resource accounting, the Accounting Standards Board now questions the acceptability of this practice. For accounting purposes, social housing properties are regarded as 'tangible fixed assets' rather than 'investment assets'. As such, they are primarily valued for their economic usefulness rather than for their potential to appreciate in exchange value. Good accounting practice requires all tangible fixed assets to be depreciated to reflect the consumption of their economic benefit. This requires the

---

12 Although a logical way of recording the asset value, and recommended by SORP, work done by the NFHA in the early 1990s indicated that EUV-SH produced a relatively low valuation in so far as repossessed dwellings often raised higher sums on disposal through sales or re-renting than that represented by this 'going concern' valuation.

social landlord to charge a depreciable amount for their housing properties to the income and expenditure account on a systematic basis over their useful economic lives.[13]

Property valuers and accountants argue that few buildings can be regarded as having a limitless life, and that a point will eventually come at which redevelopment (full replacement) rather than maintenance, repair and refurbishment will be the most economic course. A depreciation charge puts an estimated value on the wearing out, consumption or other reduction in the useful economic life of a tangible fixed asset that has occurred during the accounting period.[14] Depreciation is concerned to take account of the declining use value that occurs with the effluxion of time (wear, tear and obsolescence). The principle here is that an increase in the exchange value of a property does not justify ignoring depreciation. (Refer to Chapter 1 for a discussion on the distinction between use value and exchange value).

The depreciation charge is based on the balance sheet carrying value. Freehold land should not be depreciated and so the current value of the land should be deducted from the carrying value before assessing the need to depreciate. In different cases different methods of calculating depreciation may be deemed appropriate. There are several acceptable depreciation methodologies. The two most commonly used are:

- *the straight line (annuity) method* – where the asset is written off in equal instalments over its estimated economic useful life; and,
- *the reducing balance method* – where a standard percentage of depreciation is applied to the reducing depreciable amount of the asset.

The reducing balance method has more economic logic in that it assumes that the consumption benefits of the assets diminish as they age. However, in order to prevent undue fluctuations and avoid the expense of continually having to value properties, the straight line method is often employed. We will return to the question of depreciation when we consider the issue of stock management (see below).

Impairment of the value of housing assets
The notion of depreciation has to be distinguished from that of impairment. With the passage of time, factors other than condition obsolescence (wear and tear) can come into play that 'impair' the utility of a tangible fixed asset such as a dwelling and thus reduces its value. In other words, events or changed circumstances may

---

13   The useful economic life of an asset is defined as the period over which the organisation expects to derive economic benefits from that asset. A traditionally built new building is assumed to have an economic life of 60 years.

14   The structure of a building and items within the structure, such as central heating boilers, lifts and general fittings, may have substantially different useful economic lives and, if material, may need to be depreciated separately.

occur that cause the value of the assets to decline at a faster rate than that allowed for by the depreciation methodology. This is a problem because good accounting practice requires the landlord to ensure that properties are not shown in the books at an amount exceeding their exchange value, called the 'recoverable amount'.[15] For this reason social landlords are required to address the issue of impairment of housing properties in addition to depreciation.

The landlord should instigate an impairment review where there is an indication that carrying values may not be recoverable. The following are illustrative examples of events or changed circumstances that might prompt an impairment review.

- A change in demand for social housing in the area with consequential high void rates and transfer requests. There are many social, demographic, economic and environmental changes that might affect the demand in a particular area.
- Significant adverse changes in the statutory or regulatory environment.
- A current or anticipated operating deficit or net cash outflow.
- Where consumption standards have changed making a particular type of housing functionally obsolete. In other words, the buildings themselves might still have a long remaining economic life but fashions and attitudes have changed to bring about functional obsolescence, as against condition obsolescence. Examples might include houses without parking spaces, built at a time before the car was so dominant, and sheltered schemes with shared facilities, built at a time when large communal areas were favoured.

3. Stock management: resource accounting, depreciation and the planning and paying for repairs, renewals and reinvestments

The shift in local authority accounting practices towards resource accounting is being mirrored in the RSL sector. Under a new SORP, effective from April 1999, associations will have to calculate the capital depreciation of their non-investment properties and charge this against income and expenditure in their accounts. As we have seen above, depreciation is a charge that reflects the loss in value resulting from wear and tear.[16] Neither the grant funded element of a property's value nor the land is included in the depreciation calculation. The basic idea is that the published accounts should be in line with modern plc accounting conventions so as to make the 'true' costs of running the 'business' more transparent. This will involve accounting for the life-cycle costs of each asset as they occur so that their true costs in use can be estimated.

---

15 The recoverable amount is defined as the higher of their net realisable value and value in use.
16 If the rent earning capacity falls for other reasons, not related to wear and tear, it is referred to as 'impairment'.

In Chapter 13 we explained that, since 1989, English RSLs have not been entitled to receive major repair grants to help cover the costs of repairing, renewing or improving their housing assets. This sort of work now has to be funded either by taking out a loan or by establishing a sinking fund for the purpose, or a combination of both.

The assessment of future major repair needs forms part of sensible financial planning, and accounting policies should reflect the needs of the organisation. It is financially prudent to set aside amounts regularly to ensure that sufficient funds are available when the costs are due to be incurred. Until recently, the amount a landlord set aside into a sinking fund to cover future renewal and improvement costs tended to be a notional figure that was set formulaically. The Housing Corporation used to recommend that the annual contribution to such a fund should be between 0.8 and 1.0 per cent of scheme cost, depending on whether the scheme was a new build or a refurbishing project. Research in the mid-1990s by Cambridge University's Department of Land Economy[17] indicated that when associations were under budgetary pressure, it is often the maintenance expenditure that suffered. This research looked at the behaviour of a sample of representative associations, and it showed that a majority underspent in this area in relation to the Housing Corporation allowances. The findings indicated that in the sector as a whole, there has been a lack of long-term planning for the provision of finance for future major repairs. Recent consultancy work carried out by the Building and Construction Research Centre based in the University of the West of England reinforces these findings and suggests that sinking funds established by many RSLs will not adequately deal with future repairs and refurbishments.[18] Social landlords concerned to establish good financial management practices should abandon the simple formulaic approach and seek to make provision that is in line with an informed estimate of future requirements.

Exactly how provisions and reserves are designated and set aside is for each association to decide in accordance with its own policies, external regulatory requirements and legal/contractual commitments. The over-riding objective is to prevent undue fluctuations in costs that will damage long-run financial plans or drain free revenue reserves to a point where lenders' loan covenants are breached (see above section on *Status and legal and financial competence*).

Using component life-cycle cost data and techniques of property profiling, built asset managers can establish theoretical models of future repair and renewal

---

17 Chaplin, R. *et al.*, 'Rents and Risks', (1995), *Investing in Housing Associations*, Joseph Rowntree Foundation.
18 Holmes, R. and Marshall, D., (1996),'Property Profiling and Data Collection for Housing Repairs and Improvements: Part 2. Applications', Chartered Institute of Building, *CIOB Construction Papers No. 62*. Also, Marshall, (1996), 'Condition Surveys for Housing Associations: Some Potential Pitfalls and a Survey of Client Experience', *CIOB Construction Papers No. 68*. Editor: Harlow, P.

costs for new build schemes. For existing properties, cost models can be produced that are informed by condition surveys. Although there are many variables and uncertainties associated with life-cycle data, this form of rational planning is likely to lead to better stock management decisions than the mechanistic application of a standard formula. By using the 'stock management planning' approach clear forecasts of future requirements can be presented to decision-makers. To encourage strategic thinking, benchmarks can be produced that distinguish between the RSL's *condition obligations* and its *condition aspirations*. By the use of computer modelling, it is possible to build in assumptions about component life spans and future building costs so that decision committees can be presented with graphic representations of possible optimistic and pessimistic cost futures. This can help the manager or committee to clarify the risks of taking one financial decision as against another.

Reinvestment is an important financial aspect of long-term stock management. Until recently the principle of public financial accountability carried more weight than that of rational asset management. Regulations required the capital grant element to be repaid on disposal or demolition and this acted against associations developing strategic plans for the overall management of their housing stocks. The provisions of the Housing Act 1996 gave RSLs in England and Wales the ability to dispose of or demolish SHG funded properties without having to repay grant. Restrictions in Scotland were also eased where some disposals now do not lead to grant repayment and abatement of grant applies in demolition. This easing of the regulations allows landlords to sell or demolish properties and reinvest the proceeds without financial penalty so long as it can be shown that this is part of an active asset management plan that generates 'best value'.

4. Risk assessment and management

The relationship between risk, enterprise and sound management

The CIPFA code of practice for treasury management emphasises the point that the effective employment of money always involves a degree of risk and that treasury management decisions need to be explicit about the relationship between financial risks on the one hand and returns and benefits on the other. Enterprising organisations necessarily operate in a risk environment because risk is implicit in all areas of commercial activity. Well managed housing agencies will inevitably take risks both in pursuing their corporate plans and also in adapting their plans in response to changing external circumstances. An organisation pursuing a policy of total risk avoidance would soon experience corporate stagnation and decline – 'nothing ventured, nothing gained'. This means that the enterprising housing association should not be seeking *total risk avoidance* so much as *effective risk management*.

Although, for reasons of analysis, we are here considering the question of risk as a distinct issue, in practice, risk management is an integral part of good general management. Everything we have said so far in this chapter about the presentation of financial information, borrowing strategies, and built asset management, underlines the importance of an approach to management that minimises unnecessary risk and reduces uncertainty. Having said this, risk planning and management is increasingly seen as a subject in its own right. In recent years it is a topic that has come to the fore both in housing management practice and housing management training and education. In no small measure this has been a consequence of the 1989 reforms discussed in Chapters 12, 13 and 14. Since the introduction of the 1989 regime, there has been an explicit requirement that the financial risks associated with the provision and management of social housing should be taken by associations and their funders rather than by the Exchequer. With this relocation of the commercial risks has come the need to establish sound risk management principles and practices.

A strategic approach to risk management

In developing a coherent risk management strategy the organisation needs to be aware of the four broad approaches for dealing with specific risks (Baldry, 1998). These are risk transfer, risk retention, risk reduction, and risk avoidance.

Risk transfer. Insurance is the most obvious way of transferring risk. Decisions have to be made about which risks should be moved to an insurance company in return for an annual premium. Some insurance companies specialise in providing defect insurance for housing agencies.[19] Although this is very much a matter of judgement, balancing insurance costs against probabilities and impacts, the general principle is that when the impact is likely to be catastrophic, serious consideration should be given to taking out insurance cover. In recent years, housing associations have developed other ways of transferring risks. In attempting to minimise the additional commercial risks imposed by the new financial regime, many associations have moved to contractual arrangements that specifically off-load some of the jeopardy to others. As a result, housing association developments in the 1990s were typically conducted under fixed price design-and-build contracts and/or involved purchasing 'off-the-shelf' designs. Such arrangements afford the association less detailed control over the nature of the scheme and inhibit the association from experimenting with designs and materials or from negotiating 'improvements' in detail once the scheme is underway. Interference from any in-house officials, such as the association's own architect, could undermine the shift in development risk to the builder that was the whole purpose of the chosen contractual arrangement. Extended product liability deals might also be struck with manufacturers and suppliers as a way of passing on the risk of early product failure.

---

19 The National House-Building Council, Zurich Municipal and Housing Association Property Mutual (HAPM), are dominant in the market. HAPM was specifically set up by a group of housing associations in response to the 1988 Act and is owned by them jointly and works exclusively for them.

Risk retention. A decision might be made to retain risks that _could_ be insured on the assumption that the organisation's reserves and control frameworks are so sound that the probability of problems arising is insignificant and the consequences of failure are in any event covered by resources. Some risks are difficult or impossible to transfer: significant amongst these are the disruption risks arising from postponement or cancellation of projects, a change in corporate policy, unexpected external changes in interest rates, the costs of production, or the regulatory framework.

Risk reduction and avoidance. Risk avoidance is synonymous with a refusal to take risks. Certain risks can only be avoided by non-activity. However, we have already made the point that social housing agencies are obligated to deliver certain functions and that any activity necessarily involves risk-taking. The objective should be to achieve a defined outcome with minimum risk. There is no one technique for achieving this optimum position. It involves the cultivation of a general management culture that at all times and at all levels demonstrates an awareness of the need to (a) avoid exposure to unnecessary risks and (b) be clear about defensive procedures and contingencies. Risk reduction strategies can be particularly important at certain times. For example, they come to the fore when negotiating or renewing a contractual relationship.

One way of reducing risk is to negotiate a degree of stability into contracts. Given its significance, this may be deemed particularly important in the field of loan management. Well over 60 per cent of the rent on new grant aided housing association schemes is typically spent on loan interest. This figure has increased as the capital grant element has been reduced. This is potentially the most variable element of the association's costs. Variability leads to uncertainty and uncertainty makes overall financial planning difficult. In particular, projecting future rent levels becomes difficult when future loan costs are uncertain. To bring a degree of stability into the cost structure, social landlords often seek to negotiate loans on a fixed interest basis. Under these arrangements the interest is fixed for a proportion of the loan's term. It may also be possible to hedge a variable rate loan by holding other assets (financial instruments) as a protection against unexpected interest rate fluctuations. Because social landlords are adverse to uncertainty, in recent years they have sought either to borrow funds on a fixed rate basis or to hedge against high fluctuations when taking out variable rate loans. They have also shown a preference for long dated finance rather than short-term loans (refer section _Private sources of capital finance_).

Putting the risk management strategy into operation
The total approach to risk management. Social landlords have to take a variety of decisions involving both insurable and non-insurable risks. Some major decisions associated with strategic and business planning carry self-evident risks. For example, major shifts in policy are inevitably embedded in uncertainties about the future. Similarly, decisions involving the raising of private finance are risk sensitive. Major contracts to develop land and buildings or to provide services are

also seen to carry significant risks. However, we need to make the point that focusing on such major decisions can give a misleading impression about the nature and scope of risk management. Activities at all levels carry risks.

> *'Almost all activities can go wrong. Poor maintenance could result in an injury to a tenant or to a much more expensive repair at a later date. Sloppy procedures could encourage a fraud. Under-insurance could lead to significant loss. A development opportunity might be missed because there is no cash reserve. Vulnerable residents could be mistreated by staff.'* (Extract from the guidance notes to voluntary board members prepared by the NHF).

All of this points to the need for the organisation to take a *total approach* to risk management. A total approach requires the association's operations to be planned and managed effectively at all levels and across all planning time periods. It also requires them to give consideration to both insurable and non-insurable risk factors.

A balanced approach to risk management

It is argued (Garnett, 1995; Flynn, 1997; Baldry, 1998), that risk management in public service organisations has to take into account a wider range of considerations than is the case in private enterprise firms. This is because the values underlying the provision of public services are discretely different from those underpinning successful commercial businesses. Public service agencies are often required to consider broad questions of public policy that would be deemed to be irrelevant to most private businesses. They are also required to take more direct account of questions relating to distributional equity and social justice in their investment and management decisions (refer to Figure 2.3 and previous discussions on the topic of 'best value'). This means that risk management in public service agencies has to balance a broader range of factors than is often the case with private free-enterprise firms. Whether operating in a purely commercial or a public services environment, risk management should always begin with a systematic analysis of the risks and uncertainties confronting the organisation.

A systematic approach to risk analysis: risk mapping. Effective risk management requires the association to have a systematic approach to its analysis of *total balanced risks*. Registered social landlords in England are now required to undertake an annual risk appraisal or review exercise that involves the management team compiling a comprehensive list of risks to which it feels the association is exposed.[20] The exercise seeks to tackle the multi-faceted nature of risk by requiring the RSL to 'map' the areas of risk that they consider most pertinent to their organisation. It involves identifying the risks in relation to specific categories such as development, maintenance, finance, fraud, information technology, staffing, etc., and then allocating a 'risk ranking' to each one

---

20 Refer to section C1 of the *Housing Corporation's Performance Standards* entitled 'Prudence and Risk Management'.

identified. Each broad category of risk can then usually be broken down into an extended sequence of sub-categories. For example, within the specific category 'maintenance', it should be possible to identify the sub-category 'gas servicing'. Within this sub-category we can then identify a sub-sub category 'boilers': in turn this can be broken down further into 'specific model' and then 'component failure'. Decisions have to be made about the appropriate level of risk analysis. Decisions about what to itemise should be informed by reference to *probability*, *incidence* and *impact*.

The *probability factor* (the chances of occurrence) can be analysed by reference to in-house data and published research by other landlords, manufacturers, insurance companies, the professional bodies and academic institutions. *Incidence* refers to the occurrence rate (probable frequency) of the risk event. The scale of the loss (the consequences of occurrence) is referred to as the *risk impact*. The impact should be analysed and quantified in some way. If possible, an attempt should be made to place an appropriate money value on the loss. Experience from the commercial world shows that the impact of the incidence of most risk events can be measured in financial terms – e.g. as the effect on turnover, market share and profitability (Baldry, 1998, p36). Given their more complex social objectives, providing a money value may be more problematic for public service agencies such as housing associations. Even if the effect of the risk event is on some intangible (that is, difficult to measure) operational feature such as reputation, staff morale, or landlord-tenant relations, if it is felt to be important, then its impact has to be measured and recorded in some way. In risk analysis there is always a temptation to measure what is easy to quantify rather than what is relevant to the organisation's mission. The principle has to be, however, that it is better to measure the right thing in a rough and ready way than to measure the wrong thing with impressive refinement. If it is not possible, or sensible, to put a money value on the relevant loss, then it should be recorded in terms of its effect on some non-monetary performance indicator target.

Classifying and quantifying the impact

The appraisal or review exercise should make clear the appropriate managerial responses to the actual or probable occurrence of such events. These responses must seek to mitigate the damaging effects upon the corporate finances or upon specific performance indicator targets. This means that potential losses have to be clearly associated with identifiable cost centres or departments (areas of specific managerial responsibility). Any linked consequences also have to be traced. For example, in the broad managerial area 'finance' we may wish to analyse the risk sub-category 'non-compliance with loan covenants'. The consequences here might be analysed as a default that will result in the withdrawal of the loan or a financial penalty. Within the broad management category 'staffing', the consequence of unanticipated sickness and absences might be measured in terms of increased workloads for other staff, service failures and/or increases in agency costs. Having identified, quantified, and ranked the risks the appraisal or review exercise should then consider the controls (policies, procedures and practices) that will reduce the probability of occurrence or the damage impact should they occur. Where they exist, controls should be tested for adequacy and, if necessary, improved. Where they do not exist, appropriate controls should be introduced.

The danger of producing a 'risk map' is that it may lead to complacency. Risk maps tend to be complex and need to be subjected to further analysis. The organisation should resist the belief that just because a number of potential problems have been identified, its risks have been managed. Risk mapping is only a starting point and it is the quality of follow-up that determines its success as a management tool. It is only the first step in effective risk management. Any follow-up requires the application of appropriate and effective techniques.

Specific techniques for dealing with uncertainty and reducing risk

Risk appraisal and management involves the marshalling of evidence in order to make a judgement. The effectiveness of the exercise depends in large part on the appropriateness and comprehensiveness of the data and the appropriateness of the marshalling and appraisal techniques employed. Risk appraisal and management is an expansive topic and it is not the intention of this text to provide a detailed and comprehensive description of the full range of techniques and approaches that have been developed in this field.[21] We will, however, point to some key tools and ideas that are commonly used by those seeking to analyse and manage risk and uncertainty.

Effective information and feedback systems. Risk analysis should be an automatic element in decision appraisal. Any decision to invest new resources or to realign existing resources carries financial risks: the object is to take a decision that proves to be 'sustainable' through the different planning time periods identified at the start of this chapter. A sustainable decision is one that the organisation does not live to regret. It is well understood that when decisions are informed by sufficient and relevant information they are more likely to turn out to be sustainable than if they are informed by insufficient or inappropriate information. This means that an organisation's information systems, and how they are utilised, should be regularly assessed to ensure that they are effectively contributing to the association's decision processes. Well run agencies will inevitably make mistakes; the question is, 'Do we have in place identifiable mechanisms for learning from our mistakes and successes?' Of course, sound decision-making involves more than the acquisition of data and other types of information. An effective decision involves the application of judgement to information.

Optional generation, judgement and multiple criteria analysis

It has to be recognised that housing investment and management decisions are multi-faceted in that they often seek to achieve a mix of financial, technical,

---

21   For an overview of risk management issues and an extensive reading list see NHF *Living with risk*, October 1999.

social, legal, political, environmental and administrative outcomes. This means that appropriate options have to be generated that balance and reconcile different, and sometimes competing, proprietary and non-proprietary interests. Research shows that when there is a failure to generate appropriate options subsequent problems are likely to arise (Garnett, 1999). There is little point in using sophisticated option appraisal techniques on an inappropriate range of options. If we fail to present the most viable options for appraisal it is simply not possible to make a risk-efficient decision. Option generation involves ensuring that important development, reinvestment, or policy change decisions are justified at the outset by reference to a shared corporate understanding of the balance of interests being pursued, whether of tenants, other community interests, future generations, or whoever.

Option generation involves the application of judgement to information. The problem is that judgement is not an absolute quality; it is relative to the values and attitudes of the individual decision-makers. This means that project planning needs to make explicit the various personal or professional rationalities that lie behind different proposed courses of action. It may be the case that the treasurer will seek one course of action based on her understanding of the financial implications (budgetary rationality) while the estates manager is arguing for a different course of action based on his understanding of sound building practices (technical rationality). Other rationalities associated with administrative feasibility or political expediency may point to yet other ways forward. In the context of new projects or major policy changes, risk appraisal has to involve the reconciliation of these competing rationalities by some form of multiple criteria analysis.[22]

Harnessing stakeholder perceptions

It is well understood that public service organisations are subject to the influences and expectations of a diverse constituency of interested parties. Both academic research and best value philosophy indicate that the opinions and experiences of employees, clients and community stakeholders can be utilised in the appraisal and review exercise to identify and clarify the risk perception process. By widening the area of consultation we automatically widen the scope of risk identification. Conversely, a reliance on a limited range of internal managerial perceptions and professional interests may compromise the risk assessment exercise by limiting the range of objectives being considered.

Effective control frameworks

Control frameworks are essential weapons in any risk management armoury. They provide guidance, prescribe and proscribe certain actions, and set limits for a broad range of activities. These policies, standing orders and procedures typically require management processes to be monitored and appraised, regulate the nature and scope of delegated authority, and declare the corporate view of what constitutes best practice.

---

22 For further discussion on multiple criteria analysis see Garnett, D., 1995 and 1999.

To be effective, control frameworks have to be relevant to current circumstances, understood by those who are meant to use them, practical to operate, supported by training, constantly reviewed, and reinforced by a compliance culture (NHF, 1999c, p8). However, it must be understood that the emergence of unnecessary or inappropriate regulations and procedures itself constitutes a 'risk'. An organisation can be over-regulated: when this occurs, the resultant compliance culture can inhibit initiative and have a deadening effect on staff morale, energy and confidence. All quality control managers should have pinned up on their walls the old Polish proverb, 'Constantly weighing the pig doesn't make it any fatter'.[23]

Analysing cumulative and linked risks

In analysing the incidence and impact of risk occurrence, consideration should be given to the possibility of cumulative and linked risks. A general distinction should be made between one-off, or infrequent, major events (e.g. a theft, fire, etc.), and *cumulative risks*. Cumulative risks are associated with smaller scale events that may not be significant in themselves but which can have a damaging cumulative effect on the organisation's costs. These cumulative risks are sometimes referred to as 'aggregate risks' and are of particular concern to the managers of built assets.

A general distinction should also be made between *isolated* and *linked* risks. Some apparently small-scale risks can have significant knock-on effects that must be taken into account in risk assessment and management exercises. The connectedness of a *linked risk* might be technical: the failure of a small and cheap component might cause an entire system to fail causing expensive, inconvenient, or even life threatening consequences. The connectedness of a *linked risk* might be managerial: the failure of a light bulb might be regarded as a relatively insignificant event, but if the bulb is located in a dark stairwell, its failure might be highly dangerous. The connectedness of a *linked risk* might be environmental: we might develop a piece of land in a way that enhanced the organisation's productivity but which was damaging to local wildlife, or created some other third party or ecological problem. The connectedness of a *linked risk* might be political: we might instigate a policy change that increased the cost effectiveness of our operations but which contravened central or local government guidelines thereby bringing into question our entitlement to public funds. All of this points to the need to assess risks in a way that makes explicit all the possible linked consequences. Sensitivity analysis is one technique that can be used to assess the impact of particular assumptions being proved wrong.

Discounting and sensitivity analysis

Discounting is a technique that seeks to cost future money flows in terms of present values. When project appraisals and budgets cover an extended period, it may be necessary to put a present value on future costs/benefits or

---

23 They might also pin up a more modern aphorism that originated at the Harvard Business School: 'What you measure is what you get'.

expenditures/incomes. This is because we are seeking to make rational decisions now, in the present, about impacts and monetary flows that will occur sometime in the future. Put most simply, the appraisal or the budget needs to take account of two issues resulting from the relationship between time and the value of money.

1. Different costs and benefits and expenditures and incomes come on stream or impact at different times.
2. A £1's worth of income or expenditure today will not have the same real value as a £1's worth of income or expenditure in the future.[24]

Because planning involves looking to the future, and the future is uncertain, all plans have to incorporate assumptions about such things as interest and discount rates, building costs, rent projections, general levels of inflation, works completion dates, and the physical life of building components. *Sensitivity analysis* is a technique that seeks to test the plan's key incorporated assumptions about such variables. It asks the question 'How sensitive is the planned or expected outcome to the assumptions being made?' Managers and risk analysts will need some idea of the consequences that might follow from unexpected variations in these assumptions that underpin the plan's projections, conclusions or recommendations. Sensitivity analysis plots a range of possible futures, each grounded in discretely different assumptions about such things as interest rates and the life spans of building components. With modern computer technology these futures can be presented to decision managers or committees in clear charted or graphical formats. These can then be used to help devise appropriate tactics. For example, with respect to a proposed building contract, the knowledge and understanding gained from a sensitivity analysis of building cost price projections might persuade the client to reduce the risk of price rises by insisting on a fixed price contract.

The use of 'experts'

Experts provide specialist knowledge that should inform *but not determine* a decision about what constitutes best action. Consultants and professional advisors do not have a legitimate authority to make final decisions; they should be used to advise those who do have such authority. Advisors should not relieve decision-makers of the task of determining how to respond to perceptions of risk but might be used to help generate unthought-of options, or to offer new perceptions of risk, or to test, challenge and reshape the organisation's existing perceptions. The best use of consultants is made when they understand what it is that the organisation is seeking to achieve. Research shows that in the field of social housing, where there has been little or no pre-planning before briefing consultants, the 'experts' may offer rational, but inappropriate, courses of action based on their own professional values and attitudes rather than on those of the client organisation (Garnett, 1996).

---

24   For a fuller explanation of discounting and the time value of money see Garnett D; *The Theory and Practice of Cost-Benefit Analysis*, Faculty of the Built Environment Occasional Papers, UWE 1994, pp21-24.

Experts may have information and experience that the client does not possess and they may be able to provide new insights that can be drawn upon in carrying out a risk assessment exercise. By interacting with the client they may also help to clarify the organisation's aims and objectives – but they cannot know better than the organisation itself what values and interests constitute the bedrock of its function. This means that any expert advice should reinforce or reshape, but not replace, the organisation's judgements about what to do. In selecting consultants we are choosing 'expert witnesses' to give *informed opinions* rather than appointing 'judges' to give *definitive rulings*.

Dealing with long-term structural uncertainties

There are a number of established techniques specifically designed to aggregate the knowledge and judgements of experts about possible future trends.[25] Although we cannot tell for certain what the future holds, it is possible to canvass informed opinion about external political and economic trends that may affect our long-term plans. These approaches to thinking about the longer-term are referred to as Delphi techniques – after the Greek oracle at Delphi who gave riddled answers to those seeking knowledge of what the future held in store.

A particular form of sensitivity analysis called 'stress testing' can be used to consider the impact implications of different possible futures. This involves asking a variety of 'what would we do if' questions. For example, we might stress test our risk assumptions by asking 'What would we do if there was a change in government?' or, 'What would we do if an advantageous investment opportunity comes our way in two years time?' or, 'What would we do if we are suddenly required to freeze rents?'

5. Taxation and social landlords

As private sector organisations, housing associations are subject to Corporation Tax and VAT. These tax liabilities have to be allowed for in their financial management arrangements. This means that the financial planning of an RSL has to take account of any tax liabilities that will occur during the accounting period. The main taxes that affect RSLs are Corporation Tax and Value Added Tax (VAT). The detailed regulations surrounding these taxes are rather complex and constantly being changed. However, as we are simply concerned to outline how tax liabilities impinge on the organisation's financial planning, we will focus on basic principles. The basic principles of Corporation Tax and VAT are fairly straightforward.

Corporation Tax

Corporation Tax can be thought of as a sort of companies' income tax. It is charged on the profits or other 'assessable gains' accruing to the organisation during the accounting period. In the accounts of an RSL the assessable gain is

---

25   See, for example, Moore, C.M., 1987.

recorded in the Income and Expenditure Account and is usually referred to as the *surplus on ordinary activities*.[26] In determining the 'assessable gain' a deduction may be claimed for certain types of expenditure. Repairs, maintenance and replacement expenditure that restores a building to its original condition is an allowable expense for tax purposes and can be deducted from the turnover in the assessment of assessable gain. Improvement expenditure does not qualify for relief as this adds to, rather than maintains, the quality of the assets. This means that care should be taken to determine whether or not the works are an improvement. If works that are really repairs and replacements are capitalised in the books, it is unlikely that they will be allowed as a deduction from income, and this will result in an unnecessarily high tax bill. Any monies transferred to reserves do not qualify and, as the account shows, these are recorded after the tax has been deducted (refer to Figure 13.1 in Chapter 13). Relief may be given for bad debts, but only so long as a reasonable effort has been made to collect them.

Charitable organisations are not subject to Corporation Tax, which means that it is only non-charitable social landlords that are liable. Until recently, liable associations could receive grants to help meet the costs of paying the tax. However, these have now been phased out. This has resulted in a reduction of net surpluses for those landlords that do not have charitable status. This could, in turn, lead to increases in rents and/or cuts in general expenditure on the service.[27] In some associations this is leading to a debate about the possibility of changing to charitable status.

In recent years, Corporation Tax has been levied at two rates – the *full rate* and the *small companies' rate*. Where the assessable gains of a UK resident organisation do not exceed stated limits the full rate of tax is reduced. The application of the lower, small companies' rate is governed by the amount of profit or gain and not by the size of the organisation. The current rates are 30 per cent and 20 per cent (April 1999).

Value Added Tax (VAT)

In contrast to Corporation Tax, no VAT exemptions are granted to charitable organisations. This means that all registered social landlords are liable for VAT. VAT is a sort of purchase or trading tax that is charged on the value of supplies made by a registered trader. Organisations are required to register for VAT once their turnover reaches a specified threshold. The tax extends both to the supply of

---

26 This surplus is calculated by taking the operating surplus net of deductible costs, and then adding in any profits resulting from the sale of fixed assets and any income received in the form of interest payments. The net operating surplus is effectively the rental income minus allowable property expenditure costs. These allowable deductions refer to expenditures that are deemed to be necessary to provide the housing service and keep the stock in a fit condition. They include certain expenditures on repairs and maintenance, insurance, and some management functions.

27 Particularly exposed in this regard are LSVT associations, whose business plans were often written on the assumption of continuing tax relief grant.

goods and also to the supply of services. Supplies of certain goods and services are exempt from the tax. These include the provision of finance, insurance and education and burial and cremation services. The granting of a lease or licence to occupy land will usually be classified as exempt.

Non-exempt supplies are subject to tax at one of three rates.

- A zero or nil rate (e.g. most food products, water and sewerage services, books, newspapers and magazines, clothing, and transport).
- A standard rate of 17.5 per cent.
- A reduced rate of 5 per cent (e.g. domestic fuel). Since July 1998, the reduced rate also applies to the installation of energy saving material under certain government grant schemes.

In most commercial circumstances, the liability is calculated in a way that only taxes that element of value that has been contributed by that particular trader. In other words, the idea of the tax is to levy a charge on the additional value that has been added at each stage in the production process. This means that in most circumstances, a registered trader will both suffer tax (input tax)when acquiring goods and services for the purposes of a business, and charge that tax (output tax) when supplying goods and services to customers and clients. A normal commercial trader is required to calculate both the input and the output tax during the accounting period, and if the latter exceeds the former, the difference has to be paid over to Customs and Excise. In this way the tax liability is passed on 'along the line' and eventually comes to rest on individuals or organisations who are not VAT registered, or who do not themselves charge VAT on that particular good or service. When this end point is reached, it is assumed that the production process has ended and the purchaser has to pay their suppliers VAT on the full value of the goods and services without having an opportunity to pass the burden on as an output tax.

Because rents are not subject to VAT, we can say that the tax is not charged on the core outputs of social landlords. This means that as a general needs housing provider, the landlord, and not the tenant, is deemed to be at the end of the added value line (i.e. the taxable production process is assumed to have ended prior to the letting of the dwelling). Therefore, the landlord has to pay the full input tax on its supplies without being able to pass the burden on in the form of an output tax to its tenants.

Although associations and other RSLs do not charge VAT on their rents, they do have to charge output tax on specific services. For example, certain types of long-term hostel accommodation are subject to VAT at the standard rate[28] as are any management services it provides to other organisations. Heating and lighting

---

28 Where such accommodation is run by a charity and provides care and support in addition to accommodation, the total charge is exempt.

services that it provides to a tenant's private area of occupation are subject to VAT at the reduced rate. Other charged-for personal services may also be subject to VAT.

VAT and building works

At the time of writing, repair, renovation and renewal works are subject to the full standard rate of tax (2000). By contrast, supplies made in the construction of the following are zero rated.

- A new built dwelling. This includes the construction of a garage if the work is undertaken at the same time as the construction of the dwelling.
- New buildings used as children's homes, old people's homes and the provision of student accommodation – but not hotels and prisons.
- New buildings to be used by a charity for non-business purposes, e.g. a church.
- Substantial alterations to listed buildings so long as they are to be used for one of the above purposes.

The construction of other buildings, such as shops, offices and factories, are not zero rated.

Many argue that it is irrational to tax housing renovation work at the standard rate while zero rating new house-building. It is felt that this 'anomaly' positively discourages the process of housing repair and improvement.[29]

Summary

Since 1989 housing associations and other registered social landlords have experienced declining support from central government. Capital grants to this sector are now distributed on the basis of directed competition and they cover only a proportion of the total scheme costs. The remaining costs have to be met from reserves or from private sector loans. Because they are now operating in a more commercial climate, social landlords have to put more emphasis on financial planning and management.

Financial planning and management has to operate through time. A series of interrelated time profiles lies at the heart of strategic financial management. Together this series of time profiles constitutes an *integrated planning and control cycle*. This cycle links the organisation's long-term aspirations to its immediate activities. Converting the idea of the cycle into a management process involves

---

29 The 1999 Report of the Urban Task Force, *Towards an Urban Renaissance* (The Rogers Report), looked at the causes of urban decline in England. It proposed removing 'the anomaly' whereby renovation work on empty dwellings carries VAT at 'a punitive' 17.5 per cent, but house-building and conversion of commercial premises for housing are exempt.

asking different types of policy question and creating a cascade of documents differentiated by time, scale and specific detail.

In commercial settings risks have to be taken: 'nothing ventured nothing gained'. Therefore well-managed associations should seek to manage rather than avoid risks. Risk-mapping is now a standard practice.

The two main tax liabilities facing social landlords are Corporation Tax and VAT. The position of social landlords is somewhat different to that of most other trading organisations because their rents are not subject to VAT.

Further reading

HACAS Consulting, *Housing Associations – A Viable Financial Future?*, CIH, 1999.

Gray, D. (1999), *What's it all about? Registered social landlord accounts explained*, National Housing Federation, 1999.

Baldry, D., 'The evaluation of risk management in public sector capital projects', in *International Journal of Project Management*, Vol.16 No.1 pp35-41, Pergamon, 1998.

CHAPTER 16:
Private renting

In recent years, there has been much debate in Britain about whether private landlords could or should play a more prominent role in the provision of dwellings for households on or below average incomes. It is generally agreed that over the last 60 years or so political, social and economic forces have operated to diminish the role of private landlordism and if the sector is to be revitalised, some form of intervention in the market will be needed to overcome these negative forces. The main task of this chapter is to analyse critically recent attempts to support the development of this tenure and to consider what future financial measures might be needed to stimulate its further expansion.

Before setting out on this task, we will say something about the motive forces that drive consumption and investment in the tenure. To understand the part that private renting has played, does play and could play, in the provision of housing, we need to examine the proprietary interests involved.

The landlord-tenant relationship

The private rented housing sector embraces two distinctive sets of proprietary interests that are governed by contractual rights and duties. These contractual rights and obligations are set in a statutory framework that establishes such things as the broad nature of a legal tenancy agreement (e.g. the Housing Act 1988), and prescribes minimum standards of personal safety (e.g. the Furniture Safety Regulations 1993 and regulations covering gas and electrical safety). It is generally recognised however, that both the investment interests of the landlord and the consumption interests of the tenant are best served by the cultivation of an informal working relationship that does not require recourse to law. A clear understanding over things like the inventory and the deposit as well as how and when the rent will be paid, especially if it involves a claim for housing benefit, can help prevent a breakdown in this crucial landlord-tenant relationship. Many people prefer to leave the letting arrangements in the hands of an agent as a way of depersonalising what is, after all, a business relationship.

Tenants and the consumption interest

Although, at the time of writing, only about 10 per cent of British households rent their homes from a private landlord[1], it is worthy of note that since the dawn of

---

1   This percentage is significantly lower in Northern Ireland where currently the private rented sector constitutes only 3.4 per cent of the total housing stock.

industrialisation, most British people have depended on private landlords for their accommodation needs. Private renting accounted for some 90 per cent of all tenure arrangements before the First World War and even at the end of the Second World War more than 60 per cent of households rented their homes privately. Private renting remained the largest single tenure in Britain until the late 1950s.

Both the sector's historical dominance and its more recent decline can be explained in part by people's attitudes towards, and abilities to gain access to, other tenures. Arguably the most significant socio-economic characteristic of housing is that for most households it is expensive relative to disposable income. This has meant that historically even households with above average incomes have not been able to gain access to owner-occupation without inheriting or borrowing financial resources. This, together with the fact that social renting is a comparatively recent phenomenon, has meant that until the 1940s most people expected that their housing careers would begin and end in privately rented accommodation. These expectations were eventually changed in the immediate post-war period by the development of an increasingly sophisticated and aggressive mortgage finance market and a subsidised, large-scale council house building programme. From the 1960s, the tenure restructuring away from private renting was further stimulated by government policies that favoured the development of the housing association movement.

Between the late 1980s and the mid-1990s the number of households renting from the private sector grew by about a fifth to around two million[2]. However, much of this increase was due to falling house prices that caused many home owners to become trapped by negative equity. The negative equity trap produced a class of 'reluctant landlords' who rented out their homes in order to move on to new employment opportunities. It might be argued that the small revival of private renting that occurred after 1987 was not so much the result of successful policies to stimulate private renting as a failure of policies to sustain owner-occupation.

Who are the tenants?

In this text we are primarily concerned to explore the part private landlords play in the satisfaction of general housing needs. However, we must make the point that private landlords provide dwellings in response to a diverse range of demands. In addition to providing permanent family homes, private landlords are the main providers of both short-term holiday lets (and hotel bed spaces) and employment-related tied accommodation; they are also prominent providers of high class second homes to the 'mobile rich'.

As an element of general needs housing, a relatively small number of people regard private renting as a preferred first choice. It is regarded by many as a

---

2 It is estimated that the supply of rented accommodation in the UK increased by some 300,000 between 1988 and 1992 (*Housing Association Weekly, January* 1994).

temporary stop-gap until they can gain access to owner-occupation or to social renting. To others who, in the foreseeable future, cannot afford, or do not qualify for, access to other tenures it is seen as a permanent 'second-best' arrangement. In a Department of the Environment survey of a few years ago[3] some 62 per cent of private tenants declared that they expected to buy a home at some future time. This preference for owner-occupation was twice as strong among private tenants than it was among council or housing association tenants. The survey also showed that about half of the private tenants who were not expecting to become owner-occupiers said that this was because they could not afford it rather than because they did not wish to buy. Such surveys consistently show that, in terms of general levels of consumer satisfaction, fewer private tenants are satisfied with renting than council or the tenants of housing associations. Only 28 per cent of private tenants said they were 'very satisfied' with their arrangements. In short, the indications are that a majority of private tenants see their tenancy as a stepping stone to some other tenure arrangement.

Research also indicates that in recent years the average age of private tenants has been declining, with the proportion under the age of 30 increasing and the proportion aged 60 and over falling. Also, tenants in this sector are becoming more middle class, with relatively more coming from the non-manual, socio-economic groups and the proportion eligible for housing benefit falling[4].

The changing age and socio-economic profile of private tenants is one manifestation of what appears to be an emerging shift in the conditions of demand. In the late 1990s, the end of rapid house price inflation coupled with a continuous restructuring of the labour market towards more part-time jobs and temporary contracts began to shift the forces of demand away from owner-occupation and towards renting. This was particularly true with respect to younger workers at the start of their employment careers.[5] Despite these trends many households still are unwillingly locked into the tenure by virtue of their relatively low incomes.

Income augmentation

By the mid-1990s, it is estimated that, on average, private tenants spent about 27 per cent of their disposable income on rent, and that more than a quarter of tenancies were spending a third or more of their income on rent.[6] The low or

---

3   '1994/95 Survey of English Housing'. Full details in Down, D., *et al.*, (1996), *Housing in England*, Chapter 7. HMSO. See also 'Customer Satisfaction', *Inside Housing*, July 5 1996, pp14-15.

4   Rauta, I. and Pickering, A., (1994), *Private Renting in England in 1990*, HMSO.

5   Steve Wilcox has made the point that economic and labour market trends, coupled with changes in employment legislation that have extended the period before workers qualify for employment protection, have meant that by the mid-1990s only about a third of the working population had full-time secure jobs compared with well over a half in 1975. (Joseph Rowntree Foundation, *Housing Finance Review 1995-96*, pp40-41).

6   DoE Housing Research Summary No.36, p3.

---

insecure earnings of many of the actual and potential households who rely on this sector mean that many cannot afford to acquire private accommodation appropriate to their needs out of their incomes. Income augmentation in the form of housing assistance is meant to deal with this. The significant rise in the national housing benefit bill is in part due to the growth of claimants in the private rented sector. Rent allowances to private tenants rose from £900 million in 1988 to around £5 billion in 1996/97 in cash terms. By the mid-1990s, spending on rent allowances to private tenants was, for the first time, higher than the value of rent rebates paid to council tenants. This is only partly explained by a widening disparity between the growth in rents compared with the growth in incomes. It was also partly the result of the transfer of blocks of council housing to registered social landlords as part of the government's policy of *large-scale voluntary transfer*.

This assistance forms part of the housing benefit arrangements (see Chapter 17), and in recent years, since January 1996, the government has set a 'cap' on rents eligible for benefit.[7] This means that new tenants and those moving home will be entitled to assistance only up to the average for similar properties in the locality[8]. The intention is to give tenants an incentive to negotiate their rents and encourage them to choose less expensive dwellings. The idea is to prevent landlords exploiting the housing benefit system by pushing up their rents to the maximum the system will allow. This measure has had a dampening effect on the general level of supply of privately rented accommodation.

The nature and condition of the stock

In comparison with other European countries there is a lack of purpose-built private rented dwellings in the UK. In some other EC countries more private finance goes into the provision of apartments specifically designed as rented accommodation. This allows for one of the potential benefits of private renting – namely, the ability to rent modern, newly built accommodation that has just the amount of space needed at the time you need it. The British private rented stock is dominated by relatively old dwellings many of which have been converted from family residences to accommodate the needs of single people or relatively small households. Such conversions are not always carried out to high standards and often result in the need to share facilities.

Census data (1991) show that across Britain the private rented sector has the highest number of dwellings that lack amenities such as a separate bath, shower or WC. The sector also contains a relatively high proportion of dwellings that are officially classified as 'unfit'. Within the sector, furnished lets are particularly lacking in amenities and, compared with unfurnished lets, a significantly higher

---

7   Announced in the 1995 Budget and introduced by regulations from January 1996.
8   The locality is not defined but is set by rent officers. In a moderate sized town such as Exeter it will roughly correspond to the urban area, larger cities may have a number of localities.

number fail to meet the various acceptable fitness standards. The 1996 English House Condition Survey found about 18 per cent of the private rented stock to be unfit, compared with 20.5 per cent in 1991. This figure is high when compared with other sectors. Just over five per cent of owner occupied housing was judged to be unfit. The figures for local authority and housing association dwellings were 6.8 per cent and 3.9 per cent respectively. Unfitness and disrepair in Wales in 1997/98 for the private rented sector was estimated at 18.4 per cent (Welsh House Condition Survey). In Scotland official figures published in 1996 showed that of that country's 84,000 sub-standard homes, 70 per cent were in the private sector.[9] Figures taken from the Scottish House Condition Survey (1996), and Scottish Homes (1997), indicate that just over four per cent of Scottish privately rented dwellings were below the Scottish 'tolerable standard'.

In 1998 the Housing Minister announced the government's intention to introduce revised fitness standards and more regulation of the private sector. The 'home fitness rating' replaces the previous 'fitness standard' in England. The new standards will include measures of health and safety risks in an attempt to provide a more appropriate measure of sub-standard housing. The rating was finalised in the summer of 1999 and will be introduced 'as soon as possible'.

Landlords and the investment interest

Despite the sector's long-term decline, it would be wrong to describe the provision of market rented dwellings as a 'marginal' or 'insignificant' economic activity. Private landlords probably own something in excess of £150 billion worth of built assets: these generate an annual rental income of some £13 billion. The recent Green Paper (*Quality and Choice: A Decent Home for All*, April 2000) indicated that more than a quarter of all landlords only have one letting. In Britain as a whole, over half of privately rented housing is owned by unincorporated individuals, about a quarter is owned by companies and two-thirds of all lettings provide the landlords with less than a quarter of their total income. By 1993 over half of all lettings were assured or assured shorthold and two out of three who rented from a non-residential landlord did so from individuals rather than from corporate landlords.[10]

In deciding whether or not to invest in rented housing, rational landlords will consider the commercial opportunity costs involved. This means that they will take account of whether such an investment is the 'highest and best' utilisation of their limited money capital. In considering which to choose of a range of possible opportunities, the commercially motivated investor will assess, in the context of a given time frame, the price, risk and convenience of each potential investment against its expected rate of return.

---

9   Scottish Office Development Department, reported in *Public Finance*, 7 March 1997, p4.
10   Siobhan Carey, *Private Renting in England 1993/94*, HMSO.

Figure 16.1: Opportunity cost of money capital

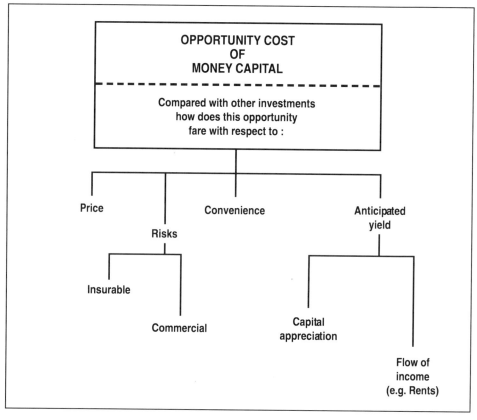

The price is simply the amount of money paid to acquire the asset. Risks fall into two broad categories – commercial and insurable. Insurable risks are, to a degree, calculable and can be under-written by an insurance company in return for regular premium payments. In this way, proprietors commonly insure against losses resulting from flood, vandalism, fire and theft. Premature failure of building components is another example of an insurable risk: to insure against such risks the under-writer might require the landlord to manage the dwellings in a prescribed way, e.g. carry out certain maintenance procedures on a regular basis. Commercial risks are normally non-insurable and refer to uncertainties associated with such things as the vagaries of the market or unforeseen changes in taxation or legislation that may affect the investment's profitability. The degree of convenience will be determined by the time, effort and worry involved in managing the investment.

The rate of return will be partly determined by the degree of capital appreciation in a given period (net of capital gains tax) and partly by the surplus of rental income over revenue costs in that period (net of Schedule A income tax). Rental returns are influenced by market conditions (e.g. demand and shortages), location, property type and condition, and whether the accommodation is furnished or unfurnished.

Deposits against loss and damage

It is typical practice for the tenant to pay an 'up front' deposit to the landlord to cover any loss or damage that may occur during the tenancy period. The basic legal position is that the landlord must return the deposit at the end of the tenancy providing the tenant has met the terms. There is evidence from Citizens' Advice Bureaux that some landlords exploit such arrangements by treating the deposits as automatic non-returnable charges or by claiming for non-existent damage.[11] In Britain these arrangements are solely governed by the terms of the contract and aggrieved tenants have to go to the trouble and expense of going to law, usually the Small Claims Court, if they wish to seek redress. In some other countries, such as Australia and New Zealand, the payment of deposits of this kind is governed by special rules that require the money to be held and administered by an independent third party. There has been some lobbying for a change in the law that might allow for the deposit to be held in a joint account or by an independent body. A number of professional associations (e.g. the Association of Residential Letting Agents), run a protected bonding scheme so that if the deposit is lodged with a member firm, it will be held in a separate client account and will be covered against loss. There is, however, resistance in the sector against moves towards compulsory schemes. The government is currently looking at how best to introduce measures to protect tenants' deposits from unscrupulous landlords.

The question of rent

Contract rent is the *price* paid by a tenant to a landlord for the temporary occupation or use of land, buildings or other property.[12] In commercial settings landlords acting rationally will seek to charge the highest rent that the market will bear. In a free-enterprise economy with no State intervention, the price a landlord can charge will be determined by market conditions. In particular, the ability to fix a rent will be affected by the degree of competition that exists.

Perfect competition and marginal cost pricing. In the extreme case of a perfectly competitive market, rents would be determined by a process called *marginal cost pricing*. In these highly competitive conditions, the rents charged would be just sufficient to cover all the costs of providing the accommodation including what economists refer to as *normal profit*. In this way, normal profit is seen as a cost of production and is defined as that amount of profit just sufficient to make it

---

11 *Unsafe Deposit: CAB clients' experience of rental deposits*, National Association of Citizens Advice Bureaux, 1998.
12 E.g. cars, telephones, televisions, etc. can be 'rented' for periods. When the use of something is acquired on an hourly or weekly basis, we normally talk of 'hire' rather than 'rent'.

worthwhile for the provider to stay trading in the market. Under perfectly competitive conditions, landlords will be able to raise their rents up to, but not beyond, the level of marginal costs. If they do attempt to put up their rents beyond the level that just covers marginal costs, then they would make higher than 'normal' profits and these 'excess' rewards would, in turn, attract extra provision of equivalent accommodation by competing landlords. This additional supply would then force rents back down to the level at which, once again, price just covered the marginal costs of provision. In this way it is argued that, in strongly competitive conditions, the power of a landlord to set a rent is limited by market forces.

Imperfect competition and real market pricing. In the real world there is no such thing as a 'perfectly' competitive housing market and for this reason landlords may be able to increase their rents to levels that enable them to make more than 'normal' profits. At a particular time and place the market for a specific type of accommodation will be more-or-less competitive. It has to be understood that perfect competition is a theoretical construct. It represents the extreme case in which there are no barriers to prevent new suppliers coming into the market to compete, and in which all the dwellings are of identical size, type and condition, and in which all the market participants have perfect knowledge of the market and the product, and none of them is large or powerful enough to do anything that will influence the price. The less the local market reflects these conditions the less competitive it will be.

In practice, within a specific market area, new landlords may be inhibited, or even prevented, from setting up in business because of planning restrictions, a scarcity of appropriate building land, or a shortage of capital finance. Within the area, dwellings will vary with respect to siting, tenancy conditions, size, form, and state of repair. Landlords and tenants will only have an imperfect knowledge of what others are charging or offering, and will not have the professional expertise to assess the precise condition of a property. At any time there may be shortages or surpluses of particular types of accommodation and some of the market participants may have some influence through their size, professional affiliations or other connections that enable them to affect the negotiated price. For all these reasons the market will be *imperfectly*, rather than *perfectly*, competitive. This means that some landlords, at some times, in some locations, will be able to set rents for some types of property above the level of marginal costs without fear of these being forced down by competition. In charging what the imperfect market will bear the landlord will receive a rent that reflects the *real market price* for that accommodation, and at that price, more than normal profits might be generated. Of course, at that price, not every household deemed to be in 'need' of that kind of accommodation will be able to afford the rent.

Real market rents and housing policy. For some years there has been a general consensus in Britain that the principal aim of housing policy is to ensure that every household is able to occupy a dwelling of a size, type, standard, and location suitable to its needs.[13] When landlords charge what the market will bear, market forces will equate supply with effective demand which means that all the properties will be let. When this occurs the market is said to be 'in equilibrium' because demand is satisfied and the market is cleared. However, when a market is in equilibrium it does not mean that every household's housing needs have been met; it simply means that those who can afford to pay the going rent are satisfied and that landlords are satisfied.

Effective demand is defined as a need or want that is satisfied by spending money in the market. Clearly, some households have insufficient income to satisfy their housing needs. In the past there have been a number of policy responses to this problem. These have included augmenting the incomes of those who cannot afford to pay commercial rents (see above and Chapter 17), controlling or regulating commercial rents, and providing incentives to invest in private rented housing. Paradoxically, this last approach, as well as providing tax breaks, has involved deregulation measures.[14]

Regulation and the private landlord

Throughout the twentieth century, governments have periodically intervened in the market to restrict the activities of private landlords. These measures have had two aspects – to control or regulate rents and to establish a degree of security of tenure. The primary motives for intervention have been to keep rents within the means of low-income households and to protect tenants from the actions of unscrupulous landlords profiteering from shortages that exist in highly imperfect local housing markets.

The distinction between 'control' and 'regulation'. The notions of 'control' and 'regulation' are grounded in specific pieces of legislation. The former is the product of the various Rent Acts from 1915[15] onwards and is an aspect of the *controlled tenancy* arrangements they established; the latter is a feature of the 'fair rent' system of *regulated tenancies* that was ushered in with the Rent Act 1965 and developed by subsequent legislation. The fair rent legislation provided for disputed rents to be set by a rent officer. If either party then disputed the officer's ruling, they could apply for a decision to be made by a Rent Assessment Committee. The members of a Rent Assessment Committee are appointed on the basis of their assumed professional expertise and knowledge of local market conditions.

---

13 Refer *NFHA Inquiry into British Housing: Report*, July 1985, p7.
14 Arguably the most significant response has been to invest public funds in the provision of 'social' housing which is then allocated to low-income households at less than real market rents. The financial arrangements associated with the provision and consumption of non-commercial ('social') housing are considered in other chapters.
15 The Increase of Rent and Mortgage Interest (War Restrictions) Act 1915 froze rents at 1914 levels for rented properties of less than £35 rateable value in London and £25 elsewhere, except where improvements had been made or the rates increased.

Control and regulation are about the management of rent increases. Under controlled tenancies specific properties, identified by reference to their rateable values, have their rents frozen, with allowances made for improvements and local tax increases. Over time the controlled rent may become fixed at a level that is significantly below that which would be set by market forces. In particular locations this may discourage new investment, lead to existing landlords withdrawing from the market, and bring about illegal 'black market' arrangements (such as 'key money'). Control has been strongest during wartime periods (after 1915 and 1939) when it was recognised that free markets had to be abandoned because normal supply activities became impossible due to construction resources being diverted into the building of munitions factories and other projects associated with the war effort. At such times these control measures were regarded as temporary and designed to protect tenants from the inflation and insecurity brought about by wartime disruptions in supply and immediate post-war shortages. After the First World War, however, the system was maintained and all except the grandest of houses were made subject to control. After the Second World War rents remained controlled until the 1957 Rent Act when the more valuable houses were released from control. Sitting tenants in less valuable properties continued to have their rents controlled until they moved, leading to a gradual decline in numbers.[16] All remaining controlled tenancies were finally converted to regulated tenancies by the Housing Act 1980.

In some parts of the country the period following the Conservative government's relaxing of controls in 1957 was characterised by the harassing and eviction of tenants by what the press termed 'slum' or 'bully-boy' landlords and has since been termed *Rachmanism* (after the activities of Peter Rachman, a petty criminal and slum landlord operating in the East End of London). The 1957 legislation allowed for capital gains to be realised as landlords sold or demolished the vacated dwellings. Contrary to the legislators' intentions, this brought about a short-term disinvestment in private accommodation and some 300,000 dwellings were lost to the sector between 1958 and 1964.[17] In addition, investment in the sector remained depressed by the findings of the Milner Holland Committee's Inquiry into the state of London's housing and the Labour Party's response which took the form of a high profile public commitment to reintroduce controls. This they eventually did through the provisions of the Rent Acts 1965, 1968 and 1974.

Regulated tenancies and fair rents. The current system of regulation stems from the Rent Acts of 1965, 1968, 1974 and 1977 and the Housing Acts 1980 and 1988. In the wake of the Milner Holland Report, the 1965 Rent Act introduced a system of regulation based on the notion of a *fair rent*. The fair rent system was designed to balance the proprietary interests of landlords and tenants and, in particular, sought to overcome the disincentive effects on investment that resulted from rent

---

16 The Rent Act 1957 decontrolled some 5 million dwellings. These included dwellings above a certain rateable value, with regional variations, all vacated dwellings, all new unfurnished dwellings and all properties with a resident landlord.

17 Balchin and Kieve, (1977), *Urban Land Economics*, p194.

control. Rent control involves market abandonment while rent regulation involves market modification. The idea behind a *fair rent* is that rent officers should regulate arrangements between landlords and tenants by fixing a rent that relates to the market without abandoning the tenant to the vagaries of unrestrained market forces.

The so-called 'fairness' of a fair rent stems from its apparent similarity, in the minds of the civil servant who designed it, to the market ideal of a *marginal cost price rent* (see above). That is, it is designed to reflect the rent that would be charged in the area in question if conditions of perfect competition prevailed (i.e. if there were no shortages and thus no super-normal profits).

The fair rent system was introduced by the Rent Act 1965 for the private sector and extended to public sector and housing association tenancies by the Housing Finance Act 1972. The provisions were consolidated in the Rent Act 1977 and subsequently amended by the Housing Acts 1980 and 1988.

Fair rents are set by independent agents of central government known as 'rent officers'. The Rent Service, formerly the Rent Officer Service, in England and Wales became an executive agency of the DETR in November 1999. The creation of the Agency did not alter the rent officers' status – they still remain independent statutory officers responsible for making 'fair rent' valuations, valuing local private sector rents for housing benefit, and advising local authorities about the effects of rent on housing renovation grants. The Agency only operates in England and Wales, but in Scotland the equivalent service is also part of the civil service system. Rent officers are required to set rents that ignore the personal circumstances of both tenants and landlords. Furthermore, the rent they set must assume that the properties are not in short supply; this means that they must not include any price element that reflects a rented dwelling's scarcity value. They must, however, take into account other relevant circumstances including the property's age, location, character and state of repair. Fair rents are registered and remain fixed for a period of two years. Either party can appeal to a rent assessment committee and subsequently to the courts if they wish to challenge the rent officer's decision. A fair rent may consist of two elements; one relating to rights of occupancy and the other to service charges. Under fair rent arrangements service charges are assessed on the basis of their value to the tenant rather than on the costs of provision.

A fair rent is not a *controlled rent* in that it is not simply frozen within bands set by rateable values.[18] It is not a *welfare rent* in that it is not determined by reference to the personal circumstances of the tenant. It is not a *real market rent* because, although it does take account of the property's character, location, age,

18 Rateable values were used to set thresholds above which properties are excluded from fair rent regulation and to set rent levels for the remaining controlled tenancies between 1957-1980.

and condition, it ignores any price effect resulting from shortages or surpluses. It is an *administrative* arrangement that seeks to 'square the circle' by regulating rents in a way that would produce a similar outcome to that which would occur in an unregulated competitive market.

The 1980 Housing Act extended the fair rent regime to cover all the tenancies previously controlled by the Rent Acts. The legislation also sought to encourage the growth of private landlordism by lowering the fair rent registration period from three to two years and by introducing two new forms of tenancy that gave landlords repossession rights after fixed terms. New protected shorthold tenancies allowed landlords to let vacant dwellings for terms ranging from one to five years. The Act also allowed certain landlords, under certain conditions, to let dwellings under the conditions of *assured* tenancy agreements. Assured tenancies began as an arrangement for letting commercial properties (Landlord and Tenant Act 1954), and the 1980 legislation extended it for the first time into the residential property field. Some years later, the idea of assured tenancies became the main mechanism of deregulation provided for by the Housing Act 1988 (see below).

Reviving the sector

In recent years there has been considerable debate about both the political desirability and practical possibility of reviving the private rented sector to a point where it could once again play a significant role as a provider of housing for people on average or below average incomes.[19]

There is evidence to suggest that the decline in private landlordism has an international dimension. In many developed countries the decline has occurred as an inevitable result of long-term political, social and commercial forces. Michael Harloe's study of private renting in Germany, Holland, France, Denmark and the United States found that, by the mid-1980s, despite attempts to ease the impact of restrictive legislation, a widespread and powerful amalgamation of political and economic circumstances was restricting the tenure to a 'marginal' and 'problematic' role.[20]

In Britain, as elsewhere, it is clear that the decline in private landlordism is in large part explained by long-run social and economic restructuring. Over the last 80 years, many new investment opportunities have emerged to compete with residential property provision and at the same time, saving and investment mechanisms have become more sophisticated and accessible. During the same period the State's commitment to the provision of various forms of social rented housing has expanded, and this commitment carried with it a range of fiscal support measures that were denied to the private landlord. Fiscal support has also

---

19   See in particular the writings of Best, R., Crook, A.D.H., Eversley, D., Gibb. K, Harloe, M., and Kemp, P.A.
20   Harloe, M., (1985), *Private Rented Housing in the United States and Europe*, Croom Helm.

reinforced the preference for home-ownership that began to emerge in the inter-war period and developed at a pace after 1950. By the 1980s most commentators were arguing that, in combination, these forces have become so powerful that it is not possible to reverse the historical trend towards decline by a simple process of deregulation, and that any government wishing to attract substantial amounts of private money into the sector will need to provide positive incentives to potential investors.

A key problem associated with the development of a residential portfolio relates to what might be termed the 'funding issue'.[21] Historically, funders have viewed residential investment as a commercial activity and as a result, landlords tend to pay higher interest charges than those available in the owner-occupation market. Recognition that funding issues could be inhibiting general growth in the sector led to the launch of the 'buy to let' scheme in 1996. This is a scheme initiated by the Association of Residential Letting Agents and a number of mortgage providers that is designed to provide preferential loans to landlords so as to encourage wider investment and participation in the market. The preferential interest rates are granted subject to specific requirements relating to such things as maximum loan to value ratios, minimum rent to interest ratios, minimum capital values and loans, and detailed criteria regarding unacceptable or ineligible properties and letting arrangements. Other sector specific investment schemes are being developed by individual lenders and groups of lenders.[22] The success of such schemes will depend, to a large extent, on general investment opportunities in the economy. In the final analysis, all housing investment has to compete for funds with the full range of other enterprises.

Recent policy initiatives

Governments have found it politically difficult to provide direct subsidy to private landlords and have therefore relied on policies of deregulation coupled with indirect subsidies in the form of tax breaks when they have wanted to stimulate the sector. The Conservative administrations of the 1980s and 1990s were ideologically predisposed in favour of private renting and their attempts to breathe new life into the sector involved the application of two contrasting, but mutually reinforcing, pressures for growth. One involved *positive incentives* in the forms of deregulation measures and tax breaks targeted directly at the private landlord. The other took the form of *negative incentives* and involved the reduction of financial and legislative support for municipal housing and reducing capital grants to housing associations which had the effect of narrowing the fiscal advantage differential between private landlords and their competitors in the social rented sector.

---

21 This phrase is taken from John Mansfield, *Inside Housing*, January 15 1999.
22 For example, in 1998 Aichisons, an Oxfordshire agent, co-ordinated the launch of the Residential Investment Centre, adding a further six institutions willing to provide funds for residential investment purposes.

A strategy for reviving the sector

By the mid-1980s, research and informed opinion indicated[23] that an effective strategy for reviving the sector needs to have the following interrelated features.

- First, there needs to be clarity about the sector's future specific contribution to satisfying housing need and demand.
- Second, a degree of deregulation needs to be realised.
- Third, fiscal incentives will need to be introduced to encourage new investment.
- Fourth, there needs to be a greater degree of tenure neutrality with respect to fiscal policy in general.
- Fifth, measures might be introduced to ease the management burden.

The role of private renting

How the sector is to be supported will depend to a large extent on an understanding of the part we wish it to play in the fulfilment of overall housing policy. Recognition of the fact that the decline in private renting is in part an inevitable consequence of wider structural changes in society has resulted in a general consensus that, in the foreseeable future, it will continue to play only a limited role compared with owner-occupation and social renting. The current debate is not about whether it should replace one of the existing primary tenure arrangements so much as whether, in the future, it should or could play a more prominent role. Arguably, the most important role that private renting could play in the future would be to provide a greater degree of flexibility within the overall system of housing provision. Many argue that it is well-suited to offer appropriate accommodation to certain groups at certain points in their housing careers including the provision of a temporary stop-gap to those seeking long-term housing solutions in other tenures.

The need for more rented accommodation is clearly indicated by recent projections of household growth that show a probable increase of between three and four million households in England alone for the 25 years up to 2021.[24] This growth will result from falling death rates, net inward migration, and new household formation through increased divorce and marital separation rates. New housing demand for relatively short stay accommodation is likely to arise from the increasing need for mobility that will result from the gradual restructuring of the labour market in a way that weakens job security and gives a greater prominence

---

23 See, for example, the various submissions to the *Inquiry in British Housing* chaired by the Duke of Edinburgh and published as 'Report' (1985), 'The Evidence' (1985), and 'Supplement (1986), NFHA.

24 Alan Holmans, (1995), 'The Rising Number of Households Requiring Homes – The National and Regional Picture', in Wilcox, S., *Housing Finance Review 1995/96*, Joseph Rowntree Foundation, pp17-24. Also Wilcox, 1999, p66.

to short-term contracts. These foreseeable trends point to a particular need for more single-person dwellings for rent that are both affordable and immediately accessible. Expected patterns of internal migration indicate that in some areas, such as London and some Northern conurbations (especially Greater Manchester) shortages of suitable accommodation to rent by the young, the single and the occupationally mobile may be very pronounced.

The present government's commitment to promote a healthy private rented housing sector was restated in the 2000 Housing Green Paper, which stated that, *'Through its flexibility and speed of access, it can also help to oil the wheels of the housing and labour markets'*.[25]

Deregulation

An early priority of the Conservative administration elected in 1979 was to begin dismantling the provisions of the Rent Acts. The Rent Act 1977 fixed rents at levels well below those that would have been determined under free market conditions and it also gave tenants a significant degree of security of tenure. Its provisions were seen by many to be inhibiting the growth of private renting and throughout the 1980s pressure grew for a less strongly controlled system that would redress the balance of proprietary interests. The idea was to allow landlords to charge market-related rents and to repossess their properties more easily. The 1980 Housing Act introduced the possibility of either letting new built domestic property with less contractual restrictions or letting new tenancies (of existing or new dwellings) as a 'shorthold' with a guaranteed right to possession at the end of a fixed-term. The effect of the new *assured* tenancy agreements was, however, limited by the requirement for the dwellings to be purpose-built (new or substantially renovated with letting in mind), and owned by an organisation approved by the Secretary of State. Protected shorthold tenancies also failed to prove popular, partly because they were still subject to rent regulation and partly because the administrative procedures required to set up and end the tenancies were complicated.

It is widely accepted that the 1987 Housing White Paper marks the point when a positive decision was made to breathe new life into private renting. The sector was substantially deregulated by the Housing Act 1988, which sought to allow market forces and landlord-tenant negotiations to be the guiding influence on rent levels and tenancy time conditions. The expansion of assured and shorthold tenancies was intended to revitalise the private rented sector. After the 1988 Act rents rose. The largest increases were in the furnished part of the sector, where net rents, after deduction of housing benefit, doubled between 1989 and 1993.[26] As far as unfurnished accommodation was concerned, between 1985 and 1988, rents were

---

25   DETR/Department of Social Security, April 2000, para.5.1, p44.
26   HMSO, *Social Trends 25*, 1995, p179.

lower, on average, than housing associations. By 1993, however, they were, on average, double that of housing associations.

The Housing Act 1988 reformed the structure of the independent rented sector.[27] It established *assured tenancies* as the main form of letting for the use of private landlords and housing associations alike. Its measures constituted a significant degree of deregulation and, in establishing the new tenancy arrangements, the Act required the phasing out of all *regulated tenancies* that had been established by the Rent Act 1977, as amended by the Housing Act 1980. In this way, although all regulated tenancies retained their security of tenure and regulated rents, from 15 January 1989, all new tenancy agreements were now assumed to be *assured* or *assured shorthold*.[28]

As mentioned above, assured tenancies were first extended to residential property by the Housing Act 1980. At that time, however, their use was restricted to private landlords who were registered with, and approved by, the DoE to provide 'new purpose-built accommodation' for rent. The 1988 legislation made *assured tenancies* the cornerstone of the new deregulated system of housing finance. From its implementation, landlords no longer had to register with the DoE and assured tenancy agreements covered all types of dwellings (not just new, purpose-built accommodation).

The provisions of an assured tenancy agreement are specifically designed to enhance the *proprietary investment interests* of the landlord while, at the same time, maintaining a degree of security of tenure which is regarded as a key *proprietary consumption interest* of the tenant. Under the reformed arrangements, rents and duration of tenancies are negotiated as in a free market, but the tenant, as well as enjoying security of tenure during the contract period, has the right to a statutory periodic tenancy at the end of that period. On the tenant's death his or her spouse has an automatic right to take over the assured tenancy. However, there is no automatic right to further successions by the spouse or any other family member.

To encourage private landlords to supply the increasing demand for short-term lets, the 1988 legislation allowed for a variant of the assured agreement called an *assured shorthold tenancy*, in Scotland called *short assured tenancies*. These arrangements allow for fixed-term tenancies that must not be less than six months duration. A tenant has the right to apply for a rent determination by a rent assessment committee if they think the contractual rent is significantly out of line

---

27 A term used to describe the wider private rented sector that includes both private landlords and housing associations.

28 The legislation does not allow an assured tenancy to be imposed on an existing protected tenant. A protected tenancy was simply the contractual tenancy set up within the remit of the Rent Act. Once the contractual period ended the statutory tenancy came into being; both protected and statutory tenancies were regulated.

with that being charged for similar properties in the locality. During the term of the tenancy a landlord can seek repossession on one of a number of specified bases (e.g. rent arrears), and at the end of the term has an absolute right to repossess the property. The Housing Act 1996 made *assured shorthold* the 'normal' or 'default' tenancy arrangement: that is, unless an assured tenancy is specifically agreed, then the arrangement is assumed to be on a shorthold basis.[29] The Act further enhanced the proprietary interests of landlords by modifying the mandatory grounds for eviction on the basis of rent arrears: the arrears period was shortened from 13 to 8 weeks.

Fiscal incentives

An established feature of the British fiscal system has been to encourage business investment by the provision of tax allowances and exemptions, commonly referred to as 'tax breaks'. In comparison with most other business activities, landlords have been treated ungenerously with respect to tax breaks and this is sometimes pointed to as an historical explanation of the relative lack of enthusiasm for investment in private rented housing.

In the UK the Inland Revenue take what is known as a 'rental business' approach to tax assessment. Under these arrangements, profits from UK land or property are treated for tax purposes as 'earnings' arising from a business activity. This means that tax liability is based on commercial accounts drawn up in accordance with correct accounting principles. It means that landlords with a portfolio of properties are assessed on earnings and expenditures that are lumped together so that expenses on one property can be deducted from the receipts of another – so long as the properties are let on commercial terms, and not cheaply to friends or relatives. It also means that a trading loss can be carried over into subsequent tax years and set off against future tax liabilities.

Income tax

Although the basic principle in the UK is that there is only one income tax, in order to facilitate the collection of that tax, different sources of income are allocated to different *schedules*. Landlords are taxed under *Schedule A* that covers rent and other income generated from the ownership of, or an interest in, land and real property.

Allowable revenue expenses. A landlord is allowed to offset certain revenue expenses against his or her liable income so long as these are incurred wholly and

---

29 The Association of Residential Letting Agents argues the need for further deregulation measures that would introduce *assured longhold tenancies*. These would run for periods in excess of three years, and the Association argues that the additional security they would afford to landlords would have the effect of attracting more investment into the sector.

exclusively for business purposes. These revenue allowances include ordinary expenditure on maintenance, repairs, insurance and management costs. The costs of major repairs to reinstate a worn out or dilapidated asset are usually deductible as revenue expenditure but extensive alterations to a building that amount to the reconstruction of the property are counted as capital expenditure and therefore are not allowed as an ordinary revenue business expense. The cost of servicing a loan taken out to acquire the property is regarded as a revenue expense and is therefore allowable.

Capital allowances. It is a general income tax principle that you cannot deduct capital expenses in computing your taxable income. This means, for example, that in calculating taxable profits, a landlord cannot deduct the purchase price of the property being let or the amount of any depreciation or any loss incurred in selling the property. This rule applies to all business activities not just rental businesses. Despite this general principle, in some cases capital expenditure on a property (but not the land) may qualify for *capital allowances*. A capital allowance effectively enables the business to claim further deductions in calculating its taxable rental profit.

Some industrial and commercial businesses can deduct a percentage of the property's overall capital value to allow for the asset's depreciation; however, this is not permitted in the case of residential accommodation. Although there are no capital allowances for the cost or depreciation of residential property, the costs of maintaining plant and machinery such as lifts and heating systems can be allowed for, and a 'wear and tear' depreciation allowance may be due for such items as fridges, freezers, furniture, furnishings, etc. that are supplied with the accommodation.

Capital gains tax

Unlike owner-occupiers, private landlords are not exempt from capital gains tax when they sell the dwellings they have been letting. Furthermore, unless they are dealing in furnished holiday lettings, landlords of residential properties do not benefit from the capital gains tax reliefs that are available to other traders. This means, for example, they cannot enjoy the benefit of roll-over and retirement reliefs.

Section 28 capital grants

Section 28 of the Local Government Act 1988 allows for the provision of production subsidies by giving local authorities discretionary powers to award capital grants to investors in new or refurbished private housing for rent. The grant must come from the authority's own resources and the risk and ownership must be lodged in the private sector.

Tax breaks: the Business Expansion Scheme and Housing Investment Trusts

The Business Expansion Scheme

In the late 1980s, the government wanted to provide a tax incentive stimulus to reinforce the parallel deregulation measures being introduced to encourage the private rented sector into more active life. Rather than introduce a new package of tax breaks with new administrative arrangements they utilised the machinery of the already existing Business Expansion Scheme. The Business Expansion Scheme (BES) was introduced in the Finance Act 1983 as an extension of the 1981 Business Start-Up Scheme. The idea was to use tax breaks as an incentive to small savers to invest in unquoted high-risk venture companies that lacked sufficient equity finance to fulfil their growth potential.

In July 1988, under the provisions of the previous year's Finance Act, the BES was extended to include investment in companies engaged with letting residential accommodation on assured tenancies. The scheme allowed a private individual to invest from £500 to £40,000 a year in a BES housing company and in so doing, they were eligible for income tax relief at their marginal rate. Capital gains tax was also exempted so long as the shares were held for a minimum of five years.

As the BES was initially targeted at small venture companies, the original legislation fixed a maximum of £500,000 equity capital on each participating company. However, in recognition of the capital intensive nature of housing enterprises, in the case of BES housing companies, this limit was increased to £5 million.

Deregulation was not seen to be enough on its own to 'kick-start' the sector back to life and the BES was introduced to reinforce the process of revivification. The idea was that after an initial period of five years they would continue to attract investors without subsidies and at the same time allow their existing shareholders to sell their shares on the assumption that by then the company would be profitable and trading on the stock market. The BES incentives ended in December 1993, which means that by 1998 the arrangement was a thing of the past.

In the 1990s the Conservative government reaffirmed its commitment to encourage and sustain a revival of private renting, and in particular it sought to attract investment from the financial institutions which, in recent years, had shown relatively little interest in residential accommodation. By allowing the formation of Housing Investment Trusts, the Finance Act 1996 sought to create a vehicle for carrying this aim forward.

Housing investment trusts

What is an investment trust? An investment trust is a company whose objective is to collect and reinvest the money capital of its shareholders in a spread of equities and other securities with a view of generating an investment income. Like any company it will issue shares and these are quoted and freely tradable on the Stock Exchange. However, unlike ordinary trading companies, the money capital raised by its own share issues will be reinvested in the share capital of other organisations. In this way, it acts as an intermediary between those wishing to invest money capital and those needing to raise money capital for commercial ventures. In recent years investment trusts have raised billions of pounds. To protect the investing public the activities of investment trusts are closely regulated. To date they have been required to invest in such a way that produces a diverse portfolio of assets and they have been required to derive the major part of their incomes from shares and securities that can be easily liquidated on the stock market.

What is a housing investment trust (HIT)? A housing investment trust is an investment trust that operates under special rules outlined in Schedule 28 of the Finance Act 1996. These rules allow a qualifying company to establish a portfolio of 'eligible residential property'. The notion of 'eligibility' exists to ensure that the qualifying trusts invest in dwellings that are appropriate to the needs of low-income households rather than in up-market speculative properties. An eligible residential property is defined as a dwelling unit acquired on or after 1 April 1996 which is either freehold or subject to a low rent/long lease,[30] at a purchase price that does not exceed a specified amount.[31] To count as 'eligible' it must also be ultimately let by the trust on an assured tenancy agreement. In return for operating within these rules the trust will qualify for two specific tax breaks.

Before an application can be made to the Inland Revenue for favourable tax treatment a potential HIT has to acquire property and gain a Stock Exchange listing. A condition of Stock Exchange listing is that 75 per cent of the company's property portfolio must be let at all times.[32] Once established, the HIT operates with two parallel management strands; one concerned with fund management and one with property management. This makes a HIT a more complicated organisation than a normal investment trust. The fund managers are required to invest all funds in suitable properties within a given period, currently two years, and it is clear that property acquisition involves more complex procedures than those associated with equity investments. The housing management functions of rent collection, service charge administration, repairs and property maintenance, etc, will normally be contracted out to a specialist managing agent.

---

30   At the start of the scheme (April 1996), maximum rent levels were fixed at £1,000 in Greater London and £250 elsewhere. The minimum length of lease was set at 21 years.

31   At the start of the scheme the maximum purchase price was set at £125,000 in Greater London and £85,000 elsewhere. These figures are to include any necessary improvements costs.

32   If the percentage of let properties falls below 75 per cent the HIT is required to notify the Stock Exchange but, at the time of writing, it is not clear what would be the consequences following such an eventuality.

What are the tax concessions enjoyed by a HIT? When first mooted the idea was to encourage investment by allowing qualifying HITs to take advantage of two tax breaks. Firstly, they were to be charged what was then the lower 'small companies' rate' of corporation tax (24 per cent) on rental income net of approved expenses. Second, any capital appreciation was to be exempted from capital gains tax. The effect of these proposed advantages were severely dented by the 1997 Budget in which the new Labour Chancellor altered the rules so that institutional investors could no longer reclaim the bulk of the tax they pay on dividends.

The lessons from the BES and HITs

Although neither the BES nor HITs are currently playing a significant part in the provision of private housing to rent, the debate that surrounds such fiscal experiments remains important. The idea of housing investment trusts was floated in the 1995 White Paper on Housing in England and Wales, *Our Future Homes*. The White Paper restated the government's commitment to see that a decent home is put in reach of every household. The White Paper looked to rented housing to play a significant part in achieving that objective. It also looked to private finance and a market-led approach to revitalise the private rented sector. The government's declared hope was that commercial investors and more competition would provide the tens of thousands of extra rented homes that will be needed. HITs were put forward as part of the mechanism for bringing this about. What is needed, they argued, is a new type of housing agency that will allow investors to buy shares (encouraged by significant tax breaks) and thereby generate the funds needed to create new homes for rent.

BES also tried to lever money into the sector but was targeted at relatively small investors. Under the scheme small private investors were encouraged to put money into small property companies created specially to take advantage of the BES tax concessions. In contrast to the BES experiment, HITs were intended to be a permanent feature in the housing investment landscape rather than a short-term 'pump-priming' exercise. Perhaps the most positive thing to say about the BES experiment is that it showed that, despite some worries to the contrary, it is politically viable to subsidise private landlords.

BES did not, and was not intended to, attract the institutional market. This, however, was the expectation of HITs. By establishing HITs it was, and perhaps still is, hoped to lever significant amounts of institutionally managed funds into housing on a basis that is both permanent and flexible. By financing housing provision through the market for equities, a system is created whereby the overall supply of funds becomes permanent but the individual investor is able to liquidise the investment if the need arises.

The difficulties of attracting institutional finance

Pension and long-term insurance funds have the sort of 'serious' money that could make a real difference to the sector. HITs were designed especially to attract them.

Unlike BES companies, there were to be no limits to the size of an HIT or how long they can continue to operate and enjoy their tax breaks – total exemption from capital gains and a reduced rate of corporation tax. To be viable an HIT would need to have a relatively large asset base[33] and property portfolio. The legislation prevents BES companies converting into trusts or trusts acquiring BES companies, since a trust is not allowed to own properties that are let on assured tenancies. One possible source of property that could have attracted the trusts is the 'starter homes' built in the boom years of the 1980s and that have since become increasingly difficult to sell on the open market. Other suggestions include enabling victims of negative equity to come to an arrangement whereby they exchange their properties for shares in an HIT.[34]

There are two key principles that underpin the idea of the HIT proposal. The first is that we need to provide tax advantages to institutional investors. Although the White Paper made it clear that it would be for the market to judge whether HITs could produce attractive returns, there is no doubt that their popularity with corporate investors would have depended in part, on their ability to be 'tax efficient'. From the start there were some doubts about the effectiveness of the tax concessions offered by HITs. The largest potential investors are the pension funds and insurance companies, both of which have long-term investment horizons and already benefit from tax concessions on their investments. Furthermore, the tax incentive aspects of HITs was significantly reduced with the election of the Labour government in 1997. When they came to office, the New Labour government brought in measures that were designed to close what they saw as a number of tax loopholes in the corporate sector. The new government's first Budget introduced measures that prevented investment trusts reclaiming the bulk of the tax they pay on dividends. This measure diminished the attractiveness of investment trusts in general and brought into question the future of the HITs idea in particular.[35]

The second key idea behind HITs is that we need to enable investors to put money into the sector at arms length – enjoying the benefits of buying and selling shares in housing without having to own property directly or get involved with the thorny

---

33 The Stock Exchange sets a minimum net asset level for a HIT; this currently stands at £30 million.

34 Coopers and Lybrand, (1996), *The Outlook for Housing Investment Trusts.*

35 Enthusiasm for HITs amongst institutional investors waned after the 1997 Budget removed some of the tax credits trusts had enjoyed. It is now generally agreed that there would have to be significant changes in the legal and fiscal framework for HITs to take off. Indeed, since 1997, plans to establish one major planned association HIT has been postponed and private landlords' representatives have put pressure on ministers to make further tax concessions. At the time of writing, the Association of Residential Letting Agents have declared their continued support to the idea in principle, and studies by Coopers and Lybrand and the Universities of Sheffield and Glasgow are analysing the reasons for the lack of development of the trusts and are examining other ideas to attract large-scale investors. The findings of research so far indicate that the key issue remains that of the opportunity cost of money capital. In other words, it is unlikely that institutions will invest in residential property so long as it is possible to invest in other activities that carry equivalent risks but give higher returns. 'While HITs are expected to provide returns of 8 or 9 per cent, investors can receive 12 to 20 per cent from commercial property.' (Julian Dobson, *Inside Housing* 30 January 1998, p1.).

problem of managing tenants. In principle, there are a number of possible routes to creating a HIT.[36] One would be to raise the money and invest it directly in housing. Another would be to raise the money, 'park' it temporarily in gilts or utility stocks to be called on as and when suitable properties become available. An existing investment trust could choose to diversify into housing, or an existing housing investment company could float as a HIT.[37] Despite these perceived benefits, early indications are that the viability of HITs is weakened by the poor reputation that social housing has amongst investors. Large-scale private housing organisations face an image problem because there is no recent tradition in Britain of such investments and the memory of earlier rent control and regulation measures lingers on.[38] Institutional investors are apprehensive both about the uncertainties associated with the possibility of some future governmental intervention and about becoming tainted by bad publicity should landlord-tenant relations break down in some scheme in which they have money invested.

Institutional investors are acutely aware of how political and financial factors impact on each other. From the institution's point of view, returns from investing in homes for rent simply have not been commercially competitive with alternative forms of investment. Despite deregulation there is still a gap between investors' expectations of private renting and what market rents actually yield. In some parts of the country the rental yield (the total rent as a ratio of the asset value of the property) is judged to be unacceptably low. This is particularly so given the risks and management costs associated with residential housing. To be competitive, the yield will have to be high enough to compensate the investor for the multiplicity of management costs associated with tenant care and disputes; depreciation on furniture and fittings; redecoration, maintenance, running repairs, future major repairs and refurbishment needs; and void and re-letting times.

All of this means that to attract significant amounts of private corporate finance into the rented housing system requires a multiple strategy of deregulation (to limit commercial risk factors), tax incentives, and partnership arrangements with the public sector (to limit political risks factors). Current research shows that there is also a need for more reliable information so that potential investors can have access to data that will enable them to track the performance of their investments (Fordham, 1998).

---

36 Coopers and Lybrand (1996), *op. cit.*
37 At the time of writing HITs are regarded as investment trusts by the government and property companies by the Stock Exchange, which may lead to some initial confusion.
38 E.g. see 'Housing Trusts Flop', comments from Dorrington Holdings reported in the *Investors Chronicle*, 24 May 1996, p14.
    Direct subsidy may be needed to overcome all the disadvantages, real or perceived, of investing in this area. Research at Sheffield points to the need for an injection of initial cash grants (£16,000 per property suggested), which would provide the sort of return that private property companies say they need. £250 million in grants is needed according to Tony Crook of Sheffield, equal to 25,000 additional properties a year. There is, however, some political reluctance to follow this route as it would probably have to come out of some other programme, such as social renting, to meet Treasury concerns about the public expenditure implications.

Some argue the need for legislation to allow a new HIT model under the umbrella of the Private Finance Initiative (PFI).[39] Such a trust would be empowered to buy homes built for local authorities in PFI schemes, allowing the developer to recover funds to invest elsewhere. It might also be possible to allow trusts to form joint ventures with councils to provide accommodation for tenants who could not afford to buy in the owner-occupied market. Suggestions like these mean that the idea of HITs is not necessarily dead. It is clear from the 2000 Green Paper that the government are still considering ways in which the tax system might be adjusted to encourage institutional investment in private rented housing.[40]

The owner-occupier landlord and the Rent-A-Room Scheme

There is a long tradition of people letting out rooms in their own homes. The lodger was a common feature of working-class domestic life in the Victorian and Edwardian periods. Lodgers have not had any of the rights that tenants have had under the Housing and Rent Acts. They have no security of tenure and can be evicted without a court order because they share a landlord's property and do not have exclusive use of its facilities (in comparison with a tenant of a self-contained flat).

A tax break was introduced in 1992 that allows home owners to let out spare rooms and pay no tax on the rental income so long as it is less than an official threshold figure.[41] In practice, the scheme is administered by the claimant simply ticking a box on his or her tax return. Landlords can elect for the excess to be taxed in full or, alternatively, they can apply for normal income tax rules for the whole income less allowable expenses. From the landlord's point of view, participating in the scheme has no implications for capital gains liabilities. Advisors usually argue that it would be sensible to draw up clear agreements about payment of council tax and other household expenses, and both sides should sign a license setting out the rights and obligations of each party. Furthermore, insurance companies should be informed about the arrangements or cover may be deemed to be invalid.

Tenure neutrality

The introduction of tenure neutrality into fiscal arrangements is seen by many as a key feature of any strategy for reviving the private rented sector. The argument here is that the sector's revival is inhibited by the lack of a 'level playing field' and, unless and until private landlords are allowed to operate under fiscal arrangements

---

39 See for example Sara Fordham, 1998.
40 See DETR/Department of Social Security, (April 2000), p47. (Ministers have intimated that any future incentive scheme would not be a 'HITs2'. It is likely that some newly conceived model will emerge. Crook and Kemp have floated the new idea of 'Terls' a new tax transparent vehicle).
41 This figure currently stands at £4,250 p.a. (since April 1997).

that are equivalent to those facing other providers, they will be unable to play their full and appropriate part in the housing system.

This argument emphasises the need to reform the system of housing taxes and subsidies in ways that do not unduly privilege or penalise one tenure in comparison with the others. One approach would be to take away the current concessions given to owner-occupiers.[42] The withdrawal of mortgage interest tax relief to owner-occupiers in 2000 has helped in this respect. Further equalisation measures might prove to be politically difficult. However, some commentators have argued for the extension of existing concessions in other tenures into the private rented sector. This could involve, for example, exempting all residential property transactions from capital gains tax and allowing private landlords to compete with social landlords for grant aid. The advocates of this argument[43] say that the equalisation of fiscal treatment need not prove expensive to the Exchequer or work to the disadvantage of tenants. They argue that the cost to the Exchequer would be modest because, the sector is relatively small and if it grew at the expense of the owner-occupied sector, the additional cost would be zero as owner-occupiers already benefit from such subsidies. Furthermore, if the private sector grew at the expense of the public sector, the public purse may actually make savings. To avoid exploitation of tenants, private landlords might have to agree to submit to regular rigorous inspection in return for the new fiscal concessions. This, however, would in itself impose an additional expense on public expenditure.

Easing the management burden of small landlords

The 2000 Housing Green Paper suggests that more investment might be attracted into private renting if the burdens of day-to-day management could be eased. In particular, it suggested that there may be a particular need in some areas of declining housing demand, where market rents may give a poor return on the landlord's original investment, for the provision of low-cost management services. Registered social landlords would be well positioned to provide such a service, either by operating as managing agents for the landlord, or by themselves taking a commercial lease on the property.[44]

Housing benefit and private renting

In the period between the mid-1980s and the mid-1990s housing benefit played a key role in underpinning a policy of allowing private renting to play a more

---

42 Since 1945 an estimated four million properties have been transferred from the private rented sector into owner-occupation. Power, A., (1993), *Hovels to High Rise: State Housing in Europe Since 1850*, London: Routledge.

43 For a clear summary of these arguments see Halifax Building Society, *Viewpoint*, spring 1992.

44 DETR/Department of Social Security, (April 2000), p46, para.5.15.

prominent role in the provision of rented accommodation to households on low incomes. Instead of investing public funds directly in the construction of new homes, housing benefit subsidy targeted funds at those in most need. The idea was that by paying benefit at market rates, rents could rise attracting private landlords to respond and provide accommodation. By concentrating support on housing benefit, the government sought to avoid the need to fund the building of expensive social homes. The cuts and restrictions in housing benefit after 1996 have effectively reversed this policy. If within the more restrictive rules governing entitlement to benefit, those in housing need are not able to gain access to appropriate accommodation in the private rented sector, then this seems to point to a greater role for the social sector.

Summary

There is currently much debate about the need to revive private renting as a means of responding to the changing nature of employment. According to the recent Green Paper the government believes that the sector is performing 'below its true potential'. This is important for three reasons.

1. For many people there is no alternative to private renting at some stage in their lives (e.g. students and young workers).
2. In some areas social rented housing is in short supply and many low-income households are forced into renting privately.
3. Private renting has a potential to be flexible and responsive and thereby able to act effectively as a stepping-stone to other tenure arrangements.

A policy to revive the sector will need a multiple strategy that combines deregulation with positive fiscal incentives and/or the provision of a low-cost management service, and/or a move to tenure neutrality.

Further reading

DETR/Social Security, *Quality and Choice: A Decent Home for All*, The Housing Green Paper, April 2000. Chapter 5.

Peter Kemp, *Private Renting in Transition*, CIH, 2000 (forthcoming).

CHAPTER 17:
Financial support measures for the vulnerable: housing benefit, the working families' tax credit, 'supporting people', and income support for mortgage interest

Introduction

In this chapter we will look at the financial support and benefit provisions that are available to help households who find it difficult to meet their housing expenses or who are in some other way 'at risk'. We will distinguish between the assistance that is given to tenants and that which is available to owner-occupiers. We will see that, while the support arrangements for renters and owners are quite different, they share a common operational rationale: that is, eligibility to both is determined by reference to a common poverty baseline. This baseline is defined in terms of entitlement to income support or the jobseekers' allowance (JSA).[1] The point to be made is that these baseline allowances are intended to help with general living expenses *excluding* those associated with housing. Assistance with housing-specific expenses is provided by *housing benefit* for those who rent and by *income support for mortgage interest* (ISMI), for those who own.

Over the years there has been a degree of confusion about how to finance accommodation-related support services provided for vulnerable groups such as the frail elderly and people with mental health problems. The current debate on this topic is explored at the end of the section describing current housing benefit arrangements.

The reader should be aware that much of the content of this chapter is necessarily technical and descriptive. What is more, many of the arrangements are currently under review. Those with a general interest in housing finance may find it helpful to concentrate on the 'overview' principles and to regard the detail as reference material. What follows is intended to provide both a description and an analysis of current arrangements that will provide a clear point of departure for those who wish to follow the unfolding debate about how best to support vulnerable people so that they can be secure and active citizens.

---

1   Throughout this chapter references to income support include references to income based jobseekers' allowance. For a short description of the differences between jobseekers' allowance (JSA) and income support see note 4 below.

The system of housing benefit

The basics: an overview

Housing benefit provides weekly means-tested assistance to low-income households to help them pay their rent. It is a housing-tied Social Security allotment that takes the form of a 'rebate' to council tenants and an 'allowance' to housing association and private tenants. It currently provides rebates for nearly three million council tenants and allowances for some one and three quarter million housing association and private tenants. It should be thought of as a demand-side, 'consumption' subsidy designed to augment the real incomes of eligible claimants so that they are able to acquire access to a form of housing that is deemed to be appropriate to their needs.

Housing benefit helps some 4.5 million households in Great Britain meet the costs of renting their homes. The largest group of recipients is the elderly who account for some 40 per cent of the total. Lone parents account for about 20 per cent, and the long-term sick and the disabled each account for about 15 per cent of the total caseload. The remaining 10 per cent include the short-term sick, those in work on low incomes (other than lone parents), widows and widowers, and asylum seekers. Given the prominence of the current debate about 'social exclusion', it is an important social fact that the majority of claimants are dependent upon other Social Security benefits for the main source of income. Nearly 60 per cent of claimants live in council housing, just under 20 per cent rent from a registered social landlord, and just over 20 per cent from a private landlord.

Housing benefit provides a supplement to real income that is related to the claimant's actual housing costs and which will meet some proportion (up to 100 per cent) of those costs. Rebates for council tenants are deducted from the rent bill whilst rent allowances to private tenants are normally made by cheque which can be paid to the tenant or direct to the landlord (the decision is normally the tenant's). For private sector or housing association rent allowance claims, the benefit is paid in arrears either to the claimant or directly to the landlord.[2] Although, broadly speaking, it is the size of the rent that determines the level of benefit, this can be reduced for rent allowance cases if either the rent or the accommodation is deemed to be excessive.

The principle of the scheme is that claimants who receive income support/JSA[3] or who have very low incomes, are entitled, with certain exceptions, to rebates on the whole amount of their eligible rent. Claimants in this category are also entitled to a rebate on up to 100 per cent of their council tax.[4] In the case of those claiming

---

2 Housing benefit rent allowances are paid four weekly, in arrears, (From October 1996).
3 From October 1996 unemployment benefit and income support were replaced by the *jobseekers' allowance* (JSA). Unemployment benefit was a flat rate payment paid on the basis of the claimants national insurance record regardless of income whilst income support was a means-tested benefit paid to unemployed claimants if their income, including any unemployment benefit, was below the State minimum. These two benefits were merged in

benefit whose incomes are higher than this level a means-tested formula, referred to as a '*taper*', is used to determine the extent of benefit entitlement. The taper reduces the maximum benefit payable by a fixed percentage for every £1 of additional income over the income support level. Detailed calculations of housing benefit entitlement can be complex because the system deals with people in a wide variety of circumstances and with more than one tenure.

Housing benefit is administered by those local authorities that have responsibilities for providing housing services – i.e. district, metropolitan, London borough, and unitary councils. (See Chapter 5 for a brief description of the structure of local government.) Most of the cost, however, is met by central government via the Department of Social Security (DSS).

This cost has rocketed in recent years as government policy shifted its emphasis away from supply-side, general 'bricks and mortar' subsidies towards demand-side, targeted 'personal' assistance. DSS figures indicate that between the time that the current arrangements were established in 1988 and the mid-1990s, the number of housing benefit claimants increased from 4 million to 4.7 million and expenditure from less than £4 billion to more than £10 billion.

The principle: satisfying merit needs

The main structure of the current means-tested arrangements for housing benefit was established between 1983 and 1988 and is designed to help low income households to consume an 'adequate' level of housing service. This minimum level of service can be thought of as a *merit need*. By this we mean that, for economic and humanitarian reasons, society has decided that a certain level of housing should be available to all irrespective of their ability to pay. The intention is that those whose incomes are too low to give them access to this minimum level should qualify for some form of assistance. Given its purpose, the following question of principle arises: 'Is housing benefit an aspect of housing finance or Social Security finance?'

---

to JSA. Consequently there are two types of JSA, 'income based' for those with incomes which are lower than the income support level, and 'contributions based' for those who qualify for a flat rate benefit payment based on their national insurance contributions regardless of income. The system works to define the qualifying poverty benchmark for those needing help because of unemployment on the same basis as income support claimants. This means that they receive the same amount of income augmentation and access to other underlying benefits including housing benefit as they would if they were on income support. The only practical difference for someone on JSA rather than on income support is that, if they fail to meet their obligations to actively seek employment, they may, at the discretion of the DSS, lose their rights to JSA. Throughout this chapter references to income support include entitlement to income based jobseekers' allowance.

4   The last Conservative Budget restricted council tax benefit so that claimants with property in bands F, G and H have their benefit restricted to that of band E, from April 1998. This was implemented by the incoming Labour government but with the concession that it would only apply to new claims.

Throughout this book we have made the point that the best way of appreciating the nature and scope of housing finance is to understand the purposes to which financial resources are put. These are summarised in simple diagrammatic form in Figure 2.1 (Chapter 2). Reference to this diagram indicates that, along with *provision* and *management, redistribution* might be considered to be one of the functions of the system of housing finance. However, it must be stressed that, unlike provision and management, redistribution should *not* be regarded as a primary function of the system. As the chapters so far have made clear, housing finance is primarily concerned with the provision and use of the capital and revenue resources that enable residential property to be produced and managed. Redistribution is concerned with income augmentation and, as such, is arguably more a matter of welfare policy than of housing finance. The main reason for redistributing real incomes is to help low income households meet those financial outgoings that are necessary to enjoy some agreed minimum standard of housing provision.

Economists have developed the concept of *merit needs* to help explain why the State may intervene to provide certain goods and services directly or to redistribute disposable incomes so as to increase the consumption of certain goods and services provided by the market. It is argued that some things are so meritorious (central to a civilised life or to the general national interest) that, even if an unregulated free market system *could* provide them, the State *should* nevertheless involve itself to ensure that a sufficient quantity of an appropriate quality at an affordable price is, in fact, provided. In contemporary Britain, for example, there is a general consensus that education, medical treatment and shelter are so crucial to the maintenance of a worthwhile life and an effective economy, that all citizens, including those with little means, should have access to some minimum level of schooling, health care, and accommodation. Without State involvement there is no doubt that the market would provide facilities in these areas, but the problem is that such provision may not be sufficient to meet all needs, or be of an appropriate standard or type, or be in the right place, or be of a price that all in need could afford. In other words, without State involvement, it is likely that there would be a degree of *under-consumption* of these 'merit goods and services': under-consumption that is, in comparison with that which society regards as being necessary and appropriate for the needs of a modern, advanced economy.

The history: from 'discretionary rebates' to 'mandatory benefits'

For many years local authorities have had the power to implement rent rebate arrangements. The Housing Act 1930 empowered council landlords to charge lower rents to poorer tenants but did not require them to do so or provide any Exchequer assistance to underpin such voluntary schemes. No such assistance was provided until 1972 which meant that between 1930 and 1972, any authority operating its discretionary power to provide rent rebates, funded them by imposing higher rents on its better-off tenants, or by utilising its general housing subsidy for the purpose, or by transferring monies from the rate fund, or by a combination of some or all of these methods.

The lack of special funding, together with the administrative complexities involved in operating such schemes meant that, in the early years, not many were established. Indeed, the very idea was unpopular with many councillors and better-off tenants who feared that such schemes would attract the 'wrong type' of tenant onto their estates. After 1936, when each authority was required to operate a unified housing revenue account, rent pooling became practicable. For most authorities rent pooling became the preferred way of providing affordable dwellings for poorer tenants.

Rent pooling operated as an internal quasi-market and allowed housing managers to make use of the significant rent differentials that existed between newly-built dwellings with relatively high associated historic costs, and older dwellings with relatively low associated historic costs. It is important to understand that these differential rents were more the result of differential historic costs than differential utilities. That is, an older dwelling had a lower burden of debt associated with it: as a 'home' it may well have functioned more-or-less as adequately as a newer property. The existence of these differentials allowed the local authority landlord to allocate the older, cheaper stock to its poorer tenants without providing them with a significantly inferior home. In this way, allocating officers were able to give low-income households access to council housing without the provision of a scheme of rent rebates.

From the 1960s onwards, the case for rebates was, however, continually being discussed. Many Conservative politicians were ideologically opposed to *bricks and mortar* subsidies that produced 'social' housing with 'low' rents for everyone irrespective of need. Rather than provision in kind, they favoured fiscal welfare arrangements, such as rent rebates: they saw these as offering a way of raising rents towards market levels and, at the same time, targeting scarce public funds on those in greatest housing need. These ideas were increasingly articulated in Conservative Party circles and they had a significant influence on the drafting of the Bill that eventually became the Housing Finance Act 1972.

The 1972 legislation introduced into the public sector the concept of 'fair rents' together with a system of deficit subsidies and rent rebates and allowances. The legislation's intention was simultaneously to raise rents and reduce general housing subsidy. A national rent rebates scheme was introduced in recognition of the need to provide assistance to low-income tenants to help bridge the gap between 'fair rents' and their ability to pay them. As well as rebates to council tenants, authorities were required to set up rent allowance schemes for private sector and housing association tenants living in unfurnished accommodation in their areas. Running in parallel with these arrangements was a system of rate rebates, which was introduced by the Rating Act 1966 and modified by the Local Government Act 1974.

The initial mandatory rebate arrangements were administered by the Department of Health and Social Security (DHSS), clearly indicating that they were seen as an aspect of welfare (income augmentation) rather than as part of the housing service. The whole arrangement was complicated by the fact that, from April 1974, rebates and allowances were not payable to recipients of supplementary benefit, the predecessor of income support. From that date the DHSS was required to assist such recipients with their rent costs by including the full unrebated charge in the calculation of entitlement, and they then recouped the rebate element back from the local authorities. This meant that, at that time (up to 1983) there were two distinct schemes running alongside each other which calculated entitlement in different ways (through rebates and allowances and supplementary benefits), and difficulties arose in as much as they overlapped, so that some people could qualify for either. As the social benefits withdrawal taper operated somewhat differently from the rebate taper, that is, the two means-test calculations were not done on the same basis, those who qualified for both housing rebate and supplementary benefit had the problem of calculating which of the two claims generated, for them, the most assistance.

In 1981, the Department of the Environment published a consultation paper[5] that pointed to the need to reform the entire system by introducing a unified housing benefit to be administered by one authority. The administrative arrangements were partially reformed by the Social Security and Housing Benefits Act 1982, but a properly unified system of housing benefit was not introduced until 1988.

Partial reform. As we have seen, up to 1983 the rebate system effectively comprised two distinctly separate benefit schemes, one of which targeted supplementary benefit claimants (the forerunner of income support), and the other aimed at claimants whose incomes fell below the supplementary benefit level. The operation of these arrangements was simplified in 1983 when local authorities became responsible for the administration of both 'halves' of the system. However, the DHSS (now DSS), retained responsibility for the formal procedure of certificating supplementary benefit claimants, so that they could go to the local authority to claim entitlement to maximum rebates in respect of their housing costs.

The establishment of the modern system. The system introduced in 1983 addressed some of the problems experienced with its predecessor. These criticisms related mainly to administrative complexity and long delays in benefit being paid out to claimants. When under the new 'unified' system, local authorities were found to be struggling under their increased workload, and frequent adjustments to the system had to be introduced, claimants quickly found that the problems the scheme had been designed to tackle did not disappear. Other pressures on the system were linked with rising unemployment during the 1980s, which was accompanied by a rise in the numbers applying for welfare benefits in general. The arrangements clearly needed further reform.

---

5   *Assistance with Housing Costs*, DOE, 1981.

The inevitable overhaul of the 1983 system of housing benefit came with the 1986 Social Security Act, the provisions of which were implemented in 1988. Along with housing benefit, the Social Security Act introduced major revisions to all the main welfare benefits. In addition to the comprehensive review of housing benefit, supplementary benefit was replaced with *income support*. Single payments, which had in the past assisted tenants meet the costs of buying essential furniture or paying deposits on rented accommodation, were replaced with loans from the social fund; and family income supplement was replaced with family credit. Family credit was paid to families with children who were working 16 hours a week or more. It was designed to boost weekly income from employment up to a fixed amount and was received by some 650,000 households prior to its reform in 1999. The maximum benefit payment increased with family size and was payable where the family income (i.e. earnings) was no greater than the income threshold (£81.95, April 2000). If the income was more than the threshold then the maximum benefit was tapered away.

Throughout the 1990s there was talk of following the practice of some other countries by converting family credit, which is delivered through the benefit system, into an earned income tax credit, which would be delivered through PAYE income tax arrangements. This reform was eventually announced in the 1998 Budget, which announced the introduction of *the working families' tax credit* in 1999. These changed arrangements are in line with the Labour government's philosophy of weakening the 'dependency culture' by linking, wherever possible, the receipt of benefit with employment.[6]

This new arrangement is operated by the Inland Revenue (from October 1999) and is designed to end a situation in which one Department of State (the DSS) distributes support to people in poverty while, at the same, another Department of State (the Inland Revenue) charges taxes to people on relatively low incomes. Under the new arrangement the credit will be offset against tax on pay from 2000, which means that it will be received through the pay packet rather than be received as a benefit cheque. The old family credit was usually paid to the mother whereas the new credit will be claimed by whichever parent is in paid employment. Under the old regime, those in receipt of family credit were automatically entitled to health benefits such as free prescriptions, under the new scheme the passport to fringe benefits will only apply to tax credits beneficiaries

---

6   Despite its attractiveness to ministers, the reform might be said to have the drawback of confusing the tax system, which is designed to collect revenue, with the welfare system, which is designed to disperse collected revenues to the poor. It also has a number of practical implications as family credit was normally paid to the mother as a Giro cheque and focused on immediate needs while the idea of a tax credit implies that the benefit is made as a tax adjustment at the end of the year to the working partner. To avoid the fear that the working families' tax credit will end the principle of independent taxation (i.e. the benefit going to the working father in the form of a tax adjustment rather than directly to the mother in the form of a benefits cheque), the Chancellor has made it clear that when the reform is fully operational, families will have their credit paid through an adjustment to their pay packet, or as a six monthly tax rebate.

with the lowest incomes. [7] Disability working allowance is replaced by disabled person's tax credit so that working people with disabilities are helped in a similar way to those receiving the working families' tax credit. The new terminology, '*working families tax credit*', has been consciously thought through. It is symbolic of the government's political commitment to shift the poverty debate away from notions of *unemployment*, *dependency* and *benefit* towards notions of *work*, *independence* and *taxation*. It reflects a political consensus that relief from tax is more in line with a policy of 'welfare to work' than is the payment of benefits. Although both a system of tax credits and a system of welfare benefits are tailored to take account of individual circumstances, the latter is symbolic of a 'dependency culture' whilst the former symbolises a 'culture of work and personal responsibility'.

The 1998 budget reforms also brought in additional help for people on income support with children under eleven years of age. This extra child support allowance recognises that there is not much difference between the costs of bringing up children under eleven as compared with older dependent children. From April 2000 all allowances for children under 16 have been equalised by raising the lower rates for younger children up to the higher rates for older children. This additional support will be included in the working families tax credit, housing benefit and council tax benefit allowances.

The introduction of the community charge (poll tax) in 1990 saw the end of an integrated housing benefit that dealt with both rent and local tax. Community charge benefit was introduced as a separate benefit requiring a separate claim. When the community charge was replaced in 1993 by the council tax this split continued with community charge benefit being replaced with council tax benefit.[8]

Claiming housing benefit

Under current arrangements, housing benefit can be claimed in one of two ways, depending on whether or not the applicant is in receipt of income support. Entitlement to income support establishes an official definition of 'poverty' and, in so doing, produces a welfare needs baseline that is used to administer a range of entitlements including housing benefit. Where a claimant receives income support they may qualify for full housing benefit and in such cases the Benefits Agency of the DSS notifies the local authority who arrange to pay housing benefit from the

---

7　Family credit recipients were automatically entitled to health benefits such as free prescriptions, help towards dental treatment and opticians' fees. Under the new arrangements only those WFTC recipients with the lowest incomes will qualify for fringe benefits. Families on WFTC with earnings of more than £217 per week (1999/00), will no longer be passported to free health benefits.

8　Community charge benefit was a separate benefit requiring, strictly, a separate claim although, in practice, authorities usually assessed both benefits from a single claim form. Technically, a claim for one was not a claim for the other. When council tax benefit replaced the community charge benefit, this arrangement continued.

date income support commences. Claimants not in receipt of income support have to apply directly to their local authority that then calculates the amount of housing benefit to which they are entitled. In such cases payments cannot predate the application unless 'good cause' can be shown as to why the claim was not made earlier.[9]

Determining eligibility

From their inception in the Tudor period, all poverty relief measures have had to address the issue of eligibility. Eligibility has always been tested against qualifying criteria relating to residency, need, and income.[10]

Claimants with the appropriate residency qualifications will have their entitlements to housing benefit calculated against criteria that are guided by notions of *reasonableness* and *appropriateness*. These criteria are translated into rather complex, and constantly changing, regulations that are used to prevent landlords exploiting the system by charging 'excessive' rents and claimants from exploiting the system by living in accommodation that is 'unnecessarily' lavish and expensive.

In this context, 'reasonableness' is judged by considering whether or not the rents they are seeking help with are reasonable when compared with local rent levels. If the claimant is a council or housing association tenant the rent is normally accepted as being reasonable. The eligible rent establishes the maximum amount of benefit that can be paid. What proportion of this maximum is judged to be appropriate for the claimant to receive will depend on the household's circumstances. These circumstances are judged by reference to household needs, incomes and savings.

Reasonableness and eligible rent

Housing benefit is paid on the *eligible rent,* which may well differ from the actual commercial rent being charged by the landlord. Service charges relating to the property's maintenance qualify as 'eligible' so long as they are reasonable, but charges for personal services, such as individual cleaning, medical care, etc., do not qualify.

9   The 'good cause' must have lasted throughout the relevant period. For guidance to a comprehensive explanation as what is accepted as good cause see *Claim in Time: Time Limits in Social Security Law*, Third Edition, Martin Partington, LAG, 1994.

10   Early Poor Law rules were designed to restrict relief to the 'deserving poor' of the parish. In the Victorian period, all but the destitute were discouraged from claiming help by restricting relief for able-bodied people to a place in a harsh and stigmatising parish workhouse. After the Second World War, the responsibility for provision moved from the parish to the welfare state and as a result, national rather than local residency qualifications were applied. The welfare state culture also brought with it an attitude shift away from the idea that benefits are a form of charity for the deserving poor, towards the idea that they are a form of Social Security entitlement, available to all citizens if and when they need it.

Eligible rent comprises the basic rent for the dwelling together with allowable service charges. Not all charges made by landlords in respect of services provided are allowable. For example, individual cleaning charges, the cost of any meals provided in conjunction with the tenancy or electricity costs are not eligible. Others, such as a share of the costs of cleaning communal areas and maintenance charges made to keep the accommodation habitable, are admissible. There is a continuing debate about the extent to which support services to special needs groups should qualify for housing benefit cover. Some argue that the benefit should be restricted to the provision of facilities that relate to the adequacy of the accommodation as a dwelling, while others argue that the ethos of 'care in the community' requires housing agencies to provide services that are connected to the special personal needs of such groups as the elderly, the disabled, and those with learning difficulties.[11] The question of how best to fund support services is currently under review and discussed more fully below (see below section *Funding support services*).

Unreasonable or 'excessive' rents are not supported by the scheme. The eligible rent has to be 'reasonable' in comparison with local rent levels and the housing benefit system makes a point of not contributing to an element of rent that is judged to be above the market level. It is possible for a particular asking rent to be judged unreasonable even though it is well below the average. This might be the case for a dwelling in a very poor state of repair or yet to be modernised with no bathroom. Market rents, which, nevertheless, are exceptionally high because the accommodation is of a luxury standard at the very top end of the market, will also be deemed unreasonable and restricted.

In an attempt to stem the growing bill for housing benefit, a system of payment capping for rent allowances was introduced in 1996 to create an incentive to claimants to seek out and negotiate less expensive accommodation. Under this arrangement, in addition to assessing the market rents for individual properties, the Rent Service[12] has to advise the local authority of what is known as the *local reference rent (LRR)*. The LRR is the mid-point of a range of rents charged for similar dwellings in a locality and represents the maximum rent that can be charged without the claimant losing a proportion of the benefit. In other words, since 1996, housing benefit is granted in full (100 per cent of rent) only up to a median market average[13] for that type of dwelling in the locality. This means that

---

11 During 1996 the Secretary of State for Social Security considered removing the right to the use of housing benefit to meet service charge costs, but eventually backed down in response to fierce lobbying.

12 The Rent Service, formerly the Rent Officer Service, was established as an Executive Agency of DETR on 1 November 1999. The service only operates in England. In Wales it is still called the Rent Officer Service and it has not yet been re-structured. The service in Scotland also operates as a centralised civil service function. Rent officers have independent statutory status. The service is discussed more fully in Chapter 16.

13 The LRR equates to the 'trimmed' median average: that is, the mid-point of an 'appropriate' spread of rents for that property type. In some areas there may be a relatively large number of luxurious dwellings let to wealthy people for very high rents. In such circumstances a trimmed rather than a true average is used to fix the LRR.

full housing benefit may now not cover the true market rent,[14] so that for some households claiming for the first time, or who move and reclaim, the assistance does not meet their full rent outgoings even if they are on income support. The local reference rent restrictions do not apply to certain specialist *exempt accommodation* in the voluntary sector where the landlord provides care, support or supervision. [15]

The maximum rent rule

Of course, the LRR may not be the same as the rent that the landlord is asking (*the contractual rent*), nor may it be the same as what the rent officer would regard as a reasonable market rent for that type of property, in that condition, in that area (*the property specific rent*). This means that the LRR may or may not represent the lowest rent calculation. If the landlord is asking for less than the LRR (if the contractual rent is below the LRR), then it is this lower figure that is used to set the maximum allowable rent. Similarly, if in the rent officer's judgement, the market rent for the particular property is less than the LRR (if the property specific rent is below the LRR), then again it is this lower figure that is used to set the maximum allowable rent.

Example 1:
Contractual rent	£80
Property specific rent	£70
Local reference rent	£75
• Maximum rent	£70

Example 2:
Contractual rent	£95
Property specific rent	£85
Local reference rent	£75
• Maximum rent	£75

Example 3:
Contractual rent	£60
Property specific rent	£85
Local reference rent	£75
• Maximum rent	£60

---

14 When first introduced, the regulations allowed authorities to meet 50 per cent of the difference between these 'average' rents and the actual market rent paid. This discretion is now withdrawn.

15 Exempt accommodation includes resettlement hostels funded by government grants or accommodation provided by housing associations, not-for-profit bodies or registered charities. Exempt accommodation can still be subject to rent capping, but at the discretion of the local authority to whatever they judge to be reasonable, rather than by the rent officer valuations. Rent officers still make valuations for these rents but these would only determine the maximum subsidy paid by the DSS to the local authority. The authority is entitled to use the Rent Service valuations to inform its judgement of what is reasonable.

In cases such as Example 2, some tenants still receive a 50 per cent top-up between LRR and property specific rent. In cases such as Example 3, the rent officer would not give the figures: they would simply state that the asked for rent was not unreasonably high. From this we can see that the LRR is only one of several possible rent officer rent limits and the limit set could be lower than the LRR. It should be noted, however, that in spite of any rent officer restriction, the authority has discretionary powers to restrict the rent still further or, in exceptional circumstances, increase the restricted rent up to a maximum of the (actual) contractual rent.

Pre-tenancy determination

Since 1996 claimants do not need to apply formally for benefit in order to have their eligible rent determined. They can receive a determination before agreeing to a tenancy. This involves submitting a form to the local authority, signed both by the landlord and the would-be tenant. Until 1997, landlords were not allowed to apply on their own for a 'test' calculation, but the Housing Act 1996 enabled them to seek pre-tenancy determinations of maximum eligible rents for benefit purposes. Once a determination is made it remains binding on the local authority for a year.

Appropriateness and the assessment of need and income

The broad guiding principle for determining entitlement is that the rent should be *appropriate* to the household's needs as well as *reasonable* by reference to local rents. The eligible rent fixes the maximum benefit payable but not necessarily the actual benefit paid. This has to be 'appropriate' to the particular circumstances of the claimant. Size is seen as a relevant criterion for all claims referred to the rent officer. Where a family is deemed to be over accommodated the rent officer will set a notional market rent for accommodation which would be of the appropriate size, known as a *size related rent*. These rules are particularly stringent with respect to people under 25 years of age. From October 1996 the regulations were altered to assume that young, single people under the age of 25 only have a need to occupy bed-sit accommodation. The new rules mean that, for the under 25s, benefit is no longer paid on the actual rent, but only on a figure that equates with the median average local market rent for *shared accommodation* (i.e. with separate bedroom and shared kitchen/ bathroom). In effect this means that the government now regards a 'bed-sit' rent as the limit of support that it is reasonable to give to young people between the ages of 16 and 25. Further benefit restrictions apply to 16 and 17 year olds who, whilst entitled to housing benefit on the same terms as others aged under 25, can only claim income support and jobseekers' allowance whilst out of work in very limited circumstances.[16]

---

16 The change disqualifying most 16 and 17 year olds from income support was introduced in September 1988. In October 1996 on the introduction of JSA, the rules were consolidated and re-codified for the unemployed. Some in this age group can still qualify, but not those, generally, who just leave school without a job. Those with disabilities or who are undergoing secondary education, but who are estranged from their parents, are two examples of those who still qualify.

There is evidence that these rules have caused a shortage of accommodation for this age group as some landlords now discriminate against the under twenty-fives[17]. Critics argue that these restrictions, together with the rules for jobseekers' allowance aggravates problems of homelessness, child prostitution, and drug abuse, and is encouraging begging on the streets.

The 1996 Budget proposed to extend the 'bed-sit' rule to every single claimant under the age of 60.[18] However, the government's Social Security Advisory Committee counselled against this proposed extension and the idea was abandoned by the in-coming Labour government in 1997.

Calculating entitlement: comparing the household's income with its needs

In determining what counts as 'appropriate' much depends on how the household's assessed weekly income compares with the amount they need to live on. For this reason a parallel assessment of the income needed by the household to meet normal non-housing costs is made. This amount is assumed to vary from household to household according to various qualifying special needs, and is called '*the applicable amount*'. The applicable amount is determined by reference to different allowances for single people under 25, single people 25 and over, couples with or without children and other circumstances, such as whether they are of pensionable age, single parent families, disabled or carers. This applicable amount is compared with the household's assessed income to determine the amount it is considered reasonable for that family to contribute towards the rent. The family's appropriate contribution is determined by a fixed percentage of their income that is in excess of their non-housing needs (the applicable amount). Ordinarily, the benefit payable will simply be the maximum rent payable less their assessed contribution. However, where there are other adults in the household, other than the claimant's dependent family, such as their adult children, it is assumed that they will be contributing to the rent.

Anyone regarded as a member of the household who is neither the claimant's partner nor a dependent child will be a '*non-dependent*'. In such cases 'non-dependent charges' are deducted from the claimant's maximum rent. Deductions are made on the basis of a sliding scale,[19] except in certain circumstances, e.g. where the claimant is registered blind. The total deductions made in respect to non-dependents may be sufficiently high so as to wipe out the claimant's entitlement to benefit completely. All benefit will be lost, even if the claimant's

---

17 DETR (1999) *Housing Benefit and the Private Rented Sector*, p72.
18 Among others, this reform would have affected the consumption interests of that growing group of people whose marriages have broken down. Although it would not have applied to an individual who is a lone parent, it would have affected the entitlement of some quarter of a million claimants.
19 The amount currently deducted varies from £7.20 a week to £46.35 a week for a non-dependent earning more than £255 a week (1999/00).

income is assessed as being insufficient to contribute to the rent, if the total non-dependent charges exceed the maximum rent. Obviously these deductions give considerable savings to the Exchequer. The temptation for government to increase these charges each year by more than inflation has proved irresistible. These rules only apply to household members. Special rules cover multiple households living in the same property such as boarders, sub-tenants, and others who pay their rent separately.

If any rent remains after non-dependent charges have been deducted from the maximum rent, an assessment is made of the claimant's ability to make a contribution towards the remainder. To assess the claimant's contribution a comparison is made between the income they require to cover their non-housing costs, their applicable amount, and their actual income. If their assessed income is less than or equal to their applicable amount then they are deemed to have insufficient income to be able to contribute and so will receive the *maximum benefit* (i.e. the maximum rent less any non-dependent charges). If the claimant's income assessment exceeds their applicable amount their maximum benefit is progressively reduced. In other words, the higher the household's income, the less its entitlement to housing benefit.

Income support and income-based JSA claimants. Claimants in receipt of these benefits are assumed to have no income (i.e. zero). The result is that their assessed income will always be less than their applicable amount, automatically qualifying them to maximum benefit. The means-test is carried out by the Benefits Agency when the claim is made for the income support/JSA, since these benefits are themselves means-tested. All other claimants not entitled to these benefits have their means-test carried out by the local authority. The point we need to emphasise here is that income support is _not_ intended to cover outgoings related to *rent* or *council tax* charges. The need for *income support/JSA* provides access to further benefits related to these outgoings. These parallel benefits are dealt with by local councils through systems of *housing benefit* and *council tax benefit*.

Other claimants. For claimants who do not receive income support an assessment is made of their capital and income which is available to contribute towards their rent. This assessment takes the form of a 'means-test' that is administered by way of an application form. If the claimant's weekly disposable income is equal to, or less than, the eligible costs, they will receive the maximum benefit, i.e. the maximum rent less any non-dependent charges.

Claimants with capital and savings valued at more than £16,000 are not entitled to housing benefit. Capital and savings are valued the same way as they are for income support.[20] Savings and capital valued at less than £3,000 are disregarded.

---

20 However, for income support and income based JSA claimants the savings limit is £8,000 rather than £16,000. Claimants with savings between £8,000 and £16,000 have to apply directly to the local authority as an ordinary claim.

All actual income earned on capital and savings is also disregarded; however, every £250 of capital and savings between £3,000 and £16,000 is assumed to produce a nominal £1 per week which is carried forward to the income assessment.

The income assessment starts with net earnings from employment, other benefit entitlements (including pensions) and rental or unearned income, including nominal income earned on savings. The assessment is based on the aggregated income of the claimant and partner net of income tax, national insurance and 50 per cent of any contributions made to a private or company pensions scheme. Some income is disregarded, referred to as the *'earnings disregard'*. This means that the system allows a certain level of earned income before operating the withdrawal taper. The current earnings disregard is £5 a week for single people and somewhat more for other categories of claimant.[21]

If the claimant's income, including any assessed income from capital, exceeds their applicable amount then their maximum benefit is progressively reduced in line with the taper, which is set at 65p for each £1 of income in excess of the applicable amount (65 per cent). So for example, if a claimant were paying rent at £70 per week, and his or her income exceeded the allowance and premium level by £20, the housing benefit payable would be £57, after a deduction of £13 had been made, representing 65 per cent of the £20 excess. If income exceeded the allowance and premium level by £110, this would be the point when no benefit would be paid, as the 65 per cent deduction exceeds the rent level itself. These deductions are akin to a high marginal rate of income tax and, as such, create a problem referred to as the 'poverty trap' (see below).

Reviews and appeals

Claimants can appeal against any determination made by the authority under a procedure called *the right to a review*. This procedure applies to any determination and can be requested on *any grounds*. Such a request has to be made by the claimant within six weeks of being notified of the decision. The authority can also review any of its decisions at *any time* if it appears that there has been a change in circumstances, they have wrongly applied the regulations, or they have new factual evidence. The local authority should complete all reviews within 14 days. Explanations of the outcome must be given. Following an 'any grounds' review the claimant may request a further review within four weeks of being notified. An oral hearing must then be held within six weeks by a review board made up of elected members. Once the board has declared its findings either side can then only appeal on points of law or breach of natural justice and these have to be

---

21 Earned income disregards are £25 for lone parents, £15 for carers and the disabled and £10 for a couple. Some claimants can claim what is known as 'the child care disregard'. Working lone parents, or couples where both are in paid work, and paying for child care, are able to have some of these child care costs ignored in the income calculation.

heard by the high court. From April 2001 the procedure for further review will be replaced by a right of appeal to the independent Social Security appeal tribunal service. Appeals against decisions of the tribunal on points of law lie with the Social Security commissioners and then to the court of appeal.

The 'poverty trap'

All means-tested benefits tend to create the problem of a *poverty trap*. Such a trap exists when entitlement is withdrawn as earnings increase. It is seen as a problem because the withdrawal of entitlement acts as a disincentive to seek work related advancement. The real income effect of an increase in earned income is diminished by a combination of deductions and withdrawals. The deductions include income tax payments and national insurance contributions. The withdrawals include working families' tax credit, housing benefit, and council tax benefit. [22]

The statutory deductions combined with the tapering off of benefit entitlements creates the so-called 'poverty trap' by diminishing the effect of any increases in earned income. The loss of benefit resulting from the withdrawal tapers has a negative *real income effect* that acts as a kind of 'poor person's income tax'. The *poverty trap* is pernicious in so far as this marginal 'withdrawal rate' (benefit loss), is high in comparison with the real income tax rates of average and high earners. Department of Social Security figures show that in 1997, in the extreme case, the benefit taper was as high as 96.7 per cent resulting in some households getting an increase in net real income of only 3p for every extra £1 earned from employment.

By the year 2001, the financial position of many low-income households will be improved by the combined effects of the minimum wage, reforms to tax and national insurance, increased child benefit payments and the working families tax credit. Taxation reforms include a restructuring of national insurance contributions, the introduction in 1999 of an initial ten pence rate of income tax (on the first £1,500 of taxable income) and from April 2001 a 'children's tax credit' for families with dependent children. The children's tax credit will be worth up to £8 per week but will be tapered away from families where at least one of the partners is a higher rate taxpayer.

After the reforms have been introduced, any gross increase in take-home pay of those in low paid employment will still be reduced by the combined effects of income taxation, national insurance payments and the combined WFTC and housing benefit withdrawals. However, it is important to realise that these reforms will not eliminate the poverty trap.[23] In some respects, the 1999 reforms help to

---

22 The housing benefit taper is set at 65 per cent of marginal net income in 1998 and the council tax benefit taper at 20 per cent, giving a combined withdrawal effect of 85 per cent for every £1 earned above the applicable amount.
23 See Wilcox, 1998b for examples of the effects of the reforms on different household make-ups. Although the reforms will reduce the number of claimants trapped on the highest withdrawal rates (i.e. in excess of 70 per cent), there will, however, still be some claimants entitled to WFTC, housing benefit and council tax benefit for whom the combined effect will be a reduction from 96.7 per cent to 92.8 per cent.

underline the lack of vertical equity in the tax and benefit system. Because the WFTC is classified relief from taxation, then its withdrawal has more of the form of a marginal tax rate. For the poorest workers in society this marginal rate is still likely to be high compared with the rates charged to higher income groups.[24]

In addition to the poverty trap the additional costs associated with moving off benefit and into work produce further disincentives. In an attempt to lessen the disincentive effect *extended payments* were introduced in April 1996 whereby housing benefit (and council tax benefit) is extended into the first four weeks of work. This effectively eases the transition into employment by smoothing over the gap created by payment of wages or salary in arrears. It also guards against interruptions in benefit should the job fall through for some reason.

Housing benefit and public expenditure

Although reasonableness and appropriateness are meant to be the underlying principles of the assessment regulations, it is clear that some of the more recent eligibility restrictions have been partly motivated by the Treasury's desire to cap the growing bill for housing benefit.[25]

To a large extent the cost of housing benefit falls on the Exchequer. Expenditure on rent allowances is reimbursed at 95 per cent by central government in the form of rebate subsidy. They are not allowed to claim it all back because the government wishes to provide an incentive to the authorities to administer the system 'tightly'. The administration costs, as against the benefit payments, are reimbursed partly in the form of a specific grant and partly in the calculation of revenue support grant. The subsidy on rent rebates is currently an element in the overall HRA subsidy (see Chapter 11).[26] Central government can penalise authorities deemed to be operating the system in a way that is judged to be inefficient by limiting or withdrawing subsidy.

Housing benefit, because it can offer tenants greater purchasing power in the rented housing market, will widen choice and stimulate consumption. Around one third of tenants in social housing rely on income support from the DSS, and are entitled to maximum housing benefit. Two thirds of all social housing tenants receive some level of housing benefit, and in 1989-90 the cost to government of this level of support was put at £4,245 million. In the late 1980s ministers seemed

---

24 Although the reforms will reduce the number of claimants trapped on the highest withdrawal rates (i.e. in excess of 70 per cent), there will, however, still be some claimants for whom the combined effect will be a reduction from 96.7 per cent to 92.8 per cent.

25 Social Security expenditure dwarfs all other expenditure categories. This means that it is always under pressure to be controlled. In particular, governments always have an eye on the fastest rising item within the Social Security budget at any one time. Hence, State pension reforms in the 1980s, housing benefit in the mid-1990s, and disability benefits in the late 1990s.

26 The government is currently giving consideration to removing rent rebates from the HRA and to place them elsewhere from 2001.

enthusiastic to push the rents for social housing upwards towards market levels (see discussions in Chapters 4 and 11). They knew that their combination of housing finance reforms would increase rents but argued publicly that this would not matter because, for the needy, those rents would be paid through housing benefit. They argued that switching subsidies from *bricks and mortar* to *people* would be more efficient because resources would be better targeted on those who really needed them.

Before the introduction of the 1989 rent deregulation measures, some 60 per cent of tenants were on housing benefit. Of new tenants coming in 1996, the figure was 83 per cent. In 1995 it was estimated that some 4.7 million households who do not own their own homes received housing benefit (*Roof*, March/April 1995). This figure represented about 12 per cent of the Social Security budget. It was estimated that, if the system were not revised, then this proportion would rise to 15 per cent by 1998.

The higher rents were brought in on the back of housing benefit but, eventually, the growing benefit bill brought about a change in government thinking. As the Conservative government's housing reforms added more and more to the consumption costs of social housing, the assumption that housing benefit should 'take the strain' was challenged. In 1994, the DoE's chief economist, Norman Glass told the Harry Simpson lecture that *'there is now a real issue about how much further the process of reducing the disparity between social rents and market rents should continue'* (*Roof*, November/December 1994, p22). This statement signalled a radical change in policy (see Chapters 11 and 13).

By the mid-1990s, the annual bill for housing benefit had topped £10 billion, reflecting just how much the public expenditure burden for supporting low income households in need of housing subsidy had shifted from the Environment Department to the DSS. It was clear that the savings made by cutting capital grants had brought about higher demands on the Social Security expenditure programme. In any one year, the cuts in general housing grant were more than proportional to the additional benefit claim bringing a net saving to the Exchequer. However, while the cutting of a capital grant represents a one-off saving to the Exchequer, the resultant addition to revenue expenditure is re-occurring and there comes a point at which the accumulated revenue costs outweigh the initial capital savings, so that over time the policy adds to total public expenditure. The issue arose partly because of a failure to calculate the displacement costs from one department of State to another and partly because of a failure to calculate the longer-term revenue consequences of short-run capital cuts. Such a policy might be termed *disconnected short-termism*. It is a basic principle of financial management that current capital decisions have future revenue consequences (refer to Chapter 1). The Labour government's Comprehensive Spending Review sought to address the question of *disconnected short-termism* by requiring the various spending departments to cross-reference the revenue consequences of their spending plans. However, interrelated problems of Social Security have proved to be particularly complicated, and were not resolved by the time the Review was published in the summer of 1998.

By the mid-1990s the additional expenditure on housing benefit led the government to change its housing policy in two ways. Firstly, it relaxed its ideological commitment to put upward pressure on social housing rent levels. Second, it began to bring in measures to restrict the eligibility criteria for housing benefit claimants. Just after the November Budget in 1994 the Social Security Secretary announced plans to introduce a cap on the rents eligible for housing benefit in an attempt to control its burgeoning cost to the Exchequer.[27] This and other measures designed to limited eligibility to benefit are described above.

Some commentators have made the point that control systems that depend on benchmarks can put upward pressure on the starting average. As Paul Walentowicz suggests, the reforms will not save the Exchequer any money if below average rents (on poorer quality accommodation) are pushed up by landlords who see the official average as the going rate. (*Roof*, January-February 1995, p10.). With RSL rents still below market rents the impact of the new rules falls hardest on the tenants in the private sector.

Pressure for future reforms

Recent changes in the housing benefit arrangements have tended to be *ad hoc* and introduced with the primary intention of limiting the burden on the public purse. The Chartered Institute of Housing believes that the regime now needs overhauling with a view to making it simpler to understand and easier to administer.[28] One issue that is currently under serious review relates to the question of how best to fund the provision of support services.

Funding support services

Over recent years, many innovative schemes have been developed to provide 'special needs' accommodation for a wide range of vulnerable people. Housing schemes often provide support services as an integral part of the accommodation packages. These additional facilities are targeted on such groups as the frail

---

27 David Curry, Housing Minister (in Hansard, 25 October 1994) reported that average housing benefit payable in 1994 to various tenures was as follows: council £28.94 per week; housing association £35.75; private rented £46.80. He reported that the average weekly rent had risen from £28.10 in 1990 to £36.60 in 1994 for council tenants, but because of housing benefit, the real rise was only £1.30 – from £15.60 to £16.90. These figures relate to households whose incomes are less than £10,000 and equates to 13 per cent of net income for such a household.

28 The Institute's proposals for reform have been brought together in a working paper entitled *Improving and Simplifying Housing Benefit*, December 1998. Further information can be obtained from the Institute's Policy Unit at Coventry.

elderly, those with mental health problems, ex-offenders, the young 'at risk' homeless, victims of domestic violence, and those recovering from drug addiction. The current provision of sheltered and supported housing seeks to help this wide range of vulnerable people to maintain stable and independent lives in the community by providing a range of specialist support services. Such services vary in scope and intensity and include general counselling and advice, assistance with administrative affairs, services provided by wardens, and liaison work with other agencies and individuals responsible for the person's welfare.

Councils and RSLs raise some of the money for running sheltered homes and other supported housing projects via a service charge payable through housing benefit. As well as housing benefit, the provision costs of these support services have been paid for by a mixture of personal payments and special grants from a variety of public sources. [29] It is now felt that this complex funding system needs to be co-ordinated and reformed to make it less complicated and more flexible. The reform proposals arose from the work of an inter-departmental review of funding for supported accommodation (1997), which concluded that there was a need to change the way in which funding arrangements are structured and expenditure managed. The key conclusion was that funding through the benefit system has failed to achieve sufficient transparency to enable provision to be planned and co-ordinated (an unknown amount of benefit was going to an unknown number of beneficiaries and providers).

Following an earlier consultation exercise, the government's reform proposals were laid out in a 1999 discussion paper entitled *Supporting People: a new policy and funding framework for support services*. This pointed out that an important part of the current funding mechanism involved the use of housing benefit and this meant that providers typically recovered support service costs in their rent charges. In the late 1990s, problems with the *ad hoc* nature of the existing funding regime were highlighted by a series of court cases that demonstrated the extent to which housing benefit, intended to meet 'bricks and mortar' costs, had unintentionally expanded to meet the costs of supporting vulnerable people in the community.[30] It is argued that, by incorporating the cost of support services into housing benefit calculations, upward pressure has been put on rents and this, in turn, has acted as a disincentive for some people to seek employment.

---

29 The complex of funding sources include Social Security payments, in the form of housing benefit and, to a lesser extent, income support, supported housing management grant provided by the Housing Corporation; supported housing revenue grant in Wales; special needs allowance package in Scotland; the probation accommodation grant funded jointly by the Home Office and the DETR; and individuals with incomes above benefit levels paying charges personally.

30 As the discussion document made clear, eligibility for housing benefit is based on criteria, which do not reflect individuals' support needs. Its availability distorts the accommodation options open to vulnerable people, and potentially inhibits the flexibility, effectiveness and efficiency with which resources can be applied.

The government felt that the funding arrangements were working against the principles of promoting independence as set out in the White Paper *Modernising Social Services* and were therefore keen to make changes. It proposes to replace the current 'arbitrary' arrangements with a new co-ordinated approach, bringing the various funding streams together to create a new single budget. It is proposed that the new co-ordinated arrangements will allocate central resources to local authorities on a local needs basis in a way that encourages consistency and value-for-money. The authorities, in partnership with probation services, and taking account of the views of voluntary organisations including RSLs, will take decisions on how the allocated monies can best be spent on the provision of support services. It is proposed that when the single budget is introduced in April 2003 housing benefit will no longer cover the costs of support services but will be restricted to bricks and mortar costs. The costs of support services previously covered by housing benefit will be funded out of the single budget, transferring demand-led funding to a cash limited one. In the meantime, between April 2000 and 2003, these services will continue to be met by housing benefit but the charges will be separately identified when benefit is assessed (rather than just as part of the rent), enabling government to estimate the size of the budget required to cover these services in 2003.[31]

Income support for mortgage interest

The Social Security legislation of the 1980s that established the basis of the modern housing benefit system specifically excluded owner-occupiers from entitlement. At the time, the idea of a unified housing benefit system embracing all tenures had been considered, but the inclusion of home owners would have involved a radical restructuring, or even the abandonment, of mortgage interest tax relief. At a time when the creation of a 'property-owning democracy' was at the heart of the government's housing policy ambitions, such an idea was soon ruled to be politically unacceptable. Therefore, another support mechanism needs to be available for this tenure; this takes the form of income support for mortgage interest (ISMI). Through ISMI the DSS provides a 'safety net' for mortgagors who run into financial difficulties that might lead to their homes being repossessed.

Assistance for mortgagors in difficulties with their repayments has been a long-standing feature of the UK housing system. This form of income augmentation dates back to the immediate post-war period and the introduction of national assistance (1948) when owner-occupation began to gain prominence as a tenure arrangement. The scheme operates to provide assistance in maintaining mortgage loans up to a fixed size (currently £100,000) to borrowers who have limited savings (currently £8,000 or below) and are in financial difficulty through loss of income brought about by redundancy, accident, illness, or retirement. A key

---

31   SSAC (1999) Press release 4 June 1999. The Housing Benefit (General) Regulations 1999.

feature of the scheme is that only the interest element of the outstanding loan (calculated on a standard rate is covered). Crucially, however, no assistance is available to those who cannot afford to keep up their mortgage because of low wages. In fact, any claimant who works 16 hours or more a week is automatically barred from any assistance. As a result, those who start back into low paid work after a period of unemployment may find that, after paying their housing costs, their disposable income is less than when they were on benefit. This is referred to as the 'employment trap'.

Rules of entitlement

1. Claimants whose assessed capital is in excess of £8,000 are excluded from benefit. For claimants with capital between £3,000 and £8,000 a tariff is carried forward into the claimant's assessment of income. The tariff is calculated in the same way as for housing benefit.[32]

2. Since 1992, the system has operated by making direct payments to lenders and regulations prevent the assistance being used to service non-mortgage debts such as buildings insurance and endowments. Any charges that are related to any second mortgages do not qualify as 'eligible' expenses for ISMI purposes.

3. *Predetermination.* From May 1994, regulations limited any increase in housing expenses while a claimant is in receipt of income support.

4. *Deferred payments.* Until October 1995, eligibility for ISMI was tied strictly to eligibility for income support. After that date waiting periods were introduced which meant that payment of benefit was deferred. The length of the waiting period depends on whether the mortgage was taken out before or after the 1995 rule changes. Existing borrowers get no help at all for the first two months of claim and, for the next four months, up to half the interest obligations are met by the scheme, and up to 100 per cent ISMI thereafter.[33] For new mortgages, all home owners on income support, with the exception of pensioners, now get no State help for some nine months (39 weeks). From

---

32   If the Benefits Agency has made a decision that somebody actually does have savings, and then that person realises, or spends, those savings to bring them below the limit, then they can still be treated as if they still possessed it. This is called 'the notional capital rule'. Under this rule action depends on the Benefit Agency's judgement about the intention of the saver. The Agency has to consider the motivation for realising the capital: they seek to determine whether or not it was for the purpose of qualifying for benefit. Even seeking advice indicates that the claimant knew of the rule and might be used as evidence of avoidance. If the claimant is able to show that the motivation was to clear a mortgage debt it will normally be allowed. In any event, it will depend on the interpretation of the officer.

33   Strictly speaking, ISMI does not pay full or half of mortgage interest, but includes this as a need element in the person's IS/JSA calculation. So, for example, if the claimant does not qualify for IS on a standard calculation (i.e. excluding housing costs), their housing costs may help them to qualify. The total IS they receive will be the difference between their eligible housing costs and any income in excess of their total needs excluding housing costs. Therefore, it may not cover the full 100 per cent of the mortgage interest.

---

week 40, payment of up to 100 per cent of ISMI can be met. To bring a degree of stability and neutrality into the scheme's operation, all payments covered by the scheme are calculated in relation to an officially determined, standard rate of interest rather than the actual rate.[34] In this way the DSS does not look at the actual payments being charged and match them but, after the waiting period, pays a rate tied to a basket of bank and building society rates.

The waiting period is calculated, not from the point at which income support/JSA is received, but from the point at which a claim is made for JSA, statutory sick pay or incapacity benefit. This provision was introduced so as not to penalise the thrifty behaviour of those who saved prior to their financial difficulties.

5. *Non-dependent charges.* As with housing benefit, a deduction will be made from ISMI if a claimant has a 'non-dependant' living with them. It is assumed that such a person (e.g. adult child), is making a contribution to the running costs of the home. The amount deducted will depend on the age, income and working status of the relative. For example, at the time of writing, no deduction is made for a non-dependant aged between 18 and 25 who is on income support, but a deduction of £7.40 (2000/01), is made for every non-dependant over the age of 25 who is on income support.

6. *Part-time work.* If a claimant works for more than 16 hours a week, or their partner works more than 24 hours a week, all entitlement to ISMI is withdrawn.

7. *Eligible interest.* Since 1992 the system has operated by making direct payments to lenders and regulations prevent the assistance being used to service non-mortgage debts such as buildings insurance and endowments.

Subject to negotiation, claimants may be able to have the interest on certain repair and improvement loans met. To qualify for support, the repair or improvement has to be shown to be necessary to maintain the home in a habitable condition. In effect, this means that only specified works, on an approved DSS list, qualify. The list includes, amongst other things; provision of a bath and necessary plumbing and hot water, home insulation, and correcting unsafe structural defects. Loans for approved repairs and improvements can be taken out whilst the claimant is already on ISMI, unlike ordinary loans where restrictions apply.

It is possible to receive help with more than one mortgage. If a second mortgage has been taken out to repay the original mortgage, that element of

---

34 The standard rate is currently based on a weighted average of the published rates of the top 20 building societies. If the actual rate is less than 5 per cent on the day ISMI is first payable then that rate applies until and unless it reaches 5 per cent when the standard rate will apply. The standard rate may be below the rate that the borrower is paying so that there is a shortfall between the help from the DSS and the payment being charged by the mortgage lender.

the latter which is repaying the original loan is eligible interest. A mortgage taken out for purposes other than acquiring an interest in a dwelling is not eligible.

The mortgage interest liability may be considered to be excessive if the accommodation is considered to be unnecessarily large for the claimant or is located in an area that is more expensive than other areas in which there is suitable accommodation or the costs of the accommodation are unreasonable in relation to other suitable accommodation in the area.

8. *Right-to-buy transferees*. Council and HA tenants on secure tenancies who become owner-occupiers for the first time whilst on income support have their ISMI tied to the amount of rent used to calculate their housing benefit when they were renting. This measure is designed to ensure that the lack of horizontal equity that exists between the system of housing benefit and ISMI does not damage the government's commitment to expand owner-occupation as a tenure (see discussion below).

Differences between housing benefit and ISMI: a question of horizontal equity

As we have intimated, ISMI to owner-occupiers is in some respects equivalent to the housing benefit paid to augment the incomes of poorer households in the private and social rented sectors. However, in contrast with housing benefit, ISMI is restricted to those on income support or income based JSA. ISMI is always paid direct to the lender[35] and is administered by the local offices of the Benefits Agency under regulations and guidance drawn up by the DSS.[36] We have already made the point that ISMI is not available to those in low paid work.

As explained above, income support/JSA entitlement is withdrawn if and when a claimant finds a job providing weekly employment of 16 hours or more a week. Under present arrangements, a further question of *horizontal equity*[37] arises because, in such circumstances, owner-occupiers lose their entitlements to ISMI while claimants who rent their homes can continue to seek help with their housing costs via housing benefit. This anomaly is known as the 'the employment trap' (see above).

To overcome the horizontal inequity that exists between tenants and owners, the Chartered Institute of Housing argues the need to create a common system of

---

35 The principle of direct payments to lenders was established in July 1992. In return, lenders' organisations introduced a voluntary agreement not to repossess the home if ISMI was being met in full on the mortgage interest obligation. However, this agreement has somewhat broken down following the changes introduced in 1995 which fixed the payment according to a standard rate of interest, although regulations still require payments to be made direct.

36 By contrast, housing benefit is administered by local authorities acting as agents of the DSS.

37 For an explanation of the notion of *horizontal equity* see pp41-42.

'housing credit' to apply across both tenures.[38] It could be argued that a housing credit system could be used to weaken the disincentive effects of the employment and poverty traps by incorporating provisions that would allow claimants in both tenures to continue to be given support as they gained employment. Work incentives could also be improved by establishing an earned income disregard that is more generous than that currently applied to housing benefit claimants and extending it to ISMI claimants. Further reforms would integrate working families tax credit and housing benefit into a 'housing credit' scheme with a single calculation and a common taper. This would allow the worst withdrawal rates (which occur when WFTC, housing benefit and council tax benefit are all in payment) to be reduced.[39]

ISMI and the 'employment trap'

The government's Social Security Advisory Committee highlighted the nature of the ISMI 'employment trap'.

> *'If the partner's work of 16 hours or more precludes either of them claiming income support but the partner's earnings are insufficient to maintain them both and pay the mortgage, the only sensible course of action is for the partner to cease work so that income support may be claimed.'* (Social Security Advisory Committee, 1994)[40]

In a limited way the government has addressed the issue of work disincentive through the family credit/WFTC schemes for households with dependent children and through the jobseekers' allowance. However, family credit/WFTC claimants cannot claim help with mortgage costs and, although the JSA does permit claimants to work less than 16 hours a week,[41] earning more than £5 will cause benefit to be reduced by £1 for every £1 earned – a marginal withdrawal rate of 100 per cent.

It has been possible to come off ISMI for a short period without the need to re-qualify for the full waiting period when the new claim is made; this is known as 'the linking period'. To encourage people to take up work, the linking period has recently been extended to 12 weeks. The 2000 Green Paper pointed to further changes.

The Green Paper recognised that current regulations may be a factor in home owners building up significant arrears, and possibly losing their homes, if they do

---

38 Alison Barker, Housing credit 'would be fair to homeowners', in *Public Finance* 31 January 1997, p4.

39 Wilcox, S. (1998), p17, *Unfinished Business*, Chartered Institute of Housing.

40 From DoE, *A Foot on the Ladder, A Study of Households on the Margins of Renting and Owning a Home*, HMSO 1994. para.2.9. Although since 1996 partners of claimants have been able to work up to 24 hours before entitlement is lost.

41 If it is the partner who is working, then the limit is 24 hours.

not have replacement income. To reduce disincentives to work two reforms will be introduced from April 2001.

1. Extending to 52 weeks the linking arrangements for benefit help for those taking but then losing a job. This will enable people who take up work but then lose it (within 52 weeks) to re-claim support without having to wait another nine months.
2. Providing in-work support for claimants of benefit help with mortgage interest payments so they have time to adjust to the new financial circumstances that follow from the move into employment. This will bring the mortgage benefit system in line with those who rent. Under these arrangements, help with mortgage interest payments will be continued to claimants for a further four weeks after they take up work.

The Green Paper points to the possibility of further changes to benefit help with mortgage interest. If introduced, these would be designed to link in better with private insurance (MPPI) and encourage home owners to make more private provision. Options being considered include allowing MPPI payments to be given more generous treatment in assessing benefit help entitlement and offering benefit help earlier to home owners who had taken out MPPI but who had suffered an uninsurable event.

ISMI and public expenditure

Owner-occupation expanded rapidly during the 1980s and this, together with the subsequent downturn in employment and job security, meant that the cost to the Exchequer of this assistance rose sharply in the ten years following 1984.[42] DSS expenditure in this area rose from £286 million in 1988 to a peak of £1,222 million in 1993.[43] These rising costs caused the government to alter the arrangements. Some 5 per cent of all mortgagors, some 550,000 people, claimed income support for mortgage interest in 1994 at a cost to the Exchequer of £1.06 billion (£31 million in 1979). Of these, 227,000 were unemployed, 98,000 over 60 years of age, and 120,000 were lone parents.[44]

Under the old system, on mortgages below £125,000, claimants received half the interest paid for the first 16 weeks of claim and full interest after that. Following an announcement in the 1994 Budget, in October 1995 the government cut income support entitlement for mortgage interest payments. The public expenditure savings are largely achieved by deferring the support to those who qualify (see above). Arguably, the 1995 reforms will cut the State's commitment to ISMI by some £200 million. This figure is a DSS estimate but is not based on any cost-

---

42　The recession and monetary policy increased the cost of ISMI in two ways; more benefit claimants and higher interest rates.
43　Liz Phelps 'Housing Costs' in *Roof*, May/June 1995 p13.
44　*Roof Briefing*, February 1995.

benefit analysis of the changes. It therefore fails to take account of the public expenditure consequences of higher levels of homelessness that might result from the new rules. Currently, of those who have their homes repossessed, some 60 per cent end up in the public sector. As a result there is an unforeseen fiscal consequence: once dispossessed of owner-occupier status, these households become eligible for housing benefit and thus are potentially an added burden on the public purse. In this way, via a process of repossession, measures designed to save public expenditure simply relocate its incidence and, in the process, create personal misery and additional work for advice bureaux and housing practitioners.

Two political motivations appear to have been behind the change in rules outlined above. The first was a concern about rising public expenditure and the second was the desire to encourage personal responsibility and increase private sector involvement in the provision of cover.

With the withdrawal of income support in this area came the assumption that new borrowers would turn to private insurance for cover, and ministers made the further assumption that as the insurance market expanded in response to the new climate, the price of private cover will fall.[45] But private insurance operates in the context of free-enterprise markets and competition between lenders is likely to result in differential charges for different categories of risk. Only about 40 per cent of ISMI recipients are unemployed[46] and the rest are people with financial difficulties resulting from marital breakdown, disablement, an accident, or illness. Because some things are easier to predict statistically than others, it is likely that competitive insurance companies will charge differential premiums.

Mortgage payment protection insurance differs significantly from the income support system (ISMI). Eligibility for the latter depends on the size of the loan, the value of the mortgagor's savings and whether they have a partner who is economically active. It will cover only the interest element of the mortgage after the elapse of a qualifying period. In contrast, private insurers will normally cover the full mortgage obligation including repayment of principal and any endowment premium – they may also cover payment of associated insurances. However, private insurers tend to limit their liabilities with a variety of restrictive clauses. It should also be noted that the whole idea of 'insurance' is to restrict cover to unforeseeable risks such as sudden disability or redundancy and not to loss of employment caused by foreseeable changes in circumstances which reflect a nominal degree of personal choice such as retirement, the winding up of a self-employed business or withdrawal from the labour market to look after children. Normal insurance agreements would also exclude loss of income resulting from voluntary redundancy, resignation and dismissal.

The realities of private payment protection are that insurance companies will use 'credit scoring' techniques to protect themselves from high risk agreements and,

---

45   *Roof Briefing*, December 1994.
46   Ibid.

as a result, some people will be excluded from private cover altogether, like some of the seriously ill and the elderly, and others will be required to pay relatively high premiums, like those in insecure employment. Mortgage insurance costs are running at about £7 per £100 of monthly repayment and the typical policy pays nothing for the first few months and then only covers the full premium for a fixed period (typically 12 months). Private insurance cover tends to be regressive in that it tends to charge higher premiums for those at greatest risk (e.g. the elderly and those in low paid, insecure employment) and lower premiums for those in least risk. In this way the reforms are likely to create a socially divisive, two-tier system of private coverage.

A two-tier system is likely to make some individuals vulnerable to commercial forces and there is some concern amongst housing practitioners and academics about the lack of statutory regulation. As welfare claimants are transmogrified into private customers they will have to rely heavily on the industry's voluntary code of practice and the industry-funded Insurance Ombudsman Bureau that operates a voluntary scheme to deal with complaints. Recent reports from the National Association of Citizens Advice Bureaux (NACAB)[47] indicate that many of their clients bought policies only to discover that, when they needed to make a claim, they had been paying premiums for a policy from which they could never benefit. Others had fallen foul of rigid qualifying conditions that could make it almost impossible to lodge a successful claim.[48] Furthermore, NACAB argue that exclusion clauses in many policies prevent some claimants from participating in government retraining schemes without losing their entitlements.

Such concerns are intensified by an awareness that fundamental changes are taking place in the structure of the mortgage industry. The deregulation of financial markets and the transformation of a significant part of the building society movement to PLC status have already led to the establishment of differential lending criteria. Such changes also bring to the fore questions about whether traditional lenders to owner-occupiers will gradually shift the balance of their investment interests to housing in general and seek new opportunities in the private rented sector (see Chapter 7).

One major new initiative has just commenced. Under a joint arrangement by the Council of Mortgage Lenders and the Association of British Insurers, a new scheme was introduced in the summer of 1999. This seeks to take on board some of the criticisms outlined above. With these criticisms in mind, they have devised a scheme that lays down minimum standards that are intended to produce policies that will pay out within sixty days and provide cover for a minimum of twelve months. Automatic exclusion clauses will not be included so that each claim will be treated individually. The success of such a scheme will largely depend on how potential clients judge the relationship between the cost, how much extra will be

---

47 *Dispossessed* (1993) and *Security at Risk* (1995).
48 Ann Abraham, Chief Executive NACAB, letter to *Inside Housing*, 26 April 1996.

added to the monthly mortgage repayments, and the protection benefits received. Herein lies a dilemma: the scheme, which could add an extra £50 or £60 a month to the mortgage costs of a household, may seem relatively unattractive to someone in secure employment with entitlement to generous sickness payments. This means that the scheme may attract a disproportionate number of people in insecure employment who are more likely to make a claim. This will keep the unit costs high and thereby limit the scheme's market appeal. The scheme may also be flawed in another way. One of the most common reasons people have for getting into difficulty with their mortgage repayments is relationship breakdown, and it would appear that the proposals do not provide cover for this eventuality.

A private, voluntary, self-regulating, unsubsidised scheme is always likely to be discriminatory and, for the most vulnerable, too expensive to join. A compulsory, universal scheme would be more affordable and encourage insurers to extend the product range. It would, however, need to be under-written by public funds. The Council of Mortgage Lenders and others are currently exploring the feasibility of a mortgage benefit scheme but at the time of writing there is no agreement within the industry about how such a scheme would be financed and operated.

The reform of housing benefit

Housing benefits cost the Exchequer well in excess of £11 billion in 1998/99. The charge to the public purse is forecast to continue to rise at 1.4 per cent a year in real terms between 1999 and 2002. Given these figures and the fact that many millions of pounds are lost in fraud, the subsidy has become an obvious target for major reform. Official statistics reveal (1998) that housing benefit is paid incorrectly to one in six people and well over £800 million is lost through clerical error and fraud. Much of the problem results from the fact that the current system is highly bureaucratic, complex, fragmented, inflexible, and confusing. Alastair Darling, the Social Security Secretary has argued that *'Reform is essential if we are to deliver a modern welfare system that is realistic about human nature, tough on fraud and high-tech in delivery'*.[49]

The 2000 Housing Green Paper, *Quality and Choice: A Decent Home for All* (DETR/Social Security, April 2000) floated the idea that the availability of housing benefit for a property should be made conditional in some way on the landlord providing decent standards of accommodation and housing management. This would involve giving additional powers to local authorities to introduce a licensing or approved accreditation scheme. To pursue this suggestion in Scotland and Wales would involve negotiations with the devolved administrations, taking account of their specific housing issues. If introduced, it is likely that 'approval' would only be given in areas of genuinely low demand, where the claimant could move readily to another home that satisfied the licensing requirements.

---

49   Reported in *Inside Housing*, 30 October 1998, p7.

In recent years academic criticism of housing benefit has concentrated on the unique structure of the British system to base the payment of benefit on the full rent. It is argued that this structure produces no incentive to the tenant to take an interest in their rent, since any increase in rent will be matched by a corresponding increase in benefit leaving the tenant with no extra to pay. Consequently, there is no incentive for tenants to shop around for accommodation that is more reasonably priced or more closely matches their needs. Proposed reforms to tackle this problem have suggested that housing benefit should only be paid on a fixed proportion of the rent, say 80 per cent, leaving the tenant to pay the rest out of their own pocket. Tenants on low incomes would be compensated by including a fixed allowance in their income support payments based on 20 per cent of average rent levels, maintaining the incentive to shop around for more reasonably priced accommodation thereby saving money from the public purse. At the time of writing it is believed that the Treasury are interested in long-term reforms along these lines. However, such a reform might undermine the financial viability of housing associations. If rents are less convincingly under-written by public subsidy, the level of rent arrears may increase, making it more difficult to service loans. This, in turn, will make it more difficult for associations to borrow cheaply from private sources.[50]

To be economically and socially coherent[51], proposals for the reform of housing benefit have to be seen in the context of a wider review of the overall tax and benefit system. Many point to the *poverty trap* as the key issue and much of the current debate centres on how to move people off benefit and into employment. The Chartered Institute of Housing has argued for a package of measures which includes the integration of working families tax credit and housing benefit into a unified housing credit scheme. An integrated housing credit scheme would enable the worst combined deductions and withdrawals to be reduced from over 95 per cent to 80 per cent. The Institute's proposals for comprehensive reform would also improve work incentives by extending benefits to working low-income home-buyers, stabilise rent levels for local authority and housing association tenants and allow people in work to keep more of their earnings before benefit is withdrawn.

Summary

Rents for housing association and local authority tenants are normally accepted as reasonable for benefit purposes. In contrast, for private sector tenants the total amount of housing benefit is fixed by reference to local rent levels. Within this ceiling, the support given to any particular household is determined by a means test that compares their income and savings with their assumed needs. Claimants

---

50 See *Housing Associations – A Viable Financial Future?*, HACAS Consulting, Chartered Institute of Housing, June 1999

51 In this context, 'coherence' means efficient, effective and equitable: see the value-for-money debate in Chapter 2.

receiving income support are entitled to maximum housing benefit which is calculated as the maximum eligible rent less any non-dependant deductions. The housing benefit for other claimants is based on a calculation that compares how much their income exceeds their applicable amount (i.e. income support level) and reduces their maximum benefit by 65 per cent of this excess.

In response to Exchequer concerns about the rising cost of housing benefit, in recent years there has been a firming up of the eligibility rules. Evidence from such organisations as Shelter and the Association of Residential Letting Agents indicates that one consequence of these changes has been that private landlords have become increasingly concerned about letting their properties to those receiving housing benefit, fearing that they may be liable to losses caused by recovered overpaid benefit or shortfalls between the claimant's full rent and the maximum benefit allowable, restricted to the rent officer assessments.[52]

Further reading

CIH, *Improving and Simplifying Housing Benefit*, CIH, January 1999.

DETR/Social Security, *Quality and Choice: A Decent Home for All*, The Housing Green Paper, April 2000, Chapters 5 and 11.

Martin Ward and John Zebedee, *Guide to Housing Benefit and Council Tax Benefit*, CIH/Shelter (updated annually).

Steve Wilcox, *Unfinished Business: Housing Costs and the Reform of Welfare*, CIH/CML/LGA/NHF and JRF, 1998.

Peter Kemp, *'Shopping Incentives' and Housing Benefit Reform*, CIH/JRF, 2000.

---

52 DETR, (1999) *Housing Benefit and the Private Rented Sector*, pp26-29 and p73.

CHAPTER 18:
Housing finance:
future directions

by John Perry

It is a theme of this book that there is a common framework for understanding housing finance, whichever tenure, sector, or part of the UK is being considered. However, in policy terms, the future looks fragmented. The most notable example is, of course, the outcome of devolved government in Scotland, Wales and potentially Northern Ireland. But equally the government's approach to the private sector, home-ownership and private renting, does not yet follow the kind of 'joined-up thinking' which it has tried to make its hallmark in social policy. Only in the prospects for social housing – councils and housing associations – does convergence towards a common approach seem likely. In policy towards the support for housing costs for those on low incomes, 'joined-up thinking' appeared to be in prospect at the time of the Chancellor's 1999 Budget, but now seems less likely.

In concluding this book with some speculation on future directions for housing finance, each of these four broad policy areas will be looked at in turn.

Devolution

The Scottish Parliament and the National Assembly for Wales have now begun to formulate their housing policies, albeit somewhat hamstrung by the resource constraints, staffing as well as finance, that devolution did not resolve, and still constrained too by decision-making on crucial areas being retained in Whitehall. (At the time of writing, the Northern Ireland Assembly has been only recently re-instated.)

In setting a policy agenda, Scotland is ahead of England, the Secretary of State having published a green paper, *Investing in Modernisation – An Agenda for Scotland's Housing* just before devolution took place. The key issues are in the social housing sector. The Scottish Executive has whole-heartedly embraced stock transfer as its route to dealing with the future of council housing, notably in pushing for the transfer of council housing in Glasgow – Britain's biggest municipal landlord. Scotland has so far eschewed other routes – such as PFI or resource accounting – to dealing with the investment backlog.

If stock transfer is set to alter the balance between councils and housing associations as social landlords in Scotland, convergence is also likely on other fronts. A common regulatory framework, a single form of tenancy and a common approach to the right-to-buy, are all to be included in a forthcoming Housing Bill. (For further analysis of recent developments in Scotland, see *'Back on the Agenda: Housing policy and devolution in Scotland'* by Michael Thain in *Housing Finance Review*, 1999/2000, CIH/CML.)

Wales is also set to adopt stock transfer as its way forward for council housing, although, as in Scotland, the policy is not uncontentious. The National Assembly has already pioneered the 'single regulator' favoured in Scotland. Wales is also ahead of both England and Scotland in the coherence and affordability of its social sector rents. The Assembly has now published its policy on private finance in social housing and has recently received reports from four task groups involving bodies such as CIH which have made more than 190 recommendations on different housing issues. (For further analysis of recent developments in Wales, see *'End of the Empire: housing policy in a devolved Wales'*, by Peter Williams in *Housing Finance Review* 1999/2000, CIH/CML, and *Housing in Wales* in the CIH Policy and Practice Series, 2000).

In England, the Housing Green Paper, *Quality and Choice: A Decent Home for All*, was published in April 2000. The rest of this chapter considers briefly the issues being raised and how housing finance might be affected both in England specifically and in the UK more generally, given that housing benefit, in particular, is a UK-wide policy decided in Whitehall.

The private sector

The heyday of government support for private sector housing can now be seen to have been the 1980s, with mortgage interest tax relief, the right-to-buy, itself responsible for a large share of the growth of home-ownership, the deregulation of private sector rents, and initiatives such as the Business Expansion Scheme, as hallmarks. The 1990s have seen both withdrawal and consolidation in government policy, which look set to continue after 2000.

For home owners, specific support such as tax relief has become much less relevant (and has now been withdrawn), whilst the effects of macro-economic policy are much more important. The low inflation/low interest rate environment looks set to continue, which means that lengthy and damaging house price booms, like that of the late 1980s, are unlikely to recur. At the margins, however, home-ownership will continue to have its difficulties, reflected in levels of mortgage repossessions which remain high compared with the early 1980s. Whilst new forms of personal subsidy are not completely out of the question (see below), the most likely response is a tightening regulatory regime for mortgage lenders.

An issue raised but not resolved in the English Green Paper is the future of the renovation grant scheme. The whole scheme is now much smaller than it was in the 1980s (see Chapter 10), and is likely to be further affected by the introduction of the 'single housing pot' and the loss of specified capital grant. Yet poor conditions in the older owner-occupied stock still persist, and it houses half of poor households. The Green Paper proposes a more flexible grant system which complements private investment.

The decline of the private rented sector appears to have halted and is unlikely to resume, but it would be rash to forecast sustained growth. Promotion of the sector through Housing Investment Trusts (see Chapter 16) has not worked, but in view of the potential for institutional finance, as the City is awash with funds, further development of this kind of vehicle seems possible. Retail lending (buy-to-rent mortgages) may also become a bigger feature. Constraints within the housing benefit system, notably the single room rent limitation and the system of local reference rents, seem to be having an effect on landlords' willingness to let to benefit dependent would-be tenants. Whether long-term reform of housing benefit will modify these adverse effects remains to be seen.

Rising rents and continued poor conditions in part of the private rented sector have led to calls for greater regulation. The government is set to introduce mandatory licensing of multi-occupied properties, and another possibility heralded in the Green Paper is the further development of local schemes of voluntary regulation.

Social housing

Much of this book has concerned issues about securing sufficient investment to meet housing need. The government's Spending Review 2000 made a welcome increase in English housing spending of 12 per cent per annum in real terms for the three years to 2003/04, and confirmed a target of tackling the £19 billion backlog of work on council housing within ten years. (Housing allocations in Scotland, Wales and Northern Ireland are set to be determined later.)

Nevertheless, the transfer of council housing out of the sector remains an essential element of policy, since even the increased level of funding will not tackle the backlog on more than one third of the remaining stock. The government has provided for up to 200,000 units being transferred each year, and clearly expects not much more than one million houses to be left in the ownership of English councils by 2010. Transfer will continue apace across Britain, with whole stock transfer in urban areas (even in cities as large as Birmingham) featuring strongly.

The Green Paper indicated for the first time that (in England) councils will be able to set up arms length management companies which will have extra borrowing freedom within the public sector, and limited funding for this has been provided in 2002-04. (See Chapters 9 and 10 for the discussion which has led to this option being put forward.) To be allowed to pursue this option, councils will have to demonstrate the excellence of their housing management services.

The Spending Review also boosted two other alternatives to transfer. PFI projects for stock renovation (see Chapter 10) now have provision for accompanying credit approvals in the next three years, signalling further schemes beyond the initial eight pathfinder projects. Councils with better quality stocks may find that the provisions for resource accounting (including a major repairs allowance at £550 per house) will enable them to both keep their houses and bring them up to standard.

The need for new affordable rented housing is now largely met by housing associations. The Housing Corporation has seen its Approved Development Programme boosted by nearly 80 per cent in cash terms over three years, and has been set a target of delivering 56,000 rented homes and 7,700 low cost home-ownership units over this period. Also new is a £250m Starter Home Initiative aimed at areas where there is pressure on housing markets.

Also competing for available ADP funding is the need for regeneration of urban areas, on which Government policy is now focussed strongly. In addition to the Housing Green Paper, a White Paper is expected on urban policy. The final outcome of the work of the Social Exclusion Unit, a National Strategy for Neighbourhood Renewal, has been published. All of these call for greater integration of housing with wider community regeneration.

Helping people with their housing costs

Another financial issue which is central to current policy development is how people pay for their housing and the extent of State help that they get. In England, social sector rents have emerged as a key area of concern in the Green Paper, with rationalisation of rents and the gradual imposition of a common approach to rents across the social sector as the outcome. The extent to which rents should reflect market values on the one hand, or be affordable on the other, is a key issue (see Chapters 3, 4, 11, 13 and 16. Also refer to the report *Evaluating Housing Affordability: Policy Options and New Directions*, LGA, 1999). The outcome seems likely to be a compromise, and one which will be phased in over a number of years so as to reduce the impact on RSLs in particular.

Reforming rents and getting a better relationship between the price of a property (its rent) and its size, quality, location and condition are seen as essential precursors of any major overall of housing benefit. One possibility heralded in the Green Paper is that the government will, in the longer-term, want to create so-called 'shopping incentives' in the benefit system, whereby tenants are more in touch with the rents they pay and may have to pay part of the rent themselves (see *'Shopping Incentives' and Housing Benefit Reform*, Kemp, P., CIH/JRF, 2000).

Another related possibility is the integration of the housing benefit scheme with the recently introduced working families' tax credit (see Wilcox, S., *Unfinished Business: Housing Costs and the Reform of Welfare Benefits*, CIH, 1998).

Both these long-term possibilities are put forward for discussion in the Green Paper, but the possibility of a flat-rate housing element which includes a new form of direct help for low-income home owners, does not yet seem to be part of government thinking. The all-party Social Security Select Committee has backed more radical reform of housing benefit, but whether this takes place in the near future will only be evident as the government takes on board reaction to its Green Paper.

Longer-term prospects for housing finance

Apart from the medium term reforms being shaped at UK level and in the devolved parliaments/assemblies, a longer-term view has been developed through a major Inquiry into the Future of Social Housing being conducted by the Institute for Public Policy Research. Published in July 2000, and likely to be influential with the government, it looks to redefine the purpose of social housing and show how housing finance should be redesigned accordingly.

One of its major concerns is what kind of future does social housing have? Is it ultimately destined to replicate the North American model, as a dwindling sector catering only for those with no job and little prospects? Or might it be reinvented as a broader sector, catering for low-cost home-ownership and market renting alongside its traditional tenants? These are concerns that are likely to dominate the housing policy debate, and ultimately have far-reaching consequences for government financial involvement in housing during the early years of the new century.

Further reading

Department of the Environment and the Regions and the Department for Social Security, *Quality and Choice: A Decent Home for All*, The Housing Green Paper, HMSO, April 2000.

Scottish Office, *Investing in Modernisation – An Agenda for Scotland's Housing*, The Scottish Housing Green Paper, HMSO, February 1999.

Putting the House in Order – Housing Professionals' Agenda for Legislation, CIH, 1999.

Housing United – the Final Report of the IPPR Forum on Social Housing, IPPR, 2000.

Perry, J., 'The End of Council Housing?' in *Housing Finance Review 2000-2001*, CIH/CML, 2000.

BIBLIOGRAPHY

General publications

Anderson, K., (1996), 'Housing Renewal and Regeneration', Chapter 8 in Currie, H. and Murie, A., *Housing in Scotland*, pp105-121, CIH (Housing Policy and Practice Series): Coventry.

Anderson, K., (1997), *Funding of Local Authority Stock Transfers (Scotland)*, CIH: Edinburgh.

Ashby, J., (1992), *Risk Management for Committee Members*, NFHA: London.

Ashley, R., (1990), *A Basic Guide to Private Finance*, NFHA: London.

Atkinson, R. and Moon, G., (1994), *Urban Policy in Britain: The City, The State and the Market*, Macmillan.

Aughton, H. and Malpass, P., (1994), *Housing Finance: A British Guide*, Shelter: London.

Balchin, P. N. and Kieve, J. L., (1977), *Urban Land Economics*, Macmillan: London and Basingstoke.

Baldry, D. (1998), 'The evaluation of risk management in public sector capital projects', in *International Journal of Project Management*, Vol.16, No.1 pp35-41, Pergamon.

Bradshaw, J., (1972), 'The Taxonomy of Social Need', in McLachlan, G., (Ed), *Problems and Progress in Medical Care*, 7th series, Nuffield Provincial Hospitals Trust, OUP.

Bramley, G. and Morgan, J., (1998), 'Low Cost Home Ownership Initiatives in the UK', in *Housing Studies*, Vol.13, No.4 pp567-586.

Brown, T. and Passmore, J., (1998), *Housing and Anti-Poverty Strategies*, CIH/JRF: Coventry.

Buckland, P., (1999), 'Private Places', in *Public Finance*, 4 June 1999.

Button, F., (1993), *Best Practice for Better Borrowing*, NFHA: London.

Chartered Institute of Housing, (1997), *Sustainable Home Ownership: New Policies for a New Government*, CIH: Coventry.

Chartered Institute of Housing, (1997), *Good Practice Briefing No.11 – Rents and Service Charges*, December 1997.

Chartered Institute of Housing, (1998), *Council Housing: Financing the Future*. Report prepared by Graham Moody Associates Ltd., Edited by John Perry, CIH: Coventry.

Chartered Institute of Housing (1999), *Good Practice Briefing No.17 – Housing and Services for People with Support Needs*, November 1999.

Chartered Institute of Public Finance and Accountancy, (1995), *Financial Reporting in Local Government: Capital*, CIPFA: London.

Chartered Institute of Public Finance and Accountancy, (1997a), *Councillors' Guide to Local Government Finance, 1997 revised edition*, CIPFA: London.

Chartered Institute of Public Finance and Accountancy, (1997b), *New Local Government: Supplement to the 1997 Councillors' Guide to Local Government Finance*, CIPFA: London.

Chartered Institute of Public Finance and Accountancy and Price Waterhouse, (1998), *In Good Company: A Guide to Local Housing Companies*, CIPFA: London.

Commission on Social Justice, (1994), *Social Justice: Strategies for National Renewal*, The Report of the Commission on Social Justice, Vintage: London.

Connolly, M. and Knox, C., (1991), 'Policy Differences within the United Kingdom: The Case of Housing Policy in Northern Ireland'. In *Public Administration*, vol. 69.

Connolly, M., (1996), 'Lessons from Local Government in Northern Ireland', in *Local Government Studies*, Vol.22, No.1, Winter 1996.

Coopers and Lybrand and Steve Wilcox, (1995), *Challenging the Conventions: Public Borrowing Rules and Housing Investment*, CIH: Coventry.

Coopers and Lybrand, (1996), *Consensus for Change – Public Borrowing Rules, Housing Investment and the City*, CIH: Coventry.

Cope, H., (1990), *Housing Associations: Policy and Practice*, Macmillan: Basingstoke and London.

Curry, D., (1999), *Lobbying Government – A Guide to Lobbying on Housing Issues*, CIH: Coventry.

Davies, M. and Niner, P., (1987), *Housing Work, Housing Workers and Education and Training for the Housing Service*, CIH: London.

Duncan, P. and Thomas, S., (2000), *Neighbourhood regeneration: Resourcing community involvement*, Rowntree/ The Policy Press: Bristol.

Dwelly, T., (Ed), (1997), *Sustainable Home Ownership – The Debate*, CIH for the Joseph Rowntree Foundation.

England, M., (1997), *The Tenants' Guide to Housing Finance*, London Housing Unit.

Flynn, N., (1997), *Public Sector Management (3rd edition)*, Prentice Hall/Harvester Wheatsheaf: Hemel Hempstead.

Ford, J. and Seavers, J., (1998), *Housing Associations and Rent Arrears: Attitudes, Beliefs and Behaviour*, CIH/JRF: Coventry.

Ford, J., (2000), 'MPPI take-up and retention: the current evidence', in *Housing Finance* No.45, February 2000, pp45-51.

Fordham, S., (1998), *Housing Investment Trusts, Moving into the Millennium*, Coopers and Lybrand, 1998.

Forrest, R., Murie, A. and Williams, P., (1990), *Home Ownership: Differentiation and Fragmentation*, Unwin Hyman: London.

Freeman, A., Holmans, A. and Whitehead, C., (1999), *Evaluating Housing Affordability – Policy Options and New Directions*, LGA: London.

Garnett, D., (1994a), *The Theory and Practice of Cost-Benefit Analysis*, Faculty of the Built Environment Working Paper WP31, UWE: Bristol.

Garnett, D., (1994b), *To Redevelop or Rehabilitate? A CBA Approach to Decision Making*, Faculty of the Built Environment Working Paper WP32, UWE: Bristol.

Garnett. D., (1995), 'Multiple rationality Analysis: An Approach to Reconciling the Competing Interests Associated with Housing Renewal Schemes'. Paper given to the Commonwealth Association of Surveying and Land Economy and the International Federation of Surveyors: *Sustainable Development: Counting the Cost – Maximising the Value*, Harare, Zimbabwe, August 1995. Copies available from the author, UWE Bristol.

Garnett, D., (1996), *Building Obsolescence*, UWE: Bristol.

Garnett, D., (1999), 'Absent Voices: Accommodating the Interests of Future Generations Through Multiple Rationality Analysis', in the *International Journal of Sustainable Development*, Vol.2, No.4.

Gibb, K. and Monro, M., (1991), *Housing Finance in the UK: An Introduction*, Macmillan: Basingstoke and London.

Gibbs, J., (1992), *Rent Levels, Rent Structures and Affordability: A Guide for Local Authorities and Housing Associations*, CIH: London.

Gibson, M. and Langstaff, M., (1982), *Introduction to Urban Renewal*, Hutchinson.

Goodlad, R., (1994), 'Conceptualising 'Enabling': The Housing Role of Local Authorities', in *Local Government Studies*, Vol.20, No.4, Winter 1994.

Goodlad, R., (1998), *Creating a new future – the strategic role of Scottish local authorities*, CIH: Edinburgh.

Goss, S. and Blackaby, R., (1998), *Designing Local Housing Strategies – A Good Practice Guide*, CIH: Coventry.

Gray, D., (1999), *What's it all about? Registered social landlord accounts explained*, NHF: London.

Hall, D., (1997), *Local Housing Companies Implementation Manual, Chapter 3: Impact of Local Housing Companies*, CIH/Chapman Hendy Associates: Coventry.

HACAS Consulting, (1999), *Housing Associations – A Viable Financial Future?* (Eds Lupton, M. and Perry, J.), CIH: Coventry.

HACAS and Trowers and Hamlins, (1999), *New Structure for Council Housing?* CIH and LGA.

Harloe, M., (1985), *Private Rented Housing in the United States and Europe*, Croom Helm: London.

Harriott, S. and Matthews, L., (1998), *Social Housing: An Introduction*, Longman: Harlow.

Hawksworth, J. and Wilcox, S., (1995), *Challenging the Conventions: Public Borrowing Rules and Housing Investment*, CIH/Coopers and Lybrand: Coventry.

Hills, J. (1991), *Unravelling Housing Finance*, Clarendon Press: Oxford.

Holmans, A., (2000), 'Owner-occupied households: recent trends in England and the USA, Australia, Canada and New Zealand', in *Housing Finance*, No.45, February 2000, pp30-35.

Holmes, R. and Marshall, D., (1996), *Property Profiling and Data Collection for Housing repairs and Improvements*, Construction Papers 61 and 62, (Ed. Harlow, P.), Chartered Institute of Building.

Imrie, R. and Thomas, H., (1993), *British Urban Policy and the Urban Development Corporations*, Paul Chapman: London.

Johnston, D. and Reid, M., (1998), *Best Value for Housing Services in Scotland*, CIH.

Joseph, D. and Terry, R., (1996), *Financing the future: and anticipating the consequences*, NFHA and Halifax Building Society, NFHA: London.

Joseph, D. and Terry, R., (1997), *Private Finance – Initiatives for Affordable Housing*, CIH: Coventry.

Kemp, P., (2000), *'Shopping Incentives' and Housing Benefit Reform*, CIH/JRF: Coventry.

Kerley, R., (1994), *Managing in Local Government*, Macmillan: Basingstoke and London.

Leather, P. and Mackintosh, S., (1993), 'Housing Renewal in an Era of Mass Home Ownership', Chapter 8 in Malpass, P. and Means, R., (Eds), *Implementing Housing Policy* pp106-126, OUP: Buckingham.

Leather, P. and Mackintosh, S., (1997), 'Towards Sustainable Policies for Housing Renewal in the Private Sector', in Williams, P., (Ed), *Directions in Housing Policy*, Paul Chapman: London.

Local Government Association, (1997), *A New Financial Framework for Local Authority Housing*, LGA Publications: London.

Local Government Information Unit, (1998), *Spotlight on best value No. 3: Equal Opportunities and Best Value*, LGIU: Warwick.

Lowndes, V., (1997), 'Change in Public Service Management: New Institutions and New Management Regimes', in *Local Government Studies*, Vol.23, No.2, Summer 1997.

Lowry, I. S., 'Filtering and Housing Standards: A Conceptual Analysis', in *Land Economics*, 1960, pp362-370.

Mackintosh, S., Malpass, P., and Garnett, D., (1988), *Most Peoples' Dream: A Study of Home Ownership and the Management of Maintenance of Older Low Cost Housing*, NAB: London.

Mackintosh, S. and Leather, P., (1993), *Renovation File: A Profile of Housing Conditions and Housing Renewal Policies in the United Kingdom*, Anchor Housing Trust: Oxford.

Malpass, P., (1990), *Reshaping Housing Policy: Subsidies, Rents and Residualisation*, Routledge: London and New York.

Malpass, P., (Ed), (1997), *Ownership, Control and Accountability: The New Governance of Housing* (Housing Policy and Practice Series), CIH: Coventry.

Marsh, A. and Mullins, D., (Eds), (1998), *Housing and Public Policy: Citizenship, Choice and Control*, OUP: Buckingham.

Marshall, D., (1996), 'Condition Surveys for Housing Associations: Some potential pitfalls and a survey of client experience'. *CIOB Construction Papers No. 68*.

Graham Moody Associates, (1998), *Council Housing – Financing the Future*, CIH: Coventry.

Moore, C. M., (1987), *Group Techniques for Idea Building*, Sage Publications.

National Federation of Housing Associations, (1986), *Inquiry in British Housing: The Evidence*, NFHA: London.

National Federation of Housing Associations/Rowntree Foundation, (1990), *Paying for Rented Housing, Research Report 12*, NFHA: London.

National Housing Federation, (1995), *Making the best use of your asset base: Private finance and security issues*, NHF: London.

National Housing Federation, (1996), *Financial Planning: a practical guide*, NHF: London.

National Housing Federation, (1997), *Rents, resources and risks: the new balancing act*, NHF: London.

National Housing Federation, (1999a), *Statement of Recommended Practice (SORP): Accounting by registered social landlords*, NHF: London.

National Housing Federation, (1999b), *Guidance on depreciation and impairment, Accounting by registered social landlords*, NHF: London.

National Housing Federation, (1999c), *Living with risk: An overview of risk for registered social landlords*, NHF: London.

National Housing Forum, (1998), *Regionalism, Devolution and Social Housing*, NHF: London.

Nettlefold, J.S., (1908), *Practical Housing*, Garden City Press: Letchworth.

Nevin, B., (1999), *Local Housing Companies – Progress and Problems*, CIH/JRF: Coventry.

Oatley, N., (1995), 'Competitive Urban Policy and the Regeneration Game', in *Town Planning Review*, 66(1).

Partington, M., (1994), *Claim in Time: Time Limits in Social Security Law*, Third Edition, LAG: London.

Power, A., (1993), *Hovels to High Rise: State Housing in Europe since 1850*, Routledge: London.

Rowntree Foundation, (1996), *More than somewhere to live: housing's impact on healthy communities*, JRF: York.

Saunders, P., (1990), *A Nation of Home Owners*, Unwin Hyman: London.

Smith, J., (2000). 'Attitudes to home-ownership and mortgage choices: 1999 market research findings', in *Housing Finance*, No.45, pp 20–24, February 2000.

Stewart, J. and Stoker, G., (Eds), (1995), *Local Government in the 1990s*, Macmillan: London.

Thomas, A., (1986), *Housing and Urban Renewal*, Allen and Unwin.

Tingley, K., (1998), *Daily Mail Income Tax Guide 1998-1999*, Orion: London.

Trott, A., (1998), *Managing Private Rented Housing*, (Good Practice Guide), CIH/RICS: Coventry.

Wilcox, S., (1995), *Housing Finance Review 1995/96*, Joseph Rowntree Foundation: York.

Wilcox, S., (1996), *Housing Review 1996/97*, Joseph Rowntree Foundation: York.

Wilcox, S., (1997), *Housing Finance Review 1997/98*, Joseph Rowntree Foundation: York.

Wilcox, S., (1998), *Unfinished Business: Housing costs and the reform of welfare benefits*, CIH: Coventry.

Wilcox, S., (1999), *Housing Finance Review 1999/2000*, Joseph Rowntree Foundation, Chartered Institute of Housing and the Council of Mortgage Lenders, 1999.

Wild, D., (1996), 'Unsafe as Houses', in *Public Finance*, 29 November 1996.

Zitron, J., (1995), *Local Housing Companies – A Good Practice Guide*, CIH: Coventry.

Zitron, J., (2000), *Winning Structures – Registered Social Landlords in a Changing World*, CIH: Coventry.

Official publications

Building Economic Development Committee, *Ways to Better Housing*, NEDO, 1986.

Department of the Environment, *Housing: The Government's Proposals*, Cm214, HMSO 1987a.

Department of the Environment, *Housing: The Government's Proposals for Scotland*, Cm242, HMSO 1987b.

Department of the Environment, *Local Authorities' Housing Role: 1990 Housing Investment Programme Round*, HMSO 1990.

Department of the Environment, *Evaluating Large Scale Voluntary Transfers of Local Authority Housing: An Interim Report*, HMSO 1992.

Department of the Environment, *Impact of the 1991 Funding Regime for Special Needs Housing*, DOE Housing Research Report, Capital Management Consultancy, HMSO 1994.

Department of the Environment, *Evaluating Large Scale Voluntary Transfers of Local Authority Housing*, HMSO 1995.

Department of the Environment, *Private Sector Renewal: A Strategic Approach*, Circular 17/96, The Stationery Office, December 1996.

Department of the Environment, Transport and the Regions, *Annual Report 1997: The Government's Expenditure Plans 1997-98 to 1999-2000*, Cm3607, 1998.

Department of the Environment, Transport and the Regions, *Modern Local Government, In Touch with the People* (White Paper), Cm4014, 1998.

Department of the Environment, Transport and the Regions, *Modernising local government: Local democracy and community leadership*, Cm6646, 1998.

Department of the Environment, Transport and the Regions, *Modernising local government: Business rates*, Cm7327, 1998.

Department of the Environment, Transport and the Regions, *Modernising local government: Improving local services through best value*, Cm6988, 1998.

Department of the Environment, Transport and the Regions, *Modernising local government: A new ethical framework*, Cm7308, 1998.

Department of the Environment, Transport and the Regions, *Modernising local government: Improving local financial accountability*, Cm7326, 1998.

Department of the Environment, Transport and the Regions, *Modernising local government: Capital finance*, Cm7257, 1998.

Department of the Environment and the Regions, *Towards an Urban Renaissance*; The Report of the Urban Task Force, Chaired by Lord Rogers of Riverside, 1999.

Department of the Environment and the Regions (with the Department for Social Security), *Quality and Choice: A Decent Home for All*, The Housing Green Paper, HMSO, April 2000.

Housing Corporation, *Procedure Guide*, Version 2, 1993.

Housing Corporation, *Grant Rates 1994/95. Guidance Notes Effective from 1st April 1994*, August 1993.

Housing Corporation, *Best Value for registered social landlords.* Guidance Note, February 1999.

Housing Corporation, *Total Cost Indicators 1994/95 Effective from 1st April 1994*, August 1993.

HM Treasury, *Public Expenditure: Statistical Analyses 1996-97* Cm3201, London: HMSO 1996.

HM Treasury, *The Government's Expenditure Plans 1997-98 to 1999-2000*, Cm3601-20, HMSO February 1997.

HM Treasury, *Economic and Fiscal Strategy Report*, Cm3978 June 1998.

Inland Revenue, *Taxation of Rents: A Guide to Property Income*, Practitioners Series IR150, Corporate Communications Office of the Inland Revenue, March 1996.

Northern Ireland Housing Executive, *Housing in the 1990s*, Belfast: NIHE 1989.

Northern Ireland Housing Executive, *Housing Strategy 1995-1998: The Case for Programme Funding*, Belfast: NIHE 1994.

Scottish Office, *An Evaluation of GRO Grant for Owner Occupation*, HMSO 1997.

Scottish Office, *Investing in Modernisation – An Agenda for Scotland's Housing*, The Scottish Housing Green Paper, HMSO, February 1999.

Useful contacts

Chartered Institute of Housing
Octavia House, Westwood Way,
Coventry CV4 8JP
Website: www.cih.org
Publications e-mail: pubs@cih.org

Chartered Institute of Housing in Scotland
6 Palmerston Place,
Edinburgh EH12 5AA
Scotland@cih.org

Chartered Institute of Housing in Wales
4 Purbeck House, Lambourne Crescent,
Cardiff Business Park, Llanishen,
Cardiff CF14 5GJ
Wales@cih.org
Cymru@cih.org

Chartered Institute of Housing in
Northern Ireland
Carnmoney House,
Edgewater Office Park,
Dargan Road,
Belfast BT3 9JQ
Ni@cih.org

Royal Institution of Chartered Surveyors
12 Great George Street,
Parliament Square,
London SW1P 3AD

Chartered Institute of Public Finance and
Accountancy
3 Robert Street,
London WC2N 6BH
www.publicfinance.co.uk

Local Government Association
Local Government House,
Smith Square,
London SW1P 3HZ.
http://www.lga.gov.uk

Convention of Scottish Local Authorities
Rosebery House, 9 Haymarket Terrace,
Edinburgh EH12 5XZ

Council of Mortgage Lenders
3 Savile Row,
London W1X 1AF

Housing Corporation
149 Tottenham Court Road,
London W1P OBN

Scottish Homes (Head Office)
Thistle House, 91 Haymarket Terrace,
Edinburgh EH12 5HE
http://www.scot-homes.gov.uk

Scottish Executive Development
Department,
Victoria Quay,
Edinburgh EH6 6QQ

Department of the Environment, Transport
and the Regions – DETR
Eland House, Bressenden Place,
London SW1E 5DU
http://www.housing.detr.gov.uk

National Assembly for Wales
Cathays Park,
Cardiff CF10 3NQ
http://www.wales.gov.uk

DoE for Northern Ireland
Clarence Court, 10-18 Adelaide Street,
Belfast BT2 8GB

National Housing Federation
175 Gray's Inn Road,
London WC1X 8UP
http://www.housing.org.uk

Scottish Federation of Housing
Associations
38 York Place,
Edinburgh EH1 3HU

Welsh Federation of Housing Associations
Norbury House,
Norbury Road, Fairwater,
Cardiff CF5 3AS

Topic index